SECOND EDITION

CRIME
Readings

TITLES OF RELATED INTEREST FROM PINE FORGE PRESS

SECOND EDITION

CRIME
Readings

EDITORS
Robert D. Crutchfield

George S. Bridges

Joseph G. Weis

Charis Kubrin
University of Washington, Seattle

with contributions by
Jon'a Meyer
Rutgers University, Camden

PINE FORGE PRESS

Thousand Oaks, California • London • New Delhi

For information:

 Pine Forge Press
A Sage Publications Company
2455 Teller Road
Thousand Oaks, California 91320
(805) 499-4224
E-mail: sales@pfp.sagepub.com

Sage Publications Ltd.
6 Bonhill Street
London EC2A 4PU
United Kingdom

Sage Publications India Pvt. Ltd.
M-32 Market
Greater Kailash I
New Delhi 110 048 India

Printed in the United States of America

Library of Congress Cataloging-in-Publication Data
Crime / edited by Robert D. Crutchfield ... [et al.].—2nd ed.
    p.   cm.
Includes bibliographical references and index.
    ISBN 0-7619-8679-0 (pbk. : alk. paper)
    1. Crime—United States.   2. Criminology—United States.   I.
Crutchfield, Robert D.
    HV6789 .C682   2000
    364.973—dc21

                                                            00-008037

This book is printed on acid-free paper.

00   01   02   03   04   05   10   9   8   7   6   5   4   3   2   1

Publisher:	Stephen D. Rutter
Assistant to the Publisher:	Ann Makarias
Production Management:	Scratchgravel Publishing Services
Copy Editor:	Linda Purrington
Typesetter:	Scratchgravel Publishing Services
Cover Designer:	Greg Draus

About the Editors

Robert D. Crutchfield is Professor of Sociology and Chair of the Department of Sociology. He served on the Washington State Juvenile Sentencing Commission and is also a former juvenile probation officer and adult parole officer. He was a Deputy Editor of *Criminology* and has published a number of papers on labor markets, crime, and racial and ethnic disparities in the administration of justice, including "Labor Stratification and Violent Crime."

George S. Bridges is Professor of Sociology and Associate Dean of Undergraduate Education. He has served as a staff member of the policy office of the Attorney General of the United States as well as deputy editor of *Criminology*. He has published many papers on racial biases in American law and is co-editor, with Martha Myers, of *Crime, Inequality, and Social Control*.

Joseph G. Weis is Professor of Sociology and the Director of the Center for Law and Justice. He served for a number of years as the Director of the National Center for the Assessment of Delinquent Behavior and Its Prevention, funded by the U.S. Department of Justice, as well as a member of the Washington State Governor's Juvenile Justice Advisory Committee. He is a past editor of the journal *Criminology* and a co-author, with Michael J. Hindelang and Travis Hirschi, of *Measuring Delinquency*.

Charis Kubrin is a Ph.D. candidate in sociology at the University of Washington. Her research interests focus on neighborhood correlates of violent crime rates and race and crime. She has taught many courses in the area of crime and criminal justice, including Deviant Behavior and Social Control, Introduction to Criminal Justice, and The Sociology of Murder. She is currently finishing her dissertation entitled "Context and the Social Ecology of Criminal Homicide."

About the Publisher

Pine Forge Press is a new educational publisher, dedicated to publishing innovative books and software throughout the social sciences. On this and any other of our publications, we welcome your comments.

Please write to:

Pine Forge Press
A Sage Publications Company
31 St. James Ave., Suite 510
Boston, MA 02116
(617) 753-7512
E-mail: sdr@pfp.sagepub.com

Visit our World Wide Web site, your direct link to a multitude of online resources:
www.pineforge.com

Dedicated to Clarence C. Schrag, colleague and friend

In memory of Marvin E. Wolfgang

Brief Contents

Detailed Contents

Foreword

About four years ago, I adopted these two volumes as required readings for my classes—*Crime* for my criminology course and *Juvenile Delinquency* for my delinquency course. At that point, I had been teaching the courses with great success for over ten years at five different universities. Despite this record of success, my courses improved substantially after I adopted these two texts, my students were learning more, and my teaching evaluations improved. Why? In no small part it was due to the quality of these two volumes, which are without question the best collection of readings on crime and delinquency today.

Each volume has managed to optimize seemingly disparate pedagogical goals: appealing to the interests of the student without compromising the scholarly presentation. The articles selected are written in clear and lively prose, address provocative and timely issues, and represent the cutting edge of theory and research in criminology. They tend to make difficult theoretical and methodological issues comprehensible even to the novice. Collectively, they cover the field in a creative and comprehensive way, providing a historical sense of what we know about crime and delinquency and showing the relationships between explanatory theory, empirical research, and public policy. Classic theoretical and empirical statements that continue to dominate the field are included, while outdated and less influential pieces are discarded. The result is a snapshot of the current state of research in crime and delinquency, as well as a window to the future.

The success of the volumes at both scholarly and pedagogical levels reflects the unique abilities of the editors, Professors Bridges, Crutchfield, Kubrin, and Weis, whose careers have bridged scholarship and teaching. Each is not only a national leader in criminological research and scholarship, but has also been recognized for outstanding undergraduate teaching with university teaching awards. Their selections of readings are based on their own experience in the field *and* in the classroom.

The field of criminology is in an exciting and dynamic state, with important new advances cropping up every year. The second editions of the two volumes have been updated to reflect these changes in the field. Articles representing important recent developments have been included, replacing those that are no longer at the cutting edge. As a result, the new volumes provide a superb overview of the most exciting and influential scholarly writing on crime and delinquency. Anyone who reads these volumes cover to cover will understand the cutting edge of scholarly research, the relationship between classical and contemporary theory, and the links between criminological theory and practice. Readers will become not only better scholars, but better citizens as well.

—ROSS L. MATSUEDA

Foreword

WHEN I was a graduate student studying the best works in criminology, my equally striving graduate student colleagues and I knew every work worth reading in the field. I mean *every work*. I could quote volumes, numbers, pages of *Journal of Criminal Law and Criminology*. I could cite chapters from Barnes and Teeters, Kinsey, Gillin. Nothing escaped us.

As we have shown in *Evaluating Criminology* (New York: Elsevier [with Robert M. Figlio and Terence P. Thornberry] 1979), there was an explosion of criminological literature in the 28 years from 1945 to 1972. Since then, there has been an even greater increase in publication of books and articles in this field. Not even the most ardent reader can keep abreast of everything. Selections have to be made.

Having made selections for publications in the past, I know the difficulties of making choices, of screening among the enormous numbers of publications for inclusion in a series. I have carefully read the table of contents and many of the articles in these volumes and am prepared to defend them as the best in the field.

These four editors have shown that age of publication is less important than substance. Some pieces are from 1938, 1958, and the early 1960s. Why? Because they are nearly timeless in the significance of their observations, theory, or empirical research. There are also very recent articles of excellence.

Within these volumes is the essence of the best we know in causation, theory, delinquency, and criminal justice. Anyone who reads and absorbs the readings of these volumes will have a full degree of knowledge to match anyone in the field of criminology.

We cannot read everything, but we can read the cream of the crop. These volumes cut across time and ideologies.

—MARVIN E. WOLFGANG

Preface

A leading "crime story" in the past few years has been the declining American crime rate. Each year the Federal Bureau of Investigation releases its *Uniform Crime Reports,* which leads to a flurry of phone calls and interviews with criminologists by those seeking to understand the decline. Despite this trend in crime, however, politicians continue to "run against crime" at election time, and the popular media remain fascinated with "true crime" shows and news of criminal events. In the academic milieu students and teachers alike spend much time and energy thinking about crime and criminals.

Although crime rates are down, no one contends that crime is no longer a major problem. In the second edition of *Crime and Justice,* Sir Leon Radzinowicz and Marvin E. Wolfgang wrote, "There can be no doubt that optimism has gone, platitudes have proven empty. We are living through a time when, more than ever before, there can be no consensus on how to tackle crime. We do not feel it our business to try to resolve the current conflicts, but we feel it our duty . . . to try to reflect it." That now classic three-volume set was first published in 1971, but those words still depict the lack of consensus in our thinking about crime, delinquency, and criminal justice. Criminologists, politicians, and the general public are no closer to consensus on how to confront the problem of crime than we were thirty years ago. Perhaps we are even more divided. We see this lack of consensus in the answers given by criminologists and criminal justice practitioners when queried about the crime rate decline. Some argue that the decline is a product of tough law enforcement, while others contend it is a result of the recent shift toward community-oriented policing. Some attribute it to the massive increases in the number of people incarcerated, while others describe changes in drug markets that have led to lower levels of drug violence. There are some who point to a strong economy while others focus on demography and an aging population. And of course there are those who suggest that all or many of these explanations are needed for a complete understanding of changes in crime rates.

In this, the second edition of *Crime,* we, like Radzinowicz and Wolfgang, do not try to resolve the important conflicts in criminology, but we do try to fairly represent the range of debate about the causes of crime and delinquency and the approaches to addressing these problems. The organizing principle for the first and this second edition of *Crime* is that the scholarly literature, both the old and the new, provides an important basis for thinking about crime for professionals, students, and the general public. As a result, we have included some of the classic works of criminology along with contemporary empirical research. In this edition, as we did in the first, we have included theoretical statements and pieces that reflect where those theories have gone since their initial statements. We believe that students will be better educated if they have the opportunity to study the diversity of the criminological literature.

Although some "theory-based" collections of readings about crime that are similar to ours have recently been published, most criminology readers focus on "types of crime." Such an approach is curious since we know that most criminals do not specialize. Much crime occurs because people are presented with opportunities to act violently, selfishly, or acquisitively. As opportunities vary, so do the types of crime individuals commit. If opportunities for different types of crime appear, the same person may well seize—with equal likelihood—the chance to victimize people, property, or institutions. Accordingly, our message in this book is simple. We obtain a much clearer picture of crime and its causes if we focus not on the specific acts that people commit, but rather on the patterns of violation, on the social and other human conditions that lead to violation, and on how groups within society control those who are defined as criminals and outlaws. As educators, we believe that students gain the greatest understanding of crime and social control from a selection of readings that focuses on theoretical explanations and research evidence advanced by criminologists. Publications that take the other approach, depicting the study of crime and criminals simply in terms of different types of illegal and bizarre acts, offer students little more than a criminological version of what Alexander Liazos described as the study of "nuts, sluts, and preverts."

The collection of readings in *Crime* began in our conversations about teaching our classes at the University of Washington. We believe that students should read the actual work of scholars who study criminology. Reading the original literature is an important part of a liberal education. The public debate about crime and what to do about it will be better informed if the public is exposed to what we know and how we have come to know it, as well as to what we do not know.

Although some articles from scholarly journals may at first seem inaccessible or of limited appeal to students, we have found that when students are asked to reach a bit beyond their grasp, more often than not, they respond positively. Our experiences, as well as those of our colleagues who used the first edition of *Crime* in their classes, confirm that students from private liberal arts colleges to research universities to community colleges can read and understand scholarly papers. We recognize that certain characteristics of some academic articles may overwhelm students—most notably, the analytic procedures and statistics. As we did in the first edition, we have edited out much of this material, as well as footnotes and references, leaving the presentation of theoretical ideas, results, discussions, and conclusions.

Nearly all the selections in *Crime* have been used in one or more of our courses. We have included, and even emphasized, a number of theoretical pieces because they form the basis of scholarship in criminology and also because most commonsense explanations of the causes of crime and delinquency have actually been captured in those theories. When we explain this to students we help them see why theory is important to criminologists and also why it can be of interest to them. The empirical pieces in this volume frequently reflect modifications and refinements in classic theories.

The second edition maintains the format that was successful in the first edition—sections on history and definitions, images of crime, measurement, correlates of crime, chronologically arranged examinations of criminological theories, and specific topics in criminology, and social control. Throughout we pay attention to both historical and contemporary efforts to understand crime.

What Is New in the Second Edition

Selected bibliography—We selected references from each reading and listed them at the end of the book. Thus students can seek out important criminological publications cited by the authors, and instructors can direct students in their search for additional literature to be used in class papers and assignments.

New articles: We have added new articles to the second edition of *Crime* for two reasons. First, we made changes where our colleagues, our students, or our own experience with the first edition suggested that a different piece might work better. Second, much research and writing have been published since the first edition was put together. We have focused particularly on keeping the contemporary selections as current as possible.

New data analysis exercises: Designed to give students hands-on experience in analyzing real data, the exercises allow students to see how the theories explain crime and the world around them. Each exercise explores the tenets of a theory and tests whether the ideas in the theory "work" to explain increases or reductions in crime. While completing the exercises, students will learn about basic methods and statistics, two skill areas that will benefit them whether they enter graduate study or the workplace. Novices in computers and statistics should be able to work through the exercises with ease.

The exercises also can be used flexibly in the classroom and in assigned work. They are divided into three sections:

- General questions are based on the guided exercises completed by the students. These fill-in-the-blank and circle-the-answer questions accommodate the needs of instructors who want to introduce students to data analysis but require assignments that are quick to score. These questions can also be assigned as extra credit.

- "Further exploration" questions are closely related to the general questions but allow the students to replicate and extend a theory on their own. The answers to these questions are fill-in, circle, and essay.

- "On your own" questions allow students to explore the theories independently, with minimal guidance. The answers are essay and may be used to generate course discussion.

Although the exercises use only frequencies and crosstabulations, some instructors may choose to introduce their students to multivariate analysis as well, using the exercises as a starting point. The exercises provide a flexible way for instructors to include data handling and interpretation skills in their courses. Both SPSS and MicroCase versions of the data sets are included on the floppy diskette at the back of the book.

Questions for discussion and writing: Two or three questions appear at the end of each reading to help students focus on the main points of the selection and better understand the reading. More questions appear in the Instructor's Manual. The reading questions provide a variety of launch points for discussion and include theoretical, methodological, and other questions. Students who answer the reading questions report a higher understanding of the text material and keep on track with class assignments.

Instructors may use the questions in class discussion as a structured presentation of the course material (this is particularly appropriate for graduate students leading discussions). Answers are provided in the Instructor's Manual for both the questions printed in the text and for the additional questions contained in the Instructor's Manual. A simple check/check-minus grading scheme would allow instructors to provide a customized learning experience for their courses with a minimum of grading overhead.

Expanded criminal justice section: We have added articles to provide more depth to the coverage of social control. At the same time we have tried to maintain the tension between competing political positions on law and justice that was represented in the selections in the first edition.

We have retained the introduction to the first edition of *Crime* prepared by James F. Short, Jr., as well as the foreword by Marvin E. Wolfgang, who has since passed away. We also added a new foreword by our colleague, Ross L. Matsueda. These three essays set the stage for the very best ideas from theory and research on crime and its control produced by criminologists over the past few decades. The readings represent different academic disciplines, with different theoretical and ideological orientations, and diverse ideas on the best ways to prevent and control crime in our society.

ACKNOWLEDGMENTS

Many persons have contributed to this volume, beyond those whose work is included in the volume itself. We are indebted to these individuals. Without their dedicated work and assistance, this edition of the book would not have been completed. The editorial staff at Pine Forge Press and Scratchgravel Publishing Services—Ann Makarias and Anne and Greg Draus—ensured that the production process went smoothly, keeping all the editors on task. We greatly appreciate their commitment to our project and their uncompromising pursuit of excellence. In particular, Steve Rutter, the president of Pine Forge Press, played an extremely valuable role with this edition of *Crime*. Steve's tireless enthusiasm for this volume and his patience with our schedules helped carry us through the demanding challenges of editing and organizing the materials for the book. We are deeply appreciative of his support of our work.

We are extremely grateful to Jon'a Meyer for her excellent contributions to this second edition, the data analysis exercises and the questions at the end of each reading. These have improved the book immeasurably.

We are also indebted to colleagues (some of whom are former students) who contributed to this volume primarily through their contributions to the first edition of *Crime*. Kristin Bates, Rod Engen, Randy Gainey, Eddie Pate, and Sara Steen all helped with the development of the book. We continue to deeply respect and appreciate their judgment. Among these, Eddie Pate deserves the greatest recognition because he worked most closely with us in locating and assembling the original set of readings for the book. Eddie did the "heavy lifting" early on, and his work helped carry us through the first and second editions of *Crime*.

We are also deeply appreciative of the helpful comments supplied by reviewers of earlier drafts of the manuscripts, including:

Q. Akin Adesun, *Pennsylvania State University*
Larry L. Bench, *University of Utah*

Eugene Bouley, *Georgia College & State University*
Susan Brinkley, *University of Tampa*
James W. Burfeind, *University of Montana*
Barbara Costello, *University of Rhode Island*
Lauren Dundes, *Western Maryland College*
Helen Taylor Greene, *Old Dominion University*
Denise Herz, *University of Nebraska, Omaha*
James W. Kanan, *Western Kentucky University*
Joanne Kaufman, *Emory University*
Christopher Krebs, *Florida State University*
Celia Lo, *University of Akron*
Daniel Mears, *University of Texas at Austin*
Robert F. Meier, *Iowa State University*
Jon'a Meyer, *Rutgers University, Camden*
Frank Mungel, *State University of New York, Buffalo*
Mahesh K. Nalla, *Michigan State University*
Amie L. Nielsen, *Bowling Green State University*
Randi Rosenblum, *Hunter College*
Gene T. Straughan, *Lewis-Clark State College*
Pamela Tontodonato, *Kent State University*
Charles Walton, *Radford University*

Despite the important comments these reviewers provided, we alone are responsible for the editing of the manuscripts and for any errors or omissions in the editing process.

Finally, we want to acknowledge the contributions that our undergraduate students at the University of Washington have made to this effort. They have toiled through many earlier versions of this book, commenting on the books and our teaching over the years. We have benefited immensely from their reactions, both positive and negative. Without their insightful comments and suggestions, we would be much less effective as teachers and learners.

—THE EDITORS

Introduction
On Crime, Criminals, and Criminologists

CRIME is a controversial concern in all modern societies. It is controversial, as well, among those who study crime and criminals. Politicians must not be seen to be "soft on crime," lest they incur the displeasure of a fearful electorate. Criminologists trained in scientific disciplines often skirt difficult issues such as the racial and ethnic distribution of crime for a variety of reasons, among them fear of being branded "racist" or otherwise prejudiced against minorities, or concern that their analyses maybe translated by politicians into ideologically or politically motivated counterproductive crime control policies.

These fears feed on one another. Even "enlightened" (by acquaintance with scientific analyses of the crime problem) politicians feel obligated to support control measures that are "tough on crime," as well as measures designed ostensibly (on the basis of scientific analyses) to prevent crime. Criminologists struggle with their scientific consciences to support crime prevention measures that are unproven because they fear harsh political responses to crime that are devoid of the input of scientific knowledge and carefully evaluated experience.

Among criminologists, priority is given to issues that are fundamental to understanding the nature of crime and criminals, rather than to issues of "toughness" or "softness" in the control of crime. The latter are derivative, distorted versions of the former, though crime control policies and their implementation are important to the etiology of *crimes and their control,* for crime is far from homogeneous, in law, in behavior, or in affects on victims (and offenders), as individuals, families, communities, or nations.

The selections reprinted in this collection shed much light on these controversies, beginning with John Hagan's searching examination of the relationship between crime and morality. Criminology arguably begins with the sociology of law, though restriction of the concerns of criminology to behavior defined in the criminal law has been objected to on several grounds, as Hagan's paper makes clear. Beyond the concerns reviewed in Hagan's fine paper (and beyond the concerns of criminology, per se), the task of developing "a theory of the distinctively legal" remains elusive.

This volume organizes criminology's concerns and controversies in 10 sections, beginning with the history and definitions of crime and criminology, and with scholarly attempts to understand public views and fears of crime. These are followed by selections concerned with the measurement of crime and with the distribution of crime among social categories. Explanations of crime occupy the next three sections, again beginning historically with theories that were first advanced half-a-century or more ago, and that continue to influence scholarly and public concerns with crime problems. More recent theories and research are then examined, including relatively new theoretical developments. The final two sections examine different patterns of criminality: white collar crime, organized crime, gangs, and criminal careers and the vexing problems of the social control of crime. Suggested readings and review questions conclude each section.

The selections reprinted here are heavily weighted toward traditional *sociological* concerns with crime, criminals, and their control. Sociologists, more than adherents of other social and behavioral sciences, focus on fundamental questions of measurement, sampling, and on *contextualizing* forces and processes of etiology. We tend to focus, that is, on the *macrosocial* level of explanation, seeking to understand what it is about social systems (such as economic and political systems, communities, and families) that produce different *rates* of behaviors of interest. The most immediate of these contexts of human activity—ongoing interaction among persons—often exert critical influences on behavioral outcomes, as studies at the *microsocial* level of explanation demonstrate. As will be seen in the selections that follow, sociologists also focus on the *individual* level of explanation, seeking to explain what it is about individuals that lead them to behave of sundry ways.

In the course of the inquiries criminologists address profound questions regarding human behavior: the relationship between broad social forces and individual experience, the relationship between hard objective realities and how they are subjectively experienced, and the problem of deriving general behavioral principles from individual (and in some respects inevitably unique) perceptions and experience. Criminology can be viewed through many social and behavioral science lenses: psychology and social psychology, for example, and through principles of organizational and group behavior. Similarly, these social and behavioral science specialties can be viewed with profit through the lenses provided by criminological inquiry.

Criminologists have not been immune to ideological concerns, though in most cases these, also, have been perused within broad scientific principles. When they are not, disciplined inquiry suffers as does criminology as a discipline. The selections in this volume reflect both the diversity of approaches to the study of crime and criminals and some of the best examples of research and theory within these approaches.

Few serious scholars claim to be "experts" concerning crime and criminals, yet we are often viewed as authorities, based on our inquiries and our experience. As such, we face many challenges, not least of which is building and maintaining the credibility of criminology and the trust of those who rely upon our knowledge, insights, and proposals for the control of crime. The selections in this and other volumes in the series offer an excellent sampling of the best that criminology has to offer. I am happy to commend them to those who wish to know what it is that we are about.

—JAMES F. SHORT, JR.

I

WHAT IS CRIMINOLOGY?

The History and Definitions of Crime and Criminology

ALTHOUGH many people may be content to accept a definition of crime as "behavior that violates the law," modern criminologists have come to believe that defining crime is a more complex enterprise. Criminologists are acutely aware that what is considered a crime is a product of moral, political, and social processes. At times those processes work smoothly and easily; at other times there is substantial controversy and disagreement. How those processes work has become an important area of scholarship.

Some of the most interesting questions in criminology focus on the central issue of defining crime. For example, no one will disagree that murder is a vile and contemptible act, rightfully considered criminal, but we do not always agree on which instances of taking human life should be considered "murder." When toxic dumping results in death, is that murder? When the state practices capital punishment, is that murder? There are those who would say yes, others no, to both questions; still others would argue that only one of these acts constitutes murder. Other acts, such as abortion and drug possession, have provoked heated public debate and illustrate the lack of consensus in our society about which behaviors should be considered criminal.

Additionally, definitions of crime vary across societies, and it is important to understand how and why societies differ in what they choose to criminalize. Every society develops rules, and complex modern societies have intricate and comprehensive systems of law. The fact that these laws, and the behaviors they define as criminal, are not uniform in all societies underscores the point that definitions of crime are not inevitable or universal, but depend heavily upon the social contexts in which they evolve. For criminologists, it is essential to understand both those contexts and the definitions of crime that emerge in them as a critical component in the scientific study of crime.

How criminologists define crime also affects their conceptions of the "criminal." Both are important factors in developing explanations for why people break the law and how society responds to these offenders. If, for example, we define crime as illegal behavior in which people choose to engage, explanations will focus on why some choose to commit crime and others choose to obey the law. With that definition of crime, society would respond to crime by trying to change the individual's "crime calculus," making it more costly to engage in crime by increasing punishment. Alternatively, if crime is conceptualized as a product of forces outside the individual's control (such as biological, psychological, or social forces), crime control would attempt to address the "root causes" of criminality.

In the first selection, John Hagan addresses some of the complexities involved in defining crime. We have led with this piece to emphasize the notion that defining crime is not a simple exercise. Anyone who wants to understand crime—whether professional criminologist, student of criminology, president of the United States, parent, or criminal—must be aware of the many ways in which crime is defined. Students should use this selection to focus on the connection between morality and law. In some areas, law and morality are closely aligned. In these instances, both compliance with the law and effective enforcement are more readily accomplished. Problems arise when laws are inconsistent with the morality of a segment of the population. In those instances, people are less likely to comply with the law, acting instead in accord with their moral beliefs, and they are less likely to assist the criminal justice system in enforcement.

We do not offer one definition of crime that we believe the student should accept. However, students should, as they move through this text, consider critically how authors define crime and what implications these definitions have for theory and empirical research.

Ronald Huff, in "Historical Explanations of Crime: From Demons to Politics," provides an overview of the history of modern criminology. Many people believe that criminologists make their living by solving crimes. The members of the American Society of Criminology do not solve crimes—and rarely commit them. Instead, criminologists try to explain why people commit crimes and how societies respond to control crime. In this piece, the student will get a sense of the distance we have covered, and have yet to go, in our quest to understand crime. In reading this selection, look for the implied definitions of crime that theorists have used and assess how those definitions shape their explanations of crime. Also, this selection will give students a useful overview of issues discussed later in this volume. Reading Huff will give you a sense of the major theoretical traditions in criminology, as well as some of the major issues that criminologists wrestle with. Use this selection to frame your study of criminological theories and explanations.

Together, Hagan and Huff set the stage for considering the modern state of criminology. Although neither answers the great questions of criminology, they both raise some of them. And in the asking, we have a most important place to begin.

DEFINING CRIME

Defining Crime: An Issue of Morality

JOHN HAGAN

THE ISSUE: WHAT SHOULD BE CALLED "CRIMINAL"?

The act of defining crime is often, but not always, a step toward controlling it; that is, the ostensible purpose of defining some behaviors as criminal is to make them liable to public prosecution and punishment. However, being *liable* to prosecution and punishment is clearly not the same as actually *being* prosecuted and punished. During the twilight of the prohibition era in America, there was little attempt to enforce temperance legislation and, when arrests and convictions did occur, the sentences imposed were light. Eventually, the production and distribution of alcohol was decriminalized. Attempts to prosecute and punish Selective Service violators produced similar problems during the last stages of the Vietnamese war. This law was never repealed, and it undoubtedly will be used again in the future. Meanwhile, there are many statutes that define white-collar crimes, but they are only infrequently enforced. This is not to say that such laws have no use; their mere existence at least serves the purpose of condemning certain unethical business practices. Thus, each of the above laws serves (or served) the purpose

of making a moral statement, a statement about how citizens *should* behave. Yet each of these laws has proved problematic, making explicit the issue of how the criminal law can and should be used to legislate morality. In one sense, this issue is moot because the criminal law is always and everywhere used to legislate morality. However, in another sense, the issue is very much alive, because the *way* in which the criminal law is used to legislate morality is constantly changing. And in the process of changing, the criminal law expands and contracts, forcing us regularly and concretely to answer the question: what should be called a crime? Should the criminal law contract and make homosexuality and some kinds of drug use legal? Should the criminal law expand and make acts of racism and sexism crimes? These are the kinds of questions this chapter is about.

THE LINK BETWEEN LAW AND MORALITY

The lengths to which the law should go in officially defining and enforcing morality has been the subject of philosophical debate for centuries. In the nineteenth century, the noted participants in this debate were John Stuart Mill and Sir James Fitzjames Stephen. In the twentieth century, the principals have been H. L. A. Hart and Lord Patrick Devlin. It is important that we begin by grounding ourselves in the opposing premises of this debate.

On one side, Mill argued in his famous essay *On Liberty* that the primary function of criminal law is to prevent individuals from doing harm to *others*.

The only purpose for which power can be rightfully exercised over any member of a civilized community against his will, is to prevent harm to others. His own good, either physical, or moral, is not sufficient warrant, he cannot rightfully be compelled to do or forbear because it would be better for him to do so, because it will make him happier, because, in the opinion of others, to do so would be wise or even right.

In other words, Mill regarded the criminal law as an improper instrument for regulating the private moral conduct of individuals that caused no direct harm to others. In contrast, Stephen saw the criminal law as serving a much broader function in the cultivation of personal responsibility, arguing that "the meaning of responsibility is liability to punishment." Thus, Stephen regarded the criminal law as a fundamental means for developing a sense of individual responsibility, and he considered the use of criminal law as essential for this purpose.

The debate has been focused most clearly in this century in Britain around the work of the British Governmental Committee on Homosexual Offenses and Prostitution. This body, known for its chairman as the Wolfenden Committee, issued a report in 1957 that renewed the classic debate by recommending that private and consensual homosexual behavior on the part of adults no longer be considered a criminal offense. Behind this recommendation lay a broader assumption, explicitly acknowledged by the committee, that the criminal law should not intrude on the private lives of individual citizens beyond what is absolutely necessary—to maintain public order and decency, to protect individuals from offensive and injurious behavior, and to prevent exploitation and corruption—particularly

of those unable to protect themselves. The committee put the matter succinctly when it concluded that "there must remain a realm of private morality and immorality which is, in brief and crude terms, not the law's business." The committee was quick to emphasize that it did not condone these forms of behavior, but neither did it see it as the proper role of the law to condemn them. These were simply not matters for legal control.

Lord Devlin, a prominent British jurist, objected to the committee's position. Devlin argued that "the criminal law as we know it is based upon moral principle" and furthermore that "in a number of crimes its function is simply to enforce a moral principle and nothing else." Thus, Devlin's position was that "the suppression of vice is as much the law's business as the suppression of subversive activities." In other words, Devlin, like Stephen, believed that it was a proper and necessary function of the law to regulate private morality.

Another prominent British philosopher of law, H. L. A. Hart, defended the committee's work against Devlin's critique. Like Mill before him, Hart based his defense on principles of individual liberty, arguing that a right to be protected from the distress which is inseparable from the bare knowledge that others are acting in ways you think wrong cannot be acknowledged by anyone who recognizes individual liberty as a value. The extension of the utilitarian principle that coercion may be used to protect men from harm, so as to include their protection from this form of distress, cannot stop here. If distress incident to the belief that others are doing wrong is harm, so also is the distress incident to the belief that others are doing what you do not want them to do. To punish people for causing this form of distress would be tantamount to punishing them simply because others object to what they do, and the only liberty that could coexist with this extension of the utilitarian principle is liberty to do those things to which no one seriously objects.

To read the debate as it has been presented thus far, one might think the issue involved is one of simple and absolute principle: whether the criminal law should be used to control private morality. However, things are seldom so simple in law, and this debate is no exception. First, each side of the debate we have presented involves rather different assumptions about the sources and purposes of law. That is, rather different assumptions are made about where law comes from, about how law evolves and develops in primitive and modern societies, and about the purposes to which law is put. Second, the line between private morality and the concerns of the surrounding society is not clear. For example, it can be argued that while drug use imposes its most direct consequences on drug-taking individuals, there are consequences (e.g., lost productivity) for society as well. Third, part of what is at issue is not only the *propriety* of using the criminal law to control individual morality, but also the *efficacy* of trying to do so. In other words, can the criminal law be used *effectively* to control individual morality? Fourth, there is a concern with the costs and harms involved for those who are subject to control. One concern here is that such laws may have the effect of creating a permanent class of criminals, that is, a class of persons whose options for leaving a lifestyle defined as criminal are few. To fully understand the Hart-Devlin debate and the link between law and morality, it is necessary to address these several dimensions of the problem. We turn next, then, to a discussion of the sources of law, followed by a discussion of each of the additional concerns raised above.

THE ORIGINS OF LAWS

Anthropologists, philosophers, and political scientists, as well as sociologists, have pondered the question of where laws come from. Although this question is raised and addressed in a variety of ways, and will be discussed in greater detail in the following chapter, two discernible kinds of answers can be considered briefly here. The first kind of answer sees the law largely as a source of social order that resolves and prevents disputes, thereby allowing individuals to live more harmoniously together. The law is seen here as a product of consensus, evolving as a means of maintaining this consensus. The second kind of answer sees the law primarily as an instrument of social conflict that is used to maintain the power and privileges of one group over another. The law is seen here as having evolved out of a conflict between interest groups. These two different kinds of answers can be understood best as they have been offered by their various proponents.

Law as a Product of Consensus

According to the consensus point of view, law is a natural product of the informal rules of interaction of a society. For example, William Seagle, a lawyer, argues that the law is simply a product of custom. Indeed, for Seagle, "custom is king," and "while there is no automatic *submission* to custom, there is an automatic *sway* of custom." Similarly, Frederick von Savigny asserts "that all law . . . is first developed by custom and popular faith," and Julius Stone concludes that laws "are generalized statements of the tendencies actually operating, of the presuppositions on which a particular civilization is based." From this viewpoint, then, there is no easy division between morality and law: customary morality is the very source of law.

With Devlin, it is assumed that to deny this would be to deny the very foundations of law. "The folkways are the 'right' ways," wrote William Sumner, and these customs or folkways are seen as giving law both its force and its purpose. From this perspective, any separation of the law from this foundation would be both artificial and perilous.

Law as a Product of Conflict

In contrast, there is another point of view that sees the emergence of law as a very selective process. This view argues that there are many moralities representing a variety of group interests in a society. The issue, then, is whose morality will get expressed in law, and with what consequences? The answer given from this perspective is that the law is a "weapon" and that it will be used as such by any group that can do so to its advantage. Chambliss and Seidman argue that this is particularly the case in complex, highly stratified societies like our own. They note that as societies become more complex in their economic division of labor, it becomes necessary to have rules, and ultimately laws, that regulate the encounters of individuals who occupy different roles. At the same time, as societies become more stratified, it is argued that it becomes necessary for those who are economically advantaged to use the law as a means of maintaining and protecting their position. In Chambliss and Seidman's terms, "The more economically stratified a society becomes, the more it becomes necessary for the dominant groups in the society to enforce through coercion the norms of conduct which guarantee their supremacy." From this viewpoint, the connection between law and morality is partial, both in the sense that the enforcement of morality is selective and in the sense that the morality enforced will be to the advantage of one group over another. In particular, this viewpoint notes that it is the alleged immorality of the poor that is much more likely to be called "criminal" than the presumed immorality of the rich. "What this means in modern times," writes Richard Quinney, "is that there is a moral basis to capitalism, a morality that supports the interests of the ruling class and, at the same time, underlies the legal system that maintains the prevailing social and economic order." Like Mill, then, those who see law as a product of conflict are usually wary of the attempt to link conventional morality closely to the law. When the closeness of this tie is preserved, they note, it is usually to the disadvantage of the less advantaged. We will have much more to say about this perspective in

later parts of this chapter. Our purpose here is simply to present these viewpoints, not to arbitrate between them.

PRIVATE MORALITY AND THE PUBLIC INTEREST

A second dimension of the debated link between law and morality involves the thin line that may divide considerations of private morality and the societal interest. The problem is that while many matters that could be considered only issues of private morality, including some kinds of drug use, prostitution, and pornography, may have their most direct and immediate effects on the individuals who pursue them, there may nonetheless be less direct but no less significant effects on surrounding communities and their members. A particularly poignant illustration of this point is provided by Donald Clairmont in his description of the development of a "deviance service center"—a whole community adjacent to Halifax, Nova Scotia, that was given the "functional autonomy" to provide a whole range of illicit services to the adjoining city.

Clairmont notes that this community, called "Africville" by its residents, was founded around 1850 by the descendants of refugee blacks who fled slavery in the United States during the War of 1812. Initially, Africville was a viable community with a few fine houses, some small-scale businesses, plenty of space, and a strong community spirit based on a stable kinship system. However, Africville soon began to experience the problems of a sluggish surrounding economy, and this, combined with two other factors, led to its development as a deviance service center. The first of these factors was that Africville was located close to the adjoining city's dockyards and port activity. The second factor was that the city's ruling circles gave the community the functional autonomy to develop an alternative economy: "that is, not sharing fairly in society's wealth, they . . . [were] allowed by the authorities a range of behavior, that would not be countenanced elsewhere." These two factors came together during World War I when visiting seamen added to the clientele of an expanding bootlegging trade. Fearing growing crime problems and the ultimate demise of their community, residents of Africville petitioned the city council of Halifax in 1919, requesting police surveillance and protection. However, no police assistance was provided, and in the period that followed World War I, Africville continued to grow as a deviance service center. Gradually, bootlegging gave way to more hazardous forms of deviance, and, as the younger and better educated members of the community began to leave, the fears of the petitioners of 1919 eventually were confirmed. The entire community was finally designated for harbor development and urban renewal nearly a half century later. This meant that the problems of the community finally were "solved," literally, through demolition, and the few remaining residents were "relocated."

It can be argued that the problems that residents of Africville experienced would not have existed if the deviant services provided were not illegal elsewhere and therefore concentrated in that particular community. There is no clear way of evaluating how valid this argument may be. Nonetheless, this example makes it clear that the pursuit of "disreputable pleasures" can have consequences beyond the individuals who are immediately involved.

THE (IN)EFFECTIVENESS OF LAW AS AN INSTRUMENT OF MORALITY

Aside from the issue of whether the law *should* try to control private morality, there is additionally the question of whether the law *can* do so. Social scientists and students of the law have long been skeptical about what the law itself can do. Sumner asserts that the mores of a society always take precedence over the law and that it is impossible to change the mores "by any artifice or device, to a great extent, or

suddenly, or in any essential element." Similarly, Sutherland and Cressey argue that "when the mores are adequate, laws are unnecessary; when the mores are inadequate the laws are ineffective." In other words, laws that are unsupported by widely shared moral beliefs are unlikely to accomplish what their legal architects would wish. This is particularly true of crimes of private morality. In addition, it is difficult to get the information and evidence necessary to control such behaviors, not only because the behaviors are not widely and/or harshly enough condemned to generate public cooperation but also because they customarily take place with some measure of privacy and because they are often only known to the persons whose behavior is involved. These problems are most notable at the level of police enforcement.

Skolnick makes this point in his study of a police department on the west coast of the United States. Skolnick notes that the narcotics officers of a police force often play a very central, although often corrupting, role in departmental operations. This is because the character of their work makes narcotics officers an important source of information and influence. To begin, narcotics offenses, like other crimes of private morality, rarely involve victim-complainants. As a result, information and evidence must be obtained in other ways, including the use of informers, entrapment techniques, and undercover work. Each of these techniques is potentially corrupting: the use of informers involves questionable use of cash and drugs as inducements; entrapment techniques can encourage crimes that might otherwise never occur; and undercover work provokes tempting possibilities for bribery and collusion. Nonetheless, in the course of these types of activities, narcotics officers develop sources of information that are important not only to the prosecution of narcotics cases but for other kinds of cases as well. Thus, narcotics officers become central actors in police departments, valuable to prosecutors and to other officers. Among the results of this type of law enforcement are ineffective efforts to control drug use and the corruption of narcotics and related areas of policing. In sum, crimes without complaints are difficult, if not impossible, to control. Worse still, however, efforts to control such crimes often corrupt the controllers.

LAW, MORALITY, AND THE CREATION OF CRIME

A final concern about using the law to control private morality involves the implications for persons whose behaviors are controlled. There are some alarming indications that attempts to legally control private morality have the unfortunate tendency of creating permanent classes of deviants, who must organize their lives around criminal roles. The best example of this involves the problems of drug addicts. Well into the second decade of this century, addicts in America were able to buy most opiates across the drug counter. One result was that "our grandmothers used many home remedies and patent medicines whose ingredients would shock us today." Coincidentally, early surveys of opiate drug addicts in America reveal that the majority of addicts were white women. The watershed event that changed this pattern was the passage of the Harrison Act in 1914. While it was originally only a tax measure, the effect of this law and its enforcement by the federal Bureau of Narcotics was gradually to make opiate addiction a crime. The result was the emergence of a black market in drugs and the development of a whole new sector of the criminal underworld. Opiate addiction, therefore, shifted from being acceptable and respectable to being criminal and disreputable in a rather brief period of time, and the involvement of individuals in this world shifted as well. Cuskey et al. note that "in many ways the period from pre–Civil War to immediate post–World War I was like a film negative of the present." White American women substituted the use of various legal painkillers, barbitu-rates, and amphetamines for the newly illegal opium. At the same time, black American men, gradually, and in increasing numbers, were pulled into this criminal underworld, a world that proved extremely difficult to leave. Access to the drug required increasing amounts of money, which usually could only be obtained through crime, and access to medical treatment became very difficult to obtain. Drug addiction became stereotyped as a black American problem that was to be the subject of policing more than treatment. The persistence of this crime problem and the scale of the other kinds of criminal activities associated with it are ominous indications that making a form of behavior criminal can create as many, and sometimes more, problems than it can solve.

VICTIMLESS CRIME AND THE LIMITS OF LAW

Because of the above kinds of concerns, social scientists and students of law have spent considerable time and effort trying to draw an effective line between the aspects of private morality that should and should not be made a part of the criminal law. One of the best known of these efforts involves Edwin Schur's discussion of "victimless crimes." "Crimes without victims," Schur writes, "may be limited to those situations in which one person obtains from another in a fairly direct exchange, a commodity or personal service which is socially disapproved and legally proscribed." After considering several victimless crimes (e.g., abortion, homosexuality, and drug addiction) in detail, and after weighing a number of the dimensions of the link between law and morality, Schur argues that public education about the problems of enforcing these laws, and the possibility of reforming them, is needed. Schur does not argue that all criminal laws relating to these crimes should immediately be abolished. In fact, he concludes that "legalization is not automatically or invariably to be preferred to criminalization."

A more provocative position is taken by Morris and Hawkins in their book, *The Honest Politician's Guide to Crime Control*. Morris and Hawkins argue that there is an "overreach of the criminal law" that contributes to the larger "crime problem" in the following ways that echo and extend our earlier discussion:

1. Where the supply of goods or services is concerned, such as narcotics, gambling, and prostitution, the criminal law operates as a "crime tariff" which makes the supply of such goods and services profitable for the criminal by driving up prices and, at the same time, discourages competition by those who might enter the market were it legal.

2. This leads to the development of large-scale, organized criminal groups which, as in the field of legitimate business, tend to extend and diversify their operations, thus financing and promoting other criminal activities.

3. The high prices which criminal prohibition and law enforcement help to maintain have a secondary criminogenic effect in cases where demand is inelastic, as for narcotics, by causing persons to resort to crime to obtain the money to pay the prices.

4. The proscription of a particular form of behavior (e.g., homosexuality, prostitution, drug addiction) by the criminal law drives those who engage or participate in it into association with those engaged in other criminal activities and leads to the growth of an extensive criminal subculture, which is subversive of social order generally. It also leads, in the case of drug addiction, to endowing a pathological condition with the romantic glamour of a rebellion against authority or some sort of elitist enterprise.

5. The expenditure of police and criminal justice resources involved in attempting to enforce statutes in relation to sexual behavior, drug taking, gambling, and other matters of private morality seriously depletes the time, energy, and number of personnel available for dealing with the types of crime involving violence and stealing, which are the primary concern of the criminal justice system. This diversion and overextension of resources results both in failure to deal adequately

with current serious crime and, because of the increased chances of impunity, in encouraging further crime.

6. These crimes lack victims, in the sense of complainants asking for the protection of the criminal law. Where such complainants are absent, it is particularly difficult for the police to enforce the law. Bribery tends to flourish; political corruption of the police is invited. It is peculiarly with reference to the victimless crimes that the police are led to employ illegal means of law enforcement.

Based on these arguments, Morris and Hawkins conclude that a range of behaviors should be decriminalized. They suggest that public drunkenness should cease to be a crime; that neither the acquisition, purchase, possession, nor use of any drug should be a criminal offense; that no form of gambling should be prohibited by criminal law; that vaguely stated disorderly conduct and vagrancy laws should be replaced; that private sexual activities between consenting adults should not be subject to criminal law; and that juvenile courts should only retain jurisdiction over adolescents for conduct that would be criminal if committed by adults. This is obviously a sweeping set of changes. We offer these proposals here not because we believe they should all necessarily be adopted, but because they illustrate the point that what is to be called "criminal" is open to review and reform.

Thus, the significance of the debates and proposals we have been considering is the possibility they represent for contraction and expansion in conceptions of the proper content of criminal law. It is precisely this potential for variable content that poses problems for social scientists who wish to define crime for the purposes of identifying the subject matter of their work. On the one hand, it might seem desirable to simply confine our attention, and therefore our definition of crime, to what is called "criminal" in any particular jurisdiction. On the other hand, it is desirable that we remain sensitive within and between jurisdictions to the shifting divisions between what is called "criminal" and what is not, and why. This may be more apparent when it is noted that thus far in this chapter we have only considered this problem as it relates to our own culture, conveniently even ignoring the fact that each American state has its own criminal code, with significant variation between states in what is called "criminal." Our view is that the only effective way of responding to the problem of variability is to conceptualize crime as a specific instance of a broader range of deviant behavior.

QUESTIONS FOR DISCUSSION AND WRITING

1. What two answers are given to the question regarding the origin of law?
2. What do sociologists like Sumner, Sutherland, and Cressey believe about the effectiveness of criminal law to regulate morality?
3. How can law "create" crime?

CRIMINOLOGICAL HISTORY

Historical Explanations of Crime: From Demons to Politics

C. RONALD HUFF

M AN's historical concern with the existence of crime has been reflected in his diverse attempts to explain how and why crime occurs. Long before there was a scientific approach to the crime problem, there were speculative "explanations" of criminal behavior. Some of these earlier views concerning the nature of crime may seem absurd according to contemporary standards, but they must be viewed as symbolic expressions of the prevailing ideas and concerns of their own era. Similarly, it would be surprising if our currently fashionable theories of crime are not viewed as naive and unsophisticated in the next century.

Before discussing the major historical explanations of crime, it seems appropriate to ask what, if any, relevance such a discussion can have for students of criminology and criminal justice. While intellectual inquiry is justifiable for its own sake, the current discussion has contemporary relevance in at least two ways: (1) it presents an overview of the development of criminological theory, which should permit a greater understanding of con-

temporary explanations and their place in the continuity of thought on the subject of crime; and (2) since society's responses to crime depend, to a large extent, on its theories and its assumptions about the nature of crime, an understanding of those views is useful in attempting to analyze the numerous attempts to "prevent . . . control," "deter," "cure," or otherwise contain criminal behavior. The operations of the various components of the criminal justice system (such as the police, the courts, and the prisons) can perhaps best be viewed by understanding the various assumptions which underlie their policies and procedures. Every major theory, explanation, or assumption about the nature and causes of crime may be viewed as having important implications for the strategies of social control which society elects to implement. The following discussion examines the existence of such connections between theory and practice.

SUPERNATURAL EXPLANATIONS

Primitive man's basic explanation of "criminal" behavior was that of diabolical possession. Criminal behavior was viewed as evidence that the culprit was under the control of evil spirits, or demons. This view of deviant behavior was simply an extension of the

From *Crime and the Criminal Justice Process* (pp. 208–220) by C. R. Huff, 1978, Dubuque, Iowa: Kendall Hunt Publishing Company. Edited by J. Inciardi and K. Haas. Copyright © 1978 by Kendall Hunt Publishing Company. Reprinted by permission of James A. Inciardi.

prevailing view of nature—that is, that every object or being was controlled by spiritual forces. Obviously, such an explanation requires *belief or faith,* since it does not lend itself to scientific verification. Nevertheless, demonology had important implications for man's responses to crime.

Given such an explanation of crime, the only sensible solution was to try to exorcise the demons which were responsible for the behavior or, failing that, to do away with the criminal, either by exile or by execution. In a society where the gods were perceived as omnipotent and omnipresent, it was clearly a matter of the highest priority to appease them, no matter what the costs. Thus, the fate of the criminal was less related to the protection of society than to compliance with the will of the gods. The failure of the group to punish the wrongdoer was believed to leave the tribe open to the wrath and vengeance of the gods. As the noted historian and criminologist Harry Elmer Barnes noted:

Not only does this transgression of the customary code expose the offending individual to untold woes, but it also renders his whole social group liable to the vengeance of the gods, for in early days, responsibility is collective from the standpoint of both the natural and supernatural world. In primitive society a crime and a sin are practically identical. Hence, to supplement the individual fear of violating the prescribed modes of conduct on account of danger from unseen powers, there is the certain knowledge on the part of the offender that his group will summarily avenge themselves upon him for rendering it open to destruction from the intervention of both human and spiritual forces. . . . [T]he most generally accepted way of wiping out a crime and sin in primitive society is "to wipe out the sinner."

One who violated the norms dealing with endogamy, witchcraft, or treason was likely to receive the harshest punishment in primitive society. The offender might be hacked to pieces, exiled, or even eaten. All three of these sanctions accomplished the same goal—the

removal of the offender from the group. Offenses of a private, rather than public, nature were generally dealt with by the victim's clan through the process known as "blood feud." Essentially, it was the duty of each member of a clan to avenge a fellow clan member. The principle which guided this pursuit of retaliation was the well-known *lex talionis* ("an eye for an eye and a tooth for a tooth"). The idea of *lex talionis,* roughly, was that the punishment should fit the crime. Primitive obsession with making the retaliation exact was in some cases so fanatical that inanimate objects which had been instrumental in accidental deaths were actually "punished."

There was very little use of any form of incarceration in primitive society, except for periods of detention while awaiting disposition and the incarceration related to cannibalistic practices. The only other major type of punishment did not appear until the late stages of primitive society. It was a form of compensation or restitution. This practice developed in response to the failure of blood feud as a method of criminal justice. Blood feuds all too often resulted in prolonged vendettas which exacted heavy tolls on both sides. The practice of paying a fixed monetary penalty therefore evolved as an alternative to the potentially genocidal blood feuds. Later, in the feudal period, the extended families or clans established a system of *wergeld* (man-money) by which the victim's status determined the amount assessed against the offender. This concept was gradually broadened to include differences in degree of responsibility, the individualization of responsibility, and even a distinction between "intent" and "accident." Eventually, a specified value was set for each *type* of offense, and the system of restitutive fines paid by the offender to the victim came to be preferred over the blood feud. With the subsequent development of an appeal procedure whereby either party could protest an injustice, the roots of the modern-day court system emerged in embryonic form. Finally, through the absolute authority which accompanied kingships, especially in early *historic* society and during feudalism, all crimes became "crimes against the king's peace"; in other words, crimes came to be regarded as offenses against the *public* welfare. At that point, man had, in a sense, come "full circle" in his efforts to rationalize law and punishment:

The heavy fines imposed on places and people became an important source of revenue to the crown and to the barons and the lords of manors.

The State was growing strong enough to take vengeance; the common man was no longer feared as had been the well-armed Saxon citizen of old, and to the "common" criminal was extended the ruthless severity once reserved for the slaves . . . and the idea of compensation began to wane before the revenge instinct now backed by power.

RATIONALISM AND FREE WILL

Just as demonological explanations dominated the thinking of early man, the so-called classical period of criminology (roughly, 1700–1800) was characterized by its own conceptions of the nature of man. Man was seen as being rational, having free will, and seeking that which would be most productive of pleasure or happiness. Such views, of course, represented a significant departure from the idea that man was under the control of supernatural forces and that criminal behavior was a function of demons. For an understanding of the magnitude of this shift in thinking during the eighteenth century, it is best to examine the ideas of the two most influential contributors to classical criminology—Cesare Beccaria and Jeremy Bentham.

Beccaria, who was influenced by French rationalism and humanitarianism, strongly attacked the arbitrary and inconsistent "criminal justice" practices of the mid-eighteenth century. In his major work, Beccaria reacted against the secret accusations, inhumane punishments, and lack of concern for the defendant's rights that characterized criminal justice. He articulated the framework of what came to be known as the classical school of

criminology, that is, (1) that the motivation underlying all social action must be the utilitarian value of that action (the greatest happiness for the greatest number); (2) that crime is an injury to *society* and can only be measured by assessing the extent of that injury (focus on the act and the extent of damage, not intent); (3) that the prevention of crime is more important than its punishment; (4) that secret accusations and torture should be eliminated and the trial process ought to be speedy and the accused treated fairly and humanely throughout the process; (5) that the only valid purpose of punishment is deterrence, not social revenge; and (6) that incarceration should be used more widely, but at the same time, conditions for those confined must be vastly upgraded and systems of classification developed to prevent haphazardly mixing all types of inmates.

Beccaria had enormous influence on the reformation of criminal justice. For example, he proposed that the courts should mete out punishments to the offender in direct proportion to the harm caused by the crime. To accomplish this, it was necessary that all crimes be classified according to some assessment of their social harm and, further, that the penal codes must prescribe for each crime exact penalties that would be useful deterrents to crime:

A scale of crimes may be formed of which the first degree should consist of those which immediately tend to the dissolution of society; and the last, of the smallest possible injustice done to a private member of society. Between those extremes will be comprehended all actions contrary to the public good, which are called criminal. . . . Any action which is not comprehended in the above mentioned scale, will not be called a crime, or punished as such.

One need only observe the deliberations of state legislatures today during the process of revising a state's criminal code to understand and appreciate the lasting effect which Beccaria has had on our criminal laws. The arguments and considerations of lawmakers today are, for the most part, still influenced by this concept of the criminal as a rational person who acts as a result of free will on a pleasure-seeking basis. Contemporary punishments prescribed by the law are generally well defined, even though they are administered in a very inexact manner. And the widespread belief that the enactment of laws is the best method of social control clearly has at least some of its intellectual roots in the work of Beccaria.

Several of Beccaria's other ideas have contemporary significance. Perhaps the most notable of these is his assertion that the speed and certainty of punishment, rather than its severity, are the most critical factors in deterrence. The modern criminal justice system, characterized by broad discretion on the part of the police, prosecutors, judges, guards, and parole boards; discrimination against the poor and minorities; court delays and months of pretrial detainment; and the use of plea bargaining, offers neither swiftness nor certainty. Furthermore, Beccaria's advocacy of the humane treatment of incarcerated offenders has certainly never been fully realized. Indeed, many contemporary reformers claim that we have largely replaced corporal punishment with psychological and social persecution.

Jeremy Bentham, a contemporary of Beccaria, was also a major figure in utilitarian social philosophy, and he proposed that all acts must be evaluated so that "the greatest happiness for the greatest number" results. To make such assessments, one would obviously need some method of calculation; Bentham happened to have just such a method. His "felicity calculus" was a superficial, quasi-mathematical attempt to quantify the utility of all conceivable acts. Humorous in retrospect, his attempt to catalogue the almost infinite varieties of behavior was nevertheless understandable, given the uncertainties of the criminal justice system he was attempting to reform.

Bentham's theory of human motivation—that man pursues pleasure and tries to avoid pain—led him to argue that criminal penalties should prescribe a degree of punishment (pain) just sufficient to offset the potential gains (pleasure) of criminal behavior, so that the net result (negative utility) would be deterrence. Bentham further believed that the punishment should "fit the crime," and he generally seemed to favor restitution over physical punishment. Given Bentham's concept of deterrence, punishment in general was regarded as a necessary evil intended to prevent greater harm or evil.

The social control philosophy that characterized classical criminology, then, was based on the assumption that the would-be criminal could be deterred by the threat of punishment if that punishment was swift, certain, appropriate for the offense, and sufficiently unpleasant to offset any potential gains to be realized by committing the act. These principles were advocated by classicists across the entire range of available punishments, whether they involved the loss of money, the loss of freedom, or the loss of life. The impact of classical criminology on the penal codes remains clear, even though in actual practice much of the vagueness and arbitrary abuse of discretion remains problematic.

Despite the anticipated ability to administer the principles of the classical school, the fact was that enforcement and implementation were quite problematic. Especially controversial was the classical position that individual differences and particular situations were irrelevant in assigning responsibility. The focus on the act committed, rather than on any characteristics or qualities of the person, came to be regarded as imprudent as did the practice of treating persons who clearly were incompetent, for various reasons, as competent solely because of commission of a given act. These principles were criticized strongly because they did not promote justice anywhere except on paper, in an abstract sort of way.

The idealized concept of justice held by the classicists, perhaps best symbolized by the familiar image of a blindfolded Lady Justice holding scales in her hand, was regarded by neoclassical revisionists (1800–1876) as too impersonal and rigid. The classical theorists, in their indignation over the inconsistencies and other inadequacies of the criminal justice system, had overreacted. They had designed a system which was so dispassionate and "objective" that it could not deliver justice to a society of human beings not identical to one another.

The neoclassicists were successful in introducing some modifications of the free-will doctrine. Criminological thought was revised to readmit some determinism—not the magical, supernatural determinism of demonology, but rather an awareness that certain factors could operate to impair one's reason and thereby mitigate personal responsibility to an extent. While retaining the essential positions articulated by the classicists, considerations involving individual differences began to appear during the neoclassical period. Age, mental status, physical condition, and other factors which could alter one's ability to discern right from wrong were acknowledged grounds for a decision of partial responsibility.

Far from regarding their views as a general theory of human behavior, the neoclassicists were actually focusing on what they viewed as a small minority of the population. There was no attempt to assert that all persons (not even all criminals) are partially shaped and controlled by deterministic forces. On the contrary, neoclassicists continued to view man as a rational, pleasure-seeking being who was personally responsible for his behavior except in abnormal circumstances or in the case of children who were not old enough to know right from wrong.

The neoclassical revisions outlined above meant that criminology had developed a dominant theoretical perspective that viewed man as essentially rational and behavior as volitional, but allowed for some mitigation of responsibility under certain circumstances. This theoretical framework provided the foundation for many legal systems, including that of the United States. The implications for sentencing and for the criminal justice system included the recognition that a particular sentence could have different effects on different offenders and an awareness that the prison environment could affect the future criminality of the offender. This allowed for much more flexibility than did the classical school in determining the appropriate punishment. Many recent "reforms" in penology, such as probation, parole, suspended sentences, and many programs designed for certain "types" of offenders, would be inconsistent with the classical emphases on uniformity and certainty of punishment.

DETERMINISM

A book written in 1876 by an Italian psychiatrist was to provide the impetus necessary to shift the focus of criminology from the crime to the criminal. The book was called *The Criminal Man*, and its author was Cesare Lombroso; the result was the development of the "positive school" in criminology. Lacking the moralistic tones of the earliest positivist Auguste Comte, Lombroso's approach was clearly Darwinian, focusing on biological determinism.

As the title of his classic book implies, Lombroso believed that there was indeed a criminal type, or "born criminal," who was discernibly different from noncriminals in physical ways. In short, he was convinced that criminals bore bodily stigmata which marked them as a separate class of people. Following Darwin's monumental work by less than two decades, Lombrosian theory postulated that criminals had not fully evolved but were, instead, inferior organisms reminiscent of ape-like, preprimitive man, incapable of adapting to modern civilization. Specifically, Lombroso described the criminal as "atavistic" (a concept used earlier by Darwin) in that the criminal was physically characteristic of a lower phylogenetic level. From his extensive physical measurements, autopsy findings, and other observations, Lombroso concluded that criminals disproportionately possessed an asymmetrical cranium, prognathism (excessive jaw), eye defects, oversized ears, prominent cheekbones, abnormal palate, receding forehead, sparse beard, woolly hair, long arms, abnormal dentition, twisted nose, fleshy and swollen lips, and inverted sex organs. He also noted such non-physical anomalies as a lack of morality, excessive vanity, cruelty, and tattooing.

It would be misleading to imply that Lombroso held firmly to the idea that his was the sole explanation for crime. While continuing to believe that his theory explained part of the difference between criminals and noncriminals, Lombroso ultimately accepted environmental and other factors as equally valid contributing causes of crime.

While positivism, since Lombroso's day, has taken in a lot of intellectual territory, there remains a unifying framework that is visible in the work of his successors. That general framework consists of the following:

1. A general rejection of metaphysical and speculative approaches.
2. Denial of the "free-will" conception of man and substitution of a "deterministic" model.
3. A clear distinction between science and law, on one hand, and morals, on the other.
4. The application, as far as practicable, of the scientific method.

These principles of positivism have been applied to the study of the criminal from various and diverse theoretical perspectives. Although these perspectives differ in significant ways, they retain the essence of positivism as described above. The theories to be discussed range from purely individualistic approaches to more macrolevel, sociological theories.

The "Italian School"

The origins of positivism in criminology have a decidedly Italian character. Besides Lombroso, the other Italian pioneers in this school of thought were Enrico Ferri and Raffaele Garofalo. Although emphasizing different points as critical in the study of the criminal, both Ferri and Garofalo were adamant in their espousal of, and adherence to, the positivist approach.

Enrico Ferri, a pupil of Lombroso, is perhaps best known for his classification of criminals as insane, born, occasional, habitual, and drawn to criminality as a result of passion. This topology of offenders represented an attempt by Ferri to conceptualize in anthropological categories the continuum of criminality. He believed that the differences between categories were differences of degree and of the danger represented for society.

The third member of the "Italian school," Raffaele Garofalo, attempted to construct a universal definition of crime—one that would be based on the concept of "natural crime," or acts that offend the basic moral sentiments of pity (a revulsion against the voluntary infliction of suffering on others) and probity (respect for the property rights of others). Garofalo's approach to the crime problem was primarily psychological and legal. He perceived some criminals as psychological degenerates who were morally unfit. His background as a jurist led him to advocate reforms in the criminal justice system so that the criminal could be dealt with in a manner more in line with his theory. Garofalo believed that the criminal must be eliminated, citing Darwin's observations on the functions of biological adaptation as a rationale for this "remedy." Since, according to this bio-organismic analogy, the criminal was one who had not adapted to civilized life, Garofalo saw only three alternatives—all of which involved some type of elimination: (1) death, where there is a permanent psychological defect; (2) partial elimination for those suitable to live only in a more primitive environment, including long-term or life imprisonment, transportation, and relatively mild isolation; and (3) enforced reparation, for those whose crimes were committed as a result of the press of circumstances.

Physical-Biological Theories

The prototype for all physical-biological theories of crime were the early (and nonpositivist), craniologists-phrenologists, who believed that the "faculties of the mind" were revealed by the external shape of the skull. This vastly oversimplified and pseudoscientific approach nevertheless predates all other theories of a physical-biological nature.

Such theories have grown increasingly sophisticated and scientific since those earliest attempts to explain man's function by analyzing his cranial structure. In addition to the Italian school, there have been a number of other intellectual contributions to this physical-biological tradition.

Charles Goring has been widely credited with refuting Lombroso's contention that there is a criminal "physical type." However, Goring's critique was aimed at Lombroso's methodology, not necessarily his theory or his conclusions, for which Goring had a certain affinity. In Goring's famous book, *The English Convict*, he presented an analysis of 3,000 English convicts, and as a matter of fact, he did find what he regarded as a positive association between certain physical differences and the offender's crime and social class. As Mannheim noted:

In the controversy "heredity or environment" . . . he was on Lombroso's side, and perhaps even more than the latter he was inclined to underrate environmental influences: "Crime is only to a trifling extent (if to any) the product of social inequalities, of adverse environment or of other manifestations of . . . the force of circumstances."

Goring's general interpretation of the height and weight deficiencies of the criminal population he studied was that the criminal suffered from hereditary inferiority. He also believed that criminals were most different from noncriminals with respect to their intelligence, which he found to be defective. Finally, Goring added a third category—that of moral defec-

tiveness—to account for those whose criminality could not be explained by either of the first two factors. But the main thrust of Goring's theoretical position was a physiological one, thus placing him within this tradition of thought.

Not everyone agreed that Goring's criticisms of Lombroso's methodology were valid. The leading skeptic was Earnest Hooton, an anthropologist at Harvard University. In *The American Criminal*, Hooton presented data and interpretations based on a twelve-year study of 13,873 criminals and 3,203 noncriminals. After analyzing 107 physical characteristics, Hooton concluded that criminals, when compared with the control group, were "organically inferior." Describing their distinctive characteristics, he included low foreheads, high pinched nasal roots, compressed faces, and narrow jaws. These he cited as evidence for his assertion of organic inferiority, and he attributed crime to "the impact of environment upon low grade human organisms."

Hooton also constructed a topology of criminals based on physical constitution. He argued that murderers and robbers tended to be tall and thin; tall, heavy men were most likely to be killers and to commit forgery and fraud as well; undersized men were disposed to commit assault, rape, and other sex crimes; and men lacking any notable physical characteristics had no criminal specialty. The primary problem with all of this is that Hooton had considered only the offender's *current* crime, whereas in fact half or more of Hooton's prisoners had previously been imprisoned for an offense *other than* that noted by Hooton.

Studies by Ernst Kretschmer and William Sheldon are typical of the work of more recent proponents of the constitutional inferiority-body type theorists. Although differing in the details of their approaches, both men advocated the idea that body type and temperament are closely related. Both developed topologies relating body types to certain forms of behavior, including crime.

Some investigators have focused specifically on the effects of heredity, especially genetic deficiencies, in producing criminality. In this regard, the studies of "criminal families" were quite interesting. Perhaps the most well-known efforts along these genealogical lines were those of Richard Dugdale and Henry Goddard, both of whom attempted to analyze the apparently excessive criminality of entire families by relating it to feeblemindedness. The term *mental testers* has often been applied to this method of inquiry.

More recently, another line of inquiry has focused on the criminality of twins. Lange, Rosanoff, Christiansen, and others have studied twins in an attempt to determine the effect of heredity in producing criminality. The basic idea has been that if a greater percentage of monozygotic ("identical") twins than of dizygotic ("fraternal") twins are concordant in being criminal, that is, if they are both criminal, then the effect of heredity would, theoretically at least, have to be given greater weight than other factors. Although the methodological criticisms aimed at Rosanoff have been less damaging than those directed at Lange, the fact remains that neither study can be regarded as conclusive in finding that identical twins are far more likely to be concordant in terms of criminality.

Finally, some of the most sophisticated research employing a physical-biological model has been focused on the neuroendocrine system. The essential proposition of these theories has been that criminal behavior is often due to emotional disturbances produced by glandular imbalance. Often using the electroencephalogram (EEG) as a diagnostic aid, this biochemical approach to crime thus far offers more promise than clear-cut and unequivocal findings.

was, of course, Sigmund Freud. His work, along with that of his intellectual successors, has focused on man's unconscious. The explanation for criminal behavior which grew out of this approach was that such behavior is largely the result of drives which are uncontrolled because of a defective personality structure. There are a seemingly endless number of applications of psychoanalytic theory to crime. Conditions such as psychosis and neurosis have been related to criminal behavior by psychoanalysts, as have most forms of deviant behavior. The essential contention of the psychoanalytic approach is that all behavior is purposive and meaningful. Such behavior is viewed as the symbolic release of repressed mental conflict. From this perspective, the criminal is one who acts not out of free will, as the classicists believed, but as an expression of deterministic forces of a subconscious nature. Such a view, of course, leads to a theory of social control based on a clinical model of therapeutic rehabilitation.

A derivation of the psychoanalytic approach and the "mental testers" has been the emphasis on personality deviation as an explanation for crime. Relying on theoretical constructs of the "healthy" personality and the "abnormal" personality, the personality deviation approach has become increasingly popular, though not well validated. Using psychological tests such as the Rorschach, the Wechsler Adult Intelligence Scale, the Minnesota Multiphasic Personality Inventory, the Thematic Apperception Test, and many others, psychologists have led in this attempt to construct causal theory. Advocates of this approach generally attempt to diagnose the psychopathological features of one's personality and then focus on these "target areas" using a variety of interventions.

Psychopathology

A number of positivist theories of crime have used the paradigm based on individual psychopathology. The father of this approach

Economic Factors

The effects of economic inequality are undeniably instrumental in producing great variability in one's "life chances." The pervasive day-to-day realities of poverty limit the chances of millions of people in securing adequate health care, housing, education, jobs, and opportunities. The crippling effects of poverty can hardly be comprehended by those not confronted with them on a daily basis. For these and related reasons, some theorists have attempted to relate at least some crimes to economic inequality. Such a theoretical position has had a special attraction for Marxists.

Historically, the most extensive application of Marxist theory to criminology was provided by Willem Bonger. The central argument Bonger made is that capitalism, more than any other system of economic exchange, is characterized by the control of the means of production by relatively few people, with the vast majority of the population totally deprived of these means. The economic subjugation of the masses, he argues, stifles men's "social instincts" and leads to unlimited egoism, insensitivity, and a spirit of domination on the part of the powerful, and the poor are subjected to all sorts of pathogenic conditions: bad housing, constant association with "undesirable," uncertain physical security, terrible poverty, frequent sickness, and unemployment. Bonger maintained that the historical condition of this class of people was severely damaged by these conditions of economic subjugation. He attempted to demonstrate connections between certain types of crime (e.g., prostitution, alcoholism, and theft) and economic inequality. This explanation of crime suggests that the socioeconomic system is causally related to crime and would have to be restructured to reduce crime.

Although Bonger did not deny the influence of hereditary traits, he attributed no causal power to them in the absence of criminogenic environmental conditions. Throughout most of his writings, he stressed a socioeconomic view of crime and attacked the views of Lombroso and others of a physical-biological persuasion. His deterministic approach, along with his application of quantitative methods and his rejection of metaphysical, speculative "explanations" for crime, places Bonger in the positivist

school, even though his primary focus was on the social structure, rather than the individual. Bonger's theory, which illustrates the economic approach to criminal etiology, is quite near the sociological approach in many ways, especially in its macrolevel focus on the structure of society.

Sociological Explanations

The economic depression of the 1930s and the social problems which accompanied it helped further an interest in socioeconomic factors related to crime. Not only the economic condition of the nation but also the seemingly disorganized condition of many areas of major American cities were causes for great concern on the part of those seeking explanations for crime. The so-called Chicago school dominated criminological thought for a number of years, focusing on a social disorganization model. Specifically, this school of thought held that the interstitial areas of our major cities (heavily populated at the time by immigrants) reflected a high degree of sociocultural heterogeneity. This, they believed, resulted in a breakdown in social organization and norms, which made deviant behavior much more commonplace. Using analogies based on plant ecology, the Chicago school believed that rapid social change in "natural areas" of the city was undermining the basic social controls of a stable cultural heritage.

The theoretical successor to the Chicago school and its social disorganization approach was the culture conflict perspective, best articulated by Thorsten Sellin. The essential contention of culture conflict theory is that crime results from the absence of one clear-cut, consensual model of normative behavior. The increasing conflict in norms that came with immigration and the rapid pluralization of our society provided the most fertile ground for culture conflict theory. Although still applicable in nations with significant levels of immigration (such as Israel), it has largely been replaced in the United States by other perspectives.

There have been several sociological theories of cultural transmission, each of which has stressed different dynamics. One, known generally as "subcultural theory," had its general intellectual origins in the work of Emile Durkheim, but was initially applied in the United States by Robert Merton. For Merton, the explanation for crime rested in the disjunction existing for many between culturally defined success goals and the institutionalized means available to meet those goals. For some, this discrepancy results in criminal behavior, according to Merton.

Elaborations of this same general statement were made later by Albert Cohen, who saw the subculture which developed from this disjunction as a negative one that attempted to invert society's success goals and create its own, more realistic goals; and by Richard Cloward and Lloyd Ohlin, who added the idea that illegitimate, as well as legitimate, opportunity structures were differentially accessible to individuals and that one could become either a criminal or a respected citizen, depending on which means were available.

Walter Miller offered an alternative view of the lower-class subculture. He saw it as essentially characterized by its own value system and goals, not perpetually seeking to emulate the higher strata to gain status. Crime, for Miller, was a function of the normal socialization occurring in the subculture.

Another type of cultural transmission theory is that of Edwin Sutherland. Known as differential association theory, it is essentially a learning theory suggestive of the earlier work of Gabriel Tarde, a French social psychologist.

Sutherland's theory was later modified by Daniel Glaser to take into account the perceived effect of the mass media and other methods of transmitting culture. Glaser's differential identification theory substituted for Sutherland's required personal interaction the following definition of the dynamics:

A person pursues criminal behavior to the extent that he identifies himself with real or imaginary persons from whose perspective his criminal behavior seems acceptable.

The foregoing presentation of positivism has been intended to provide an overview of the various types of theories comprising this school. No attempt has been made to be exhaustive, but merely illustrative. Numerous other theoretical and empirical contributions could have been discussed; however, the above provide a representative sampling of positivist thought. Unlike either the demonologists of the preclassical period or the classical advocates of a free-will, rational view of man, the positivists' concepts of causation were deterministic and antimetaphysical. Therefore, their theories of social control have also been vastly different. They have advocated change—change of the personality, of the economic system, of the social system. Each of the positivist perspectives on crime developed its own ideas of how to deal with the crime problem, and these "solutions" were, of course, of a physical-biological, psychiatric-psychological, or social-economic nature. Their effect on penal policy is perhaps best symbolized in the name changes of our prisons—from "penitentiaries" to "correctional institutions."

But positivism is not the final chapter of this story. More recent theoretical developments have tended to concentrate on crime as a phenomenon which is determined by factors such as societal reaction (labeling), a system of laws which disproportionately reflects the interests of the wealthy and the powerful, and/or a corrupt and corrupting political system which is itself viewed as producing crime and criminals.

THE NEW EMPHASIS: "THE SYSTEM"

If positivism shifted society's focus from the crime to the criminal, then clearly that focus has shifted again with the development of the labeling and conflict perspectives, and especially with the emergence of a "radical" criminology perspective in the United States. While these theories differ substantially in their interpretations of crime, one central feature which they have in common is their emphasis on the social and political systems as factors which help to generate the crime problem. Frequently, "the system" is identified as the "cause" of crime because of its unequal distribution of social and political power. Increasingly, the criminal is viewed as a victim—a victim of class struggle, racial discrimination, and other manifestations of inequality.

While there is, to be certain, some continuity between these relatively recent theories and some earlier sociological and economic perspectives, the general thrust of these new explanations is quite different. Most important, there is a much more pervasive political emphasis in current theoretical perspectives.

Labeling, Conflict, and Radical Perspectives

The labeling or "social reaction" approach to crime is reflected in the works of Becker, Lemert, Erikson, Kitsuse, and Schur. This approach represents a significant departure from the absolute determinism of the positivists. The essence of labeling theory is its assertion that crime is relative and is defined (and thus *created*) socially. The often-quoted statement of Howard Becker perhaps best sums up the approach:

Social groups create deviance by making the rules whose infraction constitutes deviance, and by applying those rules to particular people and labeling them as outsiders. From this point of view, deviance is not a quality of the act the person commits, but rather a consequence of the application by others of rules and sanctions to an "offender." The deviant is one to whom that label has successfully been applied; deviant behavior is behavior that people so label.

The labeling approach clearly shifts the focus of inquiry from the individual being labeled

and processed to the group and the system doing the labeling and processing.

Finally, recent contributions to what has been called "radical" or "critical" or "Marxist" criminology include Richard Quinney, Ian Taylor, Paul Walton, Jock Young, Anthony Platt, Barry Krisberg, and Herman and Julia Schwendinger. While there are some theoretical differences among these writers, they occupy common intellectual ground within this overview of the development of criminological theory. Their analysis of crime and social control, essentially Marxist in nature, is to be distinguished from the applications of conflict theory to criminology made by Austin Turk and other non-Marxian conflict theorists, as well as the positivist approach taken by the formal Marxist Willem Bonger.

The "radical Marxist" criminologists focus their analysis on the state as a political system controlled by the interests of the "ruling capitalist class," especially through the use of law as a tool to preserve existing inequalities. Much of the work of these theorists deals with the historical conditions of classes which they link, theoretically, with the development and differential enforcement of criminal law. They reject the traditional (functionalist) view that law reflects society's consensus on the norms and values which should control behavior; instead, they argue that law emerges from a conflict of competing interests and serves the interests of the elite "ruling class."

Turk, on the other hand, essentially continues the intellectual tradition of Ralf Dahrendorf and other non-Marxist conflict theorists who have analyzed crime as a result of conflict concerning the distribution of power and authority within society. Rather than isolating the economic system and the class structure related to it, this perspective takes a broader view of the structural factors which produce conflict.

The implications of these perspectives for a philosophy of social control and for the criminal justice system are dramatically different from those suggested by earlier theorists.

Again, the centrality of the political dimension is inescapable, whether one is discussing labeling theory, conflict theory, or "radical Marxist" theory. The labeling perspective, which emphasizes the discrepancy between actual criminal behavior and officially detected crime, is a societal reaction theory. It is not the deviance itself that is so important, but the way in which society reacts. This perspective generally is interpreted as advocating less intervention and less labeling of people as "criminal." The criminal justice system is viewed as one which exacerbates the problem of crime; therefore, that system should be reduced and made less powerful.

Conflict and radical Marxist theory also would suggest that there is a need for societal restructuring. However, from these perspectives the criminal justice system merely reflects broader structural arrangements (i.e., the economy, the class system, and/or the distribution of power and authority). Radical Marxists advocate the abolition of capitalism and the development of a socialist society. They tend to view anything less than that as piecemeal "liberal tinkering" with a fatally flawed system. The alternative conflict view would argue that the particular economic system (e.g., capitalism) is not the basic problem and that crime exists in noncapitalist states as well. Crime is viewed as a structural problem resulting from the distribution of power and authority and as a reflection of unstable relationships between legal authorities and subjects.

In conclusion, it should be apparent that while man's attempts to explain crime have covered a tremendous range of ideas, there are parallels among these ideas. The idea that crime is a result of demonic possession is perhaps not a great deal different than the "mental illness" explanation advanced at a much later point in history. Both are largely deterministic, even though one is "magical" and the other "scientific."

Similarly, the rationales cited by the state for the use of imprisonment have varied from "moral reform" to "deterrence" to "rehabilitation," "public protection," and "punishment." Meanwhile, the perceptions of those imprisoned by the state have also changed, from passive acceptance of society's reaction to the increasing tendency to view themselves as "political prisoners" of an unjust legal and political system. It is apparent, therefore, that the linkage between theories of crime and social control philosophies must be evaluated on two levels: (1) the connections between theoretical explanations and formal policies, and (2) the changing rationales for employing essentially similar social control practices (e.g., "punitive" imprisonment vs. "therapeutic" correctional rehabilitation).

QUESTIONS FOR DISCUSSION AND WRITING

1. Why were offenders often executed in "primitive" societies?
2. What are six tenets advocated by Beccaria?
3. What assumption underlies classical criminology?

II

HOW DO WE VIEW CRIME?

Images of Crime and Criminality

IT is always interesting for the student of criminology to listen to news broadcasts, to read newspapers and magazines, or to listen to friends, family, or others when the topic is crime. The interest lies in the sometimes considerable distance between widely held perceptions about crime and the reality of crime revealed in criminological research. For instance, everyone "knows" that in the 1980s and 1990s, crime has been spiraling upward, a perception that has caused much hand-wringing among both the media and the public. But the available evidence portrays a different reality. Crime rates fluctuated between the mid-1970s and the 1990s, and the general crime trend has been fairly flat or downward.

Another widely held view is that "crime is everywhere and anyone can be a victim." Technically, this statement is true; it is hard to imagine anyone who is completely free of possible victimization. The statement is also misleading. It is used to argue that the nature of crime and victimization has changed dramatically, so that people, neighborhoods, and communities that used to be safe (generally those of relatively high socioeconomic status) are now in danger. Again, this assertion is inconsistent with what we know about crime. Research, both old and new, indicates that the nature of crime has not really changed very much. Those most likely to be the victims of crime tend to be similar to those who commit crimes, and they tend to live in the neighborhoods that have long had higher rates of crime and victimization.

"The reason we have crime problems in America is because we are soft on crime." Every reader has heard this statement from a politician in a recent election campaign. Unlike the first two examples, however, we cannot tell you that most criminologists would disagree with this assertion, or that the gulf between perception and reality is wide and clearly visible. This statement has provoked interesting and sometimes heated conversations among criminologists. Combatants on both sides of the debate agree, however, that the "soft on crime" argument is overly simplistic and hides important complexities that need to receive more attention in our public discourse about crime and punishment.

The point is that perceptions about crime and criminals do not always fit with the facts. Even incorrect or inaccurate perceptions are important because they affect how people behave in daily life, in making important choices such as where to live or go to school, or for whom to vote.

This section contains three articles that bear on perceptions and crime. In "Racial Composition of Neighborhood and Fear of Crime," Ted Chiricos, Michael Hogan, and Marc Gertz examine some of the factors that cause fear to increase. Most people would presume that the level of fear expressed by people in neighborhoods would be determined by the amount of crime that occurs in close proximity to them. What we find from the research reported in this article, however, is that fear of crime is determined less by the actual variation in crime across neighborhoods than it is by the racial makeup of the residents. More interestingly, Chiricos, Hogan, and Gertz find that it is not even the actual racial composition, but what residents—and in particular, white residents—perceive. When whites think that a lot of blacks live in their neighborhood, they are more likely to be afraid of crime. This study is a useful starting point because it highlights how our perception of crime, even our fear of crime, is not simply a consequence of crime or changes in crime. Other factors, such as perceptions of a stereotyped minority, affect fear independently of the actual amount of crime.

Philip Jenkins has written about a topic that is regularly a headline grabber—serial murder. An incredibly small portion of the already small group of people who are murdered each year are victims of serial killings, but few threats are as frightening as the knowledge that a serial killer is about. Jenkins has systematically studied the patterns of occurrence of serial homicides in the United States for the fifty-year period between 1940 and 1990. This is difficult to do, because police agencies cannot always agree on whether a homicide is part of a serial group of victimizations. Jenkins has used available data to conclude that serial killings have increased in the United States. However, we would caution readers not to become hermits hiding from the second coming of Ted Bundy. After all, it has been estimated that the chance of becoming a serial murder victim is less than that of being struck by lightning . . . twice. Besides, such a strategy is self-defeating, because anything short of complete isolation merely makes one a better target, because the support of family, neighbors, and friends can afford some protection against crime. The central question regarding serial murder is, What social changes have taken place that have caused this kind of crime to increase?

Another kind of "scare" is the subject of Craig Reinarman and Harry Levine's study of the role of politics and the media in our concern about crack cocaine. Reinarman and Levine offer evidence that there is not and was not a "crack problem" to the extent that the American public has been led to believe. The public perceptions about crack in the 1980s were similar to earlier "drug scares," including LSD in the late 1960s, marijuana in the 1930s, and gin in nineteenth-century Britain. We are left here with the question, If crack was not the problem that we were led to believe it was, why was it such a focus of public attention, and why did the federal government and many states spend millions of dollars on a war against this drug?

Criminologists may not have conclusive answers to the questions provoked by these articles. But the studies, the results they report, and the questions they leave us with make a convincing case for the importance of studying both the realities and the perceptions of "the crime problem." Students should take from these selections the lesson that how we perceive crime, and thus how we react to crime, is a complex combination of actual crime and other social factors. They should look for other examples in public and political debates in which the public is reacting to crime based on erroneous or flawed information and perceptions.

Racial Composition of Neighborhood and Fear of Crime

TED CHIRICOS

MICHAEL HOGAN

MARC GERTZ

B LALOCK'S seminal hypothesis linking "discrimination" against minorities to their relative proportion in a population was mediated by two presumed consequences of increasing minority presence—economic competition and a "power threat" to the majority group. In recent years, researchers have extended that hypothesis to interpret the relationship between racial composition and criminal justice activity—mediated substantially by the ostensible fear of crime (Fear) associated with minority males, especially black males.[1]

The mere *presence* of black males increasingly is identified with crime and the fear of crime in popular and political culture. In 1992, Senator Bill Bradley observed that "fear of black crime covers the streets like a sheet of ice." In 1993, the Rev. Jesse Jackson—in a speech decrying black-on-black crime—admitted feeling "relief" when the person walking up behind him on an isolated street is not a young black male. Jerome Miller argues that the "war on crime" has become "rhetorical code" for "locking up more and more black men."

Referring to the Rodney King beating, James Q. Wilson noted that "fear can produce

behavior that is indistinguishable from racism." He argues that

It is not racism that makes whites uneasy about blacks moving into their neighborhoods, it is fear. It is not racism that leads white parents to pull their children out of schools with many black students, it is fear. Fear of crime, of drugs, of gangs, of violence.

In this article we examine the widely assumed but seldom tested relationship between fear of crime and the racial composition of place. Interviews conducted with a random sample of adults ($N = 1,850$) residing in a major state capital in the early months of 1994—at the height of a media-driven panic about violent crime—are used to test the proposition that as the minority proportion of neighborhoods increases, so too will fear. We use objective and perceptual measures of racial composition, and we examine the effects of racial composition and minority status on fear of crime for black and white respondents. We distinguish between perceived safety or risk of victimization (Risk) and Fear, with the former used as an intervening variable in path models of fear of crime. . . .

This study measures Fear, rather than Risk, but we have taken several important ideas from previous studies linking perceived risk to racial composition. From Liska et al., we take the issue of victimization risk as a possible mediating factor between racial composition and fear. From Moeller, we take the approach of assessing *perceived* racial composition and a sensitivity to her conclusion that whites in predominantly black neighborhoods may be the most fearful. From Covington and Taylor, we borrow the issues of racial concentration and diversity as innovative additions to the standard approach to racial composition. We borrow, as well, the possibility that blacks and whites may be more fearful in neighborhoods where they are the minority race.

SAMPLE

Between January 1993 and January 1994, the percentage of Americans ranking crime/violence as the nation's foremost problem jumped from 9% to 49%. At the peak of that rising national concern—between January and March of 1994—we surveyed 1,850 adults in Tallahassee, Florida—a state featured prominently in media accounts of the purported burgeoning menace. Respondents were randomly chosen from adults (18 years or older) having the most recent birthday in households accessed by random digit dialing.[2]

The sampling frame—Leon County (1994 population: 212,107), where the state capital and two major state universities are located—was stratified by telephone trunk numbers to ensure proportional representation from all community areas. The demographics of the sample and sampling frame (in parentheses) are as follows: female, 57% (52%); black, 18% (24%); median age, 37 (29) years; median household income, $30,000 ($30,512) per year. The slight overrepresentation of women, white, and older respondents is not uncommon in telephone surveys.

DEPENDENT VARIABLE: FEAR OF CRIME

As suggested by Ferraro, Ferraro and LaGrange, Warr, and others, we operationalize Fear in a manner that is direct and crime specific. Respondents were asked,

On a scale of one to ten with ten representing the most fear and one representing the least fear, how much do you fear being robbed by someone who has a gun or knife . . . (someone breaking into your house to steal things; someone stealing your car; someone attacking you physically).

Three of the four items (robbery, assault, and burglary) were effectively combined into a Fear index with an alpha of .81 and this three-item index is employed as our measure of fear of crime.

INTERVENING VARIABLE: PERCEIVED VICTIMIZATION RISK

Victimization risk is a factor that Ferraro and Liska et al., among others, have shown to be a significant intervening variable in the relationship between Fear and other predictors. Liska's research, with cities as the unit of analysis, employed an objective measure of risk—the National Crime Survey rate of interracial robbery. Ferraro used an objective indicator of risk—Uniform Crime Report (UCR) crime rates by county for the respondents in his fear survey—and perceived risk as reported by those same respondents. In this analysis, because crime rates are unavailable on a neighborhood (census block) basis, we use a two-item measure of perceived risk (Risk): "How safe would you say you feel being out alone in your neighborhood at night? . . . (home alone at night)." Responses ranging from "very safe" (least risk) to "not at all safe" (most risk) were combined (alpha = .70) as an index of this concept.

INDEPENDENT VARIABLES

Racial composition of neighborhood is operationalized several ways. The first (PCTBLACK) is an objective measure based on 1990 census data and indicates the percentage of a *census block* population that is black. Because the population density of Leon County is relatively low—318 per square mile—census tracts tend to cover too large an area to be a meaningful neighborhood referent. Even the lower level of aggregation—census block—includes several that are as large as a mile square.

We also measured *perceived* racial composition (PRCBLACK) with responses to the following question:

I would like to ask you about the neighborhood you live in. If you think of the people living within a mile of your house, what percentage of the people living there are white—black—latino?

The relevance of such a perceptual approach is underscored by recent survey data showing the extent to which the perception of racial composition distorts reality. For example, while blacks are 12% of the U.S. population, "the average American thinks that America is 32% black." Nedau et al. report that more than half of politically active (and presumably informed) respondents think blacks make up at least 30% of the population. Those who "feel threatened by minorities [due to preferential hiring or the pace of civil rights activity] perceive greater numbers of them." . . .

Finally, on the premise that the *affective* state of fear could be influenced by *cognitive* perceptions related to *risk*, we include several respondent perceptions in our models. These include responses to the Gallup question, "What would you say is the most important problem facing the country today?" (PROBLEM), and estimates of whether crime in one's neighborhood (CRMHOOD) and the county (CRMCTY) have increased, stayed the same, or decreased. . . .

. . . The actual racial composition of a respondent's neighborhood is unrelated to fear of crime in this multivariate context. Though related to Fear at the bivariate level, perceived racial composition has no significant effect when AGE, FEMALE, BLACK, and other relevant predictors are taken into account. It should be noted that the relationship of PRCBLACK to Fear is positive, indicating greater fear of crime for those perceiving more

blacks living nearby. . . . In both Fear equations, older respondents are less fearful and women and blacks are more fearful, as are those perceiving an increase of crime in their neighborhood or county. None of the latter results is surprising in the context of prior Fear research. . . .

. . . When key factors are controlled—such as experience as a victim, perception of crime in one's neighborhood, age, income, and sex—perceived racial composition is significantly related to fear of crime among white respondents, but not among blacks. This is consistent with Moeller's findings regarding perceived racial composition and with Skogan's findings concerning perceived residential proximity of blacks to whites. Given the low bivariate correlation (.16) between [racial composition of a respondent's neighborhood] and [perceived racial composition of the neighborhood] for whites and the nonsignificance of the objective measure, these results underscore the relative importance of approaching this issue from a perceptual vantage point.

To explore further the issue of racial difference in response to racial composition, we examine it for black and white respondents in neighborhoods with varying degrees of perceived racial diversity. Our objective is to address the possibility that diversity per se matters more than racial composition. Specifically, we assess whether patterns of fear of crime vary when blacks constitute a minority, a "substantial minority," or a majority in a neighborhood. Because the objective measure of racial composition (PCTBLACK) had no effect, this analysis is limited to perceptual measures. . . .

. . . When no other factors are taken into account, fear of crime among whites increases consistently as the percentage of blacks in the neighborhood is perceived to increase—with the highest levels reported for neighborhoods with a black majority. Among African-Americans the pattern is less clear. The highest levels of Fear occur in neighborhoods that are perceived to be predominantly white (< 25% black) and drop slightly as blacks become a substantial minority (26%–50%). This is consistent with observations made by Covington and Taylor. However, as blacks achieve majority status, (50% +), Fear among black respondents increases slightly. In neighborhoods with a substantial majority (90% +) of black residents . . . , Fear among blacks is almost as high (18.8) as in predominantly white neighborhoods (18.5). . . .

Finally, we have attempted to model the fear of crime in a way that considers perceived risk of criminal victimization as an intervening variable in the relationship with perceived racial composition of neighborhood (PRCBLACK). When Liska et al. controlled for an objective measure of risk of crime, the effect of racial composition on fear of crime was substantially diminished for whites. Ferraro, though not concerned with racial composition, showed that perceived risk substantially and significantly mediates the effects of a number of factors on fear of crime. . . .

It is not surprising that for whites Risk has a substantial direct effect on Fear. It is also not surprising that actual racial composition of a respondent's neighborhood does not enter the model. However, for white respondents, perceived racial composition of the neighborhood has no direct effect on Fear once Risk is taken into account. That is, all effects of perceived racial composition are indirect and mediated by Risk. This is entirely consistent with findings reported by Liska et al. showing that the effect of (objective) racial composition greatly diminished for whites when victimization risk was controlled. The only other variables to have a direct effect on fear of crime for whites are AGE, FEMALE, CRMHOOD, CRMCITY, and PROBLEM.

. . . For African-Americans, neither actual [racial composition of a respondent's neighborhood] nor perceived [racial composition of the neighborhood] has a significant effect, direct or indirect, on Fear. Perceived risk of victimization is the most powerful predictor of Fear, and once it is controlled, only AGE and FEMALE have significant direct effects on fear of crime. . . .

DISCUSSION

In this research, we have examined fear of crime among blacks and whites in relation to objective and perceptual measures of the racial composition of neighborhoods. We measure fear directly, in a manner not confounded by the cognitive assessment of risk, and we ask whether minority status per se—regardless of race—is instrumental in the understanding of Fear. In sum, the racial composition of neighborhood matters—but only to whites who perceive themselves to be in the racial minority. Among such whites, the effect of that perception on fear is indirect and mediated by the perceived risk of crime. Objective racial composition at the census-block level has no consequence and fear of crime among blacks is unrelated to racial composition—however measured.

It is widely assumed that racial polarities have intensified in the 1990s as have popular concerns about crime and the typification of crime as a black male phenomenon. Thus, when these results from 1994 are compared with earlier research using data from the 1970s and early 1980s, several questions come readily to mind. Why, for instance, is there no effect of actual racial composition [of a respondent's neighborhood] on Fear? Why is even the effect of perceived racial composition [of the neighborhood] limited to whites? Why are African-Americans not more fearful in predominantly black or predominantly white neighborhoods?

One relevant factor may be the temporal context of our research. Specifically, a 400% increase in media coverage of violent crime had accompanied a more than 400% increase in concern about crime in the months immediately preceding the data collection. A central theme in that media blitz was that violence is no longer contained in the urban ghetto, but was spreading to places previously considered safe and was both everywhere and random. If such messages achieved public resonance, the threat of crime could appear less patterned and systematic and so less connected to putative sources of threat—such as the presence of blacks in one's neighborhood.

The fact that Fear among African-Americans in this sample is unrelated to racial composition, despite being consistently higher than white fear, is a departure from the findings of Covington and Taylor. But their data from 1982 involve very urban neighborhoods in Baltimore, and ours from 1994 involve a less intensely urban environment in a government and university town. Indeed, the black community in our research site involves substantial numbers of professionals and students. It is clear that some predominantly black neighborhoods in this setting involve many fewer of the "incivilities" that Covington and Taylor show to be significant in their research setting. Vacant lots; abandoned and boarded buildings; substantial graffiti and litter; and large numbers of idle, publicly drinking, and drug-using males—all are certainly less common in our research site than in many large urban centers.

What this research may principally suggest is the need to consider the relationship between racial composition and fear of crime as geographically and temporally contingent. The dynamics of race, crime, and fear are undoubtedly different in a place like Baltimore, with 10 times the population and 3 times the population density as our research site. Beyond size, communities with large numbers of tenements and projects, whose residents rely heavily on public transportation, undoubtedly generate different patterns of interaction and fear than communities configured otherwise. If a community—like our research site—has a substantial African-American middle class, questions relating fear of crime to the characteristics of one's neighborhood will not have the same resonance or results as the same questions asked in an inner-city project. Remember, we did not ask respondents if they feared black men. We asked them to characterize their neighborhood and to describe their crime fears.

Also, despite the considerable racial typification linking criminality to black males in popular and political stereotypes, and notwithstanding the media hyping of violent crime, the context of the 1990s, both criminally and racially, differs substantially from that of the 1980s and 1970s, when most of the data addressing this question were gathered. In fact, whereas UCR measures of violent crime increased 64% in the 1970s and 23% in the 1980s, they have been unchanged in the 1990s. As the urban underclass becomes increasingly isolated residentially and socially, the frequency of interracial contact and intraracial contact between classes has likely diminished. In 1994, society was a generation removed from the intense racial unrest—both urban "race riots" and civil rights protest—that threatened many whites. Today, much racial anger and fear among whites are directed toward the "gains" that African-Americans have made in the workplace as a result of affirmative action, and resonate the economic insecurities of a changing "global economy."

In short, the increase in racial residential segregation, the expansion of popular fears to include economic insecurity, the movement of civil rights conflict to the courts and the workplace, and the media-driven images of a ubiquitous crime threat—these are just part of a changing historical context in which relationships among race, residence, and fear of crime are grounded. Still, with all of these changes and notwithstanding the kind of community we have studied, our data show once again that fear of crime among whites is significantly linked to the perception that African-Americans live nearby in substantial numbers.

The fact that white Fear is significantly increased by this perception is consistent with the earlier findings of Moeller and Skogan. The weak correlation between subjective and objective measures of racial composition, especially for whites, further underscores the importance of perceptual approaches to this issue. That an apparent threshold is reached when whites see themselves in the minority and that the effect on fear is mediated by the perceived risk of crime could mean at least two things. First, whites who see themselves in a predominantly black neighborhood could simply feel a greater risk of victimization. But they could also see themselves and their black neighbors as less well protected by law enforcement. In short, they could be reflecting some of the same bases of fear of crime that traditionally have affected African-Americans.

Whether the perception of more blacks living nearby leads to fear or that fear leads to the perception of more blacks nearby, or whether fear of crime and the perception of large numbers of blacks are tied simultaneously to an underlying racism, are important theoretical questions these data cannot adjudicate. Solving such intellectual puzzles may be of little practical consequence, if, as James Q. Wilson contends, the outcomes of fear and racism such as avoidance, exclusion, discrimination, and violence are indeed indistinguishable.

NOTES

1. This approach has been applied to the size and funding of police departments; rates of arrest; the likelihood of an individual's incarceration; and rates of incarceration.
2. The survey was conducted by The Research Network, Inc., a public opinion polling firm located in Tallahassee, Florida. A two-stage Mitofsky-Waksberg sampling design was utilized and a 10 call-back rule was employed before permitting placement. This yielded a response rate of just over 80%.

QUESTIONS FOR DISCUSSION AND WRITING

1. Why did the authors include perceived racial composition of neighborhood?
2. Which respondents were most fearful in the two fear equations used by the authors?
3. What happens to fear of crime among whites as the percentage of black residents is perceived to increase? Among blacks?

A Murder "Wave"?
Trends in American Serial Homicide, 1940–1990

PHILIP JENKINS

It is widely agreed that the frequency of serial murder in the contemporary United
States is very high in comparison with other
similar societies, and probably in relation to
most historical periods. It is common to write
of an American "wave" of serial murder that
began in the late 1960s. Murder sprees and serial homicide careers were by no means new
in the 1960s, but events of this sort now
seemed to occur with greater frequency and
severity, establishing a macabre trend which
continues unabated. Holmes and DeBurger
suggest a "surge" in "multicide" dating from
about 1960. Norris comments, "Since 1960 not
only have the number of individual serial killers increased but so have the number of victims per killer, and the level of savagery of the
individual crimes themselves." Leyton suggests that reported acts of multiple homicide
in the United States were ten or twelve times
more frequent after the 1960s than before. On
a related topic, Fox has remarked that 1966
marked "the onset of the age of mass murder."

However widespread, perceptions of an
"epidemic" leave a number of unanswered
questions about the reality of the phenomenon and its causation. First, recent conditions
are not without parallel in American history:
in an earlier study, it was suggested that serial
homicide little below the present scale and frequency did in fact occur in the United States
in the early twentieth century, between about
1900 and 1940. On the other hand, repeat homicide appears to become much rarer in the
mid-century, between about 1940 and 1965.
This is a matter of some importance for our
understanding of recent developments. If the
frequency of serial murder activity fell in mid-
century and then increased sharply during the
1960s, this suggests that this type of crime is
connected to wider social conditions that require explanation. We might explore factors
that affect either the prevalence of extremely
violent behavior, the nature of criminal justice
responses, or the availability of a victim population. Alternatively, we might hypothesize
that apparent changes in multiple homicide
merely reflect fashions in recording or reporting, rather than behavior. The increase of reported cases from the late 1960s onward
would thus reflect new perceptions by the police or the mass media, and the "wave" might
be a myth or an artificial construct.

Whichever approach proves most accurate,
the historical study of serial murder offers significant theoretical lessons. It is particularly
useful for examining the constructionist ap-

From "A Murder 'Wave'? Trends in American Serial Homicide 1940–1990" by P. Jenkins, 1992, *Criminal Justice Review* 17 (1):1–19. Copyright © 1992 by *Criminal Justice Review*. Reprinted with permission.

proach in sociology, which stresses that social problems are rarely as novel as they sometimes appear. In this view, behaviors like the use of violence against children or the elderly are endemic in society, until they come to be perceived and defined as new problems with a name such as "child abuse" or "elder abuse." The task of the sociologist is to determine the social, political, and bureaucratic forces that lead to this new recognition and definition and to identify the claims-makers who shape the debate. A constructionist approach would favor the view that serial murder activity remained high throughout the century, but that the phenomenon was only recognized (or rediscovered) in the mid-1960s. If indeed these years marked a real and significant increase of the behavior itself, this would provide an important exception to the constructionist model.

If there was a real and sudden growth in multiple homicide after 1960, then explaining it offers a challenge for sociologists and criminologists, and it is disappointing that so few of the current accounts have attempted a systematic explanation. One notable exception is Leyton, who presents an ambitious chapter titled "Towards an Historical Sociology of Multiple Murder." This accepts the idea of a "surge," which is attributed to the changing life opportunities of certain social groups and classes. The growing "closure" of avenues of opportunity in the 1960s led some to frustration and consequent outbursts of violent protest, of which multiple murder was one dramatic manifestation. The theory may or may not have substance, but at least it attempts to place the observed phenomenon in a context of known social theory. It also marks a vital shift away from the largely individualistic and psychodynamic explanations that have long dominated the analysis of multiple homicide. An authentic increase in serial murder in the 1960s would have significance for policymakers no less than academics. Understanding the social context of offenders like Ted Bundy or John Wayne Gacy might provide an opportunity for intervention, with the goal of removing or re-ducing the factors that promote this sort of crime.

These questions can only be answered by tracing the frequency of serial murder in the United States over a lengthy period before and after the apparent upsurge of the offense in the mid-1960s. Obviously, there are major methodological difficulties in such an endeavor, and a comprehensive history would be impossible. However, it will be argued that the resources do exist for an admittedly tentative account, which favors the objectivist approach to this problem. It will be argued that serial homicide was indeed rare in the mid-century and has become much more frequent in recent years; a change that will be explained chiefly in terms of the weakening of social control mechanisms from the mid-1960s onward.

METHODOLOGY

The most important stage of this research involved compiling a list of all serial murder cases recorded in the United States between 1940 and 1990. Each case involved an offender associated with the killing of at least four victims, over a period greater than 72 hours. Excluded are cases where the offender acted primarily out of political motives, or in quest of financial profit. Organized and professional criminal activity is thus excluded, a limitation that would not be accepted by all researchers. Of course, the list cannot include cases that did not come to the attention of law enforcement, or where neither police nor media recognized a linkage in a series of homicides. Also, the exact number of cases in a particular series is highly controversial.

The issue of "association" poses a large and probably insurmountable problem. It is rare for any serial killer to be formally charged and convicted in all the cases in which he or she is a strong suspect, and we thus have to rely on much less certain evidentiary criteria to assess the real number of victims. In one well-known case, Ted Bundy was executed in 1989 for a murder committed in Florida, and the same state had tried and sentenced him for two other homicides. However, it has been suggested that Bundy was guilty of anywhere between 25 and 100 other murders across the United States. In the present study, an individual is included if law enforcement and mainstream media sources consistently reported that the offender was believed to be implicated in four or more deaths. Clearly, this evidence is far from satisfactory, especially where it is based on confessions. These might be a major source in some cases, but there are many factors that could lead a suspect to portray his criminal activity as either more or less serious than it truly was. It is also likely that media and police estimates are sometimes exaggerated or simply wrong, but such a reputational approach is perhaps the only means of proceeding in such a contentious area.

Cases were listed from three major sources. The first involved three well-indexed and authoritative newspapers, the *New York Times, Los Angeles Times,* and *Chicago Tribune.* This material was supplemented from a variety of secondary sources on serial murder. Finally, a number of references were acquired from Michael Newton's recent "encyclopedia" of serial murder, *Hunting Humans,* an important source which requires discussion. Unfortunately, the book lacks a scholarly apparatus, and sources are cited only very generally, but the author's use of those sources is cautious and scholarly.

Hunting Humans is by far the most comprehensive available listing of serial murder cases, including the vast majority of references that had been found in the search of media and secondary sources. In fact, one of the major criticisms which can be levied against the book is that it is overcomprehensive, including many cases with only two or three victims. Although there are omissions—including some spectacular cases like Stephen Nash—Newton provides an excellent basis for the analysis of trends in American serial murder (less confidence can be placed in its reliability on other nations). Combined with the evidence of newspapers and

secondary sources, Newton permits us to compile a thorough list of reported serial murder cases in the last half century.

CHANGES IN REPORTING PRACTICE

The crucial issue, then, arises whether the rate of reporting is fairly constant over time. If a study of media sources in the 1940s or 1950s produces far fewer cases than we find in the 1980s, can we safely assume that this reflects a change in the frequency of the offense, or might this simply reflect changes in the practices and interests of the mass media? There is some evidence that metropolitan newspapers like the *New York Times* or *Los Angeles Times* did expand their coverage of regional news from the 1950s onward. This arose not from changes in the marketing or journalistic practices of those newspapers in particular, but from wider changes in the newspaper industry as a whole.

From the 1950s, local newspapers were increasingly likely to form part of large chains or corporate groupings, and those chains themselves grew from statewide or regional concerns to national status. About 29 percent of American newspapers were owned by chains in 1960, compared to 63 percent in 1988. In the same period, the proportion of chains that were national in scope rose from 11 percent to 33 percent. One consequence of this was that stories of any sensational value were less likely to be confined to a purely local market and would instead be disseminated throughout the chain. Stories would thus reach a national audience and would be picked up (or at least referred to) by other major journals like the *New York Times.* As the trend toward chain ownership was most marked in the late 1960s, it is possible that the increased reporting of serial murder might in part reflect a growing "nationalization" of news.

On the other hand, this would not in itself be a sufficient explanation for any perceived changes. Throughout the century, a major serial murder case has usually been viewed as a story of great journalistic interest, and the *New York Times* between about 1900 and 1940 had reported extensively and enthusiastically on serial murder cases as far afield as Colorado, Iowa, Alaska, and South Dakota. There is no reason to believe that media practices or public taste changed suddenly during the 1940s. Even so, the danger of missing cases before the 1960s is reduced by using Newton's *Hunting Humans*, which draws on regional and local newspaper files from no less than 25 states, newspapers such as the *Eagle-Beacon* of Wichita, Kansas; the *Daily News* of Anchorage, Alaska; or the *Clarion-Ledger* of Jackson, Mississippi. Even a search as wide as this apparently failed to find a large number of mid-century cases that escaped the attention of the major metropolitan press.

Also, newspapers, magazines, and books in the mid-century all devoted abundant attention to spectacular crimes such as multiple homicide when they did occur, suggesting that public interest remained high throughout the period. Magazines along the lines of *True Crimes* and *True Detective* were popular throughout the period. Moreover, cases that today might seem comparatively minor or commonplace would then have received enormous attention in terms of column inches in the newspapers, or in numbers of published books. Some of the most celebrated and widely discussed cases of these years involved three or four victims, as with Harvey Glatman, William Heirens, or Charles Howard Schmid, whereas modern studies tend to focus instead on extreme serial cases that claimed ten or twenty casualties. The suggestion is that had more cases occurred in earlier years, they would have been reported at length. If a case like that of Ted Bundy had occurred in, say, the early 1950s, it is hard to believe that its sensationalistic potential would have been overlooked.

It might also be suggested that cases were as likely to be reported in the mid-century, but that police agencies interpreted crimes differently before announcing their conclusions to the media. We might hypothesize that a police agency arresting a suspect in the late 1940s

might be slow to investigate the suspect's involvement in a series of crimes over many years in a number of states, whereas their modern counterparts would be more familiar with patterns of serial homicide and would thus tend to speculate with greater freedom. Modern agencies also have superior record-keeping techniques, and more experience of interagency cooperation, enhancing the likelihood that a suspect could be linked to a large number of earlier offenses.

This view is superficially attractive, but the contrast with earlier eras is too sharply drawn. Between 1900 and 1940, American police agencies often demonstrated their familiarity with the concept of serial murder and pursued investigations accordingly so that such offenders were frequently detected and apprehended. As a matter of course, investigators traced the earlier movements of suspects, and they attempted to link them with crimes in other jurisdictions. There is no evidence that police agencies in the mid-century were any less aware of these issues and problems, especially in the aftermath of widely publicized affairs like the Cleveland Torso murders of the 1930s. In 1941, police from several states interrogated the newly arrested multiple murderer Jarvis Catoe in an attempt to link him with crimes in their jurisdictions. Moreover, the attention focused on the "sex maniac" in the 1950s ensured that police and media were continually aware of the possibility that a sexually motivated attack might well be one of a lengthy series.

The reported cases analyzed below can only represent a proportion of the real total, but apparent changes over time do not simply reflect differences in police or media reactions to homicide. A significant growth in the number of reported incidents is likely to reflect a real change in the frequency of the behavior itself.

THE FREQUENCY OF SERIAL HOMICIDE, 1940–1990

On first impressions, it seems that serial murder in the 1940s and 1950s followed patterns quite like those of more recent years. If we consider a multiple homicide like Melvin D. Rees, his actions closely resemble those of sex killers of the 1980s, especially those who operated on or near college campuses. He raped and killed a Maryland woman in 1957, and he massacred a family of four in Virginia in 1959. He was also believed to have carried out four other "sex slayings" near the University of Maryland. Equally "modern" in character was the case of Jake Bird, a drifter who killed two women in Washington State in 1947. When arrested, he confessed to over 40 homicides in the previous decade, with confirmed offenses recorded in Illinois, Kentucky, Nebraska, South Dakota, Ohio, Florida, and Wisconsin. The reconstruction of his travels and crimes bears obvious resemblances to the investigation of more recent itinerant killers, like Henry Lee Lucas or Gerald Stano. Stephen Nash of California, meanwhile, resembles other homosexual serial killers of later years (*Los Angeles Times,* August 22, 1959).

And yet these resemblances would be misleading. There were serial killers of this sort, but they were far fewer than in more recent years. Between 1940 and 1969, there were a maximum of forty-nine serial murder cases recorded in the United States, and the real number might be smaller. Between 1970 and 1990, there was an absolute minimum of 187. An acceleration of activity is therefore indicated, and the change can be dated with some precision. We can therefore break the figures down into three periods: the age of very low serial murder rates between 1940 and 1964; a transitional period between 1965 and 1969; and the "murder wave" since 1970.

For the era between 1940 and 1964, Newton cites about fifty American cases of serial murder, but this total is substantially reduced when we remove cases with fewer than four victims. Several of the remainder should also be dismissed because of the clear profit motive underlying the offenses, which brings the crimes into the realm of organized fraud or professional criminal activity. Examples include the cases of Alfred Cline, Louise Peete,

Martha Beck, and Raymond Fernandez, or the medical rackets of Roland E. Clark.

Using these criteria, there remain about thirty cases for the whole twenty-five-year period. Seven of the total are believed to be "extreme" cases involving eight or more victims. (These offenders were Jake Bird, Albert DeSalvo, Jarvis Catoe, Nannie Doss, Stephen Nash, Melvin Rees, and Charlie Starkweather.) This is assuredly not a comprehensive list of cases, even of those which came to the notice of the media or the authorities, but the sources used would have recorded any case which attained even limited or short-lived notoriety. The list of extreme cases is more likely to be valid, as these phenomena were especially likely to draw regional or national attention.

This is not a large number of incidents for a twenty-five-year period. It is by no means certain that Ed Gein killed as many as four people, although some sources have estimated far higher figures, while Gary Krist's inclusion here is particularly tenuous. Also, several of the cases here involved at least partial motives of profit and property crime and might thus be excluded.

This research confirms once again that serial murder as such was uncommon in these years, and "pure" serial murder—lust murder or "berserk" and irrational crime—was especially rare. (The limited number of cases makes it extremely difficult to discuss multiple homicide *rates,* except to say that this type of offense represented a tiny fraction of all murders.) The relative lack of cases in the mid-century contrasts dramatically with the experience of more recent years. Between 1970 and 1990, there was a minimum of 187 cases, 94 of which were "extreme" in the sense of involving eight or more victims. This number could easily be expanded by including other cases with a strong link to robbery or professional crime.

In summary, a serial murder case was recorded on average every ten months or so between 1940 and 1964, and one "extreme" case every forty-three months. Between 1971 and 1990, a serial case could be expected to emerge in the media every thirty-nine days, and an extreme case every seventy-seven days. By this coarse measure, serial murder cases overall were eight times more likely in the later period than the earlier, and extreme cases were reported over sixteen times as frequently. The conclusion seems inescapable: serial murder has become far more frequent in recent years, and offenders tend to kill larger numbers of victims.

SERIAL HOMICIDE IN THE LITERATURE

The relative scarcity of serial murder in mid-century is confirmed by an examination of the contemporary literature on homicide and violent crime. The dominant intellectual trend of this period within criminology was psychiatric and psychoanalytic, and there was considerable interest in the life-histories of strange or bizarre offenders who might illustrate unusual aspects of the human mind. In addition, public concern about sex offenders and "sex psychopaths" led to widespread legislative action. In 1955, Tappan suggested that in popular mythology, "tens of thousands of homicidal sex fiends stalk the land." Collections of case studies were published by highly reputable scholars who devoted great attention to psychopathy. There were numerous accounts of serial homicide and lust-murder, while the important distinction between mass and "series" murder was beginning to enter the literature.

Many offenders were described, but overwhelmingly, they were drawn from countries other than the United States. The classic case studies were mainly German murderers of the 1920s and 1930s like Fritz Haarman, Karl Denke, and Peter Kürten, each of whom claimed ten or twenty victims in circumstances of extreme brutality and sexual perversion. A similar emphasis on European cases is also found in the sensationalistic literature which recounted gruesome homicide cases in prurient terms. When the Cleveland Torso murders became notorious, the affair was seized on by Nazi propagandists anxious to show that the

Western nations too had crimes like those which had become so firmly linked to German cities like Hanover and Berlin.

Modern accounts of multiple homicide would probably draw all their examples from American cases, but domestic examples did not then exist in anything like comparable numbers. In a sentence that today seems quite remarkable, Bromberg could write in 1948 that "the paucity of lust-murderers in modern criminologic experience makes an analysis of the basic psychopathology difficult." There were "few actual cases" to compare with "Jack the Ripper or other legendary sex-fiends," and the author had to return to 1913 to find an American parallel.

This is not to suggest that no American cases attracted interest, but the same small group of incidents was described repeatedly. Albert Fish occupied a central place in the literature for many years after his execution in 1936, due in large part to the detailed analysis of the case published by Fredric Wertham. Kittrie suggests that it was this case in particular which helped form public perceptions of the sex offender as multiple child killer. In later years, Ed Gein, Charlie Starkweather, and Albert DeSalvo all earned a like celebrity, and a spate of books and articles began to stimulate renewed interest in multiple homicide. The most comprehensive study of specifically American offenders was that of Reinhardt, who described Starkweather; Melvin Rees; Dudley and Gwyn; Brown and Kelly; and Nannie Doss. In addition, writers on extreme violence often referred to the cases of William Heirens and Caryl Chessman, neither of whom falls within our definition.

One remarkable point about such a list is that it omits some of the most spectacular killers, who bore the closest resemblance to the "classic" German cases. We look in vain for extensive discussion of Jarvis Catoe, Jake Bird, or Clarence Hill, and this lacuna may suggest a political element in the selection of case studies. All three were black, and in the context of these years, it might well have been thought inappropriate or tasteless to focus on their acts. If unduly publicized, these events could have given ammunition to racists and segregationists anxious to justify their opinions about black violence and criminality. Whatever the reason, the consequence was to limit the range of cases available to contemporary criminologists.

The lack of concern about serial murder as a major American problem can be illustrated in a number of ways, but one of the most striking involves the numerous official reports and investigations published in the 1960s on the topics of violence and criminality. In the aftermath of political assassinations and racial disturbances, and against a background of rising crime rates, it became common to express concern about the prevalence of violence in the United States. There were several major investigations into different aspects of the perceived crisis, most comprehensively by the National Commission on the Causes and Prevention of Violence. This examined many aspects of violence, political and otherwise, but mass and serial homicide were conspicuous by their near absence. While some cases are mentioned in the context of different theories of the causation of crime, the subject of multiple homicide occupies nothing like the role that it might be expected to play in a contemporary discussion. It is not even mentioned in the commission's influential final report.

THE EVIDENCE OF POPULAR CULTURE

Also suggestive here is the relative absence of multiple homicide as a theme in American popular culture in mid-century. The celebrated serial cases of the 1920s were recalled in early 1940s films like *Stranger on the Third Floor* and even *Arsenic and Old Lace,* but later treatments rarely referred to contemporary cases. *The Sniper* was one powerful exception in the next decade. It addressed the topic of serial murder with a sophisticated and sympathetic awareness of contemporary psychoanalytic and criminological theories, but the main real-life example chosen to illustrate the phe-

nomenon was still Albert Fish, after so many years. The compulsive nature of the "sniper's" violence also bears an explicit resemblance to the Heirens case, which formed the basis of *While the City Sleeps.*

Only in the 1960s did real-life events once more attract attention, with films based on the careers of Ed Gein (*Psycho,* 1960), Albert De Salvo (*The Strangler,* 1964 and *The Boston Strangler,* 1968), and Charlie Starkweather (*Badlands,* 1973), while *Dirty Harry* (1971) freely synthesized the stories of Gary Krist and "Zodiac." Authentic incidents of mass murder similarly inspired *In Cold Blood* (1967) and *Targets* (1968). The resurgence of interest in multiple homicide was fueled by the steadily increasing reports of actual cases, and "Ripper" or "mad slasher" films have been a profitable if controversial genre in the last two decades. The recent vogue provides a dramatic contrast to the apparent absence of notable American cases in the 1940s and 1950s.

THE YEARS OF TRANSITION, 1965–1969

In the mid-1950s, the United States enjoyed very low rates of serial homicide, while two decades later, the country would be in the midst of an apparent "murder wave," and the transition between the two stages can be dated with fair precision to the mid-1960s. The increase of extreme and seemingly irrational homicide was frequently remarked on during these years, and many writers focused on a short period during 1966. In July, Richard Speck killed eight nurses in a Chicago hostel, an act which may have been the culmination of an already lengthy career of murder; and in August, Charles Whitman killed sixteen people during a shooting spree in Texas. Less celebrated were the murder sprees later in the year, by Robert B. Smith in Arizona, and by Kelbach and Lance in Utah.

The media enjoy finding such symbolic events which can be claimed as the harbingers of wider social trends, but there seems little doubt that these events were indeed significant. Between 1965 and 1969, Newton offers a total of twenty-three cases of serial murder. Applying the same criteria as to the earlier list, we find that several of these should be removed from consideration as involving three or less victims, while several other incidents can be added from other sources. Finally, we are left with nineteen serial murder cases that were reported in these five years, or an average of one every ninety-six days.

While below the rates of the 1970s, this was a sharp increase from conditions of the previous two decades, and as the rate of serial murder intensified, so its nature changed. The new cases include fewer marginal or debatable incidents than in earlier years. There was an especially sharp rise in the number of "Ripper" crimes or "lust murders" of the sort that had been dismissed as so rare in the 1940s, but which would become so commonplace after 1970. Between 1940 and 1964, only eleven cases could be classified as "lust murders," but an additional eleven can be categorized thus between 1965 and 1969 alone. These were the years of notorious offenders like John Norman Collins, Jerry Brudos, Antone Costa, "Zodiac," and others. The picture was even worse than it appears, because several offenders now began careers of "lust murder" and serial homicide that would not be detected until the 1970s or later.

The frequency of serial homicide was accelerating at the end of the 1960s, but still more cases came to light in the following years. To take the single year of 1973, there were at least ten arrests of serial killers as well as two incidents that remain unsolved, and the cases in this year included several extreme offenders such as Dean Corll, Herbert Mullin, Edmund Kemper, and Girard Schaefer.

A constructionist approach to the problem of serial murder might seek to emphasize the continuity in activity from the 1940s onward and attempt to understand the moral and political pressures which led commentators to describe an artificial "upsurge" from the late 1960s. By contrast, this case study supports the "objectivist" view that a genuine phenom-

enon was occurring, and no creative stereotyping was required to define the problem. Of course, constructionism might still stress that the real scale of the problem was blown out of proportion, or that the debate was shaped to benefit certain interests or ideologies, but a new problem was there. There simply were more serial killers, more of whom could be categorized as "lust murderers." A new problem was identified because a new problem had come into being.

SOCIAL DIMENSIONS

We must then address the social factors which gave rise to this change. It is a commonplace that the mid-1960s marked a dramatic transition in many aspects of American life, and any attempt at explaining the growth of serial homicide must deal with an embarrassing surfeit of possible reasons. It would be rash to dismiss the status frustration postulated by Leyton, although additional factors can be suggested. It is often difficult to isolate any one type of causation, as the various elements so often are intertwined. Fundamental was the changing demographic composition of the population, and the relative growth of the proportion of people in their teens and twenties. This in itself contributed to a sharp rise in overall violence rates, and it may be asked whether the increase in serial homicide was merely a facet of the general growth in crime.

Almost certainly, this was not the case. U.S. homicide rates did rise between the 1940s and the 1980s, but may only have doubled over the whole period. From 1945 to 1965, the rate per hundred thousand fluctuated between about 4.5 and 6.0, but it then began a rapid rise, from 6.0 in 1968 to 8.8 in 1974–75, and exceeded 10.0 by 1981. It then fell below 8.0 by the mid-1980s. There were particular regions and cities with far higher growth rates in homicide, but few could match the eight- or ten-fold increases suggested for reported serial homicide.

Simple demographics may have contributed a little to the upsurge in serial murder after 1965, but additional explanations are required. Some can be found in aspects of the distinctive youth counter-culture evolved by the "baby boom" generation. Although avowedly pledged to peace and nonviolence, this culture may inadvertently have promoted overtly aggressive behavior, especially with sexual motivations. Only a small number of people might have been affected in this way, but the number of multiple homicide offenders is only in the hundreds nationwide. A vast increase in the availability and consumption of a wide range of drugs presumably had effects that are still difficult to quantify, but which would have been especially severe in individuals already prone to violent or disinhibited behavior. From the mid-1960s, there was also a rapid increase in the availability of sexually stimulating imagery both through the media and in everyday life.

It is plausible that greater access to pornography or extremely violent visual material might have shaped the fantasies and consequent actions of some offenders, but neither drugs nor pornography would in itself be an adequate explanation of the changes we observe. As has been argued elsewhere, the act of homicide may arise from any number of circumstances peculiar to the offender, but serial murder also presupposes social conditions that permit the creation of a victim population. Such a population is accessible to the offender, and several victims can disappear or be found dead before the authorities become seriously concerned. The nature of responses by police or other justice agencies plays an important role in shaping such opportunities for victimization.

In this view, the vital changes in the 1960s might have been the greater independence of the younger generation, and changes in their sexual behavior and attitudes. This greatly enhanced the opportunities for a potential offender to find himself in intimate circumstances with a victim, while the increased physical mobility in these years made it less likely that a young person's disappearance

would be immediately noticed. Similarly, the range of "acceptable" deviancy was greatly expanded in these years. Changes in mores increased willingness to experiment with alternative belief systems and lifestyles, and made many less prepared to reject or suspect individuals who might appear strange or deviant. The sum total of these changes was to facilitate encounters between strangers that might have been far more difficult only a few years previously. Meanwhile, the political fragmentation of the late 1960s discouraged young people from invoking police assistance in what might have been seen as suspicious circumstances.

THE MENTAL HEALTH SYSTEM

Other possible factors do not directly involve the "baby boom" generation, but they would similarly have encouraged a growth in both potential offenders and their victims. In the forefront were changes in the mental health system. The 1960s were marked by a reluctance to institutionalize deviants and the mentally ill for long periods, and it became difficult to commit a person on the strength of his or her outrageous or threatening acts. The average number incarcerated in state mental hospitals on any given day fell from 550,000 in 1955 to 200,000 in 1974, a decline of 65 percent (and the fall was still greater as a proportion of the overall population). Despite the generally laudable intentions of the movement, the effects of decarceration have often been disastrous, and one tragic effect was to release on the streets some genuinely dangerous offenders who would hitherto have been in secure institutions. This was also an incidental effect of the shortening of prison sentences and actual time served and the new emphasis on community care facilities.

Decarceration was part of a more general attack on therapeutic responses to crime and violence, and great skepticism about the possibility of predicting and preventing future acts. The assault was seen most clearly in the area of "sexual psychopath" laws, which faced increasingly successful courtroom challenges. In discussing this movement, Kittrie even writes of the notion of "the illusive psychopath," almost suggesting that the condition itself was mythical. It is ironic that this new legal environment coincided with a probable increase in the number of seriously disturbed offenders, in the aftermath of the rapid growth of drug abuse.

The notorious serial killers of the decade following 1965 included many individuals who had been committed or incarcerated periodically for acts of extreme violence, but who were released with what proved to be too little regard for public safety. To take a specific case, it is difficult to believe that a flamboyantly psychotic offender like Richard Trenton Chase would have escaped lengthy incarceration had he lived in the 1940s. However, the mental health system he encountered was that of 1970s California, where compulsory commitment was much more difficult, and he remained at liberty until the 1978 murder spree which earned him the title of the "Vampire of Sacramento."

In one of the most tragic examples of this sort, Carroll E. Cole (also from California) made repeated attempts to warn doctors and law enforcement authorities of his sadistic and violent impulses toward women, and he was committed to mental institutions sporadically in the 1960s and early 1970s. However, he remained at large and carried out the first of his thirteen murders in 1970. Chase and Cole may have represented extreme failures on the part of the courts and the medical profession, but very serious mistakes were made in the cases of killers like Jerry Brudos, "Buster" Putt, Herbert Mullin, Ed Kemper, Charlie Hatcher, John Wayne Gacy, and many others. All were at some stage diagnosed as showing strong tendencies to future violence, yet all were released from youth institutions or psychiatric custody, often on several occasions. Attempts at predicting violent behavior have a long and

controversial history, but in the 1960s, it appears that even the most extreme warning signs failed to cause official intervention.

CONCLUSION

It would be tempting to draw facile political conclusions. If the upsurge in multiple murder from the mid-1960s was in a sense an outgrowth of the political and social liberalism which characterized that era, then one conceivable policy response would be to limit or reverse those trends, to emphasize traditional moral views on issues like drug use and sexuality. Against this view, it is important to stress the limited scale of the multiple homicide problem within the broad spectrum of violent crime, and to avoid overemphasizing the purely negative changes associated with the 1960s. In addition, it remains uncertain how far any government could shape moral attitudes and beliefs, if that attempt ran against existing social currents. Similarly, it would be misleading to concentrate entirely on the bad effects of changes in the mental health system, such as the decline of compulsory commitment laws. Most would agree that due process values were long overdue in the area of psychiatric confinement and treatment, even though the actual process of decarceration left a great deal to be desired.

Perhaps the most important lesson concerns the state of academic research in the area of multiple homicide. It appears that social, legal, and environmental factors play a major role in determining the prevalence of this crime, although the scholarly emphasis continues to focus on the individual offender. If the rate of serial murder is to be reduced, then these underlying factors must be understood, and this can only be achieved if the killer is seen not merely as a disturbed individual, but as an actor within a changing social context.

Serial killers appear to fall into several distinct psychiatric categories, with paranoid schizophrenics and sexual psychopaths both being frequently recorded, and some authorities would emphasize the role of biological no less than psychological factors in causing acts of extreme violence. It may be that conditions which give rise to irrational violence occur to a similar degree in all human societies, or else social and developmental factors may make this behavior much more common in some societies rather than others. In the 1950s, for example, psychiatrists would strongly have emphasized the role of factors such as child-rearing practices, which would be peculiar to a particular society at a given time. In this view, changes in family structure or attitudes to children could account for variations in extremely violent behavior, as could changes in media depictions of violence or sexuality. It is quite possible that the frequency of aggressive behavior might indeed vary between societies, but that is a different matter from the specific phenomenon of *serial* homicide. An individualistic approach might account for how one person came to kill, but cannot explain how he or she found the opportunities to evade detection until several murders had been committed, and it is this latter which makes an aggressive offender into a serial killer.

If the average number of victims claimed by serial killers rises or falls in a particular era or society, this is less a comment on the changing dynamics of the individual offenders themselves than of the social, moral, and bureaucratic context in which all operate. It would be impossible to understand the murders of the medieval baron Gilles de Rais, "Bluebeard," without discussing the society in which he existed and the means by which he was able to entrap and murder so many innocent victims: it should be equally unthinkable to omit the social context of a modern case in Seattle or Houston. There is thus a crying need for scholarly studies not merely of single offenders but of all the cases of a particular region or decade, and of how they exploited the opportunities in their particular situation or milieu.

In summary, an effective strategy against multiple homicide must draw on research from both social and individual perspectives. The social perspective will explore the broad victim environment, while psychological analysis aids investigators by profiling offenders and seeking more sophisticated means of predicting future violence. But both approaches must be used if serial homicide is to be reduced.

QUESTIONS FOR DISCUSSION AND WRITING

1. For what would a study of serial homicide be "particularly useful"?
2. Did the author find an increase in the rate of serial homicide?
3. Was the increase in serial homicide related to an increase in violence in general?

Crack in Context: Politics and Media in the Making of a Drug Scare

CRAIG REINARMAN

HARRY G. LEVINE

"Two summers ago," began a 1988 *New York Times* editorial, "America discovered crack and overdosed on oratory" (October 4, 1988). In fact, in the spring of 1986 American news media and politicians began an extraordinary antidrug frenzy. Newspapers, news magazines, and television networks regularly carried lurid stories alleging that an "epidemic" or "plague" of drug use was literally destroying the nation. Politicians from both parties made increasingly strident calls for a "war on drugs" and even challenged each other to take urine tests to provide chemical proof of their moral purity and fitness for high office.

In 1988 and 1989, the drug war commanded more political and media attention than the cold war. A *New York Times*/CBS poll has periodically asked Americans to identify "the most important problem facing this country today." In January 1985, 23 percent answered war or nuclear war; fewer than 1 percent believed the most important problem was drugs. In September 1989, shortly after the president's speech and the blizzard of media stories about drugs, 54 percent of those polled believed that drugs were now the most important problem, and only 10 percent thought that war or nuclear war was most important. Even the *New York Times* itself, in a lead editorial (September 28, 1989, p.A26), declared that reversal to be "incredible" and gently suggested that problems such as war, "homelessness and the need to give poor children a chance in life" should perhaps be given more attention. In short, by the end of 1989, America's latest drug scare was still going strong.

We use the term "drug scare" to designate periods when antidrug crusades have achieved great prominence and legitimacy. Drug scares are a phenomenon in their own right, quite apart from drug use and drug problems, and have recurred throughout American history. During "Red scares," like the McCarthy period in the 1950s, leftists have been perceived as seriously threatening to destroy the American way of life. Similarly, during drug scares all kinds of social problems are blamed on one chemical substance or another. Drug scares have typically linked drugs with a subordinate group—especially working-class immigrants, racial or ethnic minorities, and youth. This latest drug scare has tied cocaine, and especially its derivative, "crack," with inner-city black and Hispanic young people.

From "Crack in Context: Politics and Media in the Making of a Drug Scare" by C. Reinarman and H. G. Levine, 1989, *Contemporary Drug Problems* 16:535–577. Copyright © 1989 Federal Legal Publications. Reprinted with permission.

COCAINE AND CRACK
IN THE PUBLIC EYE

The use of cocaine in powdered form by affluent people in music, film, and sports has been common since the 1970s. According to surveys by the National Institute on Drug Abuse (NIDA), by 1985 more that twenty-two million Americans in all social classes and occupations also reported having tried cocaine.

Crack use originated with "freebasing," which was already increasing by the late 1970s. Back then, most cocaine users bought cocaine powder for intranasal use (snorting), but many had begun to "cook" it down to crystalline or "base" form for smoking. All phases of this form of use, from selling to smoking, tended to take place in the privacy of the homes and offices of middle-class or well-to-do users, who typically purchased cocaine in minimum units of grams costing $80–$100. These relatively affluent "basers" had been discovering the dangers of smoking cocaine for several years before the term "crack" was coined. But such users tended to have a stake in conventional life that gave them something to lose; they had the incentives and the resources to cut down, quit, get private treatment, or otherwise control or conceal their use.

The orgy of media and political attention did not begin in the late 1970s, when the prevalence of cocaine use jumped sharply, or even after users began to experience trouble with freebasing. Rather, it began when smokable cocaine in the form of crack made its appearance in a few poor urban neighborhoods. As did basers, crack users report that this mode of cocaine ingestion produces a much more intense but far shorter "high" by getting more of a purer form of cocaine into the brain far more directly and rapidly than does snorting. Many crack users say it is crack's intense yet brutally brief "orgasmic rush" combined with the painful "low" or "down" immediately following that yields a powerful desire to immediately repeat use. This helps account

for the consensus that crack has high abuse and addiction potential.

However, politicians and the media focused on crack *not* because the cocaine was ingested in a more direct, dangerous manner, for freebasing had been going on for years; rather, crack attracted their attention because of its downward mobility to and increased visibility in ghettos and barrios. The new users had a different social class, race, and status. Crack was sold in smaller, cheaper, precooked units, on ghetto street corners, to poorer, younger buyers (see, e.g., *New York Times,* August 30, 1987; *Newsweek,* November 23, 1987; *Boston Globe,* May 18, 1988). Crack spread cocaine smoking into poor populations already beset with a cornucopia of troubles. These people tend to have fewer bonds to conventional society, less to lose, and far fewer resources to cope with or shield themselves from cocaine problems. The current drug scare thus began in earnest when crack use became visible among this "threatening" group.

The earliest mass media reference to the new form of cocaine may have been in a *Los Angeles Times* article at the end of 1984 (November 25, 1984). The article discussed the use of cocaine "rocks" in ghettos and barrios in Los Angeles. By late 1985, the *New York Times* made the first specific reference to "crack" in the national media in a story about three teenagers seeking treatment for cocaine abuse (November 17, 1985, p. BI2). At the start of 1986, crack was known only in a few impoverished neighborhoods in Los Angeles, New York, Miami, and perhaps a small number of other large cities.

When two celebrity athletes died in what news stories called "crack-related deaths" in the spring of 1986, news coverage skyrocketed, and crack became widely known. In July 1986 alone, the three major TV networks offered seventy-four evening news segments on drugs, half of these about crack. In the months leading up to the November elections, a handful of national newspapers and magazines alone produced roughly 1,000 stories discussing crack. *Time* and *Newsweek* each devoted five 1986 cover stories to the "crisis."

In the fall of 1986, the CBS news show *48 Hours* aired a heavily promoted documentary called "48 Hours on Crack Street," which Dan Rather previewed on his *Evening News* show: "Tonight, CBS News takes you to the street, to the war zone for an unusual two hours of hands-on horror." Among the many shots from hidden cameras was one of New York Senator Alphonse D'Amato, incognito, purchasing a vial of crack in order to dramatize the brazenness of street-corner sales in the ghetto. All this was good business for CBS: the program earned the highest Nielsen rating of any similar news show in the previous five years—fifteen million viewers. (Three years later, after *48 Hours* was nearly killed by poor ratings, the series kicked off its 1989 season with a three-hour special, "Return to Crack Street.")

Three days after the original CBS show on "Crack Street," NBC followed with its own prime-time special, "Cocaine Country," which asserted that cocaine and crack use had gone beyond epidemic to become pandemic. This was only one of over 400 separate stories on crack and cocaine by NBC alone—an unprecedented fifteen hours of air time—in the seven months leading up to the 1986 elections. By mid-1986, *Newsweek* claimed that crack was the biggest story since Vietnam and Watergate June 16, 1986, p. 15). The words "plague," "epidemic," and "crisis" had become routine. *Time* called crack the "Issue of the Year" (September 22, 1986, p. 25).

President and Nancy Reagan were only the most prominent of leaders to join in asserting that drugs, especially crack, were "killing . . . a whole generation [of] . . . our children." Drugs, they said, are "tearing our country apart" (*Time*, September 22, 1986, p. 25). Crack got far less attention in 1987, but beginning with the 1988 presidential primaries, more and more politicians again claimed that crack was destroying American youth and causing much of the crime, violence, prostitution, and child

abuse in the nation. Democrats and Republicans, liberals and conservatives alike called repeatedly for an "all-out war on drugs."

In April of 1988, an ABC News "Special Report" again termed crack "a plague" that was "eating away at the fabric of America." This documentary, like others before and since, made a long series of provocative claims: that Americans spend "twenty billion a year on cocaine"; that American businesses lose "sixty billion" dollars a year in productivity because their workers use drugs; that "the educational system is being undermined" by student drug use; and that "the family" was "disintegrating" in the face of this "epidemic." In forty-eight minutes of air time, millions of viewers were given a powerful *vocabulary of attribution: "drugs,"* especially crack, were destroying virtually every institution in American life—jobs, schools, families, national sovereignty, community, law enforcement, and business.

From the opening shots in 1986 to this 1988 television show and President Bush's 1989 address, crack cocaine was defined as supremely evil—the most important cause of America's troubles. Thus, one of the core features of drug war discourse was what we call the *routinization of caricature*—worst cases framed as typical cases, the episodic rhetorically recrafted into the epidemic.

THE OFFICIAL STATISTICAL EVIDENCE FROM THE U.S. GOVERNMENT

In almost every other category, the trends in official drug use statistics had been down even before the scare began. Prevalence figures for cocaine in particular were dropping sharply just as crisis claims were reaching a crescendo, and they had dropped still further precisely when the Bush/Bennett battle plan was being drawn up. Indeed, as White House officials anonymously admitted a few weeks after the president's speech, the new plan's "true goals" were far more modest that its rhetoric: the Bush plan was "simply to move the nation 'a little bit' beyond where current trends would put it anyway" (*New York Times*, September 24, 1989, p. 1).

CRACK

Tom Brokaw reported on *NBC Nightly News* (May 23, 1986) that crack was "flooding America" and that it had become "America's drug of choice." His colleagues at the other networks and in the print media had all made similar claims. An ordinarily competent news consumer might well have gathered the impression that crack could be found in the lockers of most high school students. Yet, at the time of these reports, there existed only anecdotal information about this new dangerous form of cocaine use; there were no prevalence statistics at all on crack; and no evidence of any sort showing that smoking crack had come to be even the preferred mode of cocaine use, much less of drug use.

In short, the official evidence on cocaine and crack available during the first three years of the crack crisis gave a rather different picture than we received from the media and politicians. The sharpest rise in the statistics on cocaine use occurred several years before the scare began and even cocaine smoking was extant long before the term "crack" was coined. Moreover, as media attention to crack was burgeoning, the extent of crack use was virtually unknown, and almost all official measures of other cocaine use were actually decreasing. In fact, claims of a "crack crisis" actually preceded the spread of crack use, at least as measured by official data.

Crack as an Epidemic and a Plague

The media and politicians have routinely talked about an "epidemic" and a "plague" of crack in America. Because both words have been used imprecisely and rhetorically—as words of alarm, warning, and danger—it is difficult to determine if there is any legitimacy

in the description of crack use as an epidemic or a plague.

It is worth noting the unintentionally ironic mixing of metaphors, or of diagnoses and remedies, when advocates for the war on drugs describe crack use as an "epidemic" or a "plague." Although disease terminology has been used to call attention to the consequences of crack use, most of the federal government's domestic responses have centered on using police to arrest users. The Bush administration now encourages arresting even occasional users of nonnarcotic drugs and plans on building more prisons to incarcerate drug users. Treatment and prevention receive only a small percentage of the funding to handle the "epidemic." On the one hand, if crack use is primarily a crime problem, then would not a term like "wave" (as in "crime wave") be more fitting? On the other hand, if this truly is an "epidemic"—a widespread disease—is a policy based primarily upon police, prisons, and the military really appropriate? Should efforts to cope with the epidemic of crack addiction, as with the epidemics of alcohol and tobacco addiction and of AIDS, not be handled primarily by public health agencies, self-help groups, and medical treatment personnel?

In short, since 1986, when politicians and the media have talked about cocaine, alcohol, and other drug use, abuse, and addiction, they have not used "epidemic" and "plague" as ordinary descriptive or technical terms. Rather, the words have been used exclusively and rather effectively as rhetoric or propaganda for the war on drugs.

We have suggested in this chapter that claims about a pandemic "crisis" endangering the lives of "a whole generation" of youth are at odds with the best official data. We are left, therefore, with the question of what else, besides extant drug use, is animating the new war on drugs. We will suggest in what follows that the answer to this question does not hinge on the emergence of a dangerous new form of drug use alone. The crack "crisis," like previous drug scares, is in part the product of the association of "dangerous drugs" with a "dangerous class" and of the peculiarly fertile features of politics in the current context.

This current drug scare also must be understood in terms of its political context and its appeal to important groups within American society. The mass media and politicians, however, have not talked about drugs this way; they have decontextualized the drama, making it appear as if the story has no authors aside from cocaine users. The crack drama has kept abusers, dealers, crimes, and casualties under spotlights while other important factors have remained hidden in shadows. We will suggest that over and above the real difficulties people are experiencing with cocaine, and especially with crack, the rise of the "New Right" and the competition between politicians and political parties in a conservative context contributed significantly to the making of the current drug scare.

Liberals and Democrats, too, found in cocaine and crack not only a means of recapturing Democratic defectors by appearing more conservative but also a convenient scapegoat for deteriorating conditions in the inner cities—and all this at a historical moment when the liberals' traditional solutions to the problems of the poor were stigmatized by a successful Right as ineffective and costly. Thus, in addition to the political capital to be gained by waging the war, the new chemical bogeyman afforded politicians across the ideological spectrum both an explanation for pressing public problems and an excuse for not doing much about them.

In the 1980s, the conservative-led drive to reduce social spending exacerbated the enduring problems of poor black and Latino city residents. In turn, their growing numbers, visibility, and desperation made them appear more and more menacing to the white middle-class majority. At the same time, inner-city churches, local organizations, and parent groups tried to defend their children and communities from further assault from drug dealers on the one hand and from conservative social policies on the other. Unfortunately, the crack scare has not thus far inspired politi-

cians to address the worsening conditions and growing needs of poor and working-class blacks and Hispanics—to begin the often-called-for "Marshall Plan for cities." However, the drug war has given local and federal authorities a justification for increasing ghetto police surveillance and for putting more people in prison. Despite their best efforts, the enlarged drug squads are unable to reduce the crime and seaminess of urban poverty neighborhoods. But the crack crisis has increased police, court, and parole system supervision of urban underclass minorities, and it has made the jails and prisons bulge. All the while, unemployment, poverty, and homelessness remain untouched. As a result, a visible minority of the urban poor, and especially the youth, turn to crime and attempt to escape from lives of despair and deprivation into the fleeting pleasures of hard drugs.

CONCLUSION

Crack, we agree, *is* an especially dangerous way to use an already risky drug, and despite all the exaggeration, it *has* made life more difficult for many people, especially the poor. More than enough families have been touched by drug-related tragedies, so why do we bother with criticizing the war on drugs? If even a few people are saved from crack addiction, why should anyone care if this latest drug scare has been in some measure concocted by the press, politicians, and moral entrepreneurs to serve their other agendas? Given the damage that drugs can do, what's the harm in a little hysteria? We suggest two answers to such questions.

First, drug scares blame individual immorality and personal behavior for endemic social and structural problems, and they divert attention and resources from those larger problems. Drug scares have long linked drug use with racial minorities, the poor, or wayward youth and have blamed economic problems—and often other real and imaginary problems in society—on their use of drugs.

Obscured or forgotten in all the political rhetoric on and media coverage of crack are the social and economic problems that underlie drug abuse, and that are much more widespread—especially poverty, unemployment, and the prospects of life in the permanent underclass. Dealing drugs, after all, is often quite accurately perceived by poor city kids as the highest-paying job they will ever get.

Liberal Democrats denounced the Reagan administration's hypocrisy in declaring war on drugs and then cutting the budgets for treatment, prevention, and research. However, they usually missed the more important point: the "just say no" administration had just said no to virtually every social program aimed at creating alternatives for inner-city young people and improving their lawful life chances. Unfortunately, these kids cannot "just say no" to poverty and unemployment. Thus, there is harm in drug scares, first, for what they do to democratic discourse on and popular understanding of public problems: they falsely attribute to drugs alone a wide array of problems that have little to do with drugs and much to do with U.S. economic and social policy.

Second, we strongly suspect that drug scares do not work very well to reduce drug problems and that they may well promote the behavior they claim to be preventing. For all the repression that successive drug wars have wrought (almost exclusively upon the poor and the powerless), they have yet to make a dent either in drug problems or in any of the other problems affecting those vulnerable to drugs. More than simply not succeeding, there is the risk that all of the exaggerated claims made to mobilize the population for war will arouse interest in drug use. The *New England Journal of Medicine* recently reported that the frequency of teenage suicides increases after news reports and TV shows about them. Drug abuse, especially of new and exotic drugs or methods like crack, may work the same way. In his classic "How to Launch a Nationwide Drug Menace," Edward Brecher shows how exaggerated newspaper reports of dramatic police raids in 1960 functioned as advertising for glue sniffing. The arrests of a handful of sniffers led to an anti-glue-sniffing hysteria that actually spread this hitherto unknown practice across America.

In the current crack scare, the media's desire for dramatic drug stories interacted with politicians' desire for safe election-year issues so that news about crack spread to every nook and cranny of the nation far faster than dealers might have spread word on the street. In order to claim, as literally thousands of media reports and political speeches did, that crack is "the most addictive substance known to man," there was some commonsense obligation to explain why. Therefore, alongside all the statements about "instant addiction" the media also reported some very intriguing things about crack: "intense rush," "whole body orgasm," "better than sex," and "cheaper than cocaine." For those people apt to be experimenting with various consciousness-altering substances anyway—for example, young people, members of the underclass—all the attention given to crack may well have functioned as a massive advertising campaign.

After months of being bombarded with such accounts, the question is not why 4 percent of America's young people try crack, but rather why many more of the other 96 percent do not. One college student who had some modest experience with drugs offered a telling anecdote along these lines to Professor Arnold Trebach. After reading a *Newsweek* story in which the editor-in-chief likened crack to medieval plagues and the attack on Pearl Harbor, the student said, "I had never heard of it until then, but when I read that it was better than sex and that it was cheaper than cocaine and that it was an epidemic, I wondered what I was missing. I questioned why I seemed to be the only one not doing the drug. The next day I asked some friends if they knew where to get some."

QUESTIONS FOR DISCUSSION AND WRITING

1. What did the *New York Times* polls reveal?
2. Does the official evidence on crack and cocaine concur with the media depiction?
3. What are two problems with drug scares?

III

HOW IS CRIME MEASURED?

The Observation and Measurement of Crime

IN the previous section, we pointed out several inconsistencies between perceptions of crime and what we referred to as the "reality" of crime. The obvious question is, "How do we know what the reality of crime is?" It is easy to argue that as a consequence of credentials or professional position, criminologists know the truth about crime. It is equally easy to identify the weakness in this approach. Many people are prepared to believe some assertions about crime if they are made in print (newspapers, national magazines, and popular books included); disseminated via electronic media; or shouted loudly by politicians, demagogues, or even professors. The fact is, however, that the only legitimate basis for concluding that one assertion about crime or criminals is more correct than others is systematic research, particularly research based on empirical observation.

Here we should take care because there is often an unfortunate confusion of the terms *empirical* and *quantitative* research. Although quantitative research done by professional criminologists is empirical research, so too are studies that do not count or tally. Qualitative observations, too, are empirical studies and extremely valuable in understanding certain aspects of crime.

So our earlier statement that some perceptions are inconsistent with the reality of crime is based on our interpretation of the criminological research literature. There remain several important issues to consider. First, some would argue that published research tends to leave out ideas and styles of scholarship that do not fit with the dominant traditions of academic publishing. Second, like all readers of this literature, our interpretations are colored by our training and personal histories. Finally, the data upon which modern research is based are not without complications and weaknesses, and criminologists differ in their assessments of the utility of these data and the methods that produce them. The readings in this section focus on this last point.

The methods that yield the major sources of crime data are, first, official data, or data produced by the criminal justice system. The most widely used data on crime in the United States are the Uniform Crime Reports

(UCR), published annually by the Federal Bureau of Investigation. Second, victimization surveys question a representative sample of a population about experiences of victimization. Since 1973, the National Institute of Justice and the Bureau of the Census have collaborated on the National Crime Victimization Survey (NCVS), the most widely used example of victimization data. Third, self-report studies of crime and delinquency have gained in importance in criminological research over the past fifty years. Self-report studies ask people about their own involvement in illegal acts. This approach may strike many students as silly, because the confessions of criminals cannot possibly be trusted. Strange as it may seem, however, criminologists do get useful data from these studies. Fourth, secondary data sources can provide extremely useful information about crime. Examples are records from insurance companies (excellent for tallying car theft) and the reports of medical examiners, coroners, or the Centers for Disease Control (all good sources when studying homicide). And finally, observational studies of a variety of criminals have a rich tradition in criminology, and they continue to be important sources of knowledge about criminality.

Unfortunately, we cannot simply say that one of these methods is the best. All have strengths and weaknesses, and because they can reveal different aspects of crime, they may be complementary. An important task for a criminologist contemplating a research project is to decide which method is most appropriate for the question at hand. At times, criminologists disagree about which method is best.

This section includes both samples of published research using these methods and discussions of what happens when criminologists use multiple methods in research. Readers will see how different data sources are used and will also be exposed to the controversy that occurs as a by-product of using methods that can yield different, perhaps even contradictory, research results.

Darrell Steffensmeier and Miles Harer, in their paper "Did Crime Rise or Fall During the Reagan Presidency?" use UCR and NCVS data to examine crime trends during the 1980s. Among their important findings are that, contrary to popular belief, crime did not increase during those years and, contrary to political rhetoric, observed decreases had little to do with government policies. This selection provides a good illustration of why it is important to think about how crime is measured. Using the UCR, based on the number of crimes reported to police, yields very different conclusions than using the NCVS, based on the number of crimes reported by victims of crime. Students should not conclude that it is impossible to estimate crime trends, nor should they throw up their hands in exasperation and decide that they can never know what is really going on. They should be aware, however, that sometimes some people or groups have a vested interest in the public's drawing particular conclusions. As citizens, their best protection against this kind of manipulation is to examine critically statements such as "crime is increasing" or "crime is decreasing," asking what type of data are being used and how a different conclusion might be drawn if other data were used. They may not be able to answer the question themselves, but when more citizens ask such questions, those who publicly comment on crime may be less prone to simple manipulations.

In "Reconciling Race and Class Differences in Self-Reported and Official Estimates of Delinquency," Delbert Elliott and Suzanne Ageton address two of the most interesting correlates of crime. Discussion of these correlates—race and social class—also has the potential for being highly socially charged; that is, people frequently get upset when the relationships between race and crime and between social class and crime are brought up. The next section includes two selections that specifically address issues of race, social class, and crime. Here, Elliott and Ageton focus on what appear to be substantively important differences reported in various studies of race and class. Some studies, based on official records—ordinarily arrest records—reported considerable differences between blacks and whites, as well as between lower and middle classes, in crime involvement. When early self-report studies were published, however, they reported either smaller differences between races and classes or no differences at all. Obviously, if we found that minorities and the lower classes did not commit more crime than others, these findings would have a major effect on both our perceptions about crime and our efforts to explain crime. Elliott and Ageton describe how the particular means of collecting self-reported crime data exaggerated the difference between the findings using these data and those using official sources. These important differences, and questions about why they exist, will be explored in subsequent sections.

"You Can Get Anything You Want If You've Got the Bread" is from William Chambliss's larger work On the Take, an important study of organized crime in an American city. It is included here because it is one of the most important pieces of observational research in modern criminology. The fruits of this research could only have been obtained by going out to talk to people and observe their behavior. Chambliss could not have collected these data from any of the other sources discussed here.

When some students think of criminological research, they imagine a sleuth—usually a cop or private eye, less frequently a scholar—out in the street observing, like Chambliss, the seedier side of life. Or, like the authors of the next selection, Richard Wright, Scott Decker, Allison Redfern, and Dietrich Smith, talking to actual "bad guys." Of course, Chambliss as well as Wright and his colleagues are in fact scholars. In "A Snowball's Chance in Hell: Doing Fieldwork with Active Residential Burglars," the authors describe how some criminologists decline to do fieldwork with active criminals because they perceive it to be impractical. In their article, they demonstrate that this kind of data collection does have its difficulties, but it is doable. Most important, there are things that we can learn about crime and criminals only by doing this kind of research.

As we have suggested, the appropriate method for studying crime should be determined by the research question. The papers in this section show how criminologists work to achieve the right match between questions and data sources. As you read other selections in this volume, consider how authors have succeeded in making that match.

Did Crime Rise or Fall During the Reagan Presidency?

DARRELL STEFFENSMEIER

MILES D. HARER

I N an earlier article that appeared in the *Journal of Research in Crime and Delinquency*, we used age-standardization methods to determine whether the 1980 to 1984 drop in the nation's index crime rate was due to changes in the age structure of the U.S. population, by specifying how the downward trend in index crimes is a function of shifts in the population, on the one hand, toward proportionately fewer young or high-crime-prone persons and toward more elderly or low-crime-risk persons, on the other hand. Our analysis included the two main sources of national crime data, the Uniform Crime Reports (UCR) and the National Crime Survey (NCS)—both of which reported that the nation's crime rate fell about 15 percent from 1980 to 1984. The rate adjustments performed revealed that age effects explained about 40 percent of the drop in the 1980–84 crude index rate in both the UCR and the NCS reporting programs.

In this report, we update our earlier analysis to cover the 1980–88 period, the years of the Reagan presidency. Both the UCR and the NCS report that the nation's crime rate fell between 1980 and 1988 (Federal Bureau of Investigation, 1980–88; Bureau of Justice Statistics, 1980–88)—the decline in crime was 4 percent according to the UCR and 17 percent according to the NCS. Neither the UCR nor the NCS changes can be interpreted straightforwardly, however. A problem common to both reporting programs is that their crime figures are not age-specific but are based on the U.S. population as a whole.

Consequently, the "crude" crime rates that are the basis for trend comparisons do not take into account two important factors: (a) that crime is strongly age-sensitive, and (b) that an "aging out" of the U.S. population has been occurring in recent years. Index crime rates peak during adolescence or early adulthood and decline with age.

Examining specific offenses shows that the peak age is earlier and the rate of decline from the peak much steeper for property than for person crimes. Age-specific arrest rates peak in the 16- to 18-year age range for all index crimes, then drop quickly to half the peak by age 21 for the property crimes and slowly to age 35 for person crimes. The nation's crime rate, therefore, is likely to be strongly affected by the age composition of the population. The most significant age shift during the 1980s has been the decrease in the population of those aged 15 to 24; this group is most prone to committing the index crimes. This age group peaked in the mid-1970s; it then held steady until about 1980, when it declined sharply.

The article is a timely one because (a) of predictions on the part of some criminologists that crime would drop during the 1980s due to the changing demographic makeup of the U.S. population; (b) of the attention this period has received in both popular and scientific writings that has centered, in particular, on a comparison of crime trends during the Reagan and previous (e.g., Carter) administrations; and (c) the Bush presidency has avowed a "tough enforcement" stance that in part rests on the Reagan administration's perceived success in reducing crime.

In other ways, too, the movement of the nation's crime rate has both theoretical and practical significance. The police use it as a measure of their success in fighting crime and as a leverage for the allocation of resources.

The public looks at crime statistics as a gauge of the severity of the country's crime problem and as a factor in making personal decisions such as where to live, or where to send children to school. In response to public concerns, the press and politicians point to crime statistics and rate changes as evidence of the success or failure of governmental policies in combating crime. Not surprisingly, officeholders and incumbent presidents are inclined to "manipulate the crime statistics to suit the purposes at hand, and [this] has not been a bipartisan effort." A rise in crime rates is likely to be ignored or explained away, whereas a downward trend is heralded as evidence of the success of current policies or ideology. Ex-president Reagan, for example, emphasized to Congress and the nation in his 1985 Inaugural Address that "for the first time in twenty years, the [UCR] index rate has fallen two years in a row," a drop that he then proudly attributed to aggressive law enforcement and a return to traditional values. Similar claims were made by then-candidate Bush in his 1988 campaign for the presidency.

DATA AND METHODS: UCR AND NCS

The Uniform Crime Reports (UCR) and the National Crime Survey (NCS) are the two main sources of national crime statistics. Both concentrate on measuring a limited number of well-defined crimes commonly referred to as *index crimes* and that are used for evaluating changes in the volume of crime.

The nucleus of the UCR, which has appeared annually since 1930, is "crimes known to the police." These statistics are based on police department counts of citizen reports of victimization and on the number of crimes or victimizations witnessed by the police themselves. The UCR's "crimes known to the police" does not refer to all types of crime, but to seven "serious" offenses that make up the crime index. These index crimes are homicide, aggravated assault, forcible rape, robbery, burglary, larceny-theft, and motor vehicle theft. The crime index is a single number obtained by adding together all the incidents of each of these crimes, and its year-to-year fluctuations have been used to measure trends in the nation's crime rate.

Created in 1973, the NCS provides a second measure of annual crime data. Rather than using police records, this survey is based on a scientifically selected sample of households throughout the United States. All persons over 12 years of age in these households are questioned about their experience with six crimes: assault, forcible rape, robbery, burglary, larceny, and motor vehicle theft. As in the UCR, the basic counting unit in the NCS is offenses or criminal incidents. Each criminal incident is counted only once, by the most serious act that took place during the incident, ranked in accordance with the seriousness classification used by the FBI.

Each program is subject to the kinds of errors and problems typical of its method of data collection. First, the UCR counts only crime (i.e., incidents or victimizations) that comes to the attention of the police. The NCS obtains information on both reported and unreported crime. Second, the UCR counts crimes committed against all people and all businesses, organizations, governmental agencies, and the like. The NCS counts only crimes against persons age 12 or older and their households.

Third, the two series compute rates using different population bases, in some instances. The NCS base for burglary, motor vehicle theft, and household larceny is households, whereas the UCR base is population. Because of these differences, moreover, it is necessary to convert the household rates for these offenses to per capita rates to enable a comparison of the NCS with the UCR.

As a result of these limitations in the NCS data, the UCR in fact may offer the more reliable and valid measure of serious crime, for several reasons. First, the more serious the crime (within the broad index categories), the more likely the citizenry and/or the police are to report it. As Skogan states, "Most victimizations are not notable events. The majority are property crimes in which the perpetrator is never detected. The financial stakes are small, and the costs of calling the police greatly outweigh the benefits." Second, NCS data are derived from a sample which is intended to be representative of the national population, but representativeness does not appear to be constant over time; there is evidence that changes in the panel connected with residential mobility bias victimization results toward a declining trend in rates of victimization. Finally, the NCS does not include homicide, thefts from businesses (e.g., shoplifting or commercial burglaries), nor crimes against children under 12 years of age.

The most important difference between the two reporting programs is that index crimes that fall on the low end of the seriousness continuum are more likely to be counted in the NCS, and crimes that fall on the high end of the seriousness continuum are more likely to be included in the UCR. There are two main reasons for this: (a) citizens report to NCS interviewers a substantial volume of trivial of-

fenses that they fail to report to law enforcement agencies, just as the police oftentimes overlook minor offenses and do not record them; and (b) when a single event includes several crimes committed together, the NCS records all the crimes that fall into NCS categories. In contrast, UCR statistics include only the most serious crime committed within a single event. It is reasonable to conclude, therefore, that the index statistics of UCR offer the more reliable and valid measure of serious crime.

Regardless of which is the better measure, our concern is with a problem common to both reporting programs: their crime figures are not age-specific but are crude rates based on the U.S. population as a whole instead of the population at risk. Consequently, both the UCR and the NCS are flawed gauges of trends in the nation's crime rate. Adjustment procedures are needed to purge any observed changes in the crude rate that are due to shifts in the age structure of the population.

There is a fair amount of agreement between the UCR and NCS over the 1980 through 1988 trends. Both programs show a decline in crime during the early 1980s followed by an increase, so that the overall effect is one of relative stability in the nation's crime rate during the Reagan presidency. Furthermore, as reported in Steffensmeier and Harer, an analysis of the nation's crime rate backward to include the years of the Carter presidency reveals—once age effects are purged—the following: (a) the UCR shows an overall modest rise in crime during the late 1970s, and (b) the NCS shows essentially stable or slightly declining rates. The downward trend during the late 1970s observed in the NCS data is also reported in the National Youth Survey which shows declining rates of delinquency during this period, whereas the Monitoring the Future study of high school seniors shows fluctuating but fairly stable offense rates during the 1975–85 period. Thus, the findings from these two annual surveys offer supporting evidence not only that index crimes were either fairly stable or were on the decline during the period prior to the Reagan years but also that the nation's crime rate has held fairly stable during the 1980s once age effects are purged.

DISCUSSION

Because a disproportionate number of adolescents and young adults commit the index crimes that compose the nation's crime rate, it follows that a sharp decline in their numbers may dramatically lower the level of crime in a society. By the start of the 1980s, the aging of the "baby boom" generation of the 1950s, followed by the "baby bust" cohorts of the 1960s, had reduced considerably the proportion of persons in the age groups that generally commit the largest numbers of crimes. There also has been during the 1980s a continual growth of large elderly cohorts, which are the years of least active criminality. Not surprisingly, therefore, the two main sources of national crime data, the UCR and the NCS, both report that the nation's crime rate fell from 1980 to 1988. But use of UCR and NCS crime figures is likely to be misleading because changes in their crime rates are determined without adjusting for changes in the age structure of the population.

On the basis of the evidence presented, we conclude that a very sizable portion of the reported drop in the nation's crime rate (i.e., index crimes) is due to demographic change. The crude (or reported) decline in the UCR rate is about 4 percent, whereas the true (adjusted) rate of change is an actual increase of about 7 percent. For the NCS, the crude decline is about 17 percent whereas the adjusted decline is only 7 percent once age effects are purged. Thus 100 percent plus of the reported drop in the nation's crime rate as publicized through the UCR and about 60 percent of the drop as reported in the NCS are due to shifts in the age structure alone.

When divided into person and property crimes, the adjusted change in the UCR per-

son index is an increase of 28 percent as compared to 24 percent based on crude rates; for the property index, the adjusted change is a 6 percent increase that compares to a 6 percent decline based on crude rates. For NCS data, the adjusted rate changes are a 1 percent decline in the person index and a 7 percent decline in the property index, that compares to a 4 percent and a 17 percent decline as based on NCS crude figures. The effects are smaller for the person than the property crimes because, during the 1980s, the "baby boom" children are passing into their late 20s and early 30s; although these are ages at which the rates for person crimes decline some from earlier years, they still remain fairly high.

Social scientists continue to debate the reliability and validity of the two statistical series. The UCR is older and more familiar, has a stronger media image, and is favored by law enforcement officials. We are more likely to read or hear about the UCR statistics, which signal whether crime is rising or falling. The major disadvantages of the UCR are that much crime (mainly, less serious forms of lawbreaking) is not reported by citizens to the police and, because of budgetary or political pressures, published crime figures may be either inflated or shrunk. Nonetheless, although the NCS data are derived from a sample which is intended to be representative of the national population, representativeness does not appear to be constant over time; there is evidence that changes in the panel connected with residential mobility bias victimization results toward a declining trend in rates of victimization.

The major advantages of the UCR are that it provides more complete coverage of index crimes and that it tends to record crimes which are more serious on the average than those recorded in victimization surveys. In this sense, the UCR offenses known to the police are better than NCS victimization data as indicators of serious crime as defined both by the citizenry and by the police.

Nevertheless, leaving this issue aside, our analysis shows that (a) where applicable, age adjustment explains a substantial portion of the decline in the nation's crime rate as reported in both the UCR and the NCS, and (b) after age adjustment, the nation's crime rate has been relatively stable over the Reagan years and even as far back as the mid-1970s. Whichever figure one chooses to emphasize, the 7 percent rise in the UCR or the 7 percent drop in the NCS, these represent small or relatively insignificant changes in the nation's crime rate which are easily attributable to random fluctuation. This absence of significant change, moreover, prevails across all the individual crimes except aggravated assault in the UCR and motor vehicle theft in both the UCR and NCS, where increases of about 30 percent are found. In this sense, too, the two crime-reporting programs are not that far apart in what they suggest about whether rates of serious criminal behavior are decreasing, increasing, or staying about the same, thereby increasing our confidence that the overriding pattern in the nation's crime rate is one of stability rather than real change.

Forecasting Trends in the Nation's Crime Rate

Besides analyzing the past, the data allow us to forecast the future and to gauge the impact age shifts of the population will have on crime in the 1990s.

First, we expect that the crude rates for the person crimes (homicide, aggravated assault, rape) will drop more sharply in the 1990s as the "baby boom" generation passes into middle and old age. Second, we anticipate that property crime rates will continue to decline into the early 1990s, after which they will level off and even rise slightly by the late 1990s as the "mini baby boom" cohorts of the post-Vietnam period spread across the teenage years, the years of high risk for the index property crimes. This rise will continue into the next century (year 2000), at which time person crime rates also will begin to rise. Moreover, because the crime index is heavily weighted by the much larger volume of property crime (es-

pecially larceny), trends in the nation's crime rate will parallel the index property crime trends.

These predictions are jeopardized by two important caveats. First, they assume that all else is equal—that the technology, social organization, and behavior patterns that have governed the reactions of Americans to criminal risk in the past will apply in the future. Second, the predictions consider age-structure changes in the population as a whole but do not take into account age-structure changes in specific population groupings whose at-risk probability for crime may be unusually high. For example, the forecasts may be affected by differential fertility rates and immigration patterns which may bring about an increase in the proportion of young black and Hispanic males in the population who commit a disproportionate share of the index crimes.

Nonetheless, property crime rates should begin to rebound in the mid-1990s as the mini-baby boomers move through adolescence, but there is some prospect of a downward trend in violent crime in the next decade as the overall population grows older and, in effect, becomes less violence prone. Our results have some pertinence for a major theoretical issue in criminology and a principal policy debate of recent years—the effects of greater sanction severity and rising rates of imprisonment on the nation's crime rate. The principal thrust of U.S. crime-control policy in recent years has been general deterrence and incapacitation, with the UCR index rates (rather than NCS rates) used as the barometer of the success/failure of the policy. The crime problem would be met, above all, by increasing the severity of punishment to the extent that prospective offenders would refrain out of fear of the consequences and by keeping out of circulation those individuals most at risk to commit crimes.

This approach has been aimed particularly at "rapists," "muggers," and other violent offenders—who, in the eyes of the citizenry and law enforcement, symbolize the gravest element of the crime problem. Officials of the Reagan administration (and Reagan himself) steadfastly maintained that stronger enforcement and stiffer sentencing have reduced crime.

Other commentators have been less sanguine about the effectiveness of the law enforcement strategy, arguing instead that, above and beyond the penalties currently in place—which they view as already quite high—stiffer sentencing or the "piling on of punishment" will have very little, if any, deterrent effect on the level of crime in society as a whole and, at best, only a small, short-term incapacitative effect. The debate has been acrimonious at times, with some researchers even claiming that Reagan/Bush appointees have attempted to manipulate or suppress the results of empirical studies in ways that would produce data favorable to longer prison sentences.

Imprisonment rates rose far more sharply in the 1980s than in any previous decade in the nation's history. In spite of their record-setting pace, there was no discernible drop in either the nation's crime rate as a whole or in the "serious" street crime rate. Indeed, if we consider only the UCR—judged typically by public officials as the better measure of serious crime and used as their yardstick of trends in the nation's crime rate—both the index rate and especially the street crime rate have inched upward. As a group, the "serious" crimes of homicide, forcible rape, aggravated assault, and robbery increased about 17 percent since 1980. Also, some crimes not included in the crime index such as drug trafficking appear to have risen sharply (e.g., UCR arrests for drug offenses—that mostly involve drug dealing—increased 99 percent from 1980 to 1988).

It obviously is risky business to forge a causal linkage between crime rates and imprisonment rates in the absence of statistical controls for other relevant variables, especially because statistics on crime allow considerable leeway for smoke and mirrors. But taken at face value—the fact that tougher enforcement and bulging prisons have not led to the expected reduction in crime (small drop in NCS but small rise in UCR) suggests that the criminal justice system does not contain the solution to the nation's crime problem, and that no law enforcement strategy can be confidently recommended to remedy it.

CONCLUSION

Both on the campaign trail and in office, President Reagan regularly exhorted the American citizenry with the question, "Are you better off today than . . . ?" It is too soon to render a verdict on most social and economic matters touched by the Reagan presidency. As for crime, the verdict is probably mixed—not better, but not much worse, either. Controlling for age effects (and ignoring the expanding drug problem), the magnitude of the crime problem is about the same in 1988 as it was in 1980.

QUESTIONS FOR DISCUSSION AND WRITING

1. What did the UCR and NCS show happened between 1980 and 1988?
2. What is a problem common to both the UCR and NCS?
3. What do the authors conclude "on the basis of the evidence presented"?

Reconciling Race and Class Differences in Self-Reported and Official Estimates of Delinquency

DELBERT S. ELLIOTT

SUZANNE S. AGETON

PROBLEMS of conceptualization, definition, and measurement continue to plague researchers interested in the epidemiology and etiology of delinquency. While most would acknowledge the conceptual distinction between delinquent behavior and official responses to delinquent behavior, these distinctions are not clearly maintained in the measurement of delinquency or in the interpretation and analysis of specific delinquency data. This problem is clearly illustrated in the current controversy over the validity of self-reported (as compared with official) estimates of the incidence and distribution of delinquency in the general adolescent population. Put simply, there are those who argue that police and arrest records provide more accurate and reliable estimates of the social correlates of delinquent behavior than do self-report surveys; others hold the opposite view.

Self-report measures of delinquency provide a different picture of the incidence and distribution of delinquent behavior than do

From "Reconciling Race and Class Differences in Self-Reported and Official Estimates of Delinquency" by D. Elliott and S. Ageton, 1980, *American Sociological Review* 45:95–110. Copyright © Delbert Elliott and Suzanne Ageton. Reprinted by permission of The American Sociological Association.

official arrest records. Both types of data indicate significant age and sex differentials, but the magnitude of these differences is much smaller with self-reported data than with official arrest data.

At the center of the controversy, however, is the fact that self-report studies generally find no differences in delinquent behavior by class or race, while studies relying upon police and court data report significant differences by both class and race.

To date, attempts to reconcile this apparent discrepancy between official and self-reported findings have taken one of two approaches. Most recently, researchers have challenged the strength of the empirical evidence for the class differential in official data. Tittle and Villemez and Tittle et al. reviewed earlier published research findings and concluded that the class differences in official data are not clearly established and that the widespread belief in an inverse relationship between class and crime is not based upon sound empirical research findings. Hindelang et al. have also concluded that police records of juvenile offenses are not strongly or even moderately related to socioeconomic status.[1] On the other hand, the race differential in official data has not been seriously challenged, to our knowledge.

The second and most frequent approach has been to challenge the methodological adequacy of the self-report technique and the adequacy of self-report research. Specifically, critics of self-report research contend:

1. There are problems inherent in the method itself which make it inaccurate and unreliable. These problems include deliberate falsification, inaccurate recall, and forward and backward telescoping.
2. There are problems with the construction of measures used in self-report research and with the procedures for administering the measures. These problems concern the lack of representativity in items, item overlapping, imprecise response sets, and the lack of anonymity of respondents.
3. There are problems with generalizing from self-report studies, due to the almost exclusive reliance upon small, unrepresentative samples.

This paper is concerned with this second approach to reconciling official and self-reported findings with respect to class and race. We will not deal with those problems inherent in the self-report method itself, except to note that available research seems to support both the validity and reliability of the method. Instead, we will deal with the correctable problems, i.e., the construction of measures and their administration, as well as representativity and sample size. The general question we will address here is whether or not the satisfactory resolution of these methodological issues in the construction and administration of self-report measures will result in greater consistency between self-reported and official data. More specifically, will the satisfactory resolution of these problems produce race and class differentials in self-reported estimates of delinquent behavior?

The discussion that follows will focus on: (1) the methodological criticisms of previous self-report delinquency (SRD) research; (2) the use of a new SRD measure in a national youth study; (3) a comparison of the race/class findings of this study with previous SRD research and with official arrest data; and (4) the epidemiological and theoretical implications of these findings.

PROBLEMS WITH SRD RESEARCH

Instrument Construction

Much of the controversy over self-report measures involves problems with instrument construction. Primarily, criticism centers on three issues: (1) the question of the representativeness of items employed in SRD measures; (2) problems of item overlap; and (3) limited or ambiguous response sets.

The major criticism concerns the unrepresentativity of the items selected. Trivial and nonserious offenses (e.g., cutting classes and disobeying parents) are often overrepresented, while serious violations of the criminal code (e.g., burglary, robbery, and sexual assault) are frequently omitted. In addition, many SRD measures tend to overrepresent certain behavioral dimensions (e.g., theft) to the exclusion of other relevant delinquent acts. As a result of such selection processes, most existing SRD measures have a restricted focus and do not represent the full range of delinquent acts; this limits the appropriateness of these scales as general measures of delinquent behavior.

Another problem is the overlapping nature of items often included in SRD measures, which results in inaccurate estimates of frequency due to duplicate counts of certain events. For example, many SRD measures include a "shoplifting" item, a "theft under $5" item, and a "theft $5–50" item. A single theft event could logically be reported on two of these items. The presence of both a "cutting school" and a "cutting class" item represents another form of measurement redundancy since cutting school necessarily involves cutting classes. This problem is not easily overcome, since a given behavioral event in fact may involve more than a single offense. Nevertheless, item overlapping creates a potential source of error in estimating the volume of delinquent behavior from SRD measures.

The type of response sets typically employed with SRD measures has been another source of criticism. One major concern has been the frequent use of normative response categories such as "often," "sometimes," and "occasionally." This type of response set is open to wide variations in interpretation by respondents, and precludes any precise count of the actual number of acts committed.

Other response sets used to estimate the number of behaviors (e.g., "never," "once or twice," and "three times or more") have been challenged on the grounds that they are not precise categories for numerical estimation, and that numerical estimates based upon such categories may severely truncate the true distribution of responses. With the above set, for example, any number of behaviors in excess of two is collapsed into a single "high" category. While this procedure may allow for some discrimination between youth at the low end of the frequency distribution, it clearly precludes any discrimination at the high end. Thus, a youth involved in three shoplifting offenses during the specified period receives the same "score" as a youth involved in 50 or 100 shoplifting events during the period. This limited set of categorical responses appears particularly problematic when the reporting period involves a year or more and when such items as using marijuana; drinking beer, wine, or liquor; and carrying a concealed weapon are included in the SRD measure.

Administration Procedures

The manner in which the measures are administered is also a problematic area for self-report delinquency research. Here the issue concerns: (1) anonymous vs. identified respondents, and (2) questionnaire vs. interview formats.

Many researchers have argued that anonymity has to be guaranteed or youth will not admit certain offenses—probably the more serious, stigmatizing ones. Research on this question suggests that there is slightly more reporting of offenses under conditions of anonymity, but that anonymous/identified differences are slight and statistically insignificant. These findings have led Dentler to comment that the necessity for anonymity is overemphasized, and that it may in fact lead to reduced involvement by respondents and careless or facetious answers.

On the matter of interview vs. questionnaire formats, the discussion again involves the issue of anonymity, and the belief that self-administered questionnaires are more likely to produce accurate responses than personal interviews. One recent self-report delinquency research study compared results from structured interviews and self-administered checklists, where anonymity was guaranteed under both conditions. While seven of the eight offenses were admitted more often under checklist conditions than under interview conditions, none of the differences was significant at the .05 level. Even when education, sex, class, and IQ were controlled, no significant differences were obtained.

Some researchers, most notably Gold, have argued that the interview format has significant advantages for delinquency research in that it permits clarification of specific behaviors and, consequently, the ability to more correctly classify illegal acts. In general, however, there is still controversy over the effects of specific administration procedures when the research is directed toward illegal or socially disapproved behaviors.

Sampling Design and Generality

Another problematic area for self-report delinquency research is that of the generality of findings. Here the question focuses primarily on the adequacy of the sampling designs for: (1) inferences to the adolescent population, and (2) comparisons with official data.

In most cases, SRD measures have been administered to small, select samples of youth, such as high school students in a particular local community or adolescents processed by a local juvenile court. The samples are rarely probability samples, and generalizations (about the adolescent populations sampled) cannot be made with any known degree of accuracy. Only two published studies involve national probability samples.

A further concern is that few cohort studies using normal populations have incorporated a self-report measure in their instruments. This means that the age and sex gradients of SRD measures are not known, a critical fact if this measurement approach is to become more refined and useful. Furthermore, since the studies using self-report measures have almost always been cross-sectional ones, little is known about the dynamics of self-reported behavior over time.

Finally, Empey notes that national self-report studies have not been conducted on an annual basis and, as a result, it is not possible to discern trends across time or to make direct comparisons with other standard delinquency data such as the Uniform Crime Reports (UCR) or the National Crime Panel (NCP).

THE NATIONAL YOUTH SURVEY

We will now report on a national youth study in which we have attempted to deal with the previously noted methodological criticisms of self-report delinquency research. Our aim will be to see if these improvements in the quality of self-report research have any impact on self-report findings relative to findings from official data.

The National Youth Survey involves a five-year panel design with a national probability sample of 1,726 adolescents aged 11–17 in 1976. The total youth sample was selected and initially interviewed between January and March, 1977, concerning behavior during the calendar year 1976. The second survey was completed between January and March, 1978, to obtain delinquency estimates for the calendar year 1977. The third, fourth, and fifth surveys will also be conducted between each January and March of the years 1979, 1980, and 1981.

The data reported herein are taken from the first survey, completed in 1977. The estimates presented are thus for delinquent behavior during the calendar year 1976.

Construction of New SRD Measure

In constructing the SRD measure for this study, we attempted to obtain a representative set of offenses. Given our interest in comparing SRD and UCR estimates, we began by listing offenses included in the UCR. Any specific act (with the exception of traffic violations) involving more than 1% of the reported juvenile arrests for 1972–1974 is included in the SRD measure.

In addition to the list of specific offenses, the UCR contains a general category, "all other offenses," which often accounts for a high proportion of the total juvenile arrests. To cover the types of acts likely to fall within this general category, and to increase the comprehensiveness of the measure, two general selection criteria were used to choose additional items. First, items which were theoretically relevant to a delinquent lifestyle or subculture as discussed in the literature were selected for inclusion in this measure. Thus, additional items—such as gang fighting, sexual intercourse, and carrying a hidden weapon—are included. Second, a systematic review of existing SRD measures was undertaken to locate items that tapped specific dimensions of delinquent behavior not previously included.

We believe the resulting set of 47 items to be both more comprehensive and more representative of the conceptual universe of delinquent acts than found in prior SRD measures used in major, large-scale studies. The item set includes all but one of the UCR Part I offenses (homicide is excluded); 60% of Part II offenses;

and a wide range of "other" offenses—such as delinquent lifestyle items, misdemeanors, and some status offenses. The vast majority of items involve a violation of criminal statutes.

Two separate response sets are being used. Respondents initially are asked to indicate how many times during the past year they committed each act. If an individual's response to this open-ended question involves a frequency of 10 or more, interviewers then ask the youth to select one of the following categorical responses: (1) once a month, (2) once every 2–3 weeks, (3) once a week, (4) 2–3 times a week, (5) once a day, or (6) 2–3 times a day.[2] A comparison of the two response sets indicates high agreement between frequency estimates given in direct response to the open-ended question and frequency estimates based upon the implied frequency associated with the midpoint of the category selected.[3]

A specific attempt was also made to eliminate as much overlap in items as possible. None of the items contains a necessary overlap as in "cutting school" and "cutting class." Although some possible overlap remains, we do not feel it constitutes a serious problem with this SRD measure.

The SRD measure asks respondents to indicate how many times, "from Christmas a year ago to the Christmas just past," they committed each offense. The recall period is thus a year, anchored by a specific reference point relevant to most youth. The use of a one-year period which coincides almost precisely with the calendar year allows for direct comparison with UCR data, NCP victimization data, and some prior SRD data. It also avoids the need to adjust for seasonal variations, which would be necessary if a shorter time period were involved.

Administration Procedures

For the present study, the research design (a longitudinal panel design) precludes a guarantee of anonymity. Therefore, our major concern is to guarantee respondents that their answers will be confidential. This assurance is given verbally as well as being contained in the written consent form signed by all youth and their parents. In addition, a Certificate of Confidentiality from the Department of Health, Education, and Welfare guarantees all respondents that the data and the interviewers will be protected from legal subpoena.

The interview format was selected over the self-administered questionnaire format for several reasons. First, we share Gold's belief that the interview situation (if properly structured to protect confidentiality) can insure more accurate, reliable data. Second, the necessity of securing informed consents from all subjects and the complexity of the present research require, in our judgment, a personal contact with the respondents. Once this contact is made, it seems logical to use the interviewer to facilitate the data collection process and to improve the quality of the data obtained. Finally, some of our previous research suggests that the differences in responding to SRD items in a questionnaire as opposed to an interview format are not significant. . . .

Summary of New Measure

In sum, the current SRD measure addresses many of the central criticism of prior SRD measures. It is more representative of the full range of delinquent acts than were prior SRD measures and involves fewer overlapping items; it also employs a response set which provides better discrimination at the high end of the frequency continuum and is more suited to estimating the actual number of behaviors committed. The choice of a one-year time frame with a panel design involving a one-year time lag is based upon both conceptual and practical concerns. Compared with the other SRD measures, the measure involves a moderate recall period, captures seasonal variations, and permits a direct comparison with other self-report and official measures which are reported annually. And, finally, the study involves a national probability sample of youth aged 11–17.

ANALYSIS OF DATA

. . .

Race and Class Differentials

Unlike most previous self-report studies, we find significant race differences for total SRD and for predatory crimes against property. Blacks report significantly higher frequencies than do whites on each of these measures. In both cases, the differences in means are substantial. With respect to total offenses, blacks report three offenses for every two reported by whites. For crimes against property, blacks report more than two offenses for every offense reported by whites.

While there is a substantial difference in mean scores on the crimes against persons scale, it is not statistically significant. The difference in the total SRD score appears to be primarily the result of the very high level of property crimes reported by blacks.

We also observe a class differential for total SRD and for predatory crimes against persons. For total SRD scores, the difference is between lower socioeconomic status youth and others; i.e., there does not appear to be any difference between working- and middle-class group means.

The differences are greater, and the trend is more linear, for the crimes against persons scale means than for total SRD. Lower-class youth report nearly four times as many offenses as do middle-class youth and one-and-one-half times as many as working-class youth. There is also a substantial class difference in the mean number of crimes against persons, but this difference is not statistically significant. There are clearly no substantial differences in means for any of the remaining subscales. . . .

Relationship Between SRD and Official Data

In sum, it appears likely that the differences between the findings reported here and those from earlier self-report studies are, in fact, the result of differences in the specific SRD measures employed. The findings also suggest a logical connection between self-report and official measures of delinquency which, at least in part, accounts for the observed differences in the class and race distributions of these two measures.

The consistent findings of earlier self-report studies have led many sociologists and criminologists to the conclusion that race and class differences in arrests are primarily the result of processing biases and have little or no basis in behavior. The findings from the 1977 National Youth Survey suggest some behavioral basis for the observed class and race differences in official processing. In this sense, the National Youth Survey data are more consistent with official arrest data than are data from most prior self-report studies.

Further, these findings provide some insight into the mechanism whereby official actions produce exaggerated race and class (as well as age and sex) differences in delinquent behavior when compared with self-reported differences in normal adolescent populations. On both logical and empirical grounds, it seems reasonable to argue that the more frequent and serious offenders are more likely to be arrested, and that the youth population represented in official police statistics is not a representative sample of all youth.

Self-report studies are capturing a broader range of persons and levels of involvement in delinquent behavior than are official arrest statistics. Virtually all youth report some delinquent activity on self-report measures, but for the vast majority the offenses are neither very frequent nor very serious. Police contacts, on the other hand, are most likely to concern youth who are involved in either very serious or very frequent delinquent acts. Police contacts with youth thus involve a more restricted segment of the general youth population.

The findings discussed previously indicate that race and class differences are more extreme at the high end of the frequency continuum, that part of the delinquency continuum where police contacts are more likely. In fact, at this end of the frequency continuum, self-report and official correlates of delinquent behavior are relatively similar. While we do not deny the existence of official processing biases, it does appear that official correlates of delinquency also reflect real differences in the frequency and seriousness of delinquent acts.

The results of this self-report delinquency study also have implications for previous tests of theoretical propositions which used SRD data. Stated simply, earlier self-report measures may not have been sensitive enough to capture the theoretically important differences in delinquency involvement. Given the truncated frequency distributions and the restricted behavioral range of earlier self-report measures, the only distinctions possible were fine gradations between relatively nondelinquent youth.

For example, earlier distinctions were typically among (1) youth with no reported offenses; (2) those with one or two offenses; and (3) those with three or more offenses. Given the extensive frequency distribution observed in this study, there is reason to question whether or not such a trichotomy would capture meaningful distinctions among offending youth. The most significant difference may not be between the nonoffender and the one-time offender, or even between the one-time and multiple-time offender. Equal or greater significance may be found between those reporting over (or under) 25 nonserious offenses, or between those reporting over (or under) five serious offenses.

The ability to discriminate more fully among many levels and types of involvement in delinquent behavior introduces much more variance into the delinquency measure. That ability also allows for the identification of more extreme groups of offenders, and that identification may be particularly relevant for tests of theoretical propositions.

NOTES

1. Hindelang et al. have also recently studied the extent to which sex and race are differentially related to self-reported and official records of delinquency, and some of their conclusions with regard to the race discrepancy will be cited later.
2. The categorical response set has led to the identification of some highly episodic events, e.g., 20 shoplifting offenses, all occurring within a two-month period during the summer (an initial response of 20; a categorical response 2–3 times a week, and an interviewer probe revealing that the offenses all occurred during the summer).
3. The only exception involves the last two high-frequency categories. At this end of the frequency continuum, estimates based upon the midpoint of the category are substantially higher than the frequency response given directly. The open-ended frequency measure thus appears to provide a more conservative estimate of number of delinquent acts, and the estimates reported here are based upon this response.

QUESTIONS FOR DISCUSSION AND WRITING

1. What are the similarities and differences with respect to age, sex, class, and race in the incidence and distribution of delinquent behavior in self-reported and official arrest data?
2. What differences, if any, did the authors find with respect to race?
3. What differences, if any, did the authors find with respect to class?

You Can Get Anything You Want
If You've Got the Bread

WILLIAM J. CHAMBLISS

I N a very real, if surprising way my work on the crime network began with an observation of Mark Twain's. He noted that "science is a fascinating thing: we get such wholesale returns of conjecture out of such trifling investments in fact." The trifling investment in fact that characterized the study of crime in the 1960s was a major impetus for me to shed my academic stance long enough to go into the streets of the city—more precisely, down to skid row and the black ghetto—to see what was taking place.

I chose this area of the city for a good reason: 80 to 90 percent of all the arrests in every city in the United States take place in the skid-row, lower-class, slum areas. I wanted to know why the police made most of their arrests in this rather small geographical area and, more precisely, how the working policeman decided to arrest some people and not others.

In 1962, a change in the sociological weather was taking place that was affecting us all, and it made us look again at what had often been taken for granted. Sociologists began to look through the windows of police cars and behind the bars of jail cells to discover "the law in action." I was skeptical that such a practice would yield reliable results. I decided, therefore, to watch the law work from the vantage point of those it worked on.

In an earlier time, I had passed through skid rows in various cities while bumming around the country and working as a migratory laborer. I felt, therefore, that I could pass as a resident if I dressed and acted as I remembered others in those areas dressing and acting.

With two days' growth of beard, a pair of khaki pants, and an old shirt, I drove down to the edge of that magical ring that circumscribes and, in fact, effectively hides skid row from the eyes of those who do not care to see it. I walked the two blocks between the commercial center and skid row, turned a corner, and found myself there: incognito—almost. One block later two large black men stepped from doorways and moved toward me. Whoosh went my adrenaline.

"Got a buck, buddy?" It used to be a quarter, I thought.

"No, sorry." I was unnerved by the realization that they knew I was enough of an outsider to try to put the bite on me for a dollar.

It was raining this day, in that ubiquitous rain that is the hallmark of Seattle's climate. So I looked for shelter and found a seat in Tip's Amusement Parlor, where I had a cup of coffee. I didn't like coffee and would have preferred tea, but coffee, I calculated, was essential for the image.

Pinball machines stood against the wall at Tip's. After my coffee I played one, and the waitress gave me a strange look when I

From *On the Take: Petty Crooks to Presidents* (pp. 13–31) by W. J. Chambliss, 1978, Bloomington, In.: Indiana University Press. Copyright © 1978 Indiana University Press. Reprinted with permission.

walked away from the machine with four unplayed "free games."

"Hey, don't you want the money for them games you won?"

"Oh. Oh, yeah." She went to the cash register and gave me forty cents. Then she went to the machine and rang off the games I had won.

Out in the rain, I wondered about the meaning of all that. My thoughts were interrupted, however, by the sight of a patrol car moving slowly down the street. I walked in the same direction. The car, with two policemen inside, stopped at the curb and motioned to a man standing in a doorway. The man went to the car. They talked for a minute. The patrol car pulled away and the man went back to the doorway.

For the next several days I observed numerous incidents of this kind. They made little sense at first: foot patrolmen would, apparently at random, walk up and shake the handle of some closed businesses while completely ignoring many others. I saw people who appeared to be only slightly intoxicated arrested while others who were barely able to walk were either ignored or told to go home.

Once in the middle of a sunny (for a change) Friday afternoon, a very large Spanish-looking woman ran onto the street from a small hotel entrance. She was screaming, "He's gonna kill me."

She saw a foot patrolman walking by and anxiously ran up to him. He waved his hand impatiently to ward her off and continued his walk down the street. A patrol car turned the corner in the next moment and moved slowly down the street. The woman ran up to the window of the car and said, "He's gonna kill me." The patrol car pulled away from her, turned the next corner, and was gone.

After a week of observation, my only conclusion was that the arrest-nonarrest, action-nonaction decision of a policeman was totally random and irrational.

Sitting in Tip's Amusement Parlor one afternoon, I was joined by a patrolman whom I had seen several times. I started a conversation. He asked me what I did and I said, "I drive a truck." In the middle of his lunch I said, "You know something, I have always wondered how you guys decide who to pick up and who to ignore—where to look for things and where not to."

He replied, "Look, when you know a place as well as I know this one—I been on this beat for fifteen years—you just naturally know where to look, who's okay, and who needs to be watched. If a light's on when it should be off, I go see. If a broad's on this corner when she usually works uptown, I check her out. It's like when my old lady don't cook dinner, I know something is wrong."

This made sense to me so I accepted it as the start of an explanation.

Tip's was only a few minutes from the downtown business section. It stood behind an invisible wall that separated the city's skid row area of flophouses, Salvation Army relief centers, drunks, occasional workers, and amusement parlors from the rest of the city. It was a simple thing to cross the imaginary line and pass out of the respectable community. But despite the ease of access, only those with special interest in the pleasures, pains, and profits to be had behind the wall ever ventured there.

Behind the facade of banks, office buildings, and department stores, a different life pounded out a heartbeat distinct from that of the neighboring commercial district. Tip's, along with half a hundred similar establishments, was very much a part of this invisible world hidden within the city.

The outside of Tip's had the appearance of a run-down bowling alley. Two of the bulbs in the neon sign were burned out; the paint was peeling and the door was painted an offensive green that was purchased because it was outdated and therefore inexpensive. Only the large plate-glass window which provided a panoramic view of the street was new and well kept.

Inside Tip's was a long lunch counter where Millie (pseudonym), an over-the-hill ex-prostitute and sometime junkie, served coffee hot enough to take away the chill of a night spent in a cold, wet alley. Other than the long lunch counter and chair behind the cigar case beside the cash register, there were no seats in Tip's. A row of pinball machines stood where booths might have been. The un-initiated played pinball for the sheer joy of watching the flashing lights and the meaningless numbers hop around the face of the machine. The initiated played for pay—or so they hoped. These machines were part of a relatively recent innovation in pinballs; they were "multiple coin" machines. The principle is simple enough: instead of inserting one dime and playing the game, you can insert as many dimes as you can shove into the slot. The more dimes you insert the higher the odds go and the more you stand to win—or, more likely, to lose.

Naturally, the odds do not increase as a straight increment of how many dimes you put in. The machines are set to make the increase in odds something less than the increase one might expect mathematically to occur with every additional dime. Some of the players no doubt were aware of this but played anyway. Others—one suspects the majority—were really taken in by the assumption that underlies all gambling: that the "house" is in fact gambling and can be beaten. In reality the house never gambles: it only takes advantage of some well-known and clear mathematical principles of chance. The house cannot go broke and gamblers cannot beat the house no matter how much an individual may win. In the end the laws of chance are more powerful than the laws of luck.

On cold winter or rainy days, the area around the pinball machines and between the machines and the window are filled with men standing around. Since it rains more often than not, business was usually brisk. Most of the customers were unemployed, unattached men for whom the inside of Tip's offered some relief not only from the incessant drizzle but from the boredom of their cheap hotel rooms or the bad coffee of the "social clubs" set up by various charities.

One afternoon while I was having coffee at Tip's, I noticed people going in and out of a back room. I asked Millie, who had become my friend, where these people were going.

Millie: To play cards.
Me: Back there?
Millie: Yes, that's where the poker games are.
Me: Can I play?
Millie: Sure, just go in. But watch your wallet.

So I go, hesitantly, through the back door and into a large room which has seven octagonal, green felt-covered tables. People are playing five-card stud at five of the tables. I am immediately offered a seat by a hand gesture from the cardroom manager. I play—all the time watching my wallet, as I had been advised.

There is no money on the table, only small poker chips. The chips, however, are purchased from the cardroom manager. The limit on the bet varies but ranges between three and five dollars at these tables. The players are an interesting assortment of men, most of whom seem to be "down on their luck." They are mainly middle-aged men playing conservative cards with what appears to be a group of friends. Most of them are acquaintances, a few are friends. The daytime game tends to draw the same group of people together day after day barring illness or recovery from a drunk. The players are amazingly patient and remain in their chairs hour after hour watching the cards come and go and the chips move around.

Occasionally, a stranger—a sociologist dressed like a truck driver or an honest-to-God truck driver who comes by on his route to play for a half an hour—enters and leaves the game. The rhythm is only slightly jarred by these outside intrusions. Otherwise the scene has the distinct aura of a well-rehearsed play.

At noon, the tables fill to capacity as shopkeepers and workers from nearby offices step across the line into skid row and play a few fast hands of poker or rummy.

Other than the players, there are only the waitress and the cardroom manager present.

The waitress is a marvelous contrast to Millie; if Millie gives the appearance of an over-the-hill prostitute, Margaret (pseudonym) gives the distinct impression that she is not over the hill. The manager is casual and friendly without being exuberant. The atmosphere is like that found in truck stop cafes, where conversation is limited and pointed but with an undertone of easy humor focused on making fun of one another's weaknesses or strengths.

Across from the cardroom, somewhat closer to the toilets on the other side of the hall, was a small door that led to a room with a sign (in yellow and red letters) announcing PANORAMA. Tip's' panorama was filled with machines which, for only ten cents, played two-minute reels of film showing women undressing and couples copulating. There are usually two distinct groups of people at panorama. First and most obvious is a counterpart to the men standing out front by the pinball machines: a row of sleepy-looking males leaning against the back wall of the room. Second are those who come in with something specific on their minds: men in business suits with neatly trimmed hair and boys of sixteen or so who are getting some sort of education. Like the difference between the initiated and uninitiated at the pinball counter, there are the "fish" and the "insiders" of panorama as well. The businessmen and the boys are mostly fish. The men leaning against the wall are insiders.

For the uninitiated, the ten cents spent on the reel brings two minutes of viewing interest. However, what the initiated know is that the film becomes more and more explicit in its sexuality as each dime is inserted. What starts off as a film of a woman undressing ends as a film of a man and woman engaged in oral intercourse. The men leaning against the wall know that it takes five dimes to move from undressing to finale; they wait patiently for the boys to come and go with their dimes until the last reel is due, then they invest their money.

For the next several weeks, I played poker in Tip's every day. In conversations with the cardroom manager, the waitresses, and the other poker players, I learned the truth of what a taxi driver had told me the second day of my research: "You can get anything you want in Seattle if you've got the bread." Gambling, bookmaking, stud-poker games, prostitution, drugs, pornographic literature and devices, high-interest loans, stolen property, bingo parlors, and pinball machines that pay off were available on practically every street corner of the hidden city.

Bingo began at ten in the morning and went until eleven at night inside the Alpha Bingo Club, one of eleven bingo clubs operating in the city. Here you found older people, many with shopping bags beside them, whiling away a few hours. Some played an amazing number of cards all at once: as many as fifteen or twenty at a time. The room was barren, with an invisible sign that said "strictly for profit." The players were intent on the game. My field notes on one of my visits to the Alpha Club report: "At the front of the room on a slightly elevated platform an attractive woman moves a basketful of ping-pong balls with numbers on them. She reaches in and calls out `B 43.' The players quickly search their cards for that number. Each card costs ten cents. Cash and prizes go to the winners, though mostly the cash goes from the players to the bingo parlor." Enough cash goes that way to make the bingo parlor owners wealthy men. The secretary to one bingo operator explained that "normal" profits were not high enough, however, to keep the owners from cheating the customers. One of the games played is called Blackout. The idea is simple: the house pays off an extraordinarily high prize to the lucky winner, but each time a round goes by with no winner the size of the prize dwindles. When Blackout is called, there is a discernible quickening in the atmosphere.

Most often, so many rounds go by without a winner that the prize slides from five hundred to twenty-five dollars. The bingo card manufacturer informed the purchaser that there is one number which appears on all the cards and without which none will ever yield the complete line across, down, or vertically necessary for a "bingo." Thus, the lady on the elevated platform, who juggled and picked the balls, needed only to palm the one ball with the number necessary to win, and see that it did not get called until the prize had dwindled from five hundred to twenty-five dollars.

Occasionally, however, someone was allowed to win the big prize. This was done to keep the rumor around that huge payoffs were possible. Unfortunately for the customers, the "huge winner" was, more often than not, a plant: someone hired by the owners to spend an afternoon (at two dollars an hour) playing bingo and to return the five-hundred-dollar prize as soon as he or she left the room with a big smile and a satisfied air.

The stories I heard led me to visit innumerable bars, cafes, cardrooms, and bingo parlors in the area. There were some variations in clientele, some variation in games played, but the fact that gambling was conducted openly and rampantly throughout this part of the city could be observed by anyone who cared to look. The police did not *seem* to be looking. It became my self-appointed task to find out why.

At the end of the month, as I sat talking to Millie, a partial answer to some of my questions was suggested. A man dressed in civilian clothes but whom I knew to be a sergeant on the vice squad came in and went into the manager's office.

Me: Who is that?
Millie: He's the bagman.
Me: The what?
Millie: The bagman. He collects the payoff for the people downtown.
Me: Oh.

Nightfall brings many more people to the area. The cardrooms fill up, the panorama and pinballs get busier, and often there are lines of people waiting for their turn. On the street, other activities come to life. Bingo parlors that have played most of the day to "little old ladies with shopping bags" now fill up with middle-aged men and women who play three, four, or five cards at a time. The small shops specializing in pornography and sexual mechanics light their neon signs and prepare for the rush of the evening.

Now on the street are more of the same people who played cards in the day. Those who live in the area are more numerous after dark. There are the drunks, the occasionally employed, the disabled, and the retired poor who live on skid row because of its cheap housing and food. But added to this nucleus of residents is an equal, perhaps even greater, number of nocturnal visitors who steadfastly avoid the area by day. These are "square johns," whose money makes the place live and die. These are the people who come at night for the gambling, the sex, the drugs, and the liquor that may be found elsewhere but are concentrated here and brought conveniently together.

Prostitutes, who during the day are occasionally drinking coffee in cafes or hanging around bars in the late afternoon, become more visible and more aggressive with nightfall. Some walk the streets, stand on street corners, or saunter along in front of cheap hotels. Others frequent bars and amusement parlors looking for customers. I met Judy (pseudonym) in front of a hotel. It was a slow evening and she was cold. So she accepted my invitation to go have a drink. We talked: not about her but about life, drugs, and women. Women, it developed, was a subject about which Judy had done a great deal of thinking.

"In this society, women are nothing but a commodity. You buy and sell them for their sex and discard them when their sex runs out. I sell my sex openly. Most women hide the sale behind a marriage license."

The really profitable prostitution did not take place on the streets or in front of hotels. "The better girls work in houses or apartment buildings. When I'm clean [not on drugs] I can work in those places too, but lately I've been too strung out to make my way up the hill."

Prostitution is widespread and comes in an array of packages. Streetwalkers concentrate near the pockets of vice. Higher-class prostitution is located in whorehouses "up on the hill" and in apartment houses located in more respectable parts of the city where call girls live and work. In recent years, body-paint and massage parlors have emerged as fronts for prostitution. Judging from the ever-increasing number of prostitutes and customers, apparently it is a myth that with the liberalized sexual mores of the time, "amateur competition" is driving the professionals from the job.

In Seattle of the 1960s, there were at least ten whorehouses in the tradition of New Orleans, at least one of which had a madam that would make Sam Goldwyn envious. She was large, full-breasted, aristocratic in bearing, with a voice soft and cultured. The house was red-carpeted. At one time the madam was protected by a high-ranking police officer who was one of her closest friends and came to see her through a back door that no one else used.

Another part of the night scene were the high-stakes poker games that began around midnight. These games were not so visible as the small-stakes games in the backrooms of the amusement houses. A few dollars of illegal gambling money across a table is one thing, but when fifty to a hundred thousand dollars changes hands every night, players and managers become more discreet. To play high stakes necessitates making contact with someone who can get you in. Out-of-town businessmen staying in expensive hotels can find the games through hotel porters, desk clerks, or taxi-cab drivers, all of whom receive a small compensation (ten or twenty dollars) for steering customers to the games. Others must make contact with the right connections.

After hearing of the high-stakes games and gaining confidence that I could play stud poker without losing my shirt, I asked the cardroom manager, with whom I had often talked, if he could get me into a "bigger game." One night as I was leaving, he suggested that I stay a while longer. At 1:00 A.M. he closed up. I waited for him to count the money in the cash register and lock it in the safe. We then went up the street to an office building which was kitty-

corner from the police station. There, on the second floor in an otherwise empty room, was a card table. Soon there were six players (including myself) sitting at the table playing a pot-limit game. It was "a sweaty experience," as the cardroom manager would say. Most bets were for more money than I was carrying and every bet was more than I could afford. We played five-card stud.

On the first hand, I was dealt cards that were both lower than the card showing in the hand of the player immediately to my right. I had to play very cautiously because the pot and each bet could skyrocket. If it went too high too fast, I would have to drop simply because I would not have enough cash to cover the bet. With pot-limit poker each bet can be as high as the total amount of money in the pot. Since there were six players, and we were anteing five dollars each, the first bet could be as high as thirty dollars. If everyone stayed, then the next bet (on the third of five cards) could go to $30 plus (6 × $30), or $210.

Being lower than the other players, I dropped. This round of betting did not get too high so I was encouraged. In the next round of cards, I again had a low pair to begin, so I dropped again. The next round was critical for me. I had come with limited cash. I could neither afford to continue dropping (at five dollars each time) nor afford to play in a hand where the betting was extremely high. I had to calculate both the chance of winning and the chance of betting when others would not.

On the third hand, I was dealt a pair of aces. This meant that I was probably going to win the pot if I could keep others from betting too high. I bet high with the ace of hearts showing, and, as I hoped it would, this scared away three of the other players. On the next card, I bet high again and the other two dropped out. This gave me a small cushion for playing. The gods of sociology were smiling on me.

The rest of the evening I won and lost various pots; I selected those that I thought would not attract the high rollers and played cautiously. By the end of the evening I was a winner; and, in fact, I was able to finance other poker playing with the winnings from that first night.

The game broke up early—five-thirty in the morning. I had left a few minutes earlier and stood on the corner when the other players drifted downstairs. The man who ran the game and who took the cut for the house told me it had been a bad night, with only a thousand dollars for the house.

Tip's, its customers, managers, and waitresses are bland compared to the more intrigue-, violence-, and profit-infested cardrooms and gambling dens. The New Caledonia Bridge Club was located at 611 Union Street, above Bob's Chili Parlor. The front for this operation was a social club where people could gather to play bridge. Some people actually did play bridge—for money, with the owner taking a share of the stakes. Others played poker, and pan, and some shot dice. During a dice game on April 2, 1968, Robert Kevo, a well-known local gambler, was shot and killed. The person who shot him was agitated, according to observers, because he had been waiting too long for a seat at the table and Kevo refused to give up his seat.

Six-eleven Park Avenue was the home of a cardroom and high-stakes poker games. It was rumored that the man who ran this cardroom also worked as an enforcer when someone who owed some of the gamblers or loan sharks money needed persuading. It was said he could break a man's legs more efficiently than he could cut a deck of cards. And he was very adept at card cutting.

Cardrooms, bridge clubs, chili parlors, and restaurants were also the scene of other illegal enterprises: the distribution of drugs, the handling of stolen merchandise, the acquisition of illegal liquor (where taxes had been circumvented, for example), and the arranging of illegal, high interest loans. People who ran some of these establishments were also called upon from time to time to serve as collecting agents for outstanding loans; steerers to put people in touch with gambling, prostitution, and drugs; and, last but not least, handmaidens to those above them who needed special jobs done.

During my night sojourns, I saw the skid row scene repeated over and over again in various pockets of the city. The black ghetto had its own versions, while the Japanese, Chinese, and Filipino communities had theirs. The management shifts, the games vary, and the sex differs, but the formula is the same: money for crime.

On Capitol Hill in the black ghetto, one of the oldest established whorehouses in the country was still flourishing in the mid-1970s. The owner and manager had been arrested for procuring, dealing in drugs, having gambling on his premises, white slavery, and a host of other offenses. He has yet to be convicted of anything.

In the Filipino community a prominent man in the rackets is a good old American success story. He came to Seattle in the 1930s when, I am told, police had an undeclared racist war against the Filipinos.

"If you were a Filipino youth it was worth a night in jail to simply be standing on the corner or walking slowly down the street."

Shortly after arriving in Seattle, he saw an opportunity to help his fellow Filipinos and, incidentally, to make a profit from benevolence. He established the Filipino Community Club (pseudonym). The club provided a place for Filipino men to come in out of the rain. It kept them from the visibility of police and the arrests that attended that visibility. It gave them a place to while away the endless hours of unemployment in a community which, because of its historical roots in the importation of male-only labor immigrants, was populated by few women. The owner installed card games and served as the community's principal informal and illegal moneylender. The card games were supplemented by various forms of lottery and numbers rackets modified to resemble similar games from the Filipinos' homeland.

All of these innovations pleased not only the owner and his customers but the police as well. Having Filipinos off the street meant less trouble for the police. Having a reliable associate who would, if need be, provide the police with information about troublemakers or, more specifically, someone who had committed an unsolved crime made their work easier and more efficient. Furthermore, the police shared the profits from the Community Club, which paid them off regularly and handsomely for the privilege of remaining open and doing business.

The Filipino Community Club thrived; the police payments increased. In time, dealing in drugs and women augmented everyone's income. In addition, there were contributions to various politicians' campaign expenses and some influence over the Filipino vote.

People working out of the club ran a nice little usury business on the side. Filipino immigrants arrived impoverished. They were provided room and board for a few weeks and given enough cash to get started. When seasonal work came, the loan sharks would be paid back at 80 and 90 percent interest. The same system could be used, with carefully chosen customers, to enable people out of cash to gamble in the social club with loans made at high, illegal interest rates.

Many of the men in the Filipino community work summers in the canneries of Alaska and are unemployed the remainder of the year. With an accumulation of surplus capital, some enterprising capitalists came to invest in usury. Seasonal workers were loaned money in the spring, when last summer's earnings were running out. They paid back the loans with their first month's pay. These were high-risk loans which led to the creation of a "collection agency" which employed people to convince debtors it was time to repay the loan or have their legs broken.

There are large profits to be had from the poor and the occasionally employed, but the lifeblood of high-stakes gambling and usury is the money spent by members of "respectable" society, particularly people whose incomes can be concealed from the Internal Revenue Service: medical doctors, dentists, and lawyers, whose fees can be readily hidden. For them, gambling with money they do not have to claim on their income-tax return is gambling with money most of which they would otherwise have to pay in taxes.

A frequent participant in the high-stakes games whom I had noticed losing substantial sums of money on several occasions explained it to me this way: "I can afford these games because I'm only betting 10 or 15 percent of what I actually wager. I have a large income but one which I can hide from the Revenue people by taking my fees in cash or in personal checks. If I report all my income, I would have to pay 80 to 90 percent in taxes of everything I earn over sixty thousand dollars. So, say I end the year with twenty-five thousand dollars in unreported income. If I spend it on houses or vacations, they could establish that I was living better than my reported income would allow and thus hold me liable. But if I gamble with it there's none to know. So when I bet a thousand dollars I'm really only betting one or two hundred. If I should win a large sum in a year, then I could even report that as income, pay the 80 to 90 percent and still come out ahead. Meanwhile, I have a really good trip because I love to play poker for high stakes. And I can always tell my wife I'm on night duty at the hospital. She stopped checking on me years ago."

Another frequent player supported this viewpoint. A lawyer who lost and won large sums said succinctly: "There may be better tax dodges than gambling, but no other way is half so much fun."

Poker games go on all over the city in hotel rooms, office buildings, and fraternal organizations. In the middle-class neighborhoods, card games flourish at the Elks Club, the American Legion, the Moose lodge, and the city's leading country clubs. These games are organized by some of the same people who own and run the cardrooms in skid row. They are different in significant ways, however; the players are mostly upper-middle and upper class; and the amount of money bet is infinitely greater than what can be seen at Tip's' open tables.

Recently, a national survey on gambling showed that the average amount of money spent gambling in the United States by a representative group of people was thirty dollars a year. Although this figure may be an accurate estimate of the average, it clearly does not tap the amount spent by those who seek and find gambling. For not only were these high-stakes games well attended, but the local fraternal organizations all contracted out to the high-stakes games for them to provide "fun nights" for club members.

Fun nights were ostensibly limited to members only, but in most instances one could obtain a temporary membership, good for the one night, by paying two dollars at the door. On such nights, the club or house where the event was held looked startlingly like a Las Vegas casino. There were roulette, dice, cards of all kinds, blackjack, cocktail waitresses, and, in adjoining rooms, skinflicks and live striptease.

For the really wealthy who are reluctant or unable to venture to skid row, high-stakes games were available in surroundings more amenable. In the better hotels, the bellhops and desk clerks served as steerers to get wealthy, out-of-town people into high-stakes games that were often located in the hotel where they were registered.

Or, for those who knew the city, there were amusement parlors and there were amusement parlors. The two most famous clubs in the downtown area, The Ram and The Turf, were scenes of high-class games where lovely women entertained customers with smiles and promises. There were games where contact could be made for sex, drugs, or whatever the customer wanted. And in the backrooms, telephones rang often but the conversations were short. Bookmaking operations of considerable magnitude were conducted in these high-class amusement centers.

Here the customers all wore business suits or flashy sportcoats. Many were from out of town. Conventions that bring thousands of people a year to the city bring millions of dollars to the gambling tables, thousands of dollars to prostitution, and an inestimable amount of money for drugs, liquor, usury, and other illegal businesses.

Winter set in. Tourism declined, and the size of the pots in the high-stakes games grew smaller. It was a good time to spend talking instead of observing. It was also time to find some people who were deeply involved in the rackets. These people could tell me how it all worked so smoothly with so many different facets apparently coordinated into a workable enterprise. Thus, I began searching for those in the know who were willing to talk.

QUESTIONS FOR DISCUSSION AND WRITING

1. Why did the author study skid row and the black ghetto?
2. Why didn't the police "seem to be looking" for gambling?
3. Where does the "profitable" prostitution take place?

A Snowball's Chance in Hell: Doing Fieldwork with Active Residential Burglars

RICHARD WRIGHT

SCOTT H. DECKER

ALLISON K. REDFERN

DIETRICH L. SMITH

CRIMINOLOGISTS long have recognized the importance of field studies of active offenders. More than 2 decades ago, for example, Polsky observed that "we can no longer afford the convenient fiction that in studying criminals in their natural habitat, we would discover nothing really important that could not be discovered from criminals behind bars." Similarly, Sutherland and Cressey noted that:

Those who have had intimate contacts with criminals "in the open" know that criminals are not "natural" in police stations, courts, and prisons, and that they must be studied in their everyday life outside of institutions if they are to be understood. By this is meant that the investigator must associate with them as one of them, seeing their lives and conditions as the criminals themselves see them. In this way, he can make observations which can

hardly be made in any other way. Also, his observations are of unapprehended criminals, not the criminals selected by the processes of arrest and imprisonment.

And McCall also cautioned that studies of incarcerated offenders are vulnerable to the charge that they are based on "unsuccessful criminals, on the supposition that successful criminals are not apprehended or at least are able to avoid incarceration." This charge, he asserts, is "the most central bogeyman in the criminologist's demonology."

Although generally granting the validity of such critiques, most criminologists have shied away from studying criminals, so to speak, in the wild. Although their reluctance to do so undoubtedly is attributable to a variety of factors, probably the most important of these is a belief that this type of research is impractical. In particular, how is one to locate active criminals and obtain their cooperation?

The entrenched notion that field-based studies of active offenders are unworkable has been challenged by Chambliss who asserts that:

From "A Snowball's Chance in Hell: Doing Fieldwork with Active Residential Burglars" by R. Wright, S. Decker, A. Redfern and D. Smith, 1992, *Journal of Research in Crime and Delinquency* 29 (2):148–161. Reprinted by permission of Sage Publications, Inc.

The data on organized crime and professional theft as well as other presumably difficult-to-study events are much more available than we usually think. All we really have to do is to get out of our offices and onto the street. The data are there; the problem is that too often [researchers] are not.

Those who have carried out field research with active criminals would no doubt regard this assertion as overly simplistic, but they probably would concur with Chambliss that it is easier to find and gain the confidence of such offenders than commonly is imagined. As Hagedorn has stated: "Any good field researcher . . . willing to spend the long hours necessary to develop good informants can solve the problem of access."

We recently completed the fieldwork for a study of residential burglars, exploring, specifically, the factors they take into account when contemplating the commission of an offense. The study is being done on the streets of St. Louis, Missouri, a declining "rust belt" city. As part of this study, we located and interviewed 105 active offenders. We also took 70 of these offenders to the site of a recent burglary and asked them to reconstruct the crime in considerable detail. In the following pages, we will discuss how we found these offenders and obtained their cooperation. Further, we will consider the difficulties involved in maintaining an ongoing field relationship with these offenders, many of whom lead chaotic lives. Lastly, we will outline the characteristics of our sample, suggesting ways in which it differs from one collected through criminal justice channels.

LOCATING THE SUBJECTS

In order to locate the active offenders for our study, we employed a "snowball" or "chain referral" sampling strategy. As described in the literature, such a strategy begins with the recruitment of an initial subject who then is asked to recommend further participants. This process continues until a suitable sample has been "built."

The most difficult aspect of using a snowball sampling technique is locating an initial contact or two. Various ways of doing so have been suggested. McCall, for instance, recommending using a "chain of referrals":

If a researcher wants to make contact with, say, a bootlegger, he thinks of the person he knows who is closest in the social structure to bootlegging. Perhaps this person will be a police officer, a judge, a liquor store owner, a crime reporter, or a recently arrived Southern migrant. If he doesn't personally know a judge or a crime reporter, he surely knows someone (his own lawyer or a circulation clerk) who does and who would be willing to introduce him. By means of a very short chain of such referrals, the researcher can obtain an introduction to virtually any type of criminal.

This strategy can be effective and efficient, but can also have pitfalls. In attempting to find active offenders for our study, we avoided seeking referrals from criminal justice officials for both practical and methodological reasons. From a practical standpoint, we elected not to use contacts provided by police or probation officers, fearing that this would arouse the suspicions of offenders that the research was the cover for a "sting" operation. One of the offenders we interviewed, for example, explained that he had not agreed to participate earlier because he was worried about being set up for an arrest: "I thought about it at first because I've seen on TV telling how [the police] have sent letters out to people telling 'em they've won new sneakers and then arrested 'em." We also did not use referrals from law enforcement or corrections personnel to locate our subjects owing to a methodological concern that a sample obtained in this way may be highly unrepresentative of the total population of active offenders. It is likely, for instance, that such a sample would include a disproportionate number of unsuccessful criminals, that is, those who have been caught in the past. Further, this sample might exclude a number of successful offenders who avoid associating with colleagues known to the police. Rengert and Wasilchick used a probationer to contact active burglars, observing that the offenders so located "were often very much like the individual who led us to them."

A commonly suggested means of making initial contact with active offenders other than through criminal justice sources involves frequenting locales favored by criminals. This strategy, however, requires an extraordinary investment of time as the researcher establishes a street reputation as an "all right square" who can be trusted. Fortunately, we were able to short-cut that process by hiring an ex-offender (who, despite committing hundreds of serious crimes, had few arrests and no felony convictions) with high status among several groups of Black street criminals in St. Louis. This person retired from crime after being shot and paralyzed in a gangland-style execution attempt. He then attended a university and earned a bachelor's degree, but continued to live in his old neighborhood, remaining friendly, albeit superficially, with local criminals. We initially met him when he attended a colloquium in our department and disputed the speaker's characterization of street criminals.

Working through an ex-offender with continuing ties to the underworld as a means of locating active criminals has been used successfully by other criminologists. This approach offers the advantage that such a person already has contacts and trust in the criminal subculture and can vouch for the legitimacy of the research. In order to exploit this advantage fully, however, the ex-offender selected must be someone with a solid street reputation for integrity and must have a strong commitment to accomplishing the goals of the study.

The ex-offender hired to locate subjects for our project began by approaching former criminal associates. Some of these contacts were still "hustling," that is, actively involved in various types of crimes, whereas others either had retired or remained involved only peripherally through, for example, occasional buying and selling of stolen goods. Shortly thereafter, the ex-offender contacted several street-wise law-abiding friends, including a youth worker. He explained the research to the contacts, stressing that it was confidential and that the police were not involved. He also informed them that those who took part would be paid a small sum (typically $25.00). He then asked the contacts to put him in touch with active residential burglars. . . .

Throughout the process of locating subjects, we encountered numerous difficulties and challenges. Contacts that initially appeared to be promising, for example, sometimes proved to be unproductive and had to be dropped. And, of course, even productive contact chains had a tendency to "dry up" eventually. One of the most challenging tasks we confronted involved what Biernacki and Waldorf have termed the "verification of eligibility," that is, determining whether potential subjects actually met the criteria for inclusion in our research. In order to take part, offenders had to be both "residential burglars" and "currently active." In practice, this meant that they had to have committed a residential burglary within the past 2 weeks. This seems straightforward, but it often was difficult to apply the criteria in the field because offenders were evasive about their activities. In such cases, we frequently had to rely on other members of the sample to verify the eligibility of potential subjects.

We did not pay the contacts for helping us to find subjects and, initially, motivating them to do so proved difficult. Small favors, things like giving them a ride or buying them a pack of cigarettes, produced some cooperation, but yielded only a few introductions. Moreover, the active burglars that we did manage to find often were lackadaisical about referring associates because no financial incentive was offered. Eventually, one of the informants hit on the idea of "pimping" colleagues, that is, arranging an introduction on their behalf in exchange for a cut of the participation fee. This idea was adopted rapidly by other informants and the number of referrals rose accordingly. In effect, these informants became "locators," helping us to expand referral chains as well as vouching for the legitimacy of the research, and validating potential participants as active residential burglars.

The practice of pimping is consistent with the low level, underworld economy of street culture, where people are always looking for a way to get in on someone else's deal. One of our contacts put it this way: "If there's money to make out of something, I gotta figure out a way to get me some of it." Over the course of the research, numerous disputes arose between offenders and informants over the payment of referral fees. We resisted becoming involved in these disputes, reckoning that such involvement could only result in the alienation of one or both parties. Instead, we made it clear that our funds were intended as interview payments and thus would be given only to interviewees.

FIELD RELATIONS

The success of our research, of course, hinged on an ability to convince potential subjects to participate. Given that many of the active burglars, especially those located early in the project, were deeply suspicious of our motives, it is reasonable to ask why the offenders were willing to take part in the research. Certainly the fact that we paid them a small sum for their time was an enticement for many, but this is not an adequate explanation. After all, criminal opportunities abound and even the inept "nickel and dime" offenders in the sample could have earned more had they spent the time engaged in illegal activity. Moreover, some of the subjects clearly were not short of cash when they agreed to participate; at the close of one interview, an offender pulled out his wallet to show us that it was stuffed with thousand dollar bills, saying:

I just wanted to prove that I didn't do this for the money. I don't need the money. I did it to help out [the ex-offender employed on our project]. We know some of the same people and he said you were cool.

Without doubt, many in our sample agreed to participate only because the ex-offender assured them that we were trustworthy. But other factors were at work as well. Letkemann, among others, has observed that the secrecy inherent in criminal work means that offenders have few opportunities to discuss their activities with anyone besides associates—which many of them find frustrating. As one of his informants put it: "What's the point of scoring if nobody knows about it?" Under the right conditions, therefore, some offenders may enjoy talking about their work with researchers.

We adopted several additional strategies to maximize the cooperation of the offenders. First, following the recommendations of experienced field researchers, we made an effort to "fit in" by learning the distinctive terminology and phrasing used by the offenders. Here again, the assistance of the ex-offender proved invaluable. Prior to entering the field, he suggested ways in which questions might be asked so that the subjects would better understand them, and provided us with a working knowledge of popular street terms (e.g., "boy" for heroin, "girl" for cocaine) and pronunciations (e.g., "hair ron" for heroin). What is more, he sat in on the early interviews and critiqued them afterwards, noting areas of difficulty or contention and offering possible solutions.

A second strategy to gain the cooperation of the offenders required us to give as well as take. We expected the subjects to answer our questions frankly and, therefore, often had to reciprocate. Almost all of them had questions about how the information would be used, who would have access to it, and so on. We answered these questions honestly, lest the offenders conclude that we were being evasive. Further, we honored requests from a number of subjects for various forms of assistance. Provided that the help requested was legal and fell within the general set of "norms governing the exchange of money and other kinds of favors" (Berk and Adams) on the street, we offered it. For example, we took subjects to job interviews or work, helped some to enroll in school, and gave others advice on legal matters. We even assisted a juvenile offender who was injured while running away from the police, to arrange for emergency surgery when his parents, fearing that they would be charged for the operation, refused to give their consent.

One other way we sought to obtain and keep the offenders' confidence involved demonstrating our trustworthiness by "remaining close-mouthed in regard to potentially harmful information" (Irwin). A number of the offenders tested us by asking what a criminal associate said about a particular matter. We declined to discuss such issues, explaining that the promise of confidentiality extended to all those participating in our research.

Much has been written about the necessity for researchers to be able to withstand official coercion and we recognized from the start the threat that intrusions from criminal justice officials could pose to our research. The threat of being confronted by police patrols seemed especially great given that we planned to visit the sites of recent successful burglaries with offenders. Therefore, prior to beginning our fieldwork, we negotiated an agreement with police authorities not to interfere in the conduct of the research, and we were not subjected to official coercion.

Although the strategies described above helped to mitigate the dangers inherent in working with active criminals, we encountered many potentially dangerous situations over the course of the research. For example, offenders turned up for interviews carrying firearms including, on one occasion, a machine gun; we were challenged on the street by subjects who feared that they were being set up for arrest; we were caught in the middle of a fight over the payment of a $1 debt. Probably the most dangerous situation, however, arose while driving with an offender to the site of his most recent burglary. As we passed a pedestrian, the offender became agitated and demanded that we stop the car: "You want to see me kill someone? Stop the car! I'm gonna kill that motherfucker. Stop the fuckin' car!" We refused to stop and actually sped up to prevent him jumping out of the vehicle; this clearly displeased him, although he eventually calmed down. The development of such situations was largely unpredictable and thus avoiding them was difficult. Often we deferred to the ex-offender's judgment about the safety of a given set of circumstances. The most notable precaution that we took involved money; we made sure that the offenders knew that we carried little more than was necessary to pay them.

CHARACTERISTICS OF THE SAMPLE

Unless a sample of active offenders differs significantly from one obtained through criminal justice channels, the difficulties and risks associated with the street-based recruitment of research subjects could not easily be justified. Accordingly, it seems important that we establish whether such a difference exists. In doing so, we will begin by outlining the demographic characteristics of our sample. In terms of race, it nearly parallels the distribution of burglary arrests for the City of St. Louis in 1988, the most recent year for which data are available. The St. Louis Metropolitan Police Department's Annual Report reveals that 64% of burglary arrestees in that year were Black, and 36% were White. Our sample was 69% Black and 31% White. There is divergence for the gender variable, however; only 7% of all arrestees in the city were female, while 17% of our sample fell into this category. This is not surprising. The characteristics of a sample of active criminals, after all, would not be expected to mirror those of one obtained in a criminal justice setting.

Given that our research involved only currently active offenders, it is interesting to note that 21 of the subjects were on probation, parole, or serving a suspended sentence, and that a substantial number of juveniles—27 or 26% of the total—were located for the study. The inclusion of such offenders strengthens the research considerably because approximately one third of arrested burglars are under 18 years of age. Juveniles, therefore, need to be taken into account in any comprehensive study of burglars. These offenders, however, seldom are included in studies of burglars located through criminal justice channels because access to them is legally restricted and they often are processed differently than adult criminals and detained in separate facilities.

Prior contact with the criminal justice system is a crucial variable for this research. . . .

More than one-quarter of the offenders (28%) claimed never to have been arrested. (We excluded arrests for traffic offenses, "failure to appear," and similar minor transgressions, because such offenses do not adequately distinguish serious criminals from others.) Obviously, these offenders would have been excluded had we based our study on a jail or prison population. Perhaps a more relevant measure in the context of our study, however, is the experience of the offenders with the criminal justice system for the offense of burglary, because most previous studies of burglars not only have been based on incarcerated offenders, but also have used the charge of burglary as a screen to select subjects. Of the 105 individuals in our sample, 44 (42%) had no arrests for burglary, and another 35 (33%) had one or more arrests, but no convictions for the offense. Thus 75% of our sample would not be included in a study of incarcerated burglars.

We turn now to an examination of the patterns of offending among our sample. In order to determine how many lifetime burglaries the offenders had committed, we asked them to estimate the number of completed burglaries in which they had taken part. We "bounded" this response by asking them (a) how old they were when they did their first burglary, (b) about significant gaps in offending (e.g., periods of incarceration), and (c)

about fluctuations in offending levels. The subjects typically estimated how many lifetime burglaries they had committed in terms of a range (e.g., 50–60), then were prompted with questions about the variation in their rate of offending over the course of their burglary career. We recorded what offenders agreed was a conservative estimate of the number of lifetime burglaries. More than half of the sample (52%) admitted to 50 or more lifetime burglaries. Included in this group are 41 offenders (40% of the total) who have committed at least 100 such crimes.

The measure of lifetime burglaries, of course, does not provide an estimate of the *rate* of offending. For that, we calculated "lambda"—that is, the annual number of lifetime burglaries—for each subject by using our interview data. We arrived at this figure by subtracting age at first burglary from age at time of initial interview; from this, we subtracted the number of years each offender spent "off the street" in a secure residential facility (prison, jail, secure detention, or treatment center). This gave us the denominator for the lambda measure, the number of years at risk. The number of lifetime burglaries was divided by years at risk to get lambda. Approximately two thirds of the sample (68%) averaged 10 or fewer burglaries a year over the course of their offending careers—a finding not out of line with lambda estimates for burglary derived from arrest data. It should be noted, however, that there was great variability in the rate of offending among our sample; 34% committed, on average, less than 5 burglaries a year while, at the other extreme, 7% committed more than 50 such crimes yearly. This subgroup of exceptionally high rate offenders accounted for 4,204 of the 13,179 residential burglaries (32%) reported by our subjects. This result complements previous research based on self-reports by prison inmates that has shown great variability in individual crime rates, with a small group of very active criminals being responsible for a disproportionate number of offenses. . . .

CONCLUSION

By its nature, research involving active criminals is always demanding, often difficult, and occasionally dangerous. However, it is possible and, as the quantitative information reported above suggests, some of the offenders included in such research may differ substantially from those found through criminal justice channels. It is interesting, for example, that those in our sample who had never been arrested for anything, on average, offended *more* frequently and had committed *more* lifetime burglaries than their arrested counterparts. These "successful" offenders, obviously, would not have shown up in a study of arrestees, prisoners, or probationers—a fact that calls into question the extent to which a sample obtained through official sources is representative of the total population of criminals.

Beyond this, researching active offenders is important because it provides an opportunity to observe and talk with them outside the institutional context. As Cromwell et al. have noted, it is difficult to assess the validity of accounts offered by institutionalized criminals. Simply put, a full understanding of criminal behavior requires that criminologists incorporate field studies of active offenders into their research agendas. Without such studies, both the representativeness and the validity of research based on offenders located through criminal justice channels will remain problematic.

QUESTIONS FOR DISCUSSION AND WRITING

1. Why were the authors pleased that more than a quarter of their sample had never been arrested before and that an additional 42% had no arrests for burglary?
2. Is it true that all of the burglars committed about the same number of burglaries each year?
3. What was true about the number of burglaries committed by those who had never been arrested for anything?

Data Analysis Exercise

An Exploration of Fear of Crime

INTRODUCTION

Welcome to the world of data analysis! In the data analysis exercises, we will be exploring some of the theories you have read about in this book. This first exercise is designed to introduce you to the student version of SPSS and to allow you to do some data exploring. The setup of these exercises is consistent throughout the book. After completing a number of guided activities, you will be able to conduct similar analyses on your own. There are three homework assignments at the conclusion of each exercise. The first is a general assignment that asks questions about the guided activities. The second assignment ("Further Exploration") is designed to facilitate further exploration of the researched relationships. The third assignment ("On Your Own") allows you to expand on the material and further extend your understanding of the theories about which you have read. In short, these exercises add a "hands-on" component to the study of theories of crime. Our first exercise involves using the General Social Survey to look at public perceptions of crime and criminality.

DESCRIPTION OF THE DATASET

The General Social Survey (GSS) had been administered to a representative sample of Americans nearly every year since 1972. This survey asks a wide variety of questions about people's opinions and behaviors. The GSS also obtains many demographic descriptors. The data we will be using in the exercises for Part III are from the 1996 GSS. Because the student version of SPSS can only handle 50 variables, a subset of 46 variables was chosen from the many hundreds of GSS variables for you to include in your research. You will find that the subset allows you to explore many relationships.

SPSS for Windows is not very difficult to operate, even if you have never used a computer before. One essential concept is coding. Coding is actually a form of translation from "computerese" to English, because most humans don't think in terms of numbers. In computer language, strings of numbers are used. Thus if the number 2 were coded to mean "female," then the computer would read the 2 and tell the researcher that a given respondent answered "female." Researchers need codebooks to be able to make the computer understand what they want and also to decipher what the computer prints out.

Consider a coding example from the 1996 GSS, respondent's sex, which has three possible answers: male, female, or no response (a respondent could have chosen not to answer the question at all). If a respondent was male, the response was coded 1. Females were coded 2. If the respondent did not answer the question at all, the response was left blank. Luckily, we don't have to worry much about coding, because labels are already included to make the data we'll be using easier to work with. If the labels were not included in the file, we would need a codebook that would help us decipher the computer's printouts. For now, we can put the idea of coding on the back burner because we will not need to use codes unless we use the Data Editor or try to transform the data (for example, recoding a variable into smaller categories). If you open the Data Editor, you will see all the numbers that SPSS uses to generate its outputs.

Before we start, we'll need to load up the dataset and get ready to run our numbers. To do this, launch/run SPSS and click *OK* to *open an existing file* (words in italics indicate commands that you need to click on). When given the opportunity, click on "GSS96TAB" to open the dataset. If you don't see it listed, you might have to locate the subdirectory in which GSS96TAB is located. You will notice that a "viewer" is opened, with a toolbar along the top, a navigator along the left-hand side, and a large window for outputs. Right now, all it says is that it opened the GSS96TAB dataset (the SAV extension merely identifies the dataset as being in SPSS for Windows format).

GETTING A HANDLE ON THE DATA

Now, let's take a quick look at some demographic factors before getting into some serious analyses. Running some preliminary frequencies helps us "get a handle on the data" so that we better understand where our data came from. First, run frequencies on SEX, RACE, AGE, and INCOME. Those four tables appear below the directions for running frequencies in SPSS.

Blueprint 1: How to Run Frequencies in SPSS

1. Click on *Analyze* (on the tool bar along the top of your screen), then *Descriptive Statistics*, then *Frequencies*.
2. Highlight the variables you want, one at a time, or in groups by holding down your right mouse button and dragging your mouse pointer down until you have highlighted the whole group. If you want to pick variables further down on the list, simply hit the scroll button to move around the list. To read a whole label, merely position your mouse over the visible part of the label and you will be able to read the entire label with its variable name in parentheses at the end of the text. The variables are listed in order by variable name, but the variable labels are what is shown in the listing on the left-hand side of the dialog box, making it a tad tricky to negotiate the list. Don't worry, you'll get the hang of it.
3. Click on the arrow to the right of the variable list to move your selection into the right-hand box labeled "Variable(s)." You will get frequencies for each variable listed in this box.
4. Continue selecting variables until you have all the ones you want in the "Variable(s)" box.
5. If you accidentally include a variable you do not want, highlight its name and click on the arrow to move it back into the variable list. Notice that the direction of the arrow tells you the box into which your selection will be moved.
6. Click on the *OK* button in the upper right-hand corner of the command box to run your frequencies. You will notice that your frequencies appear in the large viewer window.

Step-by-Step Example 1: Running Frequencies

1. Click on *Analyze,* then *Descriptive Statistics,* then *Frequencies.*
2. Highlight "RESPONDENTS SEX (sex)," then click on the arrow.
3. Highlight "RACE OF RESPONDENT (race)," then click on the arrow.
4. Highlight "AGE OF RESPONDENT (age)," then click on the arrow.
5. Highlight "TOTAL FAMILY INCOME (income)," then click on the arrow.
6. Click *OK* to run the frequency tables.

Here are the four frequency tables. You can look at them in the viewer by using the scroll bars on the right-hand side and bottom of the viewer window, or you can use the handy SPSS student version navigator along the left-hand side of the viewer window. Simply click on the output you want and, voilà, you're there in a flash!

RESPONDENTS SEX

		Frequency	Percent	Valid Percent	Cumulative Percent
Valid	MALE	662	44.1	44.1	44.1
	FEMALE	838	55.9	55.9	100.0
	Total	1500	100.0	100.0	

This is the frequency table for SEX.

RACE OF RESPONDENT

		Frequency	Percent	Valid Percent	Cumulative Percent
Valid	WHITE	1211	80.7	85.6	85.6
	BLACK	203	13.5	14.4	100.0
	Total	1414	94.3	100.0	
Missing	System	86	5.7		
Total		1500	100.0		

This is the frequency table for RACE. Notice that one category has been coded as missing to make our analysis easier.

AGE OF RESPONDENT

		Frequency	Percent	Valid Percent	Cumulative Percent
Valid	18-33	417	27.8	27.8	27.8
	34-49	542	36.1	36.1	63.9
	50 and older	541	36.1	36.1	100.0
	Total	1500	100.0	100.0	

This is the frequency table for AGE. Notice that there are three categories; the respondents' exact ages were recoded to make our analysis easier.

TOTAL FAMILY INCOME

		Frequency	Percent	Valid Percent	Cumulative Percent
Valid	LOWER	470	31.3	35.9	35.9
	MIDDLE	435	29.0	33.3	69.2
	HIGHER	403	26.9	30.8	100.0
	Total	1308	87.2	100.0	
Missing	REFUSED	98	6.5		
	DK	71	4.7		
	NA	23	1.5		
	Total	192	12.8		
Total		1500	100.0		

This is the frequency table for INCOME. Notice that three categories have been coded as missing to make our analysis easier: refusals to answer the question, those who didn't know the answer, and some for whom the question was not applicable.

The first thing many students notice about the frequencies produced by SPSS is the columnar format in which they are printed. Don't let this overwhelm you. The first column contains the value labels for the variable we want to study, one for each category (for example, "Male" and "Female"). Categories that have been coded as missing appear at the bottom of the frequency table so that we can see which categories have been coded as missing and how many respondents fall into each of those categories. The "valid" cases are those that will be included in any analyses we complete.

The second column contains the frequency, or number, of cases that fall into each category (for example, 662 of the 1500 respondents in this sample were male).

The third column contains the percentage of cases falling into each category (for example, 44.1% of the 1500 respondents in this sample were male). This is sometimes called the "raw percent" because it has not been transformed in any way.

The fourth column presents the "Valid Percent," which is the percentage of all cases for which data exist. To illustrate, suppose that I polled my class last week about whether they would like to get an A in my course. Every student in the room agreed, but only half of my students were in class that day because of bad weather. The raw percent of my students who said they wanted an A would be 50% (because only half were in the room, so only half could say they wanted an A), but the valid percent would be 100% (since everyone who answered the question wanted an A). When we are looking at frequencies of variables that have missing data, we need to be careful that we use the appropriate percentage.

The fifth and final column contains the "Cumulative Percent"—the percentage of cases falling in all the value categories up to and including the value category in question. To illustrate cumulative percentages, look briefly at the table for AGE. The table shows that 27.8% of the respondents were aged 33 or younger, 63.9% of the respondents were younger than age 49 (27.8% + 36.1% = 63.9%), and 100% (all) of the respondents were in the three categories combined. Cumulative percentages are most useful when the variable in question has many sequential categories (such as ages in exact years instead of the categories used in this dataset). Cumulative percentages are meaningless when used with nominal data (data that cannot be rank ordered, such as sex or race).

From the frequency tables, we can see that slightly more than half of our sample is female. We can also see that our dataset contains responses from a large percentage (80.7%) of Whites, a smaller number (13.5%) of Blacks, and some (5.7%) cases that are "missing." Missing cases are those for which no data are included for a variable for a particular individual. In this dataset, 86 individuals do not have a value for RACE. These individuals will be excluded from any analysis that involves the variable RACE.

Looking at AGE, we can see that our sample contains responses from a nice cross-section of individuals; roughly one-third fall into each of the three age categories. INCOME is also divided into somewhat equal categories. Unlike the prior three variables, some individuals refused to answer the question (6.5%), some did not know the answer to the question (4.7%), or the question was not applicable (1.5%). These individuals have been coded as missing, so they will be excluded from any analyses including the variable INCOME. You can run frequencies on other respondent characteristics if you wish to get a better handle on the data.

EXPLORATION THROUGH CROSSTABULATION TABLES

Now let's run some analyses of our own to explore a little about how Americans view crime. For this exercise, we'll look at fear of crime (FEAR).

Fear of crime was measured by asking respondents if they were afraid to walk at night in their neighborhoods. To see the breakdown, use the directions in Blueprint 1 to run a frequency table for FEAR. The frequency table is replicated below.

AFRAID TO WALK AT NIGHT IN NEIGHBORHOOD

		Frequency	Percent	Valid Percent	Cumulative Percent
Valid	YES	404	26.9	41.6	41.6
	NO	568	37.9	58.4	100.0
	Total	972	64.8	100.0	
Missing	DK	12	.8		
	System	516	34.4		
	Total	528	35.2		
Total		1500	100.0		

This is the frequency table for FEAR. Notice that two categories will be excluded from the analyses: the 12 people who didn't know an answer to the question and the 516 who did not answer the question.

As you can tell, more than one-third (37.9%, valid percent = 58.4%) of the respondents said they were not afraid to walk in their neighborhoods at night, compared to only one-fourth (26.9%. valid percent = 41.6%) who said they were afraid. Let's see if women are more fearful than men about walking in their neighborhoods at night. Let's also check to see if fear is related to a person's race, age, or socioeconomic status as measured by income.

How can we tell if any of our four demographic variables plays a role in fear of crime? A good technique for examining differences between groups is the crosstabulation table. You've seen many of these before, but may not have known the name for them. When you see political polls broken out by party or gender, you're actually examining crosstabulation tables. Most crosstabulation tables, including all of the ones we will look at in this chapter's exercises, present two variables; one variable appears at the top of the table and the other variable is on the left-hand side.

Crosstabulation tables are easy to make. Just follow the directions in Blueprint 2.

Blueprint 2: How to Run Crosstabulation Tables in SPSS

1. Click on *Analyze* (on the tool bar along the top of your screen), then *Descriptive Statistics*, then *Crosstabs*.
2. Highlight your dependent variable (the variable you want to "predict").
3. Click on the arrow to the left of the "Row(s)" box to move your selection into that box. You will get one crosstabulation table for each variable you list in the "Row(s)" box, so continue selecting variables until you have all the variables you want in the box.
4. If you accidentally include a variable you do not want, highlight its name and click on the arrow to move it back into the variable list. As with the *Frequencies* command, the direction of the arrow tells you the box into which your selection will be moved.
5. Highlight your independent variable (the variable that you want to use to "predict" your dependent variable). An easy way to remember which variable is which is that the value of the dependent variable "depends" on the values of the independent variable. For example, likelihood of getting an A in your course depends on how much you study. Hours spent studying is the independent variable, and course grade is the dependent variable. A diagram would look like this: STUDY → GRADE. (Note that the arrow does not imply causality; it merely proposes a relationship in which grades are related to the number of hours studied.) Demographic descriptors of respondents are almost always independent variables.
6. Click on the arrow to the left of the "Column(s)" box to move your selection into that box. You will get one crosstabulation table for each variable you list in the "Column(s)" box, so continue selecting variables until you have all the variables you want in the box.
7. Click on the *Statistics* button at the bottom of the command box, then put a check mark in the box labeled "Phi and Cramer's V" to get tests of significance for nominal variables, then click *Continue* to return to the command box. (Although Phi and Cramer's V were designed for nominal data, they are useful for testing any relationship where there are relatively few categories.)
8. Click on the *Cells* button at the bottom of the command box, then put a check mark in the box labeled "Column" to get column percentages, then click *Continue* to return to the command box.
9. Click on the *OK* button in the upper right-hand corner of the command box to run your crosstabulation tables.

Step-by-Step Example 2: Running Crosstabulation Tables

1. Click on *Analyze*, then *Descriptive Statistics*, then *Crosstabs*.
2. Highlight "AFRAID TO WALK AT NIGHT IN NEIGHBORHOOD (fear)," then click on the arrow beside the "Row(s)" box. This is our dependent variable.
3. Highlight "RESPONDENTS SEX (sex)," then click on the arrow beside the "Column(s)" box. This is the first of our four independent variables.
4. Do the same for "RACE OF RESPONDENT (race)," "AGE OF RESPONDENT (age)," and "TOTAL FAMILY INCOME (income)," making sure each moves to the "Column(s)" box. These are our other three independent variables.
5. Click on the *Statistics* button at the bottom of the command box, then put a check mark in the box labeled "Phi and Cramer's V," then click *Continue* to return to the command box.
6. Click on the *Cells* button at the bottom of the command box, then put a check mark in the box labeled "Column," then click *Continue* to return to the command box.
7. Click *OK* to run the crosstabulation tables.

The tables are replicated below, followed by an explanation of each. This is the table for SEX; the statistics appear below the table.

Crosstab

| | | | RESPONDENTS SEX | | |
			MALE	FEMALE	Total
AFRAID TO WALK AT NIGHT IN NEIGHBORHOOD	YES	Count	103	301	404
		% within RESPONDENTS SEX	23.8%	55.8%	41.6%
	NO	Count	330	238	568
		% within RESPONDENTS SEX	76.2%	44.2%	58.4%
Total		Count	433	539	972
		% within RESPONDENTS SEX	100.0%	100.0%	100.0%

Symmetric Measures

		Value	Approx. Sig.
Nominal by Nominal	Phi	-.323	.000
	Cramer's V	.323	.000
N of Valid Cases		972	

a. Not assuming the null hypothesis.

b. Using the asymptotic standard error assuming the null hypothesis.

From the first crosstabulation table, we learn that 55.8% of women say they are afraid to walk at night in their neighborhoods compared to only 23.8% of men. The difference between the two percentages is 32.0%, so the finding is potentially interesting (had the difference been only a few percentage points, we would say the difference is negligible). In fact, women are more than twice as likely to report fear. That sounds like a real finding, but we need to look at the statistics to make sure our finding isn't due to chance or random fluctuations in our data. The Phi value is −.323, which means that we can do 32.3% better predicting fear when we know a respondent's gender. Alternatively, we can say that 32.3% of the variance in fear can be explained by gender. We can classify the strength of a relationship based on the Phi value. One rule of thumb says that a Phi less than .10 indicates a weak relationship, a Phi between .10 and .30 indicates a moderate relationship, and a Phi larger than .30 indicates a strong relationship (Cramer's V is interpreted the same way). In the case of SEX and FEAR, the relationship would be considered strong. We used Phi rather than Cramer's V for this table because it is a 2 × 2 table (that is, it has two columns and two rows, excluding the "total" column and row).

Looking to the "Approx. Sig." column, we can see that the Phi value is significant at the .000 level (NOTE: this is not zero; the computer rounded it off to .000, but it's probably something like .0001). Significance values sound scarier than they are. All they do is alert the researcher (that's you) to the possibility that his/her findings are due to chance rather than to a real relationship between two variables. Significance ranges from 0 to 1. A significance value of 1 means there is a 100% chance that the finding is due to chance, so it cannot be trusted. A significance value of 0 means there is almost no chance the finding is due to chance, so it can be trusted. Very few relationships have significance values of 1 or 0, however, so researchers had to develop a scale of when they would trust their findings. Many years ago, they decided that they would accept any finding with a significance level of .05 or lower because that would mean there is only a 5% chance (or lower) that the finding is due to chance. In our SEX → FEAR crosstabulation, there is almost no chance that our observed relationship (that women report more fear than men) is due to chance.

POINTS TO PONDER: What are some explanations for this finding? Make sure you consider information from the readings from Part II in your explanations.

Now let's look at our crosstabulation table for RACE.

This is the table for RACE.

AFRAID TO WALK AT NIGHT IN NEIGHBORHOOD * RACE OF RESPONDENT
Crosstabulation

| | | | RACE OF RESPONDENT | | Total |
			WHITE	BLACK	Total
AFRAID TO WALK AT NIGHT IN NEIGHBORHOOD	YES	Count	310	73	383
		% within RACE OF RESPONDENT	39.7%	53.7%	41.8%
	NO	Count	470	63	533
		% within RACE OF RESPONDENT	60.3%	46.3%	58.2%
Total		Count	780	136	916
		% within RACE OF RESPONDENT	100.0%	100.0%	100.0%

Symmetric Measures

		Value	Approx. Sig.
Nominal by Nominal	Phi	-.100	.002
	Cramer's V	.100	.002
N of Valid Cases		916	

a. Not assuming the null hypothesis.

b. Using the asymptotic standard error assuming the null hypothesis.

The first thing we notice is that Blacks are much more likely than Whites to report being afraid to walk in their neighborhoods at night (53.7% vs. 39.7%). The difference between the two percentages is 14%, so the finding is potentially interesting. The Phi value is –.10, indicating that we do 10% better predicting fear when we know a respondent's race, and the significance level is .002, well within the statistically significant range. According to the Phi value, this relationship would be considered moderate. This crosstabulation shows that race and fear of crime are related.

POINTS TO PONDER: What are some explanations for this finding? Make sure you consider information from the readings from Part II in your explanations.

Now it's your turn to examine and interpret the remaining two tables. The easiest way is to look at each value of the dependent variable, one at a time. So, in the AGE → FEAR crosstabulation, you would want to look at the percentages of individuals who said they were fearful. First, note what percentage of respondents aged 18–33 said they were fearful, then the percentage of individuals aged 34–49, then the percentage of people aged 50 and older. Do the percentages differ? If so, is the difference substantial enough to warrant our interest? What is the Cramer's V value (NOTE: we use Cramer's V for this table because there are three columns, which makes it larger than a 2 × 2 table)? Is the finding significant/meaningful? If you have problems with this table, go back and go over the first two crosstabulation tables, using the text to check your work.

This is the table for AGE. Notice that nasty significance value; this one is so close to .05 that it requires a judgment call! Usually, we say it's not significant (since it's not .05 or less), but we can tell readers the exact value so they know it was a close call. Either way, the relationship is weak because it's less than .10.

Crosstab

			AGE OF RESPONDENT			
			18-33	34-49	50 and older	Total
AFRAID TO WALK AT NIGHT IN NEIGHBORHOOD	YES	Count	105	139	160	404
		% within AGE OF RESPONDENT	37.4%	40.1%	46.5%	41.6%
	NO	Count	176	208	184	568
		% within AGE OF RESPONDENT	62.6%	59.9%	53.5%	58.4%
Total		Count	281	347	344	972
		% within AGE OF RESPONDENT	100.0%	100.0%	100.0%	100.0%

Symmetric Measures

		Value	Approx. Sig.
Nominal by Nominal	Phi	.077	.054
	Cramer's V	.077	.054
N of Valid Cases		972	

a. Not assuming the null hypothesis.

b. Using the asymptotic standard error assuming the null hypothesis.

Now, look at the INCOME → FEAR crosstabulation table and interpret it. What can we say about fear of crime based on these four tables?

Following is the table for INCOME. Do you see the downward trend indicating that those with higher incomes are less likely to be afraid to walk at night in their neighborhoods?

Crosstab

| | | | TOTAL FAMILY INCOME | | | |
			LOWER	MIDDLE	HIGHER	Total
AFRAID TO WALK AT NIGHT IN NEIGHBORHOOD	YES	Count	159	105	92	356
		% within TOTAL FAMILY INCOME	50.5%	37.1%	34.3%	41.1%
	NO	Count	156	178	176	510
		% within TOTAL FAMILY INCOME	49.5%	62.9%	65.7%	58.9%
Total		Count	315	283	268	866
		% within TOTAL FAMILY INCOME	100.0%	100.0%	100.0%	100.0%

Symmetric Measures

		Value	Approx. Sig.
Nominal by Nominal	Phi	.146	.000
	Cramer's V	.146	.000
N of Valid Cases		866	

a. Not assuming the null hypothesis.

b. Using the asymptotic standard error assuming the null hypothesis.

FURTHER EXPLORATION

What else might influence fear of crime? There are plenty of other variables in the dataset for you to look at. Maybe you think that how often respondents read the newspaper (NEWS) or the level of urban development where they live (SRCBELT) has some effect on their fear of crime. For the "further exploration" homework assignment, you will pick one of these variables (or one of your own choosing) and explore its effects on fear of crime using the same procedures we used for SEX, RACE, AGE, and INCOME.

ON YOUR OWN

Now that we have explored fear of crime, you can look at other opinions regarding crime and criminality. Two such variables in the 1996 GSS dataset are support for the death penalty for murder (CAPPUN) and support for the legalization of marijuana (GRASS). Try running the analyses we ran for fear of crime, and try adding some independent variables of your own. Perhaps you think that people's religion (RELIG) or the strength of their affiliation with their religion (RELITEN) affects their support for the death penalty. Take a look and find out. While you are exploring Americans' opinions on crime and criminality, think about the readings and how they help explain people's opinions. The possibilities are endless, so have fun!

Homework for Part III: General Questions
(Fear of Crime)

Name: _____   Date: _____

Directions: Complete the following exercises by filling in the blanks or circling the appropriate responses. A couple of answers have been filled in for you to make sure you're on the right track.

GETTING A HANDLE ON THE DATA

1. In the 1996 GSS sample, there were <u>662</u> males, and they comprise _____% of the sample. There were _____ females; they were _____% of the sample.

2. In the 1996 GSS sample, _____% of the sample was White; _____% were Black. This division *is / is not* roughly equal.

3. In the 1996 GSS sample, there were _____ individuals aged 50 and older, comprising _____% of the sample. There were _____ people aged 34 to 49, comprising _____% of the sample. The _____ youngest respondents, those aged 18 to 33, comprised _____% of the sample.

4. In the 1996 GSS sample, there were _____ higher-income individuals, and they comprise _____% of the sample. There were _____ middle-income people; they were _____% of the sample. Finally, there were _____ lower-income individuals, comprising _____% of the sample.

EXPLORATION THROUGH CROSSTABULATION TABLES

1. In the 1996 GSS sample, _____% of the sample were afraid to walk at night in their neighborhoods, compared to _____% who were not afraid to walk at night in their neighborhoods.

2. In the SEX → FEAR crosstabulation, <u>103</u> (_____%) of the male respondents said they were afraid to walk at night in their neighborhoods, compared to _____ (_____%) of the female respondents. The difference between the two percentages is _____%,

which appears to be *negligible / potentially interesting*. The *Phi / Cramer's V* value is _____, which means that we can do _____% better predicting FEAR when we know a respondent's gender. This relationship is *weak / moderate / strong*. The approximate significance is _____, which means there is a <u>negligible</u> % chance that the relationship between SEX and FEAR is due to chance. [*Note*: When SPSS says the significance is .000, we label it "negligible" rather than "zero" because we recognize there is an infinitesimal possibility of error due to chance.] This relationship *is / is not* statistically significant.

In their article in Part II, Chiricos, Hogan, and Gertz found that *men / women* reported a higher fear of crime, similar to other studies that they reviewed. The relationship between gender and fear of crime found using the 1996 GSS data *is similar to / differs greatly from* the findings regarding sex reported by Chiricos, Hogan, and Gertz.

3. In the RACE → FEAR crosstabulation, _____ (_____%) of the White respondents said they were afraid to walk at night in their neighborhoods, compared to _____ (_____%) of the Black respondents. The difference between the two percentages is _____%, which appears to be *negligible / potentially interesting*. The *Phi / Cramer's V* value is _____, which means that we can do _____% better predicting FEAR when we know a respondent's race. This relationship is *weak / moderate / strong*. The approximate significance is _____, which means there is a _____% chance that the relationship between RACE and FEAR is due to chance. This relationship *is / is not* statistically significant.

In their article, Chiricos, Hogan, and Gertz reported that *Whites / Blacks* were more fearful of crime, similar to past studies on race and fear of crime. The relationship between race and fear of crime found using the 1996 GSS data *is similar to / differs greatly from* the findings reported by Chiricos, Hogan, and Gertz.

4. In the AGE → FEAR crosstabulation, _____ (_____%) of the young (aged 18–33) respondents said they were afraid to walk at night in their neighborhoods, compared to _____ (_____%) of the middle category (aged 34–49), and _____ (_____%) of the oldest respondents (aged 50 or older). The largest difference between the three percentages is _____%, which appears to be *negligible / potentially interesting*. The *Phi / Cramer's V* value is _____, which means that we can do _____% better predicting FEAR when we know a respondent's age category. This relationship is *weak / moderate / strong*. The approximate significance is _____, which means there is a _____%

chance that the relationship between AGE and FEAR is due to chance. This relationship *is / is not* statistically significant.

In their article, Chiricos, Hogan, and Gertz reported that research by others regarding the effects of age on fear has been *consistent / inconsistent*. Historically, research showed that *older / younger* individuals are more afraid of crime. Newer studies show that this *may / may not* be true. The research by Chiricos, Hogan, and Gertz showed that *older / younger* people reported higher levels of fear. The relationship between age and fear of crime found using the 1996 GSS data *is similar to / differs from* the findings reported by Chiricos, Hogan, and Gertz.

5. In the INCOME → FEAR crosstabulation, _____ (_____%) of the lower-income respondents said they were afraid to walk at night in their neighborhoods, compared to _____ (_____%) of the middle-income group, and _____ (_____%) of the highest-income respondents. The largest difference between the three percentages is _____%, which appears to be *negligible / potentially interesting*. The *Phi / Cramer's V* value is _____, which means that we can do _____% better predicting FEAR when we know a respondent's income category. This relationship is *weak / moderate / strong*. The approximate significance is _____, which means there is a _____% chance that the relationship between INCOME and FEAR is due to chance. This relationship *is / is not* statistically significant.

In their article, Chiricos, Hogan, and Gertz found that wealthier individuals were *more / less* afraid. The relationship between income and fear of crime found using the 1996 GSS data *is similar to / differs greatly from* the findings reported by Chiricos, Hogan, and Gertz.

Homework for Part III: "Further Exploration" Questions
(Fear of Crime)

Name: _____ Date: _____

Task: Expand your list of variables that may affect fear of crime (for example, NEWS and SRCBELT). Run the same type of analyses we ran above.

Directions: Complete the following exercises by answering the questions.

Note: Please print out and include your tables with these questions so your work can be graded.

1. Which variables did you choose as your independent variables?

2. How did your first independent variable affect fear of crime? Make sure to provide a description that includes the percentages, Phi or Cramer's V value, the strength of the relationship, and the significance value.

3. How did your second independent variable affect fear of crime? Make sure to provide a description that includes the percentages, Phi or Cramer's V value, the strength of the relationship, and the significance value.

If you included more than two independent variables, you may summarize the findings here for future reference.

Homework for Part III: "On Your Own" Questions
(Fear of Crime)

Name: _____   Date: _____

Task: Explore some criminal justice opinions in addition to fear of crime (for example, GRASS or CAPPUN). Run the type of analyses we ran above (crosstabulation tables using SEX, RACE, AGE, and INCOME as independent variables). Expand your list of independent variables to include other factors that might be related to your chosen criminal justice opinion.

Directions: Complete the following exercises by answering the questions.

Note: Please print out and include your tables with these questions so your work can be graded.

1. Which variable did you select as a dependent variable, and why did you choose that variable?

2. How did SEX affect your dependent variable? Make sure to provide a description that includes the percentages, Phi or Cramer's V value, the strength of the relationship, and the significance value.

3. How did RACE, AGE, and INCOME affect your dependent variable? Make sure to provide a description that includes the percentages, Phi or Cramer's V value, the strength of the relationship, and the significance value.

4. What other independent variables did you choose and how did they affect your dependent variable?

POINTS TO PONDER: When I ran crosstabulation tables for SEX → CAPPUN and then for RACE → CAPPUN, I noted that women and Blacks are less likely to support capital punishment for murder. Both relationships were moderate. From our analysis of fear of crime above, I remember that women and Blacks were most afraid to walk at night in their neighborhoods. What could explain the fact that the most afraid individuals are least likely to support the death penalty?

IV

WHO ARE THE CRIMINALS?

The Distribution and Correlates of Crime

ONE of the most perplexing problems faced by any person with a basic knowledge of statistics is the confusion of correlation with cause. What statisticians mean when they say that two variables are "correlated" is that they are associated or vary together. For example, if unemployment goes up when crime goes up, then the two variables are positively correlated. If one of them increases and the other decreases, the correlation is negative. So, if we are looking at a sample of young people and find that those from families from the higher social classes have lower rates of delinquency than those from lower-class families, then social class and delinquency can be said to be negatively correlated.

In neither of these examples, however, can the simple observation of a correlation be interpreted to mean that one of the variables *caused* a change in the other. In the first example, all we know is that there is a pattern indicating that when unemployment goes up, crime tends to be higher. We should not conclude that the fluctuations in unemployment have caused the fluctuations in crime. Similarly, even though some studies report a negative relationship between social class and delinquency, this should not be interpreted to mean that the class positions of the young people studied cause their delinquency (in the case of the lower-class children) or inhibit their delinquency (the upper class).

Sociologists are fond of parading a host of "cute" examples past their students to make the point that "correlation does not equal causality." For example, there is a positive correlation between the number of storks in an area and birthrates, but few college students believe that more storks cause more births (storks live in rural areas rather than in cities, and rural areas tend to have higher birthrates than do cities). Similarly, there is a positive correlation between the presence of fire trucks and fires, but most people will not confuse correlation and causality in this type of obvious case. It is when the distinction is not so obvious that confusion and controversy arise.

Criminologists make the step from observing correlations to interpreting them with the help of theory. Theories not only provide a framework for interpreting the meaning of correlations (as well as other observed patterns), but they also help us determine when those correlations are meaningful and when they are not.

A number of variables have been shown to be correlated with crime, but this section focuses on "the big four": social class, race, age, and sex. Although patterns associated with each of these four variables have been central to criminology for a very long time, there continue to be major controversies surrounding each of them.

For most of criminological history, going back to at least the "classical school" of the mid-18th century, we have taken it as an article of faith that those from the lower social classes are more criminal than those from higher positions on the social ladder. Over the past fifty years, however, many criminologists have raised important challenges to this "fact." First, some have argued that lower-class people do not actually commit more crime; they are simply more likely to be arrested and punished for committing crimes than are law violators from the middle or upper classes. More recently, criminologists using self-reports of involvement in crime and delinquency have continued the argument by suggesting that "class doesn't matter," at least not as much as we have been led to believe. John Hagan, in his presidential address to the American Society of Criminology in 1991, argues for "bringing class back in" to the more central role that it played in empirical research and theory before its demise as one of the central variables in criminology. The research that has accumulated over the past hundred years on the relationship between class and crime rates at the societal level, and between one's class position and involvement in crime at the individual level, shows a multilevel, multidimensional, and complex relationship—one that is not easily defended or dismissed. As with many social phenomena, whether there is or is not a meaningful relationship between class and crime depends on how you look at it.

A paper by Michael Hindelang, originally published in 1978 and considered one of the most important empirical papers in criminology, concluded that blacks were more likely than whites to have engaged in violent crimes. That paper was a challenge to those who argued in the 1960s and 1970s that blacks did not commit more crimes, but were the objects of an oppressive criminal justice system. Hindelang described a relationship between race and violent crime, but did not attempt to explain it. In their article, "Toward a Theory of Race, Crime, and Urban Inequality," Robert Sampson and William Julius Wilson offer an explanation of this relationship, and specifically of the disproportionate involvement in violence (as both perpetrators and victims) of young black males living in large urban areas. They propose a slight twist on one of the oldest theoretical perspectives in criminology—social disorganization theory. They see the differences in crime as reflections of the different community contexts within which blacks and whites grow up, live, work, and play. Broad social forces that produce residential inequality, based on the interaction between race and socioeconomic status, create social isolation and the residential concentration of disadvantaged minorities. The result is a weakening of community-based social organization and social control mechanisms, leading to the increased likelihood that crime will establish a strong foothold in those communities, and sustain itself generation after generation.

Age is a correlate of crime that few, if any, criminologists would question. The observation that crime peaks between the ages of 14 and 18 and drops precipitously after the mid-20s, nearly disappearing among those past the mid-30s, is virtually universal among those who study crime. Controversy comes from attempts to relate this "invariant pattern" to theories and public policy. According to Travis Hirschi and Michael Gottfredson, arguments that this age/crime pattern validates some theories over others are not substantiated, and attempts to focus criminal justice policy on a small group of hard-core offenders who do not "age out of crime" are misguided.

Gender is a strong correlate of crime that few criminologists would quibble with. In every social system that has been studied, more males engage in more crime, and in more serious crime, than females. This pattern is so consistent as to be uninteresting in itself; it is in the attempt to explain the relationship that interesting questions arise. In the mid-1970s, criminologists began the first sustained focus on female criminality. Some speculated that, because of social changes that were occurring then, in particular the changes in sex roles and opportunities for women, female criminality would begin to look more like that of men. There is an ongoing debate over whether this has in fact occurred. Another, perhaps more important, issue is *why* there is such a substantial difference between males and females, whether juveniles or adults, in their involvement in crime. Daniel Mears, Matthew Ploeger, and Mark Warr suggest that the dramatic gender difference in juvenile delinquency can be attributed to the difference between boys and girls in their exposure to delinquent peers. Boys are more likely to come under delinquent peer influence than girls, who are at a higher level of moral development and, therefore, more likely to disapprove of delinquency and of delinquent peers. One might say that girls are more prudent in their choice of friends and associates than boys.

The identification of important correlates of crime can answer many questions for criminologists. But, as is the case with these four correlates of crime, the observation of patterns is really only another step toward understanding *why* they exist. It is only by building and testing theories that criminologists can begin to make sense of these observed correlations.

The Poverty of a Classless Criminology: The American Society of Criminology 1991 Presidential Address

JOHN HAGAN

WHEN criminologists write of the "Myth of a Social Class and Criminality" or ask "What's Class Got to Do With It?" they express a skepticism about the connection of class with crime that distinguishes them from other scholars as well as laypersons. Popular discourse of earlier eras included frequent references to the "dangerous" and "criminal classes," and scholarly discourse today features discussions of an "underclass," which is assumed to prominently include criminals.

The dangerous and criminal class concepts probably are heard infrequently today because they were used in such an invidious and pejorative fashion. The underclass conceptualization has the potential to be used in the same way, even though it was invented to call attention to processes of disadvantagement and subordination. Thus, new as well as old depictions of class and crime can prove problematic, and their uses demand careful scrutiny. However, the simple omission of class from the study of crime would impoverish criminology.

CONVERSATIONS ABOUT CLASS AND CRIME

Riesman describes sociology as a "conversation between the classes." Although "conversations" linking class and crime predate both modern sociology and criminology, this metaphor usefully highlights the layers of meaning that are often communicated in discussions of class and crime.

Discussions of criminal or dangerous classes are traced by Silver to eighteenth- and nineteenth-century Paris and London, and they were common as well in nineteenth- and twentieth-century Canada and the United States. Daniel Defoe wrote of eighteenth-century London that "the streets of the City are now the Places of Danger," and Charles Brace warned nearly a century and a half later, in *The Dangerous Classes of New York*, that

let but law lift its hand from them for a season, or let the civilizing influences of American life fail to

From "The Poverty of a Classless Criminology – The American Society of Criminology 1991 Presidential Address" by J. Hagan, 1992, *Criminology* 30 (1):1–16. Copyright © 1992 The American Society of Criminology.

reach them, and, if the opportunity afforded, we should see an explosion from this class which might leave the city in ashes and blood.

As Silver makes clear, the dangerous or criminal classes referred primarily to the unattached and unemployed, and to their associations with crime.

Historians continue to write about conceptions of the dangerous and criminal classes of earlier periods and places, while popular and scholarly discussions of contemporary affairs refer to the "underclass." Myrdal introduced discussion of the underclass to draw attention to persons driven to the economic margins of modern society. Marks has detailed the development of the concept of the urban underclass, calling particular attention to the place of crime within it.

Marks notes that Auletta distinguishes four distinct elements of the underclass: "hostile street and career criminals, skilled entrepreneurs of the underground economy, passive victims of government support and the severely traumatized," while Lemann characterizes this class in terms of "poverty, crime, poor education, dependency, and teenage out-of-wedlock childbearing." Often race also is embedded in these characterizations, leading to debate about the extent to which the U.S. underclass is a black underclass. But what is most striking in these discussions is the extent to which the modern underclass, like its historical predecessors described by Silver, is defined by the association of the unattached and unemployed with crime. Marks asks, "Is . . . criminality the major ingredient of . . . underclass status?" Her concern is that "the underclass has been transformed from surplus and discarded labor into an exclusive group of black urban terrorists."

DECLASSIFYING CRIME

There are scientific as well as ideological reasons to be skeptical of the modern linkage between class and crime in the concept of the underclass. Gans argues that this new concept is itself "dangerous" because by focusing on crime and other nonnormative behaviors in discussing the underclass, "researchers tend to assume that the behavior patterns they report are caused by norm violations on the part of area residents and not by the conditions under which they are living, or the behavioral choices open to them as a result of these conditions." Gans concludes that the effect is to identify and further stigmatize a group as "the undeserving poor."

However, this criticism surely is unfounded in its association with William Julius Wilson's discussion of the underclass in *The Truly Disadvantaged*. This book focuses on concentrations of joblessness among the ghetto poor as explicit causes of crime and violence in these communities. Wilson is also careful to make clear that his thesis is not confined to black American ghettoes, noting that "the concept 'underclass' or 'ghetto poor' can be theoretically applied to all racial and ethnic groups, and to different societies if the conditions specified in the theory are met." Wilson's work has stimulated important new research on urban crime and poverty, and he worries that "any crusade to abandon the concept of underclass, however defined, could result in premature closure of ideas just as important new studies on the inner-city ghetto, including policy-oriented studies, are being generated." Wilson interchanges the term "ghetto poor" for "underclass" in his recent writing.

Meanwhile, the scientific utility of some uses of the underclass concept is also open to question, at least for the purposes of theorizing about crime. Insofar as the conceptualization of the underclass includes within it the cultural (e.g., attitudes and values) and structural (e.g., joblessness) factors assumed to cause crime, as well as crime itself, it may be little more than a diffuse tautology. And it may indeed be this feature of some discussions of the underclass, like the dangerous and criminal class conceptualizations before it, that has engendered skepticism in criminology and limited our understanding of connections between class and crime.

FROM CLASS AND CRIME TO STATUS AND DELINQUENCY

Prominent theories of criminogenesis also emphasize the harsh class circumstances experienced by the most desperate and disreputable segments of the population, and they causally connect these adverse class conditions with serious crime. However, in so doing these theories separately identify class conditions and criminal behavior as distinct and independent phenomena. The correlation proposed in these theories is largely taken for granted in ethnographic research, and it also is observed in most if not all areal studies.

But the correlation of class and crime is only weakly if at all reflected in self-report analyses based on surveys of individual adolescents attending school, which has led to calls for the abandonment of class analyses of crime. Since the latter self-report studies are at variance not only with lay and scholarly theories of criminogenesis, but also with ethnographic and areal research, there might seem grounds to simply reject the former method and its results as artificial. However, doing so risks underestimating the valuable role that self-report studies have played in the advancement of criminological theory. Self-report methodology has facilitated systematic and extensive measurement of explanatory variables, while freeing researchers from reliance on official records of criminality; and this methodology has underwritten classic contributions to theory testing in criminology.

In such efforts, self-report survey researchers have usefully disentangled the concepts of class and crime. In doing do they implicitly have questioned the taken-for-granted nature of associations of crime and poverty in the densely descriptive ethnographic studies, as well as the mixtures of measures of poverty and crime that sometimes tautologically and ecologically have confounded areal studies. Self-report survey researchers rightly insist on independent measures of class and crime that can provide the building blocks for testing explanations of crime. Literary or statistical descriptions of crime-prone areas, the modern sociological analogues to Dickens' and Mayhew's early depictions of the dangerous and criminal classes of London, are not enough for the purposes of theory testing. In their place, self-report researchers moved into the schools of America (and later other countries) to collect extensive information on family, educational, community, and other experiences of adolescents. Three substitutions characterized this process: (1) schools replaced the streets as sites for data collection; (2) delinquency replaced crime as the behavior to be explained; and (3) parental-status origins replaced criminal actor's more immediate class conditions as presumed exogenous causes of delinquency.

In some ways, these substitutions enhanced the scientific standing of criminological research, but they also distanced self-report studies from the conditions and activities that stimulated attention to the criminal or underclass in the first place. For example, while sampling frames could more accurately be established from schools than from the streets, it was street youths who were more likely than school youths to be involved in delinquency and crime. Further, while adolescent self-reports of delinquency might be free from some kinds of mistakes and biases involved in official record keeping about adolescents and adults, the more common self-reported adolescent indiscretions were also less likely to be the crimes of more general concern to citizens. Parental status could be indexed (with attractive measurement properties for persons regularly employed in conventional occupations) independently of the adolescent behaviors that researchers were seeking to explain. However, the status continua underlying these measures assumed that the parents had occupations, and the measures were not actually measures of the position of those whose behavior were being explained. These substitutions made self-report survey research more systematic, but they also produced the unintended result that less theoretically relevant characteristics (i.e., status in place of class) were used to explain the less serious behaviors (i.e., common delinquency in place of serious crime) of less criminally involved persons (i.e., school youths rather than street youths and adults).

RECLASSIFYING CRIME

Serious attempts have been made to improve on these features of the self-report paradigm. These efforts most significantly have involved the use of parental and youth unemployment measures, which better represent class positions and conditions, instead of or in addition to the occupational statuses of parents.

Wright explains why this kind of reconceptualization is important when he notes that definitions of specific classes can be understood as a particular form of proposition. He writes that, "all things being equal, all units within a given class should be more like each other than like units in other classes *with respect to whatever it is that class is meant to explain*" (emphasis in original). The key to defining a class in this way is to identify relevant linking conceptual mechanisms. For example, in economics or sociology, when income is the theoretical object of explanation, educational attainment, whether as an indicator of certification or skill transmission, is an obvious linking mechanism that must be incorporated in the measurement of class.

In criminology, our theoretical objects of explanation—delinquency and crime—demand their own distinct conceptual consideration. So we need to more directly conceptualize and measure our own linking causal mechanisms. These mechanisms may involve situations of deprivation, desperation, destitution, degradation, disrepute, and related conditions. Tittle and Meier speak to the importance of such factors when they suggest that "it would

make more sense to measure deprivation directly than to measure SES, which is a step removed from the real variable at issue."

That is, when serious street crime is the focus of our attention, the relevant concern is with class more than status—especially as the former operates through such linking mechanisms as deprivation, destitution, and disrepute. These linking mechanisms are more directly experienced when actors themselves are, for example, hungry, unhoused, ill educated, and unemployed, but they may also operate indirectly through parental unemployment and housing problems, for example, involving associated family disruption, neglect and abuse of children, and resulting difficulties at school. Youth and parental unemployment experiences are important exogenous sources of these kinds of direct and indirect class effects, and some survey researchers therefore have focused on these measures in self-report studies.

However, Brownfield reports that efforts in school surveys to identify class circumstances in terms of parental joblessness (perhaps the most promising of parental class measures) reveal that "researchers have considerable difficulty finding and studying the disreputable poor." Consider briefly the few studies that are available. By counting any spell of unemployment over three preceding years, 16% of the family heads in Hirschi's Richmond study were designated unemployed. By oversampling multiple dwelling units and depressed neighborhoods, Hagan et al. produced a Toronto sample in which 9% of the family heads were unemployed. Johnson also focused on parental joblessness and selected three Seattle high schools, "in order to obtain a sufficient number of underclass students," who constitute 8% of this sample. The Research Triangle Institute oversampled ethnic communities and produced a sample in which about 7% of the youth lived in a household with an unemployed head. Finally, the Arizona Community Tolerance Study overrepresented rural families, 3% of which had unemployed heads, including many "miners who were temporarily laid off." These are the only self-report studies I can find that report parental joblessness as a measure of underclass position. All use samples stratified on exogenous variables intended to overrepresent jobless parents, and all still find relatively few underclass families.

The limited study of, and variance in, parental unemployment diminishes the likelihood of finding stable or substantial parental class-of-origin effects on adolescent delinquency. And there is the further and possibly more important factor that the influence of class of origin on delinquency is from a distance. For example, the class-of-origin effect is assumed to operate over as long as a three-year lag in the case of the Richmond study described above. Furthermore, the parental class effect is presumably also indirect, operating through the variety of family, school, and other mediating variables noted above. This combination of factors suggests that the impact of parental class of origin on delinquency *should* be weak. And it is therefore not surprising that this indirect class effect is elusive and uncertain in self-report research.

This shifts our attention to the potentially more immediate and direct class effects of youth unemployment on crime and delinquency. Although there are many aggregate-level studies of crime and unemployment, and even some attempts to disaggregate neighborhood-level effects on individuals, there are again surprisingly few studies that focus on individuals. However, these individual-level studies reveal higher levels of youth unemployment than is present in the studies focused on parents; and, perhaps most important, these studies report the expected correlation between youth unemployment and involvement in delinquency and crime, even if the full nature of this correlation is only beginning to be understood.

For example, Farrington et al. report that nearly half of the sample of 411 London males followed in their panel research from ages 8 to 18 experienced some unemployment, and the youths self-reported more involvement in delinquency during the periods of their unemployment. This study (and further research reported below) allows some consideration of the timing of crime and unemployment, and as well attempts to remove concerns about spuriousness arising from joint causes. However, this study (like others) does not definitively determine the *direction* in which the causal influence between unemployment and crime flows. A problem is that the relationship between unemployment and crime may be instantaneous or simultaneous, as well as lagged. Farrington et al. consider the simultaneous occurrence of crime and unemployment during coterminous periods, making it uncertain whether crime or unemployment can be identified as coming first.

This issue is salient because there are several classic studies which show that juvenile delinquency is nonspuriously correlated with later *adult* unemployment. Perhaps the best-known study is Robins's *Deviant Children Grown Up.* This study followed a clinic-based sample of predominately low-status, "severely antisocial children" into adulthood and compared them with a "control group," who were without adolescent behavior problems and matched with the clinic sample on race, age, sex, IQ, and socioeconomic status (SES). As adults the clinic sample experienced more frequent and longer spells of unemployment.

The Gluecks used a similar matched-group design to study white males from Boston who, because of their persistent delinquency, were committed to one of two correctional schools in Massachusetts. In their reanalysis of these data, Sampson and Laub find greater adult unemployment among the delinquent sample.

Two of the most systematic efforts to establish the direction of influence between youth unemployment and delinquency and crime are by Bachman et al. and Thornberry and Christenson. Bachman et al. analyze self-report panel data gathered through a nationally representative sampling of 87 public high schools in the United States. They ask, "Does unemployment really heighten aggression and drug use?" They conclude, "Our findings in this area are suggestive, but not definitive. In each case an alternative path of causation is possible."

Similarly, Thornberry and Christenson use a linear-panel model to analyze unemployment and crime among 567 subjects from a 1945 Philadelphia birth cohort; they conclude that unemployment and crime mutually influence one another over the individual's life span, with no indication of which problem occurs first.

The importance of these studies is that they are unified in indicating that there is a non-spurious correlation between unemployment and crime that endures over the life course. Much important work remains to be done in establishing the direction and dynamic of this relationship, as I discuss further below. However, insofar as unemployment is a core component of class, and insofar as unemployment and crime form important causal components in the formation of life course trajectories, there can be little doubt that the relationship between class and crime is a key element in criminological research.

HIGH-CLASS CRIMES AND MISDEMEANORS

Thus far I have focused exclusively on delinquency and crime at the lower end of the class hierarchy. However, too much criminological theorizing and research have operated from the simplistic assumption that the relationship between class and crime is linear and monotonic, as if with each step down a class or status hierarchy, the likelihood of crime could be expected to increase along a fixed gradient. This is unlikely. Individual-level class locations are connected to crime in different ways in different settings. For example, we do not expect to find complicated securities schemes undertaken by unemployed street youths, or street muggings and robberies performed by corporate executives. However, this does not mean that the relationship between class and crime is nonexistent or unimportant, but again that our conceptualization and operationalization of class and crime must be linked to the context in which they are applied.

It is in this sense that Sutherland's rejection of the relationship between poverty and crime has often been misunderstood. Gaylord and Galliher note of Sutherland that

he accepted the official criminal justice statistics as being more or less accurate in gauging the extent of criminality in the lower classes. His complaint was that the official statistics gave an appearance of the concentration of crime in the lower class only because middle- and upper-class crime systematically escaped official notice.

The challenge is to conceptualize and operationalize class and crime to capture the distinctiveness of these different class connections.

One way of doing this is to more generally focus on socially organized resource relationships in the conceptualization of class. Access to resources can determine the power relationships that are central to modern conceptions of class. Lack of food, shelter, and employment define one extreme of class-structured power relationships, while ownership, authority, and access to money define another. Depending on the setting and purpose involved, one or another of these conditions and relationships may be most relevant. I have already discussed research on the relationship between youth unemployment and crime. There is increasingly important research at the other end of the class hierarchy as well.

For example, Stanton Wheeler and his colleagues have undertaken a series of studies that isolate and identify the ways in which corporate resources are used to perpetrate white-collar crimes. They demonstrate that individuals operating through formally organized associations and businesses perpetrate larger-scale crimes than individuals acting alone; and these crimes are further linked into the ownership and authority structures of corporate settings. The class-specific nature of these high-class crimes is nicely captured by Wheeler and Rothman when they note that the corporation and its resources are "for white-collar criminals what the gun or knife is for the common criminal—a tool to obtain money from victims." The point of such an observation, of course, is that the relationship between class and crime is class and crime specific.

Research is also emerging on the importance of access to resources among adolescents. For example, Cullen et al. have demonstrated that having access to money is correlated with delinquency. Tanner and Krahn find that part-time employment among adolescents still in school is associated with delinquency. Hagan and Kay show that male children of employer-class parents are more likely to engage in the copyright violations that involve, for example, copying audio cassettes. And Agnew shows that under specified conditions the weekly pay of employed adolescents is positively related to delinquency. These studies indicate that access to, as well as denial of, class-structured sources of power can be causally related to delinquency and crime, so that delinquency and crime are causally linked to high as well as low positions in the class structure.

CLASS CONDITIONS AND CRIME

Finally, it is important to note that class is relevant to the study of crime not only for its main effects, but also through its interaction and conditioning effects. From this perspective, class contexts set conditions and parameters within which other factors influence and are influenced by delinquency and crime.

One of the most interesting examples of potential conditioning effects of class involves the linkage between juvenile delinquency and adult employment outcomes noted above. Two of the studies I mentioned, Robins and Sampson and Laub, find lasting negative effects of delinquency. However, both of these studies are based on samples of subjects drawn from predominantly lower-class backgrounds. Jessor et al.'s recent panel analysis based on more representative samples of middle- and upper-class subjects involved in less serious activities finds fewer long-term effects, and no effects on occupational out-

comes. This research suggests that class origins in part condition the effects of delinquency on life course trajectories.

This conditioning process could occur in several ways. On the one hand, in the middle and upper classes, the openness of the opportunity structure, processes of community absorption, and access to second chances may mitigate the effects of early involvements in delinquency. On the other hand, restricted legitimate opportunities and alternative illegitimate opportunities, as well as labeling effects, may increase the salience of early involvements in delinquency in underclass settings.

Freeman points out that contexts of low legitimate earnings can give rise to criminal activity in several ways. He cites micro-level data on inner-city youths analyzed by Viscusi, which reveal a clear relationship between illegal activity and expectations of relative earnings in legal and illegal work. The rational choice implication, of course, is that those who expected higher earnings "on the street" were more likely to participate in crime than those who did not. Similarly, Freeman reports that despite a booming labor market in the greater Boston area in the 1980s, the fraction of black males in the inner city who perceived higher earnings potential in crime relative to legitimate earnings rose substantially. Freeman and Holzer observe that this perception is consistent with the declining earnings of the less educated, and perhaps with the growing market for illicit drugs as well, leading to the conclusion that "criminal activity among young and less-educated blacks should hardly be surprising in this light."

Meanwhile, at least from the pioneering work of Schwartz and Skolnick, there is evidence that contacts with the criminal justice system have especially negative effects for underclass males. Even if most underclass males who are arrested do not go to jail, the experience of arrest can have long-term, even intergenerational repercussions. Both Freeman and Grogger report that a criminal arrest record has detrimental consequences for labor market outcomes, with negative effects on employment as much as eight years later. Presumably, some of this is due to the reluctance of employers who check for criminal records to employ ex-offenders. However, there are other possibilities as well. Incarceration, or even prolonged processing through the criminal justice system, can date job skills and networks of contacts for employment. As well, the attitudes and interests that signal employability to prospective employers may be chronically undermined. Freeman writes that, "either way, declining labor market opportunities for the less-educated and participation in crime seem to reinforce each other for growing fractions of less-educated young males." These less-educated males are the core of the underclass.

The latter discussion acknowledges the further relevance of class to juvenile and criminal justice processing decisions. One of the classic findings of research on the policing of adolescents indicates the influence of class- and race-related demeanor on arrest decisions. More direct effects of class are a part of juvenile and criminal court processing decisions when, for example, unemployment is incorporated into the legal criteria used to make bail and probation decisions. The embedment of demeanor and employment considerations in statutory guidelines makes the meaning of these effects moot for some legal purposes, but not for the theoretical purposes of understanding and explaining criminal justice operations.

Meanwhile, perhaps equally important are the ways in which these police and court experiences are perceived by citizens. Such experiences recently have been brought to public attention by graphic videotapes and audio recordings of police–citizen encounters replayed by the media. Yet we know relatively little about the ways in which these messages about our justice system are received by the public.

However, two possibilities seem likely. One possibility is that personal as well as vicarious experiences with the justice system are a part of the process by which ghetto youths develop hostile attitudes and perhaps also behaviors that impair transitions to adult employment. Another possibility is that minorities who have escaped poverty and moved into more advantaged class locations remain uniquely sensitive to these early experiences and continuing intrusions into their lives. A quarter century ago, the star center of the Boston Celtics basketball team, Bill Russell, wrote in his autobiography of the continuing harassment he had experienced in encounters with the police. A year ago, the Boston Celtics' first-round draft pick, Dee Brown, received an apology from suburban Boston police for "racial implications" in his search by officers looking for a black bank robber. Research confirms that black professionals more generally have an acute sensitivity to criminal injustice that is reflective of Russell's and Brown's experiences. This interaction of class with race in the perception of criminal justice is likely an important and continuing base of support for criminal justice reform in America.

ADVANCING THEORIES OF CLASS AND CRIME

Some of the greatest advances of criminology over the past several decades have involved its evolution into a more systematic and precise science. These advances have demanded greater clarity and testability of our theories, and these advances have occurred through the dedicated efforts of some of our field's most practiced contributors. However, some of these efforts risk being regarded as irrelevant by other scholars, policymakers, and the general public when they are interpreted as moving from the identification of flaws in conceptualizations and operationalizations of class and crime, to the dismissal of this relationship and its significance for the study of crime.

A better starting point is to acknowledge the variety and complexity of the relationship between class and crime. We need to know more about the ways in which our ideology as well as our science influences our conceptualizations and operationalizations of class and crime. Once they are conceptualized and operationalized, we need to learn more about the ways in which class and crime relationships vary across time and place, within the life course, between historical periods, as well as across societies. But perhaps most important, we need to better understand the ways in which cultural and structural forces operate to change as well as conserve relationships between class and crime. An example may help to clarify the kinds of cultural and structural processes I have in mind.

Earlier in this essay I discussed results from Sampson and Laub's fascinating reanalysis of the Gluecks' data that follow adolescents of predominately lower-class backgrounds into adulthood. Further results from this research reveal evidence of change as well as persistence in behavioral trajectories across the life course. The evidence of change is especially exciting: Former delinquents who obtained stable employment and established strong marriages were less likely to persist in adult crime. Since the Gluecks' Massachusetts sample is predominately lower class, and since several studies suggest that it is in the lower class that negative effects of delinquency on adult employment are most likely to be found, Sampson and Laub's results are especially noteworthy. One of the most valuable features of this research is that it stimulates further questions, contributing to a new agenda of criminological research.

For example, we need to learn more about how and why many formerly delinquent youths are able to find stable adult employment and form strong marriages, often despite disadvantaged backgrounds. How are many of these youths able to develop the kinds of social and cultural capital that are necessary to establish successful adult lives? Disadvantaged class origins imply little access to the forms of social and cultural capital that seem so essential in the life course. Yet when those youths who reform, as well as those who are never involved in serious delinquency, are traced into adulthood, it becomes obvious that most youths, even from significantly disadvantaged circumstances, do succeed in adulthood. We need a theory of social and cultural capital that is sensitive to issues of class disadvantage and that can account for successful life trajectories, as well as careers in crime.

Meanwhile, we also know that contacts with the juvenile justice system are associated with the kinds of impaired employment prospects, and probably impaired marriage prospects as well, that are also associated with the persistence in crime observed in the Gluecks' Massachusetts data, as well as in Farrington's panel data from working-class London. The juvenile justice system must occupy a central place in *a theory of class reproduction* that accounts for persistence in these career trajectories. Again, we need to learn more about how this process operates and accounts for persistence in crime—for example, whether it is the stigma of a police or court record, interruptions in employment and job seeking caused by police, court, and/or detention experiences, or attitudes and behaviors associated with system contacts that are most salient in determining adult outcomes.

Of course, theories of cultural capital and class reproduction will often, if not usually, be complementary. For example, police and court contacts are one way in which the cultural capital of ghetto youths is diminished, reproducing intergenerational problems of unemployment as well as crime, with attitudinal as well as behavioral ramifications. But we have much to learn about how these processes work, especially in the underclass. The advancement of our knowledge about such processes will not be enhanced by dismissing simplifying connections between class and crime for ideological or other purposes.

QUESTIONS FOR DISCUSSION AND WRITING

1. Is the idea of criminal or dangerous classes new?
2. What unintended results were produced by the move to systematic self-report research?
3. Why must our conceptualization and operationalization of class and crime be linked to the context in which they are applied?

RACE

Toward a Theory of Race, Crime, and Urban Inequality

ROBERT J. SAMPSON
WILLIAM JULIUS WILSON

OUR purpose in this [article] is to address one of the central yet difficult issues facing criminology: race and violent crime. The centrality of the issue is seen on several fronts. The leading cause of death among young black males is homicide; the lifetime risk of being murdered is as high as 1 in 21 for black males, compared with only 1 in 131 for white males. Although rates of violence have been higher for blacks than whites at least since the 1950s, record increases in homicide since the mid-1980s in cities such as New York, Chicago, and Philadelphia also appear racially selective. For example, while white rates remained stable, the rate of death from firearms among young black males more than doubled from 1984 to 1988 alone. These differentials help explain recent estimates that a resident of rural Bangladesh has a greater chance of surviving to age 40 than does a black male in Harlem. Moreover, the so-called drug war and the resulting surge in prison populations in

From "Toward a Theory of Race, Crime and Urban Inequality" by R. Sampson and W. J. Wilson, from *Crime and Inequality,* (pp. 37–54) edited by J. Hagan and R. D. Peterson, Stanford, CA: Stanford University Press, 1995. Reprinted with the permission of the publishers, Stanford University Press. © 1995 by the Board of Trustees of the Leland Stanford Junior University.

the past decade have taken their toll disproportionately on the minority community. Overall, the evidence is clear that African Americans face dismal and worsening odds when it comes to crime in the streets and the risk of incarceration.

Despite these facts, the discussion of race and crime is mired in an unproductive mix of controversy and silence. At the same time that articles on age and gender abound, criminologists are loath to speak openly on race and crime for fear of being misunderstood or labeled racist. This situation is not unique, for until recently scholars of urban poverty also consciously avoided discussion of race and social dislocations in the inner city lest they be accused of blaming the victim. And when the topic is broached, criminologists have reduced the race–crime debate to simplistic arguments about culture versus social structure. On the one side, structuralists argue for the primacy of "relative deprivation" to understand black crime, even though the evidence on social class and crime is weak at best. On the other side, cultural theorists tend to focus on an indigenous culture of violence in black ghettos, even though the evidence there is weak too.

Still others engage in subterfuge, denying race-related differentials in violence and focusing instead on police bias and the alleged invalidity of official crime statistics—this in spite of evidence not only from death records but also from survey reports showing that blacks are disproportionately victimized by, and involved in, criminal violence. Hence, much like the silence on race and inner-city social dislocations engendered by the vociferous attacks on the Moynihan Report in the 1960s, criminologists have, with few exceptions, abdicated serious scholarly debate on race and crime.

In an attempt to break this stalemate, we advance in this article a theoretical strategy that incorporates both structural and cultural arguments regarding race, crime, and inequality in American cities. In contrast to psychologically based relative deprivation theories and the subculture of violence, we view the race and crime linkage through contextual lenses that highlight the very different ecological contexts that blacks and whites reside in—regardless of individual characteristics. The basic thesis is that macrosocial patterns of residential inequality give rise to the social isolation and ecological concentration of the truly disadvantaged, which in turn leads to structural barriers and cultural adaptations that undermine social organization and hence the control of crime. This thesis is grounded in what is actually an old idea in criminology that has been overlooked in the race and crime debate—the importance of communities.

THE COMMUNITY STRUCTURE OF RACE AND CRIME

Unlike the dominant tradition in criminology that seeks to distinguish offenders from non-offenders, the macrosocial or community level of explanation asks what it is about community structures and cultures that produces differential rates of crime. As such, the goal of macrolevel research is not to explain individual involvement in criminal behavior but to isolate characteristics of communities, cit-

ies, or even societies that lead to high rates of criminality. From this viewpoint the "ecological fallacy"—inferring individual-level relations based on aggregate data—is not at issue because the unit of explanation and analysis is the community.

The Chicago School research of Clifford Shaw and Henry McKay spearheaded the community-level approach of modern American studies of ecology and crime. In their classic work *Juvenile Delinquency and Urban Areas*, Shaw and McKay argued that three structural factors—low economic status, ethnic heterogeneity, and residential mobility—led to the disruption of local community social organization, which in turn accounted for variations in crime and delinquency rates.

Arguably the most significant aspect of Shaw and McKay's research, however, was their demonstration that high rates of delinquency persisted in certain areas over many years, regardless of population turnover. More than any other, this finding led them to reject individualistic explanations of delinquency and focus instead on the processes by which delinquent and criminal patterns of behavior were transmitted across generations in areas of social disorganization and weak social controls. This community-level orientation led them to an explicit contextual interpretation of correlations between race/ethnicity and delinquency rates. Their logic was set forth in a rejoinder to a critique in 1949 by Jonassen, who had argued that ethnicity had direct effects on delinquency. Shaw and McKay countered:

The important fact about rates of delinquency for Negro boys is that they, too, vary by type of area. They are higher than the rates for white boys, but it cannot be said that they are higher than rates for white boys in comparable areas, since it is impossible to reproduce in white communities the circumstances under which Negro children live. Even if it were possible to parallel the low economic status and the inadequacy of institutions in the white community, it would not be possible to reproduce the effects of segregation and the barriers to upward mobility.

Shaw and McKay's insight almost a half century ago raises two interesting questions still relevant today. First, to what extent do black rates of crime vary by type of ecological area? Second, is it possible to reproduce in white communities the structural circumstances in which many blacks live? The first question is crucial, for it signals that blacks are not a homogeneous group any more than whites are. Indeed, it is racial stereotyping that assigns to blacks a distinct or homogeneous character, allowing simplistic comparisons of black–white group differences in crime. As Shaw and McKay recognized, the key point is that there is heterogeneity among blacks in crime rates that correspond to community context. To the extent that the causes of black crime are not unique, its rate should thus vary with specific ecological conditions in the same way that the white crime rate does. As we shall now see, recent evidence weighs in Shaw and McKay's favor.

Are the Causes of Black Crime Unique?

Disentangling the contextual basis for race and crime requires racial disaggregation of both the crime rate and the explanatory variables of theoretical interest. This approach was used in recent research that examined racially disaggregated rates of homicide and robbery by juveniles and adults in over 150 U.S. cities in 1980. Substantively, the theory explored the effects of black male joblessness and economic deprivation on violent crime as mediated by black family disruption. The results supported the main hypothesis and showed that the scarcity of employed black males relative to black females was directly related to the prevalence of families headed by women in black communities. In turn, black family disruption was substantially related to rates of black murder and robbery, especially by juveniles. These effects were independent of income, region, density, city size, and welfare benefits.

The finding that family disruption had stronger effects on juvenile violence than on adult violence, in conjunction with the inconsistent findings of previous research on individual-level delinquency and broken homes, supports the idea that the effects of family structure are related to macro-level patterns of social control and guardianship, especially for youth and their peers. Moreover, the results suggest why unemployment and economic deprivation have had weak or inconsistent direct effects on violence rates in past research—joblessness and poverty appear to exert much of their influence indirectly through family disruption.

Despite a tremendous difference in mean levels of family disruption among black and white communities, the percentage of white families headed by a female also had a large positive effect on white juvenile and white adult violence. In fact, the predictors of white robbery were shown to be in large part identical in sign and magnitude to those for blacks. Therefore, the effect of black family disruption on black crime was independent of commonly cited alternative explanations (e.g., region, density, age composition) and could not be attributed to unique cultural factors within the black community given the similar effect of white family disruption on white crime.

To be clear, we are not dismissing the relevance of culture. As discussed more below, our argument is that if cultural influences exist, they vary systematically with structural features of the urban environment. How else can we make sense of the systematic variations *within* race—for example, if a uniform subculture of violence explains black crime, are we to assume that this subculture is three times as potent in, say, New York as in Chicago (where black homicide differs by a factor of 3)? In San Francisco as in Baltimore (3:1 ratio)? These distinct variations exist even at the state level. For example, rates of black homicide in California are triple those in Maryland. Must whites then be part of the black subculture of violence in California, given that white homicide rates are also more than triple the rates for whites in Maryland? We think not. The sources of violent crime appear to be remarkably invariant across race and rooted instead in the structural differences among communities, cities, and states in economic and family organization.

The Ecological Concentration of Race and Social Dislocations

Having demonstrated the similarity of black–white variations by ecological context, we turn to the second logical question. To what extent are blacks as a group differentially exposed to criminogenic structural conditions? More than 40 years after Shaw and McKay's assessment of race and urban ecology, we still cannot say that blacks and whites share a similar environment—especially with regard to concentrated urban poverty. Consider the following. Although approximately 70 percent of all poor non-Hispanic whites lived in nonpoverty areas in the ten largest U.S. central cities (as determined by the 1970 census) in 1980, only 16 percent of poor blacks did. Moreover, whereas less than 7 percent of poor whites lived in extreme poverty or ghetto areas, 38 percent of poor blacks lived in such areas. In the nation's largest city, New York, 70 percent of poor blacks live in poverty neighborhoods; by contrast, 70 percent of poor whites live in nonpoverty neighborhoods. Potentially even more important, the majority of poor blacks live in communities characterized by high rates of family disruption. Poor whites, even those from "broken homes," live in areas of relative family stability.

The combination of urban poverty and family disruption concentrated by race is particularly severe. As an example, we examined race-specific census data on the 171 largest cities in the United States as of 1980. To get some idea of concentrated social dislocations by race, we selected cities where the proportion of blacks living in poverty was equal to or less than the proportion of whites, *and* where the proportion of black families with children headed by a single parent was equal to or less than that for white families. Although we knew that the average national rate of family disruption and poverty among blacks was two to four times higher than among whites, the number of distinct ecological contexts in which blacks achieve equality to whites is striking. In not one city over 100,000 in the United States do blacks live in ecological equality with whites when it comes to these basic features of economic and family organization. Accordingly, racial differences in poverty and family disruption are so strong that the "worst" urban contexts in which whites reside are considerably better than the average context of black communities.

Taken as a whole, these patterns underscore what W. J. Wilson has labeled "concentration effects"—that is, the effects of living in a neighborhood that is overwhelmingly impoverished. These concentration effects, reflected in a range of outcomes from degree of labor force attachment to social deviance, are created by the constraints and opportunities that the residents of inner-city neighborhoods face in terms of access to jobs and job networks, involvement in quality schools, availability of marriageable partners, and exposure to conventional role models.

The social transformation of the inner city in recent decades has resulted in an increased concentration of the most disadvantaged segments of the urban black population—especially poor, female-headed families with children. Whereas one of every five poor blacks resided in ghetto or extreme poverty areas in 1970, by 1980 nearly two out of every five did so. This change has been fueled by several macrostructural forces. In particular, urban minorities have been vulnerable to structural economic changes related to the deindustrialization of central cities (the shift from goods-producing to service-producing industries; increasing polarization of the labor market into low-wage and high-wage sectors; relocation of manufacturing out of the inner city). The exodus of middle- and upper-income black families from the inner city has also removed an important social buffer that could potentially deflect the full impact of prolonged joblessness and industrial transformation. This thesis is based on the assumption that the basic institutions of an area (churches, schools, stores, recreational facilities, etc.) are more likely to remain viable if the core of their support comes from more economically stable families in inner-city neighborhoods. The social milieu of increasing stratification among blacks differs significantly from the environment that existed in inner cities in previous decades.

Black inner-city neighborhoods have also disproportionately suffered severe population and housing loss of the sort identified by Shaw and McKay as disrupting the social and institutional order. Skogan has noted how urban renewal and forced migration contributed to the wholesale uprooting of many urban black communities, especially the extent to which freeway networks driven through the hearts of many cities in the 1950s destroyed viable low-income communities. For example, in Atlanta one in six residents was dislocated by urban renewal; the great majority of those dislocated were poor blacks. Nationwide, fully 20 percent of all central-city housing units occupied by blacks were lost in the period 1960–1970 alone. As Logan and Molotch observe, this displacement does not even include that brought about by more routine market forces (evictions, rent increases, commercial development).

Of course, no discussion of concentration effects is complete without recognizing the negative consequences of deliberate policy decisions to concentrate minorities and the poor in public housing. Opposition from organized community groups to the building of public housing in their neighborhoods, de facto federal policy to tolerate extensive discrimination against blacks in urban housing markets, and the decision by local governments to neglect the rehabilitation of existing residential units (many of them single-family homes), have led to massive, segregated housing projects that have become ghettos for the minorities and disadvantaged. The cumulative result is that, even given the same objective socioeconomic status, blacks and whites face vastly different environments in which to live, work, and raise their children. As Bickford and Massey have argued, public housing is a federally funded, physically permanent institution for the isolation of black families by race and class and must therefore be considered an important structural constraint on ecological area of residence.

In short, the foregoing discussion suggests that macrostructural factors—both historic and contemporary—have combined to concentrate urban black poverty and family disruption in the inner city. These factors include but are not limited to racial segregation, structural economic transformation and black male joblessness, class-linked out-migration from the inner city, and housing discrimination. It is important to emphasize that when segregation and concentrated poverty represent structural constraints embodied in public policy and historical patterns of racial subjugation, notions that individual differences (or self-selection) explain community-level effects on violence are considerably weakened.

Implications

The consequences of these differential ecological distributions by race raise the substantively plausible hypothesis that correlations of race and crime may be systematically confounded with important differences in community contexts. As Testa has argued with respect to escape from poverty:

Simple comparisons between poor whites and poor blacks would be confounded with the fact that poor whites reside in areas which are ecologically and economically very different from poor blacks. Any observed relationships involving race would reflect, to some unknown degree, the relatively superior ecological niche many poor whites occupy with respect to jobs, marriage opportunities, and exposure to conventional role models.

Regardless of a black's individual-level family or economic situation, the average community of residence thus differs dramatically from that of a similarly situated white. For example, regardless of whether a black juvenile is raised in an intact or single-parent family, or a rich or poor home, he or she will not likely grow up in a community context similar to that of whites with regard to family structure and income. Reductionist interpretations of race and social class camouflage this key point.

In fact, a community conceptualization exposes the "individualistic fallacy"—the often-invoked assumption that individual-level causal relations necessarily generate individual-level correlations. Research conducted at the individual level rarely questions whether obtained results might be spurious and confounded with community-level processes. In the present case, it is commonplace to search for individual-level (e.g., constitutional) or group-level (e.g., social class) explanations for the link between race and violence. In our opinion these efforts have largely failed, and so we highlight contextual sources of the race–violence link among individuals. More specifically, we posit that the most important determinant of the relationship between race and crime is the differential distribution of blacks in communities characterized by (1) *structural social disorganization* and (2) *cultural social isolation*, both of which stem from the concentration of poverty, family disruption, and residential instability.

Before explicating the theoretical dimensions of social disorganization, we must also expose what may be termed the "materialist fallacy"—that economic (or materialist) causes necessarily produce economic motivations. Owing largely to Merton's famous dictum about social structure and anomie, criminologists have assumed that if economic structural factors (e.g., poverty) are causally relevant it must be through the motivation to commit acquisitive crimes. Indeed, "strain" theory was so

named to capture the hypothesized pressure on members of the lower classes to commit crime in their pursuit of the American dream. But as is well known, strain or materialist theories have not fared well empirically. The image of the offender stealing to survive flourishes only as a straw man, knocked down most recently by Jack Katz, who argues that materialist theory is nothing more than "twentieth-century sentimentality about crime." Assuming that those who posit the relevance of economic structure for crime rely on motivational pressure as an explanatory concept, however, is itself a fallacy. The theory of social disorganization *does* see relevance in the ecological concentration of poverty, but not for the materialist reasons Katz presupposes. Rather, the conceptualization we now explicate rests on the fundamental properties of structural and cultural organization.

THE STRUCTURE OF SOCIAL (DIS)ORGANIZATION

In their original formulation Shaw and McKay held that low economic status, ethnic heterogeneity, and residential mobility led to the disruption of community social organization, which in turn accounted for variations in crime and delinquency rates. As recently extended by Kornhauser, Bursik, and Sampson and Groves, the concept of social disorganization may be seen as the inability of a community structure to realize the common values of its residents and maintain effective social controls. The *structural* dimensions of community social disorganization refer to the prevalence and interdependence of social networks in a community—both informal (e.g., the density of acquaintanceship; intergenerational kinship ties; level of anonymity) and formal (e.g., organizational participation; institutional stability)—and in the span of collective supervision that the community directs toward local problems.

This social-disorganization approach is grounded in what Kasarda and Janowitz call the "systemic" model, where the local community is viewed as a complex system of friendship and kinship networks, and formal and informal associational ties are rooted in family life and ongoing socialization processes. From this view social organization and social *disorganization* are seen as different ends of the same continuum of systemic networks of community social control. As Bursik notes, when formulated in this way, social disorganization is clearly separable not only from the processes that may lead to it (e.g., poverty, residential mobility), but also from the degree of criminal behavior that may be a result. This conceptualization also goes beyond the traditional account of community as a strictly geographical or spatial phenomenon by focusing on the social and organizational networks of local residents.

Evidence favoring social-disorganization theory is available with respect both to its structural antecedents and to mediating processes. In a recent paper, Sampson and Lauritsen reviewed in depth the empirical literature on individual, situational, and community-level sources of interpersonal violence (assault, homicide, robbery, and rape). This assessment revealed that community-level research conducted in the past twenty years has largely supported the original Shaw and McKay model in terms of the exogenous correlates of poverty, residential mobility, and heterogeneity. What appears to be especially salient is the *interaction* of poverty and mobility. As anticipated by Shaw and McKay and Kornhauser, several studies indicate that the effect of poverty is most pronounced in neighborhoods of high residential instability.

In addition, recent research has established that crime rates are positively linked to community-level variations in urbanization (e.g., population and housing density), family disruption (e.g., percentage of single-parent households), opportunity structures for predatory crime (e.g., density of convenience stores), and rates of community change and population turnover. As hypothesized by Sampson

and Groves, family disruption, urbanization, and the anonymity accompanying rapid population change all undercut the capacity of a community to exercise informal social control, especially of teenage peer groups in public spaces.

Land et al. have also shown the relevance of *resource deprivation, family dissolution,* and *urbanization* (density, population size) for explaining homicide rates across cities, metropolitan areas, and states from 1960 to 1980. In particular, their factor of resource deprivation/affluence included three income variables—median income, the percentage of families below the poverty line, and the Gini index of income inequality—in addition to the percentage of population that is black and the percentage of children not living with both parents. This coalescence of structural conditions with race supports the concept of concentration effects and is consistent with Taylor and Covington's finding that increasing entrenchment of ghetto poverty was associated with large increases in violence. In these two studies the correlation among structural indices was not seen merely as a statistical nuisance (i.e., as multicollinearity), but as a predictable substantive outcome. Moreover, the Land et al. results support Wilson's argument that concentration effects grew more severe from 1970 to 1980 in large cities. Urban disadvantage thus appears to be increasing in ecological concentration.

It is much more difficult to study the intervening mechanisms of social disorganization directly, but at least two recent studies provide empirical support for the theory's structural dimensions. First, Taylor et al. examined variations in violent crime (e.g., mugging, assault, murder, rape) across 63 street blocks in Baltimore in 1978. Based on interviews with 687 household respondents, Taylor et al. constructed block-level measures of the proportion of respondents who belonged to an organization to which coresidents also belonged, and the proportion of respondents who felt responsible for what happened in the area surrounding their home. Both of these dimensions of informal social control were significantly and negatively related to community-level variations in crime, exclusive of other ecological factors. These results support the social-disorganization hypothesis that levels of organizational participation and informal social control—especially of public activities by neighborhood youth—inhibit community-level rates of violence.

Second, Sampson and Groves's analysis of the British Crime Survey in 1982 and 1984 showed that the prevalence of unsupervised teenage peer groups in a community had the largest effects on rates of robbery and violence by strangers. The density of local friendship networks—measured by the proportion of residents with half or more of their friends living in the neighborhood—also had a significant negative effect on robbery rates. Further, the level of organizational participation by residents had significant inverse effects on both robbery and stranger violence. These results suggest that communities characterized by sparse friendship networks, unsupervised teenage peer groups, and low organizational participation foster increased crime rates.

Variations in these structural dimensions of community social disorganization also transmitted in large part the effects of community socioeconomic status, residential mobility, ethnic heterogeneity, and family disruption in a theoretically consistent manner. For example, mobility had significant inverse effects on friendship networks, family disruption was the largest predictor of unsupervised peer groups, and socioeconomic status had a significant positive effect on organizational participation in 1982. When combined with the results of research on gang delinquency, which point to the salience of informal and formal community structures in controlling the formation of gangs, the empirical data suggest that the structural elements of social disorganization have relevance for explaining macrolevel variations in crime.

Further Modifications

To be sure, social-disorganization theory *as traditionally conceptualized* is hampered by a restricted view of community that fails to account for the larger political and structural forces shaping communities. As suggested earlier, many community characteristics hypothesized to underlie crime rates, such as residential instability, concentration of poor, female-headed families with children, multiunit housing projects, and disrupted social networks, appear to stem directly from planned governmental policies at local, state, and federal levels. We thus depart from the natural market assumptions of the Chicago School ecologists by incorporating the political economy of place, along with macrostructural transformations and historical forces, into our conceptualization of community-level social organization.

Take, for example, municipal code enforcement and local governmental policies toward neighborhood deterioration. In *Making the Second Ghetto: Race and Housing in Chicago, 1940–1960*, Hirsch documents in great detail how lax enforcement of city housing codes played a major role in accelerating the deterioration of inner-city Chicago neighborhoods. More recently, Daley and Mieslin have argued that inadequate city policies on code enforcement and repair of city properties contributed to the systematic decline of New York City's housing stock, and consequently, entire neighborhoods. When considered with the practices of redlining and disinvestment by banks and "block-busting" by real estate agents, local policies toward code enforcement—that on the surface are far removed from crime—have in all likelihood contributed to crime through neighborhood deterioration, forced migration, and instability.

Decisions to withdraw city municipal services for public health and fire safety—presumably made with little if any thought to crime and violence—also appear to have been salient in the social disintegration of poor communities. As Wallace and Wallace argue based on an analysis of the "planned shrinkage" of New York City fire and health services in recent decades: "The consequences of withdrawing municipal services from poor neighborhoods, the resulting outbreaks of contagious urban decay and forced migration which shred essential social networks and cause social disintegration, have become a highly significant contributor to decline in public health among the poor." The loss of social integration and networks from planned shrinkage of services may increase behavioral patterns of violence that may themselves become "convoluted with processes of urban decay likely to further disrupt social networks and cause further social disintegration." This pattern of destabilizing feedback appears central to an understanding of the role of governmental policies in fostering the downward spiral of high crime areas. As Wacquant has recently argued, federal U.S. policy seems to favor "the institutional desertification of the urban core."

Decisions by government to provide public housing paint a similar picture. Bursik has shown that the planned construction of new public housing projects in Chicago in the 1970s was associated with increased rates of population turnover, which in turn were related to increase in crime. More generally, we have already noted how the disruption of urban renewal contributed disproportionately to housing loss among poor blacks.

Boiled down to its essentials, then, our theoretical framework linking social-disorganization theory with research on urban poverty and political economy suggests that macrosocial forces (e.g., segregation, migration, housing discrimination, structural transformation of the economy) interact with local community-level factors (e.g., residential turnover, concentrated poverty, family disruption) to impede social organization. This is a distinctly sociological viewpoint, for it focuses attention on the proximate structural characteristics and mediating processes of community social organization that help explain crime, while also recognizing the larger historical, social, and political forces shaping local communities.

SOCIAL ISOLATION AND COMMUNITY CULTURE

Although social-disorganization theory is primarily structural in nature, it also focuses on how the ecological segregation of communities gives rise to what Kornhauser terms *cultural* disorganization—the attenuation of societal cultural values. Poverty, heterogeneity, anonymity, mutual distrust, institutional instability, and other structural features of urban communities are hypothesized to impede communication and obstruct the quest for common values, thereby fostering cultural diversity with respect to nondelinquent values. For example, an important component of Shaw and McKay's theory was that disorganized communities spawned delinquent gangs with their own subcultures and norms perpetuated through cultural transmission.

Despite their relative infrequency, ethnographic studies generally support the notion that structurally disorganized communities are conducive to the emergence of cultural value systems and attitudes that seem to legitimate, or at least provide a basis of tolerance for, crime and deviance. For example, Suttles's account of the social order of a Chicago neighborhood characterized by poverty and heterogeneity supports Thrasher's emphasis on age, sex, ethnicity, and territory as markers for the ordered segmentation of slum culture. Suttles found that single-sex, age-graded primary groups of the same ethnicity and territory emerged in response to threats of conflict and community-wide disorder and mistrust. Although the community subcultures Suttles discovered were provincial, tentative, and incomplete, they nonetheless undermined societal values against delinquency and violence. Similarly, Anderson's ethnography of a bar in Chicago's South-side black ghetto shows how primary values coexisted alongside residual values associated with deviant subcultures (e.g., hoodlums), such as "toughness," "getting big money," "going for bad," and "having fun." In Anderson's analysis, lower-class residents do not so much "stretch" mainstream values as "create their own particular standards of social conduct along variant lines open to them." In this context the use of violence is not valued as a primary goal but is nonetheless expected and tolerated as a fact of life. Much like Rainwater, Suttles, and Horowitz, Anderson suggests that in certain community contexts the wider cultural values are simply not relevant—they become "unviable."

Whether community subcultures are authentic or merely "shadow cultures" cannot be resolved here. But that seems less important than acknowledging that community contexts seem to shape what can be termed *cognitive landscapes* or ecologically structured norms (e.g., normative ecologies) regarding appropriate standards and expectations of conduct. That is, in structurally disorganized slum communities it appears that a system of values emerges in which crime, disorder, and drug use are less than fervently condemned and hence expected as part of everyday life. These ecologically structured social perceptions and tolerances in turn appear to influence the probability of criminal outcomes and harmful deviant behavior (e.g., drug use by pregnant women). In this regard Kornhauser's attack on subcultural theories misses the point. By attempting to assess whether subcultural values are authentic in some deep, almost quasi-religious sense, she loses sight of the processes by which cognitive landscapes rooted in social ecology may influence everyday behavior. Indeed, the idea that dominant values become existentially irrelevant in certain community contexts is a powerful one, albeit one that has not had the research exploitation it deserves.

A renewed appreciation for the role of cultural adaptations is congruent with the notion of *social isolation*—defined as the lack of contact or of sustained interaction with individuals and institutions that represent mainstream society. According to this line of reasoning, the social isolation fostered by the ecological concentration of urban poverty deprives residents not only of resources and conventional role models, but also of cultural learning from mainstream social networks that facilitate social and economic advancement in modern industrial society. Social isolation is specifically distinguished from the culture of poverty by virtue of its focus on adaptations to constraints and opportunities rather than internalization of norms.

As Ulf Hannerz noted in his seminal work *Soulside*, it is thus possible to recognize the importance of macrostructural constraints—that is, avoid the extreme notions of the culture of poverty or culture of violence, and yet see the "merits of a more subtle kind of cultural analysis." One could hypothesize a difference between, on the one hand, a jobless family whose mobility is impeded by the macrostructural constraints in the economy and the larger society but nonetheless lives in an area with a relatively low rate of poverty and, on the other hand, a jobless family that lives in an inner-city ghetto neighborhood that is influenced not only by these same constraints but also by the behavior of other jobless families in the neighborhood. The latter influence is one of culture—the extent to which individuals follow their inclinations as they have been developed by learning or influence from other members of the community.

Ghetto-specific practices such as an overt emphasis on sexuality and macho values, idleness, and public drinking are often denounced by those who reside in inner-city ghetto neighborhoods. But because such practices occur much more frequently there than in middle-class society, largely because of social organizational forces, the transmission of these modes of behavior by precept, as in role modeling, is more easily facilitated. For example, youngsters are more likely to see violence as a way of life in inner-city ghetto neighborhoods. They are more likely to witness violent acts, to be taught to be violent by exhortation, and to have role models who do not adequately control their own violent impulses or restrain their own anger. Accordingly, given the availability of and easy access to firearms, knives, and other weapons, adolescent experiments with macho behavior often have deadly consequences.

The concept of social isolation captures this process by implying that contact between groups of different class and/or racial backgrounds either is lacking or has become increasingly intermittent, and that the nature of this contact enhances effects of living in a highly concentrated poverty area. Unlike the concept of the culture of violence, then, social isolation does not mean that ghetto-specific practices become internalized, take on a life of their own, and therefore continue to influence behavior no matter what the contextual environment. Rather, it suggests that reducing structural inequality would not only decrease the frequency of these practices; it would also make their transmission by precept less efficient. So in this sense we advocate a renewed appreciation for the ecology of culture, but not the monolithic and hence noncontextual culture implied by the subculture of poverty and violence.

DISCUSSION

Rejecting both the "individualistic" and "materialist" fallacies, we have attempted to delineate a theoretical strategy that incorporates both structural and cultural arguments regarding race, crime, and urban inequality in American cities. Drawing on insights from social-disorganization theory and recent research on urban poverty, we believe this strategy provides new ways of thinking about race and crime. First and foremost, our perspective views the link between race and crime through contextual lenses that highlight the very different ecological contexts in which blacks and whites reside—regardless of individual characteristics. Second, we emphasize that crime rates among blacks nonetheless vary by ecological characteristics, just as they do for whites. Taken together, these facts suggest a powerful role for community context in explaining race and crime.

Our community-level explanation also departs from conventional wisdom. Rather than attributing to acts of crime a purely economic motive springing from relative deprivation—an individual-level psychological concept—we focus on the mediating dimensions of community social organization to understand variations in crime across areas. Moreover, we acknowledge and try to specify the macro-social forces that contribute to the social organization of local communities. Implicit in this attempt is the incorporation of the political economy of place and the role of urban inequality in generating racial differences in community structure. As Wacquant observes, American urban poverty is "preeminently a *racial poverty* . . . rooted in the *ghetto* as a historically specific social form and mechanism of racial domination." This intersection of race, place, and poverty goes to the heart of our theoretical concerns with societal and community organization.

Furthermore, we incorporate culture into our theory in the form of social isolation and ecological landscapes that shape perceptions and cultural patterns of learning. This culture is not seen as inevitably tied to race, but more to the varying structural contexts produced by residential and macroeconomic change, concentrated poverty, family instability, and intervening patterns of social disorganization. Perhaps controversially, then, we differ from the recent wave of structuralist research on the culture of violence. In an interesting methodological sleight of hand, scholars have dismissed the relevance of culture based on the analysis of census data that provide no measures of culture whatsoever. We believe structural criminologists have too quickly dismissed the role of values, norms, and learning as they interact with concentrated poverty and social isolation. In our view, macrosocial patterns of residential inequality give rise to the social isolation and concentration of the truly disadvantaged, engendering cultural adaptations that undermine social organization.

Finally, our conceptualization suggests that the roots of urban violence among today's 15- to 21-year-old cohort may stem from childhood socialization that took place in the late 1970s and early 1980s. Consider that this cohort was born between 1970 and 1976 and spent its childhood in the context of a rapidly changing urban environment unlike that of any previous point in U.S. history. As documented in detail by W. J. Wilson, the concentration of urban poverty and other social dislocations began increasing sharply in about 1970 and continued unabated through the decade and into the 1980s. As but one example, the proportion of black families headed by women increased by over 50 percent from 1970 to 1984 alone. Large increases were also seen in the ecological concentration of ghetto poverty, racial segregation, population turnover, and joblessness. These social dislocations were, by comparison, relatively stable in earlier decades. Therefore, the logic of our theoretical model suggests that the profound changes in the urban structure of minority communities in the 1970s may hold the key to understanding recent increases in violence.

CONCLUSION

By recasting traditional race and poverty arguments in a contextual framework that incorporates both structural and cultural concepts, we seek to generate empirical and theoretical ideas that may guide further research. The unique value of a community-level perspective is that it leads away from a simple "kinds of people" analysis to a focus on how social characteristics of collectivities foster violence. On the basis of our theoretical framework, we conclude that community-level factors such as the *ecological concentration of ghetto poverty, racial segregation, residential mobility* and population turnover, *family disruption*, and the dimensions of local *social organization* (e.g., density of friendship/acquaintanceship, social resources, intergenerational links, control of street-corner peer groups, organizational participation) are fruitful areas of future inquiry, especially as they are affected by macrolevel public policies regarding housing, municipal services, and employment. In other words, our framework suggests the need to take a renewed look at social policies that focus on prevention. We do not need more after-the-fact (reactive) approaches that ignore the structural context of crime and the social organization of inner cities.

QUESTIONS FOR DISCUSSION AND WRITING

1. How do the authors' ideas differ from psychologically based relative deprivation theories and the subculture of violence?
2. What are "concentration effects," and which race experiences them in greater degrees?
3. How does the authors' perspective view the link between race and crime, "first and foremost"? What do the authors emphasize second? "Taken together," what do these facts suggest?

AGE

Age and the Explanation of Crime

TRAVIS HIRSCHI

MICHAEL GOTTFREDSON

ACCORDING to a recent criminology text-book, age is the easiest fact about crime to study. In one sense, the statement is true: the age of the offender is routinely recorded, and age distributions of crime covering a variety of contexts over a long period are not hard to find. As a result, no fact about crime is more widely accepted by criminologists. Virtually all of them, of whatever theoretical persuasion, appear to operate with a common image of the age distribution. This distribution thus represents one of the brute facts of criminology. Still, the statement that age is an easy fact to study is decidedly misleading. When attention shifts to the meaning or implications of the relation between age and crime, that relation easily qualifies as the most difficult fact in the field. Efforts to discern the meaning of the large amount of research on the topic in terms supplied by those doing the research have turned out to be futile, as have efforts to explain the relation in statistical terms.

Faced with this intransigent fact, the response in criminology has been generally sci-entific and logical. Theorists are frequently reminded that their explanations of crime must square with the age distribution, and theories are often judged by their ability to deal with "maturational reform," "spontaneous remis-sion," or the "aging-out" effect. Although some theories fare better than others when the age criterion is invoked, no theory that focuses on differences between offenders and nonoffen-ders avoids altogether the complaint that it provides an inadequate explanation of the age distribution. Given the persuasiveness of the age criticism of traditional theories, it is not surprising to find recent explanations of crime explicitly tailored to fit the accepted variability in crime by age. In fact, there is reason to believe that age could replace social class as the master variable of sociological theories of crime.

On the research side, the age effect has been instrumental in the rise of the longitudinal study to its current status as the preferred method of criminological research. The major studies of the past decade, including several still under way, have used this design. This re-search emphasis gains much of its attractive-ness from the association between age and such concepts as "career criminal," "recidi-vism," and "desistance," all of which are thought to be of considerable theoretical and practical import and all of which are thought

From "Age and Explanation of Crime" by T. Hirschi and M. R. Gottfredson, 1989, *American Journal of Sociology* 89:553–584. Copyright © 1989 The University of Chicago Press. Reprinted by permission of The University of Chicago Press.

to require, by definition, longitudinal designs for their study.

Given the increasing role of age in criminological theory and research, and the widely accepted critique of sociological theories on the basis of the age effect, it seems to us that those in the field should consider the possibility that current conceptions of the age effect and its implications for research and theory are misguided. To that end, in this chapter we advance and attempt to defend the following thesis: the age distribution of crime is invariant across social and cultural conditions. We recognize the difficulty in establishing our thesis. Nevertheless, we find nothing in the available research literature inconsistent with our position, and we find a good deal to support it.

THE AGE EFFECT IS INVARIANT

Theoretical and textbook discussions of the age effect often presuppose or flatly assert (the former is more common) variations in this effect over time, place, demographic subgroups, or type of crime. Typically, the current age distribution of crime in the United States as revealed by the Uniform Crime Reports (UCR) is shown and the reader is left with the impression that this distribution is only one of many such distributions revealed by research.

Time and Place

We can consider three age distributions of criminality: one from England and Wales in 1842-44 as reported by Neison in 1857, another from England in 1908 as reported by Goring in 1913, and another from the most recently available UCR for the United States. Looking at one of these distributions, Goring concluded that the age distribution of crime conformed to a "law of nature." The similarity between the three distributions is sufficient to suggest that little or nothing has happened to Goring's law of nature since he first discovered it. The shape or form of the distribution has remained virtu-

ally unchanged for about 150 years. Recent data, the basis for many desertions of variability in the age distribution, force the same conclusion: while population arrest rates have changed in absolute magnitude over time (almost doubling between 1965 and 1976), the same pattern has persisted for the relative magnitudes of the different age groups, with 15- to 17-year-olds having the highest arrest rates per population of any age group.

We do not know how England and Wales in the 1840s differed from the United States in the 1980s. Presumably, the differences are large across a variety of relevant dimensions. We do know, however, that in the 1960s, the age distribution of delinquency in Argentina was indistinguishable from the age distribution in the United States, which was in turn indistinguishable from the age distribution of delinquency in England and Wales at the same time. If the form of the age distribution differs from time to time and from place to place, we have been unable to find evidence of this fact.

Demographic Groups

Most discussions of the age distribution in a theoretical context assume important differences for demographic subgroups. Textbooks often compare rates of increase in crime for boys and girls for particular offenses, thus suggesting considerable flexibility in the age distribution by sex. "Age-of-onset" studies easily suggest that, say, black offenders "start earlier" than white offenders; such a suggestion gives the impression that the age distribution of crime varies across ethnic or racial groups. Such suggestions tend to obscure a basic and persistent fact: available data suggest that the age-crime relation is invariant across sex and race.

Type of Crime

A consistent difference in the age distribution of person and property offenses appears to be well established, at least for official data. In such data, person crimes peak later than property crimes, and the rate declines more slowly with age. The significance of this fact for theories of criminality is, however, problematic. For one thing, self-report data do not support the distinction between person and property offenses; they show instead that both types of offense peak at the same time and decline at the same rate with age. The peak years for person and property offenses in self-report data are the mid-teens, which are also the peak years for property offenses in official data. In contrast, person offenses in official data peak in the late teens or early 20s.

If the self-report results are taken as indicative of the level of criminality, the difference in the peak years for person and property offenses in official data may be accounted for by age-related differences in the *consequences* of person and property crimes. One of these differences lies in the seriousness of offenses. Wolfgang and his colleagues report that "injury seriousness scores advance dramatically at each offense rank number," while the increase in seriousness for theft offenses is negligible. Offense rank is correlated with age (as a group, second offenders are older than first offenders). It should follow that age is positively correlated with the seriousness of injury offenses but not with the seriousness of theft offenses. By extension (and this is consistent with everyday observation), "injury" offenses by the very young are unlikely to be sufficiently serious to attract the attention of officials. Indeed, as long ago as 1835, Quetelet presented data on the correlation between physical strength and age alongside data on the age distribution of crime, the idea being that some crimes appear only when the strength necessary to inflict injury or coerce others has been attained. Apparently, the tendency to commit criminal acts, as reflected in theft offenses, however measured, and in violent offenses, as measured by self-reports, peaks before the physical ability necessary for serious violent offenses. The peak age for person offenses is thus a consequence of the confluence of the "tendency" and "ability"

curves. Since strength continues to increase after the peak age of criminality has been reached, the person-crime curve declines from a later point. For a brief period, increases in the dangerousness of offenders more than offset their declining tendency to commit offenses.

The slower decline of person offenses in official data may reflect the fact that a greater proportion of such offenses involve primary group conflicts. Primary group conflicts may be assumed to be relatively constant over the age span and to produce a relatively stable number of assaultive offenses during the period of capability (i.e., among those neither very young nor very old). If these offenses were subtracted from the total number of person offenses, the form of the age curve for person offenses would approximate more closely than for property offenses. These speculations are consistent with the self-report finding of no difference between person and property crimes with respect to the long-term effects of age.

Since our thesis is that the age effect is invariant across social and cultural conditions, it may appear that our explanation of the apparent difference between person and property crimes requires modification of our thesis. Actually, in some social conditions, the effects of age may be muted. As people retreat into the primary group context with increasing age, the relatively rare criminal events that occur in this context continue to occur. Outside the primary group context, the effects of age on person offenses show themselves even more clearly. So, while we may find social conditions in which age does not have as strong an effect as usual, the isolation of such conditions does not lead to the conclusion that age effects may be accounted for by social conditions. On the contrary, it leads to the conclusion that in particular cases the age effect may be to some extent obscured by countervailing social processes.

Life-Course Explanations

Age is correlated with important events thought to be related to crime, such as leaving school, marriage, and gainful employment, but its effects on crime do not appear to depend on these events. Age affects crime whether or not these events occur; research indicates that marriage does not affect delinquency:

Marriage has often been invoked as the reason for the observed decrease in convictions after age 18, and indeed as the most effective treatment for delinquency. The Cambridge study found that both official and self-reported delinquency decreased between 18 and 21. Men who married during this period were compared with those who stayed single, to see if the married group decreased more. The groups didn't differ in official or self-reported delinquency at age 21, even after attempts were made to match them up to the date of the marriage.

Although not designed as direct tests of life-course questions, studies of crime during military service are, in our view, also consistent with the argument that life-course change cannot account for the age effect. The persistence of the age effect in incarcerated populations casts doubt on the assumption that such status changes as marriage, parenthood, or employment are responsible for decreases in criminality associated with age. Perhaps more fundamentally, the stability of the age effect across societies and demographic groups would not be expected were life-course factors responsible for an "apparent" age effect.

Theories that try to explain the age effect by relying on life-course events will always sound plausible. Their plausibility stems from the fact that the age effect is confounded with the effects of its correlates (e.g., marriage and "settling down" do go together because age predicts them both). Age is correlated with beliefs and practices themselves correlated with crime—for example, respect for authority, punitiveness toward offenders, church attendance—but we believe that these correlates are not responsible for the age effect. Although crime-relevant beliefs and practices indeed vary greatly over the life cycle, the data suggest the effects of age will be found in all categories of these beliefs and practices. Once again, the plausibility of explanations of the age effect based on such correlates results from the universal tendency to assign the effects of age to its correlates. The statistical difficulties inherent in this tendency are obvious once it is realized that none of these correlates can compete with age in predicting criminality.

Implications

Age is everywhere correlated with crime. Its effects on crime do not depend on other demographic correlates of crime. Therefore, it cannot be explained by these correlates and can be explained without reference to them. Indeed, it must be explained without reference to them.

Although correlated with crime, age is not useful in predicting involvement in crime over the life cycle of offenders. For predicting subsequent involvement, to know that a child of 10 has committed a delinquent act is no more useful than to know that a child of 15 has done so. The implications of this fact for contemporary research practice are profound. It denies, for example, the suggestion (at the heart of the longitudinal survey and the career criminal notion) that "prevention and treatment efforts should be concentrated on those boys who begin their criminal careers early in life."

Our argument also implies that the traditional division of the etiological problem into juvenile and adult segments is unlikely to be useful. Because the causes of crime are likely to be the same at any age, the choice of sample should depend on the complexity of the theoretical argument and the causal analysis it presupposes. Resources should not be devoted to establishing the effects of a variable whose influence on crime is noncontroversial and theoretically uninteresting, especially when, almost by definition, examination of the effects of this variable precludes adequate examination of the effects of theoretically intriguing variables.

QUESTIONS FOR DISCUSSION AND WRITING

1. Do time and place affect the age distribution?
2. Do sex and race affect the age distribution?
3. Does type of crime affect the age distribution?

SEX

Explaining the Gender Gap in Delinquency: Peer Influence and Moral Evaluations of Behavior

DANIEL P. MEARS

MATTHEW PLOEGER

MARK WARR

G ENDER is one of the strongest and most frequently documented correlates of delinquent behavior. Males commit more offenses than females at every age, within all racial or ethnic groups examined to date, and for all but a handful of offense types that are peculiarly female. Unlike some putative features of delinquency that are method-dependent (e.g., social class differences), sex differences in delinquency are independently corroborated by self-report, victimization, and police data, and they appear to hold cross-culturally as well as historically. So tenacious are sex differences in delinquency, in fact, that it is difficult to argue with Wilson and Herrnstein's conclusion that "gender demands attention in the search for the origins of crime."

Explanations for gender differences in offending have been promulgated at least since

From "Explaining the Gender Gap in Delinquency: Peer Influence and Moral Evaluations of Behavior" by D. Mears, M. Ploeger and M. Warr, 1998, *Journal of Research in Crime and Delinquency* 35 (3):251–66. Reprinted by permission of Sage Publications, Inc.

the time of Lombroso, who opined that the female criminal is "of less typical aspect than the male because she is less essentially criminal." Lombroso's observations notwithstanding, efforts to explain the gender/crime relation have not fared well, and some sharp philosophical and methodological differences have arisen as to how investigators ought to proceed. Some analysts argue that conventional theories of delinquency were largely designed to explain male delinquency and that separate theories are required to account for male and female delinquency. Smith and Paternoster, however, strongly warn against premature rejection of existing theories: "Since most empirical tests of deviance theories have been conducted with male samples, the applicability of these theories to females is largely unknown. Moreover, the fact that most theories of deviance were constructed to account for male deviance does not mean that they *cannot* account for female deviance."

Rather than postulating separate etiological theories for males and females, Smith and Paternoster join a number of investigators in suggesting that males and females differ in their rates of delinquency because they are *differentially exposed* to the *same* criminogenic conditions. In a close variant of this position, other investigators have suggested that males and females are *differentially affected* by exposure to the same criminogenic conditions. If such arguments are correct, then it is pointless to construct entirely separate theories to explain the delinquent behavior of males and females.

One traditional theory of delinquency that holds promise for a unified explanation of gender differences in offending is Sutherland's theory of differential association. In this classic sociological theory, Sutherland argued that delinquency is learned behavior and that it is learned in intimate social groups through face-to-face interaction. When individuals are selectively or differentially exposed to delinquent companions, Sutherland argued, they are likely to acquire "an excess of definitions favorable to violation of law over definitions unfavorable to violation of law" and consequently engage in delinquent conduct. Sutherland's theory was subsequently recast in modern social learning terms and enjoys considerable empirical support today. Although Sutherland did not limit his theory to peer influence, tests of the theory have generally concentrated on peers, and association with delinquent peers remains the single strongest predictor of delinquent behavior known today.

Several studies suggest that differential association may be a critical factor in explaining gender differences in delinquency. Using self-report data from a sample of Iowa teenagers, Simons et al. found that males and females experienced substantially different levels of exposure to delinquent peer attitudes in their everyday lives. "Males were much more likely than females to have friends who were supportive of delinquent behavior." But although these investigators were able to establish sex-linked differences in exposure to delinquent friends, they did not isolate and quantify the effect of such exposure on sex-specific rates of delinquency.

Other studies illustrate the variant approach described earlier. Johnson tested an integrated model of delinquency containing family, school, socioeconomic, deterrence, and peer variables. Among both sexes, the effect of delinquent associates outweighed all other variables in the model. But the effect of delinquent peers on self-reported delinquency was substantially stronger among males than females. Smith and Paternoster examined the ability of strain theory, differential association, control theory, and deterrence theory to explain sex differences in adolescent marijuana use. They, too, found that association with deviant peers had the largest effect on marijuana use among both males and females, but the effect was once again stronger for males than females. Despite the strikingly similar findings of these two studies, not all investigators have obtained similar results. Most, however, have failed to employ appropriate interaction terms or tests of significance in making gender comparisons, or have used widely divergent measures of peer influence.

This article draws on Sutherland's theory on differential association with a view to explaining gender differences in delinquency. Following the logic of Sutherland's theory, the analysis is organized around three general questions: Do male and female adolescents differ in their exposure to peers, and, more specifically, in their exposure to delinquent peers? Are males and females who are exposed to delinquent peers differentially affected by those peers? And if males and females are affected differently by exposure to delinquent peers, why is this true?

The third question is the most fundamental, and it requires elaboration. Some analysts have speculated that same-sex friendships among male and female adolescents are qualitatively different, with male culture placing greater emphasis on daring or risk-taking. Without denying that possibility, the present analysis stems from a rather different premise. That is, we suspect that females ordinarily possess something that acts as a barrier to inhibit or block the influence of delinquent peers.

What might that barrier be? One possible answer lies with moral evaluations of conduct. The notion that individuals refrain from conduct because they morally disapprove of it has a long history in criminology, but it appears in a wide variety of theoretical guises (e.g., subcultural theory, religiosity and crime, deterrence theory), and research on the issue, although promising, is not systematic, comparable, or cumulative.

Nevertheless, if moral evaluations do affect conduct, how does that bear on gender differences in offending? Gilligan has suggested that females are socialized in such a way that they are more constrained by moral evaluations of behavior than are males. In her influential book, Gilligan argued that moral development in females is guided by the primacy of human relationships and by an overriding obligation to care for and to avoid harming others. This other-oriented quality of female moral development, she added, contrasts sharply with the moral socialization of males. If the moral imperative of women is "an injunction to care," Gilligan argued, men tend to construe morality in more utilitarian terms, that is, as a set of mutually acknowledged rights that protect them from *interference* from others. Thus, the driving principle of male morality is not responsibility to others, but the freedom to pursue self-interest. These gender-linked differences in socialization described by Gilligan imply that females will be more reluctant than males to engage in conduct that harms others, including criminal conduct.

Gilligan did not present direct empirical evidence for her thesis, but research on moral development in children and adolescents provides support for her argument. Although males and females evidently do not differ in the complexity of moral reasoning, there appear to be qualitative differences in such reasoning. In longitudinal and cross-sectional studies of children and adolescents, Eisenberg, Fabes, and Shea have observed that from the age of about 11 or 12, girls "are more other-oriented in their prosocial moral reasoning than are boys." Similarly, Gibbs, Arnold, and

Burkhart report that moral judgments among females rely on a greater degree of "empathic role-taking," and Bebeau and Brabek found that females display a higher degree of "ethical sensitivity" to others than do males.

If moral evaluations of conduct do function as a barrier to peer influence, and if that barrier is higher for females than for males, then we ought to observe a strong difference in the effect of delinquent peers on males and females, a difference that is itself conditioned by sex-linked differences in moral evaluations. . . .

DATA AND MEASURES

Data for this study come from the National Youth Survey (NYS), a continuing longitudinal study of delinquent behavior among a national probability sample of 1,725 persons aged 11 to 17 in 1976. The NYS sample was obtained through a multistage probability sampling of households in the continental United States. In each wave of the study, respondents were asked a series of questions about events and behavior that occurred during the preceding year. Although the first wave of interviews was conducted in 1976, data for the present analysis come from Wave III of the NYS ($N = 1,626$), which captured respondents during the period of adolescence (ages 13 to 19).

The NYS collects self-report data on a wide range of delinquent behaviors, using the general question, "How many times in the last year have you [act]?" In addition to their own behavior, respondents are asked questions about the friends who they "ran around with," friends who they are asked to identify by name and who they are requested to think of whenever answering questions about peers. For our purposes, the crucial variable of interest is the number of delinquent friends reported by the respondent, measured by the question, "Think of your friends. During the last year how many of them have [act]?" (1 = *none of them*, 2 = *very few of them*, 3 = *some of them*, 4 = *most of them*, 5 = *all of them*). Respondents' moral evaluations of each act were measured by responses to the following question: "How wrong do you think it is for someone your age to [act]?" (1 = *not wrong at all*, 2 = *a little bit wrong*, 3 = *wrong*, 4 = *very wrong*).

Although the NYS collects data on a large number of offenses, questions concerning peer delinquency, respondents' delinquency, and moral evaluations are asked about different sets of offenses, sets that only partially overlap. Precisely comparable data on all three of these dimensions are available for only a small number of offenses. Three of these—marijuana use, alcohol use, and cheating—exhibit only minimal sex differences (the smallest, in fact, of any offenses measured in the NYS). Another three—burglary, grand theft, and selling hard drugs—are among the most highly sex-differentiated offenses, but they are so rare among females that virtually none of the females in the sample committed the offenses. Fortunately, there is one offense—theft of property worth less than $5—that exhibits a large sex difference (a male/female ratio of 2.0) and is sufficiently common among both sexes to afford statistical analysis. The analysis will therefore concentrate on this offense, but we have taken care to include data on other offenses in the analysis whenever possible.

FINDINGS

The first aim of the analysis is to describe sex differences in delinquent behavior using data from the NYS. . . . Gender differences in delinquency are quite pervasive, but they vary a good deal from one offense to the next. The largest differences are found among the most serious offenses, where the ratio of male to female offenders exceeds 5:1 (grand theft) and even 8:1 (burglary). By contrast, drug offenses (alcohol and marijuana use), as stated earlier, exhibit little or no sex difference in prevalence, as does cheating on school tests. These patterns are evident regardless of whether one considers the prevalence of offenders . . . or the mean incidence of offending.

. . . Are males and females differentially exposed to delinquent peers? The data . . . show that, compared to females, males spend more time on average with their friends (delinquent or not) on weekday afternoons and evenings, but not on weekends. The differences are not large, however, amounting to less than half an afternoon or evening per week. A much more stark contrast between the sexes, however, is evident . . . [when looking at] the percentage of male and female respondents who reported that at least some of their friends had committed each offense. The differences are once again minimal for cheating and for drug and alcohol use. Among the remaining offenses, however, the proportion of males who have delinquent friends exceeds that of females by factors of approximately 1.5 to 2.5, or by differences in the range of about 10 to 25 percent. The most general or inclusive item, simply "break the law," has a male/female ratio of roughly 2:1.

Males, it seems, are substantially more likely than females to be exposed to delinquent friends. . . .

Now recall the second major question: Are males and females *affected* differently by delinquent friends? . . .

The evidence . . . points to an initial conclusion: males are more strongly affected by delinquent friends than are females. Why is this true? As we postulated earlier, the answer may lie in the constraining effect of moral evaluations. Before turning to a direct test of that hypothesis, let us first consider some preliminary evidence. [Concerning] the percentage of male and female respondents who rated each offense in the NYS as "very wrong," [t]he difference between the sexes in these ratings is statistically significant in every case, with females more apt than males to rate the offenses as very wrong. But consistent though these differences may be, . . . sex differences in moral evaluations are not in themselves sufficient to explain sex differences in delinquency. The sex effect . . . remains strong and statistically significant even after controlling for differences in moral evaluations of the offense. . . .

Much more critical is the role of moral evaluations in regulating or conditioning the effect of delinquent peers. . . . A close look at the [data] reveals that the effect of delinquent peers diminishes very rapidly as moral disapproval increases. Moral evaluations, then, do appear to mitigate or counteract the influence of delinquent peers.

Having laid the necessary foundation, we may now turn to the central hypothesis of this study: Do moral evaluations of conduct provide a stronger barrier to peer influence among females than among males? . . .

. . . Among both males and females, moral evaluations act to regulate or restrain the effect of delinquent peers. . . . But the impact of those evaluations is different for the two sexes. Among males and females who show little or no disapproval of the act . . . , the effect of delinquent peers is very similar; both groups exhibit strong sensitivity to peers. As moral disapproval increases, however, males and females diverge from one another, with females showing less susceptibility than males to peer influence. In fact, among females who strongly disapprove of the offense . . . , the effect of delinquent friends is effectively *eliminated* . . . , meaning that females in this category are essentially immune to peer influence. But the same cannot be said of males, for whom peers continue to have a statistically significant effect even when moral disapproval is strong.

CONCLUSION

The findings of this study point to several tentative conclusions. Males and females differ in exposure to delinquent peers, with males substantially more likely than females to have delinquent friends. This differential exposure contributes to sex differences in delinquency, but it is not the sole source of those differences. Quite aside from differences in exposure to peers, males appear to be more strongly affected by delinquent peers than are females. This fact, in turn, evidently reflects the greater effect of moral evaluations in counteracting peer influence among females. Although the number of delinquent peers an adolescent has is the strongest known predictor of delinquent behavior, the moral judgments of females are apparently sufficient to reduce and even eliminated the impact of delinquent peers.

Why are moral evaluations of behavior so effective in combating peer influence among females? Given the results of our analysis, it would be difficult to reject the argument by Gilligan and others that the primary socialization of women instills moral values that strongly discourage behavior that hurts or harms others. To be sure, our analysis is not a direct test of Gilligan's thesis, if only because it focused on the intensity rather than the quality of moral evaluations and did not examine the socialization process itself. Nevertheless, the results of this analysis clearly attest to the power of moral evaluations among females, and they demonstrate that the consequence of those evaluations is to reduce the frequency of antisocial behavior among females.

Our analysis also suggests that it is fruitless to construct utterly different theories to explain the delinquency of males and females. As we have seen, both males and females are affected—though to different degrees—by a common factor: association with delinquent friends. What differs between the sexes, it seems, are not the *generative* factors that give rise to delinquency, but rather the *inhibitory* factors that prevent or counteract it. Although we have focused on peer influence in this analysis, it may be the case that, among females, moral evaluations counteract a variety of criminogenic conditions, from economic deprivation to dysfunctional family organization. If the present analysis is any indicator, there may be few, if any, generative factors that can overcome the moral constraints of most females. Viewed that way, the enormous sex ratios in offending observed in these and other data seem less startling or inexplicable.

There is at least one factor, however, that may neutralize the moral evaluations of females, one that bears directly on the phenomenon of peer influence. Several studies conducted during the past two decades suggest that, for some females, delinquency is a consequence of exposure to delinquent males. Giordano, for example, reported that girls who spend time in mixed-sex groups are significantly more likely to engage in delinquency than are girls who participate in same-sex groups. Warr found that females were much more likely than males to report that the instigator in their delinquent group was of the opposite sex. Stattin and Magnusson discovered that elevated levels of delinquency among females who experience early menarche is attributable to their tendency to associate with older males, and Caspi et al. observed that New Zealand girls in all-female schools were significantly less likely to engage in delinquency than were girls in mixed-sex schools.

Despite this evidence, it remains unclear just how often males contribute to the delinquency of females, and it is equally unclear whether the relations that link male and female offenders are ordinarily romantic in nature or similar to those of same-sex offenders. Nevertheless, there remains the intriguing possibility that relations with males are one of the few generative factors capable of overcoming the strong moral objections that females commonly hold toward illegal behavior.

One final theoretical issue deserves attention. Although the conceptualization of delinquency employed here borrows heavily from Sutherland's theory of differential association, it nonetheless differs from that theory in at least one respect. According to Sutherland's theory, delinquency is a consequence of attitudes or "definitions" acquired from others, attitudes that ostensibly include moral evaluations of behavior. Individuals, in short, become delinquent by adopting the attitudes of significant others. Tests of differential association. however, consistently indicate that attitude transference among peers is not the primary mechanism by which delinquency is transmitted, implying that other, more direct, mechanisms of social learning (e.g., imitation, direct and vicarious reinforcement) may be at work. Our findings, too, cast doubt on the notion of attitude transference that undergirds Sutherland's theory. It appears from our analysis that the moral evaluations of adolescents—especially females—are frequently a barrier that restrains peer influence rather than a conduit that transmits it. If that interpretation is correct, then Sutherland's theory may require modification.

QUESTIONS FOR DISCUSSION AND WRITING

1. Which gender commits more offenses at every age, within all racial or ethnic groups examined to date?
2. For which gender do moral evaluations of conduct provide a stronger barrier to peer influence?
3. What is one of the few generative factors capable of overcoming the strong moral objections that females commonly hold toward illegal behavior?

V

HOW DO WE
EXPLAIN CRIME?

Theories That Emerged in the 1930s
That Have Continuing Vitality

IN the first four sections of this volume, we have addressed definitions of crime, examined the variability of perceptions of criminality, traced the historical development of criminological methodology, and looked at correlates of crime. In examining each of those topics, we were always led back to the importance of theory in the criminological enterprise. As we pointed out in Part I, for example, a theorist's selection of a particular definition of crime indicates that certain assumptions have been made about crime and criminals. As criminology instructors have been saying in lectures for decades, the beginnings of answers to the "Why do they do it?" questions are in our theories.

Some students may have found it surprising that we did not more fully elaborate the observation that blacks engage in more personal crimes than whites. Over the past thirty years, data from a variety of sources have confirmed this pattern. We would argue that the interesting debate is no longer whether there are race differences in criminality, but why there are race differences. In short, criminology has moved from a debate about data and measurement to one about theory.

This section is the first of four that consider modern criminological theory. When we say "modern," we are not speaking only of new theories. We have instead included older theories that contemporary criminologists are still using to explain crime. The first three of the theory sections (Parts V through VII) focus on older theories, while Part VIII presents new theoretical developments. The format of Parts V through VII presents an original statement of a theoretical perspective, which is then accompanied by an example of contemporary research in that tradition. These theories, particularly the oldest of them, have changed considerably between the publication of the original theoretical statements and the contemporary research pieces. So with each combination of theory and contemporary research, the student will see the evolution of the core ideas of the theory.

Whenever criminologists try to classify theories, there is disagreement on how to "cut" them. There is general agreement on the major theoretical approaches, but more disagreement on which theories should be grouped within each approach and on the theory and category names. We believe that, past the point of that initial broad agreement, much of the difference in how we divide theories is simply a matter of taste. Because we cannot agree on the finer distinctions, we have organized these sections chronologically.

Part V focuses on three theories that emerged or were prominent in the mid-twentieth century: social disorganization theory, differential association theory, and anomie theory. Social disorganization theory was formulated in the 1920s by University of Chicago sociologists Robert Park and Ernest Burgess. The selection included here is by Clifford Shaw and Henry McKay, who are often associated with the "Chicago School." They were not on the faculty of the University of Chicago, but were doing research in Chicago based on the ideas of their colleagues at the university. Focusing on the importance of the urban setting as a factor affecting delinquency rates, they showed in their empirical research and in their version of the theory that community breakdown or "social disorganization" led to increases in juvenile delinquency. The contemporary research example included here, by Paul Bellair, attempts to specify those social interaction processes among neighborhood networks that foster and sustain community-based social organization. This study finds that interaction among neighbors, as infrequent as once a year, has a deterrent effect on crime. It seems that the extent to which you get to know your neighbors is an effective crime control strategy that is powerful enough to impact the crime rate regardless of the type of community.

Edwin Sutherland's differential association theory attempted to correct what he saw as problems with the theory of social disorganization being proposed by his colleagues at the University of Chicago. He tried to explain why only some individuals, even in high-crime-rate areas characterized by social disorganization, actually become criminals. Sutherland wrote not only about the social psychological processes of differential association but also about differential social organization, which he saw as similar to social disorganization but modified to take into account intra-community conflicts in the degree of organization for or against crime. Ross Matsueda, in his contemporary work, assesses the current state of differential association and shows how it has been used in the development of other criminological theories, especially those that propose the importance of cultural influences or social learning processes for involvement in crime.

Anomie theory, or "strain theory," was initially advanced by Robert Merton in the late 1930s. Based on Durkheimian conceptions of normative disruption, Merton argued that crime, and deviance more broadly, is a consequence of a disjunction between the legitimate goals and means of a society. This *structural* strain theory has been refined in a number of subsequent theories, including the "differential opportunity" theory of Cloward and Ohlin and the "status deprivation" theory of Cohen. More recently, Agnew has proposed an individual-level, social psychological version of strain theory, reminiscent of psychological frustration–aggression theory. This "general strain theory" attributes an individual's involvement in crime to the accumulation of stressors, some produced by structural forces but most by common daily problems and frustrations. Testing this theory with a longitudinal sample of adolescents, Raymond Paternoster and Paul Mazerolle discover that generalized strain has a direct effect on delinquency, while at the same time it weakens social bonds, increasing the likelihood that a juvenile will become involved with delinquent peers. In effect, they elaborate a combination of social control theory and general strain theory.

These three theories (social disorganization, differential association, anomie) dominated criminological thought into the 1960s. Criminologists were largely divided into camps that favored one over the other—although to be sure, a number of criminologists tried to integrate aspects of these competing explanations. After many years of dominance, these theories fell out of favor. However, recent research has produced a resurgence of interest in their basic ideas. Modern criminologists have taken the good ideas of those pioneering theories and, mindful of the weaknesses identified by critics, are using them to improve our understanding of crime.

SOCIAL DISORGANIZATION THEORY

Juvenile Delinquency and Urban Areas

CLIFFORD R. SHAW

HENRY McKAY

T HIS chapter is concerned with the geographic distribution of delinquent or alleged delinquent boys and the manner in which rates of delinquent boys vary from area to area in the city of Chicago. Questions pertaining to the total number of such boys in the city at any given time or to the trend in the total number during a given period of years are extraneous to the primary purpose of this discussion. The data presented serve as a means of indicating the pattern of distribution of delinquency in the city and the extent to which this pattern has changed or remained constant during a period of forty years. As an initial step in this study it is important to make clear the sense in which the term "delinquency" is used.

Definitions. The term "male juvenile delinquent," as used in the studies reported in this chapter, refers to a boy under 17 years of age, who is brought before the juvenile court, or other courts having jurisdiction, on delinquency petition; or whose case is disposed of by an officer of the law without a court appearance. "Alleged delinquent" is the more

accurate term, since it sometimes happens that charges are not sustained. Legally, a boy is not a delinquent until he is officially known to have violated some provision of the law as currently interpreted. Only in terms of this official definition can the data here presented be considered as an enumeration of male juvenile delinquents.

Several different types of series will be analyzed in the following pages—school truants, alleged delinquents as above defined, and repeated offenders or recidivists—representing in various degrees of inclusiveness boys who have been dealt with either by the juvenile police officers or by the court. Although these are official cases only, it is assumed that their utility in differentiating areas extends beyond the limits of the legal definition. Many boys commit serious offenses, yet are not apprehended. In recent years, there has been a tendency to extend the term "delinquent" to include all boys engaging in the type of activities which, if known, would warrant action by official agencies. The White House Conference of 1930 adopted as its definition of delinquency: "Any such juvenile misconduct that might be dealt with under the law." In the present chapter, the term "delinquent" will be restricted to those boys dealt with officially, while those defined as delinquent according to the more inclusive use of the term will be referred to as boys engaging in "officially proscribed activity." The data presented here, therefore, may be considered as a sample or index, but not as a complete enumeration, of the total number of boys engaging in officially proscribed activity in any given area.

The total amount of officially proscribed activity in a community, recorded and unrecorded, and the number of children involved are, of course, difficult to estimate and practically impossible to measure exactly at the present time. This fact underscores the need for a workable index—data which are available and which are known, or believed, to vary in close association with the series of events inaccessible to direct measurement. Such an index may be also a sample or incomplete enumeration of the whole, as are the data of this chapter. Where two or more series of official delinquents exhibit close geographical association and covariance, even though separated in time by 10, 20, or 30 years and regardless of changes in nativity or nationality composition of the population, it seems reasonable to consider any one of them as a probable index of the more inclusive universe—the total number of boys within the area engaging in officially proscribed activity.

It is not possible to test conclusively the validity of any of the indexes of proscribed activity presented in this chapter, since there is no satisfactory measure of such activity or complete enumeration of those who engage in it. Experience in various Chicago communities, however, furnishes a basis for confidence that the official cases do constitute an adequate and useful indication of the relative numbers of boys engaging in similar activity in various types of urban areas.

It is necessary, finally, to distinguish "officially proscribed activity," as above defined, from the still broader category of "problem behavior," including mischief, aggression, and personality problems of the type which often bring about a child's referral to a behavior clinic or other agency. The authors do not feel that rates of delinquents based on official cases can be used as indexes of this type of behavior. It is entirely probable that, in spite of overlapping, the distribution of these problem cases is quite different from the distribution of boys who are officially delinquent or who engage in activity similar to that engaged in by official delinquents.

The present series of data, then, are offered as fairly accurate measures of the relative numbers of delinquents living in contrasted types of areas in the cities studied, and also as probable indexes of the total number of boys engaging in officially proscribed activity within these communities.

Series Studied. Traditionally, police arrests, court appearances, and convictions have been used to indicate the amount of adult crime. In the present study of the distribution of juvenile delinquents throughout the city, it was possible to secure variations of each of these types of data, but since conviction is not a juvenile court concept, commitments were substituted. The data fall into three groups: (1) series of alleged delinquents brought before the juvenile court on delinquency petition; (2) series of delinquents committed by the juvenile court to correctional institutions; and (3) series of alleged delinquents dealt with by police probation officers with or without court appearance.

Probably any one of these series would serve to establish the facts of distribution and variation in rates of official delinquents, because in no one of them are any apparent selective factors operating which would seriously distort this geographic distribution. Yet there are many advantages in using all three. In the first place, the three types of series will present the facts more adequately than would any one type alone, since the whole range of cases, from arrests through commitments, will be represented. Second, findings based upon the three will be more conclusive and convincing than those based upon a single index, provided, of course, that the findings are uniform and consistent. Finally, comparison of the findings of the police and commitment series with the findings of the juvenile court series will serve to check the validity of the latter as an index of the total number of boys engaging in officially proscribed activity.

In this Chicago study, the distribution of delinquents, based upon juvenile court cases and commitments, will be presented for periods roughly centered about 1900, 1920, and 1930; and series of police cases, for three different years around 1930. These studies of the distribution of delinquents at different periods of time afford a basis for comparisons and for analysis of long-time trends and processes that could not be made for a single period. Likewise, it will be possible to compare the rates of delinquents in the same areas at different periods, not only in those areas which show significant variations either in physical and economic characteristics or in the nationality and racial composition of the population but also in those where there has been comparatively little change. This comparison furnishes a basis for an evaluation of the relative importance of physical and economic conditions, as contrasted with race and nationality, in relation to delinquency.

In Chicago, all boys who are arrested or who come to the attention of the police for investigation are dealt with by juvenile police probation officers, one of whom is assigned to each police district in the city. The individuals dealt with by these officers comprise our police series and include, as would be expected, some boys guilty of serious offenses, many guilty of lesser offenses, and also those held only for investigation, for identification, or for some other reason. On the average, about 85 percent of the cases dealt with by the police probation officer are disposed of by him without court action, while the remaining 15 percent are taken before the juvenile court on petitions alleging delinquency. The fact that such a large percentage of the boys are dealt with without court action does not mean that these boys are not delinquent. It suggests, rather, that the police probation officer, who has broad discretionary power, has decided that they should not be taken into court, either because they are too young, because they are first offenders, because the offenses with

which they are charged do not appear to him to be serious, or for other reasons best known to himself. The 15 percent taken to court are, presumably, either those who have committed the most serious offenses, who are recidivists, or who for any other reason are assumed by the officers to present serious problems.

The juvenile court, in turn, ultimately commits to training or correctional schools somewhere between one-quarter and one-half of the boys against whom delinquency petitions have been filed. These boys are, for the most part, guilty of serious delinquencies, and most of them are recidivists. The numerical relationship between this group, the boys who are brought before the juvenile court, and the boys dealt with by the police probation officers over a period of years is roughly expressed by the ratio 30:5:2. This means that, of every 30 boys dealt with by the police probation officers, 5 are taken to court on delinquency petition and 2 are ultimately committed by the court to correctional institutions.

Because of Chicago's size, a rather large sample of cases is needed. Just what the minimum could be is not known, but from experience it seems that series including several thousand individuals show the facts of distribution most clearly. The number of individuals dealt with by the police probation officers in a single year approaches 10,000; therefore, a year was taken as a unit in the police series. It is evident, however, that the number of boys taken to court in a year would not furnish an adequate sample. Accordingly, the three juvenile court series were based on the boys brought to court on delinquency petition during a 7-year period. Similarly, the commitment series cover 7-year periods. Logically, the latter should extend over a longer period than the juvenile court series, since fewer boys are included. In this study, however, the same periods were used for both, with the result that the commitment series contain fewer cases than either the juvenile court or the police series.

In the calculation of rates of delinquents, the basic assumption as to population is the same in a series extending over several years as in a series for a single year. The population for any given area, although stated in the census volumes as the population for a year, is actually the population as of the census date only. Thus, the 1930 population is the population as of April 1, 1930, the only day on which the exact population of an area is known, and the only day, therefore, for which exact rates of delinquents might be calculated. Since it is impossible to calculate rates of delinquents for this one day, an assumption must be made as to the average population in a given period. If the population is changing very little, it can be assumed that at any other day, month, year, or period of years it will be about the same as on the day of enumeration. For a changing population, adjustments can be made if the rate of increase or decrease is known.

Since the same assumptions as to the constancy of population are made for a month, a year, or a period of years, the period of time covered by a series of cases is not important, providing the date of the known population is near the midyear of the series. The only advantage in a short period is that there is less probability of change in the rate of population growth or decline in local areas. On the other hand, there are advantages in having rates of delinquents for series covering a longer period of time. In this study, rates are calculated for series covering from 1 to 7 years; accordingly, the reader can make his own comparisons and draw his conclusions as to the advantages and disadvantages of each time interval.

A. THE DISTRIBUTION OF ALLEGED DELINQUENTS BROUGHT BEFORE THE JUVENILE COURT OF COOK COUNTY

1. The 1927–33 Juvenile Court Series

Series Studied. These 8,411 different alleged male delinquents were brought before the Juvenile Court of Cook County from Chicago on petitions alleging delinquency during the 7-year period between January 1, 1927, and December 31, 1933. They are all separate indi-

viduals, as duplications from year to year, as well as within the separate years, have been eliminated from the series.

Distribution of Delinquents. Map 1 shows the distribution by place of residence of the 8,411 different male delinquents. Each dot represents the home address of one delinquent boy; only one dot was used for each individual, regardless of the number of times he appeared in court from any area.

Upon inspection, Map 1 reveals some very interesting characteristics. It will be observed immediately that there are areas of marked concentration of delinquents, as compared with other areas where the dots are widely dispersed. These concentrations are most obvious immediately north and northwest of the Loop along the North Branch of the Chicago River, in the areas some distance south of the Loop along State Street, and in the areas immediately outside and extending westward from the northern part of the Loop. In addition to these major concentrations, lesser clusters of dots will be noted in several outlying areas, in the Back of the Yards and the South Chicago steel-mill districts.

This distribution of delinquents is closely related to the location of industrial and commercial areas and to the composition of the population. In the first place, as has already been noted, the areas of heaviest concentration are, in general, not far from the central business district, within or near the areas zoned for light industry or commerce. As one moves outward, away from these areas into the residential communities, the cases are more and more scattered until, near the periphery of the city, they are, in general, widely dispersed.

The concentrations of delinquents not adjacent to the central business district are, for the most part, near outlying heavy industrial areas, especially along the two branches of the Chicago River and in the Stock Yards and South Chicago districts. The alleged delinquents are concentrated mainly in areas characterized by decreasing population and low

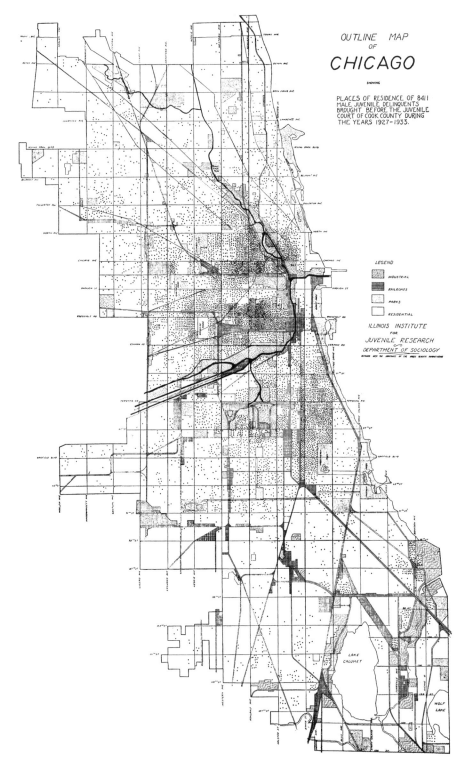

MAP 1 *Distribution of male juvenile delinquents, Chicago, 1927–33.*

rentals, with high percentages of families on relief. Here, too, industrial workers predominate. The population in these neighborhoods was, during 1927–33, largely foreign born, with high proportions of recent arrivals, aliens, and migrants from the rural South.

As to national heritage, the area of concentration of delinquents on the Near North Side was, during the period covered, predominantly Italian; the lower Northwest Side, mainly Polish; the Near West Side, Italian and American Negro; and the Lower West Side, chiefly Czechoslovakian. Among the more outlying areas, the Humboldt Park population included Poles, Swedes, Italians, and Russian Jews; the Back of the Yards district was Polish and Lithuanian; while the predominant nationalities in South Chicago were Polish, Italian, Hungarian, Mexican, and Yugoslavian.

This scattering of delinquents among many national groups is characteristic of each of the three periods studied, although the disproportions in each nationality vary. The groups producing the most alleged delinquents are, in every instance, those most recently segregated into the areas of lower economic status, as a result of the ongoing processes of American city life.

In order to compare the number of delinquents by areas and to relate this number in each instance to the population of the same age and sex, the city was divided into 140 areas. Most of these are square miles, bounded on all four sides by the section lines of the government survey. In some instances, where much of the territory was occupied by industry or where, for other reasons, the population was sparse, it was necessary to combine several contiguous square- mile areas. In our discussion, however, these units, regardless of size, will be referred to as "square-mile areas."

When the distribution of the 8,411 delinquents is analyzed in terms of these 140 square-mile areas, wide differences are evident. In each of 3 areas there are more than 300 delinquents, while 8 have more than 150 each. At the other extreme, there is 1 area from which only 3 delinquents were taken to court,

15 with fewer than 10, and 25 with fewer than 15 delinquents. Moreover, the actual difference in concentration is greater than these comparisons suggest, since many areas with large numbers of delinquents have less residential space and population than those with fewer. The theoretical significance of these facts is at least twofold. First, they reveal the wide variation in distribution; second, they indicate, quite apart from density of population, the differential probability of a boy's having contact with other delinquent boys in the same area or of observing their activities.

Rates of Delinquents. Map 2 shows the rates of delinquents in each of the 140 square-mile areas. These rates represent the number of alleged delinquents taken to the juvenile court from each area during 1927–33, per hundred of the aged 10–16 male population in that area as of 1930. It should be borne in mind that the 7-year rate here presented is less than the sum of 7 yearly rates, since all duplications have been eliminated.

The range in this series is from 0.5 to 18.9. The median is 2.5 and the rate for the city as a whole, 4.2. Three of the 140 areas have rates above 17.0, and 14 below 1.0. Similarly, there are 12 areas where the rates are more than 10.0, and 50 where they are less than 2.5. This comparison brings out two fundamental facts, namely, that there are wide differences among areas and that the number of areas with low rates far exceeds the number where they are high. The areas with the highest rates are located directly south of the central business district, and the areas with the next highest rates north and west of the Loop. At the other extreme, low rates of delinquents will be noted in many of the outlying areas.

Most of the areas characterized by high rates of delinquents, as well as by a concentration of individual delinquents, are either in or adjacent to areas zoned for industry and commerce. This is true not only for areas close to the central business district but also for outlying areas, such as those near the Stock Yards, the South Chicago steel mills, and other

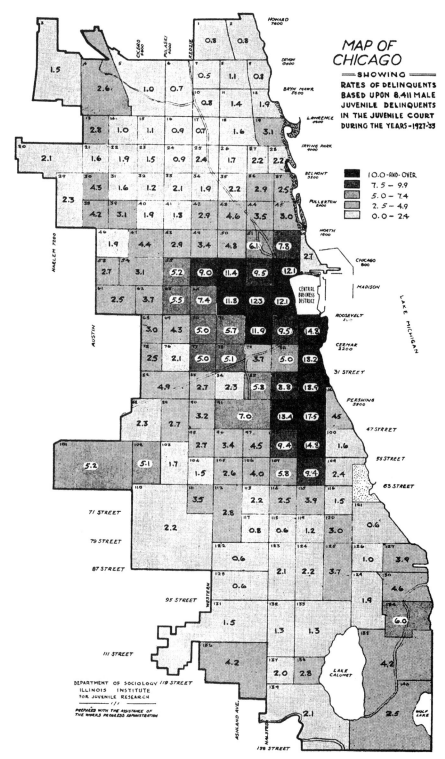

MAP 2   *Rates of male juvenile delinquents, Chicago, 1927–33.*

industrial sections. On the other hand, the areas with low rates are, for the most part, those zoned for residential purposes.

Between the center of the city and the periphery the rates, on the whole, show a regular decrease. There are, of course, deviations from this general tendency. In some outlying sections, there are areas of high rates, especially in the Stock Yards and Southwest manufacturing districts and adjacent to the South Chicago steel mills. On the other hand, not all areas close to the central business district have high rates. Area 60, for example, located just north of the Loop and including the "Gold Coast," has a rate of 2.7; and Areas 37 and 45, not far to the north, have comparatively low rates. It may be noted, however, that the physical and social characteristics of these areas differ from those of the surrounding areas.

One apparent exception to the general tendency of the rates to decrease from the center of the city outward may be noted south of the central business district, between Areas 74 and 115. Here the highest rates are in the second, third, and fourth areas (81, 87, and 93). When rates were calculated separately for the Negro and white delinquents in these areas, however, it was found that both decreased uniformly, in contrast to the combined rate. The rates for white boys, calculated necessarily on small samples, followed with some irregularities the common radial pattern, ranging from 13.4 in Area 74, the highest rate, to 2.5 in Area 115. The corresponding range for Negro delinquents was from 21.2 in the first area south of the Loop to 6.0 in the seventh area. This drop is significant because it shows that the rates of delinquents for Negro boys, although somewhat higher than those for the whites, exhibit similarly wide variations among different communities.

It was for the purpose of reducing the fluctuations resulting from chance that square-mile areas were selected for the presentation of rates of delinquents, in place of the smaller census tracts into which the city of Chicago is divided. There are, however, some advantages in considering the rates of delinquents by cen-

sus tracts or even by smaller units. In an area as large as a square mile there may be many different types of neighborhoods. On the other hand, it is difficult to ascertain whether the variations in rates in the smaller areas within a square mile represent actual differences which would be sustained by subsequent studies or whether they are purely chance variations.

In order to illustrate the variations for small units within square-mile areas, rates are presented for the census tracts combined in the construction of three areas. These variations are given in Table 1. The variations in Area 2, as shown in the table, are proportionately great, but they are not significant, since the sample of delinquents on which they were based was very small.

Square-mile Area 51 is relatively homogeneous, since rates for the tracts within it do not vary widely from the rate for the area as a whole. The critical ratio for the most widely separated rates in this area is 1.66.

There is reason to believe that in Area 97, however, the rates in the north half are significantly higher than in the south half. This is supported by the fact that the critical ratio of the rate in one of the tracts in the north half and the rate in a tract in the south half is 3.42. The critical ratio of the rate of delinquents in the entire north half of this square mile (6.2) and the rate in the south half (2.6) is 4.34.

These data indicate that, in some instances at least, the differences between rates of

TABLE 1

Rates of delinquents for census tracts included in areas 2, 51, and 97.

Area 2	Area 51	Area 97
0.0	5.0	2.1
0.3	5.5	2.1
0.4	6.1	3.0
0.5	7.2	6.0
1.1	9.5	6.7
1.3		6.7
1.4		7.0

delinquents within areas are statistically significant. For the study as a whole, the rates for small areas may be said to conform, in a general way, to those for the square-mile areas, but as indicated above, they exhibit some variation and irregularities, both because they reflect actual differences among local neighborhoods and because of the chance fluctuations due to small samples. The rates by square miles smooth out some of these variations, give a more general picture of the delinquency situation, and reveal more clearly the general trends and tendencies. Rates for successively larger areas smooth the picture more and more and present with increasing clarity the general trends. This is clearly indicated in the zone rates presented at the end of this section. It should be evident from this discussion that rates both of delinquents calculated for small areas and of those for large areas have their advantages and disadvantages and that the size of area best suited to the calculation of rates depends upon the purposes for which the calculations are made.

It should be noted that on the South Side of Chicago the rates of delinquents decrease to a low point about 7 or 8 miles from the central business district and that beyond this point, as in South Chicago and the Pullman industrial districts, they are noticeably higher. From the standpoint of city growth these South Chicago areas are independent centers, not related to the radial expansion of Chicago proper. They may be said, therefore, to confirm the radial pattern, being, in effect, secondary industrial and business centers—from each of which, in turn, the rates of delinquents tend to decrease as distance outward increases.

A. DISTRIBUTION OF MALE JUVENILE DELINQUENTS, CHICAGO, 1934–40

1. The 1934–40 Juvenile Court Series

The most recent data available comprise a series of 9,860 Chicago boys brought before the Juvenile Court of Cook County during the 7-year period 1934–40. Map 3 presents the distribution of these alleged delinquents by census tracts, each dot being placed within the tract in which the boy's home was located, but not at the exact address. Rates have not been computed, as the necessary population totals, by age groups, of the 1940 census were as yet unavailable.

Map 3 reveals a configuration quite similar to that for the 1927–33 series, except for increased concentration in the deteriorated areas south of the Loop and more dispersion into the outlying sections to the north and west, reflecting, no doubt, the movement of population away from the city's center.

2. The 1917–23 Juvenile Court Series

In the foregoing section, the distribution of delinquents and the variation in rates for Chicago were studied by analyzing a series of cases brought into the Juvenile Court of Cook County during the years 1927–33 in relation to the 1930 census data. In the present section, a similar series covering a period centered about the 1920 census will be presented. This series includes the 8,141 alleged male delinquents brought before the Juvenile Court of Cook County from Chicago on delinquency petition in the 7-year period 1917–23.

Series Studied and Types of Offenses. The 1917–23 juvenile court series was secured in the same manner and from the same sources as the 1927–33 series. With the exception of the changes in the number of areas for which rates of delinquents were calculated, the data will be analyzed in the same way. Since no important change has taken place in the basic procedure of taking boys to the juvenile court, these boys also represent those charged by police probation officers with relatively serious offenses.

The nature of the offenses committed by these 8,141 individuals is indicated by the classification of the 12,029 petitions filed against them in the juvenile court. This classification

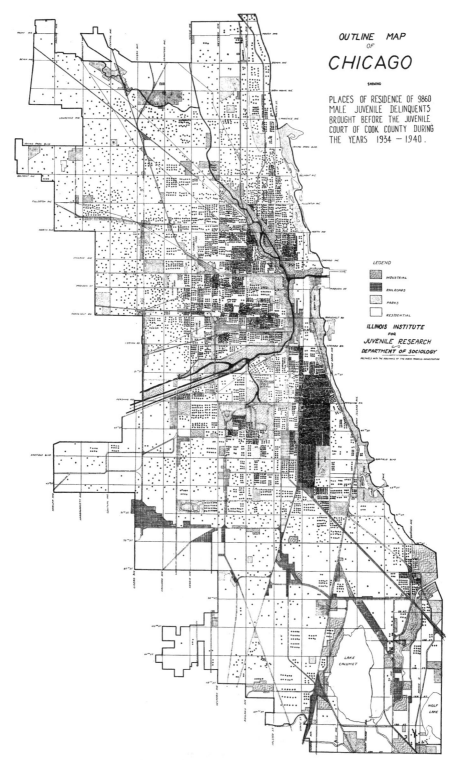

Inside the map:

OUTLINE MAP
of
CHICAGO

SHOWING

PLACES OF RESIDENCE OF 9860
MALE JUVENILE DELINQUENTS
BROUGHT BEFORE THE JUVENILE
COURT OF COOK COUNTY DURING
THE YEARS 1934 – 1940.

LEGEND

INDUSTRIAL
RAILROADS
PARKS
RESIDENTIAL

ILLINOIS INSTITUTE
FOR
JUVENILE RESEARCH
&
DEPARTMENT OF SOCIOLOGY

PREPARED WITH THE ASSISTANCE OF THE WORKS PROGRESS ADMINISTRATION

LAKE
CALUMET

WOLF
LAKE

MAP 3   *Distribution of male juvenile delinquents, Chicago, 1934–40.*

shows that 29.4 percent of the alleged offenses were burglary, 12.2 percent larceny of automobiles, and 20.4 percent petty stealing. These offenses, together with a total of 7.5 percent for other stealing offenses, such as holdup, shoplifting, and purse-snatching, give a total of 69.5 percent classified as "all stealing." The remaining 30.5 percent included incorrigibility, 17.1 percent; disorderly conduct, 4.4 percent; and all sex offenses, 2.1 percent. There can be little doubt that these boys were, on the whole, involved in serious delinquency.

In this series, 16.7 percent of the boys were under 13 years of age, 12.7 percent were 13, and 18.3 percent were 14. The highest frequencies are in the 15- and 16-year age groups, these two comprising 51.9 percent of the total.

Distribution of Delinquents. Map 4 shows the distribution by place of residence of the 8,141 boys in this series. This map indicates that the distribution is very similar to that previously presented and that the areas of concentration coincide quite closely with similar areas on the 1927–33 map. The one distinctive difference is that the concentrations in the areas later occupied by Negroes are much less evident in the 1917–23 series. Otherwise, the areas of heavy concentration, as in the previous series, are adjacent to the central business and industrial districts and to certain outlying industrial centers, while the areas in which the dots are widely dispersed fall in the outlying sections of the city.

The distribution indicates that this series also presents very great geographical variations in the number of delinquents. One of the 113 square-mile areas contains 6 delinquents, while another contains 312. Four areas contain fewer than 10 delinquents each, while 5 contain more than 250 each. When the distribution is analyzed further, it is found that 11 areas contain fewer than 15 delinquents, and 18 fewer than 20 delinquents each. At the other extreme, a total of 7 areas contain more than 200 delinquents each, and 14 contain more than 150.

Rates of Delinquents. The area rates for the present series are given on Map 5. These represent the number of boys brought to the juvenile court from each of the 113 square-mile areas during the 7-year period, per 100 of the aged 10–16 male population in each of these areas as of 1920. The range of rates is from 0–8 to 19.4; the median for the series is 4.3 and the rate for the city, 5.4. Three areas have rates of less than 1.0, and a total of 19 areas less than 2.0. At the other extreme, 4 areas have rates of 15–0 or over, and 8 areas of 12.0 or over. In other words, 8 areas have rates of delinquents that are more than twelve times as great as those in 3 other areas, and more than six times as great as the rates in 19 other areas.

Map 5 reveals variations in the rates of delinquents quite similar to those of the previous series. The range between high- and low-rate areas is not so great, however, and the areas with high rates of delinquents extend only about 4 miles south from the Loop in the present series, as compared with 6 or 7 miles in 1927–33.

3. The 1900–06 Juvenile Court Series

Series Studied and Types of Offenses. Third in this sequence is the series of 8,056 male delinquents brought into the Juvenile Court of Cook County from Chicago during 1900–06 (the first 7 years of the juvenile court's existence). By comparing this series with that for 1927–33 it will be possible to determine the extent to which variations in the rates correspond and the extent to which changes in rates can be related to changes in the physical or social characteristics of the local areas.

The age distribution of the boys in the 1900–06 series indicates that, on the whole, they were a little younger than those in the more recent series. At that time, the upper age limit in the juvenile court was 15 instead of 16, and a somewhat larger number of boys were under 15 years of age (6.1 percent). The highest frequencies were in ages 13, 14, and 15. With regard to

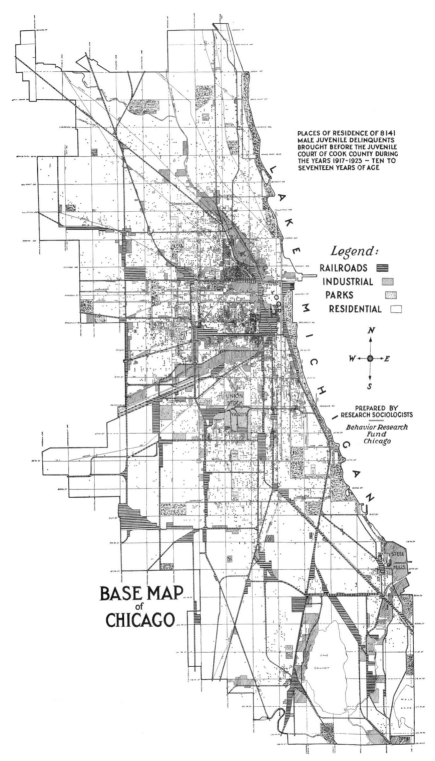

PLACES OF RESIDENCE OF 8141
MALE JUVENILE DELINQUENTS
BROUGHT BEFORE THE JUVENILE
COURT OF COOK COUNTY DURING
THE YEARS 1917-1923 — TEN TO
SEVENTEEN YEARS OF AGE

Legend:
RAILROADS
INDUSTRIAL
PARKS
RESIDENTIAL

N
W ← → E
S

PREPARED BY
RESEARCH SOCIOLOGISTS
Behavior Research
Fund
Chicago

BASE MAP
of
CHICAGO

MAP 4   *Distribution of male juvenile delinquents, Chicago, 1917–23.*

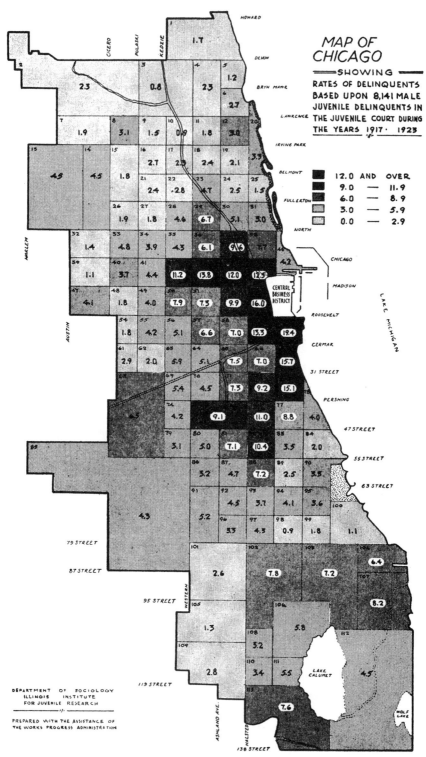

Map 5   *Distribution of male juvenile delinquents, Chicago, 1917–23.*

offenses, it seems probable that some boys were taken to court in these earlier years on charges for which no petitions would be filed by the police probation officers at the present time. This is indicated both by the fact that the number of cases in court was greater in proportion to the population than at present and by the fact that the classification of offenses indicated a somewhat higher proportion of less serious charges.

DISTRIBUTION OF MALE JUVENILE DELINQUENTS, CHICAGO, 1900–06

Distribution of Delinquents. Map 6 shows the distribution by home address of the 8,056 boys brought to court in the 7-year period 1900–06. In this series, as in those previously discussed, it will be noted that a preponderance of the delinquent boys lived either in areas adjacent to the central business and industrial district or along the two forks of the Chicago River, Back of the Yards, or in South Chicago, with relatively few in other outlying areas.

While this series exhibits the same general configuration found in the others, there are two noticeable variations. First, the concentrations are somewhat more restricted and closer to the central business district and to the industrial centers than in the later series. This is to be expected, since many of the areas used for residential purposes in this early period have since been depopulated by expanding industry and commerce. Second, on this map there are relatively few delinquents in the areas east of State Street, south from the Loop. These areas, it will be remembered, contained many delinquents in the 1917–23 map and were also areas of heavy concentration in 1927–33.

Rates of Delinquents. Map 7 shows the rates of delinquents in the 106 square-mile areas used for this 1900–06 series. The population upon which these rates were calculated was secured by combining into 106 comparable areas the 1,200 enumeration districts of 1900 and the

431 census tracts of 1910 and computing the yearly increase or decrease of population in each. The population for the midyear of this series was then estimated from the aged 10–15 male population in 1910. The areas for which rates are presented are practically the same as those used in the 1917–23 juvenile court series, except that in 7 instances it was necessary to construct combinations of the 113 areas in order to secure a larger population in districts which were sparsely settled at that time.

The rates in this series range from 0.6 to 29.8. The median is 4–9 and the rate for the city as a whole 8.4. Four areas have rates of 20.0 and over; 7 have rates of 15.0 or over; and 12 have rates of 12.0 or over. At the other extreme, 3 areas have rates of less than 1.0, and 12 of less than 2.0.

Rates of Male Juvenile Delinquents, Chicago, 1900–06. Map 7 indicates that the variation in rates of delinquents is quite similar to the variations presented previously. The 4 areas with highest rates are all immediately adjacent to the Loop, and other high-rate areas are in the Stock Yards district and in South Chicago. The areas with low rates, on the other hand, are located, for the most part, near the city's periphery. As compared to rate maps for subsequent series, it can be seen that the areas with very high rates are somewhat more closely concentrated around the central business district. This is especially noticeable south from the Loop and east of State Street, where, after the first 2 miles, the rates of delinquents are below the average for the city as a whole.

4. Comparisons Among Juvenile Court Series, 1927–33, 1917–23, and 1900–06

Three methods will be employed to determine the extent to which the variations in rates of delinquents in the several time series correspond: (1) comparisons by zones, (2) area comparisons and correlations, and (3) extent of concentration.

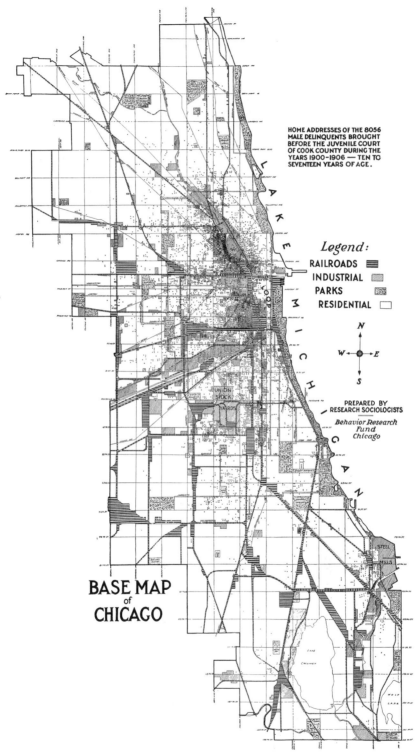

HOME ADDRESSES OF THE 8056
MALE DELINQUENTS BROUGHT
BEFORE THE JUVENILE COURT
OF COOK COUNTY DURING THE
YEARS 1900-1906 — TEN TO
SEVENTEEN YEARS OF AGE.

Legend:
RAILROADS
INDUSTRIAL
PARKS
RESIDENTIAL

N
W E
S

PREPARED BY
RESEARCH SOCIOLOGISTS
*Behavior Research
Fund
Chicago*

UNION
STOCK
YARDS

STEEL
MILLS

BASE MAP
of
CHICAGO

MAP 6   *Distribution of male juvenile delinquents, Chicago, 1900–06.*

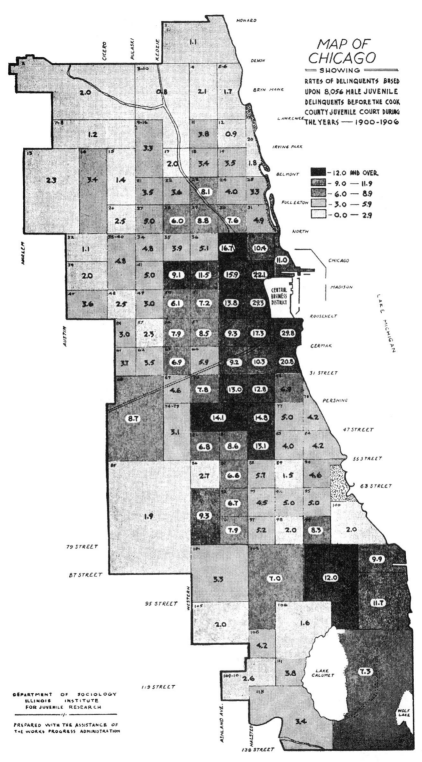

MAP 7 *Rates of male juvenile delinquents, Chicago, 1900–06.*

Rates by Zones. Rates of delinquents were calculated for each of 5 zones drawn at 2-mile intervals, with a focal point in the heart of the central business district. These rates were computed on the basis of the number of delinquents and the total aged 10–16 male population in each zone.

It should be borne in mind that zone rates of delinquents are presented chiefly because of their theoretical value. They show the variations in rates more conceptually and idealistically than do the rates for smaller units. The number of zones used for this purpose is not important, as it is not assumed that there are actual zones in the city or sharp dividing lines between those presented. It is assumed, rather, that a more or less continuous variation exists between the rates of delinquents in the areas close to the center of the city and those outlying and that any arbitrary number of zones will exhibit this difference satisfactorily.

There are wide differentials among the rates of delinquents for the square miles within each zone, just as there are among rates for census tracts within each square-mile area. These fluctuations do not greatly affect the general trend, however; in fact, it is because the zone rates eliminate the fluctuations evident for smaller areas and present the general tendencies that they are interesting and important.

Area Comparisons and Correlations. Of the 24 areas with the highest rates of delinquents in the 1927–33 series, 20 are among the 24 highest also in 1917–23. On the other hand, a few areas where significant changes took place in community characteristics show also marked changes in rates of delinquents. When the 1917–23 and 1927–33 rates are correlated by the 113 areas used for the earlier series the coefficient is found to be .70 ± .02. This coefficient is greatly reduced by the fact that the rates in 6 areas have changed so much that the points representing them fell entirely outside the line of scatter on the correlation sheet.

Most of the areas of high rates in the 1900–06 series also correspond with those ranking highest in the two later series. Of the 12 high-

est in 1900–06, 9 were among the 12 highest in 1927–33. Three of the 5 highest-rate areas in the latter series, but not in the former, are the same 3 found among the high-rate areas as of 1917–23. Although some new areas appear among those with high rates in the more recent series, it is significant to note that all 12 of the areas of highest rates in the 1900–1906 series are among the areas of high rates in 1927–33. Because of these areas, the correspondence between the series is even more clearly seen when comparisons involving a larger number of areas are made. Of the 25 areas with the highest rates of delinquents in the 1900–06 series, 19 are included among the 25 highest in the 1917–23 series, and 18 among the 25 highest in 1927–33, even though these series are separated by approximately two and three decades, respectively. This is especially significant in view of the fact that the nationality composition of the population has changed completely in some of these neighborhoods.

A more general statement of the relationship is found when the rates in the 1900–06 series are correlated with those for each of the other juvenile court series. To accomplish this, it was necessary to calculate rates in the two later juvenile court series for the same 196 areas used in the early series. The coefficient secured for 1900–06 and 1917–23 was .85 ±.04, and that for 1900–06 and 1927–33 was .61 ±.04. In the latter case, the coefficient was reduced by the few values which fell far out of the line of scatter, indicating areas where considerable change had occurred.

These coefficients are remarkably high when it is recalled that the series are separated by about 20 and 30 years, respectively. They reveal that, in general, the areas of high rates of delinquents around 1900 were the high-rate areas also several decades later. This consistency reflects once more the operation of general processes of distribution and segregation in the life of the city.

Extent of Concentration. The distribution of delinquents in relation to male population 10–16 years of age for each of the three juvenile court

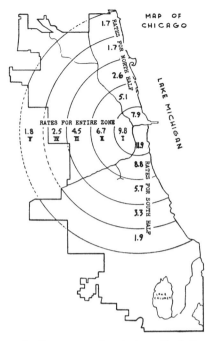

A. Zone rates of male juvenile delinquents, 1927–33 series

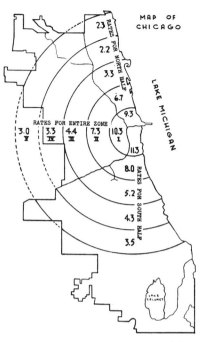

B. Zone rates of male juvenile delinquents, 1917–23 series

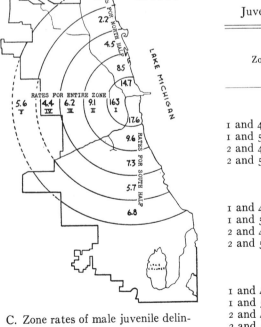

C. Zone rates of male juvenile delinquents, 1900–1906 series

CRITICAL RATIOS OF SELECTED ZONE RATES

Juvenile Court Series (Individuals)

Zones	Difference	Standard Error of the Difference	Critical Ratio
A. 1927–33			
1 and 4	7.3	.301	24.2
1 and 5	8.0	.302	26.5
2 and 4	4.2	.142	29.6
2 and 5	4.9	.142	34.5
B. 1917–23			
1 and 4	7.0	.293	23.9
1 and 5	7.3	.314	23.2
2 and 4	4.0	.162	24.7
2 and 5	4.3	.196	21.9
C. 1900–1906			
1 and 4	11.9	.371	32.1
1 and 5	10.7	.467	22.9
2 and 4	4.7	.241	19.5
2 and 5	3.5	.371	9.4

FIGURE 1   *Zone maps for three juvenile court series.*

TABLE 2

Percentage of delinquents and of city area for quartiles of male population aged 10–16, when areas are ranked by rate of delinquents: Three juvenile court series.

Quartiles of Population	Percentage of Delinquents			Percentage of City Areas		
	1927–33	1917–23	1900–06	1927–33	1917–23	1900–06
Upper one-fourth, in high-rate areas	54.3	46.1	47.3	19.2	17.8	13.1
Second one-fourth	23.9	27.3	26.6	19.4	24.8	12.1
Third one-fourth	14.6	17.7	17.4	32.3	27.1	21.7
Lower one-fourth, in low-rate areas	7.2	8.9	28.7	9.1	30.3	53.1

series has been further analyzed by dividing the population into four equal parts on the basis of the magnitude of rates of delinquents, then calculating the percentage of the total number of delinquents and total city area for each population quartile, as shown in Table 2.

It is apparent that the quarter of the population living in the areas of highest rates occupied only 19.2 percent of the geographic area of the city in the 1927–33 series, 17.8 percent in 1917–23, and 13.1 percent in 1900–06. Yet in each instance this quarter of the population produced about one-half of the delinquents.

B. THE DISTRIBUTION OF COMMITTED DELINQUENTS

This section is concerned with the least inclusive enumeration of delinquent boys in Chicago, namely, those committed to correctional institutions by the Juvenile Court of Cook County. Three series will be presented: (1) the 1927–33 commitment series, (2) the 1917–23 commitment series, and (3) the 1900–06 commitment series.

As has been noted, roughly two-fifths of the boys taken to the juvenile court on delinquency petition are ultimately committed to correctional institutions. Since these series cover the same periods as the juvenile court delinquency series, it follows that they will contain only about two-fifths as many boys. On the other hand, these boys committed to

institutions are the most serious delinquents known to the court. Most of them are recidivists, since few boys are committed on their first appearance, and some have served time previously in institutions for delinquents.

The graphic presentation of these commitment series will be limited to rate maps and zone maps.

1. The 1927–33 Commitment Series

This series includes 2,593 individuals committed by the juvenile court to correctional institutions during the 7-year period 1927–33. The majority of these boys had committed serious offenses and were recidivists. With respect to age they were, on the whole, somewhat above the average for boys appearing in the juvenile court.

Distribution. When distributed by home address, wide areal variations are found in the number of committed delinquents. There were 7 areas from which more than go boys were committed. At the other extreme, no delinquents were committed from 3 areas, and 1 boy only from each of 9 others, while not more than 2 boys were committed from each of 19 areas.

Rates. Map 8 shows the rate of committed delinquents in each of the 140 areas. These are 7-year rates, as were those in the corresponding

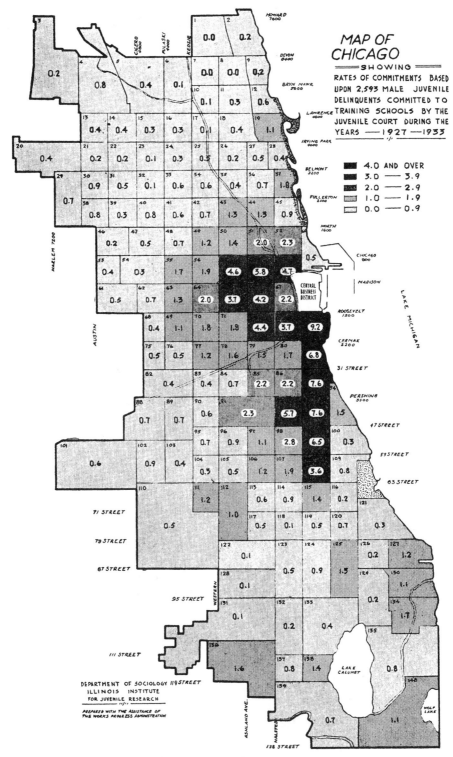

MAP 8   *Rates of committed delinquents, Chicago, 1927–33.*

juvenile court series, and calculated by the same method, on the basis of the same population. They represent in each area, therefore, the number of boys committed in a 7-year period per 100 of the aged 10–16 male population as of 1930. To distinguish them from the rates of juvenile court delinquents, these will be referred to as "rates of commitments" or "rates of committed delinquents."

Although the separate rates in this series are low because of the relatively small number of committed delinquents, the variation is even greater than in the juvenile court series. The range is from 0.0 to 9.2, the median is 0.7, and the rate for the city as a whole is 1.3. Three areas have rates of 7.0 or over, and 6 of 5.0 or over. At the other extreme, 3 areas have rates of 0.0, and 12 of 0.1 or less.

Map 8 reveals the same general configuration that was found in the juvenile court series. The areas with highest commitment rates surround the Loop and extend directly south, with relatively high rates also in the Stock Yards areas, near the Southwest manufacturing district, and in South Chicago. Low-rate areas, on the other hand, are to be noted in the outlying districts.

2. The 1917–23 Commitment Series

The second series of committed delinquents includes the 2,639 Chicago boys committed to institutions by the Juvenile Court of Cook County during the 7-year period 1917–23. Since the boys in this series appeared in the 1917–23 juvenile court series and were committed, they include the most serious delinquents known to the court for this period.

Distribution. When these committed delinquents were tabulated on the basis of the 113 areas into which the city was divided for this series, it was found that there were 3 areas from each of which more than 50 boys had been committed, 6 with 1 commitment, and 14 with less than 5 commitments each.

Rates. When rates of committed delinquents were calculated, it was found that the range extended from 0.1 to 6.9. The median area rate for the series is 1.2 and the rate for the city 1.8. Four areas have rates of 5.0 or over, and 17 of 3.0 or more; while at the lower end of the range 14 areas have rates under 0.5, and 46 of less than 1.0. Map 9 shows clearly that the geographic distribution and variation of rates in this series closely resemble the two series previously presented.

3. The 1900–06 Commitment Series

This series includes the 3,224 boys committed to correctional schools during the first 7 years of the existence of the juvenile court (1900–06), out of the total number included in the corresponding juvenile court series.

Distribution. When distributed by home address, wide variations were found among the 106 areas into which Chicago was divided for this early series. More than 150 boys were committed from each of 3 areas, and more than 1900 from each of 8. At the other extreme, only 3 boys were committed from each of 8 areas, and 2 from each of 4; while 10 areas showed 1 commitment each, and 2 areas none.

Rates. The rates of committed delinquents range from 0.0 to 12.5, the median is 1.7, and the rate for the city as a whole 3.4. Six areas have rates under 0.5, and 26 under 1.0. Four areas, on the other hand, have rates above 9.0, and 10 above 6.0. Map 10 shows the configuration.

4. Comparisons Among Commitment Series

The extent to which the variations in rates of committed delinquents correspond for the three time series will be stated in terms of zone comparisons 7 area comparisons and correlations, and extent of concentration.

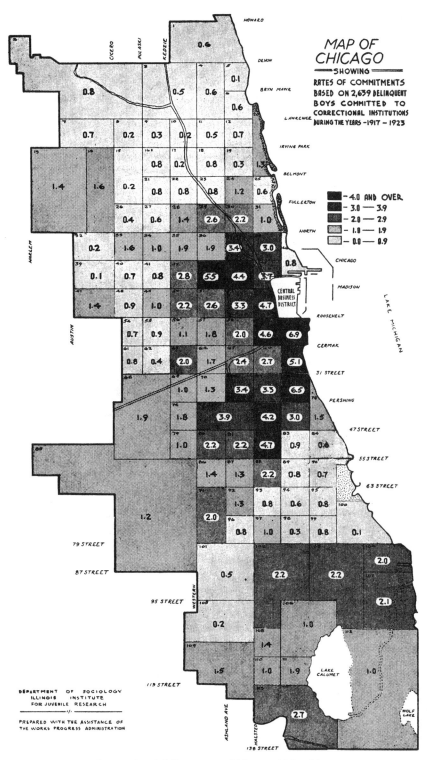

MAP 9   *Rates of committed delinquents, Chicago, 1917–23.*

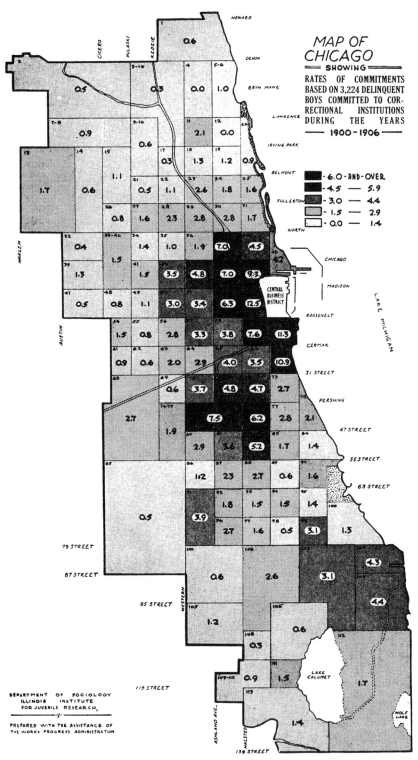

MAP 10 *Rates of committed delinquents, Chicago, 1900–06.*

Rates by Zones. Since the rates in these three series of committed delinquents are based on smaller samples than were those for the juvenile court delinquency series, the variations are somewhat less regular. When zone rates are calculated, however, these irregularities are smoothed out and the general trends revealed. As Maps A, B, and C, Figure 2, show these trends based on juvenile court commitments correspond closely to the trends based on rates of all individuals brought before the court.

In the 1927–33 series, the city rates vary from 3.4 in Zone 1 to 0.4 in Zone V, a decrease of 88 percent, as compared with a drop of nearly 75 percent in the 1917–23 series and of 70 percent for the 1900–06 data.

The zone rates for the north and south halves of the city also exhibit variations corresponding to those in the broader delinquency series. As indicated previously, the South Chicago industrial district constitutes a new locus from which, in turn, analysis might be made on a zonal basis.

Area Comparisons and Correlations. The same general configuration of rates is seen for 1900–06 as has been noted for the two other series. The most important difference is in the areas south from the Loop. In 1900–06, it will be seen, only the first 2 areas to the south are characterized by high rates; whereas in the 1917–23 series the rates are high in the first 4 areas, and in 1927–33 these areas of high rates extend southward 6 or 7 miles.

When the 1917–23 and 1927–33 series are compared, it is found that of the 25 areas with the highest rates in the former series, 20 are included among the 25 highest a decade later. As in the juvenile court delinquency series, 3 of the 5 areas among the highest in 1927–33, but not in the earlier series, are areas where marked changes in community characteristics have occurred.

When the rates of delinquents in the 113 areas of the 1927–23 series are correlated with the corresponding rates for 1927–33, $r = .74 \pm .03$. For 1927–33 and 1900–06, by 106 areas, the coefficient is $.66 + .04$; and for 1917–23 and 1900–06 it is $.81 \pm .02$.

Extent of Concentration. The concentration of committed delinquents in each series has been analyzed by ranking the areas by rate of committed delinquents, then dividing the aged 10–16 male population into four equal parts and computing the proportion of total committed delinquents and of city area for each population quartile.

It will be noted that more than half of the committed delinquents in each of the three series come from the quarter of the population living in areas of highest rates, although these constitute less than one-fifth of the total city area. At the other extreme, the quarter of the population in lowest-rate areas produced 7.3 percent of the committed delinquents in 1900–06, 7.2 percent in the 1917–23 series, and only 4.3 percent during 1927–33.

This concentration is again evident when the total number of committed boys in each series is divided into quartiles according to rate of committed delinquents and the corresponding percentages of population and of city area are computed (see Table 3).

It will be seen from Table 3 that the one-fourth of the committed boys living in high-rate areas represented less than 10 percent of the population and 7 percent of the city area, in each time series. On the other hand, the one-fourth in lowest-rate areas came from more than 51 percent of the population and 68 percent or over of the city area. Both tables show the greatest concentration in the 1927–33 series.

C. THE DISTRIBUTION OF POLICE ARRESTS

The third, and most inclusive, basic enumeration of delinquents or alleged delinquents and index of the number of boys engaged in officially proscribed activity in Chicago includes all boys dealt with by the juvenile police probation officers, one of whom is assigned to

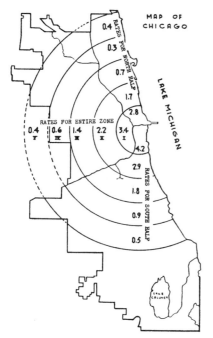

A. Zone rates of committed delinquents, 1927–33 series

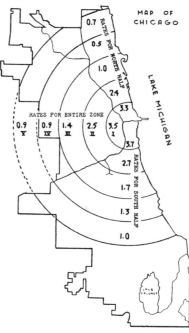

B. Zone rates of committed delinquents, 1917–23 series

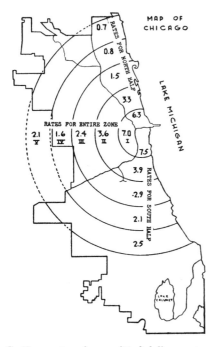

C. Zone rates of committed delinquents, 1900–1906 series

CRITICAL RATIOS OF SELECTED ZONE RATES
Commitment Series

Zones	Difference	Standard Error of the Difference	Critical Ratio
	A. 1927–33		
1 and 4.......	2.8	.182	15.4
1 and 5.......	3.0	.182	16.5
2 and 4.......	1.6	.080	20.0
2 and 5.......	1.8	.079	22.8
	B. 1917–23		
1 and 4.......	2.6	.176	14.8
1 and 5.......	2.6	.186	14.0
2 and 4.......	1.6	.095	16.8
2 and 5.......	1.6	.113	14.2
	C. 1900–1906		
1 and 4.......	5.4	.250	21.6
1 and 5.......	4.9	.306	16.0
2 and 4.......	2.0	.151	13.2
2 and 5.......	1.5	.233	6.4

FIGURE 2   *Zone of maps for three series of committed delinquents.*

TABLE 3

Percentage of male population aged 10–16 and of city area for quartiles of committed delinquents when areas are ranked by rate of committed delinquents: Three commitment series.

Quartiles of Committed Delinquents	Percentage of Population			Percentage of City Area		
	1927–23	1917–23	1900–06	1927–23	1917–23	1900–06
Upper one-fourth, from high-rate areas	5.5	9.1	9.6	4.34	6.2	4.4
Second one-fourth	10.6	15.0	15.3	6.8	10.8	4.7
Third one-fourth	21.7	22.0	24.0	14.3	15.0	12.5
Lower one-fourth, from low-rate areas	62.2	53.9	51.1	74.6	68.0	78.4

each police station. Most of the boys charged with delinquencies are brought to the attention of these officers, who decide whether the boy is to be dismissed with a warning or taken into court. In considering the seriousness of the offenses charged, it should be borne in mind that in some court systems all the boys in these series would be taken to court, although in Chicago only about 15 percent have delinquency petitions filed against them.

Since no permanent official record is made of these police cases, it has not been possible to study their distribution over widely separated periods of time. The following series, however, will be presented: (1) the 1931 police series, (2) the 1927 police series, and (3) the 1926 police series. These series will be analyzed in less detail than those preceding, as it is necessary only to determine the extent to which the findings agree.

1. The 1931 Police Series

This series includes the boys whose names and addresses appeared in the records of the police probation officers during 1931. They were, as a group, somewhat younger than the boys taken into court, about 30 percent being under 13 years. A rough classification of the offenses charged indicates that stealing; shoplifting; snatching pocketbooks; stealing automobiles; breaking into stores, residences, or factories; and similar offenses accounted for approximately half the total. The remaining half of the boys were charged with a variety of offenses, including truancy from home, assault, malicious mischief, destruction of property, trespassing, manslaughter, and sex immorality.

Distribution. When these cases were plotted by home address, the resulting configuration was quite similar to that in the 1927–33 juvenile court series (see Map 1). Analysis on the basis of 140 square-mile areas shows that 2 areas contain over 300, and 13 areas over 200, boys each. At the other extreme, fewer than 20 boys appear in each of 18 areas.

Rates. Rates of police arrests were likewise calculated by areas, on the basis of the 1930 aged 10–16 male population. These are 1-year rates and may be conveniently thought of as the percentage of all boys who were arrested during the year. The range of rates is from 0.5 to 19.4. The city rate is 5.4, and the median 4.0. The rate map for this series has been omitted because it closely resembles those previously presented.

Zone Rates. The variation in police cases from the center of the city outward is indicated by zone rates calculated for the same zones used in the other series. These are shown in Figure 3, A. Here, again, regular decreases in the rates are to be noted as distance from the Loop increases, for the two halves of the city considered separately and for both together. As in the other series, the South Side rates are considerably higher than those for corresponding zones on the North Side.

2. The 1927 Police Series

The second police series comprises the 8,951 boys who appeared in the records of the police probation officers during 1927. With respect to age and offense, these boys were not widely different from those in the 1931 series. Approximately 55 percent were charged with some form of stealing.

Distribution. The configuration resulting from the plotting of these cases on the map by home address is similar to that in the other series. Of the 113 square-mile areas, 15 contained fewer than 10 arrested boys, as compared with 12 which contained over 250 each.

Rates. A rate was calculated for each local area on the basis of the estimated aged 10–16 male population for 1927. The range of rates is from 0.0 to 21.8, the median being 3.4, and the city rate 4.9.

Zone Rates. As in the 1931 series, rates calculated by zones show a regular decrease, with one or two minor exceptions, from the central business district outward, for the two halves of the city separately and for both together.

3. The 1926 Police Series

The third police series includes the 9,243 individual Chicago boys whose names and addresses appeared in the records of the juvenile police probation officers during 1926. They correspond closely, as to age and type of offense, with the 1931 and 1927 series.

Distribution. With regard to distribution by home address, the configuration in this series is likewise similar to that of the previous series. Of the 113 local areas, 12 contain fewer than 10 arrested boys each, whereas 14 areas have more than 200 each.

Rates. Rates of police arrests were calculated by square-mile areas on the basis of the aged 10–16 population as estimated for 1926. The range of area rates is from 0.0 to 26.6, with a median of 3.4 and a city rate of 5.2. In each of 5 areas the rate is over 20.0, and in 5 additional areas it is between 15.0 and 20.0. At the other extreme, the rate is under 1.0 in 17 areas. In general, the distribution of high- and low-rate areas shows no noticeable variation from the series already presented.

Zone Rates. The decrease in rates of police arrests from the center of the city outward is indicated by Figure 3, C.

4. Recreation Survey Study

A computation of rates based on data furnished by the Chicago Recreation Survey, representing boys whose names appear in the juvenile court police records for 1935, revealed a distribution comparable both to the above police series and to the juvenile court series already analyzed. Zone rates are presented in Figure 3, D. Correlation of these data with the 1927–33 rates of delinquents yields an r of .84 ± .02. This evidence from an independent source constitutes an additional index of delinquent activity in Chicago and tends to strengthen the conclusions drawn.

5. Comparisons Among Police Series

Correlation. Nineteen of the 25 areas with highest rates in 1927 and 18 of the highest in 1926 are included among the first 25 in 1931. Correlation between the 1927 and 1931 series yields an r of .87 ± .01, and the corresponding correlation for 1926 and 1931 results in a coefficient of .83 ± .02. The correlation between the 1926 and 1927 series is much closer. The 12 areas of

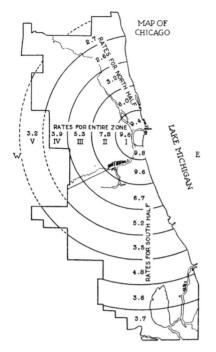

A. Zone rates of police arrests, 1931

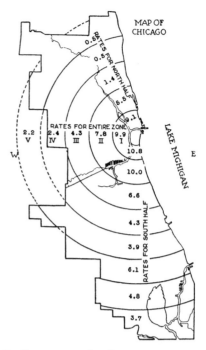

B. Zone rates of police arrests, 1927

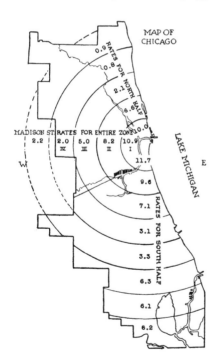

C. Zone rates of police arrests, 1926

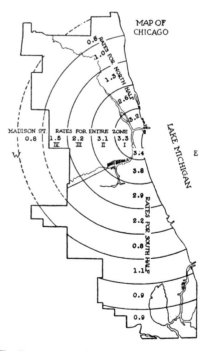

D. Zone rates of juvenile court police records, 1935

FIGURE 3   *Zone maps for police-arrests series.*

highest rates for these 2 years are the same, and the coefficient secured when the two series are correlated is .96 ± .005.

Extent of Concentration in Juvenile Police Arrests. The residential concentration of boys arrested by the police can be readily seen when their distribution is analyzed in relation to that of the total aged 10–16 male population. As in the previous series, the square-mile areas were arranged in rank order on the basis of the rate of police arrests. The population was then divided into four equal parts and the percentage of police arrests and of total city area was calculated for each population quartile.

One-fourth of the aged 10–16 male population living in the areas of highest rates produced 49.0 percent of the delinquents in the 1931 series, 58.9 percent in 1927, and 59.8 percent in 1926; while the one-fourth living in areas of lowest rates produced only 9.1, 3.1, and 3.8 percent of the delinquents, respectively.

The absolute differences among percentages in these three series should not be taken as proof of a trend in the distribution of delinquents. Such variations might be due to changes in policy in some police districts, to the fact that the population base for the 1926 and 1927 series was estimated, or to a variety of other factors. The important point is that, in spite of minor variations, all three series present the same general features.

One-quarter of the delinquents from the highest rate areas represented only 9.6 percent of the population in the 1931 series, 7.1 percent in the 1927 series, and 7.0 percent in the 1926 series; while the one-quarter of the delinquents in the low rate areas came from 49.6, 61.6, and 63.2 percent of the population in the 1931, 1927, and 1926 series, respectively.

In each series, likewise, the upper one-fourth of the delinquents came from less than 7 percent of the total city area, while the lower one-fourth represented more than 60 percent of the city area.

On the basis of the above facts, several deductions as to the relative usefulness of the different types of series can be made. It is evident, first, that the findings in the three types are so similar that any one of them might be used as an index of the others. The juvenile court series, however, show somewhat less concentration and variation in rates than either the police or commitment series. They are less inclusive than the police series, yet not limited to the serious offenders comprising the committed group; and they presumably represent, therefore, a conservative sample of the boys engaging in officially proscribed activity throughout the city. It is the authors' conclusion that, where a single set of data must serve, juvenile court series may be used safely as an index of this broader universe.

QUESTIONS FOR DISCUSSION AND WRITING

1. Where are the alleged delinquents concentrated?
2. What "characterized" the areas with high rates of delinquency?
3. How do the 25 areas in 1900–1906 compare with the highest rates in the other time periods?

Contemporary Research

Social Interaction and Community Crime: Examining the Importance of Neighbor Networks

PAUL E. BELLAIR

C URRENT social disorganization research is built on the notion that well-developed, local network structures reduce crime. This formulation is grounded in the systemic model of community organization, which views the local community "as a complex system of friendship and kinship networks and formal and informal associational ties rooted in family life and ongoing socialization processes." However, network structures have remained implicit in most of the research literature. In a common design, researchers link ecological characteristics of communities (e.g., socioeconomic status) to crime rates and argue that other social conditions (e.g., local network structures) mediate the relationship. As several community crime scholars have noted, this type of design does little to extend the research conducted by Shaw and McKay half a century ago. Indeed, in the absence of mediating variables, the potential intervening role of disorganization in the ecology–crime relationship remains largely theoretical speculation.

Although the literature is not entirely supportive, a small but growing body of research suggests the importance of measuring local networks. Perhaps the first effort to measure networks directly was carried out by Maccoby et al. in a survey study of two low-income neighborhoods in Cambridge, Massachusetts. One neighborhood had a high and the other a low rate of delinquency. Maccoby et al.'s findings indicated that the high-delinquency neighborhood was less integrated than the low-delinquency neighborhood. In the high-delinquency area, residents were less likely to know their neighbors by name, like their neighborhood, or share similar interests. However, in situations in which they were not the victim, there were only small differences (nonsignificant) in the extent to which residents took action if a child was observed committing a delinquent act.

In the next two decades, three additional studies including measures of social disorganization appeared. Warren examined riot activity in eight African American school districts in Detroit. He found that neighborhoods where a larger proportion of the residents interacted on a weekly basis and where residents perceived consensus within the community experienced

From "Social Interaction and Community Crime: Examining the Importance of Neighbor Networks" by P. E. Bellair, 1997, *Criminology* 35 (4):677–701. Copyright © 1992 The American Society of Criminology.

less riot activity and heightened counterriot activity. Kapsis examined three poor, predominantly African American communities undergoing varying levels of racial change in the San Francisco–Oakland metropolitan area. He found that residents in the low-delinquency neighborhood had extensive contact with a local settlement house, which suggested the importance of local institutions for crime control. Further, they were more likely to know at least 50 neighbors by name, to have friends in the neighborhood, and to agree that most of the families knew each other than were residents in the medium- and high-delinquency neighborhoods. However, comparison of the medium- and high-delinquency neighborhoods indicated that the latter three factors were more common in the high-delinquency neighborhood.

In the past two decades, efforts to measure disorganization directly have continued. Greenberg et al. examined informal territorial control in three high-crime and three low-crime Atlanta neighborhoods. They concluded that there were no systematic differences between the low- and high-crime neighborhoods in spatial identity, frequency and variety of neighboring, or informal control. Where differences occurred, neighboring and informal control were more common in the high-crime neighborhood. However, residents in two of the three low-crime neighborhoods belonged to a greater number of local organizations and attended meetings more frequently than residents in adjacent high-crime neighborhoods.

Simcha-Fagan and Schwartz measured community organization using general factors reflecting disorder/criminal subculture and organizational participation. The disorder/criminal subculture scale combined multiple items reflecting (low) community attachment, (low) network size and breadth, anomie, social disorder, conflict subculture, and illegal economy. The organizational-participation scale reflected average parental education and average organizational involvement. Findings indicated that the disorder/criminal subcul-

ture factor was positively associated with official and severe self-reported delinquency, and that organizational participation was inversely associated with self-reported delinquency across 12 New York City neighborhoods. Smith and Jarjoura found that community integration reduced the risk of household-level burglary, and Patterson found that it was inversely associated with burglary and violent crime. Both studies defined integration as the mean frequency of interaction within each neighborhood. Skogan reported that disorder, construed as a measure of disorganization, substantially mediated the effects of poverty, residential stability, and percent minority on robbery. Disorder was measured using an index that combined several physical and social disorder items.

Recent research by Sampson and Groves provided a convincing test of Shaw and McKay's social disorganization thesis. Using data from the British Crime Survey, they constructed community-level measures of social disorganization and linked them to victimization and offending rates in a series of multivariate equations. Further, the analysis utilized self-report and victimization data, thereby controlling for measurement error associated with citizen nonreporting and biases in police arrest procedures. Their findings indicated that the presence of teenage peer groups, greater rates of participation in local clubs and committees, and extensive friendship networks are associated with lower rates of crime. Thus, their results suggest that when the size of a community's network structure increases, informal social controls on behavior are likely to be strong and delinquency and crime relatively less likely. . . .

SOCIAL INTERACTION AMONG NEIGHBORS

. . . An unexplored issue with neighbor networks, however, is whether or not *frequency of interaction* among neighbors affects community social controls and cohesion. The social disorganization perspective traditionally assumes that social interaction among neighbors that occurs frequently, such as every day, is most effective. However, infrequent social interaction among residents may be as important as frequent interaction in building the network structure of a community for two reasons. First, infrequent interaction may signal the existence of a broader web of affiliations among neighborhood residents if a significant proportion of interaction takes place relatively infrequently. In terms of the supervisory capacity of local networks, it may matter very little whether neighbors are close friends as long as they interact with one another occasionally. Thus, the *size* of local networks may be inaccurately assessed by a narrow focus on frequent interaction. . . .

In sum, current social disorganization research asserts that community organization is reflected in local social networks. Drawing from the systemic model, the community is seen as an interwoven system of family, friendship, and formal and informal associational ties, which can be conceptualized as social networks. Communities with extensive networks are assumed to be more integrated and cohesive, and the residents more likely to engage in informal surveillance, to develop movement-governing rules, and to intervene in disturbances. The framework assumes that residents of communities with large, interconnected, and active social networks have a greater capacity to supervise social activity within the neighborhood and to socialize children and other residents toward conventional values. Moreover, the social disorganization perspective traditionally assumes that social interaction among neighbors that occurs frequently, such as every day, is most effective. This study challenges that assumption.

The analysis extends the literature in the following ways. First, to test the hypotheses developed above, I examine the effects on crime of 10 alternative measures of social interaction among neighbors. The measures vary in their inclusion of infrequent forms of interaction that have been overlooked in prior research. If frequent and infrequent interaction are both important for community control, combining them should produce a stronger negative effect on crime. Second, after demonstrating the salience of combining frequent and infrequent interaction, I examine the hypothesis that social interaction among neighbors mediates the relationship between ecological characteristics and community crime. As I noted above, such mediating relations are crucial to testing disorganization theory.

DATA AND METHODS

The data used were gathered as part of a victimization survey in the Police Services Study. This study examined citizen attitudes and satisfaction with the delivery of local police services in 60 urban neighborhoods in 1977. The neighborhoods were selected from the Rochester (New York), St. Petersburg/Tampa (Florida), and St. Louis (Missouri) Standard Metropolitan Statistical Areas (SMSAs). As such, the data are reasonably representative of neighborhoods in medium-sized U.S. cities. . . . The original sampling units were households identified and randomly selected from listings in the telephone directory. The interviewers asked respondents a series of questions about the victimization experiences of each household member that occurred within the neighborhood. In total, 12,019 households were sampled. The average number of households sampled per neighborhood was approximately 200. . . .

Crime Rate Variables

Based on availability, three index crimes are analyzed in this study: burglary, motor vehicle theft, and robbery. Data from the victimization survey are utilized to construct the measures. . . .

Exogenous Variables

Community crime research motivated by social disorganization theory typically begins with four exogenous variables thought to affect community organization: community socioeconomic status (SES), racial and ethnic heterogeneity, residential stability, and family disruption. Thus, each exogenous variable is hypothesized to affect crime through its effect on the network structure of a community.

From a systemic perspective, neighborhood SES is likely to be important for the development of local networks because it reflects the aggregate lifestyle of a locality. Research examining the role of community SES in the development of local friendship networks is conflicting. Some research suggests that social class is inversely related to community friendship networks, while other studies suggest that SES is unrelated. Community socioeconomic status is measured as the percentage of neighborhood residents whose household income is below $5,000 per year (which is the lowest income category in the response set for the family income question), the percentage of college-educated residents, and the median family income—all combined into a factor scale (principal components) with each variable weighted by its factor loading. High positive scores on this factor reflect higher SES.

The second ecological characteristic, racial and ethnic heterogeneity, is thought to disrupt local networks because racial and ethnic groups often embrace different traditions, ways of life, and stereotypes about out-group members. Within a social context characterized by heterogeneity, communication among residents is thought to be tenuous and the ability of residents to recognize and solve common problems impeded. Prior research, however, indicates that racial and ethnic heterogeneity is unrelated to local friendship networks. Respondent's racial/ethnic status was recorded in one of five categories: white, black, Latino, Native American, and other. Racial and ethnic heterogeneity is measured as the quantity one minus the sum of the squared propor-

tion of residents in each racial or ethnic group. The heterogeneity index is high when the population is evenly distributed across racial and ethnic groups and low when a neighborhood is completely homogeneous.

The systemic model posits that residential stability is the key variable for development of networks because a community is "an ongoing system of social networks into which new generations and new residents are assimilated." This hypothesis is strongly supported in the literature. Residential stability is measured as the mean number of years that respondents have resided in their neighborhoods. . . .

Social Interaction Variables

Ten measures of social interaction among neighbors are constructed from a question that asks respondents how often they, or members of their household, get together with their neighbors either in their neighbors' or their own home. Possible responses to the survey item are daily, several times a week, several times a month, once a month, once a year, and very infrequently. The first five measures are simple percentages: the percentage of residents who get together with their neighbors every day, the percentage of residents who get together with their neighbors once a week, the percentage of residents who get together with their neighbors several times a month, the percentage of residents who get together with their neighbors once a month, and the percentage of residents who get together with their neighbors once a year. . . .

The next four measures are cumulative percentages: the percentage of residents who get together with their neighbors once a week or more, the percentage of residents who get together with their neighbors several times a month or more, the percentage of residents who get together with their neighbors once a month or more, and the percentage of residents who get together with their neighbors once a year or more. . . . The final measure examined reflects the mean level of social interaction among neighbors within each neighborhood. . . . Thus, a higher score on the mean-level variable indicates that social interaction takes place more frequently, on average, in that community. . . .

ANALYSIS OF SOCIAL INTERACTION AND CRIME

. . . Traditionally the social disorganization perspective assumes that social interaction among residents that takes place frequently, such as every day, is most effective for establishing informal community controls. Based on this traditional reasoning, one may expect the percentage of neighborhood residents who get together every day to have the strongest effect on crime. . . . Taken as a whole, there appears to be no consistent pattern. The percentage of residents who get together every day has no effect on burglary, motor vehicle theft, or robbery. The percentage of neighborhood residents who get together once a week is inversely related to burglary, which suggests that relatively less frequent interaction has a stronger deterrent effect on crime. However, the results based on inclusion of the remaining simple percentage measures in the crime rate equations show no effects, with the exception of the percentage of residents who get together once a month on motor vehicle theft. In sum, measurement of social interaction using simple percentages yields no clear pattern of effects on crime rates. . . .

. . . From the traditional assumptions of social disorganization theory, one may hypothesize that higher mean levels of social interaction among neighbors would produce a stronger negative effect on crime rates than the cumulative frequencies because frequent interaction is assumed to be more effective in creating community controls on behavior. The results indicate that the mean level of social interaction has consistently negative effects on robbery only, and its inclusion explains more variance in robbery than the percentage of residents who get together once a year or more. . . .

INTERACTION AS A MEDIATING INFLUENCE BETWEEN COMMUNITY AND CRIME

This section evaluates the extent to which social interaction among neighbors mediates the effects of ecological characteristics on crime rates. Based on the results to this point, I use the percentage of residents who get together once a year or more as the principal measure of social interaction. Support for the mediation hypothesis is indicated if SES, heterogeneity, residential stability, and percent single parents are significant predictors of social interaction, and if their direct effects on burglary, motor vehicle theft, and robbery are reduced when social interaction is introduced into the equations. Further, social interaction must have a significant inverse effect on crime rates. . . .

The findings from the social interaction equation indicate that SES and heterogeneity are strong predictors. These relationships are important because they suggest an explanation for the link between affluent and homogeneous communities and the lower crime rates evident in such urban places. The systemic theory of community organization argues that ecological characteristics reflect different lifestyle or focal concerns among neighborhood residents. Residents of communities with greater social and economic resources may be more likely to interact with their neighbors because attractive recreational facilities and community activities are more likely to be built and sponsored there. Further, higher-status communities are more likely to be populated by residents with daytime work routines, which increases the proportion with leisure hours in common. Both factors may increase the likelihood of developing informal ties with neighbors. Racial heterogeneity has a moderately strong negative effect on social interaction, indicating that social interaction among neighbors is impeded by racial diversity. Surprisingly, the effect of residential stability is nonsignificant. An alternative measure of residential stability, calculated as the percentage of residents who have lived in the neighborhood for five or more years, also has no effect. . . .

. . . In sum, social interaction mediates a portion of the effects of SES, heterogeneity, and residential stability on at least one of the crime rates, thus supporting social disorganization theory.

DISCUSSION

. . . The social disorganization perspective traditionally assumes that frequent interaction among neighbors is the most effective mechanism for generating community controls. Drawing from recent research in the community literature, this study questions that assumption. The research presented examined the effect on crime rates of 10 alternative measures of social interaction, ranging from simple and cumulative percentage measures to the mean level of social interaction within a community.

The data indicate that a cumulative percentage measure that combines frequent and infrequent interaction has the most consistent and generally the strongest effect on burglary, motor vehicle theft, and robbery. Alternative social interaction measures in some cases were related to the burglary, motor vehicle theft, and robbery rates, but the data indicate that their effects are generally smaller in comparison to the effect of the percentage of residents who get together once a year or more. . . .

The data, therefore, suggest that both frequent and infrequent social interaction among neighbors is important for establishing community controls. Why are community controls strengthened even if a considerable proportion of the interaction among neighborhood residents occurs infrequently? Neighbors may be willing to engage in supervision and guardianship regardless of whether they consider themselves to be close friends with their neighbors. As noted by Freudenburg, people who know each other are more likely to work together to solve common problems. Residents of communities where a large proportion of residents know and interact with neighbors appear to be more likely to engage in surveillance, develop movement-governing rules, and intervene in local disturbances regardless of how frequently they interact (excluding extremely infrequent interaction). The findings suggest that the *size* of neighbor networks may be inaccurately assessed by an exclusive focus on frequent interaction.

Further, Granovetter suggests that weak ties strengthen community organization by creating important linkages across networks. Infrequent interaction among neighbors may signal the existence of weak ties. Thus, frequent interaction supplemented by infrequent interaction may signify a more loosely connected network structure. Both processes may increase the ability of neighborhood residents to engage in social control.

The data also provide support for the mediation hypothesis. Social interaction among neighbors that occurs once a year or more is more common in relatively affluent and homogeneous communities, and it transmits a moderate proportion of the effects of these variables on at least one of the crime rates. Thus, the analysis suggests an explanation for the link between affluent and homogeneous communities and the lower crime rates in such urban places. The systemic theory of community organization argues that ecological characteristics reflect different lifestyle or focal concerns among neighborhood residents. The positive relationship between SES and interaction may occur because communities with greater social and economic resources are more likely to build and maintain recreational facilities and sponsor various community activities. In addition, residents of higher-SES communities may be more likely to have work routines that increase the proportion of residents with leisure hours in common. The inverse relationship between heterogeneity and interaction suggests that racial diversity impedes the formation of networks. In homogeneous communities, residents are apparently more likely to perceive commonalities with neighbors, which increases the likelihood of interaction. These factors, and undoubtedly others such as racial animosity, increase or impede the potential for development of informal neighboring.

Much remains to be done in the study of the network–crime relationship. This analysis scratches only the surface of future possibilities. For instance, although I argue that infrequent interaction among neighbors in part approximates Granovetter's notion of weak ties, it is a weak measure of the strength of a social tie. A more appropriate measure might ascertain the number of different neighbors residents get together with and the frequency, intimacy, and extent of reciprocal exchange associated with each tie. Assessing the strength of network ties may also inform measurement of rates of participation in local institutions or ties between local residents and social, political, and economic institutions outside the community. The latter network characteristic may inform understanding of the capacity of neighborhood residents to acquire resources from external actors.

In sum, social disorganization research may benefit by continuing to probe carefully the dynamics of local network structures. Interaction among neighbors has rarely been studied in relation to crime. Indeed, the findings suggest that measurement of such networks may be extremely subtle. Moreover, this strategy holds promise for uncovering the basic social fabric of communities because infrequent interaction appears to be common in contemporary urban settings. Clearly, weak ties help stitch neighborhoods together and these weak ties matter when it comes to explaining levels of neighborhood crime.

QUESTIONS FOR DISCUSSION AND WRITING

1. What issue with neighbor networks is unexplored?
2. How can community controls be strengthened even if a considerable proportion of the interaction among neighborhood residents occurs infrequently?
3. Why may a positive relationship between SES and interaction occur?

DIFFERENTIAL ASSOCIATION THEORY

A Theory of Crime: Differential Association

EDWIN H. SUTHERLAND

TWO TYPES OF EXPLANATIONS OF CRIMINAL BEHAVIOR

Scientific explanations of criminal behavior may be stated either in terms of the processes which are operating at the moment of the occurrence of crime or in terms of the processes operating in the earlier history of the criminal. In the first case, the explanation may be called "mechanistic," "situational," or "dynamic"; in the second, "historical" or "genetic." Both types of explanation are desirable. The mechanistic type of explanation has been favored by physical and biological scientists, and it probably could be the more efficient type of explanation of criminal behavior. However, criminological explanations of the mechanistic type have thus far been notably unsuccessful, perhaps largely because they have been formulated in connection with the attempt to isolate personal and social pathologies among criminals. Work from this point of view has, at least, resulted in the conclusion that the immediate determinants of criminal behavior lie in the person-situation complex.

From "A Theory of Criminology: Differential Association" by E. H. Sutherland, from *Principles of Criminology, Fourth Edition*, Chicago: J. B. Lippincott, 1947. Copyright © 1989 Elaine Cressey.

The objective situation is important to criminality largely to the extent that it provides an opportunity for a criminal act. A thief may steal from a fruit stand when the owner is not in sight but refrain when the owner is in sight; a bank burglar may attack a bank which is poorly protected but refrain from attacking a bank protected by watchmen and burglar alarms. A corporation which manufactures automobiles seldom or never violates the Pure Food and Drug Law, but a meat-packing corporation might violate this law with great frequency. But in another sense, a psychological or sociological sense, the situation is not exclusive of the person, for the situation which is important is the situation as defined by the person who is involved. That is, some persons define a situation in which a fruit-stand owner is out of sight as a "crime-committing" situation, while others do not so define it. Furthermore, the events in the person-situation complex at the time a crime occurs cannot be separated from the prior life experiences of the criminal. This means that the situation is defined by the person in terms of the inclinations and abilities which the person has acquired up to date. For example, while a person could define a situation in such a manner that criminal behavior would be the inevitable result, his past experiences would for the most part determine the way in which he defined the situation. An explanation of criminal behavior made in terms of these past experiences is a historical or genetic explanation.

The following paragraphs state such a genetic theory of criminal behavior on the assumption that a criminal act occurs when a situation appropriate for it, as defined by the person, is present. The theory should be regarded as tentative, and it should be tested by the factual information presented in the later chapters and by all other factual information and theories which are applicable.

GENETIC EXPLANATION OF CRIMINAL BEHAVIOR

The following statement refers to the process by which a particular person comes to engage in criminal behavior

1. Criminal behavior is learned. Negatively, this means that criminal behavior is not inherited, as such; also, the person who is not already trained in crime does not invent criminal behavior, just as a person does not make mechanical inventions unless he has had training in mechanics.
2. Criminal behavior is learned in interaction with other persons in a process of communication. This communication is verbal in many respects but includes also "the communication of gestures."
3. The principal part of the learning of criminal behavior occurs within intimate personal groups. Negatively, this means that the impersonal agencies of communication, such as movies and newspapers, play a relatively unimportant part in the genesis of criminal behavior.
4. When criminal behavior is learned, the learning includes (a) techniques of committing the crime, which are sometimes very complicated, sometimes very simple; and (b) the specific direction of motives, drives, rationalizations, and attitudes.
5. The specific direction of motives and drives is learned from definitions of the legal codes as favorable or unfavorable. In some societies an individual is surrounded by persons who invariably define the legal codes as rules to be observed, while in others he is surrounded by persons whose definitions are favorable to the violation of the legal codes. In our American society, these definitions are almost always mixed, with the consequence that we have culture conflict in relation to the legal codes.
6. A person becomes delinquent because of an excess of definitions favorable to violation of law over definitions unfavorable to violation of law. This is the principle of differential association. It refers to both criminal and anticriminal associations and has to do with counteracting forces. When persons become criminal, they do so because of contacts with criminal patterns and also because of isolation from anticriminal patterns. Any person inevitably assimilates the surrounding culture unless other patterns are in conflict; a southerner does not pronounce "r" because other southerners do not pronounce "r." Negatively, this proposition of differential association means that associations which are neutral so far as crime is concerned have little or no effect on the genesis of criminal behavior. Much of the experience of a person is neutral in this sense, for example, learning to brush one's teeth. This behavior has no negative or positive effect on criminal behavior except as it may be related to associations which are concerned with the legal codes. This neutral behavior is important especially as an occupier of the time of a child so that he is not in contact with criminal behavior during the time he is so engaged in the neutral behavior.
7. Differential associations may vary in frequency, duration, priority, and intensity. This means that associations with criminal behavior and also associations with anticriminal behavior vary in those respects. "Frequency" and "duration" as modalities of associations are obvious and need no explanation. "Priority" is assumed to be important in the sense that lawful behavior developed in early childhood may persist throughout life, and also that delinquent behavior developed in early childhood may persist throughout

life. This tendency, however, has not been adequately demonstrated, and priority seems to be important principally through its selective influence. "Intensity" is not precisely defined but it has to do with such things as the prestige of the source of a criminal or anticriminal pattern and with emotional reactions related to the associations. In a precise description of the criminal behavior of a person, these modalities would be stated in quantitative form and a mathematical ratio be reached. A formula in this sense has not been developed, and the development of such a formula would be extremely difficult.

8. The process of learning criminal behavior by association with criminal and anticriminal patterns involves all of the mechanisms that are involved in any other learning. Negatively, this means that the learning of criminal behavior is not restricted to the process of imitation. A person who is seduced, for instance, learns criminal behavior by association, but this process would not ordinarily be described as imitation.

9. While criminal behavior is an expression of general needs and values, it is not explained by those general needs and values since noncriminal behavior is an expression of the same needs and values. Thieves generally steal in order to secure money, but likewise honest laborers work in order to secure money. The attempts by many scholars to explain criminal behavior by general drives and values, such as the happiness principle, striving for social status, the money motive, or frustration, have been and must continue to be futile since they explain lawful behavior as completely as they explain criminal behavior. They are similar to respiration, which is necessary for any behavior but which does not differentiate criminal from noncriminal behavior.

It is not necessary, at this level of explanation, to explain why a person has the associations which he has; this certainly involves a complex of many things. In an area where the delinquency rate is high, a boy who is sociable, gregarious, active, and athletic is very likely to come in contact with the other boys in the neighborhood, learn delinquent behavior from them, and become a gangster; in the same neighborhood the psychopathic boy who is isolated, introverted, and inert may remain at home, not become acquainted with the other boys in the neighborhood, and not become delinquent. In another situation, the sociable, athletic, aggressive boy may become a member of a scout troop and not become involved in delinquent behavior. The person's associations are determined in a general context of social organization. A child is ordinarily reared in a family; the place of residence of the family is determined largely by family income; and the delinquency rate is in many respects related to rental value of the houses. Many other aspects of social organization affect the kinds of associations a person has.

The preceding explanation of criminal behavior purports to explain the criminal and noncriminal behavior of individual persons. As indicated earlier, it is possible to state sociological theories of criminal behavior which explain the criminality of a community, nation, or other group. The problem, when thus stated, is to account for variations in crime rates and involves a comparison of the crime rates of various groups or the crime rates of a particular group at different times. The explanation of a crime rate must be consistent with the explanation of the criminal behavior of the person, since the crime rate is a summary statement of the number of persons in the group who commit crimes and the frequency with which they commit crimes. One of the best explanations of crime rates from this point of view is that a high crime rate is due to "social disorganization." The term "social disorganization" is not entirely satisfactory and it seems preferable to substitute for it the term "differential social organization." The postulate on which this theory is based, regardless of the name, is that crime is rooted in the social organization and is an expression of that social organization. A group may be organized for criminal behavior or organized against criminal behavior. Most communities are organized both for criminal and anti-criminal behavior and in that sense the crime rate is an expression of the differential group organization. Differential group organization as an explanation of variations in crime rates is consistent with the differential association theory of processes by which persons become criminals.

QUESTIONS FOR DISCUSSION AND WRITING

1. What are the nine propositions of differential association theory?
2. Provide an example (using people you know or have knowledge of from the media) that supports differential association theory.
3. Which is more likely to become delinquent in a high-delinquency area: a sociable, gregarious, active boy or one who is a psychopathic loner?

The Current State of Differential Association Theory

ROSS L. MATSUEDA

EDWIN Sutherland's differential association theory marked a watershed in criminology. The theory was instrumental in bringing the perspective of sociology to the forefront of criminology. Before then, criminological research and thought tended to be eclectic and unorganized, lacking a general theoretical perspective to integrate findings and guide research. Through the years, differential association theory has stimulated theoretical refinements and revisions, empirical research, and applications to programs and policy. The first two decades saw several attempts to revise the theory to explain the origin and persistence of delinquent subcultures, to incorporate principles of symbolic interaction and role theory, and to incorporate social learning principles. During the past decade, the trend of theoretical innovation has been supplanted by two distinct trends. The first focuses on testing the theory: devising methods for operationalizing the theory's concepts, deriving hypotheses from its propositions, and subjecting those hypotheses to empirical verification. The second entails rejecting the theory's principles in favor of social control or inte-

grated theories. This trend was originally stimulated by Kornhauser's theoretical critique of differential association theory, and Hirschi's empirical study supporting his social control theory.

This chapter examines the current state of differential association theory. It begins by reviewing the intellectual development of Sutherland's theory. It then assesses the evolution of the empirical test of the theory's propositions, as well as evaluating theoretical attempts to revise those propositions. Finally, the chapter outlines directions for future research, arguing that the most fruitful line of research is that which identifies the concrete historical content of the theory's abstract mechanisms, principles, and concepts. Such research would have several payoffs: enriching and perhaps modifying the theory's abstract principles, allowing the theory to make concrete predictions, and suggesting ways of translating the theory into public policy.

THEORETICAL DEVELOPMENTS AND EMPIRICAL RESEARCH

Differential association theory has spawned two major developments—one empirical, the other theoretical. Empirical research has tackled the difficult problem of operationalizing the theory's concepts, deriving hypotheses, and testing propositions. Theoretical developments have explored several crucial problems raised by the theory, such as identifying the precise mechanisms by which crime is learned and specifying a theory of the origins of delinquent subcultures.

Operationalizing and Testing the Theory

Perhaps the most serious criticism of differential association argues that the theory cannot be tested empirically. Cressey has argued that even though the theory may be untestable, it remains an important principle for organizing our knowledge about the correlates of crime. Others claim that the theory is of little value if it cannot be tested. Some versions of this criticism are on shaky ground because they fail to recognize that theories—being sets of interrelated propositions explaining a given phenomenon—are rarely testable as a whole. What are testable are specific hypotheses, propositions, or empirical implications of the theory. Another version of this criticism is on safer ground. It argues that the critical variable in the individual-level explanation—an excess of definitions favorable to crime—cannot be observed or measured. Sutherland noted that implicit in the abstract theory of differential association is the possibility of deriving a mathematical formula expressing a person's ratio of weighted definitions favorable and unfavorable to a specific crime. Even he admitted, however, to the difficulty of formulating such an expression.

Early empirical studies of juvenile delinquency operationalized differential association theory using the concept of associations with delinquent peers, and the frequency, duration, priority, and intensity of such associations. Most of these studies found general support for the theory: juveniles who reported more delinquent friends tended to commit more delinquent acts. This strategy assumes that most delinquent behaviors are learned from one's peers, that delinquent peers are

likely to transmit delinquency and nondelinquent peers nondelinquency, and therefore the concept of delinquent peers is highly correlated with the concept of associations with definitions favorable and unfavorable to delinquency. The problem with this strategy is that it fails to measure directly the crucial variable, learned definitions of law violation. It is conceivable that some definitions favoring law violation are learned from nondelinquents and some definitions favoring conformity are learned from delinquents. Furthermore, because it relies on cross-sectional data, the strategy cannot rule out a hypothesis based on the opposite causal ordering, such as Glueck and Glueck's "birds of a feather flock together."

Several researchers facilitated a more direct strategy of operationalizing the theory by identifying the content of definitions favorable to crime and delinquency. Thus, Cressey showed how verbalizations and rationalizations made up an important component of such definitions, then illustrated them with his studies of embezzlement and compulsive crimes. Sykes and Matza then developed their concept of techniques of neutralization to illustrate prodelinquent definitions used by juveniles. Researchers have taken advantage of these refinements and developed survey instruments to measure a person's learned definitions of law violation.

More recently, researchers have used advances in structural equation modeling to address three issues: response errors in measures of definitions of crime, dynamic processes inherent in the theory, and offense-specific models. Orcutt found that consistent with differential association theory, marijuana smoking is explained by definitions favorable to marijuana use and number of friends who smoke marijuana. Moreover, he found an interaction effect between the two variables, concluding that, as Sutherland suggested, predictions from differential association theory are increasingly uncertain as the ratio of definitions favorable and unfavorable to crime approaches unity.

In my own work, I conceptualize the ratio of definitions of law violation as an unobservable, latent construct, which cannot be measured perfectly, but can be measured approximately by observable indicators from surveys. Using this strategy, we found that differential association is empirically supported: for both black and nonblack males, the process of learning definitions favorable and unfavorable to delinquency is the intervening mechanism explaining the influence on delinquency of age, broken homes, socioeconomic status, neighborhood trouble, and parental and peer processes. One limitation of this line of research is that it relies on cross-sectional data to examine an inherently dynamic theory.

Tittle and his colleagues used simultaneous equation models to model the dynamic nature of the theory and to examine whether or not the differential association process is offense specific. They also examined the efficacy of several distinct operational measures, including associations with criminals, criminal attitudes, criminal normative expectations, fear of legal sanctions, and deviant motives. Using a variety of measures of the differential association process and seeking to disentangle their causal interrelationships, they found that a measure of motivation to deviate was a strong predictor, that the differential association process worked similarly for a variety of offenses, and that for some offenses, an offense-specific process appeared evident. Although this line of research addresses the dynamic nature of the theory, a better strategy would capitalize on longitudinal data, using panel or event history analysis.

Revisions of the Theory

A number of criminologists have attempted to revise the theory of differential association so it would be more amenable to empirical test. Following the spirit of Sutherland's method, these theorists drew from principles of more general social psychological theories—namely, symbolic interaction and social learning. Thus, Cressey applied the interactionist concepts of role-taking and motivation to link learned definitions of law violation to social roles, the building blocks of social structure. Glaser applied the interactionist concept of the self, arriving at his hypothesis of differential identification. He subsequently incorporated the concepts of commitment and role-taking and generalized his explanation to differential anticipation. Other researchers have built upon these principles, investigating personality and containment. This line of theorizing has great theoretical potential, but still requires additional development. Thus a more explicit conceptualization of the important elements of role-taking and cognitive processes are needed before operational measures can be located, and hypotheses derived and tested.

The second line of revision incorporates principles of operant conditioning and social learning theory to specify the precise mechanisms by which crime is learned. Early versions incorporated Skinner's principles of classical and operant conditioning, while later versions added Bandura's social learning principles. According to Akers's social learning theory, crime is initially learned through direct imitation or modeling; the subsequent likelihood of sustaining criminal behavior is determined by differential reinforcement, the relative rewards and punishments following the act. Reinforcement can be direct or vicarious, whereby simply observing another's criminal behavior being reinforced will reinforce the observer's own criminal behavior. Definitions of crime are learned through this process and affect behavior directly, as well as indirectly, by serving as cues (discriminative stimuli) for law violation. Akers and his colleagues have not only specified a social learning theory, they have also developed operational indicators of imitation, differential reinforcement, and definitions of deviance. Moreover, they find that social learning theory explains substantial variation in substance abuse and smoking. Additional theoretical work needs to identify the important reinforcers for various definitions, explicitly link these to social organization and social structure, and specify a situational model of cognition and role-taking using social learning principles.

A third set of revisions attempted to answer two important theoretical questions implied by differential association theory. The first concerned the origins of crime: "Where did normative conflict or definitions favorable to crime come from?" The second concerned the specific nature of differential social organization: "What are the social structural elements that influence rates of crime?" Both questions prompted research on the origins and persistence of subcultural delinquency as a phenomenon of lower-class adolescent males. For Cohen, working-class subcultural delinquency results when lower-class adolescents, who lack the requisite social and academic skills due to cultural and structural barriers, fail to live up to middle-class standards. Those adolescents perceive a sense of personal failure and typically find themselves together in the market for a solution. Through a tentative, probing conversation of gestures—a process best characterized as one of trial and error—a group collectively innovates a new status hierarchy, a delinquent subculture. Reaction formation explains the content of a subculture: they reduce their anxiety, exaggerating their disdain for middle-class values, leading to definitions favorable to delinquent behaviors that are impulsive, malicious, and irrational from the standpoint of the middle class.

For Cloward and Ohlin, the distribution of delinquent subcultures results from the structures of legitimate and illegitimate opportunity. Borrowing from Merton, they argue adolescents share middle-class aspirations of improving their economic status, but are structurally blocked from attaining those goals. Those who attribute their failure to a personal shortcoming are likely to adopt an isolated solution (turning to drugs) to end their frustration, while those attributing failure to the inequitable social system, are more likely to adopt a collective solution (turning to violent or criminal gangs). These solutions are structured by illegitimate opportunity—the opportunity to engage in delinquency, to learn delinquent definitions, and to learn techniques of delinquency—which varies by neighborhood organization.

Such structures constitute Sutherland's "organization in favor of crime." In integrated lower-class neighborhoods, in which bonds form between criminal and conventional roles (such as fences and fixes) and between older and younger offenders, stable subcultures of theft flourish. In unintegrated, disorganized neighborhoods, little opportunity exists to learn and execute such sophisticated crimes, and instead, frustrated youth must turn to violence to obtain status and vent hostility. Finally, in neighborhoods lacking such organization, drug subcultures develop. Most empirical research on this issue, however, has been unable to locate such distinct subcultures, finding instead a single parent subculture.

The importance of this work lies in its attempts to identify the concrete content of differential social organization and its attempt to explain the origins of definitions favorable to subcultural delinquency. Unfortunately, recent empirical research has trivialized this line of theorizing by confusing levels of explanation—reducing social structural concepts to individual-level characteristics—and by applying the explanation to explain all forms of delinquency, not merely the subcultural form. It is not surprising that such research finds the trivialized theories unsupported.

DIRECTIONS FOR FUTURE RESEARCH

Research that has operationalized, tested, and challenged differential association theory continues to be significant for understanding the strengths and limitations of the theory's principles. There is, however, a second line of research that is sorely needed: research that specifies the concrete elements of the theory's abstract principles—definitions favorable to crime, differential social organization, and normative conflict. Such research would examine the social organization of crime in a given historical and geographical context, answering questions such as, "What are the important definitions favorable to crime used by certain groups?" "What are the critical institutional elements of differential social organization?" and "What components of social structure are most important for sustaining normative conflict?" Given these abstract concepts, historical content will have enormous payoffs. It will make the propositions derived from the theory easier to operationalize and test. It will allow us to make concrete predictions based on the theory and provide implications for public policy. It will also suggest ways to revise the theory's general principles in light of the evidence. Moreover, such a strategy would enrich the theory by giving meaning to the abstract concepts—indeed by bringing them life—and revealing concrete causal mechanisms. Such concrete studies, carried out at different levels of explanation—societal, group, individual, and situational—would draw from the broader behavioral and social theories from which differential association is derived. They would not be limited to static studies but would also examine developmental processes culminating in individual changes and historical processes culminating in societal changes.

Perhaps the most fundamental research problem facing differential association theory involves identifying the content of definitions favorable to crime. Such content is likely to vary throughout history, across communication groups, and by criminal offense, such that a definition of crime pertinent to one offense, one group, and one period of time may be irrelevant for another offense, another group, and another time period. It seems clear that the preponderance of definitions favorable to crime are not oppositional values that repudiate the legitimacy of the law and make crimes morally correct. Rather, most are verbalizations that seek to fit general norms and laws to specific concrete situations. What is needed is a series of inductive studies cataloging important definitions applied to behavior by various groups, and situational studies examining the process by which individuals apply such verbalizations to conduct. This research would likely identify other variations in definitions besides Sutherland's four modalities, and perhaps lead to an alternative causal statement to the concept of a ratio of definitions. For example, the strength of a definition favorable or unfavorable to crime clearly depends in part on its persuasiveness, the rhetorical force of the underlying argument. Indeed, sociolinguistic research on the structure of arguments may be relevant. The definitions concept is likely a multidimensional construct, and research is needed to identify these dimensions.

A second problem requiring research concerns the relationships among roles, role-taking, and definitions favorable and unfavorable to crime. With the concept of role, the building block of social structure, lies the link between the social learning process specified in differential association and the broader social processes identified by differential social organization. This line of research would build on the work of Cressey, Glaser, and Weinberg in specifying a symbolic interactionist theory of role-taking, the social act, and motivation, which is consistent with Sutherland's thinking. Here, one could address the difficult problem of specifying a situational as opposed to developmental theory of crime. Sutherland first made this distinction, arguing that while differential association was a developmental theory, which explained criminality in terms of the prior life experiences of the individual, an equally important problem is explaining crime in terms of the immediate situation confronting the individual. Such an explanation could explain the mechanisms by which a person who has already learned an excess of definitions favorable to crime either engages in or refrains from crime. Thus, the explanation would include the intersection of objective opportunity, interactions or role-taking with others, and the process by which learned definitions are interpreted and applied to a developing line of action. Theoretically, this would call for use of group-process, interactional, and collective behavior theories, as well as theories of choice. Concretely, it would answer questions that Sutherland raised years ago, but did not answer: "What role does objective opportunity and alternative behaviors play in the immediate situation confronting the actor?" "To what extent do criminals learn definitions favorable to crime and then actively seek criminal opportunities and actively ignore conventional alternatives?" Furthermore, it would provide a frame of reference for examining how groups control the behavior of their members, including informal and formal sanctions.

From an interactionist perspective, individuals learn, through socialization, to take the role of the generalized other—including primarily personal groups, but also abstract groups, such as the criminal justice system—and consider their anticipated behaviors from the standpoint of the group. Thus, the definitions and sanctions of personal groups would be most important in controlling behavior. Formal sanctions would be expected to influence behavior inasmuch as the individual takes the role of the legal system, and more important, to the extent that his or her personal groups espouse the norms and fear the sanctions of the legal system, with his theories of differential social control and differential anticipation, has begun to spell out principles consistent with this framework. It is quite likely that this situational model of the criminal act would prove equally useful as a model of learning criminal behavior. The best example of research along these lines is still Short and Strodtbeck's classic study of group process and gang delinquency.

Group influences are, of course, structured by the backdrop of larger institutions and social structures. Much research has shown that neighborhood and community organization, family structures and processes, and school organization are crucial elements of differential social organization, which explain aggregate rates of crime. Such institutions can control crime by serving as conduits for anticriminal definitions, by hampering the dissemination of procriminal patterns, and by providing conventional opportunities while desiccating criminal opportunities. An important line of research would examine dynamic changes in differential social organization (including changes in these institutional contexts) on aggregate rates of crime. It would also examine the dynamic influence of the social organization of objective opportunities, as developed in the routine activities approach.

Although Sutherland did not specify a theory of social structure in differential association, he did discuss the importance of components of social structure, such as social class, for structuring group organizations and learning processes. Moreover, Sutherland presented a complex analysis of the origins of normative conflict, arguing that industrialization and the emergence of capitalism debilitated traditional forms of social control and spawned motives for crime. Specifically, with industrialization and the transition from the old feudal order to capitalism, old institutions and controls, such as the church, were weakened. Concomitantly, capitalist competition fostered an individualism and materialism that was easily transformed into criminality. And finally, the law as an agency of control was weakened by the interests of powerful business, which favored a "hands-off" government and often resorted to white-collar crimes to gain a competitive edge. Cressey later expanded this analysis, drawing explicitly on the writings of Durkheim, Weber, and Merton.

The abstract principles of differential association theory are compatible with other theories of social structure, such as Marxist theories of class structure under capitalism. In fact, differential association theory seems more compatible with a Marxist political economic theory than is social control theory, even though recent writings have attempted to combine the latter two. For any Marxian class analysis, the fundamental underlying structure of capitalist society is class conflict between capitalists and workers. Their contradictory class locations give rise to conflicting material interests; thus, history is a history of class struggle, of which the state, law, and criminal justice system play a critical role in maintaining the hegemony of capitalist institutions. Such rudimentary assumptions are consistent with the underlying model of normative conflict assumed by differential association—economic classes struggling to realize their interests, with the powerful capitalist class securing the state to promote its class interests. The seeds of political consciousness in the working class, which are revealed at times by embryonic acts of protest, strikes, and violence, consist of competing interpretations and definitions of conventional norms and laws. Social control theory, in contrast, assumes a consensual moral order, in which competing definitions, beliefs, and motives are either nonexistent or impotent to explain behavior. Even Colvin and Pauly, who claim to consider variation in both the strength and content of the social bond, fail to allow for conflicting motives and interests held by the working class. The problem is in the use of the concept of social bond, which eliminates meaning and interests, and instead focuses exclusively on conventional controls.

CONCLUSION

Fifty years ago, Sutherland outlined a series of abstract principles, derived from broader principles of social psychology and sociology, that made sense of the many concrete conditions associated with crime. The explanation was intended to arrive at a universal explanation of crime. While concrete conditions may vary across groups, societies, and history, the abstract mechanisms would remain invariant. It was a bold endeavor, bringing both fame and criticism. Although Sutherland intended his differential association theory to be a "tentative hypothesis," subject to disconfirmation and eventual revision, he viewed his methodology of searching for universal explanations as the essence of good science. I have attempted to demonstrate the strengths and limitations of Sutherland's theory, showing that his general principles and orientation are basically sound but that his explanation requires much more work. The search for abstract mechanisms, principles, and generalizations is crucial for the advancement of knowledge, revealing behavioral laws, suggesting concrete causal conditions, and implying targets for controlling crime. But we have scarcely scratched the surface; much work remains.

QUESTIONS FOR DISCUSSION AND WRITING

1. What is the most serious criticism of differential association?
2. What are two problems with assuming that delinquent peers "transmit" delinquency?
3. What is Akers' theory?

ANOMIE/STRAIN THEORY

Social Structure and Anomie

ROBERT K. MERTON

T HERE persists a notable tendency in sociological theory to attribute the malfunc-
tioning of social structure primarily to those of
man's imperious biological drives which are
not adequately restrained by social control. In
this view, the social order is solely a device for
"impulse management" and the "social processing" of tensions. These impulses which
break through social control, be it noted, are
held to be biologically derived. Nonconfor-
mity is assumed to be rooted in original nature. Conformity is by implication the result of
a utilitarian calculus or unreasoned conditioning. This point of view, whatever its other
deficiencies, clearly begs one question. It provides no basis for determining the nonbio-
logical conditions which induce deviations
from prescribed patterns of conduct. In this
[article], it will be suggested that certain
phases of social structure generate the circumstances in which infringement of social codes
constitutes a "normal" response.

The conceptual scheme to be outlined is designed to provide a coherent, systematic approach to the study of sociocultural sources of
deviate behavior. Our primary aim lies in discovering how some social structures *exert a
definite pressure* upon certain persons in the so-

From "Social Structure and Anomie" by R. K. Merton,
1938, *American Sociological Review* 3:672–682. Copyright ©
1938 by The American Sociological Association. Reprinted
with permission.

ciety to engage in nonconformist rather than
conformist conduct. The many ramifications
of the scheme cannot all be discussed; the
problems mentioned outnumber those explicitly treated.

Among the elements of social and cultural
structure, two are important for our purposes.
These are analytically separable although they
merge imperceptibly in concrete situations.
The first consists of culturally defined goals,
purposes, and interests. It comprises a frame
of aspirational reference. These goals are more
or less integrated and involve varying degrees
of prestige and sentiment. They constitute a
basic, but not the exclusive, component of
what Linton aptly has called "designs for
group living." Some of these cultural aspirations are related to the original drives of man,
but they are not determined by them. The second phase of the social structure defines, regu-
lates, and controls the acceptable modes of
achieving these goals. Every social group invariably couples its scale of desired ends with
moral or institutional regulation of permis-
sible and required procedures for attaining
these ends. These regulatory norms and moral
imperatives do not necessarily coincide with
technical or efficiency norms. Many procedures which from the standpoint of *particular
individuals* would be most efficient in securing
desired values, for example, illicit oil-stock
schemes, theft, fraud, are ruled out of the institutional area of permitted conduct. The

choice of expedients is limited by the institutional norms.

To say that these two elements, culture goals and institutional norms, operate jointly is not to say that the ranges of alternative behaviors and aims bear some constant relation to one another. The emphasis upon certain goals may vary independently of the degree of emphasis upon institutional means. There may develop a disproportionate, at times, a virtually exclusive, stress upon the value of specific goals, involving relatively slight concern with the institutionally appropriate modes of attaining these goals. The limiting case in this direction is reached when the range of alternative procedures is limited only by technical rather than institutional considerations. Any and all devices which promise attainment of the all important goal would be permitted in this hypothetical polar case. This constitutes one type of cultural malintegration. A second polar type is found in groups where activities originally conceived as instrumental are transmuted into ends in themselves. The original purposes are forgotten and ritualistic adherence to institutionally prescribed conduct becomes virtually obsessive.

Thus, in competitive athletics, when the aim of victory is shorn of its institutional trappings and success in contests becomes construed as "winning the game" rather than "winning through circumscribed modes of activity," a premium is implicitly set upon the use of illegitimate but technically efficient means. The star of the opposing football team is surreptitiously slugged; the wrestler furtively incapacitates his opponent through ingenious but illicit techniques; university alumni covertly subsidize "students" whose talents are largely confined to the athletic field. The emphasis on the goal has so attenuated the satisfactions deriving from sheer participation in the competitive activity that these satisfactions are virtually confined to a successful outcome. Through the same process, tension generated by the desire to win in a poker game is relieved by successfully dealing

oneself four aces, or, when the cult of success has become completely dominant, by sagaciously shuffling the cards in a game of solitaire. The faint twinge of uneasiness in the last instance and the surreptitious nature of public delicts indicate clearly that the institutional rules of the game *are known* to those who evade them, but that the emotional supports of these rules are largely vitiated by cultural exaggeration of the success-goal. They are microcosmic images of the social macrocosm.

Of course, this process is not restricted to the realm of sport. The process whereby exaltation of the end generates a *literal demoralization*, that is, a deinstitutionalization, of the means is one which characterizes many groups in which the two phases of the social structure are not highly integrated. The extreme emphasis upon the accumulation of wealth as a symbol of success in our own society militates against the completely effective control of institutionally regulated modes of acquiring a fortune. Fraud, corruption, vice, crime, in short, the entire catalogue of proscribed behavior, becomes increasingly common when the emphasis on the culturally induced success-goal becomes divorced from a coordinated institutional emphasis. This observation is of crucial theoretical importance in examining the doctrine that antisocial behavior most frequently derives from biological drives breaking through the restraints imposed by society. The difference is one between a strictly utilitarian interpretation which conceives man's ends as random and an analysis which finds these ends deriving from the basic values of the culture.

Our analysis can scarcely stop at this juncture. We must turn to other aspects of the social structure if we are to deal with the social genesis of the varying rates and types of deviate behavior characteristic of different societies. Thus far, we have sketched three ideal types of social orders constituted by distinctive patterns of relations between culture ends and means. Turning from these types of *culture patterning*, we find five logically possible, alternative modes of adjustment or adaptation *by individuals* within the culture-bearing society or group. These are schematically presented in the following table, where (+) signifies "acceptance," (−) signifies "elimination," and (±) signifies "rejection and substitution of new goals and standards."

		Culture Goals	Institutionalized Means
I.	Conformity	+	+
II.	Innovation	+	−
III.	Ritualism	−	+
IV.	Retreatism	−	−
V.	Rebellion	±	±

Our discussion of the relation between these alternative responses and other phases of the social structure must be prefaced by the observation that persons may shift from one alternative to another as they engage in different social activities. These categories refer to role adjustments in specific situations, not to personality *in toto*. To treat the development of this process in various spheres of conduct would introduce a complexity unmanageable within the confines of this chapter. For this reason, we shall be concerned primarily with economic activity in the broad sense, "the production, exchange, distribution and consumption of goods and services" in our competitive society, wherein wealth has taken on a highly symbolic cast. Our task is to search out some of the factors which exert pressure upon individuals to engage in certain of these logically possible alternative responses. This choice, as we shall see, is far from random.

In every society, Adaptation I (conformity to both culture goals and means) is the most common and widely diffused. Were this not so, the stability and continuity of the society could not be maintained. The mesh of expectancies which constitutes every social order is sustained by the modal behavior of its members falling within the first category. Conventional role behavior oriented toward the basic values of the group is the rule rather than the exception. It is this fact alone which permits us to speak of a human aggregate as comprising a group or society.

Conversely, Adaptation IV (rejection of goals and means) is the least common. Persons who "adjust" (or maladjust) in this fashion are, strictly speaking, *in* the society but not *of* it. Sociologically, these constitute the true "aliens." Not sharing the common frame of orientation, they can be included within the societal population merely in a fictional sense. In this category are *some* of the activities of psychotics, psychoneurotic, chronic autists, pariahs, outcasts, vagrants, vagabonds, tramps, chronic drunkards and drug addicts. These have relinquished, in certain spheres of activity, the culturally defined goals, involving complete aim—inhibition in the polar case, and their adjustments are not in accord with institutional norms. This is not to say that in some cases the source of their behavioral adjustments is not in part the very social structure which they have in effect repudiated nor that their very existence within a social area does not constitute a problem for the socialized population.

This mode of "adjustment" occurs, as far as structural sources are concerned, when both the culture goals and institutionalized procedures have been assimilated thoroughly by the individual and imbued with affect and high positive value, but where those institutionalized procedures which promise a measure of successful attainment of the goals are not available to the individual. In such instances, there results a twofold mental conflict insofar as the moral obligation for adopting institutional means conflicts with the pressure to resort to illegitimate means (which may attain the goal) and inasmuch as the individual is shut off from means which are both legitimate *and* effective. The competitive order is maintained, but the frustrated and handicapped individual who cannot cope with this order drops out. Defeatism, quietism, and resignation are manifested in escape mechanisms which ultimately lead the individual to "escape" from the requirements of the society. It is an expedient which arises from continued failure to attain the goal by legitimate measures and from an inability to adopt the illegitimate route because of internalized prohibitions and institutionalized compulsives, *during which process the supreme value of the success-goal has as yet not been renounced.* The conflict is resolved by eliminating *both* precipitating elements, the goals and means. The escape is complete, the conflict is eliminated, and the individual is socialized.

Be it noted that where frustration derives from the inaccessibility of effective institutional means for attaining economic or any other type of highly valued "success," that Adaptations II, III, and V (innovation, ritualism, and rebellion) are also possible. The result will be determined by the particular personality, and thus, the *particular* cultural background involved. Inadequate socialization will result in the innovation response whereby the conflict and frustration are eliminated by relinquishing the institutional means and retaining the success-aspiration; an extreme assimilation of institutional demands will lead to ritualism wherein the goal is dropped as beyond one's reach but conformity to the mores persists, and rebellion occurs when emancipation from the reigning standards, due to frustration or to marginalist perspectives, leads to the attempt to introduce a "new social order."

Our major concern is with the illegitimacy adjustment. This involves the use of conventionally proscribed but frequently effective means of attaining at least the simulacrum of culturally defined success—wealth, power, and the like. As we have seen, this adjustment occurs when the individual has assimilated the cultural emphasis on success without equally internalizing the morally prescribed norms governing means for its attainment. The question arises, Which phases of our social structure predispose toward this mode of adjustment? We may examine a concrete instance, effectively analyzed by Lohman, which provides a clue to the answer. Lohman has shown that specialized areas of vice in the near north side of Chicago constitute a "normal" response to a situation where the cultural emphasis upon pecuniary success has been absorbed, but where there is little access to conventional and legitimate means for attaining such success. The conventional occupational opportunities of persons in this area are almost completely limited to manual labor. Given our cultural stigmatization of manual labor, and its correlate, the prestige of white-collar work, it is clear that the result is a strain toward innovative] practices. The limitation of opportunity to unskilled labor and the resultant low income cannot compete in terms of conventional standards of achievement with the high income from organized vice.

For our purposes, this situation involves two important features. First, such antisocial behavior is in a sense "called forth" by certain conventional values of the culture *and* by the class structure involving differential access to the approved opportunities for legitimate, prestige-bearing pursuit of the culture goals. The lack of high integration between the means-and-end elements of the cultural pattern and the particular class structure combine to favor a heightened frequency of antisocial conduct in such groups. The second consideration is of equal significance. Recourse to the first of the alternative responses, legitimate effort, is limited by the fact that actual advance toward desired success-symbols through conventional channels is, despite our persisting open-class ideology, relatively rare and difficult for those handicapped by little formal education and few economic resources. The dominant pressure of group standards of success is, therefore, on the gradual attenuation of legitimate, but by and large ineffective, strivings, and the increasing use of illegitimate, but more or less effective, expedients of vice and crime. The cultural demands made on persons in this situation are incompatible. On the one hand, they are asked to orient their conduct toward the prospect of accumulating wealth and on the other, they are largely denied effective opportunities to do so institutionally. The consequences of such structural inconsistency are psychopathological personality, and/or antisocial conduct, and/or revolutionary activities. The equilibrium between culturally designated means and ends becomes highly unstable with the progressive emphasis on attaining the prestige-laden ends by any means whatsoever. Within this context, Capone represents the triumph of amoral intelligence over morally prescribed "failure," when the channels of vertical mobility are closed or narrowed *in a society which places a high premium on economic affluence and social ascent for all its members.*

This last qualification is of primary importance. It suggests that other phases of the social structure besides the extreme emphasis on pecuniary success must be considered if we are to understand the social sources of antisocial behavior. A high frequency of deviate behavior is not generated simply by "lack of opportunity" or by this exaggerated pecuniary emphasis. A comparatively rigidified class structure, a feudalistic or caste order, may limit such opportunities far beyond the point which obtains in our society today. It is only when a system of cultural values extols, virtually above all else, certain *common* symbols of success *for the population at large* while its social structure rigorously restricts or completely eliminates access to approved modes of acquiring these symbols *for a considerable part of the same population* that antisocial behavior ensues on a considerable scale. In other words, our egalitarian ideology denies by implication the existence of noncompeting groups and individuals in the pursuit of pecuniary success. The same body of success-symbols is held to be desirable for all. These goals are held to *transcend class lines,* not to be bounded by them, yet the actual social organization is such that there exist class differentials in the accessibility of these *common* success-symbols. Frustration and thwarted aspiration lead to the search for avenues of escape from a culturally induced intolerable situation; or unrelieved ambition may eventuate in illicit attempts to acquire the dominant values. The American stress on pecuniary success and ambitiousness for all thus invites exaggerated anxieties, hostilities, neuroses, and antisocial behavior.

This theoretical analysis may go far toward explaining the varying correlations between crime and poverty. Poverty is not an isolated variable. It is one in a complex of interdependent social and cultural variables. When viewed in such a context, it represents quite different states of affairs. Poverty as such, and consequent limitation of opportunity, are not sufficient to induce a conspicuously high rate of criminal behavior. Even the often-mentioned "poverty in the midst of plenty" will not necessarily lead to this result. Only insofar as poverty and associated disadvantages in competition for the culture values approved for all members of the society is linked with the assimilation of a cultural emphasis on monetary accumulation as a symbol of success is antisocial conduct a "normal" outcome. Thus, poverty is less highly correlated with crime in southeastern Europe than in the United States. The possibilities of vertical mobility in these European areas would seem to be fewer than in this country, so that neither poverty *per se* nor its association with limited opportunity is sufficient to account for the varying correlations. It is only when the full configuration is considered, poverty, limited opportunity, and a commonly shared system of success symbols, that we can explain the higher association between poverty and crime in our society than in others where rigidified class structure is coupled with *differential class symbols of achievement.*

In societies such as our own, then, the pressure of prestige-bearing success tends to eliminate the effective social constraint over means employed to this end. "The-end-justifies-the-means" doctrine becomes a guiding tenet for action when the cultural structure unduly exalts the end and the social organization unduly limits possible recourse to approved means. Otherwise put, this notion and associated behavior reflect a lack of cultural coordination. In international relations, the effects of this lack of integration are notoriously apparent. An emphasis upon national power is not readily coordinated with an inept organization of legitimate, that is, internationally defined and accepted, means for attaining this goal. The result is a tendency toward the abrogation of international law, treaties become scraps of paper, "undeclared warfare" serves as a technical evasion, the bombing of civilian populations is rationalized just as the same societal situation induces the same sway of illegitimacy among individuals.

The social order we have described necessarily produces this "strain toward dissolutions." The pressure of such an order is upon outdoing one's competitors. The choice of means within the ambit of institutional control will persist as long as the sentiments supporting a competitive system, that is, deriving from the possibility of outranking competitors and hence enjoying the favorable response of others, are distributed throughout the entire system of activities and are not confined merely to the final result. A stable social structure demands a balanced distribution of affect among its various segments. When there occurs a shift of emphasis from the satisfactions deriving from competition itself to almost exclusive concern with successful competition, the resultant stress leads to the breakdown of the regulatory structures. With the resulting attenuation of the institutional imperatives, there occurs an approximation of the situation erroneously held by utilitarians to be typical of society generally wherein calculations of advantage and fear of punishment are the sole regulating agencies. In such situations, as Hobbes observed, force and fraud come to constitute the sole virtues in view of their relative efficiency in attaining goals which were for him, of course, not culturally derived.

It should be apparent that the foregoing discussion is not pitched on a moralistic plane. Whatever the sentiments of the writer or reader concerning the ethical desirability of coordinating the means-and-goals phases of the social structure, one must agree that lack of such coordination leads to anomie. Insofar as one of the most general functions of social organization is to provide a basis for calculability and regularity of behavior, it is increasingly limited in effectiveness as these elements of the structure become dissociated. At the extreme, predictability virtually disappears and what may be properly termed cultural chaos or anomie intervenes.

This statement, being brief, is also incomplete. It has not included an exhaustive treatment of the various structural elements which predispose toward one rather than another of the alternative responses open to individuals; it has neglected, but not denied the relevance of, the factors determining the specific incidence of these responses; it has not enumerated the various concrete responses which are constituted by combinations of specific values of the analytical variables; it has omitted, or included only by implication, any consideration of the social functions performed by illicit responses; it has not tested the full explanatory power of the analytical scheme by examining a large number of group variations in the frequency of deviate and conformist behavior; it has not adequately dealt with rebellious conduct which seeks to refashion the social framework radically; it has not examined the relevance of cultural conflict for an analysis of culture-goal and institutional-means malintegration. It is suggested that these and related problems may be profitably analyzed by this scheme.

QUESTIONS FOR DISCUSSION AND WRITING

1. What two elements of social and cultural structure are important for Merton's theory?
2. How does "extreme emphasis on the accumulation of wealth" relate to crime?
3. What are Merton's five adaptations?

Contemporary Research

General Strain Theory and Delinquency: A Replication and Extension

RAYMOND PATERNOSTER

PAUL MAZEROLLE

I N a series of articles, Agnew has presented a revised version of strain theory that includes, but in important ways goes beyond, the original strain formulation. Rather than one source of strain, Agnew suggested three. In addition, he has conducted a detailed set of studies, which provided some empirical support for his theory and seemed to indicate that previous dismissals of strain theory may have been premature. Agnew's revitalized version of strain, general strain theory (GST), may therefore be a potentially important theoretical restatement that promises to complement extant criminological theory.

In the pages that follow we will briefly discuss the original strain formulation of Merton and the revisions and extensions offered by Agnew in his general strain theory. We will also review the attempts to date to empirically test GST and offer our assessment of the adequacy of these tests and what conclusions can and cannot be drawn from them. Based on the most detailed expositions of GST to date, we will then derive specific hypotheses sug-

gested by the theory. Next we will provide a detailed discussion of our indicators of GST's central theoretical constructs and how we will conduct our own empirical test of this theory.

TRADITIONAL AND GENERAL STRAIN THEORY

Traditional Strain Theories

In what we will call traditional strain theory, youths are motivated to commit delinquent acts because they have failed to achieve desired goals, such as middle-class status or economic success. In operationalizing this type of strain, most researchers have measured it in terms of conventional aspirations, conventional expectations, or as a discrepancy between the two. Moreover, initial tests of traditional strain theory have focused on long-range (educational/occupational) goals. Although some studies found that educational aspirations/expectations were positively related to delinquency, support for strain theory has not generally been particularly strong. With few exceptions, measured discrepancies between occupational/educational aspirations and expectations have generally been found to be unrelated to delinquent behavior.

Additionally, the possession of conventional aspirations has frequently been found to be inversely related to self-reported delinquency, which is contrary to theoretical expectations. Although traditional strain theory enjoyed a long tenure within the criminological community, its popularity slowly waned in large measure because of these consistently null findings. An exception to these generally null findings was a recent reconceptualization by Farnworth and Leiber. They found support for strain when it was measured as the disjunction between economic goals and educational expectations. In general, however, the empirical evidence has not been supportive of these versions of strain theory.

Rather than departing entirely from the criminological scene, however, strain theory underwent a brief reconceptualization in the 1970s. These revised strain theories adopted the traditional assumption that strain is due to the failure to achieve desired and valued goals, but altered the temporal nature of these goals. Rather than aspiring to long-range goals, adolescents were now conceived as being motivated toward the satisfaction of more short-term and immediate wants, such as athletic success, good grades, and popularity with peers. These revisions of the theory suggested that strain is produced whenever adolescents fail to achieve their more immediate goals. These revised versions of strain theory, however, met the same fate as their earlier counterpart; weak empirical support existed for the presumption that those adolescents who failed to achieve their immediate goals were more likely to be delinquent than those who were more successful.

Agnew's GST

In response to the lack of empirical support for strain theory, Agnew has developed a more comprehensive version. In his GST, Agnew suggested that previous versions of the theory have been unduly narrow in their conceptualization of the sources of strain. In addition to the failure to achieve desired goals, he contends that strain can also be brought about when others take away from us something that we value and when we are confronted with negative or disagreeable circumstances. One sense in which GST is general, then, is that the sources of strain are far more pervasive and extensive than previous strain theorists have articulated—strain is a more general phenomenon than the discrepancy between aspirations and expectations.

Although strain is a necessary cause of delinquency, it is not sufficient. A critical intervening variable in GST is the psychological state of "negative affect," which includes disappointment, frustration, and most importantly, anger. As a solution to the undesirable affective state of anger, delinquency can be instrumental (as one tries to regain what one has lost or obtain what one has been prevented from obtaining), retaliatory (as one strikes back at the source of strain), and escapist (as one attempts to seek solace from the disagreeable states of anger and strain). In response to strain and its attendant negative emotional states, therefore, adolescents can respond with acts of theft, violence, vandalism, and drug/alcohol use. A second sense in which GST is general, then, is that it can potentially explain a diverse range of delinquent behaviors.

In addition to describing the antecedent (strain) and intervening (negative affect) causes of delinquency, Agnew has offered a detailed discussion of possible conditional factors. Agnew first notes that not all strain is equally disagreeable, that is, strain is not a discrete experience but varies in its magnitude (how much discomfort is inflicted), its recency (recent events are more stressful and unpleasant than older ones), its duration (strain experienced over longer time periods is more stressful), and its clustering (many stressful events experienced over a short time period are more unpleasant because coping resources become taxed). Second, Agnew notes that in some instances strain does not result in delinquent solutions because stress and consequent negative affective states can be effectively handled or managed.

Even when strain is perceived to be a particularly unpleasant experience that one can neither cope with nor manage, there are various constraints to delinquent and nondelinquent adaptations. Agnew suggests that a delinquent adaptation to strain is more likely for those with a disposition to engage in delinquency because of "certain temperamental variables" (perhaps, self-control; see Gottfredson and Hirschi) and those with delinquent peers. Conversely, a delinquent adaptation is less likely for those high in self-efficacy, those with conventional social support, and those with strong moral restraints. Strain, then, is likely to lead to a delinquent solution when it cannot be managed, when constraints to nondelinquent solutions are strong, and when constraints to delinquent solutions are weak.

Initial Empirical Tests of GST

In addition to formulating a new version of strain theory, Agnew has been at the forefront in empirically testing his theory. In the first of several reported tests in the literature, Agnew found that negative relationships with parents and teachers and dissatisfaction with school were each positively related to adolescents' feelings of anger, which in turn were positively related to three forms of delinquent behavior (serious delinquency, aggression, school deviance). In a second, longitudinal study, Agnew found a relationship between these negative experiences and subsequent delinquency, further corroborating key features of his proposed causal model of delinquency.

The most comprehensive empirical test to date of GST was recently conducted by Agnew and White. Using longitudinal data from the Rutgers Health and Human Development Project (HHDP), they constructed eight different measures of strain, eight social control/differential association measures, and two measures of deviance (delinquency and drug use). In a cross-sectional regression analysis, they found that even with controls for social control/differential association variables, four measures of strain were significantly related to prior delinquency and drug use. They also found that a composite measure of general strain was as strongly related to prior delinquency as a composite scale of social control. They reported that this composite strain measure had a significantly stronger effect on the delinquency and drug use measures at higher levels of delinquent peers and a significantly weaker effect for youths with high levels of self-efficacy. . . .

Encouraged by Agnew and White's initial findings, in the present research we conduct what we believe to be a more comprehensive test of GST. Essentially, we attempted to both replicate and extend Agnew and White's original work. Based on Agnew's theoretical discussions, we have constructed several different types or sources of general strain, some of which directly parallel those used by Agnew and White. In addition to capturing several different types of strain, we were able to measure variations in their magnitude and duration, as well as adolescents' attempts to manage or cope with strain by diminishing its importance. We also constructed measures of several variables discussed by Agnew that could interact with strain. We are able to determine if the effect of strain on delinquency is greater for those youths with a large proportion of delinquent peers, with low self-control, with weak self-efficacy, who have weak conventional social support, and with weak moral inhibitions against offending.

Like Agnew and White, our data are longitudinal. Unlike their data, however, the recall period for our delinquency and strain items was a consistent 1-year time period. We also pursue a suggestion of Agnew's that general strain may have an indirect effect on delinquency by weakening the social bond and strengthening involvement with delinquent peers. We present and test a very rudimentary causal model that connects general strain to social control and differential association variables.

DATA AND MEASURES

Sample

The data for our empirical test come from the first and second waves of the National Youth Survey (NYS), a longitudinal study of the correlates of delinquency and drug use. The NYS employed a probability sample of households in the continental United States and drew 2,360 eligible youths ranging in age from 11 to 17. Of these 2,360 eligible youths, 1,725 (73%) agreed to participate in the study and were interviewed at the first wave. Of the 1,725 adolescents first interviewed, 1,655 participated in the reinterviews 1 year later. With a listwise deletion of missing cases, this was reduced to 1,525.

Measures of Exogenous Variables

STRAIN MEASURES It should be kept in mind that both the loss of positive stimuli and the presence of negative stimuli have a central conceptual role in Agnew's GST. In his discussion of these aversive events and experiences, Agnew has included such things as residence in an unappealing and unsafe neighborhood, stressful life events, and disagreeable relationships with adults and peers:

The loss of positive stimuli might include such things as the loss of a boyfriend/girlfriend, moving from one's neighborhood, or the death of a parent. The presentation of noxious or negative stimuli might include criminal victimization of various types; a wide assortment of stressful life events; and negative relations with parents, teachers, and others—with such relations involving insults, verbal threats, and other noxious behavior.

In our operationalization of strain, we have attempted to measure these aversive features of persons' lives. Many of our concepts are operationalized in a manner similar to Agnew's measures in his most comprehensive empirical test of the theory.

Neighborhood Problems. This is a composite, summated scale reflecting the degree to which respondents lived in a stressful physical environment. Respondents' parents were asked to estimate how much of a problem vandalism, winos and junkies, traffic, abandoned houses, burglaries and thefts, run-down buildings, and assaults and muggings were in their neighborhood. A high score indicates that these conditions were perceived to constitute more of a problem in the neighborhood. . . .

Negative Life Events. Those who score high on this 13-item scale experienced more stressful events in the past year, such as the divorce/separation of a parent, death or serious injury to a family member, parental unemployment, or changing schools. Responses to the items were binary (yes, no), and the scale is a sum of the number of yes responses.

Negative Relations with Adults. This is a 17-item summated scale that measures the degree to which respondents feel that they have poor relations with their parents ("I am an outsider with my family," "My parents think I am messed up," "My family is not interested in my problems") and teachers ("Teachers don't call on me," "My teachers think I am messed up," "Teachers don't ask me to work on projects"). Each item of this scale reflects a negative or alienated relationship with an adult.

School/Peer Hassles. This is a seven-item summated scale that measures the degree to which respondents feel hassled and isolated by peers or disappointed and dissatisfied with their daily dealings with peers, teachers, and other students. High scores on this measure reflect more daily strain due to social isolation from peers and alienation from school.

Traditional Strain. This is a summated measure of traditional strain in terms of perceived limitations on goal attainment. Respondents were asked to estimate the chance that they would "get the job you'd like" and "complete a college degree." Those who reported that their chances were poor scored high, whereas those who reported that their chances were good scored low. The higher the score on these two items, therefore, the greater the strain. This measure of traditional strain in terms of frustrated goal attainment was highly correlated ($r = .86$) with a slightly different measure of strain constructed from these data that is similar to the one successfully used by Farnworth and Leiber. This measure was operationalized in terms of a disjunction between occupational goals and educational expectations.

CONCEPTUAL OVERLAP OF GENERAL STRAIN AND OTHER THEORIES A question may arise concerning the unique standing of GST because its central theoretical concepts may overlap with other theories of delinquency. For example, our measures of Negative Relations With Adults and Negative Life Events might be seen as indicators of social attachments from Hirschi's control theory because they both concern the social bonds between persons. In addition, the measure of Neighborhood Problems might be seen as a measure derived from routine activities or social disorganization theory rather than GST.

In response to such questions, Agnew, in his own work, has devoted considerable attention to the issue. With regard to the role of social relationships with others, Agnew is explicit in distinguishing general strain from control theory in terms of the negative valence of the social attachments. In social control theory, delinquency is made possible by the absence of positive relationships with conventional others. In this case, the lack of good social experiences acts to relax inhibitions to delinquency. In contrast, general strain theory focuses on the significance of negative relationships/experiences with others. Such negative relationships do not loosen inhibitions; rather, they serve as motivators for delinquent acts. For general strain theory, then, the fact that young people have negative social experiences is more important in explaining and understanding delinquency than whether they lack favorable ones.

Regarding the more general issue of conceptual overlap with other theories Agnew believes, and we concur, that the ultimate "proof of the pudding" lies in the relationship between GST's variables that may conceptually overlap with those from other theories and its unique set of intervening variables. Although GST may share some antecedent variables with other theories, such as negative relationships with conventional others, the experience of disruptive life events, and residence in crime-filled and deteriorated neighborhoods, it has a distinctive set of intervening mechanisms that are hypothesized to lead to crime and delinquency. Strain theory, unlike social control, social disorganization or routine activities theory, stipulates that aversive experiences and relationships result in specific negative affective states (anger, frustration, disappointment) that ultimately lead to delinquency. A full account of GST (and we do not pretend that ours is such a full account) will require the measurement of all of the causal links raised by the theory. Although we do not measure these intervening mechanisms, we take the first step of measuring the relationship between antecedent variables and delinquency. If our preliminary results prove supportive, we hope it will serve to encourage even more comprehensive empirical tests. . . .

DELINQUENCY MEASURES At both Time 1 (Wave 1, 1977) and Time 2 (Wave 2, 1978) respondents were asked about their involvement during the previous 12 months in an extensive list of delinquent behaviors. The Time 1 measure of self-reported delinquency, then, reflects delinquent acts committed in the year before the first interview, whereas the Time 2 measure reflects delinquent acts committed in the year after the Time 1 interview. Because Agnew claims that GST can explain involvement in a wide range of offenses, a composite scale of general delinquency was constructed from these self-reports.

FINDINGS

Effects of Strain—Preliminary Results

. . . Four of the five measures of general strain (Neighborhood Problems, Negative Life Events, School/Peer Hassles, and Negative Relations With Adults) have a positive and significant effect on delinquency. Our panel analysis does, then, reveal support for some components of Agnew's GST. Those who live in neighborhoods beset with many social problems (including crime and physical deterioration), who have in the past year experienced stressful life events, who have problems fitting in with peers and with school, and who have bad relationships with their parents and teachers, commit significantly more delinquent acts than those experiencing less strain. It should be noted that this relationship exists while controlling for social control/differential association variables. In addition, we found that having conventional moral beliefs and earning good school grades effectively inhibits delinquent involvement whereas having delinquent peers significantly contributes to delinquency.

Variations in the Magnitude of and Coping Strategies for Strain

We have thus far found some support for Agnew's GST. Experiencing a variety of negative stimuli does have a positive effect on subsequent involvement in delinquency net of one's prior level of delinquency and other determinants. In addition to suggesting more

general sources of strain, Agnew also alluded to the fact that negative stimuli will produce more strain and presumably have a greater effect on delinquency, under particular conditions. He suggests, for example, that strain may have more pronounced effects when experienced over a long period of time (duration) and when it cannot effectively be managed by diminishing its importance. Because of data limitations (the NYS was not designed as a test of GST) our examination of these issues was not as comprehensive as we would like. Nevertheless, we were able to examine some of Agnew's hypotheses about the conditions under which the adverse conditions of strain may be amplified or muted.

For example, in addition to respondents' perceptions about problems of crime and general deterioration where they live (Neighborhood Problems), they were also asked about the length of time they have lived in their neighborhood. Agnew's notion of duration suggests that those who have lived in unpleasant neighborhoods for a longer period of time would experience more stress than recent arrivals and that this stress would produce more delinquency. There was, however, no support for this duration hypothesis. The interaction of neighborhood problems with length of time in the neighborhood was not significant; no matter how long or how recently one lived in a disagreeable neighborhood, it had a positive effect on self-reported involvement in general delinquency.

Agnew also argued that if the unpleasant effects of strain can be managed or coped with, it will be expected to have a diminished effect on behavior. One of the ways that strain can be managed, he suggests, is by individuals' minimizing the importance of the goal/value or area of life affected by the strain. With respect to the measures of strain employed here, we would expect that Negative Relations With Adults would be less strongly related to delinquency for those youths who thought that adults' approval or acceptance was unimportant; we would similarly expect that School/Peer Hassles would have a diminished effect for those youths who viewed having close friends and doing well in school as unimportant; and we would expect that Traditional Strain would be weakly related to delinquency for those who thought that achieving the two future goals (a college education and a good job) was not important. Unfortunately, none of these hypotheses were confirmed. . . . Although ours is not a comprehensive analysis, we failed to find any support for the notion that the duration or importance of strain affected its impact on delinquent behavior.

Constraints to Delinquent and Nondelinquent Responses to Strain

Like Merton, Agnew did not hypothesize that involvement in delinquent behavior was an inevitable response to strain; rather, there are both delinquent and nondelinquent adaptations. Only some strained adolescents turn to the delinquent option, and this response is affected by such factors as the availability of delinquent peers, the strength of moral inhibitions, the individual's level of self-control (delinquent disposition), coping resources (self-efficacy), and conventional social support. Supporting evidence for Agnew's hypothesis would take the form of a significant interaction effect between the indicators of strain and each relevant conditional variable. In their own empirical analysis, Agnew and White created a composite scale of general strain and employed this measure in their interaction analysis. We followed the same strategy. . . .

Relationship Between General Strain and Other Variables

Although we have not found any evidence to suggest that strain interacts with other variables in its effect on delinquency, we do have evidence to suggest that the kind of general strain theorized by Agnew is significantly related to subsequent delinquency. This is true even when there are controls for other relevant factors, such as those derived from social control and differential association theory. The next question to be addressed, then, is the relationship between the strain and social control/differential association variables. Agnew has hypothesized that one effect of strain may be to weaken the individual's social bond to conventional people and institutions and strengthen the bond with unconventional ones. If individuals find their current relationships stressful and unpleasant, it seems reasonable that they would disassociate themselves from these conventional relationships and institutions (either by breaking off the relationship or, if unable to do that, as in the case of parents and teachers, to at least distance themselves emotionally from them) and find more satisfying (although possibly more delinquent) ones. We would predict, then, that the measure of general strain would have a negative effect on the conventional social bond and a positive effect on delinquent peers. . . .

Consistent with Agnew's conjecture, general strain is negatively related to Social Control and positively related to Delinquent Peers. Strain leads to involvement in delinquency, then, because it in part weakens adolescents' ties to conventional sources of social control and strengthens their ties to delinquent others. These are not the only two factors intervening in general strain's effect on delinquency, however, because it still has a significant direct effect on delinquency with social control and Delinquent Peers controlled. It would appear, then, that general strain affects involvement in delinquency through processes in addition to its effect in weakening conventional social control and increasing ties to delinquent others. Agnew has theorized and empirically shown that two additional intervening variables between strain and delinquency are the negative affective states of anger and frustration. Unfortunately, we were not able to measure these important theoretical constructs. It is entirely conceivable that feelings of anger and resentment are an additional component of the process connecting general strain with delinquency. It should also be noted that, consistent with our cross-sectional analysis, involvement in delinquency increases both feelings of strain and participation with delinquent peers, and decreases conventional social control.

SUMMARY AND CONCLUSIONS

. . . In our article, we have attempted a more comprehensive test of the GST. With panel data from two waves of the NYS, we examined the relationship between general strain, social control/differential association variables, and measures of prior and subsequent involvement in a wide range of delinquent behaviors. In addition, we were able to determine if strain had a more pronounced effect if it was experienced over a long period of time (duration) and a less pronounced effect when respondents were able to cope with strain by diminishing its importance. We also tested for the possibility that various obstacles to delinquent and nondelinquent responses might interact with experiences of strain. Finally, we tested one preliminary causal model linking general strain with social control, associations with delinquent peers, and delinquent behavior.

Our findings provide partial support for GST. Consistent with Agnew and White's research, we found that negative relationships with adults, feelings of dissatisfaction with friends and school life, and the experience of stressful events (family breakup, unemployment, moving) were positively related to delinquency. We also found evidence that living in an unpleasant neighborhood (one where social problems and physical deterioration were perceived to be a problem) was positively related to delinquency. When conceived of more broadly as exposure to negative stimuli, then general strain is significantly related to involvement in delinquency. Contrary to Agnew's hypothesis, we found no evidence that this effect for strain was enhanced when it was experienced for a longer time period or

diminished when adolescents considered the dimension of their life in which they experienced strain as "unimportant."

We also did not find any evidence to suggest that impediments to delinquent or nondelinquent strategies interact with strain. Consistent with Agnew and White's own findings, feelings of general strain were positively related to subsequent delinquency regardless of the level of delinquent peers, delinquent dispositions, moral beliefs, self-efficacy, and conventional social support. It is possible that the feelings of distress that accompany strain can be managed by other strategies not examined here (escapism through drug use, compensatory success in school activities, athletics, or out-of-school employment).

Finally, we found some support for Agnew's conjecture that, at least in part, general strain leads to delinquent involvement by weakening the conventional social bond and strengthening the unconventional bond (with delinquent peers). In his own research, Agnew found that the strain process is mediated by a negative affective state (anger). Our findings here suggest that strain also contributes to delinquency through the mechanisms discussed by social control and differential association theory. It must be noted that ours is a very preliminary and rudimentary causal model. We were not able to measure two key intervening variables in the process leading from strain to delinquency (anger and frustration). Nevertheless, in finding support for important antecedent strain variables, as well as the mediating effects of the social bond and delinquent peers, we believe that our model is a reasonable starting point for additional research.

We see several productive avenues for subsequent empirical research and the theoretical development of GST. First of all, future research should attempt to examine the full range of the sources of strain. Although Agnew's and our research have examined some of the dimensions of negative events, others, such as the strain of more day-to-day experiences, remain unexplored. In addition, alternative measures of goal frustration that focus on the disjunction between expectations and actual outcomes or between just and fair outcomes should be investigated. The general point is that Agnew has provided a very detailed description of theoretical concepts for GST of which the relevance to delinquency has yet to be examined. Second, there may be some need to revise Agnew's original theoretical position. He had suggested several factors that he believed conditioned the effect of strain (duration, importance, presence of delinquent peers, etc.). Unfortunately, his own study with White and our own panel analysis failed to find any evidence for these predicted interactions. Strain does not appear to be conditional on any other factor, although there may be some that have not been considered. Third, additional work should be devoted to measuring the key intervening variables of GST. We have suggested that there is conceptual overlap between some of the antecedent variables alluded to by GST and other criminological theories. The critical test for the theory concerns the effect of strain on the psychological states of anger and frustration that we were unable to measure. What is perhaps most needed to advance this research agenda is a data collection effort of which the express purpose is the measurement and test of GST. Both Agnew and our research have used data collected for other purposes. Hence they provide a less than optimal empirical test. What we both have done, however, is to show that interest in the theory is not misplaced and that additional work may prove to be fruitful.

Finally, future empirical and theoretical work should explore the link between general strain and other delinquency theories. We have provided a very rudimentary causal model that connects strain with differential association and social control theory. Our model is, of course, both very modest and tentative; it is a sensible one but one best thought of as a point of embarkment. In making this final observation, we hope that we have not sealed the fate for the development of GST. That is, we hope that the expansion and development of Agnew's ideas will not be sacrificed by those wishing to incorporate general strain concepts into their own pet theory. There is a great deal of theorizing and research to do in the development of GST before any further thought and energy is devoted to integrating it with other theories. Although we have, following the suggestion of Agnew, indicated that the latter may be possible, we firmly believe that the theoretical and empirical development of GST itself is the most immediate and primary task. In expanding the scope of strain theory, Agnew has only begun an important line of both theoretical and empirical work that we wish to see undertaken.

QUESTIONS FOR DISCUSSION AND WRITING

1. What does traditional strain theory argue?
2. What is a key change made by Agnew to traditional strain theory?
3. What is a critical intervening variable in general strain theory?

Data Analysis Exercise

An Exploration of Self-Reported Delinquency and a Look at Social Disorganization Theory

INTRODUCTION

In this data analysis exercise, we will conduct two separate inquiries. First, we will use Wave VII data from the National Youth Survey (Elliott, 1996) to examine the distribution and correlates of crime that were discussed in Part IV. Then, we will use the same data to explore social disorganization theory, a theory presented in Part V.

DESCRIPTION OF THE DATASET

In 1976, a team of researchers administered the first wave of the National Youth Survey. This comprehensive survey asked juveniles about their attitudes toward and participation in deviant acts. The survey also queried the youths about their home lives, friends, and work/school activities. The seventh wave of the survey, administered in 1987, focused on events and behaviors that occurred during 1986, when the participants were in their 20s.[1]

---

[1]The original National Youth Survey Wave VII data included 1,730 variables for 1,725 individuals. Because the student version of SPSS will only accommodate 1,500 cases, the data for this exercise in this

Now, let's do some analyses. Before we start, we'll need to load up our dataset. We'll do this the same way we did for the data analysis exercise in Part III, except that we need the dataset called "NYSCRIME."

The Correlates of Crime

GETTING A HANDLE ON THE DATA

To get a handle on the data, let's take a quick look at some demographic factors. Run frequencies on MALE,[2] ETHNIC, and AGE. If you need to refresh your memory regarding how to run frequencies, see Blueprint 1 in the Part III exercise. The frequency tables appear below.

y7_2: SEX

		Frequency	Percent	Valid Percent	Cumulative Percent
Valid	Female	682	49.3	49.3	49.3
	Male	700	50.7	50.7	100.0
	Total	1382	100.0	100.0	

This is the table for sex.

y7_3: ETHNICITY

		Frequency	Percent	Valid Percent	Cumulative Percent
Valid	Anglo	1123	81.3	81.3	81.3
	Black	190	13.7	13.7	95.0
	Hispanic	48	3.5	3.5	98.5
	American Indian	6	.4	.4	98.9
	Asian	13	.9	.9	99.9
	Other	2	.1	.1	100.0
	Total	1382	100.0	100.0	

This is the table for ethnicity. Notice the Hispanic, American Indian, Asian, and Other groups.

book do not include the 343 cases for which many of the self-reported delinquency data are missing. This leaves a total of 1,382 cases. Also, the student version of SPSS can only handle 50 variables, so many interesting variables had to be cut out of the dataset. If you are interested in obtaining the entire dataset, you may do so by contacting ICPSR, the Inter-University Consortium for Political and Social Research (a quick WWW search for ICPSR will turn up a link to their homepage, from which the entire dataset may be downloaded free of charge). The variable names (short descriptors, up to 8 characters in length, that are assigned to each variable) have been changed to make the data more student-friendly, but the original names have been appended to the variable labels (longer descriptions, up to 40 characters in length, that are associated with each variable) for those students who wish to obtain and work with the full dataset. For example, y7_946 (one of the variables in the original dataset) has been renamed THEFT50 to make the name more descriptive, and the original name has been moved to the end of the variable label (THEFT50's variable label became "Stolen valued > $50 in lifetime: y7_946").

[2]To make the analyses easier, I have recoded the variable so that males are coded as "1" and females are coded as "0."

y7_7: AGE (in years)

		Frequency	Percent	Valid Percent	Cumulative Percent
Valid	21	210	15.2	15.2	15.2
	22	218	15.8	15.8	31.0
	23	214	15.5	15.5	46.5
	24	195	14.1	14.1	60.6
	25	195	14.1	14.1	74.7
	26	190	13.7	13.7	88.4
	27	160	11.6	11.6	100.0
	Total	1382	100.0	100.0	

This is the table for age. Notice the range of ages.

From the frequencies, we can see that our sample is nearly equally divided between males and females. We can also see that our data contain responses from a large percentage (81%) of Anglos and smaller numbers of Blacks, Hispanics, American Indians, Asians, and Others. In fact, there are so few Hispanics, American Indians, Asians, and Others that we will exclude them from any analyses on ethnicity because there are not enough of them to allow for meaningful analysis. Along these lines, I created a new variable WHITE that includes Anglos (coded as "1") and Blacks (coded as "0"), but codes the other ethnicities as missing so they will no longer appear in our analyses.

We can also see that our sample contains responses from individuals aged 21 to 27. This is important information; we now know that we cannot meaningfully test for age effects!

EXPLORATION THROUGH CROSSTABULATION TABLES

Now, let's get into some replication and exploration. Replication means that we will reproduce the research of other scholars; in our case, we will run some of the analyses performed by the authors whose writings are in Part IV. We will also run some exploratory analyses of our own.

For our first exploratory activity, let's see whether men are more likely than women to commit crimes. Many researchers have found this to be true. We will look at a total of three crimes: (1) whether the respondent has ever stolen something worth more than $50 (THEFT50); (2) whether the respondent has ever committed a violent offense (VIOLENCE); and (3) whether the respondent used marijuana during the past year (USEDMJ). In this section we will only look at marijuana use, leaving violent offenses and thefts for you to look at for the "further exploration" questions.[3]

---

[3] USEDMJ required modification to make it easier to use in our crosstabulations. The raw number of times that the respondent used marijuana during the previous year was recoded into two categories: those who said they did not use marijuana during the previous year ("0"), and those who said they used it one or more times ("1").

Before we see whether men are more likely than women to report having committed a crime, run a frequency table for USEDMJ to see how it is distributed because we need to make sure there are enough cases in each category to make our analyses worthwhile. If there are very few cases, statistical analyses are not valid. For example, only 7 respondents said they had ever physically hurt or threatened to hurt someone to get them to have sex. Any tables run on such a variable would be invalid due to small cell sizes. The frequency table for USEDMJ appears below.

used marijuana during past year

		Frequency	Percent	Valid Percent	Cumulative Percent	
Valid	no marijuana use	873	63.2	63.2	63.2	This is the table for USEDMJ.
	1 + times	509	36.8	36.8	100.0	
	Total	1382	100.0	100.0		

As we can see from our table, more than one-third said they had used marijuana at least once during the previous year, so both of our categories are large enough for meaningful analysis. Now, let's see if any of the correlates of crime discussed in Part IV play a role in marijuana use. To explore this possibility, we'll use our old friend, the crosstabulation table.

Race and sex are relatively straightforward variables in the NYS dataset, but I had to calculate income levels based on respondents' hourly wages (and hours worked weekly) for all jobs held during the previous year, plus income from other sources. The resulting numbers were recoded into three categories using Census Bureau data: (1) below the 1986 poverty threshold of $5,701; (2) above the poverty threshold but below the 1986 mean income of $16,908; and (3) more than the 1986 mean income. I used census data from 1986 because that's the year for which the job data were collected. Note that we cannot meaningfully test the effects of age because the respondents are too similar in age, as revealed in our frequency tables above.

Using the directions in Blueprint 2 if necessary, run crosstabulation tables with USEDMJ as the dependent (row) variable and MALE, WHITE, and INCOME as independent (column) variables. Make sure to choose "Phi and Cramer's V" under *Statistics* and check off "column percentages" under *Cells.* The tables appear below, followed by descriptions for each.

This is the MALE → USEDMJ table.

Crosstab

			y7_2: SEX		
			Female	Male	Total
used marijuana during past year	no marijuana use	Count	469	404	873
		% within y7_2: SEX	68.8%	57.7%	63.2%
	1 + times	Count	213	296	509
		% within y7_2: SEX	31.2%	42.3%	36.8%
Total		Count	682	700	1382
		% within y7_2: SEX	100.0%	100.0%	100.0%

Symmetric Measures

		Value	Approx. Sig.
Nominal by Nominal	Phi	.115	.000
	Cramer's V	.115	.000
N of Valid Cases		1382	

a. Not assuming the null hypothesis.

b. Using the asymptotic standard error assuming the null hypothesis.

First, let's consider the effects of gender. Daniel Mears and his colleagues report that women are less likely than men to commit crimes. Is this finding supported by the NYS data? To find out, look at the table for MALE. Were men more likely than women to have smoked marijuana during the past year? It seems pretty safe to conclude that women are less likely than men to commit at least this offense. The process we just completed is one part of replication—when researchers see if the findings reported by other researchers are true for their own data. Replication is a very important part of research because it shows the consistency of findings and allows for sound theories to be developed.

This is the WHITE → USEDMJ table.

Crosstab

			Respondent race: Black or Anglo		Total
			Black	Anglo	
used marijuana during past year	no marijuana use	Count	126	698	824
		% within Respondent race: Black or Anglo	66.3%	62.2%	62.8%
	1 + times	Count	64	425	489
		% within Respondent race: Black or Anglo	33.7%	37.8%	37.2%
Total		Count	190	1123	1313
		% within Respondent race: Black or Anglo	100.0%	100.0%	100.0%

Symmetric Measures

		Value	Approx. Sig.
Nominal by Nominal	Phi	.030	.273
	Cramer's V	.030	.273
N of Valid Cases		1313	

a. Not assuming the null hypothesis.

b. Using the asymptotic standard error assuming the null hypothesis.

Now, let's look at the effects of WHITE. Robert Sampson and William Julius Wilson noted that blacks are more often enmeshed in the criminal justice system, but also argued that variables describing the communities in which blacks live account for a great deal of the crimes they commit. Does their finding hold true using the NYS data? To find out, look at the table for WHITE. Were blacks more likely than whites to have smoked marijuana during the past year? It does not appear that we can easily conclude that race affects the incidence of all crimes, because this relationship does not hold true for our crime. What if we consider urban inequality or neighborhood factors, as suggested by Sampson and Wilson? You'll be doing that for the "on your own" questions.

POINTS TO PONDER: Can you think of some reasons why race might not be related to marijuana smoking?

This is the INCOME → USEDMJ table.

Crosstab

			Respondent's income category			Total
			below poverty threshold	between poverty and mean income	more than the mean income	
used marijuana during past year	no marijuana use	Count	224	414	235	873
		% within Respondent's income category	67.9%	62.3%	60.7%	63.2%
	1 + times	Count	106	251	152	509
		% within Respondent's income category	32.1%	37.7%	39.3%	36.8%
Total		Count	330	665	387	1382
		% within Respondent's income category	100.0%	100.0%	100.0%	100.0%

Symmetric Measures

		Value	Approx. Sig.
Nominal by Nominal	Phi	.056	.112
	Cramer's V	.056	.112
N of Valid Cases		1382	

a. Not assuming the null hypothesis.

b. Using the asymptotic standard error assuming the null hypothesis.

Finally, we turn our attention to INCOME. In his article, John Hagan argues that class is an important factor to consider. It seems logical that poor individuals would be more likely to commit thefts, but let's see if the NYS data support this idea. Is there a significant relationship between INCOME and marijuana use? It is important to note that the lack of findings for a given variable or variables in one dataset does not invalidate any theory. It may indicate, for example, that social class is not best measured through income alone, as we did in this example. Indeed, researchers are often frustrated by the lack of suitable variables in data collected by others who did not have their particular theory in mind!

FURTHER EXPLORATION

Are other crimes affected by the correlates we have just examined? For the "further exploration" questions, you will run the same analyses for two additional crimes: theft and violent offenses. This is an important part of research; we need to know if our findings generalize to other offenses or whether they are limited to a few select crimes.

ON YOUR OWN

What else might influence the commission of crime? Now that we have explored some correlates of crime, you can expand your list of independent variables. Try running the analyses we ran for some other potential correlates of crime, adding some independent variables of your own. Perhaps you think that the level of urban development where respondents live (RURAL) or their marital status (MARSTAT) will affect crime commission. Explore those variables and find out for yourself. You can "control" for the effects of a variable (statistically remove the effects of a variable) by listing it in the third box (labeled "Layer 1 of 1") when you run your cross-tabulations. While you are exploring the correlates of crime, reflect on the readings and how they help us understand crime.

Social Disorganization Theory

GETTING A HANDLE ON THE DATA

Part V presents some of the early theories that were developed to explain crime. Social disorganization theory is one such theory that still holds its predictive charm. Clifford Shaw and Henry McKay noted that juvenile delinquents tended to live in certain neighborhoods. It did not take long for the two researchers to begin looking at the high-delinquency neighborhoods to see what made them different from neighborhoods that had less delinquency. They found that delinquents appeared to come from neighborhoods characterized by low rents, a high incidence of individuals supported by public assistance, a high percentage of industrial (low-level blue-collar) workers, and a high rate of individuals moving into and out of the area (a population in flux). Visual clues such as boarded-up houses and buildings with broken windows indicated areas where crime and delinquents existed side by side. In Shaw and McKay's model, crime was related to the communities in which it occurred. Fortunately, the NYS has several good questions that permit testing some of the tenets of social disorganization theory.

Rather than run frequencies on the demographic factors we have already examined, we can now turn our attention to theory testing. Let's get started by matching some of the variables in Wave VII of the NYS to the ideas contained in social disorganization theory. This task involved culling through the codebook to find variables that I thought reflected Shaw and McKay's ideas, then including them in the NYSCRIME dataset so you could experiment with them.

Shaw and McKay focused on indicators of social decay, such as a high unemployment rate. They were also interested in physical neighborhood descriptors. While not providing factual data on social decay or crime rates, the NYS survey did ask questions that can address both types of measures. In one section of the survey, respondents were asked to rate how much of a problem abandoned houses and run-down buildings were in their own neighborhoods. The respondents were also asked how much of a problem high unemployment was in their neighborhoods. We'll soon see how all three of these measures affect crime.

Now, how do we measure crime? Once again, the NYS did not collect actual crime rates, but it did ask respondents how much of a problem several crimes were in their neighborhoods. Among the items on the list were two that we will examine: burglaries/thefts and assaults/muggings. We will look at burglaries first, leaving assaults/muggings for you to look at for the "further exploration" questions.

Before testing the theory, run a frequency table for our variables: UNEMP, ABANDON, RUN_DOWN, and BURGLARY.

This is the UNEMP table.

Y7_60: NEIGH PROB-HIGH UNEMPLOYMENT

		Frequency	Percent	Valid Percent	Cumulative Percent
Valid	Not a problem	771	55.8	56.0	56.0
	Somewhat of a problem	431	31.2	31.3	87.2
	Big problem	176	12.7	12.8	100.0
	Total	1378	99.7	100.0	
Missing	System	4	.3		
Total		1382	100.0		

This is the ABANDON table.

y7_67: NEIGH PROB-ABANDONED HOUSES

		Frequency	Percent	Valid Percent	Cumulative Percent
Valid	Not a problem	1190	86.1	86.2	86.2
	Somewhat of a problem	149	10.8	10.8	97.0
	Big problem	41	3.0	3.0	100.0
	Total	1380	99.9	100.0	
Missing	System	2	.1		
Total		1382	100.0		

This is the RUN_DOWN table.

y7_71: NEIGH PROB-RUN DOWN BUILDINGS

		Frequency	Percent	Valid Percent	Cumulative Percent
Valid	Not a problem	1012	73.2	73.3	73.3
	Somewhat of a problem	293	21.2	21.2	94.6
	Big problem	75	5.4	5.4	100.0
	Total	1380	99.9	100.0	
Missing	System	2	.1		
Total		1382	100.0		

This is the BURGLARY table.

y7_69: NEIGH PROB-BURGLARIES/THEFTS

		Frequency	Percent	Valid Percent	Cumulative Percent
Valid	Not a problem	764	55.3	55.4	55.4
	Somewhat of a problem	503	36.4	36.4	91.8
	Big problem	113	8.2	8.2	100.0
	Total	1380	99.9	100.0	
Missing	System	2	.1		
Total		1382	100.0		

From the frequency tables, we can see that a few of the categories are small, but they may be large enough to work with statistically. Because of the way the variables are coded, we really do not want to recode them unless we have to, because we will lose the detail that is currently present. If our individual cell sizes get too small, we'll have to recode them. Since everything looks okay for now, let's go on to our theory testing.

EXPLORATION THROUGH CROSSTABULATION TABLES

We will be running three crosstabulation tables that examine the effects of social disorganization on burglary rates: UNEMP → BURGLARY, ABAN-DON → BURGLARY, and RUN_DOWN → BURGLARY. The tables appear below.

This is the UNEMP → BURGLARY table.

Crosstab

| | | | Y7_60: NEIGH PROB-HIGH UNEMPLOYMENT | | | |
			Not a problem	Somewhat of a problem	Big problem	Total
y7_69: NEIGH PROB-BURGLA RIES/THEFTS	Not a problem	Count	518	196	49	763
		% within Y7_60: NEIGH PROB-HIGH UNEMPLOYMENT	67.2%	45.5%	27.8%	55.4%
	Somewhat of a problem	Count	242	186	75	503
		% within Y7_60: NEIGH PROB-HIGH UNEMPLOYMENT	31.4%	43.2%	42.6%	36.5%
	Big problem	Count	11	49	52	112
		% within Y7_60: NEIGH PROB-HIGH UNEMPLOYMENT	1.4%	11.4%	29.5%	8.1%
Total		Count	771	431	176	1378
		% within Y7_60: NEIGH PROB-HIGH UNEMPLOYMENT	100.0%	100.0%	100.0%	100.0%

Symmetric Measures

		Value	Approx. Sig.
Nominal by Nominal	Phi	.391	.000
	Cramer's V	.277	.000
N of Valid Cases		1378	

a. Not assuming the null hypothesis.

b. Using the asymptotic standard error assuming the null hypothesis.

This is the ABANDON → BURGLARY table.

Crosstab

| | | | y7_67: NEIGH PROB-ABANDONED HOUSES | | | |
			Not a problem	Somewhat of a problem	Big problem	Total
y7_69: NEIGH PROB-BURGLA RIES/THEFTS	Not a problem	Count	733	30	1	764
		% within y7_67: NEIGH PROB-ABANDONED HOUSES	61.6%	20.1%	2.4%	55.4%
	Somewhat of a problem	Count	403	81	19	503
		% within y7_67: NEIGH PROB-ABANDONED HOUSES	33.9%	54.4%	46.3%	36.4%
	Big problem	Count	54	38	21	113
		% within y7_67: NEIGH PROB-ABANDONED HOUSES	4.5%	25.5%	51.2%	8.2%
Total		Count	1190	149	41	1380
		% within y7_67: NEIGH PROB-ABANDONED HOUSES	100.0%	100.0%	100.0%	100.0%

Symmetric Measures

		Value	Approx. Sig.
Nominal by Nominal	Phi	.422	.000
	Cramer's V	.298	.000
N of Valid Cases		1380	

a. Not assuming the null hypothesis.

b. Using the asymptotic standard error assuming the null hypothesis.

This is the RUN_DOWN → BURGLARY table.

Crosstab

			y7_71: NEIGH PROB-RUN DOWN BUILDINGS			
			Not a problem	Somewhat of a problem	Big problem	Total
y7_69: NEIGH PROB-BURGLA RIES/THEFTS	Not a problem	Count	659	101	4	764
		% within y7_71: NEIGH PROB-RUN DOWN BUILDINGS	65.1%	34.5%	5.3%	55.4%
	Somewhat of a problem	Count	322	140	41	503
		% within y7_71: NEIGH PROB-RUN DOWN BUILDINGS	31.8%	47.8%	54.7%	36.4%
	Big problem	Count	31	52	30	113
		% within y7_71: NEIGH PROB-RUN DOWN BUILDINGS	3.1%	17.7%	40.0%	8.2%
Total		Count	1012	293	75	1380
		% within y7_71: NEIGH PROB-RUN DOWN BUILDINGS	100.0%	100.0%	100.0%	100.0%

Symmetric Measures

		Value	Approx. Sig.
Nominal by Nominal	Phi	.430	.000
	Cramer's V	.304	.000
N of Valid Cases		1380	

a. Not assuming the null hypothesis.

b. Using the asymptotic standard error assuming the null hypothesis.

Looking at the tables, what do you see? It appears that burglaries/thefts were a big problem in neighborhoods that were described as having high unemployment rates. Similarly, burglaries/thefts seem to be a problem in areas described as having a large number of abandoned houses. By now it should come as no surprise that burglaries/thefts were more of a problem in areas described as having many run-down buildings. Social disorganization appears to have at least some effects on neighborhood crime problems.

FURTHER EXPLORATION

We have now looked at the effects of social disorganization indicators on burglaries/thefts. Shaw and McKay suggested their theory explained many types of crime, so you will apply the theory to assaults/muggings for the "further exploration" questions.

ON YOUR OWN

After exploring social disorganization theory, you may have some interest in finding out whether the social decay indicators are related to the respondents' own levels of criminality. For example, do the three indicators we examined have any predictive power when considering respondents' marijuana smoking during the past year? What about the likelihood of their having been involved in violence or in stealing something worth $50 or more? You could also expand your list of social disorganization indicators to include other factors, such as the rate of vandalism (VANDAL) or the number of winos/junkies (WINOS) in the respondents' neighborhoods. Explore to your heart's content.

While you are examining social disorganization theory in depth, reflect on how it helps explain why some people break the law. Think also about the theory's weaknesses, including crimes and/or situations that it cannot adequately address. Because no one theory is able to explain all crimes by all offenders, new theories are continuously developed and tested. Maybe you'll develop a new theory during this course.

REFERENCE

Elliott, D. (1996). National Youth Survey [United States]: Wave VII, 1987 [Computer file]. ICPSR version. Boulder, CO: Behavioral Research Institute [producer], 1995. Ann Arbor, MI: Inter-University Consortium for Political and Social Research [distributor], 1996.

Homework for Part V: General Questions
(Correlates of Crime)

Name: _____   Date: _____

Directions: Answer the following questions by filling in the blanks or circling the appropriate responses. A couple of answers have been filled in for you to make sure you're on the right track.

GETTING A HANDLE ON THE DATA

1. In Wave VII of the NYS dataset, there were <u>700</u> males, and they comprise _____% of the sample. There were _____ females; they were _____% of the sample. This division *is / is not* roughly equal.

2. In Wave VII of the NYS dataset, _____% of the sample was Anglo; _____% were Black; _____% were Hispanic; _____% were American Indian; _____% were Asian; and _____% were Other. Because this division contained some small categories, only the Anglos and Blacks were included in the analysis. The breakdown of the new variable, WHITE, was _____% Anglo and _____% Black.

3. In Wave VII of the NYS dataset, the age grouping *did / did not* contain a wide range of ages.

4. In Wave VII of the NYS dataset, _____% were in the lowest income category (below the 1986 poverty threshold), _____% were in the middle income category, and _____% were in the highest income category (more than the 1986 mean income).

EXPLORATION THROUGH CROSSTABULATION TABLES

1. In Wave VII of the NYS dataset, _____% reported no marijuana use during the previous year, and _____% reported using it 1 or more times.

2. In the MALE → USEDMJ crosstabulation, <u>213</u> (_____%) of the female respondents said they had smoked marijuana during the previous year, compared to _____ (_____%) of the male respondents. The difference between the two percentages is

_____%, which appears to be *negligible / potentially interesting*. From the table, it appears that *males / females* are less likely to smoke marijuana. The *Phi / Cramer's V* value is _____, which means that we can do _____% better predicting marijuana use when we know a respondent's gender. This relationship is *weak / moderate / strong*. The approximate significance is _____, which means there is a _____% chance that the relationship between MALE and USEDMJ is due to chance. This relationship *is / is not* statistically significant.

In their article, Daniel Mears and his co-authors reported that *men / women* were more likely to break the law, similar to other studies on the gender/criminality link (by the way, this article is based on Wave III of the NYS; the authors obtained the data, tested their theory of exposure to delinquent peers, and published their work!). The relationship between gender and crime (as measured by marijuana use) found using Wave VII of the NYS data *is similar to / differs from* the findings reported by Daniel Mears and his colleagues.

3. In the WHITE → USEDMJ crosstabulation, _____ (_____%) of the Anglo respondents said they had smoked marijuana during the previous year, compared to _____ (_____%) of the Black respondents. The difference between the two percentages is _____%, which appears to be *negligible / potentially interesting*. The *Phi / Cramer's V* value is _____, which means that we can do _____% better predicting marijuana use when we know a respondent's race. This relationship is *weak / moderate / strong*. The approximate significance is _____, which means there is a _____% chance that the relationship between WHITE and USEDMJ is due to chance. This relationship *is / is not* statistically significant.

In their article, Robert Sampson and William Julius Wilson noted that Blacks are *more / less* likely to engage in violence, but that variables describing the communities in which they live account for much of that difference. The relationship between race and crime (as measured by marijuana use) found using Wave VII of the NYS data *is similar to / differs from* the findings reported by Sampson and Wilson.

4. In the INCOME → USEDMJ crosstabulation, _____ (_____%) of the lower-income respondents said they had smoked marijuana during the previous year, compared to _____ (_____%) of the middle-income group, and _____ (_____%) of the highest-income respondents. The largest difference between the three percentages is _____%, which appears to be *negligible / potentially interesting*. The *Phi / Cramer's V* value is _____, which means that we can do _____% better predicting USEDMJ

when we know a respondent's income category. This relationship is *weak / moderate / strong*. The approximate significance is _____, which means there is a _____% chance that the relationship between INCOME and USEDMJ is due to chance. This relationship *is / is not* statistically significant.

In his article, John Hagan stated that social class *has / has not* been linked to criminality. The relationship between income and crime (as measured by marijuana use) found using Wave VII of the NYS data *is similar to / differs from* the statements of Hagan.

POINTS TO PONDER: Can you come up with a possible explanation for the results we found using the NYS data?

---

5. Overall, we can say our findings regarding correlates for USEDMJ *are / are not* consistent with prior research.

Name: _____   Date: _____

Task: Run the analyses we ran for marijuana use for two additional crimes: theft and violent offenses.

Directions: Answer the following questions by filling in the blanks or circling the appropriate responses. A couple of answers have been filled in for you to make sure you're on the right track.

Note: THEFT50 is unchanged from the original dataset, but VIOLENCE was recoded. Respondents who said they had committed any of six violent offenses included in the survey[4] were coded as "2"; respondents who said they had never committed any of those offenses were coded as "1."

1. In Wave VII of the NYS dataset, _____% of the sample had ever stolen goods worth more than $50 and _____% had ever committed a violent offense.

2. In the MALE → THEFT50 crosstabulation, <u>111</u> (_____%) of the male respondents said they had stolen something worth more than $50, compared to _____ (_____%) of the female respondents. This relationship is *weak / moderate / strong*. This relationship *is / is not* statistically significant.

    The MALE → THEFT50 table *does / does not* show that men are more likely than women to report having committed a theft of an item worth more than $50.

3. In the WHITE → THEFT50 crosstabulation, _____ (_____%) of the Anglo respondents said they had stolen something worth more than $50, compared to _____ (_____%) of the Black respondents. This relationship is *weak / moderate / strong*. This relationship *is / is not* statistically significant.

    The WHITE → THEFT50 table *does / does not* show that Blacks are more likely than Anglos to report having committed a theft of an item worth more than $50.

---

[4] Those offenses were "attacked someone with the idea of seriously hurting or killing them, gotten involved in a gang fight, used force or strong-arm methods to get money or things from someone, had or tried to have sexual relations against someone's will, physically hurt or threatened to hurt someone to get them to have sex, or deliberately injured spouse/girlfriend/boyfriend."

4. In the INCOME → THEFT50 crosstabulation, _____ (_____%) of the lower-income respondents said they had stolen something worth more than $50, compared to _____ (_____%) of the middle-income group, and _____ (_____%) of the highest-income respondents. This relationship is *weak / moderate / strong*. This relationship *is / is not* statistically significant.

    The INCOME → THEFT50 table *does / does not* show that poor individuals are more likely than more wealthy people to report having committed a theft of an item worth more than $50.

POINTS TO PONDER: Can you come up with any explanations for the finding in table INCOME → THEFT50? Could white-collar crime account for some of the finding?

---

5. In the MALE → VIOLENCE crosstabulation, <u>176</u> (_____%) of the male respondents said they had committed a violent offense, compared to _____ (_____%) of the female respondents. This relationship is *weak / moderate / strong*. This relationship *is / is not* statistically significant.

    The MALE → VIOLENCE table *does / does not* show that men are more likely than women to report having committed a violent offense.

6. In the WHITE → VIOLENCE crosstabulation, _____ (_____%) of the Anglo respondents said they had committed a violent offense, compared to _____ (_____%) of the Black respondents. This relationship is *weak / moderate / strong*. This relationship *is / is not* statistically significant.

    The WHITE → VIOLENCE table *does / does not* show that Blacks are more likely than Whites to report having committed a violent offense.

7. In the INCOME → VIOLENCE crosstabulation, _____ (_____%) of the lower-income respondents said they had committed a violent offense, compared to _____ (_____%) of the middle-income group, and _____ (_____%) of the highest-income respondents. This relationship is *weak / moderate / strong*. This relationship *is / is not* statistically significant.

    The INCOME → VIOLENCE table *does / does not* show that poor individuals are more likely than wealthier people to report having committed a violent offense.

8. Overall, we can say that our findings for THEFT50 *are / are not* consistent with prior research. Overall, we can say that our findings for VIOLENCE *are / are not* consistent with prior research.

Homework for Part V: "On Your Own" Questions
(Correlates of Crime)

Name: _____ Date: _____

Task: Expand your list of independent variables to include other potential correlates of crime (for example, RURAL or MARSTAT). You may choose any variables you think make sense.

Directions: Answer the following questions.

Note: Please print out and include your tables with these questions so your work can be graded.

1. Which variables did you choose as your independent variables?

2. Why did you select these variables?

3. How did your first independent variable affect commission of crime? Make sure to provide a description that includes the percentages, Phi or Cramer's V value, the strength of the relationship, and the significance value.

4. How did your second independent variable affect criminality? Make sure to provide a description that includes the percentages, Phi or Cramer's V value, the strength of the relationship, and the significance value.

   If you included more than two independent variables, you may summarize the findings here for future reference.

Homework for Part V: General Questions
(Social Disorganization Theory)

Name: _____ Date: _____

Directions: Answer the following questions by filling in the blanks or circling the appropriate responses. A couple of answers have been filled in for you to make sure you're on the right track.

GETTING A HANDLE ON THE DATA

1. Complete the following table using percentages from the frequency tables for UNEMP, ABANDON, RUN_DOWN and BURGLARY.

| Issue | % of respondents who felt the issue was not a problem, somewhat of a problem, or a big problem in their neighborhoods | | |
	Not a problem	Somewhat of a problem	A big problem
High unemployment	55.8%		
Abandoned houses			
Run-down buildings			
Burglaries/thefts			

EXPLORATION THROUGH CROSSTABULATION TABLES

1. In the UNEMP → BURGLARY crosstabulation, 52 (_____%) of the respondents who said unemployment was a big problem in their neighborhoods also said that burglaries/thefts were a big problem, compared to 49 (_____%) who said unemployment was somewhat of a problem, and _____ (_____%) who said that unemployment was not a problem. Conversely, 518 (_____%) of those who said that unemployment was not a problem in their neighborhoods said that burglaries/

thefts were also not a problem, compared to _____ (_____%) who said unemployment was somewhat of a problem, and _____ (_____%) who said that unemployment was a big problem. Overall, it appears that as unemployment becomes more of a problem in a neighborhood, burglaries/thefts go *up / down*. This relationship is *weak / moderate / strong*. This relationship *is / is not* statistically significant.

The relationship between unemployment and crime (as measured by burglaries/thefts) found using Wave VII of the NYS data *is similar to / differs greatly from* the findings expected under social disorganization theory.

2. In the ABANDON → BURGLARY crosstabulation, 21 (_____%) of the respondents who said abandoned houses were a big problem in their neighborhoods also said that burglaries/thefts were a big problem, compared to _____ (_____%) who said abandoned buildings were somewhat of a problem, and _____ (_____%) who said that abandoned buildings were not a problem. Conversely, 733 (_____%) of those who said that abandoned houses were not a problem in their neighborhoods said that burglaries/thefts were also not a problem, compared to _____ (_____%) who said abandoned buildings were somewhat of a problem, and _____ (_____%) who said that abandoned buildings were a big problem. Overall, it appears that as abandoned houses become more of a problem in a neighborhood, burglaries/thefts go *up / down*. This relationship is *weak / moderate / strong*. This relationship *is / is not* statistically significant.

The relationship between abandoned houses and crime (as measured by burglaries/thefts) found using Wave VII of the NYS data *is similar to / differs greatly from* the findings expected under social disorganization theory.

3. In the RUN_DOWN → BURGLARY crosstabulation, 30 (_____%) of the respondents who said run-down buildings were a big problem in their neighborhoods also said that burglaries/thefts were a big problem, compared to _____ (_____%) who said run-down buildings were somewhat of a problem, and _____ (_____%) who said that run-down buildings were not a problem. Conversely, 659 (_____%) of those who said that run-down buildings were not a problem in their neighborhoods said that burglaries/thefts were also not a problem, compared to _____ (_____%) who said run-down buildings were somewhat of a problem, and _____ (_____%) who said that run-down buildings were a big problem. Overall, it appears that as run-down buildings become more of a problem in a neighborhood, burglaries/thefts go *up / down*. This relationship is *weak / moderate / strong*. This relationship *is / is not* statistically significant.

The relationship between run-down buildings and crime (as measured by burglaries/thefts) found using Wave VII of the NYS data *is similar to / differs greatly from* the findings expected under social disorganization theory.

4. Overall, we can say that our findings for BURGLARY *do / do not* support social disorganization theory.

Homework for Part V: "Further Exploration" Questions
(Social Disorganization Theory)

Name: _____ Date: _____

Task: Run the analyses we ran for BURGLARY, but with MUGGING as the dependent variable.

Directions: Answer the following questions by filling in the blanks or circling the appropriate responses. A couple of answers have been filled in for you to make sure you're on the right track.

1. In Wave VII of the NYS dataset, _____% of the sample said assaults/muggings were a big problem in their neighborhoods, _____% said they were somewhat of a problem, and _____% said they were not a problem.

2. In the UNEMP → MUGGING crosstabulation, _____ (_____%) of the respondents who said unemployment was a big problem in their neighborhoods also said that assaults/muggings were a big problem, compared to 16 (_____%) who said unemployment was somewhat of a problem, and _____ (_____%) who said that unemployment was not a problem. Conversely, 771 (_____%) of those who said that unemployment was not a problem in their neighborhoods said that assaults/muggings were also not a problem, compared to _____ (_____%) who said unemployment was somewhat of a problem, and _____ (_____%) who said that unemployment was a big problem. Overall, it appears that as unemployment becomes more of a problem in a neighborhood, assaults/muggings go *up / down*. This relationship is *weak / moderate / strong*. This relationship *is / is not* statistically significant.

    The relationship between unemployment and crime (as measured by assaults/muggings) found using Wave VII of the NYS data *is similar to / differs greatly from* the findings expected under social disorganization theory.

3. In the ABANDON → MUGGING crosstabulation, 15 (_____%) of the respondents who said abandoned houses were a big problem in their neighborhoods also said that assaults/muggings were a big problem, compared to _____ (_____%) who said abandoned buildings were somewhat of a problem, and _____ (_____%) who said that abandoned buildings were not a problem. Conversely, 1050 (_____%) of those

who said that abandoned houses were not a problem in their neighborhoods said that assaults/muggings were also not a problem, compared to _____ (_____%) who said abandoned buildings were somewhat of a problem, and _____ (_____%) who said that abandoned buildings were a big problem. Overall, it appears that as abandoned houses become more of a problem in a neighborhood, assaults/muggings go *up / down*. This relationship is *weak / moderate / strong*. This relationship *is / is not* statistically significant.

The relationship between the prevalence of abandoned houses in a neighborhood and crime (as measured by assaults/muggings) found using Wave VII of the NYS data *is similar to / differs greatly from* the findings expected under social disorganization theory.

4. In the RUN_DOWN → MUGGING crosstabulation, 21 (_____%) of the respondents who said run-down buildings were a big problem in their neighborhoods also said that assaults/muggings were a big problem, compared to _____ (_____%) who said run-down buildings were somewhat of a problem, and _____ (_____%) who said that run-down buildings were not a problem. Conversely, 922 (_____%) of those who said that run-down buildings were not a problem in their neighborhoods said that assaults/muggings were also not a problem, compared to _____ (_____%) who said run-down buildings were somewhat of a problem, and _____ (_____%) who said that run-down buildings were a big problem. Overall, it appears that as run-down buildings become more of a problem in a neighborhood, assaults/muggings go *up / down*. This relationship is *weak / moderate / strong*. This relationship *is / is not* statistically significant.

The relationship between the prevalence of run-down buildings and crime (as measured by assaults/muggings) found using Wave VII of the NYS data *is similar to / differs greatly from* the findings expected under social disorganization theory.

5. Overall, we can say that our findings for MUGGING *do / do not* support social disorganization theory.

Homework for Part V: "On Your Own" Questions
(Social Disorganization Theory)

Name: _____   Date: _____

Task: Run the analyses we ran in the text, using USEDMJ, THEFT50, or VIOLENCE as the dependent variable (instead of whether crimes are a problem in the respondents' neighborhoods).

Directions: Answer the following questions.

Note: Please print out and include your tables with these questions so your work can be graded.

1. Which variable did you select as a dependent variable?

2. Why did you select that variable?

3. How did UNEMP affect your dependent variable? Make sure to provide a description that includes the percentages, Phi or Cramer's V value, the strength of the relationship, and the significance value.

4. How did ABANDON and RUN_DOWN affect your dependent variable? Make sure to provide a description that includes the percentages, Phi or Cramer's V value, the strength of the relationship, and the significance value.

If you wish to do more exploring on your own, try to expand your list of social decay indicators to include other factors (for example, VANDAL or WINOS). You may use this space to discuss the independent variables you chose and how they affected your dependent variable(s).

VI

HOW DO WE EXPLAIN CRIME?

Theories of the 1950s, 1960s, and 1970s That Continue to Influence Research

THE major theoretical influences of the late 1950s through the 1970s have their intellectual roots in earlier criminology. This is not extraordinary. Science typically advances when scholars build on discoveries and knowledge learned by their predecessors.

The Chicago School theorists, represented in the previous section by Shaw and McKay, traced their intellectual lineage to early European sociologists who wrote about the effects of rapid social change on social life. Anomie theory likewise was based on Durkheimian ideas, as well as on conceptions of social life articulated by social disorganization theorists; Merton added his own unique contribution to these earlier explanations of crime and deviance. These works show how criticism of the original theories leads to revision and fine-tuning, as each generation of scholars takes what is valuable and moves forward. This is how knowledge advances in science, the social sciences included. The chapters in this section push our understanding of crime forward, too. Although the branches look rather different from the roots, the strong connection between them enables theorists to take the original ideas in new directions.

In "The Subculture of Violence," Marvin Wolfgang and Franco Ferracuti present an explanation of homicide and other forms of criminal violence. They argue that, although there are exceptions, the "typical" homicide most frequently is the result of a cultural system of values and beliefs that is more favorable to the use of violence than is the wider dominant culture. Carriers of this subculture of violence engage in more violence because they are more likely to approve of the use of violence and to define violence as "appropriate" in more circumstances than do carriers of the dominant culture's values and norms. Regions, areas of cities, or other places where carriers of the subculture of violence are concentrated (some criminologists have written about a "Southern subculture of violence") will therefore have higher rates of homicide and other forms of violent crime. Students should note that "culture" was an important aspect of earlier theories, but Wolfgang and Ferracuti put culture and belief systems at the forefront of their explanation of criminal violence.

Steven Messner and Reid Golden did not set out to write about the subculture of violence thesis, but they use this perspective to make sense of their observations about homicide. Their article, "Racial Inequality and Homicide Rates," is part of a debate that began when Judith and Peter Blau published a paper asserting that income inequality, and in particular income inequality based on race, is a better explanation of variation in homicide rates across cities than poverty. That is, cities in which the gap between those with higher and lower incomes is greatest, particularly when this gap is between blacks and whites, have higher rates of homicide. Messner and Golden, as well as some others, disagreed and instead asserted that it is not income inequality that explains why some cities have high murder rates, but simply the amount of poverty in cities that accounted for observed differences. They were able to take advantage of FBI data (unavailable before the 1980s) that allows criminologists not only to examine variation in homicide rates, but also to look at homicide rates among blacks and whites separately for American cities. They use the "subculture of violence" concept to make sense of their observations. Though Messner and Golden use this perspective to make sense of their findings, students should recognize that they do not explicitly measure the subculture. Rather, it is inferred from the patterns of relationships between variables that they have measured. One of the criticisms of the subculture of violence thesis is that a means of measuring or observing it has been elusive.

In "Causes and Prevention of Juvenile Delinquency," Travis Hirschi lays out an explanation of crime and delinquency that begins from a different point than others. This type of theory, control theory, begins by arguing that we have been asking the wrong question. Most criminologists have sought to answer the query, "Why do people break the laws?" Control theorists suggest that we should ask instead, "Why don't people break the laws?" The fact is that most people do not violate laws even when it may appear to be in their interest to do so. For example, we regularly wait for traffic lights to turn green even in the middle of the night when neither other cars nor police officers are around. Why do we do this? That, according to control theorists, is the behavioral pattern we should seek to understand. Obviously, if we can answer the "why don't we" question, we will gain a greater understanding of why some people are criminals or delinquents.

Hirschi was not the first control theorist; this perspective, like many others, can be traced to the work of Emile Durkheim. In the 1950s, Reckless and Nye offered their answers to the question of why most of us don't violate the rules. Reckless focused on the development of what he called "inner containment" (that which we internalize) and "outer containment" (external sources of sanctions and disapproval, including our families, law enforcement, and other institutions). Nye focused on the controlling force of the family. Hirschi's answer to the question is "social bonds." Those with well-developed social bonds are less likely to engage in acts of delinquency. He posits that we develop bonds (attachments, commitments, involvements, and beliefs) to important institutions such as families, schools, and the conventional order. Those who are not well bonded are more likely to violate the law than those who are well bonded.

In "School Delinquency and the School Social Bond," Patricia Jenkins tests an important aspect of control theory. Jenkins finds support for a basic tenet of the theory—those with strong bonds to school are less likely to be delinquent. In reading this article, students will see an important aspect of how our understanding evolves through research efforts. In addition to affirming control theory, Jenkins clarifies and adds specification to the theory. Her research makes it clearer how bonds to school inhibit delinquency.

Finally, we have included labeling theory in this section. Some criminologists might argue that labeling theory belongs more appropriately with other "oppositional theories" discussed in Part VII. But we have included it here because it surged in popularity in the mid-1960s, a turbulent time for criminological theory. By then, social disorganization had been pretty much discarded (to be revived again in the 1980s and 1990s); differential association and strain theories, which had dominated criminological discussion for decades, were suffering from the publication of several important conceptual and empirical critiques (although they, too, would be revived in the 1980s and 1990s). The theories discussed in this section began filling that void. Labeling theory was the least traditional of these emerging dominant theories.

Labeling theory, like differential association, traces its intellectual ancestry to symbolic interactionists such as Cooley and Mead. Labeling theorists argue that the societal reaction to behavior affects the identity of the person whose behavior is being judged, and subsequent behavior reflects this change in identity. Edwin Schur's "Labeling Criminals," taken from his book *Our Criminal Society*, describes how societies create deviance and criminality through their efforts to control it. When we react to individuals as "violators," we set in motion a continuing series of interactions that eventually change their identity. They come to see themselves as criminals, which then affects their behavior—leading to more criminal action.

Leslie Margolin's "Deviance on Record: Techniques for Labeling Child Abusers in Official Documents" looks at the other side of labeling theory (the labelers, as opposed to the person being labeled). She shows how a criminal label is constructed by caseworkers and how the label "child abuser" comes to be attached to accused individuals. She argues that bureaucratic and institutional forces (such as caseload size) contribute importantly to this process.

The three theories presented in this section have been and continue to be important in criminological research. Their influence has ebbed at times, but we believe that they continue to be important influences in criminology. This is especially true of control theory, which, although not unchallenged, is considered by many scholars to be the dominant theoretical perspective in criminology.

SUBCULTURE OF VIOLENCE THEORY

The Subculture of Violence

MARVIN E. WOLFGANG
FRANCO FERRACUTI

THE analysis of violent aggressive behavior has been the focus of interest of many social and biological researches, and psychology has attempted to build several theories to explain its phenomenology, ranging from the death-aggression instinct of the psychoanalytic school to the frustration-aggression hypothesis. The present discussion is the result of joint explorations in theory and research in psychology and in sociology, using the concept of subculture as a learning environment. Our major area of study has been assaultive behavior, with special attention to criminal homicide. The following chapter will present a more detailed analysis of the pertinent literature, but some of the main trends in criminological thinking related to this topic must now be anticipated for the proper focus of the present discussion.

Isolated sectional studies of homicide behavior are extremely numerous, and it is not our intention to examine them here. There are basically two kinds of criminal homicide: (1) premeditated, felonious, intentional murder; and (2) slaying in the heat of passion, or killing as a result of intent to do harm but without intent to kill. A slaying committed by one recognized as psychotic or legally insane, or by a psychiatrically designated abnormal subject involves clinical deviates who are generally not held responsible for their behavior, and who, therefore, are not considered culpable. We are eliminating these cases from our present discussion, although subcultural elements are not irrelevant to the analysis of their psychopathological phenomenology.

Probably fewer than 5 percent of all known homicides are premeditated, planned intentional killings, and the individuals who commit them are most likely to be episodic offenders who have never had prior contact with the criminal law. Because they are rare crimes often planned by rationally functioning individuals, perhaps they are more likely to remain undetected. We believe that a type of analysis different from that presented here might be applicable to these cases.

Our major concern is with the bulk of homicides—the passion crimes, the violent slayings—that are not premeditated and are not psychotic manifestations. Like Cohen, who was concerned principally with most delinquency that arises from the "working-class" ethic, so we are focusing on the preponderant kind of homicide, although our analysis will include much of the available data on homicide in general.

THE CULTURAL CONTEXT

Like all human behavior, homicide and other violent assaultive crimes must be viewed in terms of the cultural context from which they spring. De Champneuf, Guerry, and Quetelet early in the nineteenth century, and Durkheim later, led the way toward emphasizing the necessity to examine the *physique sociale*, or social phenomena characterized by "externality," if the scientist is to understand or interpret crime, suicide, prostitution, and other deviant behavior. Without promulgating a sociological fatalism, analysis of broad macroscopic correlates in this way may obscure the dynamic elements of the phenomenon and result in the empirical hiatus and fallacious association to which Selvin refers. Yet, because of wide individual variations, the clinical, idiosyncratic approach does not necessarily aid in arriving at Weber's *Verstehen,* or meaningful adequate understanding of regularities, uniformities, or patterns of interaction. And it is this kind of understanding we seek when we examine either deviation from, or conformity to, a normative social system.

Sociological contributions have made almost commonplace, since Durkheim, the fact that deviant conduct is not evenly distributed throughout the social structure. There is much empirical evidence that class position, ethnicity, occupational status, and other social variables are effective indicators for predicting rates of different kinds of deviance. Studies in ecology perform a valuable service for examining the phenomenology and distribution of aggression, but only inferentially point to the importance of the system of norms. Anomie, whether defined as the absence of norms (which is a doubtful conceptualization) or the conflict of norms (either normative goals or means), or whether redefined by Powell as "meaninglessness," does not coincide with the most empirical evidence on homicide. Acceptance of the concept of anomie would imply that marginal individuals who harbor psychic anomie that reflects (or causes) social anomie

have the highest rates of homicides. Available data seem to reject this contention.

Anomie as culture conflict, or conflict of norms, suggests, as we have in the last section, that there is one segment (the prevailing middle-class value system) of a given culture whose value system is the antithesis of, or in conflict with, another, smaller, segment of the same culture. This conceptualism of anomie is a useful tool for referring to subcultures as ideal types, or mental constructs. But to transfer this norm-conflict approach from the social to the individual level, theoretically making the individual a repository of culture conflict, again does not conform to the patterns of known psychological and sociological data. This latter approach would be forced to hypothesize that socially mobile individuals and families would be most frequently involved in homicide, or that persons moving from a formerly embraced subvalue system to the predominant communal value system would commit this form of violent deviation in the greatest numbers. There are no homicide data that show high rates of homicides among persons manifesting higher social aspirations in terms of mobility. It should also be mentioned that anomie, as a concept, does not easily lend itself to psychological study.

That there is a conflict of value systems, we agree. That is, there is a conflict between a prevailing culture value and some subcultural entity. But commission of homicide by actors from the subculture at variance with the prevailing culture cannot be adequately explained in terms of frustration due to failure to attain normative-goals of the latter, in terms of inability to succeed with normative-procedures (means) for attaining those goals, nor in terms of an individual psychological condition of anomie. Homicide is most prevalent, or the highest rates of homicide occur, among a relatively homogeneous subcultural group in any large urban community. Similar prevalent rates can be found in some rural areas. The value system of this group, we are contending, constitutes a subculture of violence. From a psychological viewpoint, we might hypothesize that the greater the degree of integration of the individual into this subculture, the higher the probability that his behavior will be violent in a variety of situations. From the sociological side, there should be a direct relationship between rates of homicide and the extent to which the subculture of violence represents a cluster of values around the theme of violence.

Except for war, probably the most highly reportable, socially visible, and serious form of violence is expressed in criminal homicide. Data show that in the United States rates are highest among males, nonwhites, and the young adult ages. Rates for most serious crimes, particularly against the person, are highest in these same groups. In a Philadelphia study of 588 criminal homicides, for example, nonwhite males aged 20-24 had a rate of 92 per 100,000 compared with 3-4 for white males of the same ages. Females consistently had lower rates than males in their respective race groups (nonwhite females, 9-3; white females, 0-4, in the same study), although it should be noted, as we shall discuss later, that nonwhite females have higher rates than white males.

It is possible to multiply these specific findings in any variety of ways, and although a subcultural affinity to violence appears to be principally present in large urban communities and increasingly in the adolescent population, some typical evidence of this phenomenon can be found, for example, in rural areas and among other adult groups. For example, a particular, very structured subculture of this kind can be found in Sardinia, in the central mountain area of the island. Pigliaru has conducted a brilliant analysis of the people from this area and of their criminal behavior, commonly known as the *vendetta barbaricina*.

In Colombia, the well-known *violencia* has been raging for the past fifteen years, causing deaths of a total estimated between 200,000 and 300,000. The homicide rate in several areas has been among the highest in the world, and homicide has been the leading cause of death for Colombian males aged between 15 and 45. Several causes, some political, initially associated with the rise of this phenomenon continue to exist, and among them, a subcultural transmission of violence is believed to play an important role.

We suggest that, by identifying the groups with the highest rates of homicide, we should find in the most intense degree a subculture of violence, and, having focused on these groups, we should subsequently examine the value system of their subculture, the importance of human life in the scale of values, the kinds of expected reaction to certain types of stimulus, perceptual differences in the evaluation of stimuli, and the general personality structure of the subcultural actors. In the Philadelphia study, it was pointed out:

The significance of a jostle, a slightly derogatory remark, or the appearance of a weapon in the hands of an adversary are stimuli differentially perceived and interpreted by Negroes and whites, males and females. Social expectations of response in particular types of social interaction result in differential "definitions of the situation." A male is usually expected to defend the name and honor of his mother, the virtue of womanhood . . . and to accept no derogation about his race (even from a member of his own race), his age, or his masculinity. Quick resort to physical combat as a measure of daring, courage, or defense of status appears to be a cultural expression, especially for lower socioeconomic class males of both races. When such a culture norm response is elicited from an individual engaged in social interplay with others who harbor the same response mechanism, physical assaults, altercations, and violent domestic quarrels that result in homicide are likely to be common. The upper-middle and upper social class value system defines subcultural mores, and considers many of the social and personal stimuli that evoke a combative reaction in the lower classes as "trivial." Thus, there exists a cultural antipathy between many folk rationalizations of the lower class, and of males of both races, on the other.

This kind of analysis, combined with other data about delinquency, the lower-class social structure, its value system, and its emphasis on aggression, suggest the thesis of a violent subculture, or, by pushing the normative aspects a little further, a *subculture of violence.* Among many juvenile gangs, as has repeatedly been pointed out, there are violent feuds, meetings, territorial fights, and the use of violence to prove "heart," to maintain or to acquire "rep."

Physical aggression is often seen as a demonstration of masculinity and toughness. We might argue that this emphasis on showing masculinity through aggression is not always supported by data. If homicide is any index at all of physical aggression, we must remember that in the Philadelphia data nonwhite females have rates often two to four times higher than the rates of white males. Violent behavior appears more dependent on cultural differences than on sex differences, traditionally considered of paramount importance in the expression of aggression. It could be argued, of course, that in a more matriarchal role than that of her white counterpart, the Negro female both enjoys and suffers more of the male role as head of the household, as parental authority and supervisor; that this imposed role makes her more aggressive, more male-like, more willing and more likely to respond violently. Because most of the victims of Negro female homicide offenders are Negro males, the Negro female may be striking out aggressively against the inadequate male protector whom she desperately wants but often cannot find or hold.

It appears valid to suggest that there are, in a heterogeneous population, differences in ideas and attitudes toward the use of violence and that these differences can be observed through variables related to social class and possibly through psychological correlates. There is evidence that modes of control of expressions of aggression in children vary among the social classes. Lower-class boys, for example, appear more likely to be oriented toward direct expression of aggression than are middle-class boys. The type of punishment meted out by parents to misbehaving children is related to this class orientation toward aggression. Lower-class mothers report that they or their husbands are likely to strike their children or threaten to strike them, whereas middle-class mothers report that their type of punishment is psychological rather than physical; and boys who are punished physically express aggression more directly than those who are punished psychologically. As Martin Gold has suggested, the middle-class child is more likely to turn his aggression inward; in the extreme and as an adult he will commit suicide. But the lower-class child is more accustomed to a parent-child relationship which during punishment is for the moment that of attacker and attacked. The target for aggression, then, is external; aggression is directed toward others.

The existence of a subculture of violence is partly demonstrated by examination of the social groups and individuals who experience the highest rates of manifest violence. This examination need not be confined to the study of one national or ethnic group. On the contrary, the existence of a subculture of violence could perhaps receive even cross-cultural confirmation. Criminal homicide is the most acute and highly reportable example of this type of violence, but some circularity of thought is obvious in the effort to specify the dependent variable (homicide), and also to infer the independent variable (the existence of a subculture of violence). The highest rates of rape, aggravated assaults, persistency in arrests for assaults (recidivism) among these groups with high rates of homicide are, however, empirical addenda to the postulation of a subculture of violence. Residential propinquity of these same groups reinforces the sociopsychological impact which the integration of this subculture engenders. Sutherland's thesis of "differential association," or a psychological reformulation of the same theory in terms of learning process, could effectively be employed to describe more fully as impact in its intensity, duration, repetition, and frequency. The more thoroughly integrated the individual is into this subculture, the more intensely he embraces its prescriptions of behavior, its conduct norms, and integrates them into his personality structure. The degree of integration may be measured partly and crudely by public records of contact with the law, so high arrest rates, particularly high rates of assault crimes and high rates of recidivism for assault crimes among groups that form the subculture of violence, may indicate allegiance to the values of violence.

We have said that overt physical violence often becomes a common subculturally expected response to certain stimuli. However, it is not merely rigid conformity to the demands and expectations of other persons, as Henry and Short seem to suggest, that results in the high probability of homicide. Excessive, compulsive, or apathetic conformity of middle-class individuals to the value system of their social group is a widely recognized cultural malady. Our concern is with the value elements of violence as an integral component of the subculture which experiences high rates of homicide. It is conformity to *this* set of values, and not rigid conformity per se that gives important meaning to the subculture of violence.

If violence is a common subcultural response to certain stimuli, penalties should exist for deviation from this norm. The comparatively nonviolent individual may be ostracized, but if social interaction must occur because of residential propinquity to others sharing in a subculture of violence, he is most likely to be treated with disdain or indifference. One who previously was considered a member of the in-group, but who has rebelled or retreated from the subculture, is now an out-group member, a possible threat, and one for the group to avoid. Alienation or avoidance takes him out of the normal reach of most homicide attacks, which are highly personal offenses occurring with greatest frequency among friends, relatives, and associates. If social interaction continues, however, the deviant from the subculture of violence who fails to respond to a potentially violent situation may find himself a victim of an adversary who continues to conform to the violence values.

It is not far-fetched to suggest that a whole culture may accept a value set dependent upon violence, demand or encourage adherence to violence, and penalize deviation. During periods of war, the whole nation accepts the principle of violence against the enemy. The nonviolent citizen drafted into military service may adopt values associated with violence as an intimately internalized reinforcement for his newly acquired rationalization to kill. War involves selective killing of an out-group enemy and in this respect may be viewed as different from most forms of homicide. Criminal homicide may be either "selective" or nondiscriminate slaying, although the literature on homicide consistently reveals its intragroup nature. However, as in wartime combat between opposing individuals when an "it-was-either-him-or-me" situation arises, similar attitudes and reactions occur among participants in homicide. It may be relevant to point out that in the Philadelphia study of criminal homicide, 65 percent of the offenders and 47 percent of the victims had previous arrest records. Homicide, it appears, is often a situation not unlike that of confrontations in wartime combat, in which two individuals committed to the value of violence came together, and in which chance, prowess, or possession of a particular weapon dictates the identity of the slayer and of the slain. The peaceful noncombatant in both sets of circumstances is penalized, because of the allelomimetic behavior of the group supporting violence, by his being ostracized as an out-group member, and he is thereby segregated (imprisoned, in wartime, as a conscientious objector) from his original group. If he is not segregated, but continues to interact with his original group in the public street or on the front line that represents the culture of violence, he may fall victim to the shot or stab from one of the group who still embraces the value of violence.

An internal need for aggression and a readiness to use violence by the individual who belongs to a subculture of violence should find their psychological foundation in personality traits and in attitudes which can, through careful studies, be assessed in such a way as to lead to a differential psychology of these subjects. Psychological tests have been repeatedly employed to study the differential characteristics of criminals, and if a theoretical frame of reference involving a subculture of violence is used, it should be possible to sharpen the discriminatory power of these tests. The fact that a subject belongs to a specific subculture (in our case, a deviant one), defined by the ready use of violence, should, among other consequences, cause the subject to adopt a differential perception of his environment and its stimuli. Variations in the surrounding world, the continuous challenges and daily frustrations which are faced and solved by the adaptive mechanism of the individual, have a greater chance of being perceived and reacted upon, in a subculture of violence, as menacing, aggressive stimuli which call for immediate defense and counter-aggression. This hypothesis lends itself to objective study through appropriate psychological methodologies. The word of Stagner on industrial conflict exemplifies a similar approach in a different field. This perceptual approach is of great importance in view of studies on the physiology of aggression, which seem to show the need of outside stimulation in order to elicit aggressive behavior.

Confronted with many descriptive and test statistics, with some validated hypotheses and some confirmed replications of propositions regarding aggressive crime in psychological and sociological studies, interpretative analysis leading to the building of a theory is a normal functional aspect of the scientific method.

But there are two common and inherent dangers of an interpretative analysis that yields a thesis in an early stage of formulation, such as our thesis of a subculture of violence. These are (a) the danger of going beyond the confines of empirical data which have been collected in response to some stated hypothesis and (b) the danger of interpretation that

produces generations emerging inductively from the data and that results in tautologous reasoning. Relative to the first type of danger, the social scientist incurs the risk of "impressionistic," "speculative" thinking, or of using previous peripheral research and trying to link it to his own data by theoretical ties that often result in knotted confusion typically calling for further research, the *caveat* of both "good" and "poor" analyses. Relative to the second danger, the limitations and problems of tautologies are too well known to be elaborated here. We hope that these two approaches to interpretation are herein combined in degrees that avoid compounding the fallacies of both, but that unite the benefits of each. We have made an effort to stay within the limits imposed by known empirical facts and not to become lost in speculative reasoning that combines accumulated, but unrelated, facts for which there is no empirically supportive link.

We have said that overt use of force or violence, either in interpersonal relationships or in group interaction, is generally viewed as a reflection of basic values that stand apart from the dominant, the central, or the parent culture. Our hypothesis is that this overt (and often illicit) expression of violence (of which homicide is only the most extreme) is part of a subcultural normative system, and that this system is reflected in the psychological traits of the subculture participants. In the light of our discussion of the caution to be exercised in interpretative analysis, in order to tighten the logic of this analysis, and to support the thesis of a subculture of violence, we offer the following corollary propositions:

1. *No subculture can be totally different from or totally in conflict with the society of which it is a part.* A subculture of violence is not entirely an expression of violence, for there must be interlocking value elements shared with the dominant culture. It should not be necessary to contend that violent aggression is the predominant mode of expression in order to show that the value system is set apart as subcultural. When violence occurs in the dominant culture, it is

usually legitimized, but most often is vicarious and a part of fantasy. Moreover, subcultural variations, we have earlier suggested, may be viewed as quantitative and relative. The extent of difference from the larger culture and the degree of intensity, which violence as a subcultural theme may possess, are variables that could and should be measured by known sociopsychological techniques. At present, we are required to rely almost entirely upon expressions of violence in conduct of various forms—parent-child relationships, parental discipline, domestic quarrels, street fights, delinquent conflict gangs, criminal records of assaultive behavior, criminal homicides, and so on—but the number of psychometrically oriented studies in criminology is steadily increasing in both quantity and sophistication, and from them a reliable differential psychology of homicides should emerge to match current sociological research.

2. *To establish the existence of a subculture of violence does not require that the actors sharing in these basic value elements should express violence in all situations.* The normative system designates that in some types of social interaction a violent and physically aggressive response is either expected or required of all members sharing in that system of values. That the actors' behavior expectations occur in more than one situation is obvious. There is a variety of circumstances in which homicide occurs, and the history of past aggressive crimes in high proportions, both in the victims and in the offenders, attests to the multisituational character of the use of violence and to its interpersonal characteristics. But, obviously, persons living in a subcultural milieu designated as a subculture of violence cannot and do not engage in violence continuously, otherwise normal social functioning would be virtually impossible. We are merely suggesting, for example, that ready access to weapons in this milieu may become essential for protection against others who respond in similarly violent ways in certain situations and that the carrying of knives or other protective devices becomes a common symbol of willingness to

participate in violence, to expect violence, and to be ready for its retaliation.

3. *The potential resort or willingness to resort to violence in a variety of situations emphasizes the penetrating and diffusive character of this culture theme.* The number and kinds of situations in which an individual uses violence may be viewed as an index of the extent to which he has assimilated the values associated with violence. This index should also be reflected by quantitative differences in a variety of psychological dimensions, from differential perception of violent stimuli to different value expressions in questionnaire-type instruments. The range of violence from minor assault to fatal injury, or certainly the maximum of violence expected, is rarely made explicit for all situations to which an individual may be exposed. Overt violence may even occasionally be a chance result of events. But clearly this range and variability of behavioral expressions of aggression suggest the importance of psychological dimensions in measuring adherence to a subculture of violence.

4. *The subcultural ethos of violence may be shared by all ages in a subsociety, but this ethos is most prominent in a limited age group, ranging from late adolescence to middle age.* We are not suggesting that a particular ethnic, sex, or age group all share in common the use of potential threats of violence. We are contending merely that the known empirical distribution of conduct, which expresses the sharing of this violence theme, shows greatest localization, incidence, and frequency in limited subgroups and reflects differences in learning about violence as a problem-solving mechanism.

5. *The counter-norm is nonviolence.* Violation of expected and required violence is most likely to result in ostracism from the group. Alienation of some kind, depending on the range of violence expectations that are unmet, seems to be a form of punitive action most feasible to this subculture. The juvenile who fails to live up to the conflict gang's requirements is pushed outside the group. The adult male who does not defend his honor or his female companion will be socially emasculated. The

"coward" is forced to move out of the territory, to find new friends and make new alliances. Membership is lost in the subsociety sharing the cluster of attitudes positively associated with violence. If forced withdrawal or voluntary retreat are not acceptable modes of response to engaging in the counter-norm, then execution, as is reputed to occur in organized crime, may be the extreme punitive measure.

6. *The development of favorable attitudes toward, and the use of, violence in a subculture usually involve learned behavior and a process of differential learning, association, or identification.* Not all persons exposed—even equally exposed—to the presence of a subculture of violence absorb and share in the values in equal portions. Differential personality variables must be considered in an integrated social-psychological approach to an understanding of the subcultural aspects of violence. We have taken the position that aggression is a learned response, socially facilitated and integrated, as a habit, in more or less permanent form, among the personality characteristics of the aggressor. Aggression, from a psychological standpoint, has been defined by Buss as "the delivery of noxious stimuli in an interpersonal context." Aggression seems to possess two major classes of reinforcers: the pain and injury inflicted upon the victim and its extrinsic rewards. Both are present in a subculture of violence, and their mechanism of action is facilitated by the social support that the aggressor receives in his group. The relationship between aggression, anger, and hostility is complicated by the habit characteristics of the first, the drive state of the second, and the attitudinal interpretative nature of the third. Obviously, the immediacy and the short temporal sequence of anger with its autonomic components make it difficult to study a criminal population that is some distance removed from the anger-provoked event. Hostility, although amenable to easier assessment, does not give a clear indication or measure of physical attack because of its predominantly

verbal aspects. However, it may dispose to or prepare for aggression.

Aggression, in its physical manifest form, remains the most criminologically relevant aspect in a study of violent assaultive behavior. If violent aggression is a habit and possesses permanent or quasi-permanent personality trait characteristics, it should be amenable to psychological assessment through appropriate diagnostic techniques. Among the several alternative diagnostic methodologies, those based on a perceptual approach seem to be able, according to the existing literature, to elicit signs and symptoms of behavioral aggression, demonstrating the existence of this "habit" and/or trait in the personality of the subject being tested. Obviously, the same set of techniques being used to diagnose the trait of aggression can be used to assess the presence of major psychopathology, which might, in a restricted number of cases, have caused "aggressive behavior" outside, or in spite of, any cultural or subcultural allegiance.

7. *The use of violence in a subculture is not necessarily viewed as illicit conduct and the users therefore do not have to deal with feelings of guilt about their aggression.* Violence can become a part of the lifestyle, the theme of solving difficult problems or problem situations. It should be stressed that the problems and situations to which we refer arise mostly within the subculture, for violence is used mostly between persons and groups who themselves rely upon the same supportive values and norms. A carrier and user of violence will not be burdened by conscious guilt, then, because generally he is not attacking the representatives of the non-violent culture, and because the recipient of this violence may be described by similar class status, occupational, residential, age, and other attribute categories which characterize the subuniverse of the collectivity sharing in the subculture of violence. Even law-abiding members of the local subculture area may not view various illegal expressions of violence as menacing or immoral. Furthermore, when the attacked see their assaulters as agents of the

same kind of aggression they themselves represent, violent retaliation is readily legitimized by a situationally specific rationale, as well as by the generally normative supports for violence.

Probably no single theory will ever explain the variety of observable violent behavior. However, the subculture-of-violence approach offers, we believe, the advantage of bringing together psychological and sociological constructs to aid in the explanation of the concentration of violence in specific socioeconomic groups and ecological areas.

Some questions may arise about the genesis of an assumed subculture of violence. The theoretical formulation describes what is believed to be a condition that may exist in varying manifestations from organized crime, delinquent gangs, political subdivisions, and subsets of a lower-class culture. How these variations arise and from what base are issues that have not been raised and that would require research to describe. Moreover, the literature on the sociology of conflict, derived principally from Simmel, on the social psychology of conflict, and on the more specific topic of the sociology of violence would have to be carefully examined. That there may be some universal derivatives is neither asserted nor denied. One could argue (1) that there is a biological base for aggressive behavior which may, unless conditioned against it, manifest itself in physical violence; (2) that, in Hegelian terms, each culture thesis contains its contraculture antithesis, that to develop into a central culture, nonviolence within must be a dominant theme, and that therefore a subtheme of violence in some form is an invariable consequence. We do not find either of these propositions tenable, and there is considerable evidence to contradict both.

Even without returning philosophically to a discussion of man's prepolitical or presocietal state, a more temporally localized question of genesis may be raised. The descriptions current in subcultural theorizing in general sociology or sociological criminology

are limited principally to a modern urban setting, although applications of these theories could conceivably be made to the criminal machinations in such culture periods as Renaissance Florence. At present, we create no new statement of the genesis of a subculture of violence, nor do we find it necessary to adopt a single position. The beginning could be a Cohen-like negative reaction that turned into regularized, institutionalized patterns of prescription. Sufficient communication of dominant culture values, norms, goals, and means is, of course, implicitly assumed if some subset of the population is to react negatively. The existence of violent (illegitimate) means also requires that some of the goals (or symbols of goals) of the dominant culture shall have been communicated to subcultural groups in sufficient strength for them to introject and to desire them and, if thwarted in their pursuit of them, to seek them by whatever illegal means are available. The Cloward-Ohlin formulation is, in this context, an equally useful hypothesis for the genesis of a subculture of violence. Miller's idea of a "generating milieu" does not assume—or perhaps even denies—the communication of most middle-class values to the lower class. Especially relevant to our present interest would be communication of attitudes toward the use of violence. Communication should, perhaps, be distinguished from absorption or introjection of culture values. Communication seems to imply transmission cognitively, to suggest that the recipients have conscious awareness of the existence of things. Absorption, or introjection, refers to conative aspects and goes beyond communication in its power to affect personalities. A value becomes part of the individual's attitudinal set or predisposition to act, and must be more than communicated to be an integral element in a prepotent tendency to respond to stimuli. It might be said that both in Cohen's and in Cloward-Ohlin's conceptualizations, middle-class values are communicated but not absorbed as part of the personality or idioverse of those individuals who deviate. In Miller's schema, communication from middle to lower class is not required. A considerable degree of isolation of the latter class is even inferred, suggesting that the lower-class ethic had a developmental history and continuity of its own.

We are not prepared to assert how a subculture of violence arises. Perhaps there are several ways in different cultural settings. It may be that even within the same culture a collective conscience and allegiance to the use of violence develop into a subculture from the combination of more than one birth process, that is, as a negative reaction to the communication of goals from the parent culture, as a positive reaction to this communication coupled with a willingness to use negative means, and as a positive absorption of an indigenous set of subcultural values that, as a system of interlocking values, are the antithesis of the main culture themes.

QUESTIONS FOR DISCUSSION AND WRITING

1. Among which groups are homicides "the most prevalent"?
2. According to the Philadelphia study, were the offenders or victims those who had no prior contact with the criminal justice system?
3. What are the seven propositions of the authors' theory?

Contemporary Research

Racial Inequality and Homicide Rates

STEVEN F. MESSNER

REID M. GOLDEN

L AND et al. review the macrolevel studies of homicide that have been published during the past two decades. They discover that the findings in this literature are highly inconsistent across different time periods and units of analysis. They also demonstrate in a multilevel, multiyear analysis that the inconsistencies can be attributed, at least in part, to the problem of high levels of collinearity among some of the independent variables. After simplifying the dimensional structure of the covariates by principal components analysis, Land et al. are able to produce more consistent findings. Substantively, their models point to the importance of a "resource deprivation/affluence" component, population structure, and divorce rates as major determinants of levels of homicide for cities, standard metropolitan statistical areas (SMSAs), and states in the United States.

Land et al. do not consider explicitly the effects of racial inequality in socioeconomic status in their regression analyses because they limit attention to variables for which data are available for three types of geographical units (states, cities, and SMSAs) over the 1960–1980

time period. They speculate, however, that measures of racial inequality would probably "cluster" along with the other variables that constitute the resource deprivation/affluence index. If this is correct, efforts to assess the distinctive effects of racial inequality on homicide rates are likely to encounter problems of statistical estimation irrespective of any theoretical or substantive interest in the effects of this variable.

One purpose of our analysis is to attempt to construct a measure of racial inequality in socioeconomic status that is sufficiently distinct from other aspects of social structure to permit the reliable estimation of its effect on city homicide rates. We combine several indicators of relative disadvantages for blacks in income, education, employment, and housing with the measures of resource deprivation/affluence considered by Land et al. in a factor analysis. Our results indicate that a racial inequality dimension can in fact be differentiated from the resource deprivation/affluence dimension and that meaningful factor scales can be computed to represent both of these aspects of social structure.

At least four causal processes linking racial inequality with criminal violence can be postulated on the basis of the theoretical literature. Moreover, the different processes imply distinctive effects of racial inequality on homicide rates disaggregated by racial characteristics of those involved. We accordingly examine the effects of racial inequality not only on total homicide rates but also on homicide rates disaggregated by race of offender and on rates disaggregated by both race of offender and race of victim. These analyses of total and racially disaggregated homicide rates thus facilitate an examination of the various ways in which racial inequality might exert causal effects on city homicide rates.

THEORY AND HYPOTHESES

The most influential statement of a theoretical link between racial socioeconomic inequality and violent crime has been formulated by Blau and colleagues. The arguments put forth by these researchers are actually rather complex, and different causal processes are suggested at different places. A common theme, however, is the emphasis on *ascriptive* forms of social differentiation. Blau et al. speculate that inequality in any form is a potential source of conflict and violence, but "inborn" inequalities are especially conducive to such behaviors.

One of the ways in which ascriptive inequality allegedly generates conflict and violence is by its effect on the overall social climate of the community. Blau and Blau hypothesize that in a society with a formal commitment to democratic principles, inequality based on race interferes with social integration. The essence of the argument is that "inborn" inequalities generate hostile sentiments and at the same time weaken support for social norms that operate to restrain such sentiments. In their words,

Ascriptive socioeconomic inequalities undermine the social integration of a community by creating multiple parallel social differences which widen the separations between ethnic groups and between social classes, and it creates a situation characterized by much social disorganization and prevalent latent animosities.

Such a situation is "akin to Durkheim's concept of anomie," especially if the lack of regulation of passions is de-emphasized in favor of "the prevalent disorganization, sense of injustice, discontent, and distrust generated by the apparent contradiction between proclaimed values and norms, on the one hand, and social experiences, on the other."

This particular argument might be labeled a "social disorganization/anomie" explanation of the criminogenic effects of racial inequality. The primary causal mechanism leading to increased criminal violence is the poor integration and widespread anomie that accompany high levels of racial inequality. Insofar as this process does in fact operate, racial inequality should have a positive effect on the total homicide rate; it should also have positive effects on the offending behavior of racial subgroups. These predictions follow because social disorganization and anomie presumably have an impact on all segments of the population.

Another, slightly different, causal mechanism is suggested elsewhere in the theoretical arguments of Blau and colleagues. In particular, Blau and Schwartz focus attention more directly on the racial minority. They emphasize the extent to which overt conflict over the distribution of resources requires an awareness of common economic interests. This awareness, they postulate, is more likely to emerge when inequalities are associated with group characteristics. Under such circumstances, the underprivileged are likely to become "aware of their collective interest in redistribution." The opportunity to pursue any such redistribution, however, may be blocked, with important consequences for the way in which conflict is expressed:

If a minority's endeavors to obtain a fair share of resources are consistently frustrated, it means their attempts to give realistic expression to their conflict of interest are blocked. . . . The blocking of realistic conflict produces the pent-up aggression, which manifests itself in diffuse hostility and violence.

The most important feature of this argument for our purposes is the clear implication that racial inequality is problematic primarily for the racial minority. This is the group with an objective interest in redistribution but without resources to bring about such a redistribution. The racial minority presumably experiences relative deprivation, which engenders frustration leading ultimately to aggression. This explanation for the criminogenic effects of racial inequality can thus be called a "relative deprivation/frustration aggression" explanation. It implies that racial inequality should have a significant positive effect on the offending rates of the racially disadvantaged group, that is, blacks.

Although Blau et al. do not explicitly consider distinctive effects of racial inequality on the white population, the logic underlying their arguments for the racial minority suggests such a possibility. If it is in everybody's interest to maximize resources, as Blau and Schwartz argue, then a condition of racial inequality is beneficial to the racial majority, at least when considered from the standpoint of immediate self-interest. Whites might, accordingly, derive certain benefits—both material and psychological—from being relatively advantaged vis-à-vis blacks, and this situation of advantage might reduce the frustrations that would otherwise promote aggressive impulses. In short, a "relative gratification/reduced aggression" explanation can be posed as an analogue to the relative deprivation explanation. The distinctive prediction here is that the level of racial inequality should be *inversely* related to the offending rate of whites.

A final prediction about the effects of racial inequality on levels of homicide can be derived from Blau's macrostructural theory of intergroup relations. Whereas the arguments presented above deal with the potential sources of *motivation* for homicide, Blau's theory of intergroup relations shifts attention to *opportunities* for intergroup contact. The fundamental premise of this theory is that an intergroup contact is required for the emergence of any meaningful intergroup association and that basic structural features of communities influence the probability of intergroup contacts.

For our purposes, Blau's theorems about racial inequality are most relevant. Blau hypothesizes that racial inequality in various forms will reduce opportunities for fortuitous contacts between members of different races. This, in turn, reduces the probability of interracial associations. Blau's theory thus implies an "opportunity" effect of racial inequality that is different from the motivational effects elaborated above. Racial inequality should be negatively related to rates of *interracial* homicide, that is, whites killing blacks and blacks killing whites.

To summarize, various theoretical explanations of the link between racial inequality and criminal violence have either implicitly or explicitly invoked different causal mechanisms. These causal mechanisms imply, in turn, distinctive associations with homicide rates disaggregated by the race of the participants. The social disorganization/anomie explanation implies a positive effect of racial inequality on the total homicide rate and on racially disaggregated offending rates. The relative deprivation/frustration aggression explanation and the relative gratification/reduced aggression explanation suggest positive effects on black offending rates and negative effects on white offending rates, respectively. Finally, the macrostructural opportunity perspective predicts that racial inequality will exhibit a significant negative effect on rates of interracial homicide.

PREVIOUS RESEARCH

Studies that have examined the relationship between racial inequality and violent crime rates have yielded highly inconsistent results. The preponderance of evidence suggests that racial inequality does not have strong, positive effects on aggregate levels of criminal violence, but there are several studies with contrary findings. Research that examines racially disaggregated crime rates also offers mixed support for the hypothesis of an appreciable positive effect of racial inequality on black offending rates. However, the validity of this literature is suspect given the persistent problem of multicollinearity, a problem that is often acknowledged but rarely resolved. There is also some evidence suggesting that certain forms of racial inequality reduce levels of interracial crime, but this research is rather sparse. In the analyses to follow, we move beyond previous studies by systematically examining total and racially disaggregated homicide rates with models that are not flawed by high levels of multicollinearity.

DATA AND METHODS

Dependent Variables

The data for the dependent variables come from two sources. Total homicide rates are taken from the Federal Bureau of Investigation's Uniform Crime Reports (1980–1984). These rates refer to the number of murders and nonnegligent manslaughters per 100,000 resident population.

The other source for homicide data is the Comparative Homicide File (CHF). The CHF is based on the annual Supplementary Homicide Reports collected as part of the FBI's Uniform Crime Reporting program. The CHF is particularly valuable for our purposes because it contains information on the race of the victim and the offender in homicide incidents. This permits the computation not only of race-specific offending rates but also of rates of homicides defined in terms of the race of the victim and the offender.

The complete city sample in the CHF includes the 168 cities with populations of 100,000 or more in 1980. Given our interest in computing race-specific measures of various variables, we follow the lead of previous researchers and impose a selection criterion of a minimum black population of 1,000. This criterion, along with some missing data on independent variables, yields a sample of 154 cities. Finally, to minimize the impact of random year-to-year fluctuations, we aggregate the homicide data for the years 1980–1984. The selection of a five-year period, rather than the more customary three-year period, is dictated by our interest in estimating events that in some cities are likely to be highly infrequent.

Measures of Racial Inequality

Four indicators of racial inequality have been selected to reflect racial differentials in income, education, employment opportunities, and residential patterns. Racial inequality in income is operationalized by the ratio of white to black median family income. The income data are taken from the 1980 Census tapes (STF-3). Educational inequality is measured in a similar manner as the ratio of white to black median years of schooling attained by the population aged 25 and over. Both measures indicate the *relative* position of the two racial groups and, more specifically, the extent to which whites enjoy advantages in comparison with blacks.

A third indicator of racial inequality is the ratio of unemployment levels. Unemployment is measured in the conventional way as the percentage of the civilian labor force that is officially unemployed. To maintain consistency in the polarity of the indicators of racial inequality, the black unemployment rate is divided by the white rate. Thus, high values represent greater relative disadvantage for blacks and greater advantage for whites.

The final indicator of racial inequality is residential segregation. Previous research indicates that segregation may be a particularly pernicious form of racial inequality, one that is highly resistant to change despite gains by blacks in other arenas. Our measure of racial residential segregation is the index of dissimilarity, which is computed on the basis of block-level data from the 1980 Census.

SUMMARY AND CONCLUSIONS

Our findings indicate that, at least for certain samples of large cities in the United States, indicators of relative, racial disadvantage cluster together to form a dimension of social structure that can be conceptualized as distinct from a general resource deprivation dimension. Moreover, by employing factor-analytic scaling techniques, it is possible to specify models that include measures of racial inequality and general socioeconomic disadvantage but that are not hampered by the confounding effects of multicollinearity. The partial effects of racial inequality on homicide rates in these samples thus can be assessed with conventional regression techniques.

The results of such an assessment lend differing support to four theoretical explanations for the link between racial inequality and violent crime. The hypothesis that racial inequality might actually decrease levels of offending for the racial majority is clearly disconfirmed. The effect of racial inequality on the white offending rate is significantly positive rather than negative. Accordingly, the notion that racial inequality might induce feelings of relative gratification among whites, feelings that might lessen aggressive impulses, is inconsistent with the data.

We also find no support for a prediction derived from macrostructural opportunity theory, namely, that racial inequality will reduce rates of *interracial* homicide because of reduced opportunities for contacts between members of the different racial groups. The coefficient for racial inequality in the equation predicting the interracial homicide rate is essentially zero. We can offer a speculative interpretation of this finding. Perhaps this null effect reflects countervailing processes. Racial inequality might indeed reduce opportunities for interracial contact, as postulated by macrostructural theory, but it might also increase the likelihood that the contacts that do occur will eventuate in a violent encounter. In other words, "motivational effects" of racial inequality (which are reflected in our results for the total homicide rate and the race-specific rates) might conceivably counterbalance "opportunity effects," yielding no appreciable overall relationship on the interracial homicide rate.

We do find some support for the relative deprivation/frustration aggression explanation. As expected, racial inequality has the predicted positive effect on the black offending rate. Interestingly, however, the effects of racial inequality on the white offending rate and the total rate are also significantly positive. The explanation that is most compatible with the full range of results is thus the social disorganization/anomie explanation. Racial inequality evidently affects the social order in some generalized way that increases criminogenic pressures on the entire population.

Several cautions are in order concerning these conclusions. First, the magnitude of the effects of racial inequality are modest at best. This may, of course, be due to random measurement error. Nevertheless, racial inequality does not emerge in our analysis as a particularly strong predictor of intermetropolitan variation in homicide rates.

Second, although our findings are most consistent with the social disorganization/anomie explanation, the precise processes linking racial inequality and homicide have not been fully explicated. Indeed, the social disorganization/anomie explanation advanced by Blau and Blau is probably the vaguest of the four explanations considered in the analysis. Blau and Blau have not explicitly defined their key concepts, and it is not clear that those concepts are being used in conventional ways. As Bursik has asked, is "social disorganization" being employed in the classical sense of "the inability of local communities to realize the common values of their residents or solve commonly experienced problems"? If so, precisely how does racial inequality impede this ability? Does "anomie" refer to the kind of normative situation depicted by Merton, that is, a situation wherein "the rules once governing conduct have lost their savor and their force"? If so, what are the mechanisms through which racial inequality engenders this delegitimation of norms? In short, there is much theoretical work yet to be done to explain the observed generalized effect of racial inequality on homicide offending.

Third, there are limitations associated with our scaling procedures. The covariance structure of the independent variables yields some troubling ambiguities. This is particularly apparent in the analyses of the total and interracial homicide rates, analyses that use the total population matrix for estimating the effects of the predictor variables. The factor analysis for the total population matrix reveals that racial composition loads very highly on the dimension that has been labeled "resource deprivation/affluence." This creates obvious problems for the interpretation of the corresponding resource deprivation/affluence scale because economic aspects of social structure are confounded with purely demographic features.

A related ambiguity emerges in the analysis of black offending rates, although the problem is not as severe because the loading of racial composition on the resource deprivation/affluence dimension (.431) is not as strong.

In the prediction of white offending rates, these kinds of interpretive problems are more pronounced for the racial inequality scale than for the resource deprivation/affluence scale. The loading of racial composition on the racial inequality dimension for the white matrix (.496) is not extremely strong, but it is not trivial either. Accordingly, the observed effect of the racial inequality measure on white offending rates necessarily confounds aspects of racial composition with those of relative socioeconomic disadvantage. The requirements for statistical estimation unfortunately conflict with the objectives of theoretical interpretation in commonly used samples of population aggregates such as cities, and any solution to the statistical problem is likely to generate interpretive difficulties. Perhaps the only way to avoid this dilemma completely is to identify different types of data that are not characterized by such serious empirical overlap among theoretically strategic variables.

We also make no claim that our specific scaling procedure for racial inequality is the theoretically correct one; the theoretical arguments are too vague to provide unambiguous guidelines for the operationalization of relevant features of urban social structure. Nor do we assert that alternative procedures would necessarily yield comparable results. To the contrary, additional analyses (not reported) reveal that the use of different factor-analytic algorithms can yield different results. Our basic claim is simply that it is possible to generate meaningful scales that are relatively independent of one another in a statistical sense and that yield results compatible with theoretically derived predictions. Once again, however, definitive conclusions about the role of racial inequality as a structural determinant of levels of homicide must await the development of a more refined theoretical framework within which these empirical findings can be located.

We close with a final comment on the issue of "units of analysis." There has been a heated controversy in criminology about the appropriate type of population aggregate to employ in macrolevel research on crime. The position that "smaller is better" seems to be gaining increasing support, although the work by Land et al. suggests that the choice among three common units—states, cities, and SMSAs—may be less critical than some have contended. In properly specified models, a number of invariant relationships can in fact be observed across these different types of subnational entities.

When considering a phenomenon such as racial inequality, however, subnational units of any type may not be the most meaningful aggregates for research purposes. Race is such a highly salient characteristic in U.S. society that the criminogenic consequences associated with racial disadvantage might be diffused evenly throughout the nation. Accordingly, even if racial inequality proves to be a rather modest predictor of variation in homicide rates across jurisdictions within the United States, as suggested in this analysis, it might still be a major factor responsible for the high homicide rate of the United States when considered in international perspective. This argument implies that in addition to efforts to test more theoretically sophisticated models of the effects of racial inequality on homicide with data on jurisdictions within the United States, cross-national studies are needed to assess the criminogenic potential of this ascriptive form of social inequality.

QUESTIONS FOR DISCUSSION AND WRITING

1. What effect did racial inequality have for the majority (white) group?
2. What effect did racial inequality have on the black homicide rate?
3. How do the authors explain the change in both minority and majority groups' rates?

CONTROL THEORY

Causes and Prevention of Juvenile Delinquency

TRAVIS HIRSCHI

A RESTRAINT OR CONTROL THEORY OF DELINQUENCY

Delinquent acts are acts contrary to law. Since the law embodies the moral values of the community (and insofar as it does not, the task of explaining delinquency is even easier), it follows that (1) delinquent acts are contrary to the wishes and expectations of other people; (2) they involve the risk of punishment, both formal and informal; (3) they take (and save) time and energy; and (4) they are contrary to conventional moral belief.

If these assumptions are true, it follows further that those most likely to engage in delinquent acts are (1) least likely to be concerned about the wishes and expectations of others; (2) least likely to be concerned about the risk of punishment; (3) most likely to have the time and energy the act requires; and (4) least likely to accept moral beliefs contrary to delinquency.

This, in brief form, is an example of control theory. It asserts that the delinquent is "relatively free of the intimate attachments, the aspirations, and the moral beliefs that bind most people to a life within the law." Such theories

assume that the potential for asocial conduct is present in everyone, that we would all commit delinquent acts were we not somehow prevented from doing so. Put another way, they assume that we are born amoral, that our morality has been added by training and is maintained by ties to other people and institutions.

In control theories, the important differences between delinquents and nondelinquents are not differences in motivation; they are, rather, differences in the extent to which natural motives are controlled. Control theories thus focus on the restraints on delinquent behavior, on the circumstances and desires that prevent it. Factors traditionally viewed as causes of delinquency, such things as poverty or "learning disabilities," remain potential causes and retain whatever significance their statistical relation with delinquency allows. They are not seen, however, as producing delinquency in the same way that friction produces heat. Instead, they are interpreted as factors that weaken the conscience or reduce the effectiveness of controlling institutions. Such causes do not require that the individual become delinquent; instead, they affect the likelihood that he will be exposed and that he will give in to temptation.

While these theories do not imply that the delinquent act is produced by any single cause, they retain the assumption that it is determined by all causes present at the moment it is committed. Some of these causes are the calculations and desires of the actor himself. It is he who wants sex, money, or peace; it is he who decides they may be had by robbing a liquor store; it is he who concludes that no policeman is near the scene. If he miscalculates the risk–benefit ratio, so does everyone, once in a while. If he is "compelled" to commit the act, it is not by forces peculiar to him, but by forces common to all of us. These theories thus locate the immediate causes of delinquent acts in the desires of the actor and his evaluation of the situation. While such causes provide reasons and motives, they cannot be interpreted as forcing the actor to act against his will or as freeing him from responsibility, since they originate with him.

Control theories come in a variety of forms and borrow from several social science disciplines. Since all of them agree that people require training, guidance, and at least a little supervision if they are to become and remain law abiding, no useful purpose is served by suggesting that one is superior to the others.

One important variant considers the effectiveness of child rearing or the adequacy of socialization as the key to delinquency. Learning theories of the control variety assume that the purpose of socialization is to teach law-abiding conduct, that the delinquent has been *improperly* trained or *inadequately* socialized. They assume that we must learn to be law abiding, that some lessons are more to the point than others, and that some of us are better teachers and better pupils than others. Theories that focus on learning are *not* control theories insofar as they assume that crime is a product of socialization, that the delinquent has been properly trained or adequately socialized from the point of view of those training him. Such a view makes crime social rather than asocial behavior, the product of positive rather than negative causes. On the whole, psychologists have favored learning theories of the control variety, while sociologists have preferred theories based on quite different assumptions about the nature of crime and the value structure of American soci-

ety. It goes without saying that the choice between these views should be a matter of evidence rather than disciplinary allegiance or policy advantage.

A second way to account for delinquency from a control perspective is to consider the effectiveness of institutions, such as the family and the school, and the extent to which they work together or at cross purposes in the control of delinquent conduct. Such an analysis may follow groups through the life cycle, noting variation *over time* in the likelihood that they will commit delinquent acts, or it can compare groups *at one point in time* with respect to their institutional affiliations and loyalties. Such explanations assume that all individuals are equally well socialized. They therefore concentrate on external rather than internal controls. Although they cannot explain all variation in delinquency among individuals, they are often effective in accounting for differences in delinquency rates across groups and over time. These were once known as *theories of social disorganization*. They assume that delinquency is evidence of institutional breakdown and failure. Their competitors are theories that deny that some institutions are more effective than others in meeting human needs and in controlling the behavior of their members.

Let us explore some of the traditional causes of delinquency from this perspective.

The Family and Attachment to Others

Sociologists use terms such as "significant others" or "reference groups" to refer to those people we consider important, to those whose good opinion we value, to those capable of influencing our behavior. These ideas correctly imply that there are still other people not very important to us. The danger with such concepts as applied to delinquency is that they suggest that each of us *has* significant others or important reference groups, which may or may not be the case. Thus sociologists sometimes say that "behavior is an attempt to maintain and enhance favorable judgments from our reference groups," which implies that delinquency, as behavior, has similar sources. Control theory reminds us that while we are all closer to some people than others, it does not follow that we are all equally close to someone. It reminds us that some of our behavior must be interpreted as reflecting lack of interest in the opinion of others.

One set of people we are expected to be close to, at least in childhood, is parents. *Parents do not want their children to be delinquent* (although they may in some cases want the product of the child's delinquency, such as the color television set "found" on the way home). We may therefore assume that delinquency often says something about the quality of relation between parent and child.

And, indeed, those least attached to their parents are most likely to commit delinquent acts. Evidence for this assertion comes from a variety of sources and cultures. However this dimension is measured, whether by asking the parent or child or by observing their behavior with each other, and whatever it is called, whether "cohesiveness," "respect," or "love," the results are the same. Academic opinion differs about whether the father or the mother is more important as a controlling agent. As of now, the best guess is that they are equally important, partly because the child tends to view them as a "team," a view that is often correct.

Those who do not care or think about the reactions of their parents are more likely to commit delinquent acts because they have less to lose. Risking the good opinion of some other person is easy when that person's opinion is not valued anyway. There are, to be sure, many sources of lack of concern for parental opinion. Some parents are simply less "worthy" of respect: They have fewer resources with which to coerce or buy conformity; they do not live up to the adolescent's standards of appearance and demeanor; they are easily fooled and manipulated. (Put more objectively, they have less money and educa-

tion.) Still others do not care to earn the love or respect of their children, being consistently cruel to or neglectful of them.

Lack of attachment to parents easily spills over into lack of "respect" for teachers and the police, for adults in general. This spillover is both psychological and structural. A good deal of the controlling power of adults outside the family lies in the threat of reporting the child's misbehavior to his parents. When this threat is removed by parental impotence, the sanctioning power of all institutions is reduced. By the same token, when relatives, friends, neighbors, and teachers do not or cannot report the misbehavior of the child, whatever control his parents might exercise is no longer possible.

Given the centrality of the family in the system of internal and external (psychological and structural) control, its absence from most sociological theories of delinquency is something of a mystery. The mystery is deepened by recent efforts to justify the absence: "We do not accept . . . that delinquency may result from differential attachment to parents, and learning processes which result in children being differentially attached to moral authority in general—especially at a time when the hold of the nuclear family is, by all accounts, being weakened." One way of reading such statements is that the family is no longer important in the control of delinquency because the family is no longer important in anything. However, when we look at adolescents whose allegiance to their families is profound (the vast majority), we see the error in assuming that because the hold of the family has weakened for some it has weakened for all. In fact, once we admit variation in the effectiveness of family control, it becomes apparent that the family may become more important as a cause of delinquency as the number of "weak" families grows.

Variations in the effectiveness of family control help account for many of the major correlates of delinquency. Girls are more closely supervised by their parents than boys and are more likely to be emotionally dependent on them, as well as on other adults. (As a consequence, there is evidence that girls are more likely than boys to "suffer" from family disruption.) Low-income and ethnic minority families are less able to control their children, for the variety of reasons mentioned earlier. In addition, such families are more likely to be disrupted and to live in neighborhoods where control is made difficult by the lack of support from the community at large.

In a much-quoted statement on the policy implications of these facts, Wilson says, "If a child is delinquent because *his family made him so* . . . it is hard to conceive what society might do about *his attitudes.*" Such enlightened pessimism being the order of the day, it may be worth repeating that control theory does not suggest that the family *makes* the child delinquent in a way contrary to the implications of deterrence "theory." (Nor does it suggest that all the families that will ever be exist now—a suggestion admired by those wishing to conclude it is too late to do anything about the family anyway.) In fact, there is no reason to believe that those wishing to increase the costs and decrease the benefits of crime may not do so as well (and as cheaply) by strengthening the family as by increasing the number of policemen.

*The School: Commitment to
or Stake in Conformity*

Perhaps the best predictor of delinquency in American society is difficulty in school. For three quarters of a century, there has been a large grain of truth in the statement that "truancy is the kindergarten of delinquency." The school is expected to engage the attention and maintain the interest of the child for some ten to fifteen years. Yet, for many, it is quickly clear that education is not their game, that proficiency in reading, writing, and arithmetic is not going to come. Given the hours and years such "students" are expected to remain

in school, we should perhaps wonder at how so many manage to avoid serious involvement in delinquency. In any event, those who do poorly in school are considerably more likely than those who do well to end up in trouble with the law. There are several ways to explain these differences from a control perspective.

One line of thought suggests that, in the school as in the family, the bond of affection or respect is crucial. The poor student simply learns to dislike school and therefore to deny the legitimacy of the school's authority. While true, such analysis is incomplete, since the school has other resources at its disposal. Institutions that prepare adolescents for the future may rely on their interest or investment in that future as a means of controlling them. The student who aspires to be a doctor or lawyer and who has worked long and hard to attain the grades required for access to these professions will presumably not want to risk his investment by engaging in delinquent acts. He is committed to, or has a stake in, conformity.

The student with low grades in the "prevocational track" does not have such an investment. His prospects for future status are not bright; there appears to be little connection between his present behavior (inside or outside the classroom) and his adult life. He will end up in a low-paying (or a high-paying) manual job, virtually regardless of what he does during the school years. He therefore has no stake in conforming to the rules; the risks from engaging in delinquent acts are slight; he is therefore more likely to engage in them.

Another consequence of the school's lack of relevance to the student is that it frees him from the shackles of childhood. Completing one's education, whether by graduation or by simply giving up, is to become in one sense an adult. Consistent with this premise, those who complete their education while still in school are much more likely to adopt attitudes and behavior patterns normally reserved for adults. They are more likely to smoke, drink, date, and be interested in automobiles. It is wrong to conclude that such freedom to behave in adult ways, coupled as it is with the normal freedom of childhood magnified by lack of concern for school, is particularly painful. It is not. In fact, it is a species of happiness. It is also highly conducive to delinquency.

In sum, the poor student is less likely to be concerned about the good opinion of the adults who run the system; he is unlikely to accept the argument that education is the royal road to success; and he is more likely to behave like an adult. Adult behavior on the part of children comes close to being delinquent in its own right and is, in any event, conducive to actual delinquency.

As might be expected, school performance is also an important key to many of the other correlates of delinquency. As of now, it appears to account for the marked differences in intelligence between delinquents and nondelinquents. It accounts for much of the differences by class and race, and it helps us understand part of the effects of family disruption. If "learning disability" turns out to be important in delinquency, it stands ready to account for that relation, too. (Actual school performance explains only a little of the considerably lower delinquency rate of girls. Girls are, however, much more likely than boys to be sensitive to the opinion of teachers, so that "school" in general explains still more of this difference.)

In general, it appears that the school has become the major institution of social control in American society. Or perhaps it has become the major generator of delinquency in American society. Which of these views is more nearly correct? Or are they identical? Again, control theory suggests that the former view is appropriate, that school failure represents not a motive for auto theft, but instead a reduction in the potential cost of apprehension for this crime. The school may "fail" to win the interest and loyalty of many of its pupils, but it does not *make* them delinquent. And there is no good evidence that efforts to pretend that all students are equal in academic ability (by eliminating IQ tests, tracking, and by inflating grades) fool anyone but the pretenders.

The Peer Group or Gang

The adolescent free of such adult institutions as the school and the family is free to take up with others in a similar situation, and he clearly tends to do so. The peer group, or gang, has thus for a long time been correctly seen as a concomitant of delinquency. At one period in American theorizing, the gang came to be seen as the key link in the chain, the most important cause of delinquency. The attitudes and values that produce delinquent behavior, it was said, are a product of gang membership. This image of delinquent behavior as a product of group membership was especially appealing to sociologists, partly because it suggests that delinquency too is social rather than asocial behavior. If true, control theory would be in trouble: Delinquency would be a product of training rather than a consequence of lack of training; it would result directly from strong rather than weak bonds to others; it would be moral rather than amoral behavior (at least from the perspective of the group in question).

Fortunately for the theory, the image of the gang as an "intimate group" bears little resemblance to the facts. Delinquents do tend to associate with delinquents, just as kids interested in chess tend to associate with each other, but the ties among delinquents are not equal in quality to those among other peer groups. On the contrary, there is now considerable evidence that gang members tend to see each other as unpredictable and untrustworthy, that their ties to each other reflect their weakened ties to other social groups.

Consistent with this revised image, it is now clear that gangs organized around or for delinquent activity, if they exist at all, are extremely rare. The bases of gang membership are age, sex, ethnicity, and territory; the sources of cohesion in the gang are external rather than internal—all members are caught in a common situation, they are to some extent forced together rather than attracted to each other. And, indeed, gang members are only slightly more likely than non–gang members to commit delinquent acts.

Belief

Belief has played a major role in sociological theories of delinquency. In perhaps the most famous of these theories, the person becomes delinquent because of "an excess of definitions favorable to violation of law over definitions unfavorable to violation of law." The basic assumption in some theories is that we cannot act contrary to our beliefs unless forced to do so. This means that criminals and delinquents either have beliefs or values that require delinquency or that they are under considerable pressure to act contrary to beliefs that forbid delinquency. Control theory offers an alternative to these views: The belief system of the delinquent neither requires nor forbids delinquency. Rather, it makes the choice between law-abiding and delinquent behavior a matter of expediency. This amoral or instrumental belief system asserts that "It is okay to get around the law if you can get away with it," that "Everybody does it, so you have to do it first," and that "Suckers deserve what they get."

These beliefs are consistent with (or effects of) the delinquent's alienation from conventional persons and institutions. That is, they reflect and rationalize the position of the unattached. Such beliefs are reasonably seen as "causes" of delinquency in the sense that those holding them are as a consequence more likely to commit delinquent acts. Now consider the following: "If causal theories explain why a criminal acts as he does, they also explain why he *must* act as he does, and therefore they make any reliance on deterrence seem futile and irrelevant." We have at least partially explained why a criminal acts as he does, but we have not implied that he *must* act as he does, nor have we suggested that deterrence is futile and irrelevant. On the contrary, the theory suggests that deterrence should be effective, that in the extreme case it is *all* that stands between the crime and the potential criminal. Wilson and others who would use deterrence *against* causal explanation have both the logic of causation and its implications for deterrence simply wrong.

Age

One of the most troublesome correlates of delinquency, both in terms of accurate measurement and explanation, is age. The tendency of delinquency as measured by official records to increase rapidly in early adolescence is clearly established. This increase is not readily explained by changes in the adolescent's beliefs, his attitudes toward or performance in school, or by changes in family structure. Rather, it appears to be a function of the increasing responsibility granted and required of the child at this time.

That greater responsibility is required is evident: The law allows a child of 7 to get away with things it hesitates to ignore in a youth of 14. By the same token, it is even less tolerant of the same behavior in an adult of 21. These varying attributions of criminal responsibility on the basis of age go back a long time. That they remain with us is clear in statistics on criminality and in the provision of separate legal institutions for juveniles and adults. And, whatever the trends in the juvenile court, it seems safe to assume that in one form or another they will remain with us always.

In this case, the law again presumably reflects the sentiments of the community as a whole. Thus it seems reasonable to assume that at the same time the requirement of legal responsibility is increasing, the granting of social responsibility is increasing at the same rate. In other words, as the child becomes more accountable to the law, he becomes less accountable to adults in general, especially to his parents. Delinquent behavior is thus most likely to *occur* and is most likely to be defined as *delinquent* at the point where the line of decreasing tolerance (by the law) crosses the line of increasing freedom from adult supervision. This point of maximum likelihood of "delinquency" is probably the point at which the child first appears to be physically mature.

Such a conception helps explain how delinquency in adolescence can be predicted from school performance and from family and school "misbehavior" at an early age. It is not so much that the child suddenly "becomes delinquent" in middle adolescence as that he has in many cases been "delinquent" all along.

SUMMARY

Causes of delinquency are often interpreted as motives propelling the individual to crime. Such interpretations suggest that, once a cause has operated, not much can be done to prevent delinquent acts; that restriction, supervision, and the threat of punishment are unlikely to be effective. They also suggest a statistical relation between cause and effect sufficiently close that at least "most people" exposed to the cause should become delinquent.

Many social scientists, convinced that deterrence can be effective and certain that most people exposed to the causes of crime do not become criminals, have concluded that the concept of causation is inappropriate to the study of delinquency and that the search for causes should be abandoned.

Still, it remains true that causes of delinquency can be (and have been) discovered. It also remains true that adolescents exposed to the causes are amenable to restriction, supervision, and the threat of punishment. Since this is so, it must be that the *interpretation* of causes as supplying the motive force behind delinquency is the root of the problem.

An alternative interpretation is that the traditional causes of delinquency do not produce delinquency directly but rather by affecting the system of internal and external controls. In other words, causes free the potential delinquent from concern for the ordinary costs of crime. In this interpretation, the benefits of crime—such things as money, revenge, sex, and excitement—are available at the moment the crime is committed to anyone committing it. Crime is not a response to unusual psychological needs or the product of a profound sense of duty. It is, rather, the product of ordinary desires operating on people ill equipped to resist them.

It follows that delinquent behavior may be prevented by restoring its ordinary costs (removing its causes), by providing its benefits in other ways, and by adding extraordinary or more certain penalties. The genius of most social groups is that they are able to control the behavior of their members without frequent resort to severe penalties. Those who say this cannot now be done ignore the fact that it is being done, cheaply and efficiently, in countless collections of basically amoral creatures.

QUESTIONS FOR DISCUSSION AND WRITING

1. What do control theories assume?
2. With respect to parental attachment, which youths are most likely to commit delinquent acts?
3. How does thinking about reactions of one's parents affect delinquency?

Contemporary Research

School Delinquency and the School Social Bond

PATRICIA H. JENKINS

THE risk of violent victimization in public schools is on the rise. In 1991, personal crimes with juvenile victims occurred most often in school or on school property. Seventy-two percent of personal thefts involving juvenile victims happened in school. According to the 27th Annual Phi Delta Kappa Gallup Poll of the Public's Attitudes Toward the Public School, 68 percent of parents surveyed believe that student violence in the public schools nationwide has increased a great deal in recent years. To develop strategies that combat school-related delinquency, schools need help in identifying factors that may influence school misbehavior. This article investigates whether the school, as an instrument of socialization, can play a major role in school delinquency prevention by strengthening the bond between students and the educational process.

Previous research on the effect of the school social bond on delinquency examined misbehavior generally. The present analysis shifts the focus to an examination of the effects of the school social bond on *school* misbehavior. Using Hirschi's social bonding theory as a

From "School Delinquency and the School Social Bond" by P. Jenkins, 1997, *Journal of Research in Crime and Delinquency* 34 (3):337–367. Copyright © 1997 Sage Publications, Inc. Reprinted by permission of Sage Publications, Inc.

general framework, this study takes some initial steps in identifying the sources of the school social bond, its overall impact on school misbehavior, and the unique contribution of each component of the bond to school delinquency.

Because of the lack of research on middle school students, and because much of the misconduct directed against schools, students, and teachers begins before students enter high school, this study focused on students aged 11 to 15—the early adolescent transitional stage. According to the Task Force on Education of Young Adolescents, middle schools are society's most powerful force to recapture millions of youths adrift yet receive little attention in discussions of educational reform. Maintaining discipline appears to be more problematic in middle schools (Grades 6 to 8) because middle school students are more likely to be suspended than expelled because of laws regarding compulsory school attendance. Toby observes that middle schools contain more troublesome "involuntary" students who are disengaged from the educational process but too young to legally leave school. Students at this grade level are more likely to be crime victims than are students in higher grades and express more fear of being attacked at school or going to and from school than older students. Also, the middle school years are the time for adolescent experimentation with tobacco, alcohol, and illicit drugs.

Using data on 754 middle school students in Grades 7 and 8, the present study offers a systematic examination of some presumed sources of the school social bond (e.g., personal background characteristics, family involvement in schooling, and ability grouping) and the effects of the school social bond on three measures of school delinquency: school crime, school misconduct, and school nonattendance. Two major issues are addressed: First, what factors influence the strength of the school social bond? Second, to what extent does the school social bond influence students' involvement in school crime, school misconduct, and school nonattendance?

FACTORS AFFECTING THE SCHOOL SOCIAL BOND AND DELINQUENCY

It is hypothesized that the effects of certain personal background characteristics, family involvement with schooling, and ability grouping on school delinquency are mediated by the school social bond. The school social bond has four components: attachment, commitment, involvement, and belief. Unsatisfying social interactions in school are believed to prevent some students from developing school ties of attachment (caring about others in school and their opinions and expectations), commitment (valuing educational goals), involvement (participating in school-related activities), and belief (accepting school rules as fair and consistently enforced).

Personal Background Characteristics

FAMILY SIZE   Research on the relationship between family size and delinquency suggests that family size is an important factor in delinquent behavior. In large families (i.e., four or more children), there may be less time for parents to attend parent–teacher meetings, to check homework, or to respond to school dis-

cipline problems for each child. Also, large families may have less money available for educational games and materials or tutorial assistance. Furthermore, because parents of large families may have less time to supervise their children, older siblings and peers may set standards of school behavior rather than parents. Thus students in large families are expected to have a weaker school social bond and to be more delinquent in school than are students in small families.

FAMILY STRUCTURE   Previous studies of family structure and delinquency have emphasized that a broken home (e.g., single-parent family or stepparent family) has a critical impact on the development of delinquency. Because of added stress stemming from the lack of economic and psychological support and physical responsibilities normally shouldered by two parents, single mothers may have more negative contacts with their children and less time for monitoring and discipline, involvement with schoolwork, and supervision of social activities.

On the other hand, Rankin and Wells contended that family structure has an indirect effect on delinquency; certain intervening processes such as substitute role models and supervision affect the probability of a relationship between broken homes and delinquency. There is evidence that many single-parent mothers develop broad systems of financial and social support to meet family needs. Other relatives may serve as positive socialization agents for children of single-parent families. Evidence further suggests that the absence of parents is less important than domestic tranquility in predicting delinquency. Emery concluded that students from homes characterized by interparental conflict are at a greater risk of involvement in delinquency than are students from broken but harmonious homes or intact households.

Furthermore, studies suggest that children who live with stepparents are more likely to be delinquent than are those living with intact families. Stepchildren may feel neglected when stepparents do not attend school activities or share in the monitoring of their academic and social progress. These feelings may generalize to disrespect for teachers and administrators. According to Nye, children who lack affectional identification with their stepparents may not care whether they embarrass or hurt them by getting in trouble.

Although the evidence regarding the effect of family structure on delinquency is inconsistent, the preceding research largely supports the association. Thus it is predicted that students from single-parent families and stepparent families will have a weaker school social bond and be more involved in school delinquency than students from intact families.

MOTHER'S EDUCATION The behavior of adolescents in school has been characterized as a reflection of their parents' social position in society. Such influences may be attributed to the availability of educational resources in the home, family socialization, or expectations about future educational attainment. Parents with more education are likely to discuss the advantages of a higher education and encourage their children to be more productive in school. Furthermore, more educated parents may be more effective and less intimidated interacting with teachers and school officials than less educated parents. Thus mother's educational attainment is expected to have a positive effect on the strength of the school social bond and a negative effect on school delinquency.

RACE/ETHNICITY The evidence on racial patterns in delinquency is inconclusive. When official data such as the *Uniform Crime Reports* are used, differences in delinquency rates have been found across race and ethnic groups. Official statistics indicate that African Americans are more likely than are Whites to be arrested for serious crime. On the other hand, self-report data indicate few differences between the races in either rates or frequency of offending. The disproportionate amount of African American official delinquency has been attributed to bias on the part of the justice system and lack of economic opportunity for African Americans.

Studies suggest that aggressive and disruptive behavior of some students in school may be a collective response to unobtainable standards by which they are evaluated in middle-class schools. Hanna argued that the misbehavior of lower-income African American children is a result of their oppressive life experiences and an attempt to recapture feelings of self-worth and self-identity. In view of the preceding research, non-White students are expected to have a weaker school social bond, particularly with regard to the attachment and belief components, than White students and, therefore, are also expected to be more involved in school delinquency.

GENDER Girls have consistently been found to have lower levels of delinquency than boys. During preliminary observations at the research site, girls appeared to be less aggressive and more attentive in class and less disruptive than boys in areas outside of the classroom. Also, in the Alternative Learning Center, a self-contained classroom where troublesome students are sent for in-school suspension, although 50 percent of the school population was male, 65 percent of the students in the center were male. For these reasons, girls are expected to have a stronger school social bond and be less involved in school delinquency than are boys.

GRADE Educational studies suggest that age is positively associated with delinquency. In the present study, it was predicted that eighth-grade students, aware of their status in the school as older students, were likely to try to increase their prestige by engaging in daring and risk-taking pursuits. Seventh-grade students, on the other hand, who are not as familiar with the school policies and teachers as the eighth-grade students, were expected to be less critical of the school educational processes and more idealistic and accepting of school rules. For these reasons as well as the findings in the above research regarding the likelihood of older adolescents to be more involved in delinquency, seventh-grade students were expected to have a stronger school social bond and to be less involved in school delinquency than were eighth-grade students.

Family Involvement with Schooling

Parental involvement in schooling refers to parents' encouraging and reinforcing good study habits, maintaining contact with teachers and administrative personnel, attending school activities in which their children participate, and encouraging behavior that is appropriate in an educational setting. Previous studies suggest that parental involvement has an important influence on students' academic performance. It is reasoned that students with parents involved in schooling will have a stronger school social bond.

Having a sibling presently or previously in the same school may be another family involvement factor affecting the school social bond. According to Wilkinson, Stitt, and Erickson, older siblings may influence younger siblings through two processes—imitation and contrast. It seems likely that students with siblings in the same school or siblings who used to attend the same school would know more students (i.e., friends of siblings) and be more familiar with some teachers and administrators. Thus it was predicted that students whose parents are involved with their schooling and whose siblings attend or previously attended the same school would have a strong school social bond and be less involved in school delinquency.

Ability Grouping

A number of studies have found that student stratification by ability differentiates student involvement in delinquency. According to Hirschi, self-perceived ability is important in the causation of delinquency. Supporting this contention, Gold suggested that students in low-ability classes are provoked to commit delinquent acts by feelings of incompetence. Conforming behavior may be promoted and delinquent behavior may be prevented when youths believe their chances of success and self-image may be damaged by delinquent behavior. On the other hand, Wiatrowski et al. found that track placement in high school students does not cause delinquency. Middle school students in low-ability classes or tracks may have unsatisfying social interactions in school because of perceptions of themselves as incompetent or feelings of insecurity in class. Accordingly, these students are expected to have a weaker school social bond and be more involved in school delinquency than those in higher-ability classes.

THE PRESENT STUDY

Although previous studies have found that the elements of the social bond—attachment, commitment, involvement, and belief—have independent effects on delinquency, there has been limited investigation of the structure of the *school* social bond to assess its contribution to the explanation of *school* delinquency. To fully understand the relationship between the school social bond and school delinquency, it is important to examine the combined effects of the four elements of the school social bond on school delinquency and to recognize the differential net impact of each component. Unlike other studies, the present study considers the impact of certain predictors of the school social bond and the consequences of the bond on school delinquency in the same model.

Sample and Research Setting

The sample consisted of 754 students ranging from 11 to 15 years of age in Grades 7 and 8 who were enrolled for the 1990–91 school year in a desegregated middle school in an urban-suburban community in Delaware. About 34 percent of the students and 12 percent of the teachers are non-White, and 57 percent of the teachers are female. The neighborhood in which the school is located is predominantly White and middle-class. Twenty percent of the students attending the school qualify for free or reduced-price lunches. . . .

Data Collection

An anonymous questionnaire was administered to all students who had parental permission to participate. Students responded to questions related to personal background characteristics, family involvement in schooling, ability grouping, commitment to school, and delinquent behavior in school. Of the 911 students enrolled in the school, 754 (83 percent) completed the questionnaire. Although the response rate was not perfect, the data are fairly representative of the overall school population. . . .

Measurement of Variables

. . . Personal background variables included family size, family structure, mother's education, ethnicity, gender, and grade. . . .

Family involvement in schooling variables represent the participation of the student's family in his or her school experience. The levels and quality of parental involvement in schooling are facilitated by cultural capital—social-class positions and class cultures. These measures include parental involvement and dummy variables indicating if siblings attend or previously attended the same school. The parental-involvement measure . . . is a 7-item index of parents' participation in schooling through volunteering in the school, going on class trips, belonging to the school Parent Teacher Association, and the frequency of parents' coming to school, talking about school at home, and checking homework. Although the alpha for family involvement is not high, the

scale provides a more reliable measure than any single indicator of family involvement.

Mathematics placement was the ability-grouping factor in this study. Mathematics classes are grouped homogeneously, with students of similar tested abilities grouped together. Although the school in this study asserts that it has no tracking policy, there is justification for using mathematics placement as an indicator of ability grouping. . . .

School commitment . . . is a 10-item index indicating responses to the following questions: Do you care if your homework is done correctly? Do you think that most of your classes are important? Do you think most of your classes are a waste of time? (no) Have you been on the honor roll this year? Does it matter a lot to you what your grades are? Would you like to quit school right now? (no) Do you think an education is important? Do you think you will fail no matter how hard you try? (no) Did you fail any courses this school year? (no) How much education do you want to have before you stop going to school? (some college)

Attachment to school . . . is a 9-item index indicating responses to the following questions: Do you care a lot about what your teachers think of you? Do you have a favorite teacher in this school? Do most of your teachers like you? Do you like most of your teachers? I wish I went to a different middle school. (no) It is easy for me to talk over schoolwork problems with most of my teachers. Most teachers are not interested in anything I say or do. (no) How is your school compared to other middle schools? (better) How are your teachers compared to other middle school teachers? (better)

Involvement in school . . . is an index of 11 items indicating responses to the following questions: Do you belong to the school band? Do you participate in intramural sports? During the present school year, have you tried to sell things to help your school raise money? Do you belong to the school orchestra? Do you participate in Student Council? Do you attend school dances? Do you attend athletic events after school hours? Do you attend school concerts after school hours? Do you belong to the drama club? Did you participate in Jump Rope for Heart this school year? How much time each day (30 minutes or more) do you spend: Doing homework assignments? Studying for tests and quizzes? . . .

Belief in school rules . . . is a 17-item index indicating responses to the following questions: Most school rules are fair. The principal is tough and too strict. (no) Students are treated fairly by most teachers in this school. Rules in this school are too strict. (no) The principal is fair most of the time. The punishments for breaking rules are the same in this school no matter who you are. Teachers in this school are too strict. (no) In this school, how are the following groups treated? (the same) African Americans? Latino Americans? Asian American? Whites? Honor roll students? Male students? Female students? Students with poor grades?

School delinquency was measured by three indexes. *School crime* . . . is an index of 14 items indicating use of alcohol, sniffing glue, smoking marijuana, use of other illegal drugs (LSD or cocaine), smoking cigarettes, selling drugs, stealing from a student or teacher, vandalism, hitting a teacher or student, damaging school property, shoving a teacher, and carrying a weapon. *School misconduct* . . . is indicated by affirmative responses to questions about frequently talking in class, using inappropriate language, marking on desks or walls, cheating, refusing to do class work, copying or not doing homework, throwing something in class, wearing improper clothing, wandering the halls without a pass, being suspended, being sent out of the classroom, and being deprived of bus-riding privileges. Finally, *school nonattendance* . . . refers to positive responses about cutting class, being late for school or class, and cutting school. . . .

DISCUSSION

The general analytic model is that personal background characteristics, family involvement in schooling, and ability grouping influence the strength of the school social bond, which in turn influences whether students pursue delinquency in school. The evidence confirms the importance of bonding adolescents to school as an important step in reducing school delinquency. The data demonstrate that the elements of the school social bond play important roles in predicting delinquency for a sample of 754 middle school students.

Examination of the independent effects of the four components of the school social bond reveal that certain elements of the school social bond appear to have more impact than others in controlling the three different types of school delinquency. For example, school involvement was the weakest predictor for all three types of school delinquency. This unexpected finding is consistent with the findings of recent research. Wiatrowski and Anderson, analyzing the dimensions of the social bond, found that involvement in academically oriented activities—for example, interest in schoolwork, discussion of schoolwork with peers, and time spent on homework—are relatively unimportant in explaining delinquency. Krohn and Massey concluded that the involvement component was better conceptualized as part of commitment than as a separate element of the bond. Paternoster et al., examining the deterrence doctrine, observed that conventional involvement had no substantial effect on delinquency involvement. They suggest that substantial blocks of time are available for deviance even for those involved in many conventional activities. This is especially true in the present research because many of the indicators of involvement are activities that occur during the school day.

The commitment component explained a higher proportion of the variance for all three forms of school delinquency than the other bond components. Commitment to school and belief in the fairness and consistent enforcement of school rules were the most important predictors of school crime. The strongest predictor of school misconduct was school commitment. School commitment and school attachment were the strongest predictors of school nonattendance.

The influence of personal background characteristics, family involvement with schooling, and ability grouping had differential effects on the school social bond components. High math ability and having a more educated mother were the strongest predictors of school commitment. Being White and having parents involved in schooling were the most important predictors of school attachment and belief in the fairness and consistent enforcement of school rules.

Certain predictor variables were not mediated by any of the school social bond components, thus *directly* affecting certain types of school delinquency. For example, family size and living with a single-parent family directly affect school misconduct. And living with a large family directly influences school nonattendance. Much of the gender effect on school crime and school misconduct is also direct.

In considering how all four components of the school social bond operate simultaneously, two important findings emerge regarding the differential effects of the school social bond on the three types of delinquency. First, the theory does better in accounting for school crime . . . than for school misconduct . . . and school nonattendance. . . . Second, school involvement is the weakest element of the school social bond. School involvement was observed to have no significant independent effect on any of the three types of school delinquency.

The present study provides mixed support for social structure theorists' contention that delinquency is a function of youths' socioeconomic situation. The data are somewhat consistent in that the mother's education and race are important predictors of belief in the fairness and consistent enforcement of school rules and commitment to school, and students in lower math courses are less committed and less attached to school. However, overall, for this sample, the effects of the mother's education and math ability level on school delinquency are relatively weak and mediated by the commitment component of the school so-

cial bond. Also, the bonding variables themselves are stronger predictors than either race or social class. Moreover, other factors—gender, parental involvement, and family structure—were observed to be more important predictors of the school social bond and school delinquency than the classic predictors of race and socioeconomic status. . . .

Implications

FUTURE RESEARCH Future research should investigate the impact of school size and other school-level variables that may influence the impact of the school social bond on school delinquency. Also, further investigation into other aspects of the involvement component of the school social bond should be conducted to determine the impact of different types of school activities on school delinquency; the effect of one's status within the activity; and the differential impact of being selected, elected, or self-volunteered for the activity.

Some variables not included in this study, but important for future research, are elementary school experiences, peer influence on school delinquency, and nonschool delinquency. The effect of *prior* school delinquency on middle school delinquency is an important issue that would probably be more adequately examined in a longitudinal study rather than a cross-sectional study such as this one. The bidirectional relations between peers and the school social bond as well as between peers and school delinquency would also be more adequately addressed in longitudinal research. The effect of the school social bond on out-of-school delinquency has been addressed in previous research, but it would be useful to develop models that incorporate the relationship between in-school and out-of-school delinquency. Finally, the results of the influence of older siblings on younger siblings would be more meaningful if the school experiences (e.g., positive or negative) of the older siblings were known. . . .

QUESTIONS FOR DISCUSSION AND WRITING

1. What are the four components of school social bond?
2. Which of the four components of the school social bond was the weakest predictor of school delinquency? Was this inconsistent with prior research?
3. Which component explained a higher proportion of the variance? Which factors were the most important predictors of school crime?

LABELING THEORY

Labeling Criminals

EDWIN M. SCHUR

NOTHER important sociological perspective, in which there has been a marked renewal of interest recently, emphasizes the role played by society's reactions to offending behavior in shaping social problem situations. Sociologist Howard S. Becker has stated this view succinctly:

Social groups create deviance by making the rules whose infraction constitutes deviance, and by applying those rules to particular people and labeling them as outsiders. From this point of view, deviance is *not* a quality of the act the person commits, but rather a consequence of the application by others of rules and sanctions to an "offender." The deviant is one to whom that label has successfully been applied; deviant behavior is behavior that people so label.

This does not, of course, mean that the *acts* we commonly term homicide, theft, and drug use would never occur if they were not considered deviant or criminal. Rather the point is that their nature, distribution, social meaning, and implications and ramifications are significantly influenced by patterns of social reaction. Society, in other words, determines what we make of these acts socially.

From *Our Criminal Society: The Social and Legal Sources of Crime in America* (pp. 115–120) E. Schur, 1969, Englewood Cliffs: N.J.: Prentice-Hall. Copyright © 1969 by Prentice-Hall, Inc. Reprinted with permission of Simon & Schuster, Inc.

"Criminal" in this view is in some measure what sociologists call an "ascribed status." An individual's designation as an offender depends crucially on what *other people* do with respect to him and his behavior; it does not result simply and directly from his own acts. This means that research on crime problems must pay a good deal of attention to the substantive nature of these reactions (how and why we react to particular "offenses" as we do); the direct reactors and "labelers" (agencies of formal control, such as the police and the courts); and the typical processes of interaction between these control agents and the individuals they treat as criminals (with special reference to how this interaction may affect the development of criminal self-images and "careers" among the people so "labeled"). This point about interaction is important, because a great value of this orientation is the stress it places on *processes* involved in the development of criminal outlooks and behavior. Crime is not simply a matter of static conditions—under which some individuals clearly "are" criminals (for all time and in all places) whereas others clearly "are not." On the contrary, both the individual's behavior and his self-conceptions are constantly undergoing change, and they are highly responsive to the reactions of others.

To a large extent, this view is little more than a recasting or amplification of a classic sociological dictum of W. I. Thomas to the effect that "when men define situations as real, they are real in their consequences"—a theme developed further by Robert Merton as the "self-fulfilling prophecy." If we treat a person like a criminal, he is likely to become one. This point was nicely described by Frank Tannenbaum in an early work on crime and delinquency:

No more self-defeating device could be discovered than the one society has developed in dealing with the criminal. It proclaims his career in such loud and dramatic forms that both he and the community accept the judgment as a fixed description. He becomes conscious of himself as a criminal, and the community expects him to live up to his reputation, and will not credit him if he does not live up to it.

We have already seen how the identification of young people as "troublemakers" by teachers and school officials may backfire—rather than acting as a preventive technique, such labeling may drive the child into new trouble and progressively greater alienation. Clearly the police and the courts also have substantial power to activate and reinforce criminal careers and self-concepts. I have mentioned the ease with which we often "change" a person into a "criminal" (that is, our view of him changes) during the course of his trial on criminal charges. Indeed, the criminal trial is a prototype of what one sociologist has called the "status-degradation ceremony"—a ritualized process by which a condemned individual is stripped of his old identity and given a new (degraded) one. It is very difficult for an individual to sustain a favorable image of himself under the pressure of such public definitions. And if the defining process is clearly unfair (recall the criteria for official disposition in the "police encounters with juveniles" study), then however unwilling the "offender" may be to define himself as such, and even if harsh sanctions are not invoked in his particular case, he is likely to develop a hostility toward the official "system" that may increase the likelihood of antisocial behavior on his part in the future.

Under the impact of negative social reactions the individual may, then, be propelled from isolated acts of criminality into more complete involvement in criminal ways of life (heightened "commitment" to criminal roles), and he may come increasingly to view himself as an enemy of society (since society seems so determined to consider him one). Sociologist Edwin Lemert has suggested the distinction between "primary" and "secondary" deviation, the latter occurring when an individual comes to employ his deviance "as a means of defense, attack, or adjustment to the overt and covert problems created by the consequent societal reaction to him."

Concern with the impact of social reactions on individual self-conceptions and behavior (that is, focusing not on the pressures that initially drive the person into deviating behavior, but rather on the *consequences* for him of engaging in such behavior and being publicly identified as doing so) is but one aspect of this orientation to crime. Another involves examining the general impact, *on the society*, of defining a particular form of behavior as criminal. I have already referred to a prime example of this sort of impact—seen in the consequences of treating as criminal various borderline "offenses." As we shall note in more detail, the "criminalizing" of certain types of behavior may exacerbate the social problems in question in ways that take us quite beyond the level of individual social psychology. Thus, we may find significant economic consequences flowing from "criminalization" (as when a society's reaction to some form of deviating behavior provides the groundwork for a thriving black market) and also significant effects on the behavior and outlooks of law enforcement officials—as well as the predictable proliferation of much "secondary" crime among the "offenders" themselves.

Finally, the emphasis on social reactions suggests still another broad area of research which should increase our understanding of crime problems. This has to do with the social meaning of the "creation" of crimes (by lawmaking), both generally and with respect to particular offenses. Thus we are led to ask what general functions are served by ensuring that there are *some* crimes and "criminals" in a society (do we, in other words, really need crime?). And we are also drawn to comparative and historical analysis of rule-making in particular behavior areas (for example, what led up to our present drug laws, why do they differ from those in other Western countries, etc.). Unfortunately it will not be possible in this book to deal with such questions at any length—important as they may be for a comprehensive analysis of crime problems.

QUESTIONS FOR DISCUSSION AND WRITING

1. How can the identification of young people as "troublemakers" by teachers and school officials backfire?
2. What is the difference between primary and secondary deviance?
3. What are we led to ask after noting the emphasis on social reactions, and what are we drawn to compare?

Contemporary Research

Deviance on Record: Techniques for Labeling Child Abusers in Official Documents

LESLIE MARGOLIN

SOME sociologists believe that wrongdoers have considerable capacity to defend and mollify attributions of deviance by offering excuses, apologies, and expressions of sorrow. For example, conceptual formulations such as Mill's "vocabularies of motive," Scott and Lyman's "accounts," Sykes and Matza's "techniques of neutralization," and Hewitt and Stokes's "disclaimers" reflect a belief in the almost limitless reparative potential of talk. In the parlance of these sociologists, deviant identities are negotiable because attributions of wrongdoing are seen to depend not only on an assessment of what the wrongdoer did but on an understanding of his or her mental state during and after the violation. As Douglas observes, "An individual is considered responsible for his actions if and only if . . . he has intended to commit those actions and knows the rules relevant to them." Given these conditions, accused persons may argue that the violation in question was unanticipated, unplanned, and contrary to what they wished. Still, limited evidence exists that people win such arguments. Although account theorists claim that "the timbers of fractured sociations"

can be repaired through talk, investigators addressing the ways social control agents process putative deviants have found few instances of people talking their way out of deviant labels. On the whole, social control agents tend to pigeonhole clients fairly quickly. As Waegel has shown, the organizational demand to meet deadlines, process an expected number of cases, and turn out paperwork reduces the amount of time agents can give their clients. The more bureaucrats are hurried, the greater their need to rely on shorthand methods for dealing with clients, and thus, the greater the necessity to interpret people and situations by means of stereotypes. In this regard, stereotypical or "normal" case conceptions guide responses to homicide defendants, juvenile delinquents, clients in a public defender's office, skid-row residents, and shoplifters.

The paperwork demand has a second effect on the putative deviant's capacity to negotiate effectively. Because oral and written communication have different potentialities for conveying information and structuring argument, agencies emphasizing the creation of records place a proportional pressure on bureaucrats to note the "recordable" features of their clients' situations. By implication, the contingencies of a case which best lend themselves to being described in written language are given the most prominence in records, and those contingencies most difficult to capture on paper (those aspects of a case best understood through face-to-face interaction) are minimized or neglected.

Studies examining the types of information bureaucrats leave out of written accounts have shown that clients' feelings are often omitted because the inner life of the individual is not only difficult to defend as objective evidence, but it is difficult to defend as evidence in writing. In face-to-face encounters, however, feelings and intentions are available through a series of gestures, tonal changes, and bodily movements which accompany the other's words. There is continual exchange between words and gestures. Such reciprocity cannot be duplicated in written communication, particularly when the writing is part of an official document. This means that putative deviants' capacity to argue their cases is seriously reduced when cases must be made in writing.

While documents may be a poor medium for describing internal states, bureaucrats are also reluctant to designate deviance on something as indefinite as "feelings"—theirs or the client's. The primary risk of citing the client's mental state at the time of the violation as a criterion for labeling or not labeling is that it makes agents vulnerable to accusations of subjectivity and personal bias. Since records are permanently available to supervisory scrutiny, agents feel pressure to make written assessments defendable displays of bureaucratic competence. For this reason, agents must use records to display not only "what happened" but that they performed their jobs rationally and objectively. These practical considerations oblige agents whose decision processes are recorded to place singular emphasis on the tangible aspects of the case—what the putative deviant's behavior was and what harm resulted—at the same time giving relatively little weight to clients' excuses, apologies, and expressions of sorrow.

Conceptualizing the deviant identity, then, as a mosaic assembled out of imputations of behavior and intention, this study examines how such a mosaic is pieced together in written documents. I explore how the "deviant's"

point of view is documented and displayed and how evidence is organized on paper to create the appearance that "deviance" has occurred. These dynamics are addressed through the examination of 120 case records designating child abuse.

Since the documentary reality of child abuse provides the vehicle and substantive focus of the analysis, what follows shows how child care providers are constituted as intentionally harmful to children. Like other "dividing practices" which categorize people as either healthy/sick, law abiding/criminal, or sane/insane, the separation of child abusers from normals is seen as an accomplishment of asymmetric power relations.

This chapter focuses on the power imbalance between child abuse investigators and suspects and the means by which the former impose their version of reality on the latter. Since this imposition is an accomplishment of contemporary modes of discourse, I focus on investigators' vocabularies, the structure of their arguments, and the types of commonsense reasoning they use.

METHODS

The idea for this research emerged while I was involved in a study of child abuse by babysitters. As part of that study, I had to read "official" case records documenting that child abuse had occurred. The more records I read, the more it appeared that the social workers devoted a rather large portion of their writing to describing children's injuries, as well as the violent and sexual interactions which often preceded and followed them. By contrast, the alleged perpetrator's intentions, feelings, and interpretations of what happened appeared to occupy a relatively small portion of the documents. This imbalance roused interest in view of the agency's formal regulations that social workers satisfy two criteria to establish that a caregiver committed child abuse: (1) they must establish that a caregiver performed acts which were damaging or exploitive to a child, and (2) they must prove that the caregiver *intended* to damage or exploit the child—that the trauma was nonaccidental. In the chapter, I examine how social workers managed to label child abusers in a manner consistent with these regulations without appearing to give much weight to subjective factors such as suspects' excuses and justifications.

The sample consisted of 60 case records documenting physical abuse and 60 records documenting sexual abuse. They were randomly selected from all case records of child abuse by babysitters substantiated by a state agency during a two-year period ($N = 537$). A babysitter was defined as someone who took care of a child who was not a member of the child's family, was not a boyfriend or girlfriend of the child's parent, and was not employed in a registered or licensed group care facility.

I do not treat these records as ontologically valid accounts of "what happened"; rather, I treat them as a "documentary reality," indicating the ways the social workers who constructed them want to be seen by their superiors. As such, the records provide evidence that the social workers used the unstated yet commonly known procedures which represent "good work." The following analysis attempts to make these procedures explicit and to show how the social workers who used them "prove" that child abuse took place by constructing good (bureaucratically sound) arguments supporting the view that a specific person intentionally damaged a child. I also explore the degree to which deviants' excuses, denials, and other accounts were incorporated into these decision processes. Finally, I look at how each type of information—descriptions of the injuries and accounts of what happened—was used as evidence that child abuse occurred and could have only been performed by the person who was labeled.

Displaying Violence and Sexuality

At the beginning of each record, the social worker described the physical injuries which were believed to have been inflicted on the child by the babysitter. These descriptions did not specify how the child's health or functioning were impaired but were presented as evidence that an act of transformative social import had occurred. To illustrate this reporting style, one 3-year-old who was spanked by his babysitter was described by the physician as having "a contusion to the buttocks and small superficial lacerations." However, the social worker who used these injuries as evidence of child abuse described them as follows:

The injuries gave the appearance of an ink blot, in that they were almost mirror images of each other, positioned in the center of each buttock. The bruising was approximately four inches long by about two and a half inches wide, and was dark red on the perimeter and had a white cast to the inside of the bruise. There was a long linear line running across the bottom of both buttocks extending almost the entire width of the child's buttock. There was lighter reddish bruising surrounding the two largest bruises on each buttock and faint bluish-red bruising extending up to the lower back. The bruising would be characterized as being red turning to a deeper reddish-purple than true bright red.

This unusually graphic style of presentation gave the bruises a special status. They were no longer simply bruises but were now defined as out of the ordinary, strange, and grotesque. By removing the bruises from everyday experience, the stage was set for redefining the babysitter who supposedly did this to the child. In this manner, a person whose social status had been taken for granted could now be seen as potentially suspicious, foreign, and malevolent.

A parallel line of reportage was apparent in the sexual abuse cases. To the degree that the available information permitted, reports contained no obscurity in the descriptions of sexual interactions. No detail of what happened appeared too small to be pursued, named, and included in the records as evidence. This excerpt from a social worker's recorded interview with an 8-year-old girl illustrates:

S.W.: How did the bad touch happen? Can you think?   Child: I can't remember.

S.W.: Did you ever have to kiss?   Child: No.

S.W.: Anybody?   Child: Uh uh.

S.W.: Did you have to touch anybody?   Child: Yeah.

S.W.: Ah, you had to touch 'em. Where did you have to touch 'em?   Child: Down below.

S.W.: Oh, down below. Do you have a word for that body part?   Child: A thing-a-ma-jig.

S.W.: A thing-a-ma-jig. OK, let's look . . . Is P [the suspect] a man?   Child: Yeah.

S.W.: OK, let's take a look at the man doll. Can you show me on the man doll what part you're talking about?   Child: This part.

S.W.: Oh, the part that sticks out in front. We have another word for that. Do you know the other word for that part?   Child: Dick.

S.W.: Yeah. Dick is another word for it. Another word is penis.   Child: Penis?

S.W.: Yeah.   Child: Oh.

S.W.: Can you tell me what—did you see his body? Did you see his penis with your eyes?   Child: No.

S.W.: OK. Did he have his pants on or off?   Child: Unzipped.

S.W.: Unzipped. I see. How did his penis happen to come out of his pants?   Child: By the zipper.

S.W.: I see. Who took his penis out of his pants?   Child: He did.

S.W.: What did you have to touch his penis with?   Child: My fingers.

S.W.: I see. How did you know you had to do that?   Child: He told me to.

S.W.: What did he say?   Child: Itch it.

S.W.: Itch it. I see. Did he show you how to itch it? How did he have to itch it? One question at a time. Did he show you how to itch it?   Child: He said just go back.

S.W.: So you showed me that you're kind of scratching on it.   Child: Uh hum.

S.W.: Did anything happen to his penis or his thing-a-ma-jig when you did that?   Child: No.

S.W.: OK. When he took his penis out of his pants, how did it look?   Child: Yucky.

S.W.: Yeah, I know you think it's yucky, but um, what does yucky mean? Can you tell me with some other words besides yucky?   Child: Slimy.

S.W.: Looked slimy. OK. Was it big?   Child: Yeah.

S.W.: Was it hard or soft.   Child: Soft and hard.

S.W.: OK. Explain how you mean that. . . .

I offer this dialogue not as evidence that sexual abuse did or did not occur, but rather to display the means by which equivocal behavior is translated into the "fact" of sexual abuse. Whatever it is that "really happened" to this child, we see that her experience of it is not a concern when "documentation" is being gathered. She is an object of inquiry, not a participant. Whatever reasons compel social workers to bring her to their offices and ask these questions are their reasons not hers. And as the child learns, even features of the "event"—such as the size, hardness, and overall appearance of a penis—can assume critical importance within interviewers' frames of reference.

While social workers used these details of sexual interactions and injuries to set the stage for the attribution of deviance, I noted four cases in which the analysis of the injuries themselves played a conspicuously larger role in determining who was responsible. In these cases, the injured children were too young to explain how their injuries were caused, the babysitters denied causing the injuries, and there were no witnesses. This meant that the only way the investigators were able to label the babysitters as abusive was to argue that the injuries occurred during the time the suspects were taking care of the children. The parents of the injured children testified that the children were sent to the babysitters in good health, without any marks, but returned from the babysitters with a noticeable injury. This allowed the social workers to determine responsibility through the following method: if a babysitter cannot produce any plausible alternative explanation for the child's injuries, the babysitter must be responsible for the injuries.

Since children who had allegedly been sexually abused did not have conspicuous or easily described injuries, attributing sexual abuse on the absence of any plausible alternative explanation for the injury was, of course, impossible. This would appear to severely limit social workers' capacity to document that a babysitter committed sexual abuse when the babysitter denied the charges, when the child was too young to provide coherent testimony, and when there were no other witnesses. However, this was not always the case. Like the investigators described by Garfinkel who were able to determine the cause of death among possible suicides with only "*this* much; *this* sight; *this* note; *this* collection of whatever is at hand," child abuse investigators showed the capacity to "make do" with whatever information was available. In one case of sexual abuse, for example, there were no witnesses, no admission from the suspect, no physical evidence, and no charge from the alleged victim; still, "evidence" was summoned to establish a babysitter's guilt. Here, the social worker cited a 4-year-old girl's fears, nightmares, and other "behavior consistent with that of a child who was sexually traumatized by a close family friend." Additionally, the babysitter in question was portrayed as a "type" capable of doing such things:

Having no physical evidence, and no consistent statement from the alleged victim, I am forced to make a conclusion based on the credibility of the child as opposed to that of the perpetrator. This conclusion is supported by similar allegations against him from an independent source. It is also supported by behavioral indications and what we know of his history.

In a second case, a social worker showed that information pointing to the suspect's homosexuality and history of sexual victimization could be used to support charges of sexual abuse when other kinds of evidence were lacking:

Although the babysitter denied having sexual contact with this child when interviewed, he did leave a note to the effect that he was attracted to males and thought that he was homosexual, and records

indicate that he, himself, was sexually abused at the age of 8. Based on the interview done, the past history, and his own previous victimization, this worker feels that he did, in fact, penetrate and perpetrate himself upon the victim.

In most cases, however, portraying the suspect as a "type" was not critical to the finding of child abuse. The rationale for labeling was primarily constructed out of witnesses' testimony showing "who did what to whom."

Using Witnesses to Determine Who Did What to Whom

Since the children and alleged child abusers often had different versions of what happened (40 cases), social workers needed a decision-rule to settle the question of who had the correct story. The rule used for resolving disagreements was fairly simple: the child's version was considered the true one. The children were called "credible" witnesses when describing assaults which were done to them because it was assumed they had nothing to gain by falsely accusing the babysitter. The babysitters, on the other hand, were seen as "noncredible" (when they attempted to establish their innocence) because they had everything to gain by lying. Even children as young as 2 and 3 years old were believed in preference to their adult babysitters. In fact, the main reason given for interpreting children as superior witnesses was precisely their youth, ignorance, and lack of sophistication. As one social worker observed, "It's my experience that a 4-year-old would not be able to maintain such a consistent account of an incident if she was not telling the truth." Particularly in cases of sexual abuse, it was believed that the younger the witness, the more credible his or her testimony was. Social workers made the point that children who were providing details of sexual behavior would not know of such things unless they had been abused.

The children's accounts were rejected in only three instances. In one of these cases, two teenage boys claimed they witnessed a babysitter abuse a child as they peered through a window. Both the babysitter and the child said this was not true. The social worker did not feel it was necessary to explain why the babysitter would deny the allegations, but the child's denial was seen as problematic. Therefore, the social worker offered the following rationale for rejecting the child's account: "The child's refusal to say anything is not unusual because her mother was so verbally upset when she was informed of the allegations." A child's version of what happened (his denial of abuse) was rejected in a second case on the grounds that he was protecting a babysitter described as his "best friend." Finally, a 12-year-old female who repeatedly denied that anyone had touched her sexually was seen as noncredible because of her "modesty." As the social worker put it, "She did seem to have a very difficult time talking about it, and I feel she greatly minimized the incident due to her embarrassment about it." In general, however, testimony from children was treated as the most credible source of evidence of what happened, since most social workers believe that children do not lie about the abuse done to them. By contrast, babysitters were presented as credible witnesses only when they agreed with the allegations made against them (56 cases). When they testified to the contrary, they were portrayed as biased. What does *not* happen, therefore, is the child implicating someone, the accused saying nothing happened, and the investigator siding with the accused. This suggests an underlying idealization that precedes and supports the ones operating on the surface of most cases: *The accused is guilty.* It goes without saying that this organizational stance runs roughly opposite to the constitutional one of "innocent until proven guilty." Here it might be useful to draw an analogy between the child protection workers' "investigative stance" and that of welfare investigators responsible for determining applicants' eligibility.

In both cases, investigators adopt a thoroughgoing skepticism designed "to locate and display the potential discrepancy between the applicant's [or suspect's] subjective and 'interested' claims and the factual and objective (i.e., rational) account that close observance of agency procedure is deemed to produce." However, an important difference should be noted: during the conduct of welfare investigations, the investigated party is referred to as the "applicant," indicating that the investigation could end in a determination of either eligibility or ineligibility; by contrast, during the conduct of child abuse investigations, the investigated party is routinely identified as the "perpetrator," suggesting a previously concluded status. To illustrate, these notations documented one worker's activities during the first days of a child abuse investigation:

3/24: Home visit with police, interviewed parents, child not at home—perpetrator not in home.
3/26: Interview with Detective J at Police Station with CPI and child. Perpetrator arrested.

While babysitters accused of child abuse may in theory be only "suspects," at the level of practice, they are "perpetrators." This discrepancy between "theory" and "practice" is more than an example of how the formal structures of organizations are accompanied by unintended and unprogrammed structures. In this instance, child protection workers are formally enjoined to gather evidence about "perpetrators," not "suspects." Consider these guidelines from the agency's official handbook:

Information collected from the person [witness] should include precise description of size, shape, color, type, and location of injury. It may be possible to establish the credibility of the child, the responsible caretaker or the *perpetrator* as a source of this information. . . . The *perpetrator* and victim may be credible persons and need to be judged on the basis of the same factors as any other persons. (Italics added)

The implicit message is that the goal of the child abuse investigation is not to determine an individual's guilt or innocence but to find evidence to be used in recording or "documenting" what is already taken for granted, that parties initially identified as the "perpetrator" and "victim" are in fact the "perpetrator" and "victim." Strictly speaking, then, the goal is not to determine "who did what to whom," since that information is assumed at the outset, but rather to document that agency rules have been followed and that the investigation was conducted in a rational, impersonal manner.

Determining Intentionality

A decision-rule was also needed to determine the babysitter's intentions. While babysitters were portrayed in the allegations as malicious or exploitive, many babysitters offered a different version of their motivations. Among the babysitters accused of physical abuse, 25 acknowledged hitting the children but also claimed they intended no harm. Three said they were having a bad day, were under unusual stress, and simply "lost it." They attributed their violence to a spontaneous, noninstrumental expression of frustration. For example, one male caregiver took a 2-year-old to the potty several times but the child did not go. Later, he noticed that the child's diaper was wet, so he hurried him to the potty. However, just before being placed on the potty the child had a bowel movement. At that point, the caregiver lost his temper and hit the child.

One woman who was labeled abusive claimed she was ill and never wanted to babysit in the first place. She only agreed to take care of a 2-year-old girl because the girl's mother insisted. The mother had an unexpected schedule change at work and needed child care on an emergency basis. The abusive event occurred soon after the babysitter served lunch to the child. While the sitter rested on a couch in the living room, she observed the girl messing with her lunch. The sitter got up and tried to settle the child. When this did not work, she took away the girl's paper plate and

threw it in the garbage. At that point, the girl began to cry for her mother. The babysitter returned to the living room to lie down on the couch. But the girl followed her, wailing for her mother. When the girl reached the couch, the babysitter sat up and slapped her.

Other babysitters described their violence in instrumental terms: their goal was to discipline the children and not to hurt or injure them. They said that whatever injuries occurred were the accidental result of hitting (in one case, biting) the children harder than they meant to do. Some sitters indicated that the only reason children were injured during a disciplinary action was that the children moved just as they were being hit, exposing a sensitive part of the body to the blow. Others protested that the child's movements made it impossible to aim the blows accurately or to assess how hard they were hitting. In one case, the sitter said she was trying to hit the child across the buttocks with a stick, but the child put her hand across her buttocks to protect herself, receiving "nonintentional" bruising and swelling to the hand.

A different sitter asked that the social worker consider that at the time of the violation he did not know it was against the law to beat a child with a belt. Another said he had been given permission to spank the child by the child's mother and was only following her orders. This was confirmed by the mother. After a 2½-year-old bit another child, his sitter bit him to show him "what it felt like." The sitter argued that she had done this in the past and had even told the child's mother. Thus, she believed that this was tacitly approved. Still another babysitter claimed that he struck the 11-year-old girl who was in his care in self-defense. He said that when he told her it was time for bed she began to bite and kick him. He said her injuries resulted from his efforts to calm and restrain her.

To sift out the babysitters' "official" intentions from the versions offered by the sitters themselves, several social workers explicitly invoked the following reasoning: physical damage to the child would be considered "intentional" if the acts which produced them were intentional. Thus, a social worker wrote: "I am concluding that this injury to the child was non-accidental in that the babysitter did have a purpose in striking the child, that purpose being to discipline her in hopes of modifying her behavior."

While close examination of this logic reveals an absurdity (the injury was seen as "intentional" despite the fact that it was produced by an act aimed at an entirely different outcome, "modifying her behavior"), the practical consequence of such a formula was a simple method for determining a suspect's intentions: if a babysitter was known to intentionally hit a child, causing an injury, the social worker could conclude the babysitter intended to cause the injury. Through such a formula, the most common excuse used by babysitters to account for their actions, that the injury was the accidental result of a disciplinary action, was interpreted as a confession of responsibility for physical abuse.

To give another example of how this formula provided a short-cut to determining intentionality, one social worker concluded her recording as follows: "Physical abuse is founded in that the caretaker did hit the child on the face because she was throwing a temper tantrum and left a bruise approximately one inch long under the right eye. This constitutes a non-accidental injury. The bruise is still visible after five days."

In cases involving allegations of physical abuse, the problem of figuring out what the babysitter was really contemplating at the time of the violation never came up as a separate issue because the alleged perpetrator's motivation to injure the child was seen as the operational equivalent of two prior questions, "Does the child have an injury resulting from a blow?" and "Did the babysitter intentionally strike the child?" When each of these questions was answered affirmatively, intent to harm the child was inferred. Thus, it was possible for a social worker to observe, "It was this writer's opinion that the babysitter was surprised at the injury she left on the child by spanking the child," and later conclude, "the injury occurred as a result of a non-accidental incident."

One record included comments from witnesses which stated that a babysitter pushed a 5-year-old boy after the child socked a cat. All agreed that the injury was not a direct consequence of the push but resulted when the child lost balance and fell over. Despite the social worker's explicit recognition that the child's injury was neither planned nor anticipated (she wrote that "the injury will probably not be repeated due to the sitter's awareness of the seriousness of disciplining a child by reacting rather than thinking"), the report of physical abuse was, nonetheless, founded "due to the fact that the injury occurred in the course of a disciplinary action."

In another record, a male babysitter admitted to spanking a child, causing red marks on his buttocks. Although the child's father said he "did not believe the sitter meant to spank as hard as he did," and the police officer who was present concluded that "based on the information obtained in this investigation, I could find no intent on the sitter's part to assault this child," the social worker found the determination of physical abuse nonproblematic. Since the child received the injury in the course of a spanking, child abuse occurred.

There were only two cases of sexual abuse in which the alleged abuser acknowledged touching the child in a manner consistent with the allegations, but at the same time denied sexual intent. In one of these cases, the alleged abuser said he only touched a 10-year-old boy's genitals in the process of giving him a bath. In the other case, the alleged abuser claimed he only touched the girl's body as part of an anatomy lesson, to show her where her rib and pelvic bones were located. Both of these accounts were dismissed as preposterous. The social workers expressed the opinion that sexual intent was the only possible reason anyone would enact the types of behavior attributed to the accused in the allegations. In short, an equation was drawn between specific behaviors attributed to the accused and their states of mind. If it was established that the babysitter behaved toward the child in ways commonly understood as sexual (e.g., fondling), establishing intent, as a separate dimension of the investigation, was seen as redundant. Thus, social workers were able to conclude their investigations of sexual abuse, as one investigator did, by using the following formula: "The child, a credible witness, indicated that her babysitter did fondle her genitals. Therefore, this is a founded case of intent to commit sexual abuse."

To summarize, in cases of both physical and sexual abuse, the intent to commit these acts was seen as a necessary component of the specific behaviors used to accomplish them. Hitting which resulted in an injury was always treated as if it was a direct indicator of the motivation to injure. Similarly, behavior commonly known as "sexual" was always treated as if it was identical with the suspect's intent to sexually exploit. The fact that social workers sometimes described the suspects' surprise and horror at the physical damage their violence caused the child did not make the attribution of "intent to harm" more problematic because suspects' accounts were not organizationally defined as indicators of intent. Consistent with Mills, motives for child abuse are not features of the perpetrator's psyche, but rather of the bureaucracy and profession. That 50 of the babysitters labeled as abusive denied performing the actions imputed to them, and another 14 were not interviewed at all (either because they could not be located or refused to speak to the social worker) demonstrated that it was possible to "officially" determine babysitters' intentions without confirmatory statements from the babysitters themselves.

DISCUSSION

Sociologists have often questioned official records on the grounds of their accuracy, reliability, and representativeness. However, the methods through which and by which deviance is routinely displayed in records have rarely been investigated.

This study has treated as problematic the standardized arguments and evidence which social workers use in official documents to prove that child abuse has taken place. In this regard, child abuse is seen as an accomplishment of a bureaucratic system in which members agree to treat specific phenomena as if they were "child abuse." The proof of abuse was problematic since more than half of the suspects either denied the accusations or were not interviewed. Social workers "made do" without supportive testimony from suspects by routinely defining them as "noncredible" witnesses. Also, social workers managed to conform to agency regulations requiring proof that suspects intended to harm or exploit children by agreeing to treat specific observables as if they represented the intent to harm or exploit.

Thus, the designation of child abuse was simplified. Testimony from the person most likely to disagree with this label, the accused, did not have to be considered. This is not to say that testimony from the accused might overcome the processes of institutional sense-making.

It is to suggest, rather, that defining the accused as noncredible makes the designation of child abuse more "cut and dried," defendable, and recordable, since abuse that might otherwise be denied, excused, or justified, either in whole or in part, can then be fully attributed to suspects.

While it can be argued that simplifying the means by which suspects are labeled is desirable for a society concerned about keeping dangerous people away from children, the negative consequences should be acknowledged.

As might also be expected, the personal, social, and legal stigma resulting from designating this label is enormous. Once the impression has been formed that a person is a child abuser, the expectation exists that he or she will continue to be abusive. Moreover, there is little a person can do to remove this label. It exists as part of a permanent record that can be recalled whenever a person's child care capacities or moral standing are questioned.

While most who write about child abuse are enmeshed in that system, either as practitioners or idealogues and so are strained to defend its existence, in recent years critics have shown concern about the growing numbers of people labeled as child abusers. Most trace this "overattribution" of child abuse to professional and laypeople's "emotionally charged desire to 'do something' about child abuse, fanned by repeated and often sensational media coverage." However, Conrad and Schneider provide a more general explanation: "Bureaucratic 'industries' with large budgets and many employees . . . depend for their existence on the acceptance of a particular deviance designation. They become 'vested interests' in every sense of the term." To take their analysis one step further, "bureaucratic industries" have a vested interest not only in a label but in a labeling process—specifically, in finding ways of reducing complexity and making labeling accomplishable.

Piven and Cloward's analysis of the regulating functions of welfare programs suggests why these bureaucracies have expanded in recent years. If income support programs expand and contract to control turmoil resulting from instability in labor markets, it is possible that social agencies geared to controlling child care grow in response to instability in the child care system. This hypothesis warrants attention if for no other reason than that mothers' dramatic increases in labor force participation over the past three decades, and the commensurate increase in young children's time in nonparental care, have closely paralleled the emergence of child abuse as a major social issue. However, this single causal mode of explanation would be more compelling if it were not that history reveals other periods in which institutional momentum developed around "saving children" under a variety of different conditions. This suggests that any explanation of why such social movements wax and wane, taking their particular form at each point in history, needs to account for many interacting factors, including the prevailing moralities and family institutions as well as opportunities for effectively marketing these problems to a wide audience.

To conclude, this study has shown some of the ways in which the construction of documents labels deviance. The main findings include bureaucrats' determination to translate sex and violence into endlessly accumulated verbal detail, to "make do" with whatever information is available, to fashion proofs of child abuse based on the new "commonsense" that children's testimony is more credible than adults', and to develop simple, accomplishable ways of imputing intentionality that are unaffected by suspects' accounts.

QUESTIONS FOR DISCUSSION AND WRITING

1. In addition to their role in documenting what happened, for what else do bureaucrats use official records?
2. What "implicit message" is conveyed by an official policy of referring to suspects as "perpetrators"?
3. What does the author conclude about this study?

VII

HOW DO WE EXPLAIN CRIME?

The Loyal Opposition to Conventional Criminological Theory

W HAT do we mean by "loyal opposition?" To answer that question, we
should first address what we mean by "conventional criminological
theory"—mainstream theories of mid- to late twentieth-century American
criminology. These theories have tended to build on one another, to use legal definitions of crime (crime is behavior that violates the criminal law),
and to be compatible with official sources of crime statistics such as those
collected by the Uniform Crime Reports. With the exception of labeling
theory, the theories discussed in Parts V and VI fit this conception.

A reason for differentiating from the mainstream the theories presented
in this section is that the major theorists represented here, with the possible exception of Sellin, would characterize themselves as being in opposition to the theories that have dominated criminological discussion during the middle and late twentieth century.

Most modern sociologists believe that dividing ideas into those that reflect consensus images versus conflict images is a false dichotomy. We
agree, but at the same time, we find it useful to think in these terms when
we categorize theories—it simply makes it easier to discuss them. The assumption (or image) underlying consensus theories is contained in the answer to the question, "How is society possible?" The answer is that there is
a consensus, or broad-based agreement, among members of the society on
important norms and values. Those who reject this assumption believe
that societies are characterized not by consensus but by conflict—that societies are divided into competing interest groups, and that important cleav-
ages separate and distinguish groups within societies. These divisions
may be along the lines of class, race, gender, age, and so on. For conflict
theorists, the answer to the question "How is society possible?" is that society can exist either when one group has sufficient power to dominate its
competitors or when multiple groups share power so that they each have
an interest in maintaining a truce.

In reality, neither consensus nor conflict alone characterizes societies. Every society has aspects that are consistent with both images, and some societies are more divided than others. But in explaining crime, criminologists

have found it useful to emphasize one aspect or the other. Those theories that we have labeled "conventional criminological theories" have been more consistently based on consensus assumptions. The theories to which we will now turn are more consistent with conflict assumptions.

We have called these theories the "loyal opposition" because, although theorists of this tradition have been critical of mainstream criminologists, they continue to belong to the same scholarly associations and to publish in the same journals. Their criticisms have been important in the development of criminology. Not only have they offered important ideas of their own, but their critiques have also improved the quality of mainstream theorizing. For instance, many conventional criminologists use unofficial data sources in their research, in part because critical scholars argued convincingly that official sources may be biased by the institutionalized coercive and discriminatory practices of the criminal justice system.

The first reading in this section is by Thorsten Sellin. His concept of "cultural conflict" was an important contribution to criminology. In this selection from his monograph *Culture Conflict and Crime*, Sellin has written about the production of crime when cultures with differing value systems come into contact. An individual could become criminal, he argues, by adhering to the norms of his native culture in a situation in which another culture with different norms has the legal power to define criminality. That person then becomes a criminal, not because of pathology, or a decision to violate the norms, but because he adheres to the norms that govern life in his own culture.

Some criminologists will no doubt wonder why we've chosen to place Elijah Anderson's "The Code of the Streets" with culture conflict. We believe that the conflict Sellin discusses is a product of social structural change—migration, invasion, and close proximity—that bears a striking resemblance to the circumstances Anderson observes. In Philadelphia, where Anderson has been doing important ethnographic research, a set of norms and values that he calls the "code of the streets" has emerged, largely because of social and economic structural changes that affect inner-city life across America. Consistent with Sellin's thesis, by adhering to the norms of this oppositional culture, people at times find themselves in trouble with the dominant culture's legal system. Although not identical, we believe that it is useful to think of Anderson's work in the context of the tradition established by Sellin.

Austin Turk's "Conflict and Criminality" is an explication of basic conflict theory. Students sometimes think of conflict rather narrowly when instructors introduce it. By "conflict," criminologists do not mean fights that are later defined as assaults. Clearly the two parties in the fight are engaging in a conflict of sorts, but criminologists are referring to larger conflicts between those who wield power and are able to influence social institutions, the state, and the criminal justice system, and those who are subjects of this power. Conflict, as defined by Turk, grows out of a Weberian view of society, one in which competing groups or "parties" (not necessarily political parties) try to use power to pursue and protect their own interests. In some circumstances, this can lead to criminality among losers in the conflict of competing interests.

A good example of how this process works is the changing public conception of rape. The concept "acquaintance rape" is now widely known and is publicly defined as criminal behavior. This was not the case too many years ago. Previously rape was generally conceived of more narrowly as stranger assault. The women's movement, which represents an interest group, challenged this narrower conception of rape. In other words, there was conflict over the definition. A broadening of the public conception of rape was a product of conflict that resulted from feminists' challenge to the old conception.

Robert Crutchfield, Ann Glusker, and George Bridges' "A Tale of Three Cities: Labor Markets and Homicide" represents a different conflict-oriented approach. Dual labor market theory is a conflict perspective developed by sociologists to explain why some groups, particularly but not exclusively minority groups, are perpetually disadvantaged in the labor market and in the economic system generally. They argue that the structure of the labor market benefits some groups disproportionately, while systematically disadvantaging others. In their paper, Crutchfield, Glusker, and Bridges combine this approach with control theory conceptions of bonding and the routine activities perspective (to be discussed further in Part VIII) to explain why neighborhood homicide rates differ within cities. They also show how the structure of local labor markets affects homicide. These authors further argue that inequality in the labor market is reproduced in the educational system, which in turn has an effect on homicide rates.

Finally, we turn to Marxist criminological theory. Marxist, or radical, theory is a special case of conflict theory. Marxists propose that the important division in society is the one produced by economic class. Marx himself wrote very little about crime, but in 1916 Willem Bonger used a Marxist analysis to describe the causes of criminality. However, this perspective only began to flourish in modern criminology in the late 1960s. As the twenty-first century begins, some students may wonder why we have included a "discredited" perspective. After all, the Soviet Union has collapsed, the countries of Eastern Europe have capitalist economies, and the Berlin Wall was torn down years ago. Nonetheless, we believe it is important to discuss this theory because it still guides research and assists some criminologists in interpreting the world they are observing. We continue to learn from research in this tradition.

The selection by William Chambliss, "Crime and Structural Contradictions," outlines the basic arguments of Marxist criminology. Chambliss argues that economic interests determine what behavior is defined as crime, how the law is enforced, and the sanctions levied against violators. Much of Chambliss' work (another example appears in Part III) makes the point that we cannot fully understand crime and enforcement unless we study it in the context of the economic and political interests and forces in society.

In "Causes of Crime: A Radical View," Michael Lynch and Byron Groves describe developments in contemporary Marxist criminological theory. They too argue for the importance of analyzing crime within the context of economic power. It should be clear to the reader that we learn interesting and important things about a phenomenon by being critical of competing views and evidence. Radical criminologists have been critical of the state, the criminal justice system, and mainstream criminology itself, and the development of criminology has been moved forward as a result.

CULTURE CONFLICT

Culture Conflict and Crime

THORSTEN SELLIN

THERE are social groups on the surface of the earth which possess complexes of conduct norms which, due to differences in the mode of life and the social values evolved by these groups, appear to set them apart from other groups in many or most respects. We may expect conflicts of norms when the rural dweller moves to the city, but we assume that he has absorbed the basic norms of the culture which comprises both town and country. How much greater is not the conflict likely to be when Orient and Occident meet, or when the Corsican mountaineer is transplanted to the lower East Side of New York. Conflicts of cultures are inevitable when the norms of one cultural or subcultural area migrate to or come in contact with those of another, and it is interesting to note that most of the specific researches on culture conflict and delinquency have been concerned with this aspect of conflict rather than the one mentioned earlier.

Conflicts between the norms of divergent cultural codes may arise (1) when these codes clash on the border of contiguous culture areas; (2) when, as may be the case with legal norms, the law of one cultural group is extended to cover the territory of another; or (3) when members of one cultural group migrate to another.

From "Culture Conflict and Crime" by T. Sellin, *Culture Conflict and Crime* (Bulletin 41), 1938, New York: Social Science Research Council.

Speck, for instance, notes that "where the bands popularly known as Montagnais have come more and more into contact with Whites, their reputation has fallen lower among the traders who have known them through commercial relationships within that period. The accusation is made that they have become less honest in connection with their debts, less trustworthy with property, less truthful, and more inclined to alcoholism and sexual freedom as contacts with the frontier towns have become easier for them. Richard White reports in 1933 unusual instances of Naskapi breaking into traders' store houses."

Similar illustrations abound in the works of the cultural anthropologists. We need only to recall the effect on the American Indian of the culture conflicts induced by our policy of acculturation by guile and force. In this instance, it was not merely contact with the white man's culture, his religion, his business methods, and his liquor, which weakened the tribal mores. In addition, the Indian became subject to the white man's law and this brought conflicts as well, as has always been the case when legal norms have been imposed upon a group previously ignorant of them. Maunier, in discussing the diffusion of French law in Algeria, recently stated:

"In introducing the *Code Pénal* in our colonies, as we do, we transform into offenses the ancient usages of the inhabitants which their customs permitted or imposed. Thus, among the Khabyles of Algeria, the killing of adulterous wives is ritual murder committed by the father or brother of the wife and not by her husband, as elsewhere. The woman having been sold by her family to her husband's family, the honor of her relatives is soiled by her infidelity. Her father or brother has the right and the duty to kill her in order to cleanse by her blood the honor of her relatives. Murder in revenge is also a duty, from family to family, in case of murder of or even in case of insults to a relative: the vendetta, called the rekba in Khabylian, is imposed by the law of honor. But these are crimes in French law! Murder for revenge, being premeditated and planned, is assassination, punishable by death! . . . What happens, then, often when our authorities pursue the criminal, guilty of an offense against public safety as well as against morality: public enemy of the French order, but who has acted in accord with a respected custom? The witnesses of the assassination, who are his relatives, or neighbors, fail to lay charges against the assassin; when they are questioned, they pretend to know nothing; and the pursuit is therefore useless. A French magistrate has been able to speak of 'the conspiracy of silence among the Algerians'; a conspiracy aiming to preserve traditions, always followed and obeyed, against their violation by our power. This is the tragic aspect of the conflict of laws. A recent decree forbids the husband among the Khabyles to profit arbitrarily by the power given him according to this law to repudiate his wife, demanding that her new husband pay an exorbitant price for her—this is the custom of the lefdi. Earlier, one who married a repudiated wife paid nothing to the former husband. It appears that the first who tried to avail himself of the new law was killed for violating the old custom. The aboli-tion of the ancient law does not always occur without protest or opposition. That which is a crime was a duty, and the order which we cause to reign is sometimes established to the detriment of 'superstition'; it is the gods and the spirits, it is believed, that would punish any one who fails to revenge his honor."

When Soviet law was extended to Siberia, similar effects were observed. Anossow and Wirschubski both relate that women among the Siberian tribes, who in obedience to the law, laid aside their veils were killed by their relatives for violating one of the most sacred norms of their tribes.

We have noted that culture conflicts are the natural outgrowth of processes of social differentiation, which produce an infinity of social groupings, each with its own definitions of life situations, its own interpretations of social relationships, its own ignorance or misunderstanding of the social values of other groups. The transformation of a culture from a homogeneous and well-integrated type to a heterogeneous and disintegrated type is therefore accompanied by an increase of conflict situations. Conversely, the operation of integrating processes will reduce the number of conflict situations. Such conflicts within a changing culture may be distinguished from those created when different cultural systems come in contact with one another, regardless of the character or stage of development of these systems. In either case, the conduct of members of a group involved in the conflict of codes will in some respects be judged abnormal by the other group.

QUESTIONS FOR DISCUSSION AND WRITING

1. According to Sellin, at what three times may conflicts between norms of divergent cultures arise?
2. What may happen when new norms are followed?
3. What does Sellin conclude about the conduct of members of a group?

The Code of the Streets

ELIJAH ANDERSON

O F all the problems besetting the poor inner-city black community, none is more pressing than that of interpersonal violence and aggression. It wreaks havoc daily with the lives of community residents and increasingly spills over into downtown and residential middle-class areas. Muggings, burglaries, carjackings, and drug-related shootings, all of which may leave their victims or innocent bystanders dead, are now common enough to concern all urban and many suburban residents. The inclination to violence springs from the circumstances of life among the ghetto poor—the lack of jobs that pay a living wage, the stigma of race, the fallout from rampant drug use and drug trafficking, and the resulting alienation and lack of hope for the future.

Simply living in such an environment places young people at special risk of falling victim to aggressive behavior. Although there are often forces in the community which can counteract the negative influences, by far the most powerful being a strong, loving, "decent" (as inner-city residents put it) family committed to middle-class values, the despair is pervasive enough to have spawned an oppositional culture, that of "the streets," whose norms are often consciously opposed to those of mainstream society. These two orientations—decent and street—socially organize the community, and their coexistence has important consequences of residents, particularly children growing up in the inner city. Above all, this environment means that even youngsters whose home lives reflect mainstream values—and the majority of homes in the community do—must be able to handle themselves in a street-oriented environment.

This is because the street culture has evolved what may be called a code of the streets, which amounts to a set of informal rules governing interpersonal public behavior, including violence. The rules prescribe both a proper comportment and a proper way to respond if challenged. They regulate the use of violence and so allow those who are inclined to aggression to precipitate violent encounters in an approved way. The rules have been established and are enforced mainly by the street-oriented, but on the streets the distinction between street and decent is often irrelevant; everybody knows that if the rules are violated, there are penalties. Knowledge of the code is thus largely defensive; it is literally necessary for operating in public. Therefore, even though families with a decency orientation are usually opposed to the values of the code, they often reluctantly encourage their children's familiarity with it to enable them to negotiate the inner-city environment.

From "The Code of the Streets" by E. Anderson, 1994, originally appeared in *The Atlantic Monthly* 273 (no. 5, May 1994):81–94. Copyright © 1999 by Elijah Anderson. Reprinted by permission of W. W. Norton & Company, Inc.

At the heart of the code is the issue of respect—loosely defined as being treated "right," or granted the deference one deserves. However, in the troublesome public environment of the inner city, as people increasingly feel buffeted by forces beyond their control, what one deserves in the way of respect becomes more and more problematic and uncertain. This in turn further opens the issue of respect to sometimes intense interpersonal negotiation. In the street culture, especially among young people, respect is viewed as almost and external entity that is hard-won but easily lost, and so must constantly be guarded. The rules of the code in fact provide a framework for negotiating respect. The person whose very appearance—including his clothing, demeanor, and way of moving—deters transgressions feels that he possesses, and may be considered by others to possess, a measure of respect. With the right amount of respect, for instance, he can avoid "being bothered" in public. If he is bothered, not only may he be in physical danger but he has been disgraced or "dissed" (disrespected). Many of the forms that dissing can take might seem petty to middle-class people (maintaining eye contact for too long, for example), but to those invested in the street code, these actions become serious indications of the other person's intentions. Consequently, such people become very sensitive to advances and slights, which could well serve as warnings of imminent physical confrontation.

This hard reality can be traced to the profound sense of alienation from mainstream society and its institutions felt by many poor inner-city black people, particularly the young. The code of the streets is actually a cultural adaptation to a profound lack of faith in the police and the judicial system. The police are most often seen as representing the dominant white society and not caring to protect inner-city residents. When called, they may not respond, which is one reason many residents feel they must be prepared to take extraordinary measures to defend themselves and their loved ones against those who are inclined to

aggression. Lack of police accountability has in fact been incorporated into the status system: the person who is believed capable of "taking care of himself" is accorded a certain deference, which translates into a sense of physical and psychological control. Thus the street code emerges where the influence of the police ends and personal responsibility for one's safety is felt to begin. Exacerbated by the proliferation of drugs and easy access to guns, this volatile situation results in the ability of the street-oriented minority (or those who effectively "go for bad") to dominate the public spaces.

DECENT AND STREET FAMILIES

Although almost everyone in poor inner-city neighborhoods is struggling financially and therefore feels a certain distance from the rest of America, the decent and the street family in a real sense represent two poles of value orientation, two contrasting conceptual categories. The labels "decent" and "street," which the residents themselves use, amount to evaluative judgments that confer status on local residents. The labeling is often the result of a social contest among individuals and families of the neighborhood. Individuals of the two orientations often coexist in the same extended family. Decent residents judge themselves to be so while judging others to be of the street, and street individuals often present themselves as decent, drawing distinctions between themselves and other people. In addition, there is quite a bit of circumstantial behavior—that is, one person may at different times exhibit both decent and street orientations, depending on the circumstances. Although these designations result from so much social jockeying, there do exist concrete features that define each conceptual category.

Generally, so-called decent families tend to accept mainstream values more fully and attempt to instill them in their children. Whether married couples with children or single-parent (usually female) households, they are generally "working poor" and so tend to be better off financially than their street-oriented neighbors. They value hard work and self-reliance and are willing to sacrifice for their children. Because they have a certain amount of faith in mainstream society, they harbor hopes for a better future for their children, if not for themselves. Many of them go to church and take a strong interest in their children's schooling. Rather than dwelling on the real hardships and inequities facing them, many such decent people, particularly the increasing number of grandmothers raising grandchildren, see their difficult situation as a test from God and derive great support from their faith and from the church community.

Extremely aware of the problematic and often dangerous environment in which they reside, decent parents tend to be strict in their child-rearing practices, encouraging children to respect authority and walk a straight moral line. They have an almost obsessive concern about trouble of any kind and remind their children to be on the lookout for people and situations that might lead to it. At the same time, they are themselves polite and considerate of others, and teach their children to be the same way. At home, at work, and in church, they strive hard to maintain a positive mental attitude and a spirit of cooperation.

So-called street parents, in contrast, often show a lack of consideration for other people and have a rather superficial sense of family and community. Though they may love their children, many of them are unable to cope with the physical and emotional demands of parenthood, and find it difficult to reconcile their needs with those of their children. These families, who are more fully invested in the code of the streets than the decent people are, may aggressively socialize their children into it in a normative way. They believe in the code and judge themselves and others according to its values.

In fact the overwhelming majority of families in the inner-city community try to approximate the decent-family model, but there are many others who clearly represent the worst fears of the decent family. Not only are their financial resources extremely limited, but what little they have may easily be misused. The lives of the street-oriented are often marked by disorganization. In the most desperate circumstances people frequently have a limited understanding of priorities and consequences, and so frustrations mount over bills, food, and, at times, drink, cigarettes, and drugs. Some tend toward self-destructive behavior; many street-oriented women are crack-addicted ("on the pipe"), alcoholic, or involved in complicated relationships with men who abuse them. In addition, the seeming intractability of their situation, caused in large part by the luck of well-paying jobs and the persistence of racial discrimination, has engendered deep-seated bitterness and anger in many of the most desperate and poorest blacks, especially young people. The need both to exercise a measure of control and to lash out at somebody is often reflected in the adults' relations with their children. At the least, the frustrations of persistent poverty shorten the fuse in such people—contributing to a lack of patience with anyone, child or adult, who irritates them.

In these circumstances a woman—or a man, although men are less consistently present in children's lives—can be quite aggressive with children, yelling at and striking them for the least little infraction of the rules she has set down. Often little if any serious explanation follows the verbal and physical punishment. This response teaches children a particular lesson. They learn that to solve any kind of interpersonal problem one must quickly resort to hitting or other violent behavior. Actual peace and quiet, and also the appearance of calm, respectful children conveyed to her neighbors and friends, are often what the young mother most desires, but at times she will be very aggressive in trying to get them. Thus she may be quick to beat her children, especially if they defy her law, not because she hates them but because this is the way she knows to control them. In fact, many street-oriented women love their children dearly. Many mothers in the community subscribe to the notion that there is a "devil in the boy" that must be beaten out of him or that socially "fast girls need to be whupped." Thus, much of what borders on child abuse in the view of social authorities is acceptable parental punishment in the view of these mothers.

Many street-oriented women are sporadic mothers whose children learn to fend for themselves when necessary, foraging for food and money any way they can get it. The children are sometimes employed by drug dealers of become addicted themselves. These children of the street, growing up with little supervision, are said to "come up hard." They often learn to fight at an early age, sometimes using short-tempered adults around them as role models. The street-oriented home may be fraught with anger, verbal disputes, physical aggression, and even mayhem. The children observe these goings-on, learning the lesson that might makes right. They quickly learn to hit those who cross them, and the dog-eat-dog mentality prevails. In order to survive, to protect oneself, it is necessary to marshal inner resources and be ready to deal with adversity in a hands-on way. In these circumstances physical prowess takes on great significance.

In some of the most desperate cases, a street-oriented mother may simply leave her young children alone and unattended while she goes out. The most irresponsible women can be found at local bars and crack houses, getting high and socializing with other adults. Sometimes a troubled woman will leave very young children alone for days at a time. Reports of crack addicts abandoning their children have become common in drug-infested inner-city communities. Neighbors or relatives discover the abandoned children, often hungry and distraught over the absence of their mother. After repeated absences, a friend or relative, particularly a grandmother, will often step in to care for the young children, sometimes petitioning the authorities to send her, as guardian of the children, the mother's welfare check, if the mother gets one. By this time, however, the children may well have learned the first lesson of the streets: survival itself, let alone respect, cannot be taken for granted; you have to fight for your place in the world.

CAMPAIGNING FOR RESPECT

These realities of inner-city life are largely absorbed on the streets. At an early age, often even before they start school, children from street-oriented homes gravitate to the streets, where they "hang"—socialize with their peers. Children from these generally permissive homes have a great deal of latitude and are allowed to "rip and run" up and down the street. They often come home from school, put their books down, and go right back out the door. On school nights eight- and nine-year-olds remain out until nine or ten o'clock (and teenagers typically come in whenever they want to). On the streets they play in groups that often become the source of their primary social bonds. Children from decent homes tend to be more carefully supervised and are thus likely to have curfews and to be taught how to stay out of trouble.

When decent and street kids come together, a kind of social shuffle occurs in which children have a chance to go either way. Tension builds as a child comes to realize that he must choose an orientation. The kind of home he comes from influences but does not determine the way he will ultimately turn out—although it is unlikely that a child from a thoroughly street-oriented family will easily absorb decent values on the streets. Youths who emerge from street-oriented families but develop a decency orientation almost always learn those values in another setting—in school, in a youth group, in church. Often it is the result of their involvement with a caring "old head" (adult role model).

In the street, through their play, children pour their individual life experiences into a common knowledge pool, affirming, confirming, and elaborating on what they have observed in the home and matching their skills against those of others. And they learn to fight. Even small children test one another, pushing and shoving, and are ready to hit other children over circumstances not to their liking. In turn, they are readily hit by other children, and the child who is toughest prevails. Thus the violent resolution of disputes, the hitting and cursing, gains social reinforcement. The child in effect is initiated into a system that is really a way of campaigning for respect.

In addition, younger children witness the disputes of older children, which are often resolved through cursing and abusive talk, if not aggression or outright violence. They see that one child succumbs to the greater physical and mental abilities of the other. They are also alert and attentive witnesses to the verbal and physical fights of adults, after which they compare notes and share their interpretations of the event. In almost every case the victor is the person who physically won the altercation, and this person often enjoys the esteem and respect of onlookers. These experiences reinforce the lessons the children have learned at home: might makes right, and toughness is a virtue, while humility is not. In effect they learn the social meaning of fighting. When it is left virtually unchallenged, this understanding becomes an ever more important part of the child's working conception of the world. Over time the code of the streets becomes refined.

Those street-oriented adults with whom children come in contact—including mothers, fathers, brothers, sisters, boyfriends, cousins, neighbors, and friends—help them along in forming this understanding by verbalizing the messages they are getting through experience: "Watch your back." "Protect yourself." "Don't punk out." "If somebody messes with you, you got to pay them back." "If someone disses you, you got to straighten them out." Many parents actually impose sanctions if a child is not sufficiently aggressive. For example, if a child loses a fight and comes home upset, the parent might respond, "Don't you come in here crying that somebody beat you up; you better get back out there and whup his ass. I

didn't raise no punks! Get back out there and whup his ass. If you don't whup his ass, I'll whup your ass when you come home." Thus, the child obtains reinforcement for being tough and showing nerve.

While fighting, some children cry as though they are doing something they are ambivalent about. The fight may be against their wishes, yet they may feel constrained to fight or face the consequences—not just from peers but also from caretakers or parents, who may administer another beating if they back down. Some adults recall receiving such lessons from their own parents and justify repeating them to their children as a way to toughen them up. Looking capable of taking care of oneself as a form of self-defense is a dominant theme among both street-oriented and decent adults who worry about the safety of their children. There is thus at times a convergence in their child-rearing practices, although the rationales behind them may differ.

SELF-IMAGE BASED ON "JUICE"

By the time they are teenagers, most youths have either internalized the code of the streets or at least learned the need to comport themselves in accordance with its rules, which chiefly have to do with interpersonal communication. The code revolves around the presentation of self. Its basic requirement is the display of a certain predisposition to violence. Accordingly, one's bearing must send the unmistakable if sometimes subtle message to "the next person" in public that one is capable of violence and mayhem when the situation requires it, that one can take care of oneself. The nature of this communication is largely determined by the demands of the circumstances but can include facial expressions, gait, and verbal expressions—all of which are geared mainly to deterring aggression. Physical appearance, including clothes, jewelry, and grooming, also plays an important part in how a person is viewed; to be respected, it is important to have the right look.

Even so, there are no guarantees against challenges, because there are always people around looking for a fight to increase their share of respect—or "juice," as it is sometimes called on the street. Moreover, if a person is assaulted, it is important, not only in the eyes of his opponent but also in the eyes of his "running buddies," for him to avenge himself. Otherwise he risks being "tried" (challenged) or "moved on" by any number of others. To maintain his honor he must show he is not someone to be "messed with" or "dissed." In general, the person must "keep himself straight" by managing his position of respect among others; this involves in part his self-image, which is shaped by what he thinks others are thinking of him in relation to his peers.

Objects play an important and complicated role in establishing self-image. Jackets, sneakers, gold jewelry, reflect not just a person's taste, which tends to be tightly regulated among adolescents of all social classes, but also a willingness to possess things that may require defending. A boy wearing a fashionable, expensive jacket, for example, is vulnerable to attack by another who covets the jacket and either cannot afford to buy one or wants the added satisfaction of depriving someone else of his. However, if they boy forgoes the desirable jacket and wears one that isn't "hip," he runs the risk of being teased and possibly even assaulted as an unworthy person. To be allowed to hang with certain prestigious crowds, a boy must wear a different set of expensive clothes—sneakers and athletic suit—every day. Not to be able to do so might make him appear socially deficient. The youth comes to covet such items—especially when he sees easy prey wearing them.

In acquiring valued things, therefore, a person shores up his identity—but since it is an identity based on having things, it is highly precarious. This very precariousness gives a heightened sense of urgency to staying even with peers, with whom the person is actually competing. Young men and women who are able to command respect through their presentation of self—by allowing their possessions and their body language to speak for them—may not have to campaign for regard but may, rather, gain it by the force of their manner. Those who are unable to command respect in this way must actively campaign for it—and are thus particularly alive to slights.

One way of campaigning for status is by taking the possessions of others. In this context, seemingly ordinary objects can become trophies imbued with symbolic value that far exceeds their monetary worth. Possession of the trophy can symbolize the ability to violate somebody—to "get in his face," to take something of value from him, to "dis" him, and thus to enhance one's own worth by stealing someone else's. The trophy does not have to be something material. It can be another person's sense of honor, snatched away with a derogatory remark. It can be the outcome of a fight. It can be the imposition of a certain standard, such as a girl's getting herself recognized as the most beautiful. Material things, however, fit easily into the pattern. Sneakers, a pistol, even somebody else's girlfriend, can become a trophy. When a person can take something from another and then flaunt it, he gains a certain regard by being the owner, or the controller, of that thing. But this display of ownership can then provoke other people to challenge him. This game of who controls what is thus constantly being played out on inner-city streets, and the trophy—extrinsic or intrinsic, tangible or intangible—identifies the current winner.

An important aspect of this often violent give-and-take is its zero-sum quality. That is, the extent to which one person can raise himself up depends on his ability to put another person down. This underscores the alienation that permeates the inner-city ghetto community. There is a generalized sense that very little respect is to be had, and therefore everyone competes to get what affirmation he can of the little that is available. The craving for respect that results gives people thin skins. Shows of deference by others can be highly soothing, contributing to a sense of security, comfort, self-confidence, and self-respect. Transgressions by others which go unanswered diminish these feelings and are believed to encourage further transgressions. Hence one must be ever vigilant against the transgressions of others or even *appearing* as if transgressions will be tolerated. Among young people, whose sense of self-esteem is particularly vulnerable, there is an especially heightened concern with being disrespected. Many inner-city young men in particular crave respect to such a degree that they will risk their lives to attain and maintain it.

The issue of respect is thus closely tied to whether a person has an inclination to be violent, even as a victim. In the wider society people may not feel required to retaliate physically after an attack, even though they are aware that they have been degraded or taken advantage of. They may feel a great need to defend themselves *during* an attack, or to behave in such a way as to deter aggression (middle-class people certainly can and do become victims of street-oriented youths), but they are much more likely than street-oriented people to feel that they can walk away from a possible altercation with their self-esteem intact. Some people may even have the strength of character to flee, without any thought that their self-respect or esteem will be diminished.

In impoverished inner-city black communities, however, particularly among young males and perhaps increasingly among females, such flight would be extremely difficult. To run away would likely leave one's self-esteem in tatters. Hence people often feel constrained not only to stand up and at least attempt to resist during an assault but also to "pay back"—to seek revenge—after a successful assault on their person. This may include going to get a weapon or even getting relatives involved. Their very identity and self-respect, their honor, is often intricately tied up with the way they perform on the streets during and after such encounters. This outlook reflects the circumscribed opportunities of the inner-city poor. Generally people outside the ghetto have other ways of gaining status and regard, and thus do not feel so dependent on such physical displays.

BY TRIAL OF MANHOOD

On the street, among males these concerns about things and identity have come to be expressed in the concept of "manhood." Manhood in the inner city means taking the prerogatives of men with respect to strangers, other men, and women—being distinguished as a man. It implies physicality and a certain ruthlessness. Regard and respect are associated with this concept in large part because of its practical application: if others have little or no regard for a person's manhood, his very life and those of this loved ones could be in jeopardy. But there is a chicken-and-egg aspect to this situation: one's physical safety is more likely to be jeopardized in public *because* manhood is associated with respect. In other words, an existential link has been created between the idea of manhood and one's self-esteem, so that it has become hard to say which is primary. For many inner-city youths, manhood and respect are flip sides of the same coin; physical and psychological well-being are inseparable, and both require a sense of control, of being in charge.

The operating assumption is that a man, especially a real man, knows what other men know—the code of the streets. And if one is not a real man, one is somehow diminished as a person, and there are certain valued things one simply does not deserve. There is thus believed to be a certain justice to the code, since it is considered that everyone has the opportunity to know it. Implicit in this is that everybody is held responsible for being familiar with the code. If the victim of a mugging, for example, does not know the code and so responds "wrong," the perpetrator may feel justified even in killing him and may feel no remorse. He may think, "Too bad, but it's his fault. He should have known better."

So when a person ventures outside, he must adopt the code—a kind of shield, really—to prevent others from "messing with" him. In these circumstances it is easy for people to think they are being tried or tested by others even when this is not the case. For it is sensed that something extremely valuable is at stake in every interaction, and people are encouraged to rise to the occasion, particularly with strangers. For people who are unfamiliar with the code—generally people who live outside the inner city—the concern with respect in the most ordinary interactions can be frightening and incomprehensible. But for those who are invested in the code, the clear object of their demeanor is to discourage strangers from even thinking about testing their manhood. And the sense of power that attends the ability to deter others can be alluring even to those who know the code without being heavily invested in it—the decent inner-city youths. Thus a boy who has been leading a basically decent life can, in trying circumstances, suddenly resort to deadly force.

Central to the issue of manhood is the widespread belief that one of the most effective ways of gaining respect is to manifest "nerve." Nerve is shown when one takes another person's possessions (the more valuable the better), "messes with" someone's woman, throws the first punch, "gets in someone's face," or pulls a trigger. Its proper display helps on the spot to check others who would violate one's person and also helps to build a reputation that works to prevent future challenges. But since such a show of nerve is a forceful expression of disrespect toward the person on the receiving end, the victim may be greatly offended and seek to retaliate with equal or greater force. A display of nerve, therefore, can easily provoke a life-threatening response, and the background knowledge of that possibility has often been incorporated into the concept of nerve.

True nerve exposes a lack of fear of dying. Many feel that it is acceptable to risk dying over the principle of respect. In fact, among the hard-core street-oriented, the clear risk of violent death may be preferable to being "dissed" by another. The youths who have internalized this attitude and convincingly display it in their public bearing are among the most threatening people of all, for it is commonly assumed that they fear no man. As the people of the community say, "They are the baddest dudes on the street." They often lead an existential life that may acquire meaning only when they are faced with the possibility of imminent death. Not to be afraid to die is by implication to have few compunctions about taking another's life. Not to be afraid to die is the quid pro quo of being able to take somebody else's life—for the right reasons, if the situation demands it. When others believe this is one's position, it gives one a real sense of power on the streets. Such credibility is what many inner-city youths strive to achieve, whether they are decent or street-oriented, both because of its practical defensive value and because of the positive way it makes them feel about themselves. The difference between the decent and the street-oriented youth is often that the decent youth makes a conscious decision to appear tough and manly; in another setting—with teachers, say, or at his part-time job—he can be polite and deferential. The street-oriented youth, on the other hand, has made the concept of manhood a part of his very identity; he has difficulty manipulating it—it often controls him.

GIRLS AND BOYS

Increasingly, teenage girls are mimicking the boys and trying to have their own version of "manhood." Their goal is the same—to get respect, to be recognized as capable of setting or maintaining a certain standard. They try to achieve this end in the ways that have been established by the boys, including posturing, abusive language, and the use of violence to resolve disputes, but the issues for the girls are different. Although conflicts over turf and status exist among the girls, the majority of disputes seem rooted in assessments of beauty (which girl in a group is "the cutest"), competition over boyfriends, and attempts to regulate other people's knowledge of and opinions about a girl's behavior or that of someone close to her, especially her mother.

A major cause of conflicts among girls is "he say, she say." This practice begins in the early school years and continues through high school. It occurs when "people," particularly girls, talk about others, thus putting their "business in the streets." Usually one girl will say something negative about another in the group, most often behind the person's back. The remark will then get back to the person talked about. She may retaliate or her friends may feel required to "take up for" her. In essence this is a form of group gossiping in which individuals are negatively assessed and evaluated. As with much gossip, the things said may or may not be true, but the point is that such imputations can cast aspersions on a person's good name. The accused is required to defend herself against the slander, which can result in arguments and fights, often over little of real substance. Here again is the problem of low self-esteem, which encourages youngsters to be highly sensitive to slights and to be vulnerable to feeling easily "dissed." To avenge the dissing, a fight is usually necessary.

Because boys are believed to control violence, girls tend to defer to them in situations of conflict. Often if a girl is attacked or feels slighted, she will get a brother, uncle, or cousin to do her fighting for her. Increasingly, however, girls are doing their own fighting and are even asking their male relatives to teach them how to fight. Some girls form groups that attack other girls or take things from them. A hard-core segment of inner-city girls inclined toward violence seems to be developing. As one thirteen-year-old girl in a detention center for youths who have committed violent acts told me, "To get people to leave you alone, you gotta fight. Talking don't always get you out of stuff." One major difference between girls and boys: girls rarely use guns. Their fights are therefore not life-or-death struggles. Girls are not often willing to put their lives on the line for "manhood." The ultimate form of respect on the male-dominated inner-city street is thus reserved for men.

"GOING FOR BAD"

In the most fearsome youths such a cavalier attitude toward death grows out of a very limited view of life. Many are uncertain about how long they are going to live and believe they could die violently at any time. They accept this fate; they live on the edge. Their manner conveys the message that nothing intimidates them; whatever turn the encounter takes, they maintain their attack—rather like a pit bull, whose spirit many such boys admire. The demonstration of such tenacity "shows heart" and earns their respect.

This fearlessness has implications for law enforcement. Many street-oriented boys are much more concerned about the threat of "justice" at the hands of a peer than at the hands of the police. Moreover, many feel not only that they have little to lose by going to prison but that they have something to gain. The toughening-up one experiences in prison can actually enhance one's reputation on the streets. Hence the system loses influence over the hard core who are without jobs, with little perceptible stake in the system. If mainstream society has done nothing *for* them, they counter by making sure it can do nothing *to* them.

At the same time, however, a competing view maintains that true nerve consists in backing down, walking away from a fight, and going on with one's business. One fights only in self-defense. This view emerges from the decent philosophy that life is precious, and it is an important part of the socialization process common in decent homes. It discourages violence as the primary means of resolving disputes and encourages youngsters to accept nonviolence and talk as confrontational strategies. But "if the deal goes down," self-defense is greatly encouraged. When there is enough positive support for this orientation, either in the home or among one's peers, then nonviolence has a chance to prevail. But it prevails at the cost of relinquishing a claim to being bad and tough, and therefore sets a young person up as at the very least alienated from street-oriented peers and quite possibly a target of derision or even violence.

Although the nonviolent orientation rarely overcomes the impulse to strike back in an encounter, it does introduce a certain confusion and so can prompt a measure of soul-searching, or even profound ambivalence. Did the person back down with his respect intact or did he back down only to be judged a "punk"—a person lacking manhood? Should he or she have acted? Should he or she have hit the other person in the mouth? These questions beset many young men and women during public confrontations. What is the "right" thing to do? In the quest for honor, respect, and local status—which few young people are uninterested in—common sense most often prevails, which leads many to opt for the tough approach, enacting their own particular versions of the display of nerve. The presentation of oneself as rough and tough is very often quite acceptable until one is tested. And then that presentation may help the person pass the test, because it will cause fewer questions to be asked about what he did and why. It is hard for a person to explain why he lost the fight or why he backed down. Hence many will strive to appear to "go for bad," while hoping they will never be tested. But when they are tested, the outcome of the situation may quickly be out of their hands, as they become wrapped up in the circumstances of the moment.

AN OPPOSITIONAL CULTURE

The attitudes of the wider society are deeply implicated in the code of the streets. Most people in inner-city communities are not to-

tally invested in the code, but the significant minority of hard-core street youths who are have to maintain the code in order to establish reputations, because they have—or feel they have—few other ways to assert themselves. For these young people the standards of the street code are the only game in town. The extent to which some children—particularly those who through upbringing have become most alienated and those lacking in strong and conventional social support—experience, feel, and internalize racist rejection and contempt from mainstream society may strongly encourage them to express contempt for the more conventional society in turn. In dealing with this contempt and rejection, some youngsters will consciously invest themselves and their considerable mental resources in what amounts to an oppositional culture to preserve themselves and their self-respect. Once they do, any respect they might be able to garner in the wider system pales in comparison with the respect available in the local system; thus they often lose interest in even attempting to negotiate the mainstream system.

At the same time, many less alienated young blacks have assumed a street-oriented demeanor as a way of expressing their blackness while really embracing a much more moderate way of life; they, too, want a nonviolent setting in which to live and raise a family. These decent people are trying hard to be part of the mainstream culture, but the racism, real and perceived, that they encounter helps to legitimate the oppositional culture. And so on occasion they adopt street behavior. In fact, depending on the demands of the situation, many people in the community slip back and forth between decent and street behavior.

A vicious cycle has thus been formed. The hopelessness and alienation many young inner-city black men and women feel, largely as a result of endemic joblessness and persistent racism, fuels the violence they engage in. This violence serves to confirm the negative feelings many whites and some middle-class blacks harbor toward the ghetto poor, further legitimating the oppositional culture and the code of the streets in the eyes of many poor young blacks. Unless this cycle is broken, attitudes on both sides will become increasingly entrenched, and the violence, which claims victims, black and white, poor and affluent, will only escalate.

QUESTIONS FOR DISCUSSION AND WRITING

1. Which are the circumstances of life among the ghetto poor?
2. What is true about many of the forms that "dissing" can take?
3. How do the child-rearing practices of decent and "street" parents differ?

CONFLICT THEORY

Conflict and Criminality

AUSTIN T. TURK

RELATIONS between conflict and crime have been conceptualized in four basic ways, although any given discussion can be shown to be in some respects a unique treatment of one or more of the major ideas. The four conceptual relations are as follows, along with the principal variants of each:

1. Criminal behavior as an indicator of conflict within the person, emphasizing either
   a. failure to resolve tensions generated in the course of interaction between the organism and human figures in its environment, or
   b. tensions generated by the person's inability to satisfy the contradictory expectations of others, or else to mobilize the resources needed to perform a role assigned to him.
2. Criminal behavior as the expression of participation by the offender in a criminogenic subculture, emphasizing either
   a. a basically pathological and largely unsuccessful attempt by persons in similar circumstances and in contact to solve their adjustment problems,
   b. a partly normal and partly pathological effort by persons in similar positions and

in contact to adapt to opportunity barriers, or
   c. the trouble-making features of an established sector of the culture, such as a class culture, or of the culture itself.
3. The occurrence of criminal behavior where the offender, because of having been socialized in a different culture, either does not know or does not accept certain legal norms.
4. The violation of laws by essentially normal persons in the course of realistic conflicts of interest, emphasizing either
   a. the activities of those involved in organizations created to satisfy the demand for illicit goods and services, as well as to use illegal means to control and profit from legitimate economic activity,
   b. resistance by vested interests to legal restraints, especially where efforts are made to modify institutionalized patterns of legitimate economic activity,
   c. criminal behavior as almost entirely a function of an inequitable and unstable economic structure promoting selfishness and resulting in uncertainty for all and misery for many, or
   d. conflict between those who seek to preserve a given authority structure and those who are trying to modify or destroy it.

Thus, one finds some writers emphasizing internal psychological conflicts of which unlawful acts are taken to be symptomatic, others thinking primarily in terms of deviant group formation and/or elements of group cultures in opposition to law-abidingness, still others talking mostly about cross-cultural differences with respect to behavior norms, and a minority concerned with relations between economic and political struggles and the occurrence of criminal behavior. The first two perspectives are associated with an almost exclusive concern with explaining the behavior of deviants who are only incidentally and sometimes officially criminals. The third and especially the fourth evidence more concern with the nature of law and with nonpathological dimensions of intergroup conflict, even though these writers too view crime mainly as problem behavior. Their work suggests at the very least that while crime may be viewed sometimes as an indication that something is wrong with the person or with his social environment as it affects him, it may at other times be more usefully seen as "reasonable" behavior engaged in by individuals, with varying degrees of group support, who more or less consciously disagree with certain laws or patterns of law enforcement perceived as threats to their interests. From the latter viewpoint, that some people act contrary to statutes becomes less a problem than a fact with which analysis begins, and understanding crime becomes less a matter of unraveling social, psychological, and biological processes resulting in pathological behavior than a matter of comprehending cultural diversity and patterns of social conflict.

PROPOSITIONS FOR A THEORY OF CRIMINALIZATION

Criminological theory—as distinct from *deviant behavior* theory—is viewed as that part of general conflict theory which applies to norm conflict within political authority structures, specifically to conflicts defined by authorities in terms of the violation and enforcement of legal norms. Instead of the "criminal behav-

ior" of individual suspects, arrestees, and convicts, the focus is upon the conflict process during which some parties come to be defined as criminal. The theoretical objectives are to account for (1) variations in the probability of criminalization, that is, in crime rates, and (2) variations in the degree of deprivation associated with criminalization, including both modes of punishment and the point in the legal process at which coercive treatment is officially terminated. The following propositions comprise no more than a rough first approximation of a theory that will hopefully offer not only plausible but precise, systematic, and therefore testable explanations of criminality and punishment.

1. In regard to evaluation of any given attribute, the probability that a cultural difference between authorities and subjects will result in conflict will depend upon the extent to which this difference corresponds to a difference in social norms. In general, the greater the cultural difference, the greater the probability of conflict.

   1.1. Conflict will be most likely when there is high congruence between cultural and social norms for both authorities and subjects, and least likely where there is low congruence for both authorities and subjects.

       1.1.1. When congruence is high for one party and low for the other, conflict will be more probable for the combination of high authorities and low subjects, since authorities are less likely to tolerate cultural difference when their cultural norm is strongly supported by a corresponding social norm.

       1.1.2. While social normative conflict is conceivable, that is, conflict in which the parties have no awareness of why they are fighting, it is unlikely that such a conflict between authorities and subjects can continue for long without one or both parties interpreting the struggle in culture conflict terms. The "real" social-normative reasons for conflict will never exactly coincide with the interpretations given by the parties to the conflict. In fact, there are likely to be various sets of interpretations used, depending mainly upon whether the audience is "public" or "private." Thus, the investigator must not accept at face value any statement by party spokesmen regarding the nature and extent of the normative difference.

1.2. Authorities will tend to appeal to legal norms, or to announce new ones, in contradistinction to the cultural norms taken to be characteristic of the opposition. The opposition, on the other hand, since they are by definition more or less excluded from law-making positions, will tend to appeal to nonlegal, more abstract principles such as justice, natural law, and the right to be left alone.

1.2.1. The less distinct and established the opposition's culture, and the less the sophistication of individuals comprising the opposition party, the more likely—it seems—they are to make essentially negative appeals of the sort described by Sykes and Matza as "techniques of neutralization," implying an effort to justify violation of a norm actually shared with the authorities. The use of such techniques may, however, be due to the lack of verbal skills and the immaturity of the subjects. It is harder to articulate alternative cultural norms and justifications than to offer ad hoc excuses for not adhering, in particular instances, to cultural norms formulated by someone else. One extremely important and familiar class of unsophisti-

cated excuses is that of fictional law, in which those who resist legal restraint make an appeal to what they imagine *are* legal norms, or else voice disbelief that some rule is actually "the law."

1.2.2. It may be that the more distinct and established the opposition culture, the greater the probability of conflict, since there is more of a core of potential resistance. However, the variable of "sophistication"—meaning here knowledge of patterns in the behavior of others which is used in attempts to manipulate them— may actually determine whether or not the potential conflict develops. If the level of sophistication of opposition members is generally high, they are likely to be more successful in minimizing the chances of conflict with the authorities without making significant concessions. A solid culture combined with little sophistication is probably most likely to be associated with conflict.

1.3. The greater the extent to which the basis of legitimacy is the social norm of deference rather than norm internalization, the greater will be the probability of conflict, since

1.3.1. the less the importance of normative consensus as the basis of social order, the less likely are subjects to accept the authority structure with reference both to the right of authorities to announce norms and to the official status of the behavior enforcers.

2. When the normative conflict has been interpreted by authorities in legal terms, the probability that members of the opposition will be officially dealt with as criminals will depend upon (1) the status of the legal norm in the culture of the authorities, (2) the status of the opposing norm or illegal

attribute in the culture of the opposition, (3) the congruence of the legal norm with the cultural and social norms of those specifically charged with enforcement, (4) the relative power of enforcers and resisters, and (5) the realism of moves made by the conflict parties.

2.1. The greater the behavioral significance of the legal norm for authorities, both in regard to congruence of cultural and social norms and in regard to the relative priority of the norm over other norms, the greater the probability that violators will be assigned criminal status.

2.2. The greater the significance of the opposition's norm to them, the greater the likelihood that they will provoke the authorities sufficiently for legal sanctioning to occur. This is, of course, even more likely when the cultural norm of the authorities is also highly significant. Otherwise, the authorities may be reluctant to join the issue and may prefer either to ignore or to grant a special dispensation to the opposition. The greater the cultural difference, however, the more likely are the authorities to be forced to use their power either to criminalize members of the opposition or, if the opposition is a highly organized, strongly established group, to redefine the position of the opposition in the authority structure, that is, to come to terms with them, recognizing to some extent their right to be different. Examples would be ethnic enclaves such as Chinatowns with which authorities work out accommodations, whether or not such accommodations are "legal."

2.3. The more offensive the prohibited attribute is to the enforcers, the greater the probability of criminalization of those with the attribute.

2.3.1. If there are various levels of enforcers, that is, police, prosecutors, judiciary, and so on, the more the several levels of enforcers agree that the illegal attribute is offensive, the higher will be the probability of criminalization and the more stages of the legal process the offender will go through.

2.3.2. The more offensive the illegal attribute is to those enforcers with sentencing power, the judiciary, the more severe will be the consequences of criminalization.

2.3.3. When an attribute is highly offensive to first-level enforcers but far less offensive to higher-level enforcers, the offender will be less likely to pass beyond the first stage of the legal process but there will be greater deprivation associated with the first stage. Moreover, there will be a greater proportion of unofficial and illegal cases wherein first-level enforcers coerce norm violators.

2.3.4. When an attribute is highly offensive to higher-level enforcers but far less offensive to first-level enforcers, the offender will, if officially identified at the first (arrest) stage, very likely pass beyond the first stage. Arrest will be associated with minimal deprivation and maximal adherence to explicit regulations upon police behavior, but since there is a high probability of charge, conviction, and relatively severe sentence, arrest will imply eventual severe deprivation, given the highly negative evaluation of the attribute by higher-level enforcers.

2.3.5. When an attribute is not offensive to enforcers at any level, arrest rates will be low and offenders will seldom be processed beyond the first stage.

2.3.6. If the attribute is both inoffensive and has low visibility, the law is likely to be a dead letter. Either the law is an approximation of a social norm that no longer exists or a statute adopted for essentially "political" reasons and perhaps not even meant to be enforced.

2.4. In general, the greater the power difference in favor of the authorities, the greater the probability of criminalization of the opposition. However, the relationship seems very likely to be curvilinear if the extremes of the power differential are included in a given set of data.

2.4.1. In the absence of a power differential, the authorities are increasingly likely to perceive the opposition as threatening, the greater and more behaviorally significant the cultural difference. The more threatening the opposition, the more likely are "normal" legal procedures to be officially abrogated in order to fight effectively for survival. Criminalization will be decidedly "political," but at the same time there will be more than ordinary concern for establishing the factual basis of the opposition's "guilt," which will be an almost foregone conclusion. The "facts" may be valid, biased by the fears of the authorities, or fabricated.

2.4.2. When the opposition is virtually powerless, normal legal procedures are likely to be unofficially abrogated in favor of summary and less costly procedures, so that official criminalization rates may well be lower than for more powerful opposition parties. Procedural law is not a gift but a concession. The validity of this proposition depends upon the attribute being found in known proportions at all socioeconomic levels. If the offensive attribute is found almost exclusively at the lowest levels, the criminalization rates will obviously be highest at those levels. Even then, the ratio of official to unofficial enforcement situations will probably be lower for low- than for high-status populations.

2.4.3. The perception of offensiveness will probably be more valid in the "no power difference" case than in the no-contest case, implying a higher frequency of "miscarriages of justice" in the no-contest case, since the potential cost of honest mistakes (e.g., increasing the morale and ferocity of the enemy) is much higher in the former case.

2.5. In general, the more realistic the moves of a conflict party, the more likely the party is to be successful. In the context of normative-legal conflict, success for enforcers is the elimination of resistance; for resisters, success is ending enforcement efforts.

2.5.1. The less realistic the moves of the opposition, the higher the probability of criminalization.

2.5.1.1. Any move that increases the visibility of the offensive attribute is likely to be unrealistic.

2.5.1.2. Any move that increases offensiveness, for example, by emphasizing the initially offensive attribute, by drawing attention to additional offensive attributes, and by violating a higher-priority norm of the authorities, is likely to be unrealistic.

2.5.1.3. Any move that increases consensus among the various levels of enforcers is likely to be unrealistic.

2.5.1.4. Any move that increases the power difference in favor of the enforcers is likely to be unrealistic. The greater the power difference in favor of the enforcers, the greater the likelihood of unrealistic moves, since powerlessness is associated with ignorance. (Where both parties are fully informed and fully rational, ignorance does not have anything to do with powerlessness. An empirically relevant theory must, however, take into account the complex interaction of ignorance and powerlessness. Ignorance eventually increases powerlessness, while powerlessness, implying lack of access to resources, eventually results in ignorance. Knowledge is a long-run prerequisite of power but not a sufficient condition for the development of a power center; power provides opportunity for the extension of knowledge, but does not imply that the opportunity will be used.)

2.5.2. It might seem obvious that the less realistic the moves of the authorities or enforcers, the lower the probability of criminalization. Short-run consequences, however, must be distinguished from long-run consequences of enforcement activity. Measures aimed at victory in a short-run *power* struggle are likely to prove detrimental to the long-run effort to establish or preserve *authority* and induce norm resisters to accept the dominance-subordination relationship as legitimate. In regard to the long-run objective.

2.5.2.1. Any move that shifts the basis of legitimacy from norm internalization toward the deference norm is likely to be unrealistic. The less attention paid to "conversion" of resisters rather than unadorned coercion, the greater the likelihood that the move is unrealistic in the long run, although a temporary repression of resistance is a likely short-run result, especially when the relative power difference is great.

2.5.2.2. Any move that constitutes a departure from normal legal procedures is likely to weaken the authority structure, and therefore be unrealistic in the long run. (It may, however, be realistic in the short run through increasing the effectiveness of enforcement activity.) Unofficial departures will have more effect than official departures; less radical departures will have less effect than more abrupt ones.

2.5.2.3. Any move that tends to cause additional attributes of the opposition to become offensive is likely to be unrealistic. While it may be expedient to hate the enemy, generalized hostility will be more likely to increase unrealism. Realistic moves are likely to be associated with specification of what precisely is to be eliminated or changed, not with a vaguely formulated conglomerate of the attributes of the enemy.

2.5.2.4. Similarly, any move by authorities that increases the size, and therefore the power, of the opposition is likely to be unrealistic. Adding attributes, as mentioned above, is likely to increase the size of the offensive population.

2.5.2.5. The less agreement among the various levels of enforcers on the offensiveness of an attribute, the more likely their moves are to be unrealistic since (a) moves are less likely to reflect the full range of knowledge available to authorities, (b) moves may be made in a context of interlevel rivalry rather than in a context of norm enforcement, and (c) moves will be likely to reflect personal offensiveness norms rather than strictly legal norms.

CONCLUSIONS

The theory as it has been sketched is clearly a long way from a propositional calculus. Moreover, even as "verbal theory" it does not yet come to grips with a number of relevant problems, such as (1) the significance, in terms of effects upon the hypothesized relationships among variables, of the institutionalization of conflict; (2) the upper and lower limits of probabilities of criminalization, that is, the question, "How large a proportion of the subject population can authorities criminalize, and for how long, before the authority structure either collapses or is transformed?"; and (3) specification of the conditions under which certain changes in norms and normative structures will occur, beyond the obvious implication that changes in the values of the variables built into the propositions, especially the power difference, will probably result in *some* changes. Further elaboration of propositions requires additional exploratory and descriptive research. Transformation of the set of propositions into a formal deductive system will be undertaken when the various hypothetical relationships have been thoroughly examined in the light of empirical studies. At present, rigorous formalization would be premature.

QUESTIONS FOR DISCUSSION AND WRITING

1. What are the four conceptual relationships between conflict and crime?
2. Instead of the "criminal behavior" of individuals, on what does conflict theory focus?
3. What does Turk mean by "the upper and lower limits of probabilities of criminalization"?

Contemporary Research

A Tale of Three Cities:
Labor Markets and Homicide

ROBERT D. CRUTCHFIELD
ANN GLUSKER
GEORGE S. BRIDGES

CRIMINOLOGISTS have long argued about economic circumstances that affect crime. Among the enduring issues addressed is the relationship of employment to the probability that individuals will engage in crime. At the macro or aggregate level, questions have focused most frequently on the relationship between unemployment rates and crime rates. In recent years a number of sociological analyses have moved beyond this simplified focus on unemployment to consider the effects of other labor market variations on criminality. This approach fits into a broader sociological literature, which has traced changes in the rates of other social dislocations to, in part, labor market changes.

Crutchfield demonstrated that Seattle census tract crime rates were positively related to "labor instability," a combination of the unemployment rate and the portion of workers in secondary sector jobs in each tract. Borrowing from dual labor market theory, he argued that the stratification of labor into primary and secondary sector jobs could explain why some portions of populations are chronically disadvantaged not only in the labor market, but also in resulting spheres, including crime, that are influenced by economic well-being. Explaining chronic disadvantage, especially for racial and ethnic minorities, was one of the objectives of dual labor market theorists. According to these theorists, marginalized groups are frequently overrepresented in secondary sector jobs characterized by low pay, high turnover, poor benefits, and limited prospects for the future. Primary sector jobs, those well-paid ("family wage" jobs in the current vernacular) good-benefits jobs where employees have a reasonable expectation of future employment and perhaps even promotion, are more open to majority group members. Crutchfield observed higher crime rates in census tracts with relatively large portions of their population either unemployed or in secondary sector jobs. The hypothesized mechanisms connecting secondary sector employment and unemployment rates to crime rates are the social bonds specified in control theory. Secondary sector workers are less likely to bond to jobs that offer them little to

From "A Tale of Three Cities: Labor Markets and Homicide," by Robert D. Crutchfield, Ann Glusker, and George S. Bridges, 1999, *Sociological Focus* 32(1):65–83. Reprinted by permission.

lose, and those who are unemployed will obviously have no stake in keeping a nonexistent job. Crutchfield and Crutchfield and Pitchford found support for this hypothesis.

Crutchfield and Pitchford found that young adults who spend more time out of the labor force and who are not confident that their jobs will last into the future, two characteristics of secondary sector employment, are more likely to have committed crimes. This was especially the case for people living in counties with higher than average levels of labor force nonparticipation by adults. The implication of Crutchfield's and Crutchfield and Pitchford's findings is that the existence of a critical mass of people who are not working, or who are marginally employed, has additional criminogenic effects, beyond the effect of individual employment status.

An important aspect of dual labor market theory could not be investigated in Crutchfield's initial analysis of Seattle census tracts. In addition to the sector distribution of individual workers, variations in types of industry and the structure of the local labor market should affect crime rates. This notion is reinforced by Crutchfield and Pitchford's finding that the effects of job characteristics on crime rates are significant where labor market participation is low, but are insignificant where participation is relatively high. Also, some industries tend to employ relatively large proportions of workers in primary sector jobs while others hire more in positions with secondary sector characteristics. The blue-collar jobs of the old industrial Northeast and Midwest, big steel and the automobile industry, are good examples of the former, while tourism is a good example of the latter.

In this analysis we examine the distribution of labor in three cities. Seattle, Washington, DC, and Cleveland are selected for several reasons. First, we want to replicate Crutchfield's analysis of Seattle data using more recent census and crime data. Second, we seek to examine differences across cities in labor market variations. And third, crime data

coded by census tracts are readily accessible from the police departments in these cities. . . .

Our analysis focuses on homicide rates. The labor stratification thesis has been applied more broadly to violent crime rates, individual criminal involvement—both violent and property—and to other forms of deviance. We limit our analysis to criminal homicide because the complexity of other violent crimes warrants greater depth of attention than is possible here.

We investigate three important aspects of the "labor stratification" thesis. First, there is the already-mentioned important distinction between local labor markets and the type of industry that dominates employment locally. Second, well-documented changes in industrial composition and the social consequences of the changing world economy should affect cities differently. Wilson has made a compelling argument that the decline of blue-collar manufacturing jobs is an important element contributing to the emergence of the urban underclass since the middle to late 1970s. These conditions obviously will affect neighborhoods in cities that have had many manufacturing jobs, such as the rust belt cities of the Northeast and Midwest, including Cleveland. We hypothesize that secondary sector employment and high levels of labor market nonparticipation will affect homicide in the three cities differently. A second hypothesis is that indicators of the size of the underclass will be more important determinants of census tract homicide rates in Cleveland and Washington than in Seattle. Third, because of recently reported research findings, we seek to assess the effect of education on the capacity of the labor stratification model to predict crime variation.

LABOR MARKETS, WORK, AND CRIME

Most sociological discussions of work and crime have focused on the relationship between unemployment and crime. In general, we can conclude that there is not a consistent relationship between the rates of unemployment and crime. We take a somewhat broader view of this issue by expanding consideration to include both unemployment and marginal employment, which is consistent with dual labor market conceptions of secondary sector employment.

Our perspective on the link between work and crime is that those with intermittent employment, low income, and little chance for improving their lot will have diminished "stakes in conformity." This approach does not portray involvement in crime as necessarily utilitarian; we suspect that, for most people, the route to crime is not very calculated. Yet unemployment and poor-quality employment can *indirectly* affect crime rates because of their destabilizing effects on communities. We argue that marginal and unstable employment exposes people to, and gives them little incentive to avoid, circumstances that are likely to lead to crime.

LABOR MARKETS, EDUCATION, AND CRIME

It is important to bring education into theories which explain how the economy influences crime because many of those directly affected by economic changes, like job loss, are adults, while much urban crime is committed by juveniles. However, an important issue is whether labor-market shifts in employment opportunities are likely to affect youth in the same way they affect adults. The only jobs available to most teenagers are secondary sector jobs. While there is evidence that unstable work is related positively to criminal involvement for young adults, the thesis is strengthened to the extent that it can also show if and how labor market changes affect teenagers. Two studies have shown that the work experience of parents and other adults who live around those under 18 affects their school performance, which in turn affects their probabil-

ity of delinquency involvement. Crutchfield, Rankin and Pitchford found a small but significant indirect effect on delinquency of marginal parental involvement, and relatively high local joblessness, through the academic performance of juveniles. Wadsworth found that this link is caused in part by diminished bonding between children and parents when the parent is employed in a marginal setting.

These findings have been interpreted to mean that children invest less in education when the evidence in front of them, the work experience of parents and other adults, suggests that "playing by the rules"—or to use Merton's term, "conformity"—offers little hope for advancement or material wealth. For instance, children who grow up in an inner-city neighborhood where few adults are legally employed may be less likely to believe that getting good grades will really make a difference for their futures. While there are certainly young people who rise above this dismal image, it is not difficult to believe that children in this circumstances will have less faith in the power of education in their lives than will children whose parents' and neighbors' investments in education obviously have paid off. To explore these possibilities, this analysis includes consideration of the educational characteristics of the census tracts of the three cities studied. We hypothesize that high school dropout rates will be related positively to homicide rates and that measures of census tract labor force participation will have both direct and indirect effects on homicide rates through high school dropout rates.

STUDY METHODS

In the following analysis the dependent variable, homicide rate, is calculated from data provided by the police departments of Seattle, Cleveland, and Washington, DC, for the census tracts within each city. Here the homicide rate is the number of homicides per 1,000 people in the tract. The rates for the three years 1989, 1990, and 1991 are averaged to provide more stable measures for these small units.

The labor force measures for census tracts are: a joblessness rate—the rate of adult males who were out of the labor force (computed as the number of adult males who were out of the labor force per 1,000 people in the tract population); and a secondary sector jobs measure—the proportion of employed persons working in secondary sector jobs. The adult males out of the labor force measure is an alternative to the more widely used unemployment rate. The census category of unemployed persons includes only individuals who report that they were looking for work during a specified period. Our out-of-the-labor-force variable includes the sum of unemployed males and those who are no longer looking for work. This operationalization, then, includes "discouraged workers."

To construct the secondary sector jobs measure, the Census Bureau's occupational categories were divided into primary and secondary sector jobs according to the logic of dual labor market theory. The following occupations are defined as primary sector jobs: managers and professionals, technical, sales and administrative support, precision production, crafts, repair persons, machine operators, assemblers and inspectors, and transportation and material-moving occupations. The following occupations are defined as secondary sector jobs: service workers, machine handlers, equipment cleaners, helpers and laborers. These divisions are consistent with dual labor market conceptions of primary and secondary sector occupations.

Two measures of census tract education levels were selected for this analysis: the high school graduate rate is the number of persons over 25 years of age who are high school graduates per 1,000 people in the census tract population, and the school dropout rate is the number of persons aged 16 and older who are not currently in school and who did not complete high school per 1,000 population. . . .

. . . The other variables selected or created from data in Census Bureau publications for this paper are: a dummy variable indicating whether each census tract is within the central business district (CBD) of each city (0 = non-CBD, 1 = CBD), the divorce rate (number of divorced persons per 1,000 population), the percentage of the census tract population that is young males (14 to 25), the percent black population, the percent in poverty, and crowding—the proportion of the population living with more than one person per room. . . .

RESULTS

. . . Following the work of Sampson and Laub, we constructed a composite measure for the "underclass." The following variables were factor analyzed to produce this scale: the percent black, crowding, low-income population (the number of persons living in families with less than $5,000 per year income per 1,000 population), the percentage of the adult population that has never been married, the poverty rate, and families on AFDC (per 1,000 population). These variables are not identical to the ones used by Sampson, but we believe they are consistent with the logic of Wilson's description of the urban underclass. . . .

[We looked at] the direct, indirect, and total effects on homicide rates of the four variables of interest in this paper: the underclass scale, the high-density singles scale, the percentage of adult men out of the labor force, and the proportion of employed persons in secondary sector jobs. The differences in how these measures are associated with homicide in the three cities were obvious. . . . Three of the differences are important. First, the influence of the underclass scale varies across the cities. Underclass is not as important a predictor of homicide in Seattle as in Cleveland or Washington. Second, the high-density singles scale negatively affects homicide rates in Seattle, has a substantial positive total effect in Cleveland, and a weaker total effect in Washington. We suspect that this pattern is produced by the relatively large portion of Seattle tracts that are in and around the university district, which provides housing for a large population of students. These tracts are also close to upper-class and gentrified areas of the city, which typically have few homicides. Third, men out of the labor force is a much more important predictor of homicide in Seattle and Cleveland than in Washington.

Of interest also . . . is the consistent negative, though insignificant, direct effect of secondary sector employment in all three cities. These coefficients are opposite of the direction predicted by the theory. Despite this, the findings do not imperil the theory; rather they suggest a slight modification of the perspective. The negative effects of secondary sector employment are net of the positive indirect effect of this factor through the other variables (variously high school dropout, underclass, high-density singles) on homicide rates. We suspect that once the problems that secondary sector work causes for neighborhoods—making it more likely that they will develop underclass characteristics and increasing school dropout rates—are taken into account, having secondary sector jobs for residents is somewhat beneficial as the alternative may be no jobs at all. While the three cities are alike in that those neighborhoods with relatively high levels of workers in the secondary sector have higher homicide rates (as a result of large indirect effects), they differ in the sources of the indirect influence of this variable on murder. In Seattle, the nature of labor market participation works primarily through the high school dropout rate. In Cleveland, the rate of high-density singles and especially the underclass are important. In Washington, school dropout rates do not appear to have an important influence while the underclass measure is clearly more important.

Why might these differences exist among the cities? We began by selecting the cities to represent three different types of local labor markets. Seattle has had a vibrant growing economy that has substantial employment in modern industries, technology, and trade. Cleveland suffered a considerable economic setback during the 1970s and 1980s when it, like other older, industrial cities suffered from the ill effects of deindustrialization and an emigration of industrial jobs to the Sunbelt and overseas. Although Washington does have manufacturing jobs, its major industry is government. Washington also has a large service sector that provides services for those employed by the federal government.

Many of the jobs in the Seattle labor market are primary sector jobs. They pay well and offer relative security. The neighborhoods where primary sector workers live are likely to benefit from this security by having very low high school dropout rates that contribute to lower homicide rates. It is in those Seattle neighborhoods where secondary sector workers reside that high school dropout rates are high, and this appears to be linked to elevated levels of homicide. The strong economy in Seattle means that unemployment rates are low (the mean unemployment rate per 1,000 *total population* for census tracts in Seattle in 1990 was 28.9 whereas for the three-city group as a whole the rate was 46.0 per 1,000). High levels of employment and the presence of many primary sector jobs account in part for the diminished direct effect of the underclass scale in Seattle. As we mentioned earlier, Seattle does not have the levels of isolated and concentrated poverty and joblessness that are typical of underclass neighborhoods as described by Wilson and others. But in those neighborhoods where the proportion of secondary sector workers is higher and the bounty and good fortune of the booming economy are not shared, high school dropout rates are higher, as is homicide.

Cleveland is different. A hardworking industrial town with lots of good, blue-collar primary sector jobs, Cleveland suffered when those industries downsized or simply moved. Deindustrialization in Cleveland had effects similar to those described by Wilson for Chicago. As a consequence, there is a strong influence of disrupted neighborhoods, underclass, and high-density singles tracts on Cleveland's homicide rate. We doubt seriously that many out-of-work steelworkers turned to crime when their jobs disappeared. Perhaps some of the younger ones did, but most of those workers would have been of an age where they would have been very unlikely to be involved in crime. We have suggested that a more likely scenario is that young adults would not have the opportunity to become bonded to the good blue-collar jobs that had sustained their parents and neighbors. Further, the children of Cleveland's distressed neighborhoods would have increased likelihood of dropping out of or not doing well in school. One end product of the presence of underclass and unstable neighborhoods and resulting higher high school dropout rates is homicide.

Then there is Washington, DC. The District of Columbia, like the rest of the country including Seattle and Cleveland, no doubt suffered from the inflation of the 1970s and the recession of the 1980s. During these times, Washington's labor market was affected, but the large proportions of residents employed by the federal government had and have secure jobs. Most employed people in Washington work for government or in various service industries (retail, restaurants, domestic services, tourism, etc.). This latter group in large part consists of secondary sector jobs. Our analysis shows that in Washington only the underclass factor is an important direct determinant of homicide. Unlike Cleveland, Washington's underclass is not a product of the deindustrialization of the past twenty years. Washington's largely poor, black communities are not a product of the departure of heavy industry. Those industries were not a substantial part of Washington's local labor market. We suggest that underclass neighborhoods in Washington are a consequence of more long-term labor market stratification.

The distribution of secondary sector workers has strong indirect effects on homicide through the underclass and high-density singles, but not as we hypothesized, through high school dropout rates. To explore Washington's distinct pattern, we examined the distribution of high school dropout rates (data not shown). In Cleveland and Seattle, the distributions are normal. The average dropout rate in Seattle is low (mean dropout rate = 97 per 1,000 persons) and in Cleveland it is considerably higher (mean dropout rate = 278 per 1,000 persons). In Washington the distribution is bimodal (mean dropout rate = 186.5 per 1,000 persons). A small proportion of the tracts have very low high school dropout rates, much like Seattle's, while most of Washington's census tracts have dropout rates more similar to those in Cleveland. Washington has a small number of neighborhoods with high levels of educational attainment, while most of the city has appallingly high levels of high school dropouts. In a city where the overall economy has not suffered from the deindustrialization felt by Cleveland, a great many people nevertheless seem to suffer the despair of being marginalized from Washington's stable, high-cost-of-living economy. The "secure" economy appears to be an example of a stable dual labor market that might explain Washington's longtime high homicide rate.

In summary, labor market characteristics have very important indirect effects on census tract homicide rates. The proportion of adult male workers who are out of the labor force at times has a direct effect on murder rates. There are important differences between the three cities considered in this analysis. High school dropout rates are linked to labor market participation of census tract residents and, in Seattle and Cleveland, these rates are associated positively with homicide rates. The underclass, and high-density singles, which are both influenced by labor market stratification, have significant direct effects on census tract homicide in Cleveland and Washington, but less so in Seattle.

CONCLUSIONS

This analysis clearly illustrates important differences in how characteristics of labor market participation, community structure, and education differ in three urban locations in the U.S. In all three cities, Cleveland, Seattle, and Washington, DC, labor market participation has a significant influence on homicide rates. Also, the structure of work appears to have an important effect on the rate at which people do not finish high school. The pattern of these effects, though, differs in the three cities. In Seattle, the city with what might be called a twenty-first century industrial structure, work has a strong effect through education on murder rates. In Cleveland and Washington there is a bit more of an underclass effect. Homicide rates in Cleveland, the old rust belt city, reflect the presence of underclass communities, but here too there is an important direct influence of education on crime. Washington's homicide rate is driven in a more substantial way simply by its underclass.

We speculate that longtime labor market stratification, and the resultant economic inequality, makes Washington qualitatively different not only from newer cities like Seattle but also from older industrial centers like Cleveland. The latter always had poor neighborhoods, but economic shifts of the past twenty years have led to an expansion of poor—underclass—neighborhoods. In Washington, the stratification, much of it based on race, has been long-standing. We wonder if the structural arrangements in places like Washington, and other cities with large service sectors (secondary sectors), is more similar to caste-like circumstances in some nonindustrial nations than they are like other American cities. Obviously this is an important issues for future research.

QUESTIONS FOR DISCUSSION AND WRITING

1. What did Crutchfield find during his previous study in Seattle?
2. What is the implication of the findings of the two studies (by Crutchfield and by Crutchfield and Pitchford)?
3. What do the authors conclude about the effects on murder of education and underclass?

Crime and Structural Contradictions

WILLIAM J. CHAMBLISS

ONE conclusion to be drawn from the analysis of our knowledge about crime is that the structural tradition holds the greatest promise of leading to reliable scientific knowledge. It asks questions amenable to systematic investigation and capable of leading to reliable knowledge, for it assumes that criminal behavior is a response of groups and social classes to the resources and constraints of the social structure rather than the adaptation of individuals to personal biology, psychology, or social experiences. Our theory therefore draws from the structural tradition for its starting point. We seek to answer questions about why criminal behavior exists, why it is distributed as it is, and why it varies from place to place and from one historical period to another. We do not seek to answer why Johnny steals and Bobby makes airplanes, why one politician accepts bribes and another does not, or why one manager violates health and safety regulations and another does not. We understand that paradigms trying to explain individual criminal behavior are bound to end in either tautologies or empirically false theories. Either way, they are unsatisfactory as explanations. We wish to avoid this by focusing on questions that seek to understand the relationship between crime and social structure. Such an approach holds the most promise for the development of a reliable body of scientific knowledge.

CONTRADICTIONS AND CONFLICTS

A contradiction exists in a given set of social relationships (political, social, economic, and ideological) when, in the normal course of events, existing social relations simultaneously maintain the status quo and produce the conditions necessary to transform it—that is, when conforming to one set of demands, goals, or institutionalized processes creates situations that are fundamentally antagonistic to the existing social relations.

Under these circumstances, "contradictions tend to intensify with time and cannot be resolved within the existing social framework." Every historical era, every society, and every human group in the process of constructing ways to survive invariably creates contradictory forces and tendencies that serve as an unseen force moving the group toward new social, political, and economic relations. Change is thus an inexorable part of every human group. To understand this, it is essential that we adopt an attitude toward social life that flies in the face of conventional wisdom. We must accept the fact that social life is contradictory, that opposites exist simultaneously,

From "Toward a Political Economy of Crime," by W. Chambliss, 1975, *Theory and Society* 2:149–170. Copyright © William Chambliss. Reprinted by permission of the author.

and that people both create their own history and are created by it. "The world is not to be comprehended as a complex of ready made *things*, but as a complex of *processes*."

The contradictions lead inexorably to conflicts between groups, classes, and strata. The conflicts reflecting contradictions are manifested as antagonistic relations that reflect the struggle of people to deal with contradictory social, political, and economic relations. The following are examples: workers go on strike, women demonstrate against unequal pay, farmers march on Washington, small landowners take up arms against agribusiness, and Indians barricade themselves on their reservation against federal agents.

Every historical era has its own unique contradictions and conflicts. The most important conflicts existing in a particular time and place are those that derive from the way the social, economic, and political relations are organized. The following are the most basic characteristics of any human group: how people make a living, the work they do, the way they organize their labor to produce the things that are useful and necessary for survival, and how they distribute the results of their labor and organize power relations. People may create a political organization that strives for equality or one that creates vast differences in wealth between the rich and the poor. People may create a political structure that allows every member of the community a voice in every decision or they may organize their politics so that only a few people have the right to decide. There exists an apparently infinite number of possible combinations and permutations.

For an understanding of crime, it is the way people organize their economy, politics, and social relations that must be the starting point for constructing an adequate theory.

Criminal behavior is generated because of the contradictions that inevitably arise in the course of life. The type of crime, the amount of crime, and the distribution of crime in a particular historical period and society depend upon the nature of the existing contradictions, the conflicts that develop as people respond to

the contradictions, and the mechanisms institutionalized for handling the conflicts and dilemmas produced by the contradictions.

. . . The emergence of criminal law can be understood in just these terms. That is, criminal laws emerge, change, and develop as people attempt to respond to conflicts generated by contradictions in the political and economic organization of their world. It will be recalled, for example, that in capitalist economies there is a basic contradiction between the public nature of production and the private ownership of the means of production. Goods cannot be produced unless people can be forced, coerced, encouraged, cajoled, or persuaded to do the necessary work. This is the public nature of production. Under capitalism, however, the ownership of the goods produced does not reside with those who produce them but with those who own the means of production—the tools, the factories, and the necessary knowledge. This leads inexorably to conflict, which invariable changes the existing relationships. As workers struggle to increase their share of what they produce and owners struggle to maintain or increase their share, workers and owners are locked in conflict, each seeking to increase their share of the surplus.

The public production–private ownership contradiction—combined with a political organization of democratic, electoral politics—led in the formative years of industrialization in the United States and Europe to ubiquitous conflict between workers and owners. These conflicts were responded to politically by the passage of innumerable laws making it a crime for workers to organize collectively against owners, to strike, to refuse to work, and so forth. The attempted solution, it must be stressed, was *not* attending to the contradictions that generated the conflicts, it was focusing solely on the conflicts created by the contradictions. This attempted "solution" to the conflict did *not* suffice to silence worker demands. Indeed, the more oppressive the laws became, the more virulent the workers' rebellion. In the 1930s, another political tack was tried—laws giving workers the right to bargain collectively and to strike under certain circumstances were passed. Other laws restricted these rights and gave the government the right to arbitrate and, under certain circumstances, to intervene. [Also,] the behavior of women seeking the vote, the right to determine their own economic role in society, and even their right to decide whether or not to bear children were defined as criminal.

One way to resolve the conflicts generated by a class society is to define some groups or classes of people as less than human. This resolution, however, generates its own contradictions on an ideological level. To convince people that they live in a just and fair society, ideologies of equality, and freedom, and the inherent integrity of the individual may be promulgated. Yet the treatment of some people as less than human is a useful way of maintaining a compliant labor force. If some people—because of their race, gender, or age—are treated as though they are less human than others, then conflicts are inevitable. Dealing with these conflicts then becomes part of the state apparatus. Laws are passed that institutionalize differential access to the resources. Some people are legally prohibited from full participation in what are ideologically touted as the fundamental rights and privileges of all. Thus, when slaves or women are defined as less than human and denied their rights, the structure of political and economic relations is ripe for the emergence of conflicts. The criminal law will respond in an attempt to resolve these conflicts; some responses will be increasingly repressive, others will be ameliorative. In time, slaves were freed, women got the vote, and workers earned the right to strike. But, in the interim, there was conflict defined by law as criminal.

As Sutherland once pointed out, an understanding of the processes by which the criminal law is created is also an answer to the question of why there is crime. There is crime, in this sense, because there is law that defines certain acts as criminal.

We want to go beyond this, however. We want also to be able to answer why the types of crime differ between sexes, social classes, ethnic groups, and age groups in a particular society, and we want to be able to know why crime varies by type, frequency, and intensity from one society or historical period to another. . . .

CRIME IN CAPITALIST SOCIETIES

The capitalist economy depends upon the production and consumption of commodities by large numbers of people. There is, then, at the outset a twofold problem to be solved: How do we make people work to produce the commodities and how do we create a desire for the commodities on the part of large numbers of people?

Some commodities—food, clothing, and shelter—are essential for survival. If the only means available for obtaining these essentials is to work for someone who owns them, people will generally choose to work rather than starve or freeze to death. But capitalism does not depend upon the production and consumption of necessities alone. It also depends upon the production and consumption of goods and services that have little or nothing to do with survival. For capitalism to develop, people must be motivated to work in order to purchase unessential commodities.

There are many ways that people are taught to want nonessential commodities—advertising, socialization into a world in which the acquisition of nonessential commodities bestows status and a sense of personal integrity on those who can display them, and the necessity to accumulate property in order to stave off the possibility of falling below the level of consumption necessary for survival.

Creating the desire to consume, though, simultaneously creates the seeds of discontent and the possibility that people will discover ways of being able to increase consumption without working. If—instead of spending 8 hours at a boring, tedious, and sometimes dangerous occupation—a person can obtain the money necessary for purchasing commodities by theft, fraud, trickery, or bribery, then some people will choose that option. In an effort to avoid this possibility, the people who own the means of production and those who manage the state pass laws making such acts illegal. In this way, they try to reduce the attractiveness of alternative routes to consumption.

There are other forces at work that push people to discover alternative ways of accumulating capital. Not all people have an equal opportunity to consume the products they are taught to want. Different kinds of work pay different wages. Some jobs pay only enough for survival. In capitalist economies, there are vast differences in the wages people receive and in the wealth they can accumulate.

How, then, can a set of social relations be sustained that requires the vast majority of people to spend their lives working at tasks they find unsatisfactory in order to be able to have a large enough population of consumers to fuel the engines of capitalist production and consumption? There are many possible solutions to this dilemma, and most of these have been tried at one time or another in the history of capitalism. One solution to this contradiction is to create a class of people who can be forced to work but do not form an essential part of the consuming population. This was the solution tried during the period of capitalism that depended on slavery. Slaves were not a major part of the consuming population, but they did provide most of the essential labor for a minimum expense. This solution, however, created its own contradictions: "The system could justify slavery only by defining the Black as inhuman—but the system depended on mutual obligations, duties, responsibilities and even rights, that implicitly recognized the slave's humanity."

Today, capitalism depends upon wage labor. People must work for wages in order to have the power to consume and must consume in order for the economy to survive. This, too, creates its own contradictions. There is only one source of profit for the capitalist: the difference between the wage that the capitalist pays the worker and the price for which the product of that worker's labor is sold. If the worker is paid the full amount for which the product is sold, then there is no profit, and the economic system comes to a grinding halt. Without an accumulation of surplus to reinvest, the economy collapses. If, on the other hand, the worker is not paid enough to survive, then the population is decimated, and there is no one to purchase the commodities produced. Thus there is a fundamental *wages, profits, and consumption contradiction* in capitalist economies. Dealing with that contradiction explains a large part of the history of modern capitalism. Workers seek to earn higher wages and owners seek to pay the minimum amount. When workers do not have high enough wages to buy cars, houses, luxury items, and products of new technologies, the economy is sluggish. When workers are paid high wages that cut into the profits of the owners, there is less money to reinvest in new technologies and improved production. Foreign competition then cuts even further into the profits. This contradiction creates different conflicts and attempted resolutions: economists argue over whether it is better to increase profits to encourage investment in new productive capacities or to increase wages to encourage more consumption. Government policy vacillates in an attempt to accommodate these contradictory tendencies.

From the point of view of crime, the conflicts culminate in criminal behavior on the part of both workers and owners. Owners cut corners, violate health and safety regulations, illegally deal in the stock market, and violate securities and exchange regulations; workers steal from employers, supplement their wages by selling illegal drugs, illegally strike and organize, and join illegal political groups. The state sits squarely in the midst of the contradiction: Although generally influenced more by owners than workers, it cannot allow the ongoing conflict to disrupt social, political, and economic relations to the point of destroying the existing economic system (capitalism) or the existing political system (democracy). It responds by passing laws to keep workers from disrupting production or stealing property and owners from disregarding the health and safety of workers and consumers. It also passes laws prohibiting certain economic activities that undermine the state's own interests (avoiding taxes by laundering money through overseas banks) or give one group of capitalists an advantage over another (insider trading on the stock market, which disenfranchises those who are not privy to secret corporate information, or forming monopolies). State and government officials work to block efforts by extranational bodies (such as the United Nations) to establish codes of conduct for multinational corporations in developing nations. Another tactic is to maintain laws that allow the reserve labor force available in less-developed countries to enter the country for temporary jobs (such as in agriculture) where it can be employed at low wages without accruing any benefits from state-supported institutions such as welfare, education, and unemployment.

Under capitalism, there is also a fundamental *wages–labor supply contradiction*. The owners pursuing the logic of capitalist economies will strive to pay as little as possible to the workers. It is not possible, however, to pay nothing, unless there is an overabundance of labor that allows workers to be used up and discarded and then replaced with others flowing in. In advanced industrial societies, such a solution is impossible (as is slave labor) because much of the labor needed requires skills that take time to learn. However, if there is full employment under capitalism, workers have an advantage in the struggle for increased shares of profits with owners. If there is a reserve labor force— that is, a significant proportion of the labor force that is unemployed or underemployed— then, when the demands of labor threaten the profits of the owners, the owners can turn to the reserve army of labor to replace the workers. The reserve army, though, forms an underclass that cannot consume but nonetheless is socialized into a system in which consumption is the necessary condition for happiness. Criminal behavior offers a solution for the underclass: What they cannot earn legitimately they can earn illegitimately. . . .

Public Corruption

The corruption of public officials in capitalist societies is as much a part of the landscape as the air we breathe. Politicians from local aldermen to Presidents and Congresspeople are exposed throughout the capitalist world as having accepted bribes, payoffs, and illegal campaign contributions. In Puerto Rico in 1968, the FBI indicted a former San Juan police lieutenant colonel and three detectives (one of whom was a lawyer) for the murder of seven people and the theft of over a million dollars in jewelry and gems. In New York City during the same period, a borough president committed suicide when it was revealed that he was taking bribes from companies seeking contracts from the government. Dozens of other New York City politicians and government officials were indicted in the same probe—including a former deputy director of New York City's Parking Violations Bureau and an assistant to the mayor in charge of letting hospital and health-care contracts. The companies themselves were indicted and fined $600,000. At the federal level, every administration since George Washington's has experienced a rash of resignations and criminal indictments of high-level officials, a pattern that some thought reached its peak when Vice-President Agnew was indicted and pleaded "no contest" to a charge of soliciting and accepting bribes for giving contracts and President Nixon was threatened with impeachment for criminal acts. Under the administration of Ronald Reagan, over 200 high-level appointees were forced to resign either because they were indicted or suspected of criminal acts.

The widespread corruption of public officials suggests that choosing between administrations in terms of a propensity for corruption may be as difficult as choosing the healthiest stalk in a stack of rotten hay.

Electoral politics demands that candidates for office spend huge sums of money on political campaigns—for the presidency, over $100 million; for a seat in Congress, between $500,000 and $3 million. Governor Rockefeller of West Virginia spent over $10 million in a re-election campaign in which he was unopposed in the Democratic primary and his Republican opponent was given no chance whatsoever to win. Electoral politics combined with a capitalist economy create a seedbed for corruption. Politicians must amass huge amounts of money to compete successfully for elected office. People with the money to contribute do so in order to gain favorable treatment in dealing with the government, whether it be in legislative decisions or in obtaining contracts, licenses, and franchises. If contributions to political campaigns are allowed, the possibility and probability of corruption is omnipresent. If campaign contributions are not allowed, the electorate may not have maximum exposure to the candidates. Resolving that dilemma in the United States led to a system of campaign financing that guarantees corruption.

America is not alone in generating political corruption as a result of financing campaign contributions. Helmut Kohl, the chancellor of West Germany, admitted that, while he was chairman of the Christian Democratic Union (1974–1980), he accepted illegal political contributions from the Friedrich Flick Industrieverwaltung. To make matters worse, Chancellor Kohl apparently lied about his knowledge of the illegal campaign contributions before a parliamentary committee. The Bonn public prosecutor's office investigated the allegations that Kohl perjured himself and the possibility of pursuing criminal charges against him. Some capitalist countries limit the funds for campaigning to those that are supplied by state taxation. That system, however, produces its own contradictions and does not solve the problem, as the case of Chancellor Kohl indicates. There may be better or worse ways of encouraging or discouraging corruption in politics, but electoral politics—in which money influences success or failure—is bound to breed varying degrees of corruption.

In a similar vein, the corruption of the police is institutionalized in capitalist countries. Basically the problem is that, for the police to appear to do their job most efficiently, they must (1) permit some forms of criminality (gambling, drug dealing) to take place in order (2) to manage crime better in the community and keep the citizenry from being aware of what is taking place.

The law-enforcement system is placed squarely in the middle of two essentially conflicting demands. On the one hand, the job obligates police to enforce the law, albeit with discretion; at the same time, considerable disagreement rages over whether or not some acts should be subject to legal sanction. This conflict is heightened by the fact that some influential persons in the community insist that all laws be rigorously enforced, while others demand that some laws not be enforced, at least not against them. Faced with such a dilemma and such an ambivalent situation, the law enforcers to what any well-managed bureaucracy would do under similar circumstances. They follow the line of least resistance. Using the discretion inherent in their positions, they resolve the problem by establishing procedures that minimize organizational strains and that provide the greatest promise of rewards for the organization and the individuals involved. Typically this means that law enforcers adopt a tolerance policy toward the vices, selectively enforcing the laws when it is to their advantage to do so. [By] limiting the visibility of such activity as sexual deviance, gambling, and prostitution they appease those who demand the enforcement of applicable laws. At the same time, since controlling visibility does not eliminate access for persons sufficiently interested to ferret out the tolerated vice areas, those demanding such services are also satisfied.

The contradiction between appearance and reality leads to cooperation between some criminals and the police, which leads in turn to institutionalized corruption.

Street Crime

The forces that lead to street crime are not very different. As we have seen, capitalism produces a large class of people unable to consume the commodities they are taught to want. These people live with a constant dilemma, to accept failure by conventional standards and do without the "good things of life" or even necessities, or discover alternative ways of getting the money to buy the commodities they desire. Alternative ways are available to the lower classes as well as to the white-collar workers, corporate executives, and government officials. But lower-class people cannot engage in insider trading, embezzlement, "long firm" fraud (unless they learn the skills from someone experienced in the trade), or bribery. They can steal from grocery stores, traffic in drugs, pick pockets, run a crap game, or burgle houses. These activities require some skill, but they are not dependent upon having a particular occupation or position. Like the factory owner who commits violence against workers by refusing to adhere to factory safety and health regulations, lower-class crime also may involve violence to avoid detection or to commit the criminal act. Street crimes are less profitable, probably more likely to lead to detection, and certainly, if the criminal is caught, more likely to culminate in criminal sanctions. To protect themselves from being caught and punished, it may be necessary for criminals to engage in violence. The specifics change, but the overall pattern of responding to contradictions in the political, economic, and social relations of our historical moment remain the cause of the criminality. This applies whether it is the criminality of middle-class women who shoplift, lower-class women who prostitute themselves or sell drugs, street-gang members who steal and fight, or bankers who launder money for organized criminals. . . .

CONCLUSION

In this chapter, we have set forth a theory of crime and criminality that attempts to answer why crime exists and why different types of crime are distributed as they are. The theory suggests that every society contains within it ubiquitous contradictions that generate conflicts accounting for the emergence of criminal laws and the propensity of different social classes and groups to violate those laws. We do not pretend to explain why individual A commits crime and individual B does not. The history of criminology, combined with the facts we know about crime, proves the futility of asking that question. To be scientific requires that we ask questions that focus not on the individual but on the social structure and how different social structures generate different types of criminality. Crime in both socialist and capitalist societies reflects the particular contradictions of those societies.

QUESTIONS FOR DISCUSSION AND WRITING

1. What is a "basic contradiction" in capitalist economies?
2. What is "one way" to resolve the conflicts generated by a class society?
3. What is the "fundamental wages, profits, and consumption contradiction" in capitalistic economies?

Contemporary Research

Causes of Crime: A Radical View

MICHAEL J. LYNCH
W. BYRON GROVES

CRITIQUES of early radical theories of crime causation offer the following observations: first, radicals, like conflict and labeling theorists, have seen crime simply as the mirror image of control, thus ruling out questions of causation, or succumbing to tautological reasoning where the only cause of crime is law. A second criticism is that radicals have limited themselves to an oversimplified, "unicausal" approach where the only source of crime is capitalism. And third, many have argued that avoiding the issue of causation has resulted in a neglect of empirical research among radicals.

In recent years, radicals have addressed each of these criticisms. Specifically, they have added to the insights drawn from conflict and labeling theories; have qualified the depiction of capitalism as the "source of all evil" without de-emphasizing the structuring power of capitalism's political economy; and have undertaken a number of important empirical studies. Thus, the criticisms listed above may have been legitimate in 1975. They no longer apply today.

From *A Primer in Radical Criminology, Second Edition* (pp. 51–71) by M. J. Lynch and B. Groves, 1989, New York: Harrow and Heston. Copyright © 1989 by Harrow and Heston. Reprinted by permission.

The following four propositions relate Marx's views on class conflict, materialism, and the dialectic to the issue of causation:

1. The capitalist system has at its core a conflict between labor and capital, which means that capitalism is one in a long sequence of historical systems based on inequalities between those who own and those who work.
2. Through this fundamental structural inequality between labor and capital, society becomes stratified into social classes characterized by tremendous differences in wealth, status, power, and authority.
3. Taken together, these differences constitute variable material conditions of life which offer persons in different social classes vastly different opportunities in terms of life chances and life choices.
4. Among these opportunities are the chance or choice of becoming criminal.

Class is an important category for radicals. Social stratification accounts for the unequal distribution of chances and choices available to persons at different locations in the class structure. It also accounts for the differential allocation of incentives and motivations for both criminal and noncriminal behavior. To support these claims, radicals emphasize the causal connection between political economy, inequality, and crime.

SOCIAL CLASS, STRATIFICATION, AND INEQUALITY

Marx defined social classes in terms of their relation to the means of production, and since then social theorists (e.g., Max Weber) have expanded Marx's conception to include unequal distributions of socially valued items such as power, prestige, wealth, or income. By focusing on how class position affects life chances, political power, and socialization patterns, radicals reaffirm the causal influence of economic factors on social life.

The most dramatic and decisive factor in social stratification is wealth, which "is extraordinarily concentrated in the United States." Federal Reserve Board figures indicate that the top 20 percent of consumers own over 76 percent of the total wealth, while the bottom 20 percent hold only 0.2 percent. More dramatically, the top 1 percent of the wealthy in the United States own 42 percent of all wealth.

Income is also unequally distributed. The U.S. Bureau of the Census reports that nearly half of all income is received by 20 percent of families and individuals, while the bottom 20 percent receive only 4 percent of the total income. Putting aside political rhetoric concerning progress and equality, the fact is that distributions of income and wealth have remained fairly constant in the United States over the past fifty years. Contrary to the you-can-make-it-if-you-try ideology, this suggests that there is little chance that a significant number of lower-class persons will advance in the American class structure.

In addition, recent data on occupational stratification point to a decline in both the quality and rewards associated with white-collar work, a drop in blue-collar employment, an increase in menial labor, and permanent levels of unemployment. These trends suggest "an in-creased hardening of class lines," which particularly affect women and blacks in terms of wealth, income, and occupation. For example, women on average earn only 66 percent of what men take home in wages, and many households below the official poverty level established by the U.S. government are female-headed households. Blacks are also at a disadvantage. In 1981, the median family income for whites was $23,517, while the median family income for blacks was only $13,266. Unemployment rates for black males are twice those of white males, and blacks who have jobs are paid less on average for the same work, or are restricted to minimum wage and poorly paid service-sector employment.

To supplement our discussion of inequality, we present a few "quality of life" indicators for persons in disadvantaged socioeconomic positions. Although many such indicators exist (e.g., pertaining to illness, mental health, housing, perceived deficiencies in self-concept and happiness), we limit discussion to those which help us understand ways in which stratification and inequality bear on criminal behavior patterns.

Compared with the middle and upper classes, the American poor have far less access to quality education and, as a consequence, have lower educational levels. They are also more likely to be unemployed, or employed in secondary labor markets which offer undesirable work and inferior wages. Their families are more likely to be large, and they are less likely to remain cohesive. And last but not least, poor persons are more likely to be victims of violent crime.

Turning to the top of the class structure, it comes as no surprise that those holding positions of relative advantage are able to gain additional leverage by translating economic strength into political power. As Mills demonstrates in his *Power Elite,* wealthy people are able to lobby for their interests, purchase political power with campaign contributions, secure important positions in both the public and private sectors, involve themselves in corporate and government decisions at the highest levels, and generally use their political and economic power to shape national policy in accordance with their interests.

All of this helps explain why radicals see political economy and inequality as such important contributors to crime causation. From a radical perspective, stratification and inequality are in large part due to political and economic factors as these relate to the antagonism between capital and labor—itself a defining characteristic of capitalism. If Marx was right, if productive relationships condition social relationships, and if the relations of production vary such that different social classes relate to the system of production in different ways, then class standing should have a significant impact on social relationships, that is, familial and educational relationships. As we shall see, many social relationships are directly related to criminal behavior. Thus, the extent to which capitalism adversely influences these relationships is the extent to which it shares responsibility for generating crime.

POLITICAL ECONOMY, INEQUALITY, AND CRIME

We begin with a question: what do social class, menstruation, broken homes, race, unemployment, and lunar cycles have in common? The answer: each has been specified as a cause of crime. This tells us two things: first, criminologists have traveled far and wide in their quest to discover the causes of crime (even to the moon!). And second, that causation is no simple matter. But where does this leave the student? What allows one to choose between causes as dissimilar as IQ and capitalism?

To answer these questions, the radical criminologist uses dialectical thinking which broadens causal inquiry to include the effects of political and economic institutions as these bear on the crime problem. In practical terms, this means that radical criminologists attempt to make sense of causation by placing micro-

causal explanations in a wider sociopolitical context. By broadening the scope of criminological inquiry to include significant social, political, and economic institutions, radical criminologists simultaneously expanded the arena in which we search for causes. The goal of radical inquiry is to expand and integrate causal levels, to try and see how microlevel variables such as broken homes or defective educational institutions are "shaped by larger social structures."

With this strategy in mind, three British criminologists, Tailor, Walton, and Young, wrote a now famous book titled *The New Criminology*, in which they argued that models of crime causation must include a macrolevel analysis which incorporates a *political economy* of *crime*. Central to their argument are ways in which crime is affected by "the overall social context of inequalities of power, wealth and authority in the developed industrial society." In addition to their emphasis on political economy, which they see as constituting the "wider origins" of the deviant act, Tailor et al. argue that radical criminology must also explain the "immediate origins" of criminal behavior. Reduced to its simplest terms, Tailor et al. suggest that the wider arena of political economy will condition more immediate social milieus and that these two levels together cause crime. What follows is a review of several studies which emphasize political economy and inequality as these bear on both the wider and immediate origins of criminal behavior.

POLITICAL ECONOMY, INEQUALITY, AND CRIME: THE EVIDENCE

In specifying ways in which economic institutions and structures cause crime, Blau and Blau published an empirical study that relies explicitly on Marxian predictions. After demonstrating that socioeconomic inequalities increase rates of violence, they conclude that inequality is the root cause of both social disorganization and crime. In their view, inequality increases alienation and undermines social cohesion

by creating multiple parallel social differences which widen the separations between ethnic groups and between social classes, and it creates a situation characterized by much social disorganization and prevalent latent animosities.

Michalowski makes this same point in simpler terms when he notes that "inequality tends to increase crime by weakening the social bond." Both the Blaus and Michalowski argue that it is inequality rather than simple poverty which produces crime.

The emphasis on inequality may put some of the recent controversy regarding social class and crime into perspective. Recent statistical studies suggest a weak direct effect of social class on crime. But this does not mean that social class is unimportant. On the contrary, radical theory suggests that inequality affects other processes, which in turn impact directly on crime. Thus, for instance, Blau and Blau suggest that family disorganization (e.g., percentage divorced, percentage female-headed families) mediates the effect of inequality. Indeed, they found that percentage divorced was positively related to inequality, and that percentage divorced had the strongest direct effects on crime.

Lee Rainwater has also offered a causal framework which combines wider and immediate origins by relating crime and family disorganization to inequality and racial oppression. Adding race to his discussion of social class, Rainwater argues that the economic marginality of black men leads to tense and conflicting role relationships, which increases marital instability and ultimately leads to a pattern of female-based households and matrifocal family structure. Like Blau and Blau, he concludes that inequality, low economic status, and race interact to produce crime through social disorganization. Simply put, both studies suggest that those who are economically disadvantaged are more likely to suffer disorganized or "segregated" family structures, and that strains experienced in these types of families provide a fertile precondition for increased rates of crime and delinquency.

INEQUALITY, FAMILY DISORGANIZATION, AND CRIME

Family measures such as percentage divorced and percentage headed by women have long been powerful correlates of delinquency, and many have suggested that family disorganization is an important cause of crime. However, in line with their preference for contextual explanations, radicals view family structure as an intervening rather than an independent variable. This is the strategy adopted by both Blau and Blau and Rainwater. Others have suggested that inconsistent family socialization patterns can be traced to experiences in the workplace. Inconsistent socialization patterns have been firmly established as a cause of delinquency.

Drawing on the works of Kohn, Edwards, and Etzioni, Colvin and Pauly argue that socialization experiences in the workplace spill into socialization experiences in the home and that negative experiences in either setting increase the likelihood that children will "engage in serious, patterned delinquency."

In pursuing this claim, Colvin and Pauly conclude that stable socialization experiences in desirable white-collar professions promote internalized moral commitments to the workplace. Parents in these occupations encourage family socialization experiences which rely on *internalized control structures*, a type of control which promotes a child's attachment to the socialization sequence. As a result, socialization experiences are "positive" in that children have "initial bonds of high intensity" to the family unit.

Blue-collar employees, on the other hand, work under *utilitarian control structures*, which means that their bond to the organization depends on a calculation of extrinsic material rewards (e.g., pay increases, seniority, job security). Workers socialized in this way tend to reproduce that structure in the family, producing "calculative bonds of intermediate intensity in their children," according to Colvin and Pauly.

And finally, parents holding low-skill, low-pay, dead-end jobs are exposed to *inconsistent coercive control structures* that are externally enforced. Such parents are likely to impose inconsistent controls on their criminality. Unemployment is particularly high among young minority males, who constitute a large at-risk crime population. Bohm acknowledges the idea that unemployment is caused by the natural progression of capitalism, yet sensitizes us to forces beyond unemployment which affect all classes and also act as causes of crime.

Addressing the issue of social policy, Bohm argues that we must transcend capitalism in order to solve the crime problem. In his view, creating jobs will not reduce crime, since the overall experience of capitalism still leaves the majority of the population alienated and vulnerable to criminal incentives. Other radicals have argued that if there is a connection between unemployment and crime, creating more jobs will reduce the property crime rate here and now. Thus, there is tension in the policy recommendations suggested by radical theorists. Short-term policies which can be instituted under the current system clash with the long-term policies for altering the social order.

Box has also suggested that radicals downplay the significance of unemployment and focus instead on broader economic conditions that affect all social classes. Like Bohm, Box argues that the unemployment explanation fails to account for crimes of the powerful. He suggests that radicals examine the connection between recession and crime.

In Box's view, recessions create conditions conducive to crime which affect both the powerless and the powerful. The powerful are un-

der additional pressure to maintain or increase profits during recessions. Faced with a recession, white-collar workers confront a constellation of organizational motivations and incentives which can easily lead to violations of law. On the other hand, recessions drive the lower class further into poverty, block legitimate means to success, and reduce commitment to the conventional social order. All of this makes increases in crime more likely among the lower class.

Recessions also affect the way powerful persons view the powerless. Recessions bring with them unemployment and an enlarged surplus population. This surplus population is "viewed more suspiciously by the governing elite, not because it actually does become disruptive and rebellious, but because it might." This increased fear results in increased state coercion of the powerless in the form of rising arrest and incarceration rates. Recessionary trends also affect the way police enforce the law, and Box claims that recessions can be linked to an increased number of police crimes, including fabricating evidence, police brutality, and the killing of offenders perceived as threats to the social order.

SURPLUS VALUE AND CRIME

A recent trend in radical theory has been to examine the relationship between crime rates and the rate of surplus value. This research attempts to link the driving productive forces of capitalism to the production of criminal behavior.

Marx's clearest illustration of surplus value describes it as the ratio of paid to unpaid labor, which implies that workers produce value far in excess of what they receive in wages. This excess is appropriated by the capitalist, who uses it for capital expansion and profit. There are two primary ways to increase the rate of surplus value. First, the working day may be extended with no commensurate increase in wages (absolute surplus value). And second, more efficient machines may replace people in the production process (relative surplus value). Either of these strategies allows owners to achieve their desired goal, which is to squeeze more production from the labor process. Given that capitalists derive profit from high rates of surplus value, it is in their interest to keep that rate as high as possible.

Marx went on to argue that increases in the rate of surplus value were directly related to the economic marginalization of the labor force. For its part, the extraction of absolute surplus value means that employed laborers receive a smaller share of the surplus they produce. The extraction of relative surplus value, on the other hand, creates unemployment and underemployment as a result of workers being technologically displaced. In effect, a rising rate of surplus value affects both employed and unemployed laborers.

As the rate of surplus value rises, more and more people become economically marginal. This decreases commitment to the conventional order and increases the probability that persons will engage in crime. Lynch, along with several colleagues, Groves and Lizotte, has uncovered a statistically significant relationship between the rate of surplus value and property crime arrest rates in the United States from 1950 to 1975. This research demonstrates that Marx's key economic concept—the extraction of surplus value—is useful for explaining how capitalist economic systems generate conditions conducive to street crime—especially property crime, the most prevalent type of crime in our society.

DOES CAPITALISM CAUSE CRIME?

Several theorists use Marxist arguments to suggest that capitalism stimulates a significant proportion of all criminal behavior. They are indebted, though in different ways, to theorists such as Engels and Bonger, who argued that criminal behavior is a direct reflection of the strains associated with life under capitalism.

Engels's point is twofold. First, he points out that many technological advances associated with capitalism expel workers from production, generate unemployed populations, and result in "want, wretchedness, and crime." This theme reappears in the contemporary writings of Quinney and Gordon, who suggest that crime is a rational response to systems of inequitable distribution characteristic of capitalism. Spitzer also argues that capitalism excludes certain groups from meaningful attachment to economic and social institutions. For Spitzer, those with a reduced stake in conformity—which includes those who are economically marginal—are more likely to engage in criminal behavior.

Engels's second point is that capitalism generates competitive structural and psychological orientations which are both beneficial and harmful to society. Competition benefits capitalists when it functions to keep wages low and productivity high. On the other hand, Marx noted that in their competitive scramble to control and monopolize markets, it is often the case that "one capitalist kills many." Similarly, competition can benefit the working class when labor is scarce and owners must pay high wages to attract workers. But competition can also injure the working class; not only must they compete with owners for better working conditions, they are often forced to compete with one another for a limited number of jobs and resources. Consequently, Engels views crime as the result of competition over scarce resources and sees competition engendered by capitalism as the cause of crime by the masses, the businessman, and middle classes. Further, he sees a collective psychological component to competition, which he describes as follows:

Competition has penetrated all the relationships of our life and completed the reciprocal bondage in which men now hold themselves. Competition is the great mainspring which . . . jerks into activity our aging and withering social order, or rather disorder. . . . Competition governs the numerical advances of mankind; it likewise governs its moral advance . . . [S]tatistics of crime . . . [show] the peculiar regularity with which crime advances year by year. . . . The extension of the factory system is followed everywhere by an increase in crime. . . . This regularity proves that crime, too, is governed by competition; that society creates a demand for crime which is met by a corresponding supply.

In *Criminality and Economic Conditions,* Bonger makes a similar argument. For Bonger, however, the competitiveness created by capitalism manifests itself as egoism in individuals—and it is egoism which generates crime among all classes. While Bonger believed egoism was evenly distributed throughout the class structure, he noted that the political strength of the ruling class enabled it to perform exploitative acts without having those acts defined as crimes. This explains why more lower-class persons are processed by the criminal justice system.

Engels and Marx also claim that capitalism "creates a demand for crime which is met by a corresponding supply." Expanding on this theme, Colvin and Pauly and the Schwendingers suggest that the inequality and stratification which accompany capitalism affect educational opportunities, which in turn structure an individual's propensity to crime. Greenberg explains variations in delinquency rates in terms of the structural demands of capitalism; Barnett has analyzed criminal opportunity as it relates to capital accumulation; and Wallace and Humphries have reinterpreted the criminogenic effects of urbanization and industrialization by placing these processes within a broader Marxist perspective on investment and capital accumulation. Each of these studies employs a broad contextual approach to crime, and each is a solid contribution to the radical perspective on crime causation.

QUESTIONS FOR DISCUSSION AND WRITING

1. What are three critiques of early radical theories?
2. What do Federal Reserve Board figures and U.S. Census data show?
3. What happens as the rate of surplus value rises?

Data Analysis Exercise

▰▰▰▰▰▰▰

An Exploration of Differential Association Theory and an Exploration of Control Theory

INTRODUCTION

In this data analysis exercise, we will conduct two separate inquiries. First, we will use Wave VII data from the National Youth Survey (NYS) to explore differential association theory, a theory presented in Part V. Then, we will use the same data to test some of the ideas in control theory, which is discussed in Part VI.

DESCRIPTION OF THE DATASET

See the data analysis exercise for Part V for a description of the NYS dataset. Before we start our analyses, we'll need to load up our dataset, "NYSCRIME."

Differential Association Theory

GETTING A HANDLE ON THE DATA AND USING CROSSTABULATION TABLES

Part V presents a number of the early theories that explain crime. Although it was developed in the 1930s, differential association is still one of the most widely cited theories. In a nutshell, Edwin Sutherland argued that we become delinquents because we associate with other delinquents and learn how to commit crimes from them. Although we also learn good behaviors from others, it was delinquency that most interested Sutherland. Sutherland also argued that the more important a relationship is to a person, the stronger will be the association with what is being learned. Therefore, if I hang out with people who drink at parties, I may decide to drink at parties because there is an excess of definitions in favor of doing so. On the other hand, if I hang out with the campus ministry, I may decide to have Bible-reading meetings on Friday nights while other people are out drinking at parties. The NYS is an excellent dataset for testing some of the tenets of differential association.

Rather than run frequencies on the demographic factors that we have already examined (in the exercises for Part V), we can now turn our attention to the tenets of differential association. They are discussed in detail in Sutherland's article, so I'll just summarize the ones we're going to explore (unfortunately, some of the tenets are difficult to test with the NYS data, so we'll confine ourselves to three that we can test easily).

When we are trying to test a theory or a part of a theory, we often face the difficulty of trying to choose variables from our dataset that match the theory's propositions. We had this problem when we looked at the correlates of crime because we had to use INCOME to measure social class. Researchers often find that the "fit" of the variables included in the data collected by others may be less than ideal. In some cases, this less than ideal fit may be beneficial, as it allows us to move beyond the most basic elements in a theory into alternate measures of those elements. This form of replication can get exciting, as we'll soon see.

Now, let's turn our attention to finding some appropriate variables, as we did in the exercises for Part V when we looked at social disorganization theory. The numbers below correspond to Sutherland's original numbering of his propositions.

TENET # 3: *The principal part of the learning of criminal behavior occurs within intimate personal groups.* Basically, this tenet means that if a person's close friends view crime as acceptable, s/he may also lean in that direction. If mere acquaintances suggest violating a law, however, the person is less likely to follow along. Sutherland was quite adamant that people learned from those with whom they interacted in their lives (rather than TV or other media), but it is important to realize that TV was less common in Sutherland's day. More recent scholars have amended this tenet to reflect the strong presence of the media in today's world.

One series of questions in the NYS asked respondents how much disapproval their parents, close friends, co-workers, and domestic partners (spouses or live-in boyfriends/girlfriends) would feel if the respondent broke the law. Before we test the tenets, run frequencies on OPINPAR, OPINPEER, OPINWORK, and OPINPART in order to get a better handle on these variables. From the frequencies, we note that very few of the parents and co-workers approved of marijuana at all, while close friends and partners were more likely to approve of its use. Based on these frequencies, we would usually collapse categories (at least for parents' opinion) to ensure that all the categories had enough cases to make the analysis meaningful. Since we will be comparing the findings across the four tables, however, we will leave them in their original condition. If you wish, you can recode the variables on your own and rerun the tables.

If Sutherland's theory is right, co-workers' opinions should be less influential than those of more important/intimate individuals in the respondents' lives (parents, partners, and close friends). To see if the NYS data support this idea, run a crosstabulation with marijuana use (USEDMJ) as the dependent (row) variable and OPINPAR, OPINPEER, OPINWORK, and OPINPART as the independent (column) variables (remember to choose "Phi and Cramer's V" under *Statistics* and check off "column percentages" under *Cells*). We'll just look at marijuana use, leaving theft and violence for you to look at for the "further exploration" questions.

What do you notice about the OPINPAR → USEDMJ table? We'll ignore the first two columns ("strongly approve" and "approve") because they have too few cases to allow for valid statements; if just one case from either category were switched to another column, we would make entirely different statements about those columns. That leaves us with three valid columns to examine. The respondents who said their parents strongly disapproved of marijuana use were less likely to smoke marijuana themselves (76.7% said they had not used it during the previous year). Similarly, respondents who reported that their parents disapproved of marijuana were more likely than their counterparts with strongly disapproving parents to report that they smoked marijuana (50.7% had not used it). Those who reported more ambivalent parents, however, were likely to use marijuana (only 18.8% had not used it). To learn the strength of the relationship between parental opinion of marijuana use and respondents' actual use, look at the Cramer's V. It is a strong relationship and is statistically significant. We can say, therefore, that the two variables are related.

Now turn your attention to the OPINPEER → USEDMJ table. We notice that 92.3% of respondents whose friends disapprove of marijuana use state that they themselves do not use the drug and that the percentage of smokers increases as peer disapproval diminishes. In fact, it appears that marijuana smoking might be more strongly related to peer opinion than to parental opinion. To see if that's true, check the statistics. Our suspicions are confirmed; the Cramer's V of .53 indicates a strong relationship and it is statistically significant.

The OPINWORK → USEDMJ table shows that marijuana use is less related to co-worker opinion. We can tell by looking at the cell percentages and the Cramer's V. Of the three variables we've looked at so far, co-worker opinion seems to be the least influential.

The final table, OPINPART → USEDMJ further supports Sutherland's theory. Respondents whose domestic partners disapproved of marijuana use were the least likely of all to smoke it. Taken together, this analysis supports tenet number 3 of differential association theory. Wasn't that fun? Now, let's examine another tenet.

TENET #5: *The specific direction of motives and drives is learned from definitions of the legal codes as favorable or unfavorable.* Basically, this tenet argues that people learn from others whether laws are something to be followed (for example, laws are good or help society and should always be obeyed) or something to be broken from time to time (for example, laws are ways to oppress the poor).

The NYS asked if the respondents' friends had ever suggested that they break the law. It seems logical that such suggestions, coming from friends, could play some role in the respondents' views of whether laws are inviolable. Sutherland felt that when those close to us suggest actions contrary to the law, we may begin to agree with their recommendations. To see if this is true, first run a frequency on SUGGBLAW, then run a crosstabulation table with marijuana use (USEDMJ) as the dependent (row) variable and SUGGBLAW as the independent (column) variable. The frequency table shows that more than a fifth of the respondents reported that one or more friends suggested that they break the law.

What does the crosstabulation table show? How often is marijuana smoked by the majority of respondents who said none of their friends had suggested that they break the law? What is the general trend for marijuana smoking as more and more of the respondents' friends suggested breaking the law? What is the strength of the relationship shown in the table? Is it statistically significant? How can we summarize this table? Does this finding support differential association theory?

TENET #6: *Criminal behavior results from an excess of definitions in favor of violating a law.* In other words, if you repeatedly see the benefits of breaking a law, it will be easier for you to commit the crime yourself. Assume that you live around one or more drug dealers, through whom you see the benefits of selling drugs such as flashy cars, stylish dress, and money. Assume those around you tell you it's not bad to sell drugs, possibly by pointing out that you would only be filling a necessary niche in society. Assume your friends buy and use drugs and tell you that this is acceptable behavior. These envisioned benefits form the basis of an excess of definitions. Once a crime is no longer repulsive, potential criminals may begin to break the law. The NYS data don't have all these variables, but the survey did ask how many of the respondents' friends smoked marijuana (it also asked how many had stolen items and engaged in violence).

So, if most of your friends break a law, you may break it, too, right? Let's find out. To explore this idea, run a frequency of PEERS_MJ, then run a crosstabulation table with marijuana use (USEDMJ) as the dependent (row) variable and PEERS_MJ as the independent (column) variable. The frequency table shows that a sizable number of friends smoked marijuana themselves.

What does the crosstabulation table show? How often is marijuana smoked by those who said none of their friends smoked it? What is the general trend for marijuana smoking as more and more of the respondents' friends smoked it? What is the strength of the relationship shown in the table? Is it statistically significant? How can we summarize this table? Does this table support differential association theory?

FURTHER EXPLORATION

We have now explored three tenets of Sutherland's differential association theory as they apply to smoking marijuana. If the theory is a good one, it should apply to crimes in addition to marijuana smoking. In the "further exploration" questions, you'll apply the theory to thefts of goods valued at more than $50 and violent offenses.

ON YOUR OWN

Now that we have explored three tenets of Sutherland's differential association theory, you could devise other ways of measuring and testing the tenets. For example, importance of family could be measured through amount of time spent visiting the respondents' families (VISITFAM). This is a difficult assignment, but try to think of other ways to measure the three tenets we tested or one of the other six tenets. If any of your ideas appears in the NYSCRIME dataset, run some analyses to test it. Otherwise, run some tables for importance of family as measured through habitual visiting.

While you are further examining differential association theory, reflect on how it helps explain why some people break the law. Think also about the theory's weaknesses, including crimes and/or situations that it cannot adequately address.

Control Theory

GETTING A HANDLE ON THE DATA AND
USING CROSSTABULATION TABLES

Control theory, as posed by Travis Hirschi, assumes that people form bonds to other individuals and that these bonds control their behavior. If I am attached to my parents, I will not want to do things that would incur their disapproval. If I am psychologically distant from my parents, however, their opinions will have less of a hold on me, thus allowing me to violate laws without shame. Later researchers extended Hirschi's theory to include bonds people form with friends, teachers, and school in general.

Testing control theory will require us to find suitable measures, as we have done for the previous theories. Among the questions in the NYS survey are two that seem appropriate for our purposes. The respondents were asked how much they agreed with two statements regarding their parents: (1) "Sometimes it's necessary to lie to your parents in order to keep their trust" [LIE_PAR] and (2) "It may be necessary to break some of your parents' rules in order to keep some of your friends" [BREAKRUL]. Presumably, those who agree with these statements are more likely to act against their parents' wishes, making them more psychologically distant from their parents. Arguably, the actions taken by the respondents may appear, on the surface, to be considerate of parental wishes (such as lying to protect parents from stress), but the statements still reflect acting against the desires of one's parents. To see if the theory holds, run frequencies for LIE_PAR and BREAKRUL, then run crosstabulation tables with USEDMJ as the dependent variable and LIE_PAR and BREAKRUL as the independent variables.

What do you notice about the LIE_PAR → USEDMJ table? About a fourth (26.4%) of the respondents who strongly disagreed with the statement had smoked marijuana during the past year. Compare this to those who had less negative opinions about lying to their parents, ignoring the "strongly agree" column because it involves too few cases. Can we say that those who agree with the statement are more likely to have smoked marijuana during the previous year? To learn the strength of the relationship between opinion regarding lying to parents and marijuana use, look at the Cramer's V and the significance level.

What about the BREAKRUL → USEDMJ table? Again, about a fourth (25.1%) of the respondents who strongly disagreed with the statement had smoked marijuana during the past year. Compare this to those who had less negative opinions about breaking parental rules, ignoring the "strongly agree" column because it involves too few cases. Can we say that those who agree with the statement are more likely to have smoked marijuana during the previous year? To learn the strength of the relationship between opinion regarding lying to parents and marijuana use, look at the Cramer's V and the significance level.

FURTHER EXPLORATION

We have now explored two relationships relevant to control theory as they apply to smoking marijuana. To see if the theory helps explain crimes other than marijuana smoking, you will apply it to thefts of goods valued at more than $50 and violent offenses for the "further exploration" questions.

ON YOUR OWN

Now that we have briefly examined Hirschi's control theory, you could devise other ways of measuring and testing the ideas in the theory. For example, attachment to parents could be measured through the level of satisfaction the respondents assign to their relationship with their parents (SATISPAR). Once again, this is a difficult assignment, but try to think of other ways to measure the ideas behind control theory. If any of your ideas appears in the NYSCRIME dataset, run some analyses to test it. Otherwise, run some tables for SATISPAR.

While you are further examining control theory, reflect on how it helps explain why some people break the law and why others don't. Think also about the theory's weaknesses, including crimes and/or situations that control theory cannot adequately address. By now, you are well on your way to understanding how theories work and don't work!

Homework for Part VII: General Questions
(Differential Association Theory)

Name: _____ Date:_____

Directions: Answer the following questions by filling in the blanks or circling the appropriate responses. A couple of answers have been filled in for you to make sure you're on the right track.

Tenet #3

1. Complete the following table using percentages from the frequency tables for OPINPAR, OPINPEER, OPINWORK, and OPINPART.

Group	% of respondents within each group who . . .				
	Strongly approve	*Approve*	*Neither disapprove nor approve*	*Disapprove*	*Strongly disapprove*
Parents					56.9
Close friends					
Co-workers					
Partner	0	3.3			

2. Complete the following table using percentages of respondents who smoked marijuana during the past year and statistics from the crosstabulation tables for OPINPAR → USEDMJ, OPINPEER → USEDMJ, OPINWORK → USEDMJ, and OPINPART → USEDMJ.

Category	% of respondents who smoked marijuana during the past year, by category				
	Strongly approve	Approve	Neither disapprove nor approve	Disapprove	Strongly disapprove
Parents' opinion: Cramer's V = .367 sig = .000	ignore: not enough cases	ignore: not enough cases	81.2	49.3	23.3
Close friends' opinion: Cramer's V = ___ sig = ___					
Co-workers' opinion: Cramer's V = ___ sig = ___	ignore: not enough cases				
Partner's opinion: Cramer's V = ___ sig = ___	0 cases				

3. As parental opinion becomes more negative toward marijuana use, respondents are *more / less* likely to smoke marijuana.

4. As close friends' opinions become more negative toward marijuana use, respondents are *more / less* likely to smoke marijuana.

5. As co-worker opinion becomes more negative toward marijuana use, respondents are *more / less* likely to smoke marijuana.

6. As partner opinion becomes more negative toward marijuana use, respondents are *more / less* likely to smoke marijuana.

7. From the Cramer's V statistics, it appears that the strongest relationship is found between marijuana smoking and the opinions regarding marijuana smoking that are held by *parents / close friends / co-workers / partners*. Conversely, the weakest relationship is found between marijuana smoking and the opinions regarding marijuana smoking that are held by *parents / close friends / co-workers / partners*.

Tenet #5

8. In Wave VII of the NYS dataset, _____% of the sample had no friends suggest that they break the law, _____% had very few of their friends advocate law-breaking, _____% had some of their friends suggest they break the law, _____% had most of their friends make such a suggestion, and _____% had all of their friends advise that they break a law.

9. Complete the following table using the percentage of respondents who smoked marijuana during the past year and statistics from the crosstabulation table for SUGGBLAW → USEDMJ.

	% of respondents who smoked marijuana during the past year by number of friends who suggested that respondent break the law				
	None of them	*Vew few of them*	*Some of them*	*Most of them*	*All of them*
Cramer's V = _____ sig = ____					

10. As the number of their friends who suggest that respondents break a law increases, respondents are *more / less* likely to smoke marijuana. This relationship is *weak / moderate / strong*. This relationship *is / is not* statistically significant.

Tenet #6

11. In Wave VII of the NYS dataset, _____% of the sample had no friends who smoked marijuana, _____% had very few friends who did, _____% had some friends who used marijuana, _____% said most of their friends smoked it, _____% said all of their friends were marijuana smokers.

12. Complete the following table using the percentage of the respondents' friends who smoked marijuana and statistics from the crosstabulation table for PEERS_MJ → USEDMJ.

	% of respondents who smoked marijuana during the past year by number of friends who smoke marijuana				
	None of them	Vew few of them	Some of them	Most of them	All of them
Cramer's V = _____ sig = ____					

13. As the percentage of their friends who smoke marijuana increases, respondents are *more / less* likely to smoke marijuana themselves. This relationship is *weak / moderate / strong*. This relationship *is / is not* statistically significant.

Homework for Part VII: "Further Exploration" Questions
(Differential Association Theory)

Name: _____   Date: _____

Task: See if the measures we have developed for differential association theory (OPINPAR, OPINPEER, OPINWORK, and OPINPART) are statistically related to either THEFT50 or VIOLENCE. Make sure you substitute the opinions relevant to each crime (use OPINPAR2, OPINPEE2, OPINWOR2, and OPINPA2 for THEFT50 and OPINPAR3, OPINPEE3, OPINWOR3, and OPINPA3 for VIOLENCE). Although you only need to replicate the process for one crime (THEFT50 or VIOLENCE), you may do both.

Directions: Answer the following questions by filling in the blanks or circling the appropriate responses.

1. Which crime did you choose? *THEFT50 / VIOLENCE*

Tenet #3

2. Complete the following table using percentages from the frequency tables for opinions, being careful to choose the ones that match your crime.

| Group | % of respondents within each group who . . . | | | | |
	Strongly approve	*Approve*	*Neither disapprove nor approve*	*Disapprove*	*Strongly disapprove*
Parents					
Close friends					
Co-workers					
Partners					

3. Complete the following table using percentages of respondents who violated the law addressed by your dependent variable and statistics from the crosstabulation tables for OPINPAR2/3 → THEFT50/VIOLENCE, OPINPEE2/3 → THEFT50/VIOLENCE, OPINWOR2/3 → THEFT50/VIOLENCE, and OPINPA2/3 → THEFT50/VIOLENCE.

| Category | % of respondents who violated the law addressed by your dependent variable, by category | | | | |
	Strongly approve	Approve	Neither disapprove nor approve	Disapprove	Strongly disapprove
Parents' opinion: Cramer's V = ____ sig = ____					
Close friends' opinion: Cramer's V = ____ sig = ____					
Co-workers' opinion: Cramer's V = ____ sig = ____					
Partner's opinion: Cramer's V = ____ sig = ____					

4. As parental opinion becomes more negative toward *THEFT50 / VIOLENCE*, respondents are *more / less* likely to break that law.

5. As close friends' opinions become more negative toward *THEFT50 / VIOLENCE*, respondents are *more / less* likely to break that law.

6. As co-worker opinion becomes more negative toward *THEFT50 / VIOLENCE*, respondents are *more / less* likely to break that law.

7. As partner opinion becomes more negative toward *THEFT50 / VIOLENCE*, respondents are *more / less* likely to break that law.

8. From the Cramer's V statistics, it appears that the strongest relationship is found between *THEFT50 / VIOLENCE* and the opinions regarding that crime that are held by *parents / close friends / co-workers / partners*. Conversely, the weakest relationship is found between the crime and the opinions regarding that crime that are held by *parents / close friends / co-workers / partners*.

POINTS TO PONDER: Can you try to explain the differences between what we found for USEDMJ and what you found for your dependent variable, with respect to the "weakest" relationship? (In other words, why are the opinions of co-workers more strongly associated with marijuana than with what you found for thefts or violence?)

Tenet #5

9. Complete the following table using the percentage of respondents who violated the law addressed by your dependent variable and statistics from the cross-tabulation table for SUGGBLAW → THEFT50 or SUGGBLAW → VIOLENCE.

	% of respondents who committed theft / violence by number of friends who suggested that respondent break the law				
	None of them	*Vew few of them*	*Some of them*	*Most of them*	*All of them*
Cramer's V = _____ sig = ____					

10. As the number of their friends who suggest that respondents break a law increases, respondents are *more / less* likely to commit *theft / violence*. This relationship is *weak / moderate / strong*. This relationship *is / is not* statistically significant.

11. Complete the following table using the percentage of the respondents' friends who violated the law addressed by your dependent variable and statistics from the crosstabulation table for PEERS50 → THEFT50 or PEERSVIO → VIOLENCE:

	% of respondents who committed theft / violence by number of friends who have committed the same crime				
	None of them	*Vew few of them*	*Some of them*	*Most of them*	*All of them*
Cramer's V = _____ sig = ____					

12. As the percentage of their friends who break a law increases, respondents are *more / less* likely to break that same law. This relationship is *weak / moderate / strong*. This relationship *is / is not* statistically significant.

13. Overall, it appears that our findings using the Wave VII of the NYS *support / do not support* differential association.

Homework for Part VII: "On Your Own" Questions
(Differential Association Theory)

Name: _____ Date: _____

Task: Try to think of other ways to measure the three tenets we tested, and the other six as well. If any of your ideas appears in the dataset, run some analyses to test it. Otherwise, run some tables for VISITFAM.

Directions: Answer the following questions.

Note: Please print out and include your tables with these questions so your work can be graded.

1. Which variable did you choose as your independent variable, and which tenet does it attempt to measure/test?

2. How did your independent variable affect marijuana use? Make sure to provide a description that includes the percentages, Phi or Cramer's V value, the strength of the relationship, and the significance value.

3. How did your independent variable affect thefts of goods worth more than $50? Make sure to provide a description that includes the percentages, Phi or Cramer's V value, the strength of the relationship, and the significance value.

4. How did your independent variable affect violent offenses? Make sure to provide a description that includes the percentages, Phi or Cramer's V value, the strength of the relationship, and the significance value.

5. Can you say your tenet testing supports differential association? Why/why not?

If you included more than one independent variable, you may summarize the findings here for future reference.

Homework for Part VII: General Questions
(Control Theory)

Name: _____   Date: _____

Directions: Answer the following questions by filling in the blanks or circling the appropriate responses. A couple of answers have been filled in for you to make sure you're on the right track.

1. Complete the following table using the percentage of respondents who fell into the following agreement categories for LIE_PAR and BREAKRUL.

	% of respondents who fell into the following agreement categories				
	Strongly disagree	*Disagree*	*Neutral*	*Agree*	*Strongly agree*
"Sometimes it's necessary to lie to your parents in order to keep their trust."	29.1%				
"It may be necessary to break some of your parents' rules in order to keep some of your friends."					

2. Complete the following table using the percentage of respondents who smoked marijuana during the past year and statistics from the crosstabulation tables for LIE_PAR → USEDMJ and BREAKRUL → USEDMJ.

Variable	% of respondents who smoked marijuana during the past year by level of agreement with statements				
	Strongly disagree	Disagree	Neutral	Agree	Strongly agree
LIE_PAR Cramer's V = _____ sig = ____	26.4%				ignore: not enough cases
BREAKRUL Cramer's V = _____ sig = ____	25.1%				ignore: not enough cases

3. As their agreement with the statement about lying to their parents increases, respondents are *more / less* likely to have smoked marijuana during the previous year. This relationship is *weak / moderate / strong*. This relationship *is / is not* statistically significant.

4. As their agreement with the statement about breaking parental rules to keep friends increases, respondents are *more / less* likely to have smoked marijuana during the previous year. This relationship is *weak / moderate / strong*. This relationship *is / is not* statistically significant.

5. Overall, it appears that our findings using Wave VII of the NYS *support / do not support* control theory.

Homework for Part VII: "Further Exploration" Questions
(Control Theory)

Name: _____   Date: _____

Task: See if the measures we have developed for control theory (LIE_PAR and BREAKRUL) are statistically related to either THEFT50 or VIOLENCE.

Directions: Answer the following questions by filling in the blanks or circling the appropriate responses.

1. Complete the following table using the percentage of respondents who committed theft or acts of violence and statistics from the crosstabulation tables for LIE_PAR → THEFT50/VIOLENCE and BREAKRUL → THEFT50/VIOLENCE.

Variable	% of respondents who committed theft / violence by level of agreement with statements				
	Strongly disagree	*Disagree*	*Neutral*	*Agree*	*Strongly agree*
LIE_PAR Cramer's V = _____ sig = ____					
BREAKRUL Cramer's V = _____ sig = ____					

2. As their agreement with the statement about lying to their parents increases, respondents are *more / less* likely to have committed *theft / violence*. This relationship is *weak / moderate / strong*. This relationship *is / is not* statistically significant.

3. As their agreement with the statement about breaking parental rules to keep friends increases, respondents are *more / less* likely to have committed *theft / violence*. This relationship is *weak / moderate / strong*. This relationship *is / is not* statistically significant.

4. Overall, it appears that our findings using Wave VII of the NYS *support / do not support* control theory.

Homework for Part VII: "On Your Own" Questions
(Control Theory)

Name: _____ Date: _____

Task: Try to think of other ways to measure the ideas underlying control theory. If any of your ideas appears in the dataset, run some analyses to test it. Otherwise, run some tables for SATISPAR.

Directions: Answer the following questions.

Note: Please print out and include your tables with these questions so your work can be graded.

1. Which variable did you choose as your independent variable, and which idea does it attempt to measure/test?

2. How did your independent variable affect marijuana use? Make sure to provide a description that includes the percentages, Phi or Cramer's V value, the strength of the relationship, and the significance value.

3. How did your independent variable affect thefts of goods worth more than $50? Make sure to provide a description that includes the percentages, Phi or Cramer's V value, the strength of the relationship, and the significance value.

4. How did your independent variable affect violent offenses? Make sure to provide a description that includes the percentages, Phi or Cramer's V value, the strength of the relationship, and the significance value.

5. How does the finding for SATISPAR → USEDMJ (or whatever variable you chose) affect your assessment of control theory? Can you explain this finding?

6. Can you say your testing supports control theory? Why/why not?

If you included more than one independent variable, you may summarize the findings here for future reference.

VIII

HOW DO WE EXPLAIN CRIME?

Contemporary Theories of Crime and Social Control

S TUDENTS frequently raise two questions when their criminology instructor insists on teaching "theory." The first is, which theory gives the "right" answer? The second question comes after several "old theories" have been presented and critiqued or thoroughly debunked: If we know a theory does not give the right answer, why study it? This last question is probably easier for most teachers to answer. Simply put, "old theories" are worthy of study because we can learn from how they were wrong. But also, as we have shown by including in this volume both classic and contemporary pieces from each theoretical tradition, the original articulations of these theories contained some good ideas that are still useful.

The answer to the first question of which theory is "correct" is more difficult for some students to accept. It is unsettling for anyone searching for answers to be told that no single approach is the right one. In any intellectual pursuit, wise people will sometimes disagree. When that pursuit involves studying something very complex, such as human behavior, there is additional room to disagree. And when the behavior being studied is such that those engaging in it seek to hide and elude detection, it is easy to understand why disagreements persist among criminologists about how to explain crime.

In this section, we have selected what we believe to be important contemporary developments in criminological theory. To be sure, not all of the new and important directions are represented here. For example, an article by Ross Matsueda that we included in Part V also represents a new direction for an old theory—differential association. Inevitably, some of our colleagues will consider that we have left out something important, whereas others will question whether all of the selections included do represent significant new directions in criminological theory.

Some of the ideas presented here can be seen as complementary, yet it will be obvious to the reader that some of the writers included in this section are in wholehearted disagreement with one another. The order in which the selections appear is based on their original date of publication, not on their substantive content.

The routine activities approach presented by Lawrence Cohen and Marcus Felson in "Social Change and Crime Rate Trends" has already proved very useful in combination with a number of other criminological theories. It is used to explain macro criminological patterns of violation and victimization by showing how changes in the routine behavior of the population can increase or decrease crime rates. In "A Power-Control Theory of Common Delinquent Behavior," John Hagan, John Simpson, and A. R. Gillis combine control theory and conflict theory to explain how social class affects delinquency. Importantly, they have provided an explanation of how gender differences in delinquency vary by social class. Both of these selections make it clear that both macro forces in society and micro forces in individuals' more immediate environment are important in determining both criminality and victimization.

James Q. Wilson and Richard Herrenstein's "A Bio-Psychological Theory of Choice" is taken from their book *Crime and Human Nature*. Their explanation might best be described as a bio-psychological theory of crime and delinquency. Choice is also an important component of their explanation. After reading this selection, students may find it interesting to compare the ideas presented in it with those expressed by James Q. Wilson and George L. Kelling in Part X, which focuses on the criminal justice system. Wilson and Herrenstein's work has been quite controversial. Those who favor their approach argue that its detractors, primarily social scientists, are uncomfortable with biologically based explanations of crime. Those who disagree with Wilson and Herrenstein have argued that they have oversimplified relevant biological, psychological, and sociological research in order to support their position. Students may find it interesting to pursue the debate that flourished in the scholarly literature following the publication of *Crime and Human Nature*.

An important development over the past twenty years has been the emergence of feminist criminology. Sally Simpson's "Feminist Theory, Crime, and Justice" critiques conventional criminology as well as some early feminists' work, provides an excellent overview of contemporary feminist ideas, and suggests new directions for feminist scholars studying criminality. This selection is in the radical or critical tradition of criminological theory; students should take note of its similarities to the perspectives presented in Part VII. Students can gain a further appreciation of feminist criminology by looking back at some of the selections that were originally published before 1980 and imagining how they might have been different had they been informed by the ideas presented by Simpson.

"The Nature of Criminality: Low Self-Control" is taken from Michael Gottfredson and Travis Hirschi's *A General Theory of Crime*, published in 1990. The cornerstone of their theory is that crime, like other forms of deviance, is a product of the individual's failure to develop adequate self-control. Readers will recognize the basic features of this theory as being consistent with Hirschi's earlier conception of social control theory. Here Gottfredson and Hirschi argue that early childhood development is a critical determinant of patterns of criminal and deviant behavior later in life. Those who do not develop good self-control when they are very young ordinarily do not develop it later, and this lack of control is the cause of crime, as well as of behaviors such as alcoholism, unstable work histories, and divorce.

"Toward an Age-Graded Theory of Informal Social Control" by Robert Sampson and John Laub, from their book *Crime in the Making*, is one of the most recently published of the selections included here. As with Gottfredson and Hirschi, their perspective is derived from control theory. They argue that social bonds are important determinants of criminal involvement, and that these bonds differ over the life course. For the very young, bonds to the family of origin are most important. For adolescents, it is bonds to school and conventional peer groups that inhibit delinquency. Later in life, adult behavior is regulated by bonds such as those to a family of their own and careers. One interesting aspect of this work is that Sampson and Laub empirically test their ideas using data collected by Glueck and Glueck more than fifty years ago. They have used modern technology and contemporary analytic techniques to enhance the value of these important data.

In "The Causal Process of Control Balance Theory," Charles Tittle offers a new approach to understanding how social controls regulate deviant behavior. His work is important because he distinguishes between an individual's internally imposed self-controls and those controls externally imposed by others. Tittle believes that deviant behavior is much more likely to occur when a person's internal and external controls are out of balance—that is, when there are more of one than the other. Although Tittle recognizes that other factors are important, he concludes that when the two types of control are balanced, "people generally conform."

Earlier, we tried to convince readers that disagreement among scholars should be expected and is a positive contributor to the dynamic process of building knowledge. Rather than defining the lack of a single right answer as a source of frustration, many criminologists see the opportunity for debate as one of the things that makes scholarly life interesting. When reading the selections in this portion of the volume, students should imagine the disagreements and resulting intellectual jousting that some of these ideas produce among criminologists. It is from these disagreements, and the thrust-and-parry of scholarly discourse, that fresh and exciting ideas emerge.

Social Change and Crime Rate Trends: A Routine Activity Approach

LAWRENCE E. COHEN

MARCUS FELSON

I N its summary report, the National Commission on the Causes and Prevention of Violence presents an important sociological paradox:

Why, we must ask, have urban violent crime rates increased substantially during the past decade when the conditions that are supposed to cause violent crime have not worsened—have, indeed, generally improved?

The Bureau of the Census, in its latest report on trends in social and economic conditions in metropolitan areas, states that most "indicators of well-being point toward progress in the cities since 1960." Thus, for example, the proportion of blacks in cities who completed high school rose from 43 percent in 1960 to 61 percent in 1968: unemployment rates dropped significantly between 1959 and 1967 and the median family income of blacks in cities increased from 61 percent to 68 percent of the median white family income during the same period. Also during the same period, the number of persons living below the legally defined poverty level in cities declined from 11.3 million to 8.3 million.

Despite the general continuation of these trends in social and economic conditions in the United States, the Uniform Crime Reports indicate that between 1960 and 1975 reported rates of robbery, aggravated assault, forcible rape, and homicide increased by 263 percent, 164 percent, 174 percent, and 188 percent, respectively. Similar property crime rate increases reported during this same period (e.g., 200 percent for burglary rate) suggest that the paradox noted by the Violence Commission applies to nonviolent offenses as well.

In the present [article], we consider these paradoxical trends in crime rates in terms of changes in the "routine activities" of everyday life. We believe the structure of such activities influences criminal opportunity and therefore affects trends in a class of crimes we refer to as *direct-contact predatory violations*. Predatory violations are defined here as illegal acts in which "someone definitely and intentionally takes or damages the person or property of another." Further, this analysis is confined to those predatory violations involving direct physical contact between at least one offender and at least one person or object which that offender attempts to take or damage.

We argue that structural changes in routine activity patterns can influence crime rates by affecting the convergence in space and time of the three minimal elements of direct-contact predatory violations: (1) motivated offenders,

(2) suitable targets, and (3) the absence of capable guardians against a violation. We further argue that the lack of any one of these elements is sufficient to prevent the successful completion of a direct-contact predatory crime and that the convergence in time and space of suitable targets and the absence of capable guardians may even lead to large increases in crime rates without necessarily requiring any increase in the structural conditions that motivate individuals to engage in crime. That is, if the proportion of motivated offenders or even suitable targets were to remain stable in a community, changes in routine activities could nonetheless alter the likelihood of their convergence in space and time, thereby creating more opportunities for crimes to occur. Control therefore becomes critical. If controls through routine activities were to decrease, illegal predatory activities could then be likely to increase. In the process of developing this explanation and evaluating its consistency with existing data, we relate our approach to classical human ecological concepts and to several earlier studies.

The Structure of Criminal Activity

Sociological knowledge of how community structure generates illegal acts has made little progress since Shaw and McKay and their colleagues published their pathbreaking work, *Delinquency Areas*. Variations in crime rates over space long have been recognized, and current evidence indicates that the pattern of these relationships within metropolitan communities has persisted. Although most spatial research is quite useful for describing crime rate patterns and providing post hoc explanations, these works seldom consider—conceptually or empirically—the fundamental human ecological character of illegal acts as *events* which occur at specific locations in *space* and *time*, involving specific persons and/or objects. These and related concepts can help us to develop an extension of the human ecological

analysis to the problem of explaining changes in crime rates over time. Unlike many criminological inquiries, we do not examine why individuals or groups are inclined criminally, but rather we take criminal inclination as given and examine the manner in which the spatio-temporal organization of social activities helps people to translate their criminal inclinations into action. Criminal violations are treated here as routine activities which share many attributes of, and are interdependent with, other routine activities. This interdependence between the structure of illegal activities and the organization of everyday sustenance activities leads us to consider certain concepts from human ecological literature.

Selected Concepts from Hawley's Human Ecological Theory

While criminologists traditionally have concentrated on the *spatial* analysis of crime rates within metropolitan communities, they seldom have considered the *temporal* interdependence of these acts. In his classic theory of human ecology, Amos Hawley treats the community not simply as a unit of territory but rather as an organization of symbiotic and commensalistic relationships as human activities are performed over both space and time.

Hawley identified three important temporal components of community structure: (1) *rhythm*, the regular periodicity with which events occur, as with the rhythm of travel activity; (2) *tempo*, the number of events per unit of time, such as the number of criminal violations per day on a given street; and (3) *timing*, the coordination among different activities which are more or less interdependent, such as coordination of an offender's rhythms with those of a victim. These components of temporal organization, often neglected in criminological research, prove usual in analyzing how illegal tasks are performed—a utility which becomes more apparent after noting the spatio-temporal requirements of illegal activities.

The Minimal Elements of Direct-Contact Predatory Violations

As we previously stated, despite their great diversity, direct-contact predatory violations share some important requirements which facilitate analysis of their structure. Each successfully completed violation minimally requires an *offender* with both criminal inclinations and the ability to carry out those inclinations, a person or object providing a *suitable target* for the offender, and *absence of guardians* capable of preventing violations. We emphasize that the lack of any of these elements normally is sufficient to prevent such violations from occurring. Although guardianship is implicit in everyday life, it usually is marked by the absence of violations: hence, it is easy to overlook. While police action is analyzed widely, guardianship by ordinary citizens of one another and of property as they go about routine activities may be one of the most neglected elements in sociological research on crime, especially since it links seemingly unrelated social roles and relationships to the occurrence or absence of illegal acts.

The conjunction of these minimal elements can be used to assess how structure may affect the tempo of each type of violation. That is, the probability that a violation will occur at any specific time and place might be taken as a function of the convergence of likely offenders and suitable targets in the absence of capable guardians. Through consideration of how trends and fluctuations in social conditions affect the frequency of this convergence of criminogenic circumstances, an explanation of temporal trends in crime rates can be constructed.

The Ecological Nature of Illegal Acts

This ecological analysis of direct-contact predatory violations is intended to be more than metaphorical. In the context of such violations, people, gaining and losing sustenance, struggle among themselves for property, safety, territorial hegemony, sexual outlet, physical control, and sometimes for survival itself. The interdependence between offenders and victims can be viewed as a predatory relationship between functionally dissimilar individuals or groups. Since predatory violations fail to yield any net gain in sustenance for the larger community, they can only be sustained by feeding upon other activities. As offenders cooperate to increase their efficiency at predatory violations and as potential victims organize their resistance to these violations, both groups apply the symbiotic principle to improve their sustenance position. On the other hand, potential victims of predatory crime may take evasive actions which encourage offenders to pursue targets other than their own. Since illegal activities must feed upon other activities, the spatial and temporal structure of routine legal activities should play an important role in determining the location, type, and quantity of illegal acts occurring in a given community or society. Moreover, one can analyze how the structure of community organization as well as the level of technology in a society provide the circumstances under which crime can thrive. For example, technology and organization affect the capacity of persons with criminal inclinations to overcome their targets, as well as affecting the ability of guardians to contend with potential offenders by using whatever protective tools, weapons, and skills they have at their disposal. Many technological advances designed for legitimate purposes—including the automobile, small power tools, hunting weapons, highways, telephones, and so on—may enable offenders to carry out their own work more effectively or may assist people in protecting their own or someone else's person or property.

Not only do routine legitimate activities often provide the wherewithal to commit offenses or to guard against others who do so, but they also provide offenders with suitable targets. Target suitability is likely to reflect such things as value (e.g., the material or symbolic desirability of a personal or property target for offenders), physical visibility, access, and the inertia of a target against illegal treatment by offenders (including the weight, size, and attached or locked features of property inhibiting its illegal removal and the physical capacity of personal victims to resist attackers with or without weapons). Routine production activities probably affect the suitability of consumer goods for illegal removal by determining their value and weight. Daily activities may affect the location of property and personal targets in visible and accessible places at particular times. These activities also may cause people to have on hand objects that can be used as weapons for criminal acts or self-protection or to be preoccupied with tasks which reduce their capacity to discourage or resist offenders.

While little is known about conditions that affect the convergence of potential offenders, targets, and guardians, this is a potentially rich source of propositions about crime rates. For example, daily work activities separate many people from those they trust and the property they value. Routine activities also bring together at various times of day or night persons of different backgrounds, sometimes in the presence of facilities, tools, or weapons which influence the commission or avoidance of illegal acts. Hence, the timing of work, schooling, and leisure may be of central importance for explaining crime rates.

The ideas presented so far are not new, but they frequently are overlooked in the theoretical literature on crime. Although an investigation of the literature uncovers significant examples of descriptive and practical data related to the routine activities upon which illegal behavior feeds, these data seldom are treated within an analytical framework. The next section reviews some of this literature.

RELATION OF THE ROUTINE ACTIVITY APPROACH TO EXTANT STUDIES

A major advantage of the routine activity approach presented here is that it helps assemble some diverse and previously unconnected criminological analyses into a single substantive framework. This framework also serves to link illegal and legal activities, as illustrated by a few examples of descriptive accounts of criminal activity.

Descriptive Analyses

There are several descriptive analyses of criminal acts in criminological literature. For example, Thomas Reppetto's study, *Residential Crime,* considers how residents supervise their neighborhoods and streets and limit access of possible offenders. He also considers how distance of households from the central city reduces risks of criminal victimization. Reppetto's evidence—consisting of criminal justice records, observations of comparative features of geographic areas, victimization survey data, and offender interviews—indicates that offenders are very likely to use burglary tools and to have at least minimal technical skills, that physical characteristics of dwellings affect their victimization rates, that the rhythms of residential crime rate patterns are marked (often related to travel and work patterns of residents), and that visibility of potential sites of crime affects the risk that crimes will occur there. Similar findings are reported by Pope's study of burglary in California and by Scarr's study of burglary in and around the District of Columbia. In addition, many studies report that architectural and environmental design as well as community crime programs serve to decrease target suitability and increase capable guardianship, while many biographical or autobiographical descriptions of illegal activities note that lawbreakers take into account the nature of property and/or the structure of human activities as they go about their illegal work.

Evidence that the spatio-temporal organization of society affects patterns of crime can be found in several sources. Strong variations in specific predatory crime rates from hour to hour, day to day, and month to month are reported often, and these variations appear to correspond to the various tempos of the related legitimate activities upon which they feed. Also at a microsociological level, Short and Strodtbeck describe opportunities for violent confrontations of gang boys and other community residents which arise in the context of community leisure patterns, such as "quarter parties" in black communities, and the importance, in the calculus of decision making employed by participants in such episodes, of low probabilities of legal intervention. In addition, a wealth of empirical evidence indicates strong spatial variations over community areas in crime and delinquency rates. Recently, Albert Reiss has argued convincingly that these spatial variations (despite claims to the contrary) have been supported consistently by both official and unofficial sources of data. Reiss further cites victimization studies which indicate that offenders are very likely to select targets not far from their own residence.

*Macrolevel Analyses of
Crime Trends and Cycles*

Although details about how crime occurs are intrinsically interesting, the important analytical task is to learn from these details how illegal activities carve their niche within the larger system of activities. This task is not an easy one. For example, attempts by Bonger, Durkheim, Henry and Short, and Fleisher to link the rate of illegal activities to the economic condition of a society have not been completely successful. Empirical tests of the relationships postulated in the above studies have produced inconsistent results, which some observers view as an indication that the level of crime is not related systematically to the economic conditions of a society.

It is possible that the wrong economic and social factors have been employed in these macrostudies of crime. Other researchers have provided stimulating alternative descriptions of how social change affects the criminal opportunity structure thereby influencing crime

rates in particular societies. For example, at the beginning of the nineteenth century, Pat Colquhoun presented a detailed, lucid description and analysis of crime in the London metropolitan area and suggestions for its control. He assembled substantial evidence that London was experiencing a massive crime wave attributable to a great increment in the assemblage and movement of valuable goods through its ports and terminals.

A similar examination of crime in the period of the English industrial expansion was carried out by a modern historian, J. J. Tobias, whose work on the history of crime in nineteenth-century England is perhaps the most comprehensive effort to isolate those elements of social change affecting crime in an expanding industrial nation. Tobias details how far-reaching changes in transportation, currency, technology, commerce, merchandising, poverty, housing, and the like had tremendous repercussions on the amount and type of illegal activities committed in the nineteenth century. His thesis is that structural transformations either facilitated or impeded the opportunities to engage in illegal activities. In one of the few empirical studies of how recent social change affects the opportunity structure for crime in the United States, Leroy Gould demonstrated that the increase in the circulation of money and the availability of automobiles between 1921 and 1965 apparently led to an increase in the rate of bank robberies and auto thefts, respectively. Gould's data suggest that these relationships are due more to the abundance of opportunities to perpetrate the crimes than to short-term fluctuations in economic activities.

Although the sociological and historical studies cited in this section have provided some useful *empirical* generalizations and important insights into the incidence of crime, it is fair to say that they have not articulated systematically the *theoretical* linkages between routine legal activities and illegal endeavors. Thus, these studies cannot explain how changes in the larger social structure generate changes in the opportunity to engage in predatory crime and hence account for crime rate trends. To do so requires a conceptual framework such as that sketched in the preceding section. Before attempting to demonstrate the feasibility of this approach with macrolevel data, we examine available microlevel data for its consistency with the major assumptions of this approach.

Microlevel Assumptions of the Routine Activity Approach

The theoretical approach taken here specifies that crime rate trends in the post–World War II United States are related to patterns of what we have called routine activities. We define these as any recurrent and prevalent activities which provide for basic population and individual needs, whatever their biological or cultural origins. Thus, routine activities would include formalized work, as well as the provision of standard food, shelter, sexual outlet, leisure, social interaction, learning, and child rearing. These activities may go well beyond the minimal levels needed to prevent a population's extinction, so long as their prevalence and recurrence makes them a part of everyday life.

Routine activities may occur (1) at home, (2) in jobs away from home, and (3) in other activities away from home. The latter may involve primarily household members or others. We shall argue that, since World War II, the United States has experienced a major shift of routine activities away from the first category into the remaining ones, especially those nonhousehold activities involving nonhousehold members. In particular, we shall argue that this shift in the structure of routine activities increases the probability that motivated offenders will converge in space and time with suitable targets in the absence of capable guardians, hence contributing to significant increases in the direct-contact predatory crime rates over these years.

If the routine activity approach is valid, then we should expect to find evidence for a number of empirical relationships regarding the nature and distribution of predatory violations. For example, we would expect routine activities performed within or near the home and among family or other primary groups to entail lower risk of criminal victimization because they enhance guardianship capabilities. We should also expect that routine daily activities affect the location of property and personal targets in visible and accessible places at particular times, thereby influencing their risk of victimization. Furthermore, by determining their size and weight and in some cases their value, routine production activities should affect the suitability of consumer goods for illegal removal. Finally, if the routine activity approach is useful for explaining the paradox presented earlier, we should find that the circulation of people and property, the size and weight of consumer items, and so on will parallel changes in crime rate trends for the post–World War II United States.

The veracity of the routine activity approach can be assessed by analyses of both microlevel and macrolevel interdependencies of human activities. While consistency at the former level may appear noncontroversial, or even obvious, one nonetheless needs to show that the approach does not contradict existing data before proceeding to investigate the latter level.

DISCUSSION

In our judgment, many conventional theories of crime (the adequacy of which usually is evaluated by cross-sectional data, or no data at all) have difficulty accounting for the annual changes in crime rate trends in the post–World War II United States. These theories may prove useful in explaining crime trends during other periods, within specific communities, or in particular subgroups of the population. Longitudinal aggregate data for the United States, however, indicate that the trends for many of the presumed causal variables in these theoretical structures are in a direction opposite to those hypothesized to be the causes of crime. For example, during the decade 1960–1970, the percentage of the population below the low-income level declined 44 percent and the unemployment rate declined 186 percent. Central-city population as a share of the whole population declined slightly, while the percentage of foreign stock declined 0.1 percent, and so on.

On the other hand, the convergence in time and space of three elements (motivated offenders, suitable targets, absence of capable guardians) appears useful for understanding crime rate trends. The lack of any of these is sufficient to prevent the occurrence of a successful direct-contact predatory crime. The convergence in time and suitable targets and the absence of capable guardians can lead to a large increase in crime rates without any increase or change in the structural conditions that motivate individuals to engage in crime. Presumably, had the social indicators of the variables hypothesized to be the causes of crime in conventional theories changed in the direction of favoring increased crime in the post–World II United States, the increases in crime rates likely would have been even more staggering than those which were observed. In any event, it is our belief that criminologists have underemphasized the importance of the convergence of suitable targets and the absence of capable guardians in explaining recent increases in the crime rate. Furthermore, the effects of the convergence in time and space of these elements may be multiplicative rather than additive. That is, their convergence by a fixed percentage may produce increases in crime rates far greater than the fixed percentage, demonstrating how some relatively modest social trends can contribute to some relatively large changes in crime rate trends. The fact that logged variables improved our equations (moving Durbin-Watson values closer to "ideal" levels) lends support to the argument that such an interaction occurs.

Those few investigations of cross-sectional data which include house indicators produce results similar to ours. For example, Roncek

and Choldin and Roncek report on block-level data for San Diego, Cleveland, and Peoria and indicate that the proportion of a block's households which are primary individual households consistently offers the best or nearly the best predictor of a block's crime rate. This relationship persisted after they controlled for numerous social variables, including race, density, age, and poverty. Thus, the association between household structure and risk of criminal victimization has been observed in individual-level and block-level cross-sectional data, as well as aggregate national time-series data.

Without denying the importance of factors motivating offenders to engage in crime, we have focused specific attention upon violations themselves and the prerequisites for their occurrence. However, the routine activity approach might in the future be applied to the analysis of offenders and their inclinations as well. For example, the structure of primary group activity may affect the likelihood that cultural transmission or social control of criminal inclinations will occur, while the structure of the community may affect the tempo of criminogenic peer group activity. We also may expect that circumstances favorable for carrying out violations contribute to criminal inclinations in the long run by rewarding these inclinations.

We further suggest that the routine activity framework may prove useful in explaining why the criminal justice system, the community, and the family have appeared so ineffective in exerting social control since 1960. Substantial increases in the opportunity to carry out predatory violations may have undermined society's mechanisms for social control. For example, it may be difficult for institutions seeking to increase the certainty, celerity, and severity of punishment to compete with structural changes resulting in vast increases in the certainty, celerity, and value of rewards to be gained from illegal predatory acts.

It is ironic that the very factors which increase the opportunity to enjoy the benefits of life also may increase the opportunity for predatory violations. For example, automobiles provide freedom of movement to offenders as well as average citizens and offer vulnerable targets for theft. College enrollment, female labor force participation, urbanization, suburbanization, vacations, and new electronic durables provide various opportunities to escape the confines of the household while they increase the risk of predatory victimization. Indeed, the opportunity for predatory crime appears to be enmeshed in the opportunity structure for legitimate activities to such an extent that it might be very difficult to root out substantial amounts of crime without modifying much of our way of life. Rather than assuming that predatory crime is simply an indicator of social breakdown, one might take it as a by-product of freedom and prosperity as they manifest themselves in the routine activities of everyday life.

QUESTIONS FOR DISCUSSION AND WRITING

1. How do structural changes in routine activity patterns influence crime rates?
2. What role do capable guardians play in crime?
3. What do "daily work activities" do?

A Power-Control Theory of Common Delinquent Behavior

JOHN HAGAN

JOHN SIMPSON

A. R. GILLIS

C LASS and gender are among the most frequently analyzed correlates of delinquency today. Gender is a strong and consistent correlate, whereas class is weak and uncertain. The situation is an embarrassment to sociological theories of delinquency. Although most such theories attach great importance to class, there is doubt about the correlation on which they rest. Furthermore, although it is generally assumed that the effect of gender is socially based, there is no clear evidence that the gender-delinquency relationship can be removed when social variables are taken into account. Class apparently accounts for too little delinquency; gender stubbornly accounts for too much. Curiously, the issues of class and gender have not been joined in delinquency research. We believe that this is a crucial omission, for a combined consideration of class structure and gender is the key to a sociological understanding of the effect of gender on delinquency.

The failure to link class and gender in delinquency research betrays a neglect of classi-cal criminological theory. The father figure of Marxian criminology, Willem Bonger, offered one of the first statistical demonstrations of the strong correlation between gender and criminality. He then pointed specifically to the importance of class structure for a theoretical understanding of the social basis of this relationship: "A very conclusive proof of the thesis that the social position of woman is what explains her lower criminality, is as follows. The difference in the manner of life of the two sexes decreases as we descend the social scale. If the social position of woman is then an important determinant of her lower criminality, the figures ought to show that the criminality of men differs more from that of women in the well-to-do classes than in classes less privileged."

Of course, Bonger had neither the data nor the analytic techniques to test adequately his prediction of the interactive effect of class and gender on delinquency. Today we do, but such testing requires that we first think carefully about several issues of theory and measurement.

From "The Class Structure of Gender and Delinquency: Towards a Power-Control Theory of Common Delinquent Behavior" by J. Hagan, A. R. Gillis, and J. Simpson, 1985, *American Journal of Sociology* 90:1151–1175. Copyright © 1985 by The University of Chicago Press. Reprinted by permission of The University of Chicago Press.

TOWARD A POWER-CONTROL THEORY

Two concepts organize the classical theories of delinquency: power and control. The empirical distinction between these concepts is partly one of level of analysis. Power theories tend to be macrostructural and control theories microstructural, but they share a structural interest in relations of dominance. Power theories focus on relations of dominance that derive from control over the means of production; control theories focus on relations of dominance established within the family. In this chapter, we join parts of these two theoretical traditions to form a power theory of common delinquent behavior.

Our discussion will focus on what we have noted to be one of the strongest and most consistent correlations in delinquency research: that between gender and delinquency. Power-control theory specifies where this correlation is strongest and most difficult to remove, as well as where it is weakest and most easily explained. Relations of dominance emphasized in the power tradition, and defined in terms of class, are used to specify the conditions under which the gender-delinquency relationship rises and falls. Relations of dominance emphasized in the control tradition and explored in terms of the family are used to explain gender-delinquency relationships within specific classes.

Both the power and control traditions lead us to consider the conditions under which adolescents are free to deviate from social norms. Both the presence of power and the absence of control contribute to these conditions. It is assumed that freedom to deviate is directly related to class position, that males are freer to deviate than are females, and that males are freest to deviate in the higher classes. Note that this set of assumptions forms a basis for a prediction such as Bonger's: the relationship between gender and delinquency will increase with movement up the class structure, and it will decrease with movement down.

Our reversal of the theoretically expected, negative class-delinquency relationship is unconventional, but not unprecedented. Indeed, the proposed positive relationship is as durable as the observation that power corrupts and has found one place in sociological theory through Sorokin and Lunden's *Power and Morality*. They propose that power has an "intoxifying" effect, such that holders of power come to see themselves as above (i.e., free of) the moral and legal precepts that control ordinary persons. The expected result is that "the moral behavior of ruling groups tends to be more criminal and submoral than that of the ruled strata of the same society." Because "ruling groups" have not been meaningfully distinguished in self-report research, this proposition remains untested for delinquents as well as adults. Instead, it thrives on stories of "rich kids" and tales such as those about the young Kennedys.

A similar theme was suggested in Veblen's *The Theory of the Leisure Class*. In a passage that stimulated Matza and Sykes's theory of subterranean values, Veblen wrote that "the ideal pecuniary man is like the ideal delinquent in his unscrupulous conversion of goods and persons to his own ends, and in a callous disregard of [i.e., freedom from] the feelings and wishes of others or the remoter effects of his actions." Matza and Sykes argue that this similarity reflects a dispersion of leisure class values—the search for adventure, excitement, and thrills, or what we call a "taste for risk"—throughout society, causing delinquency at all class levels. They call special attention to common forms of "white-collar delinquency" but stop short of asserting a positive class-delinquency relationship. The dispersion they emphasize has a democratizing, and therefore diminishing, effect. Still, a small positive relationship between class position and common forms of delinquency is fully consistent with Matza and Sykes's theory: the dispersion they propose is downward through the class structure. A power-control theory of delinquent behavior proposes a class-delinquency relationship of similar size and direction.

If it is indeed relational position in the social structure, rather than type of individual, that explains delinquent behavior, it should be possible to specify and explain the gender-delinquency correlation by taking relational position fully into account. In the data analysis that follows, we consider these two kinds of relations of dominance: the controls exercised or experienced by the head of household in relation to others in the workplace and the controls exercised by parents in relation to their children. We have already discussed the role of class relations in specifying the gender-delinquency relationship. We turn now to the role of familial controls in transmitting the effects of gender on delinquency within class categories.

A fundamental instrument-object relationship structures family-based relations of dominance. The two sides of this relationship are that mothers more than fathers are the instruments of familial controls and that daughters more than sons are the objects of familial controls. This relationship is the core of what Rosabeth Kanter calls the "intimate oppression" of informal social control. This is the kind of relationship that a Marxist-feminist theory suggests is central to the "reproduction of order." There is evidence that such an instrument-object cycle even persists among working women who come to believe in "Horatia Alger as a feminist role model"—a woman who makes time to be both the primary socializer of her children and the architect of a career. In other words, even among more liberated women, the instrument-object relationship may be perpetuated. How, then, does this relationship mediate the effects of gender on delinquency?

The answer to this question ties family relations of dominance issues of deterrence and legal sanctions. Gibbs provocatively observes, "The secret scandal of the Marxist theory of criminal law is that it tacitly attributes validity to the deterrence doctrine." Gibbs makes his point by posing a rhetorical question: "How can legal punishment be used as a repressive instrument by a dominant class if the punishment does not deter?" A power-control theory of delinquent behavior asserts that threat of punishment, or at least the perception of such

a threat, does deter delinquency. This much is not new. What is new is our argument that the bases of this repressive effect are the relations of dominance established in the family. That is, adolescents, especially female adolescents, are taught to avoid risks generally and the risk of legal sanctions specifically. The testable implications of this part of a power-control theory of delinquency are that females will be deterred more by the threat of legal sanctions than males and that this effect will be produced more through maternal than paternal controls.

The class structure of the gender-delinquency relationship should be reemphasized. What a power-control theory of common delinquent behavior is saying is that in all classes males are freer to be delinquent than females but that it is in the most powerful classes that males are freest to be delinquent. The presence of power and the absence of control play a joint role in specifying and mediating this gender-delinquency relationship.

Ours is not the first theory of delinquent behavior to be informed by Marxian ideas. It is, however, the first such formulation to be empirically tested, and it is the first Marxian-based theory to address one of the most important relationships in delinquency research: that between gender and delinquency. We have demonstrated, using a power-control theory of delinquency and a prediction made by Bonger more than a half century ago, that the relationship between gender and common forms of delinquency declines with each step down the class structure. Furthermore, where this relationship is strongest, it can be statistically removed by taking theoretically predicted variables into account. A power-control theory does much to specify and explain the class structure of gender and delinquency, and in doing so it demonstrates the social bases of this relationship.

The core assumption of our theory is that the presence of power and the absence of control create conditions of freedom that permit common forms of delinquency. It is important to emphasize that this formulation is different from existing Marxian theories of delinquency. This theoretical difference may derive from the different phenomena selected for explanatory attention. Recently, Marxian theorists have followed delinquency researchers in focusing on serious forms of delinquency. For example, Colvin and Pauly announce in the first sentence of their statement of a "structural-Marxist theory of delinquency production" that their interest is in a "serious patterned delinquent behavior, defined as repeated engagement of a juvenile in the FBI's Part One Index crimes."

We have noted previously that persons high in the class structure rarely commit such offenses even once, much less repeatedly. This is, of course, the class premise of a Marxian theory of serious delinquency. The theoretical question is, What is it about conditions at the bottom of the class structure that pressures persons to commit such acts?

Our focus, however, has been on common forms of delinquency. We see no reason to assume that class, measured in Marxian terms, is related to common forms of delinquency in the same way that it is to serious delinquency. Indeed, we have argued that positions of power, defined in terms of class and gender, are conducive to higher rates of common delinquency. The theoretical question we ask is, What is it about conditions at the *top* of the social structure that *allows* persons to commit such acts?

The first kind of theory assumes that people are driven to delinquency; the second, that they are more delinquent because they are free to be so. That one theory receives empirical support need not mean that the other is wrong. The two kinds of delinquency may demand different explanations.

It is important to clarify further why we have focused on common forms of delinquency. Hindelang et al. have estimated that the annual prevalence of serious delinquency in the population is less than 2–3 percent. Given the small class fractions that interest Marxian scholars (the surplus population is smaller than 10 percent and the capitalist class smaller still) and the infrequency of such delinquencies, it will be extremely difficult to test Marxian theories of serious delinquency. The skewness of two distributions will require either exceptionally large samples or samples that are heavily stratified on the basis of known correlates of serious delinquency (e.g., known court records). The former approach will require financing on a grander scale than contemporary victimization surveys (which involve more than 100,000 screening interviews); the latter approach raises serious problems of generalization, involving a use of official data sources that has thus far proved anathema to radical criminologists. On the basis of this knowledge, we fear that empirical tests of Marxian theories of serious delinquency are unlikely to emerge soon.

Meanwhile, there is much to be learned by both Marxists and non-Marxists about the class structure of gender and more common forms of delinquency. For example, our data are in some ways quite congenial to a conventional functionalist understanding of stratification and its consequences. Consider our findings regarding one variable, "taste for risk." This variable plays a significant role in mediating the gender-delinquency relationship in the managerial and working class but not in the employer class. To the extent that risk taking is valued, at least among men in Western capitalist societies, the former findings are consistent with traditional understandings of the role of socialization in fostering attitudes that are conducive to upward mobility. Delinquency can be understood here as an unintended consequence. Nonetheless, at the top of the class structure, males in the employer class are more delinquent than females, not because they have a higher taste for risk but simply because they are less controlled by their parents and believe that they are less likely to be punished for their delinquencies. This is the stuff from which more critical theories are made.

Our findings therefore are not all of a piece. They do affirm one simple conclusion, however: Marxists and non-Marxists alike will benefit from operationalizing the concepts of class, gender, and delinquency as we have done in this chapter. Indeed, our findings indicate that to do otherwise is to obscure the class structure of gender and common forms of delinquency.

QUESTIONS FOR DISCUSSION AND WRITING

1. On what do power and control theory focus?
2. What are the authors' assumptions regarding "the freedom to deviate"?
3. Are males in the employer class more delinquent than females because of their "higher taste for risk"?

A Bio-Psychological Theory of Choice

JAMES Q. WILSON

RICHARD HERRNSTEIN

CRIME AS CHOICE: THE THEORY IN BRIEF

Our theory rests on the assumption that people, when faced with a choice, choose the preferred course of action. This assumption is quite weak; it says nothing more than that whatever people choose to do, they choose it because they prefer it. In fact, it is more than weak; without further clarification, it is a tautology. When we say people "choose," we do not necessarily mean that they consciously deliberate about what to do. All we mean is that their behavior is determined by its consequences. A person will do that thing the consequences of which are perceived by him or her to be preferable to the consequences of doing something else. What can save such a statement from being a tautology is how plausibly we describe the gains and losses associated with alternative courses of action and the standards by which a person evaluates those gains and losses.

These assumptions are commonplace in philosophy and social science. Philosophers speak of hedonism or utilitarianism, economists of value or utility, and psychologists of reinforcement or reward. We will use the language of psychology, but it should not be hard to translate our terminology into that of other disciplines. Although social scientists differ as to how much behavior can reasonably be described as the result of a choice, all agree that at least some behavior is guided, or even precisely controlled, by things variously termed pleasure, pain, happiness, sorrow, desirability, or the like. Our object is to show how this simple and widely used idea can be used to explain behavior.

At any given moment, a person can choose between committing a crime and not committing it (all these alternatives to crime we lump together as "noncrime"). The consequences of committing the crime consist of rewards (what psychologists call "reinforcers") and punishments; the consequences of not committing the crime (i.e., engaging in noncrime) also entail gains and losses.

The larger the ratio of the net rewards of crime to the net rewards of noncrime, the greater the tendency to commit the crime. The net rewards of crime include, obviously, the likely material gains from the crime, but they also include intangible benefits, such as obtaining emotional or sexual gratification, receiving the approval of peers, satisfying an old score against an enemy, or enhancing one's sense of justice. One must deduct from these rewards of crime any losses that accrue immediately—that are, so to speak, contempo-

From *Crime and Human Nature: The Definitive Study of the Causes of Crime* (pp. 43–45, 61–63) by J. Q. Wilson and R. J. Herrnstein, 1985, New York: Simon & Schuster. Copyright © 1985 by James Q. Wilson and Richard J. Herrnstein. Reprinted with the permission of Simon & Schuster, Inc.

raneous with the crime. They include the pangs of conscience, the disapproval of on-lookers, and the retaliation of the victim.

The value of noncrime lies all in the future. It includes the benefits to the individual of avoiding the risk of being caught and punished and, in addition, the benefits of avoiding penalties not controlled by the criminal justice system, such as the loss of reputation or the sense of shame afflicting a person later discovered to have broken the law and the possibility that, being known as a criminal, one cannot get or keep a job.

The value of any reward or punishment associated with either crime or noncrime is, to some degree, uncertain. A would-be burglar rarely knows exactly how much loot he will take away or what its cash value will prove to be. The assaulter or rapist may exaggerate the satisfaction he thinks will follow the assault or the rape. Many people do not know how sharp the bite of conscience will be until they have done something that makes them feel the bite. The anticipated approval of one's buddies may or may not be forthcoming. Similarly, the benefits of noncrime are uncertain. One cannot know with confidence whether one will be caught, convicted, and punished, or whether one's friends will learn about the crime and as a result withhold valued esteem, or whether one will be able to find or hold a job.

Compounding these uncertainties is time. The opportunity to commit a crime may be ready at hand (an open, unattended cash register in a store) or well in the future (a bank that, with planning and preparation, can be robbed). And the rewards associated with noncrime are almost invariably more distant than those connected with crime, perhaps many weeks or months distant. The strength of reinforcers tends to decay over time at rates that differ among individuals. As a result, the extent to which people take into account distant possibilities—a crime that can be committed only tomorrow, or punishment that will be inflicted only in a year—will affect whether they choose crime or noncrime.

THE THEORY AS A WHOLE

We assert that the chief value of a comprehensive theory of crime is that it will bring to our attention all the factors that explain individual differences in criminality and thus prevent us from offering partial explanations or making incomplete interpretations of research findings. The larger the ratio of the rewards (material and nonmaterial) of noncrime to the rewards (material and nonmaterial) of crime, the weaker the tendency to commit crimes. The bite of conscience, the approval of peers, and any sense of inequity will increase or decrease the total value of crime; the opinions of family, friends, and employers are important benefits of noncrime, as is the desire to avoid the penalties that can be imposed by the criminal justice system. The strength of any reward declines with time, but people differ in the rate at which they discount the future. The strength of a given reward is also affected by the total supply of reinforcers.

Some implications of the theory are obvious: Other things being equal, a reduction in the delay and uncertainty attached to the rewards of noncrime will reduce the probability of crime. But other implications are not so obvious. For instance, increasing the value of the rewards of noncrime (by increasing the severity of punishment) may not reduce a given individual's tendency to commit crime if he believes that these rewards are not commensurate with what he deserves. In this case, punishing him for preferring crime to noncrime may trigger hostility toward society in retaliation for the shortfall. The increased rewards for noncrime may be offset by an increased sense of inequity and hence an increased incentive for committing a crime. Or again: It may be easier to reduce crime by making penalties swifter or more certain, rather than more severe, if the persons committing crime are highly present-oriented (so that they discount even large rewards very sharply) or if they are likely to have their sense of inequity heightened by increases in the severity of punishment. Or yet again: An individual with an extroverted personality is more likely than one with an introverted one to externalize his feelings of inequity and act directly to correct them.

In laboratory settings involving both human and animal subjects, each element of the theory has received at least some confirmation and the major elements have been confirmed extensively. Extrapolating these findings outside the laboratory, into real-world settings, is a matter on which opinions differ. We propose to bring together evidence from a variety of disciplines bearing on the connection between elements of the theory and the observed characteristics of crime and criminals.

The connection between crime and impulsiveness has been demonstrated as has the link between (low) intelligence and crime. Those features of family life that produce stronger or weaker internalized inhibitions will be seen to have a connection to the presence or absence of aggressiveness and criminality. Certain subcultures, such as street-corner gangs, appear to affect the value members attach to both crime and noncrime. The mass media, and in particular television, may affect both aggressiveness directly and a viewer's sense of inequity that can affect crime indirectly. Schooling may affect crime rates by bringing certain persons together into groups that reinforce either crime or noncrime and by determining the extent to which children believe that their skills will give them access to legitimate rewards. The condition of the economy will have a complex effect on crime depending on whether the (possibly) restraint-weakening impact of affluence domi-

nates the restraint-strengthening influence of employment opportunities.

The theory is applicable to the most common crimes, but is also quite consistent with the more bizarre and unusual forms of crime. Psychopathic personalities lack to an unusual degree internalized inhibitions on crime. Persons possessed by some obsessive interest—for example, pyromania—attach an inordinately high value to the rewards of certain crimes. If everyone loved fire too much, society would try hard to teach the moral evil of fire, as well as its practical danger. As it is, what society does teach is sufficient to overcome whatever slight tendency toward pyromania every average person may have, but it is insufficient to inhibit the rare pyromaniac. One reason society punishes arsonists is not only to make it more costly for persons to use fire for material gain but also to provide extra moral education to the occasional person who loves fire for its own sake.

In addition to pathological drives, there are ordinary ones that can, under certain conditions, become so strong as to lead to crime. History and literature abound with normal men and women in the grip of a too powerful reinforcement. Many people have broken the law for love, honor, family, and country, as well as for money, sex, vengeance, or delusion. Such criminals may be psychologically unremarkable; they transgressed because as they perceived the situation the reward for crime exceeded that for noncrime, and an opportunity presented itself. The legal system often tries to minimize the punishment inflicted on such people.

QUESTIONS FOR DISCUSSION AND WRITING

1. On what assumption does the authors' theory rest?
2. What is associated with "greater tendency" to commit crime?
3. Where does the "value" of noncrime lie?

Feminist Theory, Crime, and Justice

SALLY S. SIMPSON

"WHY CAN'T A WOMAN BE MORE LIKE A MAN?"

One is tempted to respond to Henry Higgins's familiar lament with a cynical observation: criminological theory assumes a woman is like a man. As many feminist criminologists have noted, most middle-range and macro-theories of crime generously assume that what is true for the gander is true for the goose. As tempting as this simple assertion might be, however, a closer inspection reveals a more complicated picture.

Some feminist critics suggest that criminology, like other social sciences, is androcentric, that is, study of crime and the justice process is shaped by male experiences and understandings of the social world. Such studies/realities form the core of "general" theories of crime/deviance without taking female experience, as crime participant or victim, into account. According to MacKinnon:

[Men] create the world from their own point of view, which then becomes the truth to be described. . . . Power to create the world from one's point of view is power in its male form.

Not all criminological research has ignored women, but all too often, pre-1970s research on female offenders and victims of crime fell prey to unreflecting sexism and, in its more extreme form, misogyny. Females who deviated from expected roles were viewed as morally corrupt, hysterical, diseased, manipulative, and devious. Law-violating and law-conforming behaviors were believed to stem from the same etiological source—the female nature. A woman, it seemed—whether good or bad—could never be like a man.

These observations are not new, but they reflect a different voice, a feminist voice, that has been added to the criminological discourse. The purpose of this review essay is to introduce feminist criminology and its intellectual parent, feminism, to the uninitiated reader. It would be presumptuous to suggest that all relevant studies and arguments about gender and crime are included here. Such an extensive review is more appropriate for a book and depending on the topic, it has probably already been done and done well. Instead, illustrative examples of different types of feminist thinking are presented to show how feminism has reframed our points of reference, underlying assumptions, and the understandings about crime, victimization, and the justice process.

INCORPORATING FEMINIST FRAMEWORKS

The Female Offender

The stirrings of feminist criminology are nearly two decades old. Heidensohn, in a "pre-feminist" paper, bemoaned the state of knowledge about female deviance and called for a "crash program of research which telescopes decades of comparable studies of males." Later, Klein and Smart were to bring explicitly feminist perspectives to their critiques of extant theoretical and empirical work on the female offender. Klein, a Marxist feminist, noted the absence of economic and other social explanations for female crime. Smart, working within more of a radical feminist perspective, stressed the linkages among sexist theory, patriarchy, and sexism in practice—specifically identifying the relationship between stereotypical assumptions about the causes of female crime and how female offenders are controlled and treated.

Both Klein and Smart set an agenda for a new feminist criminology, but their more radical approaches were derailed by the publication of Simon's *Women and Crime* and F. Adler's *Sisters in Crime.* Claiming that a "new" female offender was emerging (white collar and/or malelike), Simon and Adler generated tremendous interest in female crime (a clear aim of incipient feminism). But tying the female offender's emergence to women's liberation brought about a "moral panic," which was viewed by some as a backlash to the women's movement. In Chesney-Lind's words, it represented "another in a century-long series of symbolic attempts to keep women subordinate to men by threatening those who aspire for equality with the images of the witch, the bitch, and the whore."

As with many social problems of our day, female crime became interesting only when it transcended the expected boundaries of class, race, and gender. As a "quasi-theory," the liberation-crime relationship had great appeal for nonfeminist criminologists. But tests of the thesis were less than supportive. In fact, most discredited it, and found evidence of a link between female crime and economic marginalization. The new offender identified by Simon and Adler was more myth than reality. These conclusions did not differ substantially from Klein's, yet they came years after her original critique—a fact that dramatically illustrates the marginality of feminist criminology at the time. Yet subsequent research on the causes of female crime has clearly buttressed the economic/class perspectives of Marxist/socialist feminists as well as the "opportunity" perspectives of the liberal feminists.

In retrospect, feminist criminology both gained and lost from the narrow focus on liberation and crime. On the plus side, we gained a better insight into the historical and cross-cultural patterns of female crime. But because the liberation thesis was so limited, it diverted attention from the material and structural forces that shape women's lives and experiences. It is in these areas that women of color and socialist and radical feminist criminologists are more apt to focus etiological attention.

WOMEN VICTIMS: THE RADICAL FEMINIST CRITIQUE

Liberal feminism has dominated studies of the female offender, but the same is not true of victimology. Shifting away from analyses that blame the victim for her victimization, radical feminists have constructed alternative interpretations of offender-victim relationships and victim experiences of criminal justice.

Brownmiller's historical and cross-cultural study of rape brought a radical feminist perspective to the center of public consciousness. Building on the argument that rape is not a crime of sex but rather an act of power and dominance, Brownmiller concluded that rape is a tool in the arsenal of all men to control all women.

Radical feminists have reframed the ways in which rape is commonly understood in our society. Rather than a crime of sex, it is more apt to be viewed as one of male power, control, and domination. Brownmiller's work, coupled with that of other radical feminists, opened a floodgate of inquiry into rape and other types of victimizations that are "uniquely feminine," such as pornography, battering, incest, and sexual harassment. Guiding much of this research is the radical feminist critique of official conceptions and definitions of violence, which are viewed as male centered and incapable of incorporating the full range of female experiences of violence (i.e., from intimidation and coercion to physical violence and death). A woman-centered definition of violence is one that portrays violence as a form of social domination rather than a random and/or non-instrumental form of expression.

Radical feminists have dominated but not monopolized feminist perspectives in this area. Socialist feminists, liberals, and women of color have also participated in the dialogue. Gordon's research of family violence is implicitly critical of some radical feminists' overly deterministic conception of patriarchy. Such an image, she argues, denies agency to women and cannot incorporate "the chronic conflict, unpredictability, and ambivalent emotions that have characterized relations between the sexes."

In another historical study, Tomes links variations in spousal abuse to changes in the economic position of the working class generally and the male's position within the family specifically. As the working class improved its economic position and males cemented greater power within the families, the official incidence of working-class battering decreased.

Based on her findings, Tomes argues that feminists may need to reconceptualize the relationship among male power, female economic dependence, and battering. Dependency is not necessarily tied to greater abuse; in fact, the opposite may be true. A wife's economic independence may exert a greater challenge to male authority within the family, thus creating a climate in which husbands resort to battering as a means to reestablish their control.

Studies that find great variety in the cross-cultural prevalence and incidence of rape and battering have forced feminists to examine patriarchal relations across different societal and situational arrangements. If female victimization is a function of changing the needs of a capitalist/patriarchal system, then male domination and its relationship to female victimization need not be viewed as inevitable or immutable.

Around the themes of rape and control of sexuality, patriarchy and racism marry and divorce in intricate ways. In the United States, white racism and fear gave rise to mythological constructions of black sexuality. Black males are perceived as sexual threats and have been hunted and hanged for their "rape potential." For black victims of rape, the justice process is not simply gendered—it is racially gendered. Data indicate that black-on-black rapes are not taken as seriously by authorities as those that involve white victims. Such findings have led one prominent black scholar, Gloria Joseph, to comment, "It must be considered an impossibility for white men to rape Black women in the eyes of justice and in the minds of many. Black women apparently are considered as something other than 'women.'"

GENDER AND JUSTICE PROCESSING

A final area to be discussed in this literature review is gendered justice. Comedian Richard Pryor once called attention to discrimination in the U.S. criminal justice system by defining justice as "just us." His concern with differential sentencing practices is one shared by feminists who primarily study the conditions under which criminal justice is gendered and with what consequences. Although liberal approaches typically dominate the gender and justice research, other feminist perspectives are gaining ground—especially in research on courts and corrections.

There are many stages in the criminal justice system at which gender may have an impact on decision making. The findings of some of the better-known studies of several strategic points in the decision-making process are summarized below.

Police

Arguments about whether and how justice is gendered must begin with police behavior. That police decisions to arrest can be influenced by extralegal factors, such as the demeanor of the offender, has been established. It is less clear how gender, either alone or in conjunction with other characteristics, may consciously or inadvertently influence police behavior.

In the liberal "equal treatment" tradition, Moyer and White test police bias in response decisions under "probable" responses to hypothetical situations. Neither gender nor race had an effect on police behavior once crime type, especially as it interacts with demeanor of the offender, was controlled. On the other hand, Feyerherm's comparison of juvenile male and female probabilities of transition from self-report incident to police contact and arrest finds males to be more likely to incur police contact and arrest than females. Both of these studies are methodologically problematic, however. Moyer and White cannot generalize their findings to real police encounters and Feyerherm does not calculate transition probabilities across individual offense categories, nor does he include status offenses. Avoiding some of these methodological traps but still working within a liberal tradition, Visher finds the interaction between race and gender to be a key factor influencing arrest decision. Visher finds police chivalry only toward white females once "legal" factors are controlled. She hypothesizes that black females are treated more harshly than their white counterparts because they are less apt to display expected (i.e., traditional) gender behaviors and characteristics when they encounter a mostly white and male police force.

Race and gender are also found to interact through victim characteristics. An analysis of 272 police-citizen encounters, in which both a suspected offender and victim were present, revealed that white female victims received more preferential treatment from police than black female victims. Thus, although chivalry may be alive and well for white women, it appears to be dead (if it ever existed) for blacks.

Courts

Police contact is not the only point in justice processing at which discrimination can occur. Women have been found to receive more lenient treatment in the early stages of court processing (i.e., bail, release on own recognizance, and/or cash alternatives to bail) and further into the process (e.g., conviction and sentencing). Other studies find no gender bias when controlling for crime seriousness and prior record or little effect from extralegal factors when legal factors and bench bias are controlled. Variation in sentencing may be related to so-called counter-type offenses, that is, women are treated more harshly when processed for nontraditional female crimes, like assault, or when they violate female sexual norms. Given variable-specification problems, however, some of these findings are potentially spurious.

Once again, race may confound these effects. Spohn et al. address the issue of paternalism in sentencing, especially for black women. Controlling for prior record and attorney type, they found that black women are incarcerated significantly less often than black men, but about as often as white men. They conclude that the apparently lenient treatment of black women is not due to paternalism in their favor but rather to the racial discrimination against black vis-à-vis white men.

Studies of court processing are not entirely dominated by liberal perspectives. More critical perspectives emphasize social power and patriarchal control as the primary mechanisms through which justice is gendered. Eaton argues that magistrate courts in Great Britain (the lower courts) reinforce the dominant imagery of justice (i.e., courts are ostensibly fair and just) while they maintain the status quo. "It is in these courts that the formal rules of society—the laws—are endorsed; it is here, too, that the informal, unwritten rules regulating social relations [e.g., gender, class, and race] are re-enacted."

When are females apt to be subjected to formal mechanisms of control? When other, more informal, constraints are lacking or disrupted. Kruttschnitt suggests that sentencing outcomes are affected by a woman's social status and/or her respectability. Differential sentencing among women is tied to the degree to which women are subjected to formal versus informal social control in their everyday lives.

Daly and Eaton offer convincing evidence that the most important factor determining sentence outcome, once prior record and offense seriousness are controlled, is marital and/or familial status. Marital status has been found to matter for women (married receive more lenient sentences) but not for men or to be as important for both.

Pretrial release and sentencing are seen to be both "familied" and "gendered." They are familied in that court decisions regarding the removal of men and women from families "elicit different concerns from the court." They are gendered in that women's care of others and male economic support for families represent "different types of dependencies in family life." Men and women without family responsibilities are treated similarly, but more harshly than familied men and women. Women with families, however, are treated with the greatest degree of leniency due to "the differing social costs arising from separating them from their families." The economic role played by familied men can, more easily, be covered by state entitlement programs, but it is putatively more difficult to replace the functional role of familied women. Judges rationalize such sentencing disparities as necessary for keeping families together.

As these latter studies suggest, much of the observed gender bias in processing may not be a case of overt discrimination for or against women relative to men. Instead, judicial decisions may be influenced by broader societal concerns about protecting nuclear families and the differing roles and responsibilities contained therein. It is not clear that such forms of justice are overtly paternalistic, nor

are they necessarily racist. Rather, in a society that stratifies other rights and privileges by gender, race, and class, "equality" in sentencing may not be just.

Eaton takes a somewhat different view of familied justice. In her opinion, the courts reflect the needs and interests of patriarchy and capitalism, in which attendant inequities are reproduced. "Family-based" justice is a visible manifestation of the patriarchal and capitalist need to maintain and protect the nuclear family—within which gender and productive/reproductive relations first emerge.

Corrections

As it became clear that, compared with males, female prisoners were treated differently (in some cases more leniently and in others more harshly), liberal feminist perspectives came to dominate research questions and policy considerations.

The linkages between female incarceration and male control of female sexuality are developed by radical feminists. Rasche, for example, describes how prostitutes with venereal disease were prosecuted and institutionalized, with the "cure" as a condition of release. Nondiseased prostitutes were less likely to go to jail or prison. Certain prison practices, such as checking for evidence of a hymen during forced physical examinations and vaginal contraband searches, have been used as techniques to control the sexuality of youthful offenders and to humiliate and degrade female inmates.

Socialist feminists emphasize how prison tenure and treatment vary by class and race. In her historical accounting of the development of women's prisons, Rafter observes how race determined whether and where a woman was sent to prison.

Comparison of incarceration rates and in-prison treatment of black women and white women demonstrates that partiality was extended mainly to whites. Chivalry filtered them out of the prison system, helping to create the even greater racial imbalances among female than male prisoner populations. And partiality toward whites contributed to the development of a bifurcated system, one track custodial and predominantly black, the other reformatory and reserved mainly for whites.

The bifurcated system of women's corrections emerges in part from two competing images of female nature. In one view, women are seen as fragile and immature creatures, more childlike than adult. Consequently, the female offender is perceived as a "fallen woman," in need of guidance but not a true danger to society. The reformatory is perfectly suited to such an offender. Primarily staffed by reform-minded middle-class women, reformatory training programs emphasized skills that would turn the white, working-class misdemeanants into proper (and class-appropriate) women, that is, good servants or wives.

In custodial prisons, however, a different archetype dominated. Women's "dark side," their inherent evil and immorality shaped prison philosophy. Here the predominantly black felons (who were perceived as more masculine, more self-centered, volatile, and dangerous) were treated like men—only, given the conditions of their incarceration (i.e., fewness of numbers and at the mercy of violent male offenders), their equality was tantamount to brutal treatment and often death.

The degree to which prisons function as something other than just places of punishment and/or treatment is a popular theme in neo-Marxist literature. Extending this interpretation to women, Marxist feminists argue that prisons, like other institutions of social control (e.g., mental health facilities), retool deviant women for gender-appropriate roles in capitalist patriarchal societies. According to Wilson:

If deviant women are more frequently assigned to the mental health system for social control than to the criminal justice system, it is perhaps because of the superior ability of the mental health system to "re-tool" worn-out or rebellious domestic workers.

Societal control of female deviance serves the needs of capital. When those needs change, so too will the mechanisms and directions of social control.

In this vein, Carlen demonstrates how "down, out and disordered" women in Scotland are disciplined through medical and judicial apparatuses. Most of the imprisoned are poor women; many have histories of alcohol and drug abuse, and a large number come from violent homes. These life experiences combine, setting into motion a cycle of deviance, imprisonment, and patriarchal and class discipline that is tenacious and defeating. According to Carlen:

Being seen as neither wholly mad nor wholly bad, [women] are treated to a disciplinary regime where they are actually infantalised at the same time as attempts are made to make them feel guilty about their double, triple, quadruple, or even quintuple refusal of family, work, gender, health, and reason.

WHERE TO GO FROM HERE?

In 1976, Carol Smart suggested a number of topics for feminist research. A decade later, feminist criminology has amassed a considerable body of knowledge in most of these areas—so much so in fact that feminists now are more self-critical—especially in the areas of policy and legislative changes. This is a positive step. It suggests not only that a feminist voice is being heard but that it is loud enough to produce disagreement and intellectual exchange. Nonetheless, certain areas in criminology either have been underexposed or are resistant to feminist concerns. Thus, some new directions for feminist criminology are discussed below.

Race and Crime

Poorly conceived offender self-report surveys provided criminologists with the empirical justification to ignore the race-crime relationship, and the prevailing political climate reinforced our myopia. There is enormous risk in ignoring that relationship, however. First, based on more sophisticated crime measures (e.g., National Youth Survey, National Crime Survey, cohort studies), it is clear that the race-crime relationship is an essential one. Second, and not unlike the gender-crime relationship, such reticence leaves the interpretive door open to less critical perspectives.

Feminist criminologists have great potential in this area, but the data are sparse and problematic and the analytic contributions few. Too often we rely on quantitative studies that dichotomize race into white and black, or the nonwhite category is broadened to include groups other than blacks. In the former instance, other ethnic/racial groups are ignored; in the latter, such inclusive categorizations assume etiological and historical/cultural invariance between groups.

Clearly, one of the first places for feminists to start is to target women of color for greater research. Available data indicate that there are significant differences between black and white female crime rates. Simpson, Miller, and Lewis argue that the unique structural and cultural positioning of black women produces complex cultural typescripts that exert push-pull pressures for crime, pressures that may not exist for white women.

Miller's ethnography of lower-class deviant networks describes how certain types of male and female criminality (e.g., hustling, pimping, and other instrumental crimes) are interdependent in minority communities. Female crime also appears to have a group-directed and group-enacted dimension. The collective nature of such minority offending may stem from the fact that it emerges, in part, from the integrated and extended domestic networks of underclass blacks and joint participation in gang activities.

These observations do not imply, however, that patriarchy is absent from these communities. Male dominance and control are reproduced within interpersonal relationships (not necessarily familial) and embodied in infor-mal organizations, like gangs and state social service agencies. Some female offending can be interpreted as challenging patriarchal control and asserting independence; much can be attributed to both economic necessity and the pull and excitement of street life. Female participation in violent crime may stem from abusive relationships between men and women and/or the frustration, alienation, and anger that are associated with racial and class oppression.

Research by Hill and Suval suggests that the causes of crime may differ for black and white women, which raises questions about whether current theories of female crime, including feminist perspectives, are white female centered. Given the paucity of data on how gender structures relationships within minority communities and families, it is impossible to say. More quantitative research is needed on minority groups other than blacks (e.g., Chicanos and other Hispanics, Asians, Native Americans) to establish a better knowledge base, but qualitative studies that probe culture and subjective differences between women of color and whites are also essential. Feminist criminologists are guilty of the "add race and stir" shortsightedness that pervades feminist thinking. We would do well to heed Spelman's reminder of how to understand and approach differences among women:

If we assume there are differences among women, but at the same time they are all the same as women, and if we assume the woman part is what we know from looking at the case of white middle-class women, then we appear to be talking only about white middle-class women. This is how white middle-class privilege is maintained even as we purport to recognize the importance of women's differences.

Elite Crime

In 1977, Harris admonished criminologists for their failure to use "the sex variable" as the empirical building block for all theories of criminal deviance. Apparently (although not surprisingly), this was interpreted to apply only to street crime. The entire area of white-collar, corporate, and organizational crime has not been examined from a feminist perspective.

Officially, women are underrepresented in white-collar crime data although recent Bureau of Justice Statistics data suggest that women have made inroads into this formerly male domain. Similar claims are made regarding female penetration of the upper reaches of organized crime. Yet Daly finds neither the crime types nor the offenders themselves to be particularly elite.

Much of our information on female participation in organized crime is anecdotal, derived from the nonsystematic observations of male crime participants. Consequently, there has been little systematic research on women's penetration of and mobility within illicit markets. The official data on corporate and other white-collar offending are equally problematic. Given that both the data and interpretation/ theory in these areas are suspect, feminist researchers must first develop an empirical base with which to answer the following types of questions. Is elite crime a male domain? What are the motivations and characteristics of women who do participate? How are they similar and different from male offenders? What explains the official increase in female participation in white-collar offenses?

At this point, feminists have barely scratched the surface of the elite crime area. Daly is providing some direction, but much more needs to be done.

Deterrence

Gender confounds the anticipated relationship between objective sanction risks and criminal activity; that is, given that female sanction risks are low, women should have high rates of law breaking. Yet, as virtually all measures of crime document, the exact opposite is true. This empirical relationship has left deterrence theorists scrambling to make sense of the inconsistency.

Richards and Tittle argue that there are at least five lines of reasoning that would predict that women perceive higher levels of risk than do men. Using measures derived from these hypotheses, they find two variables, stakes in conformity and perceptions of visibility, to be highly associated with gender differences in perceived chances of arrest:

Women may think that legal sanction is relatively certain because they are more likely to think of themselves as subject to surveillance and general social sanctions than are men. Their greater relative stakes in conformity may make deviance more threatening for them, and lead to high sanction risk estimates.

The social control literature, in general, characterizes female conformity in a stereotypical manner. Conforming females are seen as passive, compliant, and dependent. Instead, Naffine suggests that the conforming women be seen as "involved and engrossed in conventional life. But . . . also actively concerned about the effects of her behavior on her loved ones, particularly emotionally and financially dependent children." (Naffine is especially critical of Hagan.)

Naffine's image of conformity is partially influenced by Gilligan's work in moral development theory. Gilligan's research discovers that men and women use "a different voice" when they talk about moral responsibility. If the moral calculus of reasoning about crime is different between men and women, Gilligan may have identified a new way of conceptualizing gender differences in (1) perceived threat of sanction and (2) male-female crime rates. According to her theory, men often make moral decisions based on an "ethic of justice," while women employ a model of decision making based on an "ethic of care." The former is a more abstract model, expressed as a set of principles defining rights and rules. In the latter, decisions are governed by "a psychological logic of relationships, which contrasts with the formal logic of fairness that informs the justice approach."

A woman's decision to violate the law will depend on her definition of the moral domain (i.e., how will my act affect those around me, those who count on *me*). It is not surprising that in some deterrence studies women score significantly higher than men on measures of internalized guilt. Because women are responsible for the care of relationships, any act that may result in their removal from that role is apt to produce a tremendous sense of guilt. Guilt may be negated if the needs of the family (for food or other valued items) outweigh the "immorality" of breaking the law to obtain them or if others are available to take on the responsibilities of care.

Gilligan's theory can be used to explain why most women do not violate the law and why they score higher on most measures of deterrence. It can also explain class and race differences in female crime rates. Lower-class and minority women are more apt to find themselves in situations that require a renegotiation of the moral domain and, given their kinship networks, they have a greater chance of finding care substitutes. Not surprisingly, Finley and Grasmick report that blacks score lower on certainty and severity of guilt than their white counterparts.

Some critics suggest that Gilligan's findings are biased (she interviewed mostly middle-class students) or that they may be a function of subordinate female social position, not real differences in ethical philosophies. These are important criticisms that must be addressed before we proceed too enthusiastically. Gilligan's conceptualization of differences in gender-based moral reasoning, however, are an important contribution and warrant further research.

analytical development as the broader feminist movement, feminist contributions to the study of crime and justice began with more liberal approaches and have recently been giving way to more radical critiques. Liberal feminist dominance rests, in part, in ideological coherence—these approaches correspond closely with the ideas and beliefs embodied in most capitalist democracies. Thus, liberalism in any form is less threatening and more acceptable than a feminism that questions white, male, and/or capitalist privilege. Additionally, liberal feminists speak in the same voice as a majority of social scientists, that is, they are rational, objective, and (typically) quantitative. Consequently, their data and interpretations carry more weight within the scientific community and among their peers.

Although liberal/quantitative approaches offer important insights into gender as a "variable" problem, criminologists need to be more ecumenical in studying gendered society. If we emphasize qualitative, historical, and subjectivist approaches in addition to quantitative, the detail and texture of how crime and justice are gendered will lead to richer criminology theory.

There are areas in criminology into which feminists have only marginally ventured or in which their contributions have been of little consequence. In their review of feminist criminology, Daly and Chesney-Lind discuss the problems that feminists have had building and developing theories of female crime. It is not coincidental that the areas targeted for further research in this essay (e.g., race and crime, elite crime, and deterrence) all focus on this problematic area. Until we can better deal with the empirical complexities of criminal offending, it will be too easy for our critics to dismiss feminist contributions to the study of crime as facile, rhetorical, and/or atheoretical.

CONCLUSION

Feminist criminology has changed dramatically since Klein and Smart first called attention to it. Replicating the same political and

QUESTIONS FOR DISCUSSION AND WRITING

1. What do some feminists suggest?
2. How did pre-1970s research view women?
3. How does gender confound the anticipated relationship between objective sanction risks and criminal activity, and how have Richards and Tittle explained this?

The Nature of Criminality: Low Self-Control

MICHAEL GOTTFREDSON
TRAVIS HIRSCHI

THE ELEMENTS OF SELF-CONTROL

Criminal acts provide immediate gratification of desires. A major characteristic of people with low self-control is therefore a tendency to respond to tangible stimuli in the immediate environment, to have a concrete "here and now" orientation. People with high self-control, in contrast, tend to defer gratification.

Criminal acts provide *easy or simple* gratification of desires. They provide money without work, sex without courtship, revenge without court delays. People lacking self-control also tend to lack diligence, tenacity, or persistence in a course of action.

Criminal acts are *exciting, risky, or thrilling.* They involve stealth, danger, speed, agility, deception, or power. People lacking self-control therefore tend to be adventuresome, active, and physical. Those with high levels of self-control tend to be cautious, cognitive, and verbal.

Crimes provide *few or meager long-term benefits.* They are not equivalent to a job or a career. On the contrary, crimes interfere with long-term commitments to jobs, marriages, family, or friends. People with low self-control

thus tend to have unstable marriages, friendships, and job profiles. They tend to be little interested in and unprepared for long-term occupational pursuits.

Crimes require *little skill or planning.* The cognitive requirements for most crimes are minimal. It follows that people lacking self-control need not possess or value cognitive or academic skills. The manual skills required for most crimes are minimal. It follows that people lacking self-control need not possess manual skills that require training or apprenticeship.

Crimes often result in *pain or discomfort for the victim.* Property is lost, bodies are injured, privacy is violated, trust is broken. It follows that people with low self-control tend to be self-centered, indifferent, or insensitive to the suffering and needs of others. It does not follow, however, that people with low self-control are routinely unkind or antisocial. On the contrary, they may discover the immediate and easy rewards of charm and generosity.

Recall that crime involves the pursuit of immediate pleasure. It follows that people lacking self-control will also tend to pursue immediate pleasures that are *not* criminal: they will tend to smoke, drink, use drugs, gamble, have children out of wedlock, and engage in illicit sex.

Crimes require the interaction of an offender with people or their property. It does not follow that people lacking self-control will

Adapted from *A General Theory of Crime* (pp. 85–120) by M. R. Gottfredson and Travis Hirschi, 1990. By permission of the publishers, Stanford University Press. © 1990 by the Board of Trustees of the Leland Stanford Junior University.

tend to be gregarious or social. However, it does follow that, other things being equal, gregarious or social people are more likely to be involved in criminal acts.

The major benefit of many crimes is not pleasure but relief from momentary irritation. The irritation caused by a crying child is often the stimulus for physical abuse. That caused by a taunting stranger in a bar is often the stimulus for aggravated assault. It follows that people with low self-control tend to have minimal tolerance for frustration and little ability to respond to conflict through verbal rather than physical means.

Crimes involve the risk of violence and physical injury, of pain and suffering on the part of the offender. It does not follow that people with low self-control will tend to be tolerant of physical pain or to be indifferent to physical discomfort. It does follow that people tolerant of physical pain or indifferent to physical discomfort will be more likely to engage in criminal acts whatever their level of self-control.

The risk of criminal penalty for any given criminal act is small, but this depends in part on the circumstances of the offense. Thus, for example, not all joyrides by teenagers are equally likely to result in arrest. A car stolen from a neighbor and returned unharmed before he notices its absence is less likely to result in official notice than is a car stolen from a shopping center parking lot and abandoned at the convenience of the offender. Drinking alcohol stolen from parents and consumed in the family garage is less likely to receive official notice than drinking in the parking lot outside a concert hall. It follows that offenses differ in their validity as measures of self-control: those offenses with large risk of public awareness are better measures than those with little risk.

In sum, people who lack self-control will tend to be impulsive, insensitive, physical (as opposed to mental), risk taking, shortsighted, and nonverbal, and they will tend therefore to engage in criminal and analogous acts. Since these traits can be identified prior to the age of responsibility for crime, since there is considerable tendency for these traits to come together in the same people, and since the traits tend to persist through life, it seems reasonable to consider them as comprising a stable construct useful in the explanation of crime.

THE MANY MANIFESTATIONS OF LOW SELF-CONTROL

Our image of the "offender" suggests that crime is not an automatic or necessary consequence of low self-control. It suggests that many noncriminal acts analogous to crime (such as accidents, smoking, and alcohol use) are also manifestations of low self-control. Our image therefore implies that no specific act, type of crime, or form of deviance is uniquely required by the absence of self-control.

Because both crime and analogous behaviors stem from low self-control (i.e., both are manifestations of low self-control), they will all be engaged in at a relatively high rate by people with low self-control. Within the domain of crime, then, there will be much versatility among offenders in the criminal acts in which they engage.

Research on the versatility of deviant acts supports these predictions in the strongest possible way. The variety of manifestations of low self-control is immense. In spite of years of tireless research motivated by a belief in specialization, no credible evidence of specialization has been reported. In fact, the evidence of offender versatility is overwhelming.

By versatility we mean that offenders commit a wide variety of criminal acts, with no strong inclination to pursue a specific criminal act or a pattern of criminal acts to the exclusion of others. Most theories suggest that offenders tend to specialize, whereby such terms as robber, burglar, drug dealer, rapist, and murderer have predictive or descriptive import. In fact, some theories create offender specialization as part of their explanation of crime. For example, Cloward and Ohlin create distinctive subcultures of delinquency around particular forms of criminal behavior, identifying subcultures specializing in theft, violence, or drugs. In a related way, books are written about white-collar crime as though it were a clearly distinct specialty requiring a unique explanation. Research projects are undertaken for the study of drug use, or vandalism, or teen pregnancy (as though every study of delinquency were not a study of drug use and vandalism and teenage sexual behavior). Entire schools of criminology emerge to pursue patterning, sequencing, progression, escalation, onset, persistence, and desistance in the career of offenses or offenders. These efforts survive largely because their proponents fail to consider or acknowledge the clear evidence to the contrary. Other reasons for survival of such ideas may be found in the interest of politicians and members of the law enforcement community who see policy potential in criminal careers or "career criminals."

. . .

THE CAUSES OF SELF-CONTROL

We know better what deficiencies in self-control lead to than where they come from. One thing is, however, clear: low self-control is not produced by training, tutelage, or socialization. As a matter of fact, all of the characteristics associated with low self-control tend to show themselves in the absence of nurturance, discipline, or training. Given the classical appreciation of the causes of human behavior, the implications of this fact are straightforward: the causes of low self-control are negative rather than positive; self-control is unlikely in the absence of effort, intended or unintended, to create it. (This assumption separates the present theory from most modern theories of crime, where the offender is automatically seen as a product of positive forces, a creature of learning, particular pressures, or specific defect.)

At this point, it would be easy to construct a theory of crime causation, according to which characteristics of potential offenders lead them ineluctably to the commission of criminal acts. Our task at this point would simply be to identify the likely sources of impulsiveness, intelligence, risk taking, and the like. But to do so would be to follow the path that has proven so unproductive in the past, the path according to which criminals commit crimes irrespective of the characteristics of the setting or situation.

We can avoid this pitfall by recalling the elements inherent in the decision to commit a criminal act. The object of the offense is clearly pleasurable, and universally so. Engaging in the act, however, entails some risk of social, legal, and/or natural sanctions. Whereas the pleasure attained by the act is direct, obvious, and immediate, the pains risked by it are not obvious, or direct, and are in any event more greatly removed from it. It follows that although there will be little variability among people in their ability to see the pleasures of crime, there will be considerable variability in their ability to calculate potential pains. But the problem goes further than this: whereas the pleasures of crime are reasonably equally distributed over the population, this is not true for the pains. Everyone appreciates money; not everyone dreads parental anger or disappointment upon learning that the money was stolen.

So, the dimensions of self-control are, in our view, factors affecting calculation of the consequences of one's acts. The impulsive or shortsighted person fails to consider the negative or painful consequences of his acts; the insensitive person has fewer negative consequences to consider; the less intelligent person also has fewer negative consequences to consider (has less to lose).

No known social group, whether criminal or noncriminal, actively or purposefully attempts to reduce the self-control of its members. Social life is not enhanced by low self-control and its consequences. On the contrary, the exhibition of these tendencies undermines harmonious group relations and the ability to achieve collective ends. These facts explicitly deny that a tendency to crime is a product of socialization, culture, or positive learning of any sort.

The traits composing low self-control are also not conducive to the achievement of long-term individual goals. On the contrary, they impede educational and occupational achievement, destroy interpersonal relations, and undermine physical health and economic well-being. Such facts explicitly deny the notion that criminality is an alternative route to the goals otherwise obtainable through legitimate avenues. It follows that people who care about the interpersonal skill, educational and occupational achievement, and physical and economic well-being of those in their care will seek to rid them of these traits.

Two general sources of variation are immediately apparent in scheme. The first is the variation among children in the degree to which they manifest such traits to begin with. The second is the variation among caretakers in the degree to which they recognize low self-control and its consequences and the degree to which they are willing and able to correct it. Obviously, therefore, even at this threshold level the sources of low self-control are complex.

There is good evidence that some of the traits predicting subsequent involvement in crime appear as early as they can be reliably measured, including low intelligence, high activity level, physical strength, and adventuresomeness. The evidence suggests that the connection between these traits and commission of criminal acts ranges from weak to moderate.

Obviously, we do not suggest that people are born criminals, inherit a gene for criminality, or anything of the sort. In fact, we explicitly deny such notions. What we do suggest is that individual differences may have an impact on the prospects for effective socialization (or adequate control). Effective socialization is, however, always possible whatever the configuration of individual traits.

Other traits affecting crime appear later and seem to be largely products of ineffective or incomplete socialization. For example, dif-ferences in impulsivity and insensitivity become noticeable later in childhood when they are no longer common to all children. The ability and willingness to delay immediate gratification for some larger purpose may therefore be assumed to be a consequence of training.

Much parental action is in fact geared toward suppression of impulsive behavior, toward making the child consider the long-range consequences of acts. Consistent sensitivity to the needs and feelings of others may also be assumed to be a consequence of training. Indeed, much parental behavior is directed toward teaching the child about the rights and feelings of others, and of how these rights and feelings ought to constrain the child's behavior. All of these points focus our attention on child rearing.

CONCLUSIONS

Theories that cannot incorporate or account for the stability of differences in offending over time are seriously at variance with good evidence. Theories that assume specialization in particular forms of crime or deviant behavior are seriously at odds with good evidence. Theories that propose to examine the parameters of criminal careers (such as onset, persistence, and desistance) or the characteristics of career criminals are at odds with the nature of crime. Theories that assume that criminal acts are means to long-term or altruistic goals are at odds with the facts.

Our theory explicitly addresses the stability and versatility findings. It accounts for them with the concept of self-control: with deferred gratification at one extreme and immediate gratification at the other, with caution at one extreme and risk taking at the other. The mechanism producing these differences has been described as differences in child-rearing practices, with close attention to the behavior of the child at one extreme and neglect of the behavior of the child at the other.

The theory incorporates individual properties insofar as they have an impact on crime or on self-control. . . . We note that the theory is a direct response to analysis of the concept of crime and to our analysis of the failings of the theories of the positivistic disciplines. It incorporates a classical view of the role of choice and a positivistic view of the role of causation in the explanation of behavior. It produces a general explanatory concept that can be measured independently of the phenomenon it is alleged to cause, and it is thus directly testable.

QUESTIONS FOR DISCUSSION AND WRITING

1. What is a major characteristic of people with low self-control, and how does this explain criminality?
2. Throughout the first seven paragraphs, the authors describe people with low self-control. What are they like?
3. Do the authors suggest that crime is an automatic or necessary consequence of low self-control?

Toward an Age-Graded Theory
of Informal Social Control

ROBERT SAMPSON

JOHN LAUB

INFORMAL SOCIAL CONTROL
AND SOCIAL CAPITAL

Our theory emphasizes the importance of informal social ties and bonds to society at all ages across the life course. Hence, the effects of informal social control in childhood, adolescence, and adulthood are central to our theoretical model. Virtually all previous studies of social control in criminology have focused either on adolescents or on official (i.e., formal) social control mechanisms such as arrest and imprisonment. As a result, most criminological studies have failed to examine the processes of informal social control from childhood through adulthood.

Following Elder, we differentiate the life course of individuals on the basis of age and argue that the important institutions of informal and formal social control vary across the life span. For example, the dominant institutions of social control in childhood and adolescence are the family, school, peer groups, and the juvenile justice system. In the phase of young adulthood, the institutions of higher education or vocational training, work, and marriage become salient. The juvenile justice system is also replaced by the adult criminal justice system. Finally, in middle adulthood, the dominant institutions of social control are work, marriage, parenthood, investment in the community, and the criminal justice system.

Within this framework, our organizing principle derives from the central idea of social control theory: crime and deviance result when an individual's bond to society is weak or broken. As Janowitz has cogently argued, many sociologists mistakenly think of social control solely in terms of social repression and state sanctions (e.g., surveillance, enforced conformity, incarceration). By contrast, we adopt a more general conceptualization of social control as the capacity of a social group to regulate itself according to desired principles and values, and hence to make norms and rules effective. We further emphasize the role of *informal* social controls that emerge from the role reciprocities and structure of interpersonal bonds linking members of society to one another and to wider social institutions such as work, family, and school.

In applying these concepts to the longitudinal study of crime, we examine the extent to which social bonds inhibit crime and deviance early in the life course, and the consequences this has for later development. Moreover, we

From *Crime in the Making: Pathways and Turning Points Through Life* (pp. 17–23) by R. J. Sampson and J. H. Laub, 1993, Cambridge, Mass.: Harvard University Press. Copyright © 1993 by the President and Fellows of Harvard College. Reprinted with permission.

examine social ties to both institutions and other individuals in the adult life course, and identify the transitions within individual trajectories that relate to changes in informal social control. In this context, we contend that pathways to crime and conformity are mediated by social bonds to key institutions of social control. Our theoretical model focuses on the transition to adulthood and, in turn, the new role demands from higher education, full-time employment, military service, and marriage. Hence, we explore the interrelationships among crime and informal social control at all ages, with particular attention devoted to the assessment of within-individual change.

We also examine social relations between individuals (for example, parent-child, teacher-student, and employer-employee) at each stage of the life course as a form of social investment or social capital. Specifically, we posit that the social capital derived from strong social relations (or strong social bonds), whether as a child in a family, as an adolescent in school, or as an adult in a job, dictates the salience of these relations at the individual level. If these relations are characterized by interdependence, they represent social and psychological resources that individuals can draw on as they move through life transitions that traverse larger trajectories. Thus, we see both social capital and informal social control as linked to social structure, and we distinguish both concepts as important in understanding changes in behavior over time.

Recognizing the importance of both stability and change in the life course, we develop three sets of thematic ideas regarding age-graded social control. The first concerns the structural and intervening sources of juvenile delinquency; the second centers on the consequences of delinquency and antisocial behavior for adult life chances; and the third focuses on the explanation of adult crime and deviance in relation to adult informal social control and social capital. Although this model was developed in the ongoing context of our analysis of the Gluecks' data and represents

the best fit between our conceptual framework and available measures, we believe that our theoretical notions have wider appeal and are not solely bound by these data.

Structure and Process in Adolescent Delinquency

In explaining the origins of delinquency, criminologists have embraced either structural factors (such as poverty, broken homes) or process variables (such as attachment to parents or teachers). We believe such a separation is a mistake. We join structural and process variables together into a single theoretical model. In brief, we argue that informal social controls derived from the family (e.g., consistent use of discipline, monitoring, and attachment) and school (e.g., attachment to school) mediate the effects of both individual and structural background variables. For instance, previous research on families and delinquency often fails to account for social structural disadvantage and how it influences family life. As Rutter and Giller have argued, socioeconomic disadvantage has potentially adverse effects on parents, such that parental difficulties are more likely to develop and good parenting is impeded. If this is true, we would then expect poverty and disadvantage to have their effects on delinquency transmitted through parenting.

The effects of family process are hypothesized to mediate structural context in other domains as well. We argue that key factors such as family disruption, parental criminality, household crowding, large family size, residential mobility, and mother's employment have either direct or indirect effects on delinquency. All of these structural background factors have traditionally been associated with delinquency. It is our major contention, however, that these structural factors will strongly affect family and school social control mechanisms, thereby playing a largely indirect (but not unimportant) role in the explanation of early delinquency. The intervening processes of primary interest are family socialization (discipline, supervision, and attachment), school attachment, and the influence of delinquent siblings and friends.

The Importance of Continuity Between Childhood and Adulthood

Our second theme concerns childhood antisocial behavior (such as juvenile delinquency, conduct disorder, or violent temper tantrums) and its link to troublesome adult behaviors. The theoretical importance of homotypic continuity has been largely ignored among sociological criminologists. Criminologists still focus primarily on the teenage years in their studies of offending, apparently disregarding the connections between childhood delinquency and adult crime. Reversing this tide, our main contention is that antisocial and delinquent behavior in childhood—measured by both official and unofficial sources—is linked to later adult deviance and criminality in a variety of settings (e.g., family violence, military offenses, "street crime," and alcohol abuse). Moreover, we argue that these outcomes occur independent of traditional sociological and psychological variables such as class background, ethnicity, and IQ.

Although some criminologists have explored the connections among conduct disorder, juvenile delinquency, and adult crime, we argue that the negative consequences of childhood misbehavior extend to a much broader spectrum of adult life, including economic dependence, educational failure, employment instability, and marital discord. It is important to explore the adult worlds of work, educational attainment, and marriage as well as involvement in deviant behavior generally. As Hagan and Palloni argue, delinquent and criminal events "are linked into life trajectories of broader significance, whether those trajectories are criminal or noncriminal in form." Because most research by criminologists has focused either on the teenage years or on adult behavior limited to crime, this basic idea has not been well integrated into the criminological literature.

The Significance of Change in the Life Course

Our third focus, drawing on a developmental perspective and a steppingstone approach, is concerned with changes in deviance and offending as individuals age. Our thesis concerns adult behavior and how it is influenced not just by early life experiences but also by social ties to the adult institutions of informal social control (such as family, school, and work). We argue that trajectories of both crime and conformity are significantly influenced over the life course by these adult social bonds, regardless of prior individual differences in self-control or criminal propensity.

The third major theme of our research, then, is that changes that strengthen social bonds to society in adulthood will lead to less crime and deviance. Conversely, changes in adulthood that weaken social bonds will lead to more crime and deviance. This premise allows us to explain desistance from crime as well as late onset. In addition, unlike most researchers, we emphasize the quality, strength, and interdependence of social ties more than the occurrence or timing of discrete life events. In our view, interdependent social bonds increase social capital and investment in social relations and institutions. Our theoretical model rests on social ties to jobs and family as the key inhibitors to adult crime and deviance.

INTEGRATING CRIMINOLOGY AND THE LIFE COURSE

Our theoretical framework represents a challenge to several assumptions and ideas found in contemporary criminological thought. We believe that the field of criminology has been dominated by narrow sociological and psychological perspectives, coupled with a strong tradition of research using cross-sectional data on adolescents. As a result, scientific knowledge in the field has been hindered by a focus on a limited age range, a limited range of variation in crime and state sanctions, an examination of either structural or process variables, and by serious limitations found in previous research designs and analytic strategies. The overall consequence is that major gaps appear in the existing body of criminological literature.

We confront several of these knowledge gaps and, we hope, expand and enrich the focus of criminological theory and research. We do so by merging a life-course perspective on age and informal social control with the existing criminological literature on crime and delinquency. With this strategy, we believe that key issues of current debate in the field, such as the age-crime relationship and longitudinal versus cross-sectional data needs, can be resolved. Rather than pitting one view against the other in an either/or fashion, our theory of social bonding integrates what is conceptually sound and empirically correct from each perspective.

Take, for example, the issue of stability versus change. We posit that life-event transitions and adult social bonds can modify quite different childhood trajectories. Thus, our conception of change is that adult factors explain systematic variations in adult behavior independent of childhood background. This does not deny the significance of childhood. Our theory thus incorporates the juvenile period with the adult life course to provide a more unified picture of human development. The unique advantage of a sociological perspective on the life course is that it brings the formative period of childhood back into the picture yet recognizes that individual behavior is mediated over time through interaction with age-graded social institutions.

QUESTIONS FOR DISCUSSION AND WRITING

1. What have most studies of crime failed to examine?
2. How do the "important institutions of informal and formal social control" vary across the life span?
3. What do the authors argue is linked to troublesome adult behaviors?

The Causal Process of Control Balance Theory

CHARLES TITTLE

THE main assertion of control balance theory is that the overall probability of deviance of some kind, as well as the probability of a particular type of deviance, is heavily influenced by the interplay of deviant motivation with constraint. Both deviant motivation and constraint are largely functions of control, meaning whatever amount of control can be exercised relative to the amount to which the person is exposed, as well as the likelihood that potential control actually will be exercised. The process by which these variables converge to produce deviance, however, is complex, and it involves other concepts. . . .

PROBABILITIES OF DEVIANCE

The theory implies that an individual's general probability of engaging in some form of deviance is mainly a reflection of that individual's motivation toward deviance. Opportunity for deviance to occur is an essential component of any deviant act, but opportunity for *some* kind of deviance is almost always present. Further, since motivation for deviance is largely a reflection of the person's control

From *Control Balance: Toward a General Theory of Deviance* (pp. 171–200) by C. Tittle, 1995, Boulder, Co.: Westview Press. Copyright © 1995 by Westview Press, Inc. Reprinted by permission of Westview Press, a member of Perseus Books, L.L.C.

ratio, the probability of deviance, in some form, is a function of control ratios. However, these probabilities form a U-curve with respect to the control ratio. They are lowest when the control to which an individual is subject is balanced by the control he or she can exercise, and they are at maximum when the control ratio is most imbalanced, in either direction; that is, deviance is most likely when there are large deficits of control as well as when there are large surpluses.

Although the probability of deviance in general is chiefly a direct expression of motivation toward deviance, the actual commission of deviant behavior is not a mechanical manifestation of preexisting, background variables. Rather, deviant behavior stems from a proximate causal process involving several situational variables. First, the actor must be motivated toward deviance. This motivation comes from a combination of predispositions toward motivation and immediate circumstances that generate awareness of the control ratio and perceptions that deviance will help change the balance of control. Second, there must be opportunity to commit the act; opportunity is completely situational. Third, except for submissive deviance, the chances of countercontrol must not be overwhelming. Potential countercontrol is partly predetermined—by the control ratio and by the seriousness of the act—but it also reflects the situational component of risk.

Control Deficits

A person with a control deficit is predisposed toward "repressive" forms of deviance—predatory, defiant, or submissive—and the greater the magnitude of the control deficit, the greater the total chances of one or another of these deviances. First and foremost, the greater the control deficit, the greater the chances that predatory and defiant forms of deviance will help rectify the imbalance. Second, the effects of impulses toward deviance that stem from desire for autonomy and from pursuit of ordinary goals are to a large extent absorbed and reflected in the control ratio. Third, although provocations that might activate propensities toward deviant motivation are situationally variable and perceptions of their potentialities are affected by individual differences, the import of control ratios is so great that even with situational provocations varying widely, gross probabilities of deficit-generated deviance can be predicted. Fourth, constraints that might counter motivations toward deviance mainly affect the type of deviance likely to be expressed rather than the likelihood that any deviance at all will occur. This is because constraint usually causes deviantly motivated people to choose less serious forms rather than to refrain from deviance altogether.

Consider an example. Everyone has numerous primary goals, perhaps including acquisition of food and shelter, sexual gratification, group acceptance, prestige, entertainment, and so forth. Since the chances of achieving those goals are strongly influenced by control ratios, people with control deficits are sometimes doubly motivated toward deviant behavior: They are motivated by blockage of the primary goal that results from their relative control disadvantage, and they are further motivated by the debasement inherent in a control deficit. Hungry people want to get food, but the greater their control deficits, the less their capacity for soliciting, buying, or demanding it. Furthermore, if hungry people cannot get food that is readily avail-able to others, they will feel even more acutely disadvantaged. If, in addition, they are told directly that the food is only for those who are already enjoying it in abundance, they will feel hunger and disadvantage, and they will feel demeaned, insulted, or otherwise humiliated. Most such victims quickly recognize that stealing can potentially relieve their hunger—that is, it will achieve their initial goal—and at the same time it will help them conquer their feelings of abasement or ridicule, which at this point may be even more important than hunger. In addition to becoming motivated to steal, they will in all likelihood also want to slug the person, perhaps a grocer or restaurant worker, who withholds food or dispenses verbal humiliation. Hurting a grocer or restaurant manager would help balance the unfavorable control ratio implicated in this hypothetical situation because it would put the attacker in charge, at least for the moment. Assault or theft dramatically shifts the terms of control, thereby allowing those with a control deficit to overcome their feeling of debasement.

Thus the hungry individual in the example above is doubly motivated to steal because theft would permit him or her to achieve an initial *and* a situationally generated goal. Successful theft would satisfy the physiological need for sustenance, but equally important, since people are rarely actually starving, it would overcome the circumstances, at least temporarily, of denigration. Theft, therefore, is attractive in part because it affords some control over those who ordinarily control the potential thief. Hence, the person may be motivated toward theft or assault by the dynamics of the situation even when the deviant acts hold little promise of satisfying hunger. Thus, the theory takes for granted that people are propelled toward various gratifying acts, but it contends that these primary "pushes" will not lead to predatory, defiant, or submissive deviant motivation or behavior unless they are blocked, and the likelihood of blockage is closely linked to the individual's control deficit. Moreover, the blockage itself enhances potential motivation toward deviance because it keys into the desire for autonomy in a way that generates feelings of debasement or humiliation.

Although much deficit-generated deviance involves double motivation like that described above, humiliation associated with control deficits often motivates deviance even when no initial, basic need is obvious. Most of us have been in situations where someone has made us acutely aware of our relative control deficit, even when we were not actively pursuing any focused goals, but rather were doing nothing, or basically minding our own business in a nondirective sort of way. An example would be adolescents sitting around a shopping mall when a security guard approaches and tells them to leave. Even though their initial goal of resting or "goofing off" is not a particularly powerful motivator even when blocked, the action of the guard, especially if delivered in a demeaning tone, will nevertheless create a strong motivation toward acts that the youths did not previously contemplate. They want to get back at that person to show that they cannot be pushed around. In other words, they feel the urge to balance the scales of control. It may occur to them that they ought to steal something just to spite the security guard and those the guard represents or to demonstrate that they cannot be humiliated with impunity. They may also momentarily contemplate an assault. Surely most people in such circumstances will want to protest verbally, call names, defy the guard's admonition by challenging authority, or in the final analysis pretend to obey but drag their feet as a way of signifying they are not totally subordinate. The point is that the main motivation toward deviance occurs in the acute realization that one's control is less than that of others. Sometimes this motivation reinforces other motives, which are in most instances linked to the control ratio as well, but it may stand more or less alone and still exert strong influence on the probability of deviance.

Indeed, lest the hunger example cause the theory to be misinterpreted as an emphasis on material deprivations, it should be noted that the main focus of control balance theory in explaining repressive deviance is on the deprivations of control and the feelings of being "put down" that accompany comparatively rare material blockages and the more frequent blockage of trivial impulses or that often stand alone without any apparent barriers to goal achievement. Initial "ordinary needs" are of comparatively little import. Hence, the theory is consistent with the observation that much property crime is not linked to real material deprivation and that most acts of violence follow trivial insults rather than serious affronts. Control deficits sensitize people to environmental reminders of their subordinate positions regardless of, or in addition to, the usually operative motivators of action. It is the realization of relative weakness of potential control that constitutes the chief motive for deviant behavior.

Of course, a person with a serious control deficit faces the possibility of controlling reactions from others who might be affected by efforts to rectify a control imbalance through deviant acts. The greater the potentiality that the deviant acts will inconvenience, hurt, or threaten the social positions of those against whom they might be directed (the more serious the act), the greater the chances that controlling responses will be activated. Thus, individuals with a control deficit are both highly motivated and highly constrained. However, constraint is act-specific. Therefore, when a person highly motivated toward a serious form of deviance faces the possibility of massive controlling responses, that person will usually forgo that particular expression for fear of activating the potential controlling responses reflected in the control ratio and in the type of deviance being contemplated. Nevertheless, such individuals will still be motivated toward deviance, and if they can, they will fall back on a less serious form of deviant expression. Hence, deficit control ratios will always be positively linked to the total chances of committing predatory, defiant, or submissive deviance.

Control Surpluses

As explained above, predisposition toward predatory and defiant forms of deviance flowers into actual motivation when specific situations stimulate a person to recognize that deviance is a possibility and that it holds the promise of rectifying the control imbalance. The theory also contends that control "surpluses" reflecting ability to exercise more control than that to which one is subject will express themselves in "autonomous" forms of deviance—exploitative, plunderous, or decadent. Consequently, the greater the control surplus, the greater the chances of some form of autonomous deviance. This is so because (1) autonomous deviance is most likely to permit the fullest extension of control for those who already have a surplus, (2) the effects of the universal desire to escape controls on oneself and to extend one's control over others, as well as the pursuit of ordinary goals of life, are absorbed and expressed in the control surplus, (3) the effects of the control surplus are so important that they overshadow other variables, and (4) countercontrols mainly affect the type of deviance rather than the simple probability of some form of deviance occurring.

Consider again the case of hunger, but this time imagine people with control surpluses for whom severe hunger is extremely unlikely. If food is available, they can get it, and they will seldom encounter any negative reactions from grocers or restaurant workers that would humiliate or demean them. However, if resistance should appear, they can call on their resources to overcome it. Normally, however, even without activating their potential controlling abilities, individuals with a surplus of control will witness others going to extraordinary ends to accommodate the needs of people like themselves with control surpluses.

However, given the fundamental drive toward autonomy, which in this case involves a desire to extend control as far as possible, the actions that a grocery clerk or restaurant worker willingly takes to provide food for the person with superior control actually motivate deviance on the part of the superior controller. They do this by spurring the superior's awareness that deviance will further enhance his or her control advantage.

Imagine a famous, wealthy, or powerful woman entering a restaurant and nobody noticing or doing anything more to accommodate her than they would for an ordinary customer. She will feel slighted and suddenly become aware that she has not gotten the deference she deserves. Then she will be inspired to use some of the control at her disposal, by offering an advance tip, or bribe, demanding to see the manager, or using sharp words to remind the restaurant personnel of their responsibilities toward her. If there is resistance, she is likely to become motivated to use deviance to extend her control; she may contemplate threatening to have the host fired (exploitation) or storming to her favorite table and ordering anybody in the way to move out (plunder).

Suppose, on the other hand, that restaurant workers immediately recognize her and rush up to take her coat and escort her to a desirable table. Since this is expected and routine, no motivation toward deviance would be generated. However, suppose that in addition to this ordinary special attention, the restaurant host led this woman into the dining room, ostensibly pushing aside someone else in order to acquire the most desirable table for her. Since this extra deference is unusual, it also would provoke an awareness in the woman of her superior control, and it would generate motivation to use deviance to extend that control even further. The famous customer might then contemplate telling the host to order all the customers in the room to leave (exploitation) or demand that the chef drop everything and immediately prepare her a special dish (plunder).

Hence, there is double motivation in the case of a control surplus just as in the case of a control deficit—the motivation generated by blockage of the goal of obtaining food (hunger) and additional motivation generated by the realization that the controller's dominance can be extended. As with control deficits, surpluses themselves may create a motive toward deviance even in the absence of a specific, focused goal like hunger. Those with surplus control often find others seeking ways to please them even when the controllers exhibit no visible specific goal. A superior does not need to be hungry in order to induce those with less control to offer food. Control is, therefore, often exercised without direct intent simply because the potential for superior control evokes ameliorative reactions.

When control is successfully exercised, whether in response to resistance or without direct intent, it generates awareness of potential further extension, and if that potential extension involves exploitation, plunder, or decadence it constitutes deviant motivation. In the example being considered here, provocation comes from the willing acquiescence of those who possess the food. Regardless of its source, however, deviant motivation stimulates efforts to extend control as far as possible. The limit to extending control is the point at which effective resistance is encountered, which, of course, is linked to the seriousness of the deviance. Even in the face of potentially effective countercontrolling responses, those motivated to use deviance for extending control surpluses will not usually give up but instead will resort to a less serious form of autonomous deviance.

One implication of all of this is that people with control surpluses usually do not feel grateful for things, whether they are in need or not at the time and regardless of whether there is resistance to their acquisition. Instead, awareness of superior ability to control leads them to think that others should acquiesce, and they usually imply, or directly say this, to those with inferior control. This generates feelings of humiliation among those with infe-rior control. When situations allow those with relatively less control to perceive the potentiality of deviance for rectifying the control imbalance generating those feelings, repressive deviance is likely. Therefore, to some extent deviance is reciprocal. Efforts to extend control surpluses are likely to lead to efforts to overcome control deficits.

This process is evident in the restaurant example. The wealthy woman assumes superior service and food to be her right. Privileges have made her insensitive to the feelings of subordinates, and by extending her control she humiliates the restaurant workers, thereby generating awareness on their part that deviance would rectify the control imbalances under which they suffer. As a result they may contemplate spitting in her food or defecating in her car (defiance) or perhaps stealing her purse or slugging her (predation). In like manner, supervisors often lose sensitivity to the feelings of their workers and begin to perceive obedience to supervisory commands as their right. In conveying this, the line between work directives and degradation becomes blurred. The likely result is that the workers will become motivated toward defiance (as in work slowdowns) or predation (such as stealing company property) for alleviating the control imbalance that always existed but came into acute focus with the overbearing actions of the work supervisor. . . .

TYPES OF DEVIANCE

Basic Assumptions

Control balance theory asserts that various imbalances of control determine the type of deviance likely to be committed. Explanation of the type of deviance involves an additional variable not implicated in the explanation of the general probability of deviance. Whereas the probability of some act of deviance being committed depends on the strength of motivation for deviance that stems mainly from the degree to which control abilities or capacities are unbalanced, the likelihood that particular forms of deviance will be committed depends jointly upon the total volume of control that can possibly be brought into play and the probability that potential control from other entities will actually be used. The chances of actual use of potential control depend on the seriousness of the act that might be committed.

To understand how motivation and constraint intersect to influence the chances of deviant behavior of a given type occurring, we must recognize three simple assumptions. First, everybody is motivated to do some things, either because of primary needs or because of socially generated desires. Second, some of what any given person wants to do is objectionable to or disadvantageous to others, or it is difficult to do, given physical and social circumstances. Third, if what an individual wants to do is troublesome to others and those others are in a position to do so, they will limit the extent to which the things can be done. A corollary of this third assumption is that if the things that an individual wants to do are difficult, given the physical and social circumstances, that individual's options are limited (he or she is controlled) by the "structural" and physical arrangements. Since no individual is capable of totally preventing others from limiting his or her options and since everyone will at some time desire to do things that are impossible or difficult in the physical and social environment, everyone is subject to some control; that is, everyone's behavioral options are limited by potential actions of others or by the physical and social structure.

At the same time, everyone has some capacity to limit the options of others. Even seemingly helpless infants can exercise control over adults, especially their parents, by making disruptive noises. Those within earshot of such noises, whether parents or not, will almost inevitably have to make some adjustment. They may attend to the infant's needs, leave, put in earplugs, ask someone else to do something about it, learn to ignore the noise, abuse or kill the baby, and so on. Hence, without any conscious awareness of its ability, a screaming infant can control others.

Similarly, the lowest-status slave can limit the options of his or her master (as well as the options of other slaves) by working slowly, displaying insolence, or ultimately, by committing suicide. Each of these patterns has some effect on options available to the slave owner. The owner might punish or reward a slow-moving slave to induce faster work, try to persuade the slave to do better, threaten to punish others if the slave does not improve, try to get other slaves to influence the recalcitrant one, ignore the situation and accept the loss of income that the slave's labor would otherwise produce, and so forth. An insolent slave can be handled in similar ways, or ignored, but even passive acceptance requires some effort by the owner. If the slave commits suicide, the owner has to take a financial loss, make arrangements for replacement or change the expectations of those benefiting from that slave's labor, and attend to the details of disposing of the body and personal effects.

Although everyone can potentially control and is potentially controlled, the relative balance of those potentialities differs from individual to individual. Those differences are expressed in control ratios, which predict the general probability of some form of deviance. However, to understand the likelihood of specific types of deviance, we must focus on the chances that particular deviant acts will actually activate potential countercontrol. The massiveness of potential control that can come from other entities depends upon the magnitude of the imbalance of control abilities and capacities (the individual's control ratio), whereas the likelihood that potential control will actually be used depends on the seriousness of the act.

For instance, even though people may be subject to large deficits of control (by definition, abilities or capacities), they are not likely to experience the actual exercise of that controlling potential unless they do something serious. Some acts by individuals with a control deficit will almost certainly inspire use of controlling capacities or abilities by other social entities, but different acts will inspire use of those capacities only rarely. Very serious acts (those regarded as the most unacceptable, consequential, or threatening to those with capacities of control over the individual) will have a high probability of provoking the controlling responses inherent in the individual's control ratio; less serious acts are less likely to provoke the full use of controlling abilities.

Whether those motivated toward deviance actually commit specific deviant acts depends to a large extent on the chances, or perceived chances, that those acts will activate countercontrolling responses. The acts that are most appealing to people with control imbalances are usually also those most likely to activate the potential countercontrols implied by the control ratio. Individual behavior, then, represents a trade-off between motivation and constraint. Ironically, the higher the motivation for deviance, the more likely the most effective (for rectifying a control deficit or extending a control surplus) potential deviant acts are to create problems for others (i.e., they are serious acts) and the greater the likelihood that the acts will provoke countercontrol. The actual chance of a specific form of deviance occurring, then, is a reflection of the relative strengths of motivation and constraint.

Clearly, I am claiming that individual behavior is influenced by the likelihood and magnitude of anticipated controls (sanctions, limitations on future conduct, and so on), that is, that people's actions can be, and typically are, curtailed, partially curtailed, or channelled into alternative behaviors by anticipation of the likely controlling responses of others. If a specific type of deviance that an individual is likely to commit in an effort to alter his or her control balance is perceived as highly likely to evoke strong controlling reactions by others, the individual will be deterred from that act, and if strongly motivated, will turn to a type of deviant behavior perceived as less likely to evoke potential controlling responses.

Some will find this argument surprising in view of the inconsistency and weakness of evidence in support of the "deterrence doctrine." I hold to it for several reasons. First, the idea that constraint affects human behavior is eminently logical. Indeed, it is difficult to imagine how people could be totally unaffected by potentially punishing, limiting, or unpleasant responses from other entities. Furthermore, in the theory, constraint is systematically intertwined with a coherent network of processes so that the logic of the whole supports the logic of the separate parts.

Second, evidence about deterrence is not necessarily relevant to the general idea of constraint because much of it concerns only one source of potential control—formal operation of the law—and only direct punishment. The concept of constraint is far broader than this, encompassing a range of informal interpersonal, organizational, and structural sources, as well as a variety of different kinds of constraining elements. Hence, the bulk of deterrence research is tangential to the fundamental ideas of control balance theory. The most relevant extant deterrence research, although it too is narrowly focused (on interpersonal elements), has been consistent and fairly strong in support of the idea that individual perceptions of informal negative reactions from significant others affect individual behavior.

Nevertheless, the effects of constraints as conceived in this theory have never been investigated. To ascertain if constraint works as portrayed, researchers must investigate a broader range of informal controlling reactions (not necessarily sanctions in the basic sense). In addition, they will have to measure constraint in terms of the potential deviant acts that might be committed (which will be interlinked to variations in control ratios) relative to those actually committed. Constraint (or deterrence) should not express itself in straightforward variations in rates or probabilities of crime or deviance, or even in the probabilities or rates of specific offenses. Rather, its effects will be seen in choices of one form of deviance over another, varying among individuals depending on their control ratios and differing with the seriousness of the acts in question in specific contexts.

The Mechanics of Cause

Control imbalances on the deficit side imply that as the strength of motivation increases, the ability of others to exercise countercontrol also increases, but this is only one aspect of potential countercontrol. Another aspect of potential constraining response depends on the seriousness of the act in question. Since any control deficit provokes a desire to rectify the situation, all individuals with a control deficit are prone toward motivation for behaviors perceived as maximally effective for overcoming those deficits. However, such behaviors are also the ones regarded by others as most dangerous or threatening; that is, individuals with a control deficit will want to commit serious acts of deviance.

When people's overall control deficits are small, they will be able to contemplate committing serious deviant acts without excessive fear that controlling responses will be marshaled in response. Although such acts have a high probability of provoking some kind of controlling response, the abilities and capacities of others to control are not enough greater than the individual's to fully curtail the behavior. Hence, relatively small control deficits imply some probability of serious acts of deviance being committed, though most such acts will be deterred. As a result, those "marginal individuals" with relatively small negative control imbalances have low probabilities of deviance in general, but when they do commit deviance it is likely to be predatory in form. This is due to a complicated convergence of motivation and constraint. Those with marginal control deficits have less motivation for deviant solutions than those with moderate or extreme deficits, but they, like all people with control deficits, are mainly interested in predation because it is the most effective potential device for rectifying negative control imbalances. Yet, because it is

serious and stimulates countercontrol, predation is rarely used. Those most likely to employ predatory behavior in the face of greater potential counterresponses are actually the ones who suffer the least control deficit, that is, those with marginal, rather than moderate or extreme, control deficits. This is because the amount of control that can be brought to bear against a marginal individual, relative to the control that can be returned, is not great enough to discourage all predation.

As the magnitude of the control deficit increases, however, and individuals become more motivated to commit serious deviance, they are less able to imagine that such behavior will escape controlling responses from others. Hence, as the control deficit increases, people search for less serious means to help rectify the imbalance of control because less serious acts have less chance of provoking the full weight of steadily increasing potential control responses from other entities. In short, as the magnitude of a control deficit increases, the probability of some form of deviance goes up, but the seriousness of the likely behavioral response decreases. Further, since predatory deviance is regarded by most social entities as more serious than defiant acts, predation corresponds with small control deficits, and defiant acts of deviance correspond with larger control deficits. In other words, those who commit defiance would commit predation, but their control deficits are too large to allow much chance of escaping counterresponses from those with more control. However, given their relatively high motivation toward deviance, they resort to defiance as a less effective but safer ploy. Since submissive deviance is regarded as even less serious, or threatening, than either predation or defiance, it is associated with overwhelming control deficits. "Extreme" persons—those with large control deficits—are highly motivated toward deviance and would employ predation or defiance if they could. Since those forms of deviance are more likely than submission to provoke counterresponses, and by virtue of their large control deficits, extreme individuals are in the weakest position to escape countercontrolling responses. In fact, they are in such weak positions that they cannot even contemplate the possibility of an alternative.

The same processes are at work on the surplus side of the control continuum. Although people with the ability to exercise more control than they experience are motivated to extend their control as far as possible, the chances of provoking controlling responses from other social entities serve as a check. Hence, the probability of deviance of some kind varies directly with the magnitude of the control surplus, but the seriousness of the deviance likely to be committed varies directly with the magnitude of the control imbalance, rather than inversely, as it does on the deficit side. With slight surpluses of control, individuals, or social entities, can only commit less serious deviant acts to extend their control because of the possibility of provoking controlling responses from other social entities, but as the control imbalance gets larger, those with surpluses of control can anticipate less and less likelihood of generating controlling responses from others. Hence, the seriousness of the deviance likely to be committed varies directly with the extent of control surplus the individual or social entity enjoys.

Manifestations

These effects can be illustrated with two overlapping continua and their corresponding types of deviance. . . . One continuum reflects a continuous variable representing *lesser* ability to control relative to being controlled, or repression. The second reflects *greater* ability to exercise control relative to being controlled, or autonomy. These two continuous variables extend in opposite directions on the same underlying continuum, running from extreme repression on one end (the same as extreme lack of autonomy) to maximum autonomy on the other end (the same as maximum absence of repression). As already noted, autonomy and repression can be conceived as specific to particular domains of activity as well as being overarching. For instance, an individual's autonomy can be conceived of in a total sense, encompassing amounts of control experienced relative to that exercised, in all realms of human activity, or it can be conceptualized in terms of a specific domain of concern. Hence, some individuals may have medium autonomy in most realms of life, although they may have a control deficit in a particular domain such as sexual expression. Others may be repressed in terms of the totality of human activity, but nevertheless be autonomous in some sphere such as religion.

REPRESSIVE DEVIANCE   The center of the continuum represents balance—approximately equal amounts of autonomy and repression. In that zone we expect conformity (conscious recognition of the rules with studied obedience). People in other zones of the continuum are liable to commit one or another form of deviance. Consider the three zones of increasing repression (decreasing degrees of autonomy). The first one-third of that part of the continuum is a marginal zone. There people are subjected to somewhat more control than they themselves exercise, but they are not so controlled that they have no freedom of action. They have some likelihood of becoming motivated to overcome their control deficit by taking things from others or by directly forcing others to do what they want. The predisposition for this motive stems from the residual, universal disgust at being controlled, as intensified by a current situation in which individuals are subject to more control than they exercise. Because the deviance that would most effectively rectify the control imbalance is also most likely to activate countercontrolling responses, the chances of curtailment of the potential deviance are high. Nevertheless, the imbalance of control is small enough for people in this situation to sometimes be able to imagine that they can escape control from others. Such people have a low probability of deviance generally, but they are also the ones most likely to commit predation.

Predation includes such things as theft, assault, rape, or homicide, as well as any behavior in which one person directly preys upon another person or entity, such as when a mother invokes guilt in her children to gain their attention.

The second, or moderate, zone of repression contains people with modest control imbalances, and it is likely to generate defiant behavior. These people have a stronger predisposition to be motivated toward using deviance as a device that might enable them to overcome their control deficits than people with slight control deficits do, but at the same time the control to which they are subject permits them less freedom. Their relatively larger control deficit renders too great the cost of serious acts that might otherwise help rectify the imbalance. As a result, moderately repressed persons have a relatively high probability of some deviance, but they will not commit predation very often. Instead, they are liable to engage in deviant acts of protest against the sources of the control deficit they experience, or they will less dramatically register their frustration by withdrawing from participation. Defiant acts allow people to escape unfavorable control without running the risk that the full force of countercontrol will be brought down on them. The result is deviance like defiance of parental and legal curfews and other status offenses among adolescents, mocking denigrations of power holders by student rebels or striking workers, sullen obedience by children, or exaggerated overconformity by employees or students. Occupying an extremely repressed position may also lead to escape behaviors like alcoholism, drug abuse, suicide, family desertion, mental illness, or countercultural involvement.

The extreme zone of repression (the last one-third of the continuum) is associated with submissive deviance. The very large deficits of control characteristic of individuals here lead to extremely strong predispositions for motivation toward using deviance to help rectify their situations. Yet, such people are so disadvantaged that almost any deviant behavior

can activate strong counterresponses. Hence, potential predatory and defiant acts are curtailed, or deterred, and in most instances, extremely repressed people are left having to accept subordination. Repetitious subjugation dulls the human spirit and erodes cognitive creativity. The result is a high probability of slavish submission without the ability to imagine alternatives.

AUTONOMOUS DEVIANCE   There are also three zones on the autonomous end of the continuum. The first is that of minimal autonomy. Here individuals exercise slightly more control than that to which they are subject. Their motivation to deviance stems from the desire to extend their own control, which is inspired by blockage of basic human impulses and situational provocations, including circumstances where the control they already have is successfully implemented. Nevertheless, because they cannot totally escape control by others, they are restrained from direct acts of deviance that would activate such countercontrolling responses directed against themselves as individuals. Instead, they use exploitation, which involves indirect predation, as a safer means of expanding control; that is, they use their controlling positions to arrange things so that other persons or organizational units accomplish acts that enhance their control.

Such persons may mandate price-fixing (if they are corporate executives) or shakedown schemes (if they are gang leaders who can induce neighborhood gangs to sell protection to local merchants). They might also profiteer through influence peddling (legislators taking bribes to vote on legislation favorable to the briber), buy off, or injure adversarial entities (famous actors making financial settlements with complainants to escape bad publicity or athletes hiring someone to injure their competitors). Furthermore, they might use third parties to extract money or dignity from victims (estranged wives creating provocative situations between their husbands and other women to yield evidence for more favorable divorce settlements or pimps living off the earnings of prostitutes who have tricked their clients). Finally, those with minimal surplus of control are liable to contract with others to bring about the punishment or death of a troublesome person (organized crime figures having an uncooperative judge pistol-whipped or business partners using soldiers of fortune to eliminate troublesome associates).

The second zone on the positive end of the continuum is that of *medium autonomy*. Those with such control imbalances can exercise considerably more control than they experience; that is, they are relatively free of being controlled at the same time that they can control others. By observing that others generally concede to their anticipated needs and wants, individuals with medium autonomy come to perceive that there is relatively little to restrain their actions, and repeated success produces insensitivity to the absence of autonomy among those whom they can control. The freer people are from control, the less appreciation they have for the condition of others; control corrupts its wielders because they cannot relate to subordination through recent personal experience. Characteristic forms of deviance are really selfish acts—forms of plunder—that include things like environmental pollution inflicted by imperialist countries whose leaders are in search of scarce resources in underdeveloped countries, programs of massive destruction of forests or rivers for the personal gain of corporate owners or executives, unrealistic taxes or work programs imposed by autocratic rulers, enslavement of natives by invading forces for the benefit of military commanders, pillage of communities by hoods doing the bidding of crime bosses, pogroms through which political or military leaders try to exterminate whole categories of people they find undesirable (as in the Hitler-imposed holocaust or the devastation of Native Americans by any number of people during the frontier expansion in the history of this country), and acts of tyrants like Jim Jones, who ordered the suicide of hundreds of his People's Temple followers. Those occupying this medium zone of autonomy are simply in-

different to the needs of others or to their potential responses.

The maximum zone of autonomy includes those with very large control surpluses. Occupants enjoy almost total freedom to exercise control over others and to act as the mood strikes without concern for countercontrol. Even more than those with medium control surpluses, individuals here are stimulated, by the slightest provocation and by the very success of previous intended or unintended extensions, to increase their already substantial control advantages. Very few people find themselves in this situation, but those who do have a high probability of committing bizarre and jaded acts. They become bored by the ordinary in life, turning to the unusual and the atypical to find meaning. Classic examples are autocratic rulers like Nero, who fiddled while Rome burned, and a few eccentric billionaires like Howard Hughes and perhaps Michael Jackson, whose publicly known lifestyles and tastes border on the macabre. If those with medium control surpluses are insensitive, individuals with maximum control surpluses are completely oblivious to the potential of countercontrol as well as to the effects of their actions on others. The resulting patterns of behavior can best be called decadent. . . .

GENERAL SUMMARY OF THE CONTROL BALANCING PROCESS

The theory contends that deviant behavior is undertaken mainly to alter the deviant's control ratio, even if temporarily. Deviance serves a specific purpose for the individual who commits it, and this purpose is not necessarily obvious or ostensibly connected with the form of deviance. The first-person account of criminal activity by Nathan McCall, whose book *Makes Me Wanna Holler* was excerpted in *Newsweek* prior to its publication, serves to illustrate the point. McCall describes his feeling the first time he burgled a house: "As I rifled through those people's most private possessions, I felt a peculiar power over them, even though we'd never met." Later he "graduated" to stickups, and the satisfaction that this provided was clearly not the increase in income or the ease of the job. Rather, it was the exhilaration associated with a shift in control.

Sticking up gave me a rush that I never got from B&Es. There was an almost magical transformation in my relationship with the rest of the world when I drew that gun on folks. I always marveled at how the toughest cats whimpered and begged for their lives when I stuck the barrel into their faces. Adults who ordinarily would have commanded my respect were forced to follow my orders like obedient kids.

When McCall ended up actually shooting someone, he felt even more control. "I walked toward Plaz, looked into his eyes and saw something I had never seen in him before. Gone was the fierceness that made him so intimidating all those years. In its place was shock. And fear. It was more like terror. In that moment, I felt like God. I felt so good and powerful that I wanted to do it again."

From the premise that deviance serves to alter relative distributions of control, the theory reasons that motivation to commit acts of deviance will vary with the relative amount of control a person has, whereas the expression of deviant motivations in actual behavior is influenced by the amount of countercontrol that can be expected, along with the probability that it will be activated. Thus, the theory explains both the probability and type of deviance as consequences of the amount of control exercised relative to the control suffered (along with other activating variables like generation of deviant motivation, opportunity, and constraint). When the two are balanced, people generally conform. When the two are unbalanced, the probability of deviance increases directly with the degree of imbalance or by the distances from the center of the continuum in both directions. From the center, which represents a ratio of 1 as the balance of control varies along the repressive and of the continuum, there is increasing probability of deviance generally, although the seriousness (type) of likely deviance decreases. In like manner, as the degree of imbalance increases in movement from 1 on the surplus side of the continuum out to the end, the probability and the seriousness (type) correspondingly increase.

The chance of deviant behavior of some kind is mainly a function of motivation toward deviance, which increases with the degree of an individual's control imbalance and other situational provocations (though opportunity must also be present). This is because a fundamental urge for escaping and extending control interacts with the relative potentialities for control embedded in the immediate and general statuses, roles, and experiences of the individual. The type of deviance likely, however, is a function of motivation and possible countercontrol, both of which are linked to the control ratio (but not totally determined by them). An additional factor in explaining the type of deviance, however, is the seriousness of the potential act, which reflects the likelihood that the behavior will activate countercontrolling responses. Motivated individuals contemplate the most effective deviance for overcoming a control deficit or for extending a control surplus, but their actual behaviors reflect a hydraulic relationship between motivation and potential countercontrolling responses (assuming opportunity). The net effect of this is (1) a positive relationship between the magnitude of a control deficit and the likelihood of some deviance, but an inverse relationship between the magnitude of a control deficit and the seriousness of the deviance that does occur; and (2) a positive relationship between the magnitude of a control surplus and the likelihood of some deviance, as well as a positive relationship between the magnitude of a control surplus and the seriousness of the deviance that emerges. . . .

GENERAL SUMMARY

Control balance theory portrays the probability of deviance as a function of the ratio of control exercised to that experienced, and it stipulates the type of deviance likely to be committed as a joint function of the magnitude of one's control imbalance and the seriousness of potential deviant acts. The magnitude of a control imbalance is directly related to the probability of deviance of some kind. However, the seriousness of specific types of potential deviant behavior varies inversely with the magnitude of a control deficit and directly with the magnitude of a control surplus. Thus, a small control deficit portends predatory deviance, one of the most serious types, and whenever an individual enjoys a large control surplus, the chances of decadence are greatest. Moderate control deficits signify enhanced chances for defiance and whenever medium control surpluses prevail, chances of plunder are increased. Finally, with large control deficits, submissive deviance is likely, whereas those with small control surpluses will most likely exploit.

Although the probability and type of deviance are functions of control ratios and constraints, they are not straightforward consequences of those variables, nor are their effects necessarily linear. The theory implies an underlying causal process that begins with a predisposition toward deviant motivation, which is an interactive outcome of a control imbalance, a basic human desire for autonomy, and usually some blockage of a primary human impulse. Predispositions are translated into actual motivation when they converge with situational provocations, which are closely linked to feelings of degradation, to generate a perception that deviant behavior can favorably alter the control imbalance or relieve humiliation. The magnitude of motivation toward deviance, in combination with the presence of opportunity, predicts the general probability of deviance. The chances of a specific form of deviance occurring, however, stem from an alliance of the original control imbalance, the presence of motivation and opportunity, and constraint. Constraint is a con-

vergent product of a control imbalance, the seriousness of a potential act, and situational risk. The entire process is conceived as both dynamic (the values of the variables are situationally volatile) and reciprocal (deviance feeds back to alter some of its own causes).

In this theory, the control ratio is conceived as a generalized characteristic of the individual's configuration of roles, statuses, social relationships, and accommodations to the physical and organizational world. Unfortunately, the overall control ratio is difficult to measure because it includes many different elements that operate in a variety of situations. Still, even crude measurement will produce fairly good results because the bulk of the control ratio is embodied in a circumscribed set of roles and statuses.

Control balancing theory explains prevalence of general and specific deviance among individuals, the frequency of deviance for given time spans, variations in prevalence and incidence over the life course, and differences among societies, organizations, and demographic categories in rates of deviance. It makes no assertions, however, about absolute probabilities or frequencies of deviance for any ratio of control, for any individual, or for any group or category. In addition, although control imbalance is postulated as the primary factor accounting for most deviance, the theory does not contend that everybody with a particular control balance will inevitably engage in the prescribed deviant behavior. There will be instances where the control ratio suggests low likelihood of deviance that does not occur; there will be instances where the actual control ratio suggests a high likelihood of deviance that does not occur; and there will be instances where individuals commit types of deviances not predicted by their control ratios or fail to commit types of deviance that are predicted by their control ratios. In part, this is because the causal forces implicated in the theory operate with greater or lesser force under various conditions or contingencies.

QUESTIONS FOR DISCUSSION AND WRITING

1. To what do "control deficits" sensitize people, and what is the "chief motive" for deviance?
2. Through what forms of deviance will those with control "surpluses" express themselves?
3. When do we expect "conformity"?

IX

HOW ARE CRIMES DIFFERENT?

The Varying Patterns of Criminality

THE idea that criminals specialize—that is, some are burglars, others robbers, and still others car thieves—is not quite inaccurate. A more correct image is one of offenders who, for whatever reason, violate norms and laws. They are not particular about which ones they choose to violate, so we believe it is unnecessary to have a special section that describes criminals as if they are specialists. Rather, the evidence suggests they are more likely to be generalists—people who break a variety of laws, especially those that they have the opportunity to violate. A man who has a blue-collar job does not have the opportunity to engage in white-collar crime, but he may still engage in occupation-related crime made available by his own employment.

We believe, then, that it is more useful to describe patterns of criminality than types of criminals. We have selected pieces on white-collar crime, organized crime, gangs, violence, and drugs and crime, because they are of significant interest to contemporary criminologists. Although we intend for the topics in this section to be timely, we have in some instances provided a "classic" statement on a topic, for two reasons. First and foremost is their continuing value as criminological statements that describe the particular phenomenon. Second, it demonstrates how topics that are of current interest have been cycled and recycled in the discipline, sometimes in response to the ebbs and flows of he public's interest in crime control.

The first topic is white-collar crime, and we begin with a selection by Edwin Sutherland. Although we cannot be sure that he was the first to use the phrase "white-collar crime," it is his criminological concept. When other criminologists were interested exclusively in common or "street crimes," Sutherland argued that another type of crime, which took place in the high places of the corporate and government worlds, should also be studied carefully by criminologists. In fact, students should recognize that Sutherland was in general interested in crime that occurred outside of the stereotypical locations. His theory of differential association was designed to explain not only how bad behavior is produced in bad circumstances— why poor children in blighted neighborhoods might become delinquents—

but also how bad behavior is produced in apparently good circumstances. His interest in white-collar crime is consistent with this overall belief that criminologists should restrict neither their interest nor their research to the less fortunate members of society.

James Coleman's "The Criminal Elite" is a compelling description of the magnitude of the problem. By white-collar crime, criminologists do not mean "common crimes" such as homicide or rape that happen to be committed by professionals or other elites, but crimes specifically associated with their occupation or position in society. Examples are embezzlement by bank officials, or fraud committed by a corporation. Many citizens are only minimally concerned about white-collar crime, reasoning that "it doesn't hurt people as badly as street crime." Coleman shows that the losses, both economic and personal, produced by white-collar crime actually exceed those produced by common crimes.

Students should also recognize that there are other forms of elite crime, such as that committed by government officials or others involved in politics. Some criminologists, particularly those who favor conflict theories, argue that political criminal behavior is particularly insidious because it undermines the confidence of the public and threatens the very nature of the democratic order.

The two selections on organized crime represent two sides of a debate. Donald Cressey's "From Mafia to Cosa Nostra" argues that there is a large, coordinated network that dominates organized crime in America. This organization has been known by a number of names, but it is most widely recognized as the Mafia. Dennis Kenney and James Finckenauer have a different view of organized crime. In "Myths and Organized Crime: Is There a Mafia, and Does It Really Matter?" they argue that there is not really a national syndicate called the Mafia. Kenney and Finckenauer are part of a significant group of criminologists who believe that organized crime is for the most part locally controlled, its form reflecting local contexts and circumstances. This debate is particularly relevant for those interested in controlling organized crime. If the image portrayed by Cressey is accurate, it suggests the need for a nationally coordinated law enforcement effort. If Kenney and Finkenauer's description is more accurate, then perhaps a more locally centered effort would be more effective.

For the third topic, gangs, we have chosen a classic piece and an example from the contemporary gang literature. Some criminologists are perplexed at the public's image of gang delinquency. For example, there is a widespread belief that many cities have a "gang problem" because they have been invaded by gangs from elsewhere. Likewise, many people mistakenly believe that the primary reason for the existence of gangs is drug sales. The public discourse based on these kinds of mistaken beliefs run counter to much well-established knowledge about gangs.

More than seventy years ago, Frederic Thrasher wrote a wonderful description of how gangs form, and his chapter "Ganging," from *The Gang: A Study of 1,313 Gangs in Chicago*, is included here. Although his research was conducted well before the advent of modern super-gangs, we and many other criminologists consider Thrasher's work a classic, because there is good evidence that his descriptions are still valid and applicable today.

Gangs do not appear because an invading vanguard from Los Angeles or Chicago or New York sweeps over an unprotected city. Gangs form when local forces lead to crime and when, in some circumstances, the form of this criminality is "ganging." In "The Social Organization of Street Gang Activity in an Urban Ghetto," Sudhir Venkatesh uses ethnographic research to document how an inner-city gang attempts to change itself. What is important here is how the gang is affected by the social organization of the larger community in which it exists. Like other forms of criminality, gangs reflect their social environment. They can neither be understood nor eradicated without taking that environment into account.

Turning to the issue of violence, Todd Robert Gurr provides a context and the perspective of time in "Historical Trends in Violent Crime: A Critical Review of the Evidence." If we do not consider the history of violence, we have an inadequate appreciation of how current problems compare to those in the past. Historical perspective can also help us understand how some factors, such as social change, lead to increases or decreases in violence. This point is especially important in the context of recent debates over the cause of falling crime rates in the 1990s. To some extent, the increases of the 1960s and 1970s as well as the current decline are consistent with long-term trends and fluctuations.

Marvin Wolfgang and Margaret Zahn describe patterns in the most violent of crimes in "Homicide: Behavioral Aspects." This selection will help students gain an appreciation of how their country compares to others. It also presents a brief but useful description of homicide patterns within the United States, as well as a very brief review of the sociological explanations of homicide (described more thoroughly in earlier sections of this volume). Wolfgang has been the most prominent proponent of these cultural explanations (see "The Subculture of Violence" in Part VI). Wolfgang and Zahn categorize a number of theories into what they call "the structuralist position" (consider the theories described in Parts V, VII, and VIII). The theories that they refer to as "interaction theory" are discussed in Part VI under "Labeling Theory," and some aspects of conflict theory would also be included here (Part VIII).

Finally, we have included two selections on drugs and crime, primarily because of the substantial popular misunderstanding about how drug use and criminality are related. Many people fear the drug-crazed criminal, so high that he cannot control his behavior, assaulting or even killing an innocent person. This scenario does occur, but it is most likely when the drug involved is that most popular of all drugs, alcohol. Users of criminalized drugs are far less likely to behave this way, and when they do become involved in crime—prostitution, drug dealing, protecting selling areas, or drug "rip-offs"—it is most often to obtain money for their "habit."

Sam Staley presents a description of the relationships between drugs and crime "Drug Use and Abuse in America," taken from his book *Drug Policy and the Decline of American Cities*. In "The Drug Use–Delinquency Connection in Adolescence," Helene Raskin White addresses contradictions in the literature in this area. One of the major questions that she tackles is, Is the relationship between drug use and crime spurious? That is, might both be caused by some common factor, such as poverty, family breakdown, or poor education? Many people assume that drug-taking leads to crime. Others suspect that involvement in criminal lifestyles cause drug use. In this review, White begins to sort out these answers to the very important question, What is the nature of the relationship between drug use and crime?

WHITE-COLLAR CRIME

White-Collar Criminality

EDWIN H. SUTHERLAND

THIS chapter is concerned with crime in relation to business. The economists are well acquainted with business methods but are not accustomed to consider them from the point of view of crime; many sociologists are well acquainted with crime but are not accustomed to consider it as expressed in business. This chapter is an attempt to integrate these two bodies of knowledge. More accurately stated, it is a comparison of crime in the upper or white-collar class, composed of respectable or at least respected business and professional men, and crime in the lower class, composed of persons of low socioeconomic status. The comparison is made for the purpose of developing the theories of criminal behavior, not for the purpose of muckraking or of reforming anything except criminology.

The criminal statistics show unequivocally that crime, *as popularly conceived and officially measured,* has a high incidence in the lower class and a low incidence in the upper class; less than 2 percent of the persons committed to prisons in a year belong to the upper class. These statistics refer to criminals handled by the police, the criminal and juvenile courts, and the prisons, and to such crimes as murder, assault, burglary, robbery, larceny, sex of-

fenses, and drunkenness, but exclude traffic violations.

The criminologists have used the case histories and criminal statistics derived from these agencies of criminal justice as their principal data. From them, they have derived general theories of criminal behavior. These theories are that, since crime is concentrated in the lower class, it is caused by poverty or by personal and social characteristics believed to be associated statistically with poverty, including feeblemindedness, psychopathic deviations, slum neighborhoods, and "deteriorated" families. This statement, of course, does not do justice to the qualifications and variations in the conventional theories of criminal behavior but it presents correctly their central tendency.

The thesis of this chapter is that the conception and explanations of crime which have just been described are misleading and incorrect, that crime is in fact not closely correlated with poverty or with the psychopathic and sociopathic conditions associated with poverty, and that an adequate explanation of criminal behavior must proceed along quite different lines. The conventional explanations are invalid principally because they are derived from biased samples. The samples are biased in that they have not included vast areas of criminal behavior of persons not in the lower class. One of these neglected areas is the criminal behavior of business and professional men, which will be analyzed in this chapter.

From *Edwin H. Sutherland: On Analyzing Crime* (pp. 130–150) edited by K. Schuessler, 1973, Bloomington, In.: Indiana University Press. Copyright © 1973 by Indiana University Press. Reprinted by permission.

The "robber barons" of the latter half of the nineteenth century were white-collar criminals, as almost everyone now agrees. Their attitudes are readily illustrated. Commodore Vanderbilt asked, "You don't suppose you can run a railroad in accordance with the statutes, do you?" A. B. Stickney, a railroad resident, said to sixteen other railroad presidents in the home of J. P. Morgan in 1890, "I have the utmost respect for you gentlemen, individually, but as railroad presidents I wouldn't trust you with my watch out of my sight." Charles Francis Adams said, "The difficulty in railroad management lies in the covetousness, want of good faith, and low moral tone of railway managers, in the complete absence of any high standard of commercial honesty."

The present-day white-collar criminals, who are more suave and deceptive than the "robber barons," are represented by Kreuger, Stavisky, Whitney, Mitchell, Foshay, Insull, the Van Sweringens, Musica-Coster, Fall, Sinclair, and many other merchant princes and captains of finance and industry and by a host of lesser followers. Their criminality has been demonstrated again and again in the investigations of land offices, railways, insurance, munitions, banking, public utilities, stock exchanges, the oil industry, real estate, reorganization committees, receiverships, bankruptcies, and politics. Individual cases of such criminality are reported frequently, and in many periods more important crime news may be found on the financial pages of newspapers than on the front pages. White-collar criminality is found in every occupation, as can be discovered readily in casual conversation with a representative of an occupation by asking him what crooked practices are found in his occupation.

White-collar criminality in business is expressed most frequently in the form of misrepresentation in financial statements of corporations, manipulation in the stock exchange, commercial bribery, bribery of public officials directly or indirectly in order to secure favorable contracts and legislation, misrepresentation in advertising and salesmanship, em-bezzlement and misapplication of funds, short weights and measures and dishonest grading of commodities, tax frauds, misapplication of funds in receiverships and bankruptcies. These and many others are found in abundance in the business world. They are what Al Capone called "the legitimate rackets."

In the medical profession, which is here used as an example because it probably displays less criminality than some other professions, are found illegal sale of alcohol and narcotics, abortion, illegal services to underworld criminals, fraudulent reports and testimony in accident cases, extreme cases of unnecessary treatment, fake specialists, restriction of competition, and fee splitting. Fee splitting is a violation of specific laws in many states and a violation of the conditions of admission to the practice of medicine in all. The physician who participates in fee splitting tends to send his patients to the surgeon who will give him the largest fee rather than to the surgeon who will do the best work. It has been reported that two-thirds of the surgeons in New York City split fees, and that more than half of the physicians in a central western city who answered a questionnaire on this point favored fee splitting.

These varied types of white-collar crimes in business and the professions consist principally of violation of delegated or implied trust, and many of them can be reduced to two categories: misrepresentation of asset values and duplicity in the manipulation of power. The first is approximately the same as fraud or swindling; the second is similar to the double-cross. The latter is illustrated by the corporation director who, acting on inside information, purchases land which the corporation will need and sells it at a fantastic profit to the corporation. The principle of this duplicity is that the offender holds two antagonistic positions; one of them is a position of trust which is violated, generally by misapplication of funds, in the interest of the other position. A football coach permitted to referee a game in which his own team was playing would illustrate this antagonism of positions. Such situations cannot be completely avoided in a complicated business structure, but many concerns make a practice of assuming such antagonistic functions and of regularly violating a trust thus delegated to them. When compelled by law to make a separation of their functions, they make a nominal separation and continue by subterfuge to maintain the two positions.

An accurate statistical comparison of the crimes of the two classes is not available. The most extensive evidence regarding the nature and prevalence of white-collar criminality is found in the reports of the larger investigations to which reference was made. Because of its scattered character, that evidence is assumed rather than summarized here. A few statements will be presented, as illustrations rather than as proof of the prevalence of this criminality.

The Federal Trade Commission in 1920 reported that commercial bribery was a prevalent and common practice in many industries. In certain chain stores, the net shortage in weights was sufficient to pay 3.4 percent on the investment in those commodities. Of the cans of ether sold to the Army in 1923–1925, 70 percent were rejected because of impurities. In Indiana, during the summer of 1934, 40 percent of the ice-cream samples tested in a routine manner by the Division of Public Health were in violation of law. The Comptroller of the Currency in 1908 reported that violations of law were found in 75 percent of the banks examined in a three-months' period. Lie-detector tests of all employees in several Chicago banks showed that 20 percent of them had stolen bank property, and these tests were supported in almost all cases by confessions. A public accountant estimated, in the period prior to the Securities and Exchange Commission, that 80 percent of the financial statements of corporations were misleading. James M. Beck said, "Diogenes would have been hard put to it to find an honest man in the Wall Street which I knew [in 1916] as a corporation lawyer."

White-collar criminality is generally recognized as fairly prevalent in politics and has been used by some as a rough gauge by which to measure white-collar criminality in business. James A. Fairly pointed out that "the standards of conduct are as high among officeholders and politicians as they are in commercial life," and Cermak, while mayor of Chicago, said, "There is less graft in politics than in business." According to John Flynn, "The average politician is the merest amateur in the gentle art of graft, compared with his brother in the field of business." And Walter Lippmann wrote, "Poor as they are, the standards of public life are so much more social than those of business that financiers who enter politics regard themselves as philanthropists."

These statements obviously do not give a precise measurement of the relative criminality of the white-collar class. They do not mean that all businessmen and professional men are criminals, just as the usual theories do not mean that every man in the lower class is a criminal. The statements are adequate evidence, however, that crime is not so highly concentrated in the lower class as the usual statistics indicate, and they refer in many cases to leading corporations in America and are not restricted to quacks, ambulance chasers, bucket-shop operators, deadbeats, fly-by-night swindlers, and the like.

The financial cost of white-collar crime is probably several times as great as the financial cost of all the crimes which are customarily included in the "crime problem." An officer of a chain grocery store in one year embezzled $600,000, which was six times as much as the annual losses from five hundred burglaries and robberies of the stores in that chain. Public enemies numbered one to six secured $130,000 by burglary and robbery in 1938, while the sum stolen by Kreuger is estimated at $250,000,000, or nearly two thousand times as much. The *New York Times* in 1931 reported four cases of embezzlement in the United States with a loss of more than a million dollars each and a combined loss of nine million dollars. Although a million-dollar burglary or robbery is practically unheard of, million-dollar embezzlers are small fry among white-collar criminals. The estimated loss to investors in one investment trust from 1929 to 1935 was $580,000,000. This loss was due primarily to the fact that 75 percent of the values in the portfolio were in securities of affiliated companies, although the firm in question had advertised the importance of diversification in investments and had provided an investment-counseling service. In Chicago, the claim was made six years ago that householders had lost $54,000,000 in two years during the administration of a city sealer who granted immunity from inspection to stores which provided Christmas baskets for his constituents.

The financial loss from white-collar crime, great as it is, is less important than the damage to social relations. White-collar crimes violate trust and therefore create distrust, which lowers social morale and produces social disorganization on a large scale. Other crimes have relatively little effect on social institutions or social organization.

White-collar crime is real crime. It is not ordinarily called crime, and calling it by this name does not make it worse, just as not calling it crime does not make it better. It is called crime here because it is in violation of the criminal law and belongs within the scope of criminology. The crucial question in this analysis is the criterion of violation of the criminal law. Conviction in the criminal court, which is sometimes suggested as the criterion, is not adequate because a large proportion of those who commit crimes are not convicted in criminal courts. This criterion, therefore, needs to be supplemented. When it is supplemented, the criterion of the crimes of one class must be kept consistent in general terms with the criterion of the crimes of the other class. The definition should not be the spirit of the law for white-collar crimes and the letter of the law for other crimes, or in other respects be more liberal for one class than for the other. Since this discussion is concerned with the conventional theories of the criminologists, the criterion of white-collar crime must be justified in terms of the procedures of those criminologists in dealing with other crimes.

The criterion of white-collar crimes, as here proposed, supplements convictions in the criminal courts in four respects, in each of which the extension is justified because the criminologists who present the conventional theories of criminal behavior make the same extension in principle.

First, other agencies than the criminal court must be included, for the criminal court is not the only agency which makes official decisions regarding violations of the criminal law. The juvenile court dealing largely with offenses of the children of the poor is not in many states under criminal jurisdiction. The criminologists have made much use of case histories and statistics of juvenile delinquents in constructing their theories of criminal behavior. This justifies the inclusion of agencies other than the criminal court which deal with white-collar offenses. The most important of these agencies are the administrative boards, bureaus, or commissions, and much of their work, although certainly not all, consists of cases which are in violation of the criminal law. The Federal Trade Commission ordered several automobile companies to stop advertising their interest rate on installment purchases as 6 percent, since it was actually 11½ percent. Also, it filed complaint against *Good Housekeeping,* one of the Hearst publications, charging that its seals led the public to believe that all products bearing those seals had been tested in their laboratories, which was contrary to fact. Each of these involves a charge of dishonesty which might have been tried in a criminal court as fraud. A large proportion of the cases before these boards should be included in the data of the criminologists. Failure to do so is a principal reason for the bias in their samples and for the errors in their generalizations.

Second, for both classes, behavior which would have a reasonable expectancy of conviction if tried in a criminal court or in a substitute agency should be defined as criminal. In this respect, convictability rather than actual conviction should be the criterion of criminality. The criminologists would not hesitate to accept as data the verified case history of a person who was a criminal but had never been convicted. Similarly, it is justifiable to include white-collar criminals who have not been convicted, provided reliable evidence is available. Evidence regarding such cases appears in many civil suits, such as stockholders' suits and patent-infringement suits. These cases, which might have been referred to the criminal court, were referred to the civil court because the injured party was more interested in securing damages than in seeing punishment inflicted. This also happens in embezzlement cases, regarding which surety companies have much evidence. In a short consecutive series of embezzlements known to a surety company, 90 percent were not prosecuted because prosecution would have interfered with restitution or salvage. The evidence in cases of embezzlement is generally conclusive and would probably have been sufficient to justify conviction in all the cases in this series.

Third, behavior should be defined as criminal if conviction is avoided merely because of pressure which is brought to bear on the court or substitute agency. Gangsters and racketeers have been relatively immune in many cities, because of their pressure on prospective witnesses and public officials, and professional thieves, such as pickpockets and confidence men who do not use strong-arm methods, are even more frequently immune because of their ability to influence police action. The conventional criminologists do not hesitate to include the life histories of such criminals as data, because they understand the generic relation of the pressures to the failure to convict. Similarly, white-collar criminals are relatively immune because of the class bias of the courts and the power of their class to influence the implementation and administration of the law. This class bias not only affects present-day courts but to a much greater degree affected the earlier courts which established the precedents and rules of procedure of the present-day courts. Consequently, it is justifiable to interpret the actual or potential failures of conviction in the light of known facts regarding the pressures brought to bear on the agencies which deal with offenders.

Fourth, persons who are accessory to a crime should be included among white-collar criminals as they are among other criminals. When the Federal Bureau of Investigation deals with a case of kidnapping, it is not content with catching the offenders who carried away the victim; it may arrest and the court may convict twenty-five other persons who assisted by secreting the victim, negotiating the ransom, or putting the ransom money into circulation. On the other hand, the prosecution of white-collar criminals frequently stops with one offender. Political graft almost always involves collusion between politicians and businessmen, but prosecutions are generally limited to the politicians. Judge Manton was found guilty of accepting $664,000 in bribes, but the six or eight important commercial concerns that paid the bribes have not been prosecuted. Pendergast, the late boss of Kansas City, was convicted for failure to report as a part of his income $315,000 received in bribes from insurance companies, but the insurance companies which paid the bribes have not been prosecuted. In an investigation of embezzlement by the president of a bank, at least a dozen other violations of law which were related to this embezzlement and involved most of the other officers of the bank and the officers of the clearinghouse were discovered, but none of the others was prosecuted.

This analysis of the criterion of white-collar criminality results in the conclusion that a description of white-collar criminality in general terms will also be a description of the criminality of the lower class. The crimes of the two classes differ in incidentals rather than essentials. They differ principally in the implementation of the criminal laws which apply to them. The crimes of the lower class are handled by policemen, prosecutors, and judges with penal sanctions in the form of fines, imprisonment, and death. The crimes of the upper class either result in no official action at all or result in suits for damages in civil courts or are handled by inspectors and by administrative boards or commissions with penal sanctions in the form of warnings, orders to cease and desist, occasional rescinding of a license, and in extreme cases with fines or prison sentences. Thus, the white-collar criminals are segregated administratively from other criminals, and largely as a consequence of this are not regarded as real criminals by themselves, by the general public, or by the criminologists.

This difference in the implementation of the criminal law is due chiefly to the disparity in social position of the two kinds of offenders. Judge Woodward, when imposing sentence upon the officials of H. O. Stone and Company (a bankrupt real estate firm in Chicago), who had been convicted in 1933 of the use of the mails to defraud, said to them, "You are men of affairs, of experience, of refinement and culture, of excellent reputation and standings in the business and social world." That statement might be used as a general characterization of white-collar criminals, for they are oriented basically to legitimate and respectable careers. Because of their social status, they have a loud voice in determining what goes into the statutes and how the criminal law as it affects themselves is implemented and administered. This may be illustrated from the Pure Food and Drug Law. Between 1879 and 1906, 140 pure food and drug bills were presented in Congress, and all failed because of the importance of the persons who would be affected. It took a highly dramatic performance by Dr. Wiley in 1906 to induce Congress to enact the law. The law, however, did not create a new crime, just as the federal kidnapping law which grew out of the Lindbergh case did not create a new crime; the Pure Food and Drug Law merely provided a more efficient implementation of a principle which had been formulated previously in state laws. When an amendment to this law, which would have brought within the scope of its agents fraudulent statements made over the radio or in the press, was presented to Congress, the publishers and advertisers organized support and sent a lobby to Washington which successfully fought the amendment principally under the slogans of "freedom of the press" and "dangers of bureaucracy." This proposed amendment, also, would not have created a new crime, for the state laws already prohibited fraudulent statements over the radio or in the press; it would have implemented the law so that it could have been enforced. Finally, the administration has not been able to enforce the law as it has desired because of the pressures by the offenders against the law, sometimes brought to bear through the head of the Department of Agriculture, sometimes through congressmen who threaten cuts in the appropriation, and sometimes by others. A statement made by Daniel Drew describes the criminal law with some accuracy: "Law is like a cobweb; it's made for flies and the smaller kinds of insects, so to speak, but lets the big bumblebees break through. When technicalities of the law stood in my way I have always been able to brush them aside as easy as anything."

The preceding analysis should be regarded neither as an assertion that all efforts to influence legislation and its administration are reprehensible nor as a particularistic interpretation of the criminal law. It means only that the upper class has greater influence in molding the criminal law and its administration to its own interests than does the lower class. The privileged position of white-collar criminals before the law results to a slight extent from bribery and political pressures, but largely from the respect in which such men are held and without special effort on their part. The most powerful group in medieval society secured relative immunity by "benefit of clergy," and now our most powerful groups secure relative immunity by "benefit of business or profession."

In contrast, with the power of the white-collar criminals is the weakness of their victims. Consumers, investors, and stockholders are unorganized, lack technical knowledge, and cannot protect themselves. Daniel Drew, after taking a large sum of money by sharp practice from Vanderbilt in the Erie deal, concluded that it was a mistake to take money from a powerful man on the same level as himself and declared that in the future he would confine his efforts to outsiders, scattered all over the country, who would not be able to organize and fight back. White-collar criminality flourishes at points where powerful businessmen and professional men come in contact with persons who are weak. In this respect, it is similar to stealing candy from a baby. Many of the crimes of the lower class, on the other hand, are committed, in the form of burglary and robbery, against persons of wealth and power. Because of this difference in the comparative power of the victims, the white-collar criminals enjoy relative immunity.

Embezzlement is an interesting exception to white-collar criminality, in this respect. Embezzlement is usually theft from an employer by an employee, and the employee is less capable of manipulating social and legal forces in his own interest than is the employer. As might have been expected, the laws regarding embezzlement were formulated long before laws for the protection of investors and consumers.

The theory that criminal behavior in general is due either to poverty or to the psychopathic and sociopathic conditions associated with poverty can now be shown to be invalid for three reasons. First, the generalization is based on a biased sample which omits almost entirely the behavior of white-collar criminals. For reasons of convenience and ignorance rather than of principle, criminologists have restricted their data largely to cases dealt with in criminal courts and juvenile courts and these agencies are used principally for criminals from the lower economic strata. Consequently, the criminologists' data are grossly biased in respect to the economic status of criminals, and the generalization that criminality is closely associated with poverty is not justified.

Second, the generalization is inapplicable to white-collar criminals. With a small number of exceptions, they are not poor, were not reared in slums or badly deteriorated families, and are not feebleminded or psychopathic. The proposition, derived from the data used by the conventional criminologists that "the criminal of today was the problem child of yesterday," is seldom true of white-collar criminals. The idea that the causes of criminality are to be found almost exclusively in childhood is also fallacious. Even if poverty is extended to include the economic stresses which afflict business in a period of depression, it is not closely correlated with white-collar criminality. Probably at no time within the last fifty years have white-collar crimes in the field of investments and corporate management been so extensive as during the boom period of the 1920s.

Third, the generalization does not explain lower-class criminality. The sociopathic and psychopathic factors which have been emphasized doubtless have something to do with crime causation, but these factors have not been related to a general process which is found both in white-collar criminality and lower-class criminality; therefore, they do not explain the criminality of either class, although they may explain the manner or method of crime—why lower-class criminals commit burglary or robbery rather than crimes involving misrepresentation.

In view of these defects in the conventional theories, a hypothesis that will explain both white-collar criminality and lower-class criminality is needed. For reasons of economy, simplicity, and logic, the hypothesis should apply to both classes, for this will make possible the analysis of causal factors freed from the encumbrances of the administrative devices which have led criminologists astray. Shaw and McKay and others, working exclusively in the field of lower-class crime, have found the conventional theories inadequate to account for variations within the data of lower-class crime and with that difficulty in mind have been working toward an explanation of crime in terms of a more general social process. Such efforts will be greatly aided by the procedure which has been described.

The hypothesis suggested here as a substitute for the conventional theories is that white-collar criminality, just as other systematic criminality, is learned; that it is learned in direct or indirect association with those who already practice criminal behavior; and that those who learn this criminal behavior are segregated from frequent and intimate contacts with law-abiding behavior. Whether a person becomes a criminal or not is determined largely by the comparative frequency and intimacy of his contacts with the two types of behavior. This may be called the process of differential association. It is a genetic explanation both of white-collar criminality and lower-class criminality. Those who become white-collar criminals generally start their careers in good neighborhoods and good homes, graduate from colleges with some idealism, and, with little selection on their part, get into particular business situations in which criminality is practically a folkway and are inducted into that system of behavior just as into any other folkway. The lower-class criminals generally start their careers in deteriorated neighborhoods and families, find delinquents at hand from whom they acquire the attitudes toward, and techniques of, crime. The essentials of this process are the same for the two classes of criminals. This is not entirely a process of assimilation, for inventions are frequently made, perhaps more frequently in white-collar crime than in lower-class crime. The inventive geniuses for the lower-class criminals are generally professional criminals, while the inventive geniuses for many kinds of white-collar crime are generally lawyers.

A second general process is social disorganization in the community. Differential association culminates in crime because the community is not organized solidly against that form of behavior. The law is pressing in one direction, and other forces are pressing in the opposite direction. In business, the "rules of the game" conflict with the legal rules. A businessman who wants to obey the law is driven by his competitors to adopt their methods. This is well illustrated by the persistence of commercial bribery in spite of the strenuous efforts of business organizations to eliminate it. Groups and individuals, however, are more concerned with their specialized group or individual interests than with the larger welfare. Consequently, it is not possible for the community to present a solid front in opposition to crime. The better business bureaus and crime commissions, composed of professional men and businessmen, attack burglary, robbery, and cheap swindles but overlook the crimes of their own members. The forces which impinge on the lower class are similarly in conflict. Social disorganization affects the two classes in similar ways.

I have presented a brief and general description of white-collar criminality on a framework of argument regarding theories of criminal behavior. That argument, stripped of the description, may be stated in the following propositions:

1. White-collar criminality is real criminality, being in all cases a violation of the criminal law.
2. White-collar criminality differs from lower-class criminality principally in an implementation of the criminal law which segregates white-collar criminals administratively from other criminals.
3. The theories of the criminologists that crime is due to poverty or to psychopathic and sociopathic conditions statistically associated with poverty are invalid for three reasons: first, they are derived from samples which are grossly biased with respect to socioeconomic status; second, they do not apply to white-collar criminals; and third, they do not even explain the criminality of the lower class, since the factors are not related to a general process characteristic of all criminality.
4. A theory of criminal behavior which will explain both white-collar criminality and lower-class criminality is needed.
5. A hypothesis of this nature is suggested in terms of differential association and social disorganization.

QUESTIONS FOR DISCUSSION AND WRITING

1. What are the two categories of white-collar crime?
2. How do the costs of white-collar crime relate to those for other crimes?
3. Who "handles" the crimes of the lower class? Those by the upper class?

The Criminal Elite

JAMES W. COLEMAN

THE problem of white-collar crime is rooted in the social conflicts of industrial society. One of the most important of these is class conflict, and especially the struggle for power and profits waged between the dominant elite and the less privileged strata of society. Most of the laws creating organizational crimes were the product of the interaction between the efforts of farmers, consumers, workers, or the general public to limit abuses of the elite and the response of the elite to those social movements. The origins of the laws prohibiting occupational crimes such as embezzlement and employee pilferage can, on the other hand, be traced to the efforts to protect the interests of much more privileged groups by regulating the behavior of the lower classes. The same class conflicts can also be seen in the enforcement process, for example, in the success the elite has had in weakening the enforcement of legislation that threatens its interests or its use of law enforcement as a tool to suppress the political activities of its critics.

But the battle lines do not always coincide so neatly with the divisions of the class system. Environmental protection is apt to be as beneficial to the upper class as the lower. A specific antitrust action may benefit some corporate interests while harming others. And in many occupational crimes, the victims and the offenders come from the same social strata.

From *The Criminal Elite, Third Edition* (pp. 234–254) by J. Coleman, 1994, New York: St. Martin's Press. Copyright © 1994 by St. Martin's Press, Inc. Reprinted with permission of Bedford/St. Martin's Press, Inc.

The laws defining the white-collar crimes have diverse historical origins, but all of them can ultimately be traced back to the dislocations and conflicts caused by the growth of industrial capitalism. Antitrust legislation was a response to the economic squeeze put on small farmers and business people by the growth of the giant corporations. Consumer protection laws can be seen as substitutes for the informal controls that regulated commerce in small-town America. Legislation regulating political campaigns formed part of an effort to maintain and improve democratic institutions in the face of the growing centralization of economic power. Worker and environmental protection legislation can be traced to the recognition of the dangerous side effects of industrial technology. But such problems do not automatically generate new legislation. Rather, legislative change comes about as a result of the conflict between organized interest groups.

Most white-collar crime legislation has been the product of struggles between popular mass movements (with occasional support from some segments of the upper class) and entrenched elite interests. The efforts of the antimonopoly, populist, consumer, and environmental movements all fit a similar pattern. At first, the reformers encounter a stone wall of elite opposition that frustrates their efforts. But if the movement is able to take advantage of such factors as well-publicized disasters and scandals, widespread popular support, and effective organization and leadership, they may ultimately win passage of new legislation. Yet even when elite interests fail to defeat reform legislation, they still exert great influence in shaping its final form.

The prohibition of such activities as embezzlement and industrial espionage followed a different pattern, which might be called "reform from the top." Because the changes were initiated by elite interests, they did not require popular pressure for enactment. Indeed, many of these reforms arose from new judicial interpretations that involved no changes in statutory law. When new laws were created, the legislative process generally occurred with a minimum of public involvement and without great media attention.

The passage of new legislation is not, as it is so often pictured, the end of the struggle for reform—it is the beginning. The same interests continue their conflict, this time over control of the enforcement process. And in this second struggle, elite interests are in an even stronger position than they are in the legislative arena. Despite the elite's power to manipulate the media, the political process is far more open to public view than the enforcement bureaucracy, and the voting power of the masses may help counter the political influence that inevitably flows from vast concentrations of wealth and power. However, the popular appeal of reformist movements is of considerably less strategic significance in influencing the enforcement process.

A comparison of the treatment of white-collar criminals and street criminals demonstrates the justice system's double standard. For one thing, white-collar criminals are much less likely to be arrested. And even if they are arrested and convicted, white-collar criminals typically receive much lighter punishment than those who have committed street crimes of equal severity. Despite this overall pattern of leniency, many occupational criminals do receive jail sentences or other meaningful punishment, but the same is seldom true of those involved in organizational crimes. Organizational criminals are usually given nothing more than a warning or an order to stop their illegal activities. Even when punishments are meted out, in most cases they involve only small fines that do not even equal the profit the offenders made from their crimes.

The reasons for this unequal justice can be traced to the great structural advantages enjoyed by white-collar criminals. For one thing, the organization of the justice system favors the white-collar criminal. The investigation of occupational crimes is usually left in the hands of small, understaffed "fraud units" in the offices of state or local prosecutors, whereas local police departments with much greater investigative resources largely ignore the problem. Influential professions such as law and medicine have won broad powers of self-regulation that often serve as a shield against outside "interference" from the criminal justice system. And finally, most white-collar defendants in criminal or civil court enjoy the advantages of wealth, prestige, and the best legal representation.

The responsibility for most organizational crimes has been shifted away from the criminal justice system to specially created regulatory agencies that are more inclined to negotiate cooperative settlements than to pursue tough criminal sanctions. Moreover, elite interests have generally been successful in preventing the allocation of sufficient resources to those agencies to enable them to carry out their legislative mandates effectively. Regulatory agencies are almost always underfunded and understaffed, especially in comparison with the vast resources at the disposal of the corporate offenders they must police. In criminal cases, organizational offenders also benefit from the individualistic bias of our legal system, which often makes it necessary to sift through complex networks of organizational interactions in order to prove the criminal intent of each individual defendant.

Compared to other offenders, the social and political power of corporate criminals puts them in an entirely different position vis-à-vis the justice system. Corporate criminals often have the strength to fend off, wear down, or even overpower the enforcement effort. Delaying tactics have proven to be one of the corporate criminal's most effective strategies. Whereas the strength of the enforcement effort waxes and wanes with the changes in the political climate, the profit-seeking private corporation never wavers in the pursuit of its own interests. Thus, corporate criminals seek to delay legal proceedings as long as possible, while waiting for a change in the political climate that will let them off the hook. In some cases, powerful corporate criminals use direct intimidation, threatening to close a large plant or to move overseas if enforcement agencies do not adopt a more "reasonable" attitude. In others, they attempt to corrupt individual officials with the lure of highpaying jobs in private industry, big campaign contributions, or sometimes even outright bribes.

Secrecy is one tool used by white-collar and street criminals alike. But white-collar criminals, and especially organizational criminals, enjoy some important advantages in its use. For one thing, the victims of white-collar crime are often unaware of the causes of their problems and thus cannot complain to enforcement agencies. Another major advantage enjoyed by organizational criminals is the wall of secrecy that corporations and government agencies build to protect themselves from outside scrutiny. In many cases, there is a legitimate need to protect sensitive information, but the same security measures can also serve to conceal illegal activities.

It would be easy to conclude that the principal cause of white-collar crime is the offenders' knowledge that they run little risk of significant punishment, but the matter is a good deal more complex than that. It is as necessary to explain the motivations of the offenders and the structure of illicit opportunities as it is to account for the failure of the mechanisms of social control. No monocausal explanation can account for the complex interrelationships between the social-psychological and structural variables that lie at the root of the problem of white-collar crime.

On the social-psychological level, individuals are pushed toward white-collar crime by the same craving for money and success that motivates so many other crimes. Such motivations are often combined with pressures, exerted by occupational subcultures or superiors, that encourage or even demand illegal activities. The occupational subculture in many urban police departments, for example, requires officers to participate in some petty corruption if they want to be considered "one of the gang." Similar pressures are often brought to bear on government or corporate employees to carry on criminal activities for the sake of their organizations.

The combination of such motivations can create strong psychological pressure to become involved in white-collar crime; however, a belief in moral or ethical principles often generates a powerful contravening force of its own. Thus, the way an individual resolves this conflict will obviously have a great influence on his or her potential for criminal behavior. White-collar offenders use a variety of common rationalizations to neutralize those ethical standards and maintain a positive self-image despite their deviant behavior. Typically, they justify their behavior by telling themselves that no one is really being harmed by their activities, that the laws are unjust, that some criminal activities are necessary for economic survival, that everybody else is doing it, or that they deserve the extra money their crimes produce.

Although many criminologists are content with such personal explanations, the roots of these psychological forces lie in the structure of contemporary industrial society. The desire for wealth and success, more than merely an individual personality trait, is part of the culture of competition found to one degree or another in all industrial societies. These societies generate large economic surpluses and are characterized by high degrees of inequality, yet unlike agricultural societies, they also have considerable social mobility. This combination inevitably encourages the desire to outdo one's fellows in the accumulation of material goods and the symbols of success. Moreover, the competitive nature of economic organization in capitalist nations serves to further strengthen the culture of competition in its position as a dominant cultural force.

The political economy of industrial capitalism and the diverse interest groups it creates also structure the definitions of criminal behavior. And once the laws and the enforcement priorities have been set, structural variables also determine the distribution of the most attractive opportunities for white-collar crime. Thus, crime rates in the pharmaceutical and automotive industries are high because the dangers associated with their products create strong public pressure for government regulation and, thereby, the temptation to violate those regulations. In a more general way, the demand for profitability the economic system places on all private businesses is a primary motivation for organizational crime. A business must make profits in order to survive and prosper, and criminal activities often provide an effective way of making those profits.

WHAT CAN BE DONE?

Crime, as Emile Durkheim pointed out long ago, is inevitable in modern societies. The function of criminal law is to create crime by branding certain people and certain behaviors as deviant. A law that no one broke would be an unnecessary law. Thus, a certain amount of white-collar crime is inevitable in any society that bases its legal system on standards that apply to all social strata. But as we have seen, the incidence of white-collar crime goes far beyond this inevitable minimum. No other kind of crime—and indeed, few problems of any sort—can even approach the hundreds of thousands of lives and billions of dollars lost every year through white-collar crime.

The aim of this section is to explore some of the ways of dealing with this pressing problem. Although its conclusions are based on the preceding analysis, a crystal ball is not part of the standard inventory of sociological tools. The sociology of deviance has shown the unexpected damage done by past efforts to deal with such problems as drug use and prostitution through criminal law, and there are no guarantees that any of the following proposals would have the desired effects. Yet there is good reason to believe that the growing body of research into the problem of white-collar crime can help us avoid the mistakes of the moral crusaders of the past.

Ethical Reforms

One of the most common reactions to the news of some heinous crime is to ask, "What kind of a person would do such a thing?" and to blame the crime on the moral failings of the criminal. Sociologists have long opposed such one-sidedly individualistic explanations, and they are especially suspect when applied to white-collar crime. Organizations and occupational subcultures generate powerful pressures on employees to conform to their expectations, and any effort to deal with the problem of white-collar crime on this level must be aimed at changing the "ethical climate" within the corporations and the government. DeFleur argued that "because it is impossible to police everyone . . . a reduction in illegal corporate behavior depends on the development of stronger codes of ethics in business." But how can that be done? He recommended three ways in which those goals might be met: (1) courses in ethics should be made mandatory in business schools, (2) trade associations should establish uniform ethical codes for each industry, and (3) individual corporations should make systematic efforts to develop ethical codes and instill them in their employees.

To more structurally oriented sociologists, however, such proposals appear extremely naive. It is hard to imagine that a single college class, or even a series of them, would be likely to stimulate achievement-oriented young managers to defy the expectations of the organizations on whose approval their futures depend. It is equally difficult to imagine that an industry trade association would promulgate *any* standards of behavior that ran counter to the financial interests of its members, or that the members would follow the standards if they did. High-sounding codes of ethics may make for good public relations, but by themselves they are unlikely to have any effect on the "ethical climate" of the government or the business world. After a careful statistical comparison of corporations with codes of ethics with explicit penalties, corporations with codes but without penalties, and corporations with no codes at all, Marilynn Mathews concluded that "it just didn't make a difference."

A structural analysis suggests that ethical standards will change only when the structural rewards for unethical behavior change. What is necessary, then, is some way to make ethical behavior more rewarding than criminal behavior. The most obvious course of action would be to increase the civil and criminal penalties for such offenses, and we will examine those alternatives in the following section. Christopher Stone, Donald Cressey, and others have proposed another approach—the creation of a public award given to corporations that maintain proper ethical standards. Such awards would be highly publicized, and corporations would be encouraged to use them in advertising campaigns. Corporations that fail to meet ethical standards would then face negative publicity, especially since their competitors would be free to advertise their ethical superiority. This proposal still leaves many unanswered questions concerning the nature of those ethical standards and the best ways to evaluate corporate performance, but it does merit further study. A similar proposal made by W. Brent Fisse would also use publicity as a sanction against corporate offenses, but instead of a public award, he calls for new legislation requiring convicted corporate offenders to pay for advertising that would inform the public of their offenses.

Because occupational criminals are not supported by large impersonal organizations, individual ethical standards are probably more important in controlling their behavior. Tougher punishments would once again be helpful, but there are limits to the effectiveness of even a well-organized and well-financed criminal justice system. As long as the culture of competition remains a central part of our culture, the level of occupational crime is likely to remain high. There are, of course, alternative value systems, both religious and secular, that stress the ethics of cooperation. But a significant weakening of the culture of competition would have to be accompanied by changes in the structural relations that support it. Such a change is by no means impossible—and perhaps not even unlikely—but cultural evolution of this sort tends to be a painfully slow process.

Enforcement Reforms

Of all the reforms discussed here, the idea that white-collar criminals must be more severely punished is probably the most widely accepted. But there are many different proposals, and none of them has won universal acceptance by experts and political activists. Foremost among these suggestions are the calls for greater resources and new priorities for enforcement agencies, a greater effort to isolate those agencies from outside political pressures, and legislation that is less ambiguous and easier to enforce.

Regulatory agencies and prosecutors are often hopelessly outmatched by their corporate opponents, who command larger and more skilled legal staffs and much greater financial support. There are too few government inspectors to detect more than a small fraction of the pollutants illegally released into the environment, and the same is true of occupational health and safety hazards and dangerous consumer products. The regulatory agencies even lack the resources to test most potentially dangerous substances so that appropriate regulations can be promulgated. To remedy this situation, regulatory and enforcement agencies must be given very substantial increases in their budgets. Certainly, funding at five or ten times the current levels would not be out of line with the importance of the problem. The most pressing needs are for larger research budgets to permit regulatory agencies to actively search out threats to public health and safety before disaster strikes; for substantial increases in the ranks of the investigators and prosecutors; and for higher pay for the legal, medical, and scientific personnel who now are often lured away to higher-paying jobs in private industry. Greater support is also needed for the local agencies that bear the primary responsibility for dealing with occupational crimes.

An increase in resources must be accompanied by a greater effort to insulate enforcement agencies from undue political pressure. Although there appears to be no certain way to achieve that end, several possibilities have been suggested. First, along with an increase in pay, the employees of regulatory agencies could be required to sign an agreement, backed up by explicit legal penalties, promising never to work for any of the firms that fall under their regulatory jurisdiction. Currently, there is a two-year moratorium on such employment changes, but many people believe that a longer time period is necessary and that the regulatory agencies would be better off without an employee who would refuse to sign such an agreement. Second, in order to defuse the threat of punitive budgetary cutbacks for agencies that offend powerful special interests, as well as to lighten the financial burden on the public, enforcement and regulatory agencies could be made more self-supporting. This could be accomplished by legislation requiring that convicted offenders pay the full cost of the government's investigation and prosecution. This money, along with any punitive fines, would then be turned over to the agencies involved in the case.

The current system of fines and penalties needs restructuring for another reason as well. Far too often, penalties do not even equal the profits made from an organizational crime, much less pose a credible deterrent. To resolve this problem, the laws could be rewritten to require that convicted corporate offenders automatically pay a penalty at least equal to the amount of profit they made from their illegal

activities. The judge or hearing officer would also be given the authority to impose additional punitive fines as appropriate. Where violent offenses are involved, much stiffer financial penalties are called for—perhaps based on the severity of the injuries and the number of deaths the offenders caused.

Many criminologists believe that even large fines have little impact on organizational crime, because corporate offenders merely pass them on to their customers in the form of higher prices. This is indeed a problem in some cases, but it is not always so. In a competitive industry, a corporate offender may be unable to pass on the cost of the fines to its customers, thus resulting in lower profits and trouble for top management. Fines are likely to have less impact in more oligopolistic industries, but if the penalties were sufficiently large and were assessed on only a single member of the oligopoly, they might still have the desired effect.

Other critics have charged that the imposition of large financial penalties may force some offenders into bankruptcy, thus punishing the innocent along with the guilty. There is little doubt that financial penalties based on a realistic estimate of the damage done by organizational crime would indeed cause some firms to go bankrupt. But there are good grounds for believing that such an event would ultimately work to the public good. Although some workers might lose their jobs, the assets of bankrupt firms do not vanish, they are purchased by other businesses. Most of the workers probably would be quickly rehired, it is hoped, by a more reputable employer. If necessary, new legislation could be enacted mandating the bankruptcy courts to take special action to protect the interests of the workers in such cases. Stockholders would suffer a more permanent loss, but that is part of the risk investors take when they buy stocks rather than invest in more secure investments such as insured bank accounts. The example of a major corporation being forced into bankruptcy because of the penalties for its criminal behavior would certainly pose a powerful deterrent to other offenders and might also spur stockholders to monitor the activities of management more closely.

Another promising approach focuses on prevention rather than punishment. The idea here is to penetrate the organizational shell of the corporate offender by placing enforcement agents in a position to make it impossible for a corporation to repeat its crimes. For example, a firm that has committed repeated environmental violations would be required to pay the cost of hiring enough government inspectors to continually monitor the firm's compliance with the law. In order for such a system to function effectively, it would probably be necessary to rotate the inspectors periodically to prevent them from becoming too closely identified with a single firm.

There are also a number of ways in which current laws could be changed to improve the effectiveness of the enforcement effort. A simple modification of the laws concerning mergers could greatly strengthen the government's antitrust efforts. Instead of the current requirement that the government prove that a proposed merger would tend to restrain trade or create a monopoly, new legislation could simply forbid all mergers by the nation's five hundred or so largest corporations. Specific exemptions might then be granted if the firms involved could show that the proposed merger would have beneficial economic and social effects.

Under a bill introduced by Senator Edward Kennedy in 1979, corporations with over $2.5 billion in sales or $2 billion in assets would have been prohibited from merging, no matter how different their lines of business. Corporations with $350 million to $2.5 billion in sales and $200 million to $2 billion in assets would have had to prove that the proposed merger would lead to greater efficiency and more competition. Not only would such legislation simplify the current enforcement procedures and encourage competition, but it could be expected to yield other economic benefits as well. By reducing the tendency of big corporations to simply buy up an existing firm when

they want to enter a new line of business, laws of this kind would encourage U.S. firms to build new plants and buy new equipment.

Lawyers associated with Ralph Nader have drawn up a much broader piece of legislation that has been proposed for adoption in several states. Were this model legislation, titled "The Corporate Deviance Act," enacted by a significant number of states, it would certainly strike a forceful blow at corporate criminality. Among other things, it would make it a felony for a corporation to conceal any product or process that might cause death or injury, and it would also make it a crime to retaliate against "whistle-blowers" seeking to inform the public about such activities. A business license would be made contingent on the "good character" of the corporation and could be denied if the state found a consistent pattern of unethical or illegal activities. The legislation would require corporations to provide workers, consumers, and public with all available information about any hazards their activities may create.

Another approach would be to enact legislation mandating the licensing of executives of the major corporations, in the same way we license other professionals. Such a license need not be difficult to obtain. A simple test on the legal and ethical requirements of corporate management would be sufficient. The main value of this licensing system would be to create a mechanism for disbarring corporate officers who violate their ethical obligations. A special regulatory agency might be established to hear the cases against individual executives. If the evidence warranted, the hearing officer would be empowered to prohibit an offender from working for any major corporation for a fixed number of years. Although many disbarment cases would undoubtedly be appealed to the federal courts, such a procedure would provide a means of sanctioning executive misconduct without having to prove criminal intent.

One largely untapped resource in the battle against organizational crime can be found in the outside auditors whom publicly traded firms must hire to examine their financial reports. These auditors are obviously in an excellent position to uncover many types of corporate illegalities. However, the American Institute of Certified Public Accountants, along with most individual practitioners, has traditionally held that "the normal audit arrangement is not designed to detect fraud and cannot be relied upon to do so." Outside auditors face a built-in conflict of interest, for although their employer is an independent firm, it is still paid by the corporation whose books they are examining. Hence, a firm that gains a reputation for "overzealousness" in checking for corporate illegalities might find itself losing many important clients. The attitude of most accounting firms is reflected in the following statement by one member of a major firm: "We are not required to audit below the normal levels of materiality in search for illegal payments. *Our responsibility in this connection is to our clients.* It does not extend to informing the SEC [Securities and Exchange Commission] about immaterial payments if we find them. We are not police for the commission."

Auditors may not be policemen, but they are in a unique position to assist law enforcement, and a few basic reforms could greatly enhance their role in protecting the public from corporate fraud. Auditors could be legally required to search out fraud and deception in corporate financial statements and to report any suspected illegalities to enforcement agencies. But in order to carry out this new role, the accounting firms would have to be insulated from their clients' financial pressures. To achieve this goal, major corporations could be required to pay an audit fee to a government clearinghouse, which would then select the firm to do the actual audit. Thus, the auditors would feel no undue pressure to compromise the integrity of their report.

Honest employees who refuse to accept the idea that illegal activities are necessary to get the job done can be another important ally in the fight against white-collar crime. But to win their help, a strong new law protecting the whistle-blowers who report the crimes of their employers is needed. Such legislation would make it a crime to retaliate against whistle-blowers in any way and require that substantial punitive damages be paid to the victim of such an action.

According to polls, the public is most concerned about white-collar crimes that cause direct physical harm to people. It therefore makes sense to give such crimes as environmental pollution, occupational safety violations, and the manufacture of unsafe products a high priority in the enforcement effort. Those same polls show that the public believes that such violent white-collar crimes deserve punishments as severe as those given for violent street crimes. A much more vigorous effort is therefore needed to investigate, prosecute, and imprison violent white-collar offenders. For example, a greater volume of cases is necessary to establish clear legal precedents for the prosecution of negligent corporate executives for criminal manslaughter and to make such legal actions a routine and expected response to violent organizational crime.

"Supply side" economists have taken a very different approach to enforcement reform, arguing that the government ought not to be involved in economic regulation at all. They would write most white-collar crimes out of existence and allow the economic system to operate on its own. Advocates of this position have argued that consumers can regulate unsafe products by refusing to buy them, that workers can regulate occupational safety by refusing to work at unsafe jobs, and so on. In this view, environmental pollution could be controlled through some system of taxation on emissions, so that corporations can decide whether or not to install antipollution devices on economic grounds. Although such a program of deregulation would eliminate many white-collar crime by legal fiat, it is hard to imagine how it could help resolve the underlying problems that led to the creation of those laws. If it were true that an unfettered market naturally takes care of such problems, those laws would never have been enacted in the first place.

Another attack on the regulatory system came from President Reagan in February 1981, when he issued an executive order requiring a special cost/benefit analysis before any new regulation is put into effect. The goal of this cost/benefit analysis is to reduce "regulatory unreasonableness" and the burden the latter allegedly places on American business. Our previous analysis has shown, however, that the regulatory process has always been most sensitive to the interests of the businesses being regulated, and that regulatory inaction is a much greater problem than regulatory unreasonableness. The imposition of one more level of review to the already cumbersome rule-making procedure only aggravates the failures of the enforcement process.

Structural Reforms

Criminologists have long held that the best way to deal with any kind of crime is to attack it at the source rather than to rely on the criminal justice system to punish the offenders after the fact, and that is exactly what proposals for structural reforms try to do. Yet these proposals are highly controversial, both because they have strong ideological implications and because they threaten powerful vested interests. Nevertheless, this approach offers some of the most promising avenues for achieving long-range solutions to the problem of white-collar crime.

Many proposals for dealing with organizational crime involve basic changes in corporate structure to reduce the incentives for illegal activities, or at least to make them more difficult. Christopher Stone has proposed that public representatives be added to the boards of directors of all the major corporations. These directors would have their own staffs and be charged not only with representing the public interest in the boardroom but also with supervising corporate behavior, hearing complaints, and uncovering corporate illegalities. In a variation on this idea, several European nations, including Sweden and West Germany, now require worker representation on corporate boards. Such worker representatives might well be combined with Stone's public representatives to further broaden the spectrum of interests participating in corporate decision making.

How effective would these new board members be at making corporations more responsible? Studies of the European experience have shown that worker representation on corporate boards has not brought radical changes in corporate policies, for the new board members' main concerns have been in the areas of job security and working conditions. Thus, there is reason to doubt that, in itself, worker representation in corporate decision making would do much to improve the integrity of the business, discourage environmental pollution, or encourage safer products. Impetus for such reforms must come from public representatives. But as long as stockholders continue to dominate corporate boards, the likelihood of major internal reforms is obviously limited. If, however, the worker representatives and the public representatives worked together, and their combined votes exceeded those of the stockholders, some fundamental changes might then occur.

Ralph Nader's Corporate Accountability Research Group has argued that much stricter standards of corporate accountability can be imposed by means of the chartering process. But if an individual state tried to impose tough new standards under the current chartering system, major corporations would simply move their headquarters to other states that gave them a better deal. The Nader group therefore proposed a system of federal chartering that would prevent corporations from playing one state off against another. Under the Nader proposal, the federal chartering agency would require corporate boards to take a much more active role in guiding firms. The boards also would be expanded to include worker representatives, and the corporations would be required to give the public much greater access to their records on such things as product safety research, plant emissions, and plans for factory closings.

However it is achieved, a freer flow of information among top management, corporate directors, regulatory agencies, and the general public would help discourage corporate crime and make the enforcement agencies' job an easier one. Too often, top managers and directors are able to cultivate selective ignorance about the criminal activities of their subordinates, the dangerous emissions of their plants, or the hazards of their products. Today, corporate spokesmen who make false public statements that cause serious harm to others can avoid criminal liability for fraud simply by claiming that they honestly believed their statements to be true.

One way to deal with this problem would be to require corporate decision makers to review explicit reports on such things as product safety research, environmental pollution, and unethical practices. As those reports moved up the chain of command, officials at each level would be required to describe their effort to conform to legal regulations and to report any knowledge they have of possible illegalities. After the reports had been signed by the corporate board, they would be given to an appropriate federal agency for legal review. In addition to alerting enforcement agencies to possible problems, such a reporting system would make it impossible for top managers to claim that they were unaware that, for example, the statements made by the sales division were contrary to the findings of the research department.

John Braithwaite has proposed a similar program. Whether by new legislation, by court order, or by voluntary corporate reform, Braithwaite argued that those assigned the responsibility for keeping a corporation in compliance with the law must be given greater strength within the corporation. Among other things, he suggested that compliance personnel be given a more professional status; a high-level ombudsman be established to hear complaints; reports be made directly to the chief executive officer in writing (thus "tainting" him or her with the knowledge of potential criminal activities); and corporate decisions about ethical and legal matters be written down to create a kind of "corporate case law" that would then provide a guide for employees who must make a difficult decision.

A different approach to the control of corporate crime would be the selective nationalization of firms that have long records of criminal violations. Nationalization may sound like an extreme measure, but it is a common practice in many nations around the world. All the government would have to do is buy up enough stock to gain a controlling interest in the criminal firm. The old management would then be replaced by a new group of managers, who would be instructed to reform and restructure the corporation. After the reforms had been effected and the corporation was operating in a responsible manner, the government could either sell its stock and return the firm to private ownership, or continue to operate it as a public trust.

A program of nationalization might also focus on industries rather than on individual firms. The rationale behind this approach is that some industries (e.g., petroleum) have such a long history of antitrust violations that they clearly are no longer regulated by the free market, and the government therefore needs to step in to protect the public interest. This could be done in several ways. All the firms in the industry could be nationalized—but that, of course, would produce even less competition, albeit with public instead of private control.

Another alternative would be to nationalize a single large firm and to use it to reintroduce competition into the oligopolistic industry. A third alternative would be to start an entirely new, government-owned firm to compete with the existing oligopoly.

On the whole, occupational crimes are not as amenable to structural solutions as are organizational crimes. But there are two important exceptions—occupational crimes among government employees and occupational crimes in the health care professions. Analyses have shown that the fee-for-service technique of payment is a major cause of crime in the health care industry. The motivation for performing unnecessary tests and treatments, for example, comes from the fact that physicians and laboratories are paid for each service they perform; thus, they are rewarded for "over-doctoring." If the health care system paid professionals on the basis of a salary rather than on the volume of services performed, the motivation for many offenses would be eliminated. This approach has already proven successful in private health maintenance organizations, as well as in nationalized health care systems such as the one in Great Britain.

Political Reforms

White-collar crime differs from most other types of crime, in that there are so many promising proposals for dealing with it. There is little doubt that, if some reasonable combination of the proposals discussed above were vigorously applied to the problem, the incidence of white-collar crime would decline. The difficulty in dealing with white-collar crime lies not so much in discovering viable responses but in winning their implementation. In other words, this is primarily a political problem that can be solved only by reforming the political process.

The most urgent need is for radical changes in the present system of campaign financing. The fact that most politicians have to rely on campaign contributions from well-endowed special interests clearly has had a paralyzing effect on the battle against white-collar crime. An aide to former Senator Gary Hart, during his campaign to win the 1988 presidential nomination, revealed exactly what the problem was when he was asked about his candidate's position on corporate crime: "No Democratic presidential candidate has ever made corporate crime an issue," he said, because "the money will dry up."

The simplest way to resolve this problem would be to create a system of federal and state financing for election campaigns. The current provision for matching funds in presidential elections is certainly an improvement over the old system, but it is only a halfway measure for a single office. It would be far better to provide complete government funding for all major elections. Each candidate would naturally be given the same amount of money to spend, and large blocks of free television and radio time would be set aside for the candidates to discuss the issues.

The main difficulty in formulating such a system is to create a fair way to determine who is to receive government funds. On the one hand, a large number of frivolous candidates might run for office if no cost were involved. But on the other hand, the large, established parties currently in power might well write the campaign financing legislation in such a way as to exclude small-party candidates. Nonetheless, some fair system could certainly be worked out. One promising approach would be to require petitions with a minimum number of signatures to qualify for funding in the primary, and then use the primary returns as the basis for funding eligibility in the general election.

Another essential step toward reform is the provision of stronger protections for individual civil rights and the freedom of political expression. The government has not only established systematic programs for the surveillance of those who challenge the political interests of the elite, but it has actually taken direct covert action to repress such political activities. It would be helpful to have a new federal law explicitly criminalizing any activities on the part of government agents that interfere with the freedom of expression. Although most such activities are already illegal, such a law would still have an important symbolic value.

A more difficult problem is to get the government to enforce existing laws that regulate the behavior of its agents. Many observers have suggested the creation of a permanent special prosecutor's office, similar to the temporary one first created during the Watergate scandals. This office, equipped with its own investigative force, would have unrestricted access to all government records, files, and reports. The selection of the head of this office would best be left up to the Supreme Court or some prestigious, nonpartisan group. With such a strong institutional base, the effort to control the government abuse of power would seem to stand a much better chance of success than it has in the past.

But because there is some question about how effectively the government can ever police itself, it is crucial that the public be given access to the broadest possible range of information about the government's activities. When a government agency begins an investigation of a political group, it should be required to notify the group of that fact. The activities of all government agents, operatives, and informants involved in such political cases should be periodically reviewed by a panel of federal judges to make sure that the government is staying within the bounds of the law and the standards of ethical conduct. Individuals should be given speedy access to all files kept on them by public or private organizations, without having to take costly legal action. All citizens should also be able to get inaccurate information removed from their files and have the right to sue for any damages caused by the dissemination of false information.

A CONCLUDING NOTE

This must convey a rather dismal picture of the world to most of its readers. The repeated examples of respected men and women using the most unscrupulous means to enlarge already ample fortunes, of major corporations' indifference to the injuries and deaths they cause innocent people, of the government's violations of human rights, and of the weakness and corruption of the enforcement effort, certainly cast our society in a dark light.

It is the responsibility of the sociological enterprise to probe the depths of society's problems, and such an endeavor is unlikely to produce comforting results. Good sociology often contains a disquieting glimpse behind the social illusions we erect to conceal unpleasant realities. It is, nonetheless, true that there are countless honest corporate executives, diligent government servants, and dedicated professionals who have been ignored in these pages. But social problems are not created or resolved on the basis of personal moral characteristics or individual decisions, but by the objective social conditions that underlie them.

In the last analysis, the problem of white-collar crime is one strand in a seamless web of social relations that transcend the neat categories sociologists create to contain them. The kinds of changes necessary to provide a permanent solution will require a major restructuring of our social and economic relationships. If such changes are made, they will not come about because of the problem of white-collar crime alone, but because of a confluence of many social forces pushing in the same direction. The one thing that is certain is that our social relations will indeed change—but only time will tell if those changes will leave us with a more humane society.

QUESTIONS FOR DISCUSSION AND WRITING

1. What does a comparison of the treatment of white-collar criminals and street criminals demonstrate?
2. What motivates white-collar criminals?
3. How do white-collar criminals use rationalizations?

ORGANIZED CRIME

From Mafia to Cosa Nostra

DONALD R. CRESSEY

The extraordinary thing about organized crime is that America has tolerated it for so long.

—President's Crime Commission

THE threat that organized crime poses to traditional American economic and political freedoms can, interestingly enough, be determined by looking at Sicily as well as by looking at America. Because the Sicilian Mafia has been the subject of discussion and investigation, if not study, for almost a century, Americans can readily learn more about it than they can about the activities of organized criminals in their own country. While we are confident that American organized crime is not merely the Sicilian Mafia transplanted, the similarities between the two organizations are direct and too great to be ignored.

For at least a century, a pervasive organization of criminals called the Mafia has dominated almost all aspects of life—economic, political, religious, and social—in the western part of the island of Sicily. This organization also has been influential, but not dominating, in the remainder of Sicily and in southern Italy. In the early part of this century, thousands of Sicilians and southern Italians be-

came American immigrants. The immigrants brought with them the customs of their homeland, and included in those customs are psychological attitudes toward a wide variety of social relationships. At the same time, the immigration established an obvious and direct route for further diffusion of the customs of Sicily to the United States. Because the American farmland had been more or less settled by the time the Sicilians and Italians arrived, they tended to settle in the large cities of the Eastern seaboard, where they lived together in neighborhoods. The fact that they lived together enabled them to retain for some time many of the customs of the old country, unlike, say, the Scandinavians, who scattered through the upper Midwest. A certain "clannishness" contributed to the retention of the custom of "clannishness." Further, the custom of "clannishness" probably was accentuated by the move to a strange land.

In these early Sicilian and Italian neighborhoods, discussion of the workings of the Mafia and "The Black Hand" was commonplace. Violence was attributed to these organizations, and people feared the names. Men were shot on the streets but, out of fear, obvious witnesses refused to come forward. In Brooklyn, it became customary for housewives to say to

Selected excerpts from *Theft of the Nation, The Structure of Organized Crime in America* (pp. 1–18) by D. R. Cressey, 1969, New York: Harper & Row. Copyright © 1969 by Donald R. Cressey. Reprinted by permission of Harper-Collins Publishers, Inc.

each other, on the occasion of hearing the sounds of a murderer's pistol, "It is sad that someone's injured horse had to be destroyed." Fear was present, just as it had been in Italy and Sicily. No one can be sure that this fear was a product of the Old World Mafia, rather than merely the work of hoodlums who capitalized on the fear of the Mafia that existed back home.

During national Prohibition in the 1920s and early 1930s, the various bootlegging gangs across the nation were made up of immigrants and the descendants of immigrants from many countries. There were Irish gangs, Jewish gangs, Polish gangs, German gangs, Italian gangs, and many others. An organization known as *"Unione Siciliana"* was involved. Near the end of Prohibition, the basic framework of the current structure of American organized crime was established as the final product of a series of "gangland wars" in which an alliance of Italians and Sicilians first conquered other groups and then fought each other. During these conflicts the Italian-Sicilian alliance was called "the Mafia," among other things. There is no sound information about whether this "Mafia" was a branch of the Sicilian Mafia.

The Italian-Sicilian apparatus set up as a result of a 1930-1931 war between Italian and Sicilian criminals continues to dominate organized crime in America, and it is still called "the Mafia" in many quarters. The Federal Bureau of Narcotics has called it "Mafia" since the early 1930s, but the Federal Bureau of Investigation has denied the existence of an organization going by that name. While the Kefauver Committee in 1950 concluded that "there is a nationwide crime syndicate known as the Mafia," the director of the FBI as recently as 1962 stated that "no single individual or coalition of racketeers dominates organized crime across the nation." Now the director uses "Cosa Nostra" to refer to the "criminal fraternity" which others call "the Mafia":

Nostra is a criminal fraternity whose membership is Italian either by birth or national origin, and it has been found to control major racket activities in many of our larger metropolitan areas, often working in concert with criminals representing other ethnic backgrounds. It operates on a nationwide basis, with international implications, and until recent years it carried on its activities with almost complete secrecy. It functions as a criminal cartel, adhering to its own body of "law" and "justice" and, in so doing, thwarts and usurps the authority of legally constituted judicial bodies.

Whatever the "criminal fraternity" is called, there remains the question of whether it is the Mafia of Sicily and southern Italy transplanted to this country or whether it has arisen principally as the result of the response to a new cultural setting by hoodlum immigrants, some of whom happened to be Italian or Sicilian and thus knowledgeable about how to set up and control, by fear, an illicit organization. There are several reasons why this question is important.

First, it is a fact that almost all Italian and Sicilian immigrants, and their descendants, have been both fine and law-abiding citizens. They have unwittingly let criminals who are Italians or Sicilians, or Americans of Italian or Sicilian descent, be identified with them. Criminals of Italian or Sicilian descent are called "Italians" or "Sicilians," while bankers, lawyers, and professors of Italian or Sicilian descent are called "Americans." More Americans know the name "Luciano" than know the name "Fermi."

In early 1965, a group of New Yorkers formed an "American-Italian Anti-Defamation League," presumably to protect citizens of Italian descent from unwarranted attacks. From the beginning, however, it looked as though this association was designed to encourage respectable Italian-Americans to assist Italian-American criminals. A lawsuit brought by the Anti-Defamation League of B'nai B'rith caused the association to change its name first to "American-Italian Anti-Defamation Council," then to "Americans of Italian Descent." In early 1968, the group decided to stress the constructive contributions of Italian-Americans, rather than to pursue its campaign of opposition to "ethnic slurs." However, Mrs. Mary Sansone, President of the Congress of Italian-American Organizations, was skeptical that the group's shift in official policy would help matters much. She said, "It's going to take them quite a while to clean up the mess of the group's first two years of existence."

Part of "the mess" arose because members of the association's Board of Directors made speeches on "How Italians Are Persecuted" and used the Organized Crime Report prepared by the President's Commission as an exhibit. The "mess" also arose in part from the selection, in 1966, of Frank Sinatra as National Chairman of the original group. This singer, actor, and entrepreneur was to help conduct "a campaign to discourage identification of gangsters in ethnic terms." Charles Grutzner, writing in the *New York Times,* pointed out that in 1963 the Nevada Gaming Control Board revoked Mr. Sinatra's license to operate a gambling casino because he had allowed a member of "the Mafia's national commission" to participate. This was Sam Giancana of Chicago. Mr. Grutzner also referred to a 1947 Havana meeting between Mr. Sinatra and Charles Luciano, whose organizational genius, and guns, helped create the current form of organized crime in America.

Ralph Salerno, an Italian-American, was formerly with the Criminal Investigation Bureau of the New York City Police Department, and in all his twenty years of police work he specialized in the detection of the affairs of the organization sometimes called the Mafia. In commenting on the American-Italian Anti-Defamation League and, more specifically, on the appointment of Sinatra, Mr. Salerno said:

I think the Italio-American community has been following the ostrich principle of putting its head in the sand and hoping the problem will go away. These 20 million fine, decent people have failed to disassociate themselves from about 10,000 wrongdoers who enjoy a blending in with the 20 million, so that when anyone points a finger at the wrongdoers they are able to say, "You are unfairly maligning 20 million good Americans."

Because his police work led to the arrest and public exposure of many criminals with Italian names and Mafia or Cosa Nostra membership, Salerno was frequently and severely criticized by Italian-American criminals. He was rarely defended by respectable, law-abiding Italian-Americans. On one occasion, the brother of a defendant in a murder case against whom Salerno was testifying came up to him in a court corridor and said, "Why does it have to be one of your own kind that hurts you?" Salerno responded,

I'm not your kind and you're not my kind. My manners, morals and mores are not yours. The only thing we have in common is that we both spring from an Italian heritage and culture and you are the traitor to that heritage and culture which I am proud to be part of.

If the American criminal organization, which is at once a criminal cartel and a confederation of criminals, is an importation from Sicily and Italy, it should be disowned by all Italian-Americans and Sicilian-Americans because it does not represent the real cultural contention of Italy and Sicily to America. If it is an American innovation, the men of Italian and Sicilian descent who have positions in it should be disowned by the respectable Italian-American and Sicilian-American community on the ground that they are participating in an extremely undesirable aspect of American culture. This position was taken in 1963 by Paul P. Rao, Jr., the national president of the United Italian-American League, Inc. A few years later, Rao changed his position—apparently for personal reasons—and became a director of the American-Italian Anti-Defamation League. But when the McClellan Committee received the usual complaints that its hearings were casting reflections on Americans of Italian ancestry, Mr. Rao, who was then New York City Tax Commissioner and a former assistant district attorney for New York County, came forward and said:

We regret that there have been some who have irresponsibly accused the Justice Department and the

U.S. Senate subcommittee of maintaining a political smear against the Italo-Americans. . . . They who consider an exposé of racketeers dealing in narcotics, illegal gambling, prostitution, and murder as being ethnically prejudicial are either arguing illogically or are selfishly being motivated by their desire for personal publicity. We should not peremptorily dismiss the functions of the committee with diversionary cries of persecution and thereby mislead the millions of decent Americans of Italian origin who sincerely feel a personal obligation over the recent revelations, because of the coincidence of racial identification. We welcome the efforts of the committee to eliminate gangsterism, especially when involving individuals of Italian extraction. The public, however, fully realizes that other notorious names in the annals of the underworld clearly indicate that no ethnic group has a monopoly on crime. How can we eliminate criminal elements from our society if we are unenlightened as to their evil activities?

Second, many of the Sicilian and Italian peasants who emigrated to America did so precisely to escape Mafia despotism. During the early part of the current century, the Mafia dominated the economic, political, and social affairs of western Sicily, as it does today. Persons who defied the organization's leaders were injured, killed, or ruined financially. Some victims fled to the United States. These persons certainly did not bring the Mafia with them. Were they once more dominated? Are any of them, or their descendants, now members of an illicit crime syndicate?

Third, the Sicilian Mafia, like the American organization, was, and is, characterized by power struggles between individuals and factions. These struggles are most apparent when a top leadership position becomes vacant. Some of the losers in such struggles occurring in the early part of the century unquestionably fled to America. Further, in the late 1920s, Benito Mussolini, Fascist premier of Italy, had the Mafia of southern Italy and Sicily hounded to the point where some of the members found it necessary to migrate, either to avoid official prosecution or to avoid "unoffi-

cial" liquidations and executions by the police. The number entering the United States, legally or illegally, is unknown. The rulers of the principal units of the American organization are now in their late 60s or early 70s. Many of them came to this country from Sicily or southern Italy early in the 1930s, and Burton B. Turkus, once an assistant district attorney in Brooklyn, has pointed out that the major business of one New York "Mafia" leader at the time "was in smuggling alien criminals who had been chased from Sicily and lower Italy." However, it might be a mere coincidence that the Italian-Sicilian domination of American illicit syndicates and the confederation integrating them began shortly after Mussolini's eradication campaign. The American "gangland war" and peace settlement which determined the present order of things also occurred in the early 1930s.

Fourth, if the American cartel and confederation is an importation from Italy and Sicily, and if it has retained its connections with the old country, then the strategy for eradicating it must be different from the strategy for eradicating a relatively new American organization. In other words, if "Cosa Nostra" is but a branch of the Sicilian-Italian Mafia, then its "home office" abroad must be eliminated before control will be effective. Some of the amateurs and independents now selling marijuana and LSD to American college students let it be known that their work is backed by a ruthless "Cosa Nostra" or "the syndicate." This myth gives power to persons having only a very slight relationship, if any, with Cosa Nostra. By the same token, some members of the American confederation propagate the legend that their organization is a branch of the old Sicilian Mafia. This legend also confers power on the persons who cultivate it. The legend helps perpetuate the notion that the current conspiracy is ancient and therefore quite impregnable.

Fifth, there is a tendency for members of any society or group to look outside itself for the cause whenever it finds itself confronted with a serious problem or, especially, with an evil.

Any analysis of organized crime in America is affected, directly or indirectly, by this tendency. Even if all the evidence were to point to the conclusion that the American organization is merely a branch of a foreign organization, the person drawing the conclusion would in all probability be accused of "scapegoatism." As our discussion above indicated, even concluding that organized crime is dominated by Sicilians, Italians, and persons of Sicilian-Italian descent brings the accusation that the troubles of America are being tied to the back of an ethnic group, the scapegoat. Further, one who insists that there *is* an organization of criminals in America risks being accused of assigning an assortment of evils and ills to a hidden mysterious scapegoat. One who writes about organized crime risks being placed in the same category as flying-saucer fanatics and communist-conspiracy zealots, who know "they" are out there creating evils in our society even if we cannot see them.

In some cases, "looking outside" means attributing problems to the characteristics of individuals rather than to the characteristics of the society or group itself. Our society tends, both popularly and scientifically, to view the criminal's behavior as a problem of individual maladjustment, not as a consequence of his participation in social systems. It is common to maintain, for example, that criminality is strictly an individual disorder which, therefore, can be treated in a clinic, just as anemia or syphilis can be treated in a clinic. An extreme position is that criminality actually is a biological disorder, treatable by modification of the physiology or anatomy of the individual through lobotomy, castration, interference with glandular functioning, or something else. The much more popular view is that criminality is an individual psychological disorder which may or may not have a strictly biological basis. The criminal may be considered as a person who is unable to canalize or sublimate his "primitive," antisocial impulses or tendencies; or he may be considered as expressing in criminal behavior some unconscious wish or urge created by an early trau-matic emotional experience; or he may be considered as possessing some other kind of defective personality component. In any event, the implication is that crime and criminality are matters of the faults and defects of individuals, not of the society or group.

It is possible that attributing criminality to individual disorders is more scapegoatism permitting us to denounce the origins of crime without challenging any existing social conditions which we hold dear, and without assigning any blame to ourselves. James G. March and Herbert A. Simon have suggested, for example, that business managers tend to perceive conflict as if it were an individual matter, rather than an organizational matter, because perceiving it as an organizational problem would acknowledge a diversity of goals in the organization, thereby placing strain on the status and power systems. Similarly, in a family which has inadvertently but nevertheless inexorably produced a son's delinquency, it is convenient for the father to attribute the delinquency to "bad blood on the mother's side." For the same reason, the behavior of cold-blooded hired killers, and of the enforcers and rulers who order the killings, is likely to be accounted for solely in terms of the depravity or viciousness of the personnel involved, rather than in terms of organizational roles, including the roles of the victims. But during the past decade, criminologists everywhere have been increasingly shifting to the position that criminality is "owned" by groups rather than by individuals and that, therefore, attributing it to individual disorders is either mistake of fact or scapegoatism.

In other cases, looking outside the society or group for the cause of an evil means looking to another society or group and heaping our sins on it. As Gus Tyler has said, "When such a scapegoat can be found, the culture is not only relieved of sin but can indulge itself in an orgy of righteous indignation." Recent work in the sociology of deviance has shown the great contribution to delinquency, alcoholism, homosexuality, and mental disorder made by the very agencies which attempt to deal with these phenomena. Also, American society supports organized crime by demanding the right to purchase illicit goods and services. But if the Italian and Sicilian Mafia is responsible for organized crime in the United States, then documenting that fact and identifying the Mafia as the cause of our troubles is more science than scapegoatism. On the other hand, if the American cartel and confederation is a response to conditions of American life, documenting that fact is the critical problem. In a very real sense, then, deciding whether or not the American organization is a branch of the Sicilian one is a problem of deciding whether organized crime is "owned" by American society.

The problem of assigning a name to the American confederation of criminals is in part a problem of answering the five questions suggested above. If the American cartel and confederation had a specific name, like General Motors or the National Association of Manufacturers, then determining its formal organizational boundaries would be relatively simple. The fact is that no name used either by law enforcement officials or by criminals aptly characterizes the society of organized criminals in the United States. In a series of conferences at Oyster Bay, New York, some of the nation's leading experts on organized crime struggled to find a name for the organization which operates organized crime in America, and as they did so they indirectly responded to the above questions by saying that the American confederation should not be confused with the Sicilian Mafia. The conference group reviewed the names commonly used by the public and by some members of the confederation. All of them were rejected.

"Mafia" was rejected specifically because it is a Sicilian term referring to a Sicilian organization, while many participants in the American conspiracy are not Sicilian. This ground for rejection is quite tenuous. After all, "Olivetti" refers to an Italian organization but all the participants are by no means Italian. The conference group really rejected the "Mafia" terminology in order to indicate their belief that the United States does not have a "branch office" of the Sicilian-Italian firm: "This name, for many practitioners, implies that the user is naive and expects that all organized crime was exported to the United States from Sicily."

The term "Cosa Nostra" was rejected because it incorrectly implies that all members of the conspiracy speak Italian and are of Italian descent. The term is used extensively in New York, and on the Eastern seaboard, but it is seldom heard in Chicago. Further, even in New York the term is often used only in a rather indirect sense. If a member introduces a second member to a third, he is likely to identify the stranger as *"amico nostro"*—"a friend of ours." He might even use English saying, "I would like you to meet a friend of ours." The key word, in any language, is "ours." If he says *"a friend of mine,"* the stranger remains a stranger. In telling the McClellan Committee of an incident occurring in his Atlanta prison cell, the committee's star witness, a Cosa Nostra member, used this terminology, apparently without premeditation:

Chairman: Tell us what happened in the cell when you went back.

Mr. Valachi: I don't know if it was that day or the day after when the lights went out and he [Vito Genovese, a Cosa Nostra boss] said he felt like talking that night. He says, he called Ralph Wagner, he said, "Come over, Wagner."

Chairman: Who is that? Ralph Wagner? Another member of the cell?

Mr. Valachi: An inmate but *he is not a friend of ours.* He is sitting down as though he is. If I did the same thing, I would have to run out of the cell— he is the boss. He sits down, *a guy that ain't a member.* I noticed that but I made believe I didn't notice it.

If two New York, Boston, or Philadelphia members hear of an event relevant to their operations, one might say, *"Questa e' una cosa nostra,"* a phrase which is consistent with the usage of *amico nostro.* What is said here is,

"This is an affair of ours," not "I am a member of 'our thing' or 'our affair.' " Yet Italian criminals in the eastern part of the United States have corrupted the Italian, probably because they mix it with English. The bilingual ruler of an eastern "family" of the organization was heard to say, "I am in La Cosa Nostra." He really could have remained silent. All the members, all the law enforcement personnel dealing with organized crime, and most of the residents of his city know that he is the "boss" of the Sicilian-Italian apparatus in his area.

The following conversation is between a *"caporegime"* (sometimes called "captain" or "lieutenant") and one of his subordinates. Members of Cosa Nostra had assaulted a federal law enforcement agent. The guilty persons were known to the federal agency involved, but their whereabouts were not. The federal agents got in touch with the suspects' known associates in order to question them about the suspects' hiding place. After discussing the fact that the federal agents had "gone to every captain" and others, the two men used "Cosa Nostra" in the same casual way Valachi used "friend of ours." The conversation was recorded by means of an electronic "bug."

Mike: Dirty cocksuckers. Now that they bring out everything, Pete, the Cosa Nostra is a wide open thing.
Pete: Yeah.
Mike: It's an open book.
Pete: It's an open book.
Mike: Pete, you know as well as I do, familiarity with anything whatsoever breeds contempt. We've had nothing but familiarity with our Cosa Nostra . . .
Pete: It starts another trouble.
Mike: If it brings up sides, what the hell are we supposed to do? I know only one thing, Pete. The Cosa Nostra is the Cosa Nostra. You just do what the fucking bosses tell you. I mean, you can't go and do what the captain even tells you.

Since *amico nostro* or, plural, *amici nostri* is used all over the United States, one is tempted to name the organization "The Society of Friends." The Quakers would complain, or sue, as the original Anti-Defamation League complained about, and successfully sued, the American-Italian Anti-Defamation League for using its name. One organized-crime investigator, disgusted with nit-picking efforts to find a linguistically proper name, remarked in exasperation, "Aw hell, we know it exists— let's just call it the Pizza Derby." A fellow law enforcement officer objected, on the questionable ground that pizza is an American, not an Italian, dish.

The conference group noted that in Chicago the members sometimes refer to themselves as "the syndicate," sometimes as "the outfit," but these terms were rejected because they are local. Thus, the Sicilian and Italian terms were rejected because they tend to stress the relationship to the "outside," while the Chicago terms were rejected because they do not stress this relationship.

"The organization" is sometimes used by members and, while this term does not imply anything about a relationship between the American organization and the Sicilian and Italian Mafia, it was rejected because it is "not very descriptive," meaning that it does not denote the relationship between the various branches in the United States.

It is significant that there is no plural form for "syndicate," or "organization," when these terms have a national referent. Neither is there, in the language used in the United States, any indication of the existence of more than one "Mafia" or "Cosa Nostra." While a criminal might on occasion talk about "the New York Cosa Nostra" or the "Philadelphia Mafia," or the "Boston syndicate," this usage is different from that in Sicily, where one "mafia" might be said to control the construction industry, another "mafia" the fruit markets. Even rather local American terms, such as "the arm" (used in upstate New York), "the people" (used in the West), and "the mob" (used everywhere), have no plural forms. "The family" is sometimes used as a synonym for "Cosa Nostra," as well as to identify a geographically based unit under the control of one man. Thus, "I am in the family" refers to Cosa Nostra membership, while "I am in Carlo's family" refers to membership in the local section of "the family." This usage corresponds somewhat to the Sicilian usage of "Mafia" for reference to the entire organization and the usage of, say, "fruit-market mafia" for reference to a subdivision of the larger enterprise. There is no plural of the first usage of the American term ("the family"), but references to "families" in New York, Detroit, Philadelphia, and other cities are common.

In Chicago, "outfit" and "organization" seem to refer to the local apparatus, which includes both Italians and non-Italians, while "syndicate" seems to refer to the amalgamation of all the "outfits" in the country. With reference to the Chicago scene alone, there is no plural of "outfit" or "organization." For example, Chicago language does not refer to various "outfits"—such as "Salerno's outfit," "the Rogovin outfit," or "Blakey's outfit"—as it once referred to distinct bootlegging gangs. In New York, "the mob" once referred to the entire collection, "of which the New York Mafia was but a part."

The Oyster Bay group accepted "confederation" as the best term. It should be noted that this term refers primarily to the organization of a government. The word "cartel" refers primarily to the organization of a business. The conference group concluded:

All of these terms are generally applied to a single loosely knit conspiracy, which is Italian dominated, operates on a nation-wide basis, and represents the most sophisticated and powerful group in organized crime. Practically all students of organized crime are agreed that this organization does not represent the total of organized crime, but there has been almost no attempt to name those organizations which constitute the remainder.

We are satisfied that "Cosa Nostra" is as good as any other term. While this phrase does not denote the fact that not all the persons engaged in organized-crime activities are Italian or of Italian descent, an Italian organization in fact controls all but an insignificant proportion of the organized-crime activities in the United States. While Cosa Nostra still tolerates some major operations by criminals of ethnic backgrounds which are not Sicilian or Italian, if one understands Cosa Nostra he understands organized crime in the United States.

Hank Messick, who has written extensively on organized crime, is convinced that Cosa Nostra is just a new name for Mafia, and he claims that a Jewish organization he calls the "Cleveland Syndicate" welcomed the use of the Italian name because it distracted attention from them:

The income-tax investigation [of Las Vegas operations] referred to by the court was part of the "coordinated drive" on organized crime launched by Robert F. Kennedy when he became Attorney General. The campaign, while falling far short of its goal, achieved more in a short time than had ever been accomplished in the past. But before Kennedy resigned in 1964, the anticrime drive had become almost an anti-Mafia crusade. Even J. Edgar Hoover informed the FBI that there was a Mafia after all. For decades he had ignored it, but when Joseph Valachi gave it a new name, La Cosa Nostra, Hoover was able to not only admit its existence but claim his organization had known about it as far back as 1961. . . . For the Cleveland Syndicate, which hid behind the shadow of the Mayfield Road Mob for years, could not but welcome emphasis on La Cosa Nostra. Let the public and politicians assume Dalitz and Kleinman were nobodies.

It is commonly assumed, as Mr. Messick does in the above, that the term "Cosa Nostra" is somewhat the invention of Joseph Valachi, who testified at great length, in short sentences, before the McClellan Committee in 1963. This is not the case. The FBI and other federal agencies in fact heard this term used many times before Valachi used it. In 1961 and 1962 they were spelling it "Causa Nostra." Attorney General Kennedy said, "Because of intelligence gathered from Joseph Valachi *and from informants,* we know." He had the informants. There are five interlocking hypotheses concerning J. Edgar Hoover's grave concern over the operations of Cosa Nostra where he had shown little concern over the Mafia, whose operations were spelled out in fine print by the Kefauver Committee in 1951.

One hypothesis states that Hoover was jealous of Harry Anslinger, former director of the Federal Bureau of Narcotics, who worried about the Mafia as long ago as the early 1930s. Since Mr. Anslinger insisted that the Mafia existed, the idea goes, Hoover denied its existence. This is probably the hypothesis employed by Messick in the quotation above—by giving the Mafia "a new name," Valachi saved Hoover's face, and enabled him to start investigating organized crime with great vigor. I doubt this hypothesis. J. Edgar Hoover is a cop as well as a politician. There are petty jealousies among cops, even top cops, but they tend to arise over the "credit" given for investigations and arrests, not over disputes about whether crime exists.

A second hypothesis is a variation of the first. It states that the Appalachian, New York, gathering of almost a hundred organized criminals in 1957 forced Hoover to recognize that a nationwide "criminal fraternity" exists. He waited for "a new name" before taking any action.

A third hypothesis is that Attorney General Kennedy ordered Mr. Hoover to begin a drive on organized crime and he simply followed orders, as did the directors of other federal agencies. Since the information coming to him from informants indicated use of the "Cosa Nostra" terminology, he selected that title as the least desirable of many undesirable titles. From what I have read in the newspapers, however, Hoover has not been especially influenced by any of the "orders" given him by the many attorneys general who have come and gone during his long tenure. Further, as early as September 1960, before Robert Kennedy became attorney general, the FBI began to supply the Organized Crime and Racketeering Section of the Department of Justice with intelligence reports on four hundred of the nation's organized-crime figures.

A fourth hypothesis is based on the fact that in 1961 and 1962 Congress passed laws giving the FBI jurisdiction to investigate organized-crime activities for the first time. These were the laws forbidding interstate travel for racketeering purposes, interstate shipment of gambling paraphernalia, and use of interstate communications for gambling purposes. Given jurisdiction, the idea goes, Hoover immediately got down to business. This hypothesis was suggested by Hoover himself. In 1966 he wrote:

Four and a half years ago, in September, 1961, the FBI was empowered to launch a concerted drive against the organized underworld. Some of us in law enforcement knew, of course, that syndicated gambling and other vices had been organized for a number of years. But there had been no effective federal laws under which the FBI could proceed against these evils. When the FBI was charged with investigative jurisdiction of the three interstate gambling and racketeering laws passed in 1961, it moved with deliberate speed to determine who was behind these nationwide underworld operations.

A fifth hypothesis is closely related to the third and fourth. In late 1960 and early 1961, the FBI and other federal agencies greatly stepped up their employment of wiretaps and electronic bugs in organized-crime cases, and the hypothesis is that the sounds coming from these devices convinced Hoover that the United States was in grave danger. The "informants" mentioned by Attorney General Kennedy might have been bugs such as the one operating in the offices of the National Cigarette Service, Providence, Rhode Island, from March 1962 until July 1965. On October 20, 1964, this bug revealed a Cosa Nostra "boss," Raymond S. L. Patriarca, saying that "in the event he is questioned about the Mafia or Cosa Nostra he is going to reply that the only Mafia he ever heard of is the Irish Mafia the Kennedys are in charge of. Patriarca will deny that he knew about La Cosa Nostra until Valachi mentioned it at the McClellan hearings."

Of the five hypotheses, the fourth seems to have the greatest likelihood of validity. It should be noted, however, that no amount of logical discourse can be as convincing as the sounds coming from wiretaps and bugs. In fact, it is reasonable to believe that New York is said to have a more severe "organized-crime problem" than, say, Los Angeles, because, in part, New York law enforcement agencies have been authorized to use bugs while the California agencies have not. Further, New York "families" of Cosa Nostra are said to be organized along lines different from Detroit, but the difference might lie simply in the fact that we have much better information, obtained by bugs and taps, about New York. If one never heard a criminal speak, and never talked with a noncriminal informant, he could hardly convince himself that any organization of criminals exists.

Although the anthropological controversy about "diffusion versus independent invention" has largely been resolved, a look at the principal questions raised in the controversy shows that a cultural complex like organized crime could exist in both Sicily and America even if there had been no contact between the two nations. "In essence," explains Melville J. Herskovits, "the matter turns on the inventiveness of man; whether when in distant parts of the world we find similar artifacts or institutions or concepts, we must assume these to have been invented only once and diffused to the regions where they are observed, or whether we may deduce that they had originated independently in these several regions." The more extreme forms of "diffusionism" held that regardless of the distance or time between two cultural traits or complexes, these cultural elements had a single place or origin. Persons holding this view certainly would find great support in the fact that Italian immigrants used extortion to corner the New York artichoke market in the 1930s and that Italian immigrants used extortion to corner the tomato market in Melbourne in the 1950s. The appearance of the cultural trait in New York and Melbourne appears to be an obvious case of diffusion from Italy.

The matter is not so simple, however. Anthropologists also have noted that common needs and common conditions in widely separated societies will result in the invention of similar things, including ideas, even if there are no contacts between the two inventors. The "common conditions" may even be conditions of nature, which at once make for resemblances in cultural forms and limit these cultural forms. For example, anyone in need of a watercraft must fit the raw materials to the natural requirements of buoyancy and balance, with the result that the possibilities of variation in form from craftsman to craftsman, even if separated by great differences of time or space, are limited. Further, establishing that diffusion has taken place is not enough. A cultural trait or complex spread by diffusion might be accepted by one culture and rejected by another. It is accepted, in form modified by the needs and conditions of the receiving culture, only if that culture creates a "place" for it to appear. In the illustration used above, both New York and Melbourne necessarily established a place for monopoly by extortion to appear.

There is a remarkable similarity between both the structure and the cultural values of the Sicilian Mafia and the American confederation. There have been extensive contacts between Sicilians and Americans. This does not mean that the Mafia has diffused to the United States, however. Whatever was imported has been modified to fit the conditions of American life. A place has been made for organized crime to arise in the United States, just as a place has been made for the Mafia in Sicily. There is also a significant similarity between the structure, values, and even objectives of prisoners and organized criminals, but there is no evidence that these cultural traits necessarily diffused from organized criminals to prisoners, or from prisoners to organized criminals. A man steeped in the traditions of organized crime can easily adjust to the ways of prisoners, and vice versa, possibly because the conditions producing the traditions of prisoners and of organized criminals resemble each other. Similarly, a man steeped in the traditions of the Sicilian and Italian Mafia can easily find his way around American organized crime, and the behavior of American criminals returning to Italy and Sicily has shown that the reverse is also true.

As a matter of fact, if the problem of language were not present a man could with only slight difficulty move between the Sicilian Mafia and an American prison, leaving American organized crime out of the picture altogether. Further, it is highly probable that any active participant in, say, the Norwegian or French underground movement during the World War II occupation by the Nazis could move with ease in any of the other three organizations.

A few years ago, an electronic bug recorded a casual conversation taking place in an automobile repair shop. One Cosa Nostra member told another how he and a third party had deliberately refrained from acknowledging each other's presence at a public event, in the interests of security. The same kind of conversation, and the same kind of security precautions, occur daily among prisoners, Mafia members, and members of underground movements.

Willie: Hey, you know who we seen the other night down at the track? You see, I had taken my daughter Saturday night to the trotters, you know. My daughter and my niece, Patricia. But Dom was coming in later. I got reservations next to—right *next* to—Aneill. They were ahead of us. Nothing. Nothing. The other guy was with his wife. He was with his sweetheart. He didn't look at me.

Mike: Does he know you?

Willie: Yeah. He didn't look at me. I'll tell you the reason, Mike. There was a fucking guy there that looked more like the law than anything else, in my, in my, in my life. I would bet on it.

While the members of Cosa Nostra, and its affiliates, have learned a thing or two from the Sicilian Mafia, this organization is indigenous to the United States. It does things "the American way." But because the objectives of Cosa Nostra are similar to those of the Sicilian

Mafia, certain similarities between the two organizations become obvious. The potential danger of Cosa Nostra to the citizens of the United States can be observed by examining the tremendous degree of control the Mafia exercises in western Sicily. The Sicilian organization originated in peasant society, where face-to-face relations between neighbors predominated. It adapted, and it continues to adapt, as Sicily has become more industrialized and urbanized. At first it provided law and order where the official government failed to do so. It collected taxes, which were payments for protection against bandits. In the latter part of the nineteenth century, for example, one Mafia group governed a cluster of eleven mountain villages; the head and his assistants had a private police force of about 130 armed men. The leaders were well-established citizens, landowners and farmers, who supervised all aspects of local life, including agricultural and economic activities, family relations, and public administration.

Like contemporary rulers of Cosa Nostra units in the United States, the despots soon demanded absolute power. No one dared offend the chief's sense of honor. The lines between tax and extortion and between peace enforcement and murder became blurred, as they always do under despots. Today, "an overall inventory of Mafia activities leaves no doubt that it is a criminal organization, serving the interests of its membership at the expense of the larger population." Norman Lewis, among others, has shown that it has extended its influence from farms and peasant villages to the cities of western Sicily, where it now dominates commerce and government. It has a monopoly on almost all aspects of life. Mafia doctors get patients when other doctors do not, and only Mafia doctors can find vacant beds in overcrowded hospitals. Mafia lawyers have all the clients they can handle, and they have uncanny luck in winning cases. Mafia contractors get all the government contracts, even when their bids are higher than those of non-Mafia men, and despite the fact that they pay wages lower than the trade-union minimums. Mafia members, by tradition, do not run for seats in Parliament, but no man can get elected to Parliament—or anything else—without the support of "men of respect," also known as "men of honor."

Such corruption is not like "the bite" put on anyone doing business with Latin American civil servants. It is an *organized* bite, a feast by a society of cannibals. Sicily has given the Mafia a place. Both Luigi Barzini, a keen observer of the Italian scene, and Norman Lewis, a student of Mafia history, have given indications of the extent to which all economic, professional, political, and social life is dominated:

There are the cattle and pasture Mafie; citrus grove Mafie; water Mafie (who control scarce springs, wells, irrigation canals); building Mafie (if the builder does not pay, his scaffolding collapses and his bricklayers fall to their death); commerce Mafie; public works Mafie (who award contracts); wholesale fruit, vegetable, flower, and fish markets Mafie, and so forth. They all function more or less in the same way. They establish order, they prevent pilfering, each in its own territory, and provide protection from all sorts of threats, including the legal authorities, competitors, criminals, revenue agents, and rival Mafia organizations. They fix prices. They arrange contracts. They can see to it, in an emergency, that violators of their own laws are surely punished with death. This is rarely necessary. Most of the time the fact that they can condemn any man to death is enough to keep everybody toeing the line.

[By 1945], a great gathering of vulturine chiefs had collected to wet their beaks at the expense of farmers, whose produce they bought dirt cheap on the spot and carried to market in the Mafia's own beautifully decorated carts—or later, trucks. In the market only those whose place had been "guaranteed" by the Mafia were allowed to buy or sell at prices the Mafia fixed. The Mafia wetted its beak in the meat, fish, beer, and fruit businesses. It moved into the sulphur mines, controlled the output of rock salt, took over building contracts, "organized labor," cornered the plots in Sicily's cemeteries, put tobacco smuggling on a new and profitable basis through its domination of the Sicilian fishing fleets, and went in for tomb robbing in the ruins of the Greek settlement of Selinunte. . . . The Mafia gave monopolies to shopkeepers in different trades and then invited them to put up their prices—at the same time, of course, increasing their Mafia contribution. . . . The most obvious of the Mafia's criminal functions—and one that had been noted by the Bourbon attorney general back in the twenties of the last century—now became the normally accepted thing. The Mafia virtually replaced the police force, offering a form of arrangement with crime as a substitute for its suppression. When a theft, for instance, took place, whether of a mule, a jeweled pendant, or a motorcar, a Mafia intermediary was soon on the scene, offering reasonable terms for the recovery of the stolen object. . . . The Mafia intermediary, of course, wetted his beak at the expense of both parties. The situation was and is an everyday one in Sicily.

The public demand for protection against Sicilian bandits, and for other services not provided by the established government, created an illicit government which, in the long run, exploited all its members and ruled the very public that created it. The American demand for illicit goods and services has created an illicit government.

QUESTIONS FOR DISCUSSION AND WRITING

1. Why are the authors satisfied that "Cosa Nostra" is as good as any other term?
2. What five hypotheses are offered to explain Hoover's "grave concern" over the operations of the Cosa Nostra compared to his low level of concern with the Mafia?
3. Which of the five seems to have the "greatest likelihood of validity"?

Myths and Organized Crime: Is There a Mafia, and Does It Really Matter?

DENNIS J. KENNEY

JAMES O. FINCKENAUER

I F our government's policies for dealing with organized crime have been founded upon myth, as some people have charged, then certain conclusions are obvious:

- these policies will have been more symbolic than real;
- these policies will be more concerned with how things appear than with whether they actually accomplish anything; and
- the result will have been a considerable waste and misdirection of law enforcement time and resources and, ultimately, much failure and frustration.

It is to this issue that we now turn, beginning with the contention that a myth of a Mafia mystique has in fact been foisted on the American people.

Not everyone considers this to be an important issue. Charles Silberman has written widely on social problems and criticizes what he called "a heated, at times acrimonious, and often downright silly debate about the

Mafia: whether or not the Mafia really exists; whether it is called the Mafia or La Cosa Nostra; whether it is limited to Italian-Americans or includes members of other ethnic groups; whether or not there is a national syndicate, or 'crime confederation,' that controls organized crime throughout the United States; and whether or not that syndicate is controlled, in turn, by the Mafia." Similarly, Annelise Graebner Anderson dismisses the question of whether a national syndicate controls organized crime throughout the country as being a "strawman." She says that "politicians and law enforcement officials can be expected to make extreme and unqualified statements about the extent and dangers of organized crime: it gives them visibility, it develops public support for an increase in the law enforcement budget, it may discourage the citizenry from purchasing illegal goods and services." Suffice it to say that we do not consider the debate to be silly, nor do we consider it to be simply a strawman argument. Rather, this debate has serious policy implications. President John F. Kennedy once observed, "The great enemy of the truth is very often not the lie—deliberate, contrived, and dishonest—but the myth—persistent, persuasive, and unrealistic." Is there a Mafia myth that has been the enemy of the truth? Let us see if we can begin to sort this out.

THE BIRTH OF THE MAFIA MYTH

A U.S. Senate Committee, chaired by Senator Estes Kefauver of Tennessee, conducted a sweeping examination of organized crime in the United States in 1950-1951. This was not literally the first time a criminal organization loosely called the Mafia was acknowledged in the United States; the Mafia had been recognized as a part of American organized crime as early as the late 1800s. But it was the Kefauver Committee and its investigations that first put Mafia figures (so-called mafiosi) on national television. It was the Kefauver Committee that made the Mafia and organized crime one and the same thing in the minds of the American public.

Television viewers were fascinated by the confrontation of good and evil. "Good" was personified by the meek, almost schoolmaster looks of Estes Kefauver. The drawling, coonskin-capped Tennessean was the common man as hero, a kind of Gary Cooper. He stood to do battle with "evil" personified by a bunch of swarthy Italians and Sicilians named Costello, Adonis, Moretti, Luciano, Genovese, Profaci, and Anastasia, and some Jewish hoodlums named Longie Zwillman and Meyer Lansky. White, Anglo-Saxon, Protestant, middle America was going to the mat with some dark-skinned foreigners who had brought an evil conspiracy to our shores.

All of the elements of good drama—and of myth—were there. Viewers watched the nervously clenching and unclenching hands of Frank Costello, who refused to permit his face to be televised. He also refused, in a rasping and barely audible voice, to answer questions on advice of counsel. In the minds of the committee members and, of course, in the minds of the public, this confirmed his complicity in the things about which he was being questioned. America, or at least a big part of America, reveled in the spectacle of these sweating, fidgeting gangsters professing shocked surprise at being called and questioned, feigning ignorance of any wrongdoing, sometimes being sullenly silent, sometimes refusing to answer, and sometimes evading the questions. These were mafiosi, the masters of the underworld. This was organized crime—or so it seemed.

Senator Kefauver wanted answers to such questions as whether a nationwide crime syndicate existed. If so, where did its sources of power lie? To get these answers, the committee held their televised hearings in various cities around the country. These hearings brought to light a number of attributes and acts associated with organized crime: gambling (determined to be the principal source of support for big-time racketeering and gangsterism), narcotics, infiltration of legitimate business, corruption, and violence. The committee stressed the important part played by the Mafia in binding together into a national association the major criminal gangs and individual hoodlums from around the country. The Mafia was said to be dominant because it used "muscle and murder" and because it was willing and in fact did ruthlessly eliminate anyone who stood in the way of its success.

The influence of the Kefauver Committee in defining organized crime is confirmed by a study by John F. Galliher and James A. Cain, titled "Citation Support for the Mafia Myth in Criminology Textbooks." The study examined 20 criminology textbooks with chapters or sections on organized crime that were published in the United States between 1950 and 1972. The most frequently cited source for information about organized crime in these books was the Kefauver Committee report, cited in over half of the texts, followed by Kefauver's book based on the investigation. Thus, the image and understanding of organized crime conveyed to students through these textbooks was in large part the image and understanding promulgated by Senator Kefauver and his committee.

This image, the belief fostered by Kefauver that the Mafia and organized crime are synonymous, was first attacked as being false—as being a myth—by sociologist Daniel Bell. Bell identified the enforcement of public morals in America as one of the core stimuli promulgating what he criticized as being a myth. The existence of a Mafia helps resolve the "unwelcome contradiction" between our straightlaced conventional morality on the one hand and our desire for the "forbidden fruits" on the other, he said. These forbidden fruits include drugs, gambling, and sex. In other words, we are not hypocrites but are instead the victims of an alien, sinister force. Here, we see an example of the scapegoating function of myth. Myths sometimes find villains to be blamed for complicated or undesirable circumstances.

These ready explanations are popular because they offer an outlet for anger or guilt, and they absolve us of responsibility. We prefer to believe that organized crime is being imposed upon American society by a group of immoral men engaged in an alien conspiracy rather than that it is simply an indigenous product of the way American society operates—and the result of our own human weaknesses.

Senator Kefauver asserted that a "nationwide crime syndicate does exist in the United States, despite the protestations of a strangely assorted company of criminals, self-serving politicians, plain blind fools, and others who may be honesty misguided, that there is no such combine." "Unfortunately," says Bell, "for a good story—and the existence of the Mafia would be a whale of a story—neither the Senate Crime Committee in its testimony, nor Kefauver in his book, presented any real evidence that the Mafia exists as a functioning organization."

Why would Kefauver and his committee push so hard for their theory of the Mafia? Why would they, in Bell's words, be "taken in by [their] own myth of an omnipotent Mafia and a despotic Costello"? Bell says it was because they may have been misled by their own hearsay.

Senator Kefauver had begun the investigation with the attitude that with so much smoke there must be a raging fire. But smoke can also mean a smoke screen.

There is, as well, in the American temper, a feeling that "somewhere," "somebody" is pulling all the complicated strings to which this jumbled world dances. In the field of crime, the side-of-the-mouth low-down was "Costello."

Another critic of the "myth-making" by the Kefauver Committee is historian William Moore. Moore charged the committee with dramatizing organized crime more than investigating it. He says, "particularly in the case of the Mafia, the senators lacked adequate evidence for their conclusions." He accuses them of making "overblown and unfounded statements." These statements and conclusions were seemingly accepted by the public because they fit with their preconceived notions about organized crime.

The popular myths and misunderstandings grew stronger, buttressed by the "proofs" of the Kefauver Committee. Sensational journalists and publishers enjoyed a field day, explaining and enlarging upon the committee's work; gangster movies and television programs dramatized variations of the same theme. . . . Even after the initial shock and novelty of the Kefauver findings had lifted and critics began to question the more sweeping committee statements, the public at large continued to hold to the older conspiracy view, thus making more difficult an intelligent appraisal of organized crime.

Here is an example of the complicating role of the partial truth in myth. Italian-American men were leading characters in much of the mob and gangster activity in the country. They were involved in gambling, prostitution, and narcotics. But the tendency of the media to emphasize a few sensational gangsters who fit the Mafia image gave an illusion that domination of organized crime by mafiosi was much greater than was seemingly warranted by the facts.

THE MCCLELLAN COMMITTEE AND ITS STAR WITNESS: JOSEPH VALACHI

A second Senate committee, the Permanent Subcommittee on Investigations of the Senate

Committee on Government Operations, chaired by Senator John L. McClellan of Arkansas, also conducted hearings on organized crime and narcotics in 1963 and 1964. This same group had looked into organized crime and gambling two years earlier. In his opening statement before the second investigation, Senator McClellan laid out his perception of what had come to be known as La Cosa Nostra, which was loosely translated as meaning "Our Thing":

The existence of such a criminal organization as Cosa Nostra is frightening. . . . [It] attempts to be a form of government unto itself. . . . Murder has often been ordered for a variety of reasons: a grab for power, the code of vengeance, gangland rivalries, infidelity to the organization or even for suspicions of derelictions.

The featured witness before the committee was a convicted heroin trafficker named Joseph Valachi. Valachi, who was said to be the first member of La Cosa Nostra to ever testify publicly about the nature of the organization, talked for five days about his personal knowledge of the history of organized crime in New York and about his experiences as a member of the Vito Genovese crime family. Why was he willing to break the so-called code of silence and to talk to the committee and to law enforcement officials?—because he believed he had been marked for death for "ratting" to the Federal Bureau of Narcotics. After killing a fellow inmate at the federal prison in Atlanta, Georgia, whom he believed was going to kill him, Valachi negotiated a deal with federal officials to talk to them about what he knew in return for being allowed to plead guilty to the lesser charge of murder in the second degree.

Prior to his appearance before the Senate committee, Valachi had been talking to the FBI for almost a year, so the law enforcement value of his information had already been pretty much maximized. Testimony before the committee was the forum for having Valachi go public. As with the earlier Kefauver hearings, the press, the public, and the committee members found the witness to be a fascinating figure. His descriptions of the so-called Castellamarese War and of being initiated into a fraternal-like organization through a secret ritual were particularly captivating. Needless to say, these descriptions tended to fit the preconceived stereotypes the public and the senators held about the Mafia. Suspect and tenuous evidence is not a problem if we truly want to believe. Myths are not subject to ready refutation by contrary evidence. Gordon Hawkins contends that whereas acknowledgment of membership in the Mafia appeared to be accepted at face value, as in the case of Valachi, denials of such membership (as had occurred before the Kefauver Committee) were taken as evidence that the Mafia was in fact a secret society and that violation of this secrecy would be met by Mafia killings.

The McClellan Committee findings, and in particular its reliance upon Valachi's testimony, met with mixed reviews. The committee itself accepted Valachi's story of organized crime and of the character of La Cosa Nostra. Attorney General Robert F. Kennedy, the other principal witness before the committee, pointed to the importance of the intelligence information obtained from Valachi in the latter's interrogation by the FBI:

We know that Cosa Nostra is run by a commission, and that the leaders of Cosa Nostra in most cities are responsible to the commission. . . . It is an organization. It is Mafia. It is the Cosa Nostra. . . . There are other names for it, but it all refers to the same organization. . . . The members of the commission, the top members, or even their chief lieutenants, have insulated themselves from the crime itself; if they want to have somebody knocked off, for instance, the top man will speak to somebody who will speak to somebody else who will speak to somebody else and order it. The man who actually does the gun work . . . does not know who ordered it. To trace that back is virtually impossible . . . there have been large numbers of very brutal murders which have been committed by those in organized crime just over a period of the last two years. Certainly not a week goes by that somewhere in the

United States an individual is not killed or murdered in some kind of gangland battle or a witness is not garroted and killed.

Attorney General Kennedy called Valachi's testimony a significant intelligence breakthrough that enabled the Department of Justice "to prove conclusively" the existence of the nationwide organization known as Cosa Nostra. Likewise, Ralph Salerno, a noted expert on organized crime from the New York City Police Department, said that Valachi's confessions should be ranked next to Apalachin (a 1957 incident in upstate New York in which 65 alleged mafiosi were discovered in what was called a high-level conference on organized crime) "as the greatest single blow ever delivered to organized crime in the United States." Writer Peter Maas, on the other hand, in his quasi-biography of Valachi called The Valachi Papers, said Valachi's televised appearances before the committee were a disaster. This was because, according to Maas, the senators wanted to use the hearings for political purposes rather than for conducting a thorough investigation into organized crime. The testimony of Valachi has been even more heavily criticized by Bell, and by a number of others for its contributions to continuing the myth of the Mafia.

Bell's criticisms are pertinent to our earlier observations about myths and their effects on policy. Myths oversimplify and distort reality. Bell claims that La Cosa Nostra is an oversimplified and distorted picture of organized crime. Myths reflect deep-seated beliefs about such things as good and evil—in this case "good" is personified by Senator McClellan and "evil" by gangster Valachi. Myth-based policies against organized crime are likely to fail; Bell claims that whole areas of organized criminal activity have not received proper attention and focus because of this misplaced emphasis. Bell challenged Valachi's testimony as being "old hat." He questioned why no one in law enforcement had ever heard of Cosa Nostra before the Senate investigation (assuming it was as big and powerful as Valachi said it was). This same question is also raised by

Gordon Hawkins. Finally, Bell concluded that no new evidence was presented by Valachi—a very different view from that of Kennedy and McClellan.

Who was responsible for promulgating this myth? According to Bell, "the myth of the Mafia has been spread for years by a single agency of the United States government, the Bureau of Narcotics." Why? Because this bureau "has had to contend with a highly organized international racket" and could blame its lack of success on the racket being controlled by the Mafia. So, the Mafia myth could serve the useful and fairly typical purpose of explaining the otherwise unexplainable: narcotics were continuing to come into the United States despite the hard (and as the bureau would tell it, excellent) work of the bureau because narcotics were controlled by this omnipotent international organization called the Mafia, or now, La Cosa Nostra. Further, the belief in Mafia drug pushing helps resolve the "unwelcome contradiction" that there might be demand pressures in this country that kept the drug trade flourishing.

Bell also contends that the Justice Department and Attorney General Kennedy wanted to exploit Valachi and heighten public fears to gain support for new legislation to legalize wiretapping. This, too, is fairly typical of how myths may be used to influence public policy.

DOES IT MATTER AFTER ALL?

The myth of the Mafia or La Cosa Nostra, or the Mafia mystique, does exist. We will close by reiterating why such a myth exists, that is, what its social and law enforcement benefits are and its implications for organized crime control policy.

Galliher and Cain—along with Bell, Hawkins, Smith, and others—claim that the Mafia is a scapegoat that can be blamed for a lot of our crime problems. This is a social benefit. It helps get rid of some of the anxiety attendant in dealing with an unknown. What is causing our crime problem, our drug problem, our corruption? Why, the Mafia! Belief in this myth also helps relieve our sense of responsibility and guilt for availing ourselves of illicit goods and services and for the fact that we have corrupt public officials.

One law enforcement benefit is that "extreme measures are easily justified when people believe they are facing a widespread conspiratorial threat." Extensive use of wiretapping, eavesdropping, and other forms of surveillance that might otherwise be looked at askance from a civil liberties point of view become more acceptable when we are facing the "enemy within." Wiretapping is one of those law enforcement tools whose value in crime control effectiveness must be weighed against the due process concerns raised by the invasion of privacy. The same kinds of justifications and reservations can be made about the practice of seizing assets—government confiscation of houses, cars, boats, and so on determined to be the fruits of crime—permitted under the RICO statutes but which can be taken to unconstitutional extremes. This is also true of the use of scams that can tread dangerously close to entrapment, defined as inducing or encouraging criminality. In a somewhat different vein, the habit of denigrating the criminal defense lawyers that work on organized crime cases as being "mob lawyers" or "mouthpieces for the mob" or worse fails to fully recognize that even the worst criminals in our society have a constitutional right to be represented by legal counsel.

Albini and Bajon claim that the power of the Mafia myth is shown in the functions it serves:

They are to blame for all types of crime. The Mafia has been cited as responsible for controlling the American economy, for controlling unions and major corporations, for starting race riots in various American cities during the 1960s and indeed for controlling the very government of the United States which it has supposedly corrupted.

Yet it is the simplicity of the belief that makes the Mafia myth so appealing. Rather than having to accept the fact that syndicates in the United States have been operated by people from all types of ethnic and racial backgrounds, that syndicates exist because the American public has and continues to demand illicit goods, and that syndicates openly operate only because they receive protection from American police and public officials, belief in [the] Mafia allows the American public to cast its attention away from such harsh realities and place the blame on the mysterious group called Mafiosi. But we must remember that such a belief allows this public to feel more safe and comfortable. Why? Because by focalizing the blame on the Mafia there is the belief that it and its members can always be controlled. It is just a matter of time before the secret will become known, its membership list will be revealed and at last we will crush the Mafia and all crime will disappear. Does this sound too simple? Yes. But is not the belief in a myth just that—a simple answer to a complex reality?

This mythical belief has led numerous government agencies, commissions, committees, prosecutors, and the police to conduct numerous hearings and investigations, and to produce volumes of reports and other information—much of it for naught. As Smith says: "At the heart of my concern is a distinction between what is real and what we think is real and the importance of that distinction in our response to 'pictures' of organized crime. . . . Our 'pictures' of organized crime have failed to recognize [its] complexity, and we are at the mercy of preconceptions that prevent us from fully understanding the problem at hand."

Not understanding the problem, you will recall, is one of the principal dangers of adopting a myth-based explanation. Further, not understanding the problem or, worse yet, thinking we understand the problem when in fact we do not generally sets us up for failure. Have our efforts against organized crime been a failure? Here are the observations of two law enforcement officials in positions to know. The fact that these opinions were expressed nearly twenty years apart gives us an interesting time perspective on how the Mafia myth has affected organized crime policy. First, from a police official in 1966:

It's because the public and some policemen themselves have bought this crap about the Mafia that makes our work twice as tough. They figure since they're organized, all we have to do is go out, get a couple of the big guys and the castle will come tumbling down.

Next, in the words of Justin Dintino, a member of President Reagan's Commission on Organized Crime and a member of the New Jersey State Police, in 1986:

The attention given to La Cosa Nostra is fogging over the following realities: the fact that 30% of all labor racketeering is not investigated because the participants are not defined or labeled as members of La Cosa Nostra; the fact that La Cosa Nostra is made to appear the major organized crime menace to the country whereas its involvement in organized crime represents only .001 of the total of all organized crime in America; that, instead of Cosa Nostra, the number one problem in American organized crime consists of the Colombians and their involvement in cocaine distribution.

These comments should not be taken to mean that law enforcement has been ineffective against those upon whom it has chosen to focus its efforts. The .001 of the total to which Dintino refers (and we should take that figure with a grain of salt, as hyperbole) has been severely disrupted by the work of such prosecutors as Rudolph Giuliani, former U.S. Attorney for the Southern District of New York, and Samuel A. Alito, Jr., former U.S. Attorney for

New Jersey. The latter, for example, obtained convictions of a man described as "the most powerful member of the Genovese crime family in New Jersey" and two of his associates. They were convicted of plotting to kill John and Gene Gotti, reputed heads of the rival Gambino crime family in New York City. The plot allegedly arose out of a struggle for control of organized crime in the New York metropolitan area (*New York Times,* June 27, 1989).

What is relevant from our point of view is this comment made by the first assistant U.S. Attorney following the convictions: "With these convictions, we have a hope of making organized crime a historic relic rather than something that preys on people year in and year out" (*New York Times,* June 27, 1989, p. B1). They might make Italian-dominated syndicated crime a relic, but organized crime?—hardly. The real policy question is whether all this effort had any significant effect on the larger entity of organized crime.

Is there organized crime? Unquestionably. Are Italian-Americans and Sicilian-Americans involved in organized crime in the United States? Plenty of evidence suggests that these groups have been extensively involved. But are racketeers of Italian and Sicilian descent the only ones in organized crime? Clearly not. Are they as well organized, as bureaucratically structured, as nationally powerful as Kefauver, McClellan, Kennedy, and Cressey seemed to believe? In our opinion, no, no, no. So, is there a Mafia myth, and does it matter? Yes—and yes!

QUESTIONS FOR DISCUSSION AND WRITING

1. With what "contention" do the authors begin?
2. Who did sociologist Daniel Bell argue "was responsible for promulgating" the myth of the Mafia? Why?
3. Why did Attorney General Kennedy want to heighten public fears about the Mafia?

GANGS

Ganging

FREDERIC THRASHER

THE beginnings of the gang can best be studied in the slums of the city where an inordinately large number of children are crowded into a limited area. On a warm summer evening, children fairly swarm over areaways and sidewalks, vacant lots and rubbish dumps, streets and alleys. The buzzing chatter and constant motion remind one of insects which hover in a swarm, yet ceaselessly dart hither and thither within the animated mass. This endless activity has a tremendous fascination, even for the casual visitor to the district, and it would be a marvel indeed if any healthy boy could hold himself aloof from it.

In this ubiquitous crowd of children, spontaneous play-groups are forming everywhere—gangs in embryo. Such a crowded environment is full of opportunities for conflict with some antagonistic person or group within or without the gang's own social milieu. The conflict arises on the one hand with groups of its own class in disputes over the valued prerogatives of gangland-territory, loot, play spaces, patronage in illicit business, privileges to exploit, and so on; it comes about on the other, through opposition on the part of the conventional social order to the gang's unsupervised activities. Thus, the gang is faced

with a real struggle for existence with other gangs and with the antagonistic forces in its wider social environment.

Play-groups easily meet these hostile forces, which give their members a "we" feeling and start the process of ganging so characteristic of the life of these unorganized areas.

There is a definite geographical basis for the play-group and the gang in these areas. In the more crowded sections of the city, the geographical basis of a gang is both sides of the same street for a distance of two blocks. The members are those boys who have played together while their mothers and fathers, as is the custom in those regions, sat in front of their homes and gossiped during the long summer evenings. They know each other as well as brothers or sisters, and as they grow older continue to play together. An investigation showed that groups playing in the schoolyard after school hours are composed of boys living in the vicinity, many of whom do not attend that school during the day. The school is not the basis of this type of gang.

In the less crowded sections where the parks are available, the play-groups which frequent them usually live within a radius of only a few blocks. The whole group has simply transplanted itself to the park. The same thing is true of groups playing on vacant lots: they all come from nearby streets. One may see a group from one section playing against a group from another area, but never parts of two groups from different sections on the same team. From childhood up, members of these play-groups and gangs have been together; they would be in an unnatural atmosphere were they to play in any other group.

The majority of gangs develop from the spontaneous play-group. As the boys or older fellows of a block or a neighborhood come together in the course of business or pleasure, a crowd, in the sense of a mere gathering of persons, is formed.

On this basis of interests and aptitudes, a play-group's activities vary from "hide-and-go-seek" to crap-shooting.

Such a play-group may acquire a real organization. Natural leaders emerge, a relative standing is assigned to various members and traditions develop. It does not become a gang, however, until it begins to excite disapproval and opposition, and thus acquires a more definite group-consciousness. It discovers a rival or an enemy in the gang in the next block; its baseball or football team is pitted against some other team; parents or neighbors look upon it with suspicion or hostility; "the old man around the corner," the storekeepers, or the "cops" begin to give it "shags" (chase it); or some representative of the community steps in and tries to break it up. This is the real beginning of the gang, for now it starts to draw itself more closely together. It becomes a conflict group.

It would be erroneous, however, to suppose that a gang springs immediately from an ordinary street crowd like Minerva, full-grown from Jove's forehead. The gang has its beginning in acquaintanceship and intimate relations which have already developed on the basis of some common interest. These preliminary bonds may serve to unite pairs or trios among the boys rather than the group as a whole. The so-called two-boy gang is often a center to which other boys are attracted and about which they form like a constellation. Thus, the gang may grow additions of twos and threes as well as of single individuals. The notorious Gloriannas were originally a two-boy gang.

THE GANG AND THE FORMAL GROUP

Curiously enough, the gang sometimes develops within a group which is quite different from it in every way. A number of boys, perhaps entire strangers, are brought together by some interested agency and a club is formed. A conventional form of organization is imposed, and activities are directed and supervised. Friendships within the group begin to develop on the basis of common interests and lead to factions and cliques which oppose each other or incur the hostility of the directors. In either case, the clique may serve as the basis for a gang, and its members may begin to meet without supervision at other than the regular times.

It often happens that boys expelled either as individuals or as a group from some formal organization are drawn together to form a gang. They have become outlaws, and it is the old story of Robin Hood against the state.

In all cases of this type, the function of the common enemy in knitting the gangs together is clearly indicated.

INSTABILITY AND DISINTEGRATION

The ganging process is a continuous flux and flow, and there is little permanence in most of the groups. New nuclei are constantly appearing, and the business of coalescing and re-coalescing is going on everywhere in the congested areas. Both conflict and competition threaten the embryonic gangs with disintegration. The attention of the individual is often diverted to some new pal or to some gang that holds more attractions. When delinquency is detected, the police break up the group and at least temporarily interrupt its career. Some new activity of the playground or club frequently depletes its membership.

More often, the families of the boys move to other neighborhoods, and unless connections are tenacious the old gang is soon forgotten in alliance with the new. One boy joined an enemy gang when his family moved into hostile territory, because he "did not feel like walking so far."

Sometimes a quarrel splits the gang, and the disgruntled faction secedes. It is interesting to note that marriage is one of the most potent causes for the disintegration of the older groups. The gang is largely an adolescent phenomenon, and where conditions are favorable to its development it occupies a period in the life of the boy between childhood, when he is usually incorporated in a family structure, and marriage, when he is reincorporated into a family and other orderly relations of work, religion, and pleasure. For this reason, the adult gang, unless conventionalized, is comparatively rare and is the result of special selection. From this point of view also, then, the gang appears to be an interstitial group.

ROOTS OF THE GANG

Gangs represent the spontaneous effort of boys to create a society for themselves where none adequate to their needs exists. What boys get out of such association that they do not get otherwise under the conditions that adult society imposes is the thrill and zest of participation in common interests, more especially in corporate action, in hunting, capture, conflict, flight, and escape. Conflict with other gangs and the world about them furnishes the occasion for many of their exciting group activities.

The failure of the normally directing and controlling customs and institutions to function efficiently in the boy's experience is indicated by disintegration of family life, inefficiency of schools, formalism and externality of religion, corruption and indifference in local politics, low wages and monotony in occupational activities, unemployment, and lack of opportunity for wholesome recreation.

Conclusions, suggested by the present study, seem amply verified by data from other cities. New York's juvenile gangland is well illustrated where conditions of life are greatly disorganized, and gangs are typical of certain portions of the Lower East and West Sides and other interstitial areas.

The story of the early gangs, which fills such a colorful page in New York's history, bears out the same point.

The old Five Points section, described by Charles Dickens in his *American Notes* as containing slums of the utmost depravity and "all that is loathsome, drooping and decayed," was the breeding place of most of the early gangs and was the scene of many of the most famous of the gang wars.

The tenement areas in the South End of Boston have numerous gangs. In Minneapolis, the best residence districts and the better middle-class sections are free from such groups, but in the North, East, and South Town districts, industrial areas, there seem to be a good many destructive gangs. In Cleveland, the downtown business district, the lake shore east, sections of the west side near the river, the middle-east side, and the Harvard-Broadway section, which constitute disorganized interstitial areas, have been especially favorable to the development of gang life. The gangs of Los Angeles are to be found in the industrial and east-side sections where conditions of life are similar to those in Chicago ganglands. It is in the disorganized river districts of St. Louis that the city's juvenile gangs have flourished. These conditions are repeated, with variations due to local conditions, in New Orleans, Denver, San Francisco, and other American cities in which the economic, moral, and cultural frontier is in evidence.

IS THERE A GANG INSTINCT?

The traditional explanation of the gang and one supported by the older type of individual psychology has been to dismiss gang behavior as due to an instinct. "The gang instinct . . . . is a natural characteristic of our social order, and it would be impossible to uproot it or destroy it." "The gang instinct . . . is recognized in the formation of the small group clubs." "Somewhere about the age of ten, the little boy . . . begins to develop the gang-forming instinct." These are typical statements of the "gang-instinct" explanation. Other writers consider ganging as a special form of the "social instinct"—a difference in phrasing only.

Theoretical psychology no longer supports instincts as the bases of human behavior. Man has fewer instincts than other animals. His nature is plastic and he excels in his capacity to adapt himself to a multiplicity of situations for which instinct could not fit him. He is primarily of habit, but the pattern of his habits may be infinitely varied in varied circumstances.

What writers on the gang have attributed to instinct is the result of pervasive social habits arising out of the human struggle for existence and social preferment. It is apparent also that use of the phrases "gang instinct" or "social instinct" in the passages quoted is made without much attempt at a thoroughgoing analysis of the complex conditions underlying the formation and behavior of the gang.

The gang, as has already been indicated, is a function of specific conditions, and it does not tend to appear in the absence of these conditions. Under other circumstances, the boy becomes a "solitary type," enters into a relation of palship or intimacy with one or more other boys in separate pairs, or is incorporated into play-groups of a different sort or into more conventional or older groups. What relationships he has with others are determined by a complex of conditioning factors which direct his interests and his habits. It is not instinct, but experience—the way he is conditioned—that fixes his social relations.

QUESTIONS FOR DISCUSSION AND WRITING

1. What are "gangs in embryo"? Why does Thrasher use this term?
2. When does a play group become a gang?
3. What do gangs represent?

The Social Organization of Street Gang Activity in an Urban Ghetto

SUDHIR ALLADI VENKATESH

INTRODUCTION

The urban poor ghetto, the "socially isolated" inner city, and the "underclass" neighborhood have all become powerful phrases in the popular discourse on race and urbanism. They are grounded firmly in American consciousness, and they carry strong, cathected understandings of citizenship, individual responsibility, normative social behavior, and so on. One of the strongest images produced by these catchphrases is that of the street gang lurking about in dimly lit streets, preying upon the local residential population, and destroying community social fabric. Out of the extraordinary attention of media and state institutions, street gang activity has become depicted as a signature attribute of ghetto life, along with other resonant behaviors such as teenage childbearing and welfare dependency. Conventional wisdom suggests that the contribution of a street gang to its surrounding communities is largely negative and its "positive functions" minimal. Often, however, the power of such images obscures a fuller portrait, in this case, of the range of activities of a street gang—delinquent, normative, and mundane—and the complex ways it participates in the social life of a community. To date, this estimation of the street gang as a primarily destructive community actor remains based more on the weight of popular imagery and emotion than on a foundation of research and evidence.

To redress this one-sided perspective, I analyze the relations of street gangs to their broader community (hereafter referred to as the "gang–community" relation). My focus on the gang–community relation addresses both an empirical and theoretical gap in the research on street gangs. Concerning the former, in their assessments of the state of the field, researchers repeatedly single out the lack of attention to the ways in which the street gang interacts with other groups and institutions in its neighborhood. With some exceptions, scholars generally do not examine the street gang's engagement with the local neighborhood and other surrounding spaces. This includes the ways in which the street gang interacts with other social groups and institutions, how residents cope with some of the associated phenomena (e.g., patterns of symbolic expression, illicit economic activity, criminality), and, finally the patterns of change and continuity of gang and community over time. Similarly, some scholars have criticized the conventional theoretical frameworks applied to the study of street gangs because they fail to incorporate a social contextual dimension.

To explore the relations of gang and community and the theoretical relevance therein, I focus on patterns of street gang activity in Blackstone, a midsize public housing development located in a poor ghetto of a large midwestern city. Specifically, I examine a set of struggles that occurred during 1992 among tenants, street gangs, and community institutions. From May to December of that year, these actors debated with one another and engaged in political battles to control affairs that affected the social and material welfare of the housing development. Noteworthy in these interactions was the role of the street gang. Historically, despite their visibility, street gangs in Blackstone did not occupy a legitimate community presence. Their involvement in public forums, community events, and local decision making was minimal; moreover, resident interaction with street gangs was quite circumscribed, primarily in delinquent activities such as small-scale drug distribution or larceny. Both the role of the street gang and their relations with the broader population changed toward the end of the 1980s when the gangs began to "corporatize"—that is, when they directed their energies toward systematic involvement in drug distribution—and began using their illicit revenues to fulfill a range of community needs. In 1992, after the street gang's economic expansion was well underway, many of the long-standing relations between gangs, residents, and local institutions were disrupted and a historically novel social organization emerged. My main concern in this article is to analyze this process of corporatization and the ways in which it redefined the experience of street gang activity for residents of the housing development. . . .

In the analysis below, I concentrate on four actors who spoke most forcefully on behalf of the Blackstone community during the May–December 1992 period: the *Council* is a body of tenant-elected officers who act on behalf of the residential population; the *street gangs* most active during 1992 were the all-male factions; the *Grace Center* is a social service organization that provides social, recreational, and educational programs to Blackstone residents; and, the *state*, understood as an embodied social

actor, is represented by the housing authority and the municipal police department, whose roles, though formally circumscribed, are immensely significant in their scope and symbolic effect. . . .

STUDYING THE STREET GANG

The literature on street gangs is expansive and varied, but a cursory look at methodology and substantive areas of inquiry reveals particular patterns, tendencies, and gaps. Researchers employ diverse methods of data collection and analysis, including statistical analyses of rates of criminal activities among street gangs, structured interviews of gang members in institutional settings, and direct ethnographic observation. The substantive areas of focus in street gang research vary but tend to address definitional and methodological issues, patterns of gang involvement in illicit activities, organizational structure, gender and sexual relations and (sub)culture and identity. Common to most of the scholarship on street gangs is the tendency to favor social structural and attitudinal data over practice and interaction. Actual behaviors are not frequently or systematically recorded. Where lived experience *has* been documented, significant revision of extant theoretical and conceptual apparatuses ensues.

An area of relative paucity, both in terms of theory and empirical attention, is the social contextual status of the street gang, that is, its relationship to broader spaces and institutions. Jankowski clearly demonstrates the importance of the social contextual status of the street gang in his work, *Islands in the Street*. He argues that the researcher must have an appreciation for the larger sociospatial context within which the gang is embedded because part of the specificity of gang activity derives from an exigency of the "[gang] to be integrated into both the local and the larger community." In practice, this integrative process translates into a dynamism whereby the gang and other community actors (e.g., police, schools, families) engage in ongoing interaction. "Integration" becomes a contingent state that has to be continually reconstituted. And, through such engagement, social relations of power, friendship, solidarity, animosity, and so on that involve the street gang are reproduced. Thus, the street gang and those actors with whom it interacts mutually determine each other's status and identity in local community social organization.

It is precisely such processes of integration and codetermination that are not well documented in street gang scholarship. Several factors, theoretical and methodological, have directed the study of street gangs away from such phenomena. I have already alluded to one, namely the collection of primarily attitudinal data. Whether in the form of fixed-choice questionnaires or life-historical interviews, only a limited understanding of the status of the gang in community social organization has been derived through data on beliefs, values, and attitudes. A second factor is the disproportionate concern of researchers with the *origins* of gang activity, on both the individual and collective levels. Why did gangs come into being in a particular community and not another? Did nonurban street gang activity form independently or through contagion vis-à-vis the transmigration of metropolitan street gang "sets"? In this context, the reproduction of *existing* gang activity over time garners less attention, as does the gang–community relationship, since the tenure of gang activity is highly contingent on the response by others locally. Third, a study of community relations would lead street gang research into nondelinquent areas of study, a move that to date has been blocked due to the dominance of a criminological paradigm for both academic and popular inquiries.

A fourth factor, the one that I will address in greatest detail in this article, is the interplay of space and interaction that buttresses the scholarship on street gangs. This relation, theoretical in nature, has framed the possibilities both for conceptualizing the gang within a broader social and institutional context and for studying its patterns of interaction with other actors in that space. Specifically, since the mid 20th century, when Thrasher and Shaw and McKay set the tone for research on youth delinquency, researchers have acknowledged that street gangs must be understood in relation to their surrounding environment and that systemic factors can affect the character of street gang activity. To argue for this linkage between macrosocial context and locally situated behaviors, researchers typically correlate community characteristics such as demographic patterns or social structural attributes with other aggregate data such as crime rates. Thus, the link between street gang activity and systemic factors is often asserted but not well explicated either theoretically or in specific empirical areas. (An important exception to this mode of analysis is Sampson and Groves' research, which is more nuanced and incorporates community-level variables that mediate the impact of social structural forces. To date, however, their model has not been adequately incorporated by scholars of street gangs. This essay can be seen as an attempt to build on the spirit of their approach.)

A strand of ethnographic street gang research commonly referred to as the "underclass school" is noteworthy in this regard because it *has* successfully uncovered some of the spheres of social activity where street gang activity assumes its texture and force due to broader systemic transformations. Scholars adhering to this perspective appropriate William Julius Wilson's theory of the reproduction of the underclass. Wilson's theory is not intended to explain street gang activity, nor is it ostensibly an analysis of deviant behavior; nevertheless, according to Spergel, "the underclass formulation, or variations of it, has been a useful basis for explaining gang development and its sustenance by gang researchers and scholars." These researchers argue that the contemporary street gang is a product of postwar systemic factors that have deleteriously affected the economic and institutional fabric of inner cities. Specifically, the gang partially fills the void left by other community-based institutions. *Adaptation* is the central trope—a "cluster concept"—for underclass researchers to explain a range of phenomena: for example, the gang can be a substitute for poorly functioning familial structures; its value orientation offers a moral chart for those youths excluded from mainstream cultural systems.

Currently, the underclass perspective is the "most popular and influential" one used to "explain a whole range of socially disordered or deviant behaviors." However, the use of adaptation to link a wide range of social activity to macrohistorical contexts has not enabled a more detailed analysis of both interaction and gang–community dynamics. Street gang members are portrayed as active agents struggling to lead meaningful lives in impoverished contexts, yet, other community actors are often not given a voice or mention in analysis. For example, if gangs are substitutes for families in underclass communities, what is the relation of gang members to parents and siblings? Similarly, do household members and communities broadly intervene in the gangs' rising familial role? The complexity within, and differentiations among, the range of processes that are captured in the catch-all category of adaptation (and its analytic synonyms: adjustment, response, substitution, etc.) becomes erased as quickly as they are gathered together within this single analytic trope. . . .

RECONSTITUTING COMMUNITY IN BLACKSTONE

Summer 1992 proved to be a pivotal moment in Blackstone. Street gangs, tenant bodies such as the Council, and governmental agencies such as the housing authority began to act in ways that deviated from their past behavior. Stated summarily, the Council has been the dominant tenant-elected representative body in Blackstone since the early 1970s. So strong was their presence in the seventies and eighties that residents' everyday experience was

determined by their relation to the particular Council representatives in their building: that is, *a "building-centered" social space reigned whereby different buildings had different histories, reputations, levels of service, maintenance and attention by administrative agencies, rates of criminal activity, and so on.* During the mid-1980s, tenants grew frustrated because the Council could no longer procure effective physical maintenance from the housing authority, nor could they lobby law enforcement with success as in the past. As important, Council representatives were unable to dole out benefits such as part-time employment and emergency loans to residents. The Council was partially strapped because the housing authority had rescinded its own commitment to upkeep and physical maintenance, in some instances diverting budgetary resources from "maintenance" to "security" needs—a practice that provoked the ire of Blackstone residents and caused numerous protests.

In the void created by both Council and housing authority inaction, the Saints, a local street gang, channeled illicitly obtained revenues from drug economies to the general residential population. This process was part of the street gang's overall "corporatization" and had several effects on social relations within the community: (1) it enabled the Saints gang to vie for the sponsorship of resident constituencies that had previously granted their allegiance to the Council; (2) as such, the base of tenant allegiance the Councils had previously relied on was no longer self-evident, and their influence with government agencies that administered Blackstone slowly eroded because they could not unproblematically claim to be spokespersons.

To date, corporatization has been understood primarily as an *economic* process whereby the gang eschews its "territorial" or symbolic interests in favor of monetary gain. To be sure, revenue generation based on the exchange of illicit goods certainly buttressed the rising social status of the Saints street gang in Blackstone. However, their rise to economic superiority was one constitutive part of a more comprehensive social advancement that involved interaction with a broader community of actors and not only other "outlaw capitalists." In effect, the Saints consciously tried to "integrate" themselves into the social fabric of Blackstone, using economic power as their foundation to build relations with residents and local organizations. *The result of their corporatization was the emergence of a novel social space in Blackstone, that is, a new orientation to local geography in which the symbolic distinctions of local street gangs challenged the building-centered distinctions that had previously underwritten the power of the Councils. . . .*

The Impact of Corporatization

The May–December 1992 period brought to the surface many of the tensions that accompanied the Saints' historically unprecedented attempt to ground themselves in the social organization of Blackstone. According to tenant leaders such as "Ms. Willis," the most important issue brought "into the open for all to see" was the increasing acceptance of street gang resources by residents. With respect to the adaptation analytic framework the motivations of residents to accept street gang dollars and in-kind support (e.g., nightly escorts to the grocery store) can be accounted for as function of macrostructural constraints. Specifically, Blackstone's residents are generally quite poor and do not possess access to monetary, legal, social service, and other institutional resources; thus, it would not be altogether surprising that as a "survival strategy" residents would accept the offerings of the street gang. This explanation is not entirely inaccurate since it attempts to link macrosocial attributes of Blackstone with emergent social action on the part of individuals. However, it simplifies the agency exercised by residents because it cannot help explicate why some tenants preferred to reject street gang assistance, nor does it unravel why tenants' decisions to accept the gang's assistance occurred *at a particular historical juncture.* By contrast, a

more in-depth understanding of residents' attitudes toward, and historically shifting relations with, local street gangs can better account for their decision-making process.

To elaborate, in the 1980s, the Saints family of street gangs took over the power to distribute drugs in Blackstone from the Roaches family. The Saints were led in these efforts by "JT" whose set is currently the most powerful of the four Saints sets in the housing development. In May, the Roaches gang initiated a series of violent attacks on Saints members in an effort to recapture drug distribution territories. Many of these attacks were poorly planned and did little to recapture lost markets. Typically the younger members of the Roaches became drunk both with liquor and the zeal to fight the Saints; disobeying their elder leaders' commands, these "shorties" executed "drive-by" shootings in areas controlled by the Saints. On one of these drive-bys, the Roaches fatally shot a young girl and wounded her friend, both of whom were playing in front of a housing development building. This incident not only accelerated the gang war, but it prompted forthright community discussion of the deleterious effects of the increased involvement by the Saints gang in drug economies. In other words, what, on one level, signified street gangs grappling for control over drug economies, referenced on another level a crisis in community social organization.

The unexpected consequence of the gang wars was an expanded public discussion of the new behaviors and statuses being exhibited by different community actors. These discussions began in June 1992 at "community control" meetings. Here, tenants and their elected Council representatives discussed the effects of street gang activity for the safety of public spaces and semipublic areas such as stairwells and lobby areas on the first floor of buildings. For much of the three-hour dialogue, the conversation was dry, centering primarily on the possibility of diverting the Council's fiscal resources toward upgrading "tenant patrols"—these patrols are comprised of pairs of women who conduct systematic "walkabouts" within buildings in order to locate illegal or dangerous behavior. Toward the end of the meeting, tenant–police relations and resident collusion in gang-controlled drug economies were raised for discussion:

"Who's running things 'round here?" an unidentified voice from the back of the room yelled to the Council representatives sitting around the front table.

"You all don't control nothing," yelled another voice in support.

A Council member replied, "You don't either, nigger, so don't be getting all over me. We got to work together to take control of our community. If you don't feel safe walking around the building, help us out with tenant patrols."

"Tenant patrols?!" an elderly man sitting in the front row said mockingly in reference to the residents' practice of walking through their buildings each hour to identify trouble. "We need the *police* to kick these drugs out the building, tenant patrols ain't doing shit!"

"Tell 'em nigger!" yelled a voice from the back. "Police is the ones ought to be patrolling, not 50-year-old women too old to see shit."

"Women wouldn't have nothing to see if you all didn't let them gangs run up in here doing whatever they pleased," barked a Council officer in response.

"Shit, *you* the one getting they money. Don't act like you ain't. How you bought that big screen TV anyway?"

As is apparent, this exchange witnessed several accusations. Specifically, residents blamed one another for supporting street gang extortion, participating in gang-controlled drug distribution, and refusing to speak publicly against inadequate police protection.

The meeting ended when residents conceded support for a twofold intervention strategy: first, Council officers would negotiate with the street gangs to end the sale of drugs *within* buildings. As one man said, "Feeling unsafe when I go out is bad, but at least I want to feel like I ain't gonna get shot

pulling up a chair in front of my door and watching the world go by. Inside these buildings, that's where we need to be safe, that's where police gotta do something for us."

Second, Council officers would pressure law enforcement agencies to provide more responsive and effective policing inside their buildings. At a "town hall" meeting one week later, when confronted with the tenants' requests, city police officers responded by asking residents to "cooperate with law enforcement." The officers openly criticized residents who, by withholding information and refusing to allow police to enter their apartments without search warrants, were effectively lending support to street gangs. After the town hall meeting ended, Clara Davis, a prominent tenant leader, explained to me that residents of Blackstone "stopped cooperating with police a long time ago, 'cause [the police] harass us so much and they don't do a damn thing anyway: At least the gangs is giving us something, so lot of us prefers to help them 'cause we can *always* go to them and tell them to stop the shooting. Police don't do anything for us and they can't stop no shooting anyway. Call me what you want, but all I know is that [the Saints] is the ones providing security around here, not no police. And, my brother was a Saint when he was younger, so you know, it's a community thing 'cause we all niggers anyway when it comes down to it."

Davis's comments above suggest that residents' decisions to cooperate with city and housing authority police are not only a product of the perceived impotence of law enforcement agencies but are also affected by the regnant ties between residents and street gangs. For example, she points to historic relations between gangs and residents when she says, "my brother was a Saint [gang member] when he was younger." Despite their admission that gang activity is the root cause of many community instabilities, residents embrace gang members as wayward kin rather than ostracizing them completely as social deviants who need the discipline of law. At other moments, residents who have lived in Blackstone since the 1960s and 1970s will compare the ambitions of contemporary street gang factions to their predecessors, for whom community service was quite prominent (yet participation in underground economies was relatively minimal). Finally, although gang affiliation is arguably the principal public identity for many of the individual members, much of the social interaction in Blackstone occurs in situations where gang membership is not marked and where gang members are known by other roles (e.g., son, niece, neighbor's son, etc.). Thus, a great deal of everyday social life affirms common experiences for community members as opposed to differential experiences that result from gang affiliation. Witness, for example, the rebuke made by "Ms. Jackson," an elderly tenant who moved into Blackstone in 1968, of a housing authority officer's claim that gang members are the sole cause of community decline: "Keep our apartments clean. Make sure that [the] security [guards] leave the lobby and walk through the hallways and stairwells. Don't let weapons come in the buildings when the metal detector goes off! We ain't asking for much. These gang members is our kids. We'll take care of 'em. But, they need work, and we need to have [you] take care of our homes."

These strong symbolic ties between gangs and (non-gang-affiliated) residents are themselves grounded in material linkages that have formed between the two groups. In the 1980s, the Saints channeled revenues from drug economies to residents who lacked financial resources or who were simply willing to remain silent in police investigations. The most direct examples were loans and lines of credit to residents (which, depending on personal relations, could either be given interest free or offered at an exorbitant 100% rate of interest), periodic disbursements of groceries and clothing to households, and the purchase of bail bonds for jailed residents. The Saints gang also organized recreational leagues in the community at which residents would compete for trophies and bragging rights. Par-

ticipants were given clothing and uniforms (emblazoned with "Blackstone and Proud" on the back) as well as shoes and equipment.

. . . Consider, for example, "Ms. Willis's" struggle to obtain monetary support for a Council-sponsored neighborhood party during a conversation I had with her. Her reluctant acceptance of street gang resources is replicated by other tenant leaders who are unable to locate funding for their activities:

"I asked the housing authority [for the money] first, you know them? They're the ones who's supposed to give us money for these kinda things—you know little parties, community things. But, we can't get a damn dollar out of these folks. They got their little group over there, and we ain't seen a penny of the 'community' money."

"So, you want me to give you some money. . . . Well, to tell you the truth, Ms. Willis, I really don't have all that much money myself," I said.

Disbelieving what I said, she shook her head and replied, "Well, now how you gonna tell me that when you drivin' round that little sports car o' yours . . ."

"So, you won't be able to throw the party, then?" I said, trying to remain calm.

"Guess, I'll go back to Ottie [a street gang leader] again. I just don't like takin' 'dirty money' if I can avoid it. You know?! But whatcha gonna do?"

As Ms. Willis made clear, accepting street gang assistance is not only a difficult decision for residents to make but, as important, *before the early 1990s, she says many Council officers (and other tenant leaders) did not accept such gang largesse.* Only after this date could one find systematic patterns of giving whereby the Saints' leaders funded the Council's activities. Others affirm her assessment. For example, until the early 1990s Council representatives with whom I spoke stated that they did not feel threatened by local street gangs. Ms. Jackson, mentioned above, who has been an activist in Blackstone for nearly three decades, recalls that street gangs were always present in large numbers, but their status was restricted to intergang activities, and they held minimal influence in community affairs. Council officers felt little need to "use [the gang's] money, hurting our image in the eyes of other tenants" (Ms. Jackson). When the street gangs became more influential and increased their own philanthropy, Council officers and other tenant leaders felt their own power threatened: lacking the connections to city agencies, foundations, and other potential sources of monetary support, the Council turned increasingly to the Saints in order to buy goods, to plan collective activities, and to get manpower at public events. In other words, though Council members acted on the basis of perceived circumstances, their response was not simply a product of macrolevel forces but was instead mediated by their perceptions, by specific historical factors, and by emergent political dynamics at the social organizational level.

In autumn 1992, a more profound and historically unprecedented relationship between gangs and residents formed: residents used current and ex-gang members to establish social order in Blackstone. *This* gang–community dynamic, more than any other, brought to the surface the spectrum of resident opinions regarding "how much we've changed since the gangs took over the power." As a result of the cooperative relationships forming between the Council and street gangs, some tenants publicly questioned whether the Council had compromised its own vision for the community's future. The most extreme statements were skeptical of the Council's ability to serve as a representative body.

The New Law and Order

Gangs have long been a means by which "interstitial" urban communities fulfilled their need for protection, safety in intercourse, and defense against perceived threats. "Vigilante peer groups" provided white ethnic and minority urban communities with a range of regulative services that include enforcement, policing, escort, protection against social predators, and punishment. In Blackstone,

self-policing existed in varying forms since the mid-1960s. The earliest documented cases are social networks composed predominantly of women that watched over children and monitored the behavior of strangers in and around their building. Subsequent examples include tenant patrols, community watches, and militias of men who were assembled by Council officers and influential residents to chase down thieves, burglars, and perpetrators of domestic abuse. While these practices were systematic and also developed in the context of ineffective mainstream law enforcement, they could not match in breadth or intent the system of "law" that select residents were attempting to institutionalize in autumn 1992 in order to regulate gang activity. An extended account of self-policing and "indigenous" law in Blackstone is beyond the scope of this essay; therefore, I will address aspects of this process that are most relevant for the gang–community dynamism and the corporatization of the Saints street gang.

In mid-summer 1992, Council officers felt that they could no longer obtain adequate police enforcement. They needed to locate alternate methods of resolving the "gang wars" between the Roaches and Saints street gangs. Led by Carol Collins, the Council officers approached Joe Jackson, the director of the Grace Center, a local social service agency. Jackson was sympathetic to their predicament. He had been working closely with JT—the highest ranking Saints leader in Blackstone—as well as citywide, higher-ranking gang leaders to forge a peace treaty among Roaches and Saints sets based in Blackstone. His reaction was positive, and he explained his willingness to assist the Council:

Two heads are always better than one, you know. See, what we had going for us was two things. JT wanted peace and he was, you know, he was alright. I don't mean he is a priest or nothing but, he always gave us what we needed to help families 'round here, so, and he didn't want to piss off the head honchos! You know, he had to keep the money flowing in, so I figured Ms. Collins and the rest of 'em, well, talking with the Saints could only help 'em, 'cause they wasn't getting along that great. (Joe Jackson, Grace Center Director)

As Jackson makes clear in the quote above, he realized that his efforts to offer social services to the gangs could marry well with the Council leaders' interests in violence reduction and conflict resolution. Under his initiative, the Grace Center sponsored several meetings to introduce Council officers to Peace Now, an organization specializing in gang peace treaties. Peace Now was directed by an ex-gang member who had influential ties to the senior, predominantly imprisoned, leaders of the Saints and Roaches street gang families. Peace Now offered to mediate the dispute among Roaches and Saints until the fighting had been eradicated and a treaty could be formed.

Council officers wanted more, explains Carol Collins: "Peace ain't shit if they ain't respecting us every day, you know what I'm sayin. Stop beating up women, stop dealing drugs up inside the buildings, don't go shooting one another up and down Crabtree Lane—that's what we want. Peace Now agreed to add to disputes between warring gangs the many grievances issued by residents against street gangs. In doing so, their conflict resolution expanded to include mediation of gang–resident disputes. For example, residents could report incidents of domestic abuse or sexual harassment by street gang members; Peace Now officers would adjudicate these transgressions. Similarly, residents who were performing tasks for the street gangs (e.g., storing cash or drugs in their apartment) could report violations of verbal contracts; at these hearings, the party at fault would be determined, and fines and punishment would be meted out.

By November 1992, Peace Now staffers, Joe Jackson, Carol Collins, and ex-gang leaders were meeting actively with members of the Saints and Roaches to discuss complaints. At first, Blackstone's gang leader refused to allow this delegation to intervene in incidents that involved gang–community interactions. Once Peace Now produced evidence that the higher-ranking, imprisoned street gang leaders approved of this forum, the local Saints and Roaches members had no choice but to acquiesce to the issued rulings and sentencing. The following summer, JT reflected on these initial interactions and acknowledged their merit:

"I don't know why I was against all that. It reminded me of, you know court or something, and any time you get these niggers [referring to gang members] in the justice system, they gonna close up and not say shit. So why we want to have something like that again?"

"But, you think it was good, in the long run?"

"Yeah, now, 'cause all the violence is Roaches shooting at us. We don't beat up nobody, all [our] 'shorties' [adolescent members] learning to treat people with respect, we take care of our community more now, you know."

JT's resistance to the self-enforcement mechanisms, based on his distrust of the judicial system, is similar to the other street gang leaders with whom I spoke. As another Saints leader stated, "It was like going up before the judge again, and [gang members] don't like that kinda shit, you know."

During that period, resistance to the self-enforcement mechanisms came not only from the street gangs themselves but also from residents. In one of the most impassioned speeches to the Council officers, James Marcus, a 40-year-old father whose son had been shot in summer 1992 by a stray bullet (allegedly from a gang member's weapon), stated: "You all can tell [the gangs] that what goes down in that room: they gotta listen to it. But, this ain't gonna do nothing as far as getting us better police protection. You know what, the police is laughing at us: they sitting there watching us kill each other, and then, we making their jobs easier 'cause now, they don't even gotta clean up the mess we made. They laughing at you and me and all of us in this room. How you figure this is gonna help us live safer 'round here?" . . .

Several factors produced this ambivalence on the part of residents. First, as Grace Center director Joe Jackson liked to say, "Since you and I don't live here everyday, you can't predict what people will do to get them some safety and peace of mind"—that is, the willingness of an appointed body to intervene and respond to gang-related concerns had an immediate impact on a tenant body that did not have another individual or organization to help resolve street gang disputes. The impact could be measured to some degree by the high proportion of votes that tenants subsequently cast in favor of a Peace Now officer running for political office in the congressional district that included Blackstone. Whereas I heard residents frequently complain to their Council officers that the quasi-court was "turning over the community to the gangs," I watched the very same persons stand in front of the delegation and voice their complaints. One resident, whom I confronted directly regarding this contradiction, replied, "Until something better comes along, well, fuck it. I'm gonna tell them to stop them niggers from selling drugs 'round my baby. If police want to stop them, OK. But, right now, they ain't doing nothing."

The underlying material generosity of the street gangs also helped dissuade residents from actively voicing their dissent, and in this case, their bought silence proved to be a vote in favor of the Peace Now–sponsored forum. During the autumn 1992 period, the Saints' gang leaders actively lobbied to garner residential support for the "indigenous policing" procedures that were being implemented. The number of people whom JT and other Saints leaders contacted and offered money or favors "[wasn't] that many, but it was enough to get 'em to not say shit" (Ottie, another Saints gang leader). JT and Ottie also planned barbecues and basketball tournaments during the autumn 1992 months in order to demonstrate that they were interested in the affairs of the community. They replaced aging playground equipment and basketball rims, and they exercised greater discipline over the younger Saints

gang members, forcing them to minimize their truant behavior. However, in general, their benevolence was directed at Council officers because they understood that most residents were inactive in community affairs. When I asked JT why he was directing much of his lobbying at Council officers and was not waging an outright populist campaign, he replied: "It's only the Council really that we gotta worry about, 'cause they the only ones who give a fuck, so we just take care of them." . . .

Space and Social Reproduction

I have so far described some of the unprecedented material exchanges that characterized the corporatization of the Saints street gang, the novelty of which is not simply the material disbursement from street gangs to non-gang-affiliated constituencies. This practice had existed in Blackstone long before the corporatization and correlative philanthropy of the Saints began. By contrast, these 1990s exchanges assumed their unique character due to the role of the street gang as a provider of goods and services on par (or, at the very least, in competition) with the state, the Council, and legitimate labor markets. Stated differently, by "taking [the gangs'] dirty money," as one tenant leader often says, there is an implicit admission by residents that mainstream sources (e.g., income maintenance programs, part-time jobs, philanthropy) are unable to meet the community's needs. James Marcus made this point in a conversation with the director of the Grace Center and me in summer 1993: "The day when the Council—and you can blame me too, cause I took their money—the day when they started taking the gangs' money and giving it out to everybody, that's when everything changed, you dig? No way we could turn back, no way we could say no to all that cash being thrown around, man we needed that, families needed that help." Others assessed the situation in much the same manner as Marcus, reflecting on the totality of the shifts that were occurring. During a 6:00

A.M. surprise police search of apartments, several tenants—sitting in the hallway and discussing with me their decisions to withhold information in police investigations—talked openly with me as police, other residents, and housing authority representatives walked past. They remarked on their resignation to the authority of the local street gangs:

It used to be our community, we used to say what went on 'round here, but it's they community now.

We have to listen to [the Saints gang], 'cause when the police leave, [Saint gang members] are the ones who'll let you know if shootings gonna start up again, you know, they'll tell you if it's safe to go outside at night, or you can go up north [to Roaches territory] or if you should just stay in the building.

Yeah, right, [Saints] make our lives miserable, but if we piss them off, police ain't gonna come 'round here and help us out. And, shit, I gotta tell you that most of the time it's nice, 'cause they make sure I don't get robbed in here, they walk through the buildings like . . . police never did that! It's when the wars start that I don't really feel safe, you know? Most of the time, it's OK.

In these observations, residents acknowledge the gang's control over the ebb and flow of daily movements and cycles. . . .

This local omnipresence of the gang is best evidenced, not in the juridical and material offerings that I have described above, but instead in the more generic development whereby the social space formed through the territorial practices of the street gang have challenged earlier identifications of residents with their local environment. The gang's marking of "turf," its spatialization of ally and enemy relations, and its assignment of areas for exchange and consumption are articulated with, and in some cases superseded by, previously formed cultural "enunciations" that enabled residents to negotiate or make do with their physical surroundings. This is readily apparent in the reorientation of Blackstone's

non-gang-affiliated residents to the city. The manner by which they can move about in Blackstone and surrounding spaces—both *where* they can visit and *how* they get there—is effectively altered once they are forced to acknowledge and incorporate street gang inscriptions. For example, consider those residents who arrived in Blackstone before the 1980s and who often fondly recall the era when the "gangs was controlled by the community, not the other way around." Until the mid-1980s, street gang attributes were secondary for their movements in Blackstone. Instead, the building in which a person lived, the reigning Council officers, and the relative proximity to local transportation networks were some of the important indexes of social space that affected their daily intercourse. As the gang's entrepreneurialism and largesse became entrenched and as their "law and order" services became more pronounced, their geographic markings exerted a greater symbolic force. Gang-based distinctions impressed upon a social space where gang symbolism previously held minimal sway. Corey Wilson, a 40-year-old resident in a Saints-controlled building, makes this point forcefully by arguing for the relative importance of "the gang who controls the building you live in," as opposed to other symbolic attributions that determine safety, personal identity, and ease of local travel:

It's like, now I think about myself living in Saints territory. That's the most important thing, 'cause they the ones who do stuff around here, they clean up, give money to people who need food, you know, they the ones who really, you know, affect how you live. So, I tell my friends I live 'over there with the 33rd St. Saints' where before I might say 'yeah I live in this or that building, come and see me.' Now people want to know what gang controls where you living, 'cause that's more important than how far away you are from them, or if you can take the bus there, you know?

The emergent gang-laden social space has forced Blackstone residents to reconstitute their "street wisdom" in line with the new dictates imposed by street gang geography. Like the inhabitants of Village–Northton in Elijah Anderson's *Streetwise*, those in Blackstone also have "found some system for categorizing the denizens of the street and other public spaces. . . . The streetwise individual thus becomes interested in a host of signs, emblems, and symbols that others exhibit in everyday life. The general navigation of the "local and larger community" by Blackstone residents demonstrates their adherence to the contours of "gangland." For example, an individual visiting a friend living outside Blackstone may minimize travel through those areas controlled by gangs that are at war with the one in his or her own neighborhood. Within Blackstone, residents living in buildings controlled by the Saints gang will limit their visits to buildings controlled by the Roaches, calling upon friends and family only during daytime hours or when peace treaties are known to be in place between the two street gang families. "Cookie," a young adult who does not belong to a gang but who lives in a Saints-controlled building, continually expresses frustration at the constraint imposed by this "outlaw" social space. On one occasion, he was not allowed to enter a building in Blackstone by members of the Roaches who were standing guard at the building's entrance. I met him as he returned to his own apartment:

"What's wrong, Cookie, you upset at something?" I asked.

"Cookie can't go and see his old lady! Ain't that right, nigger," said Billy, a friend of Cookie's who was sharing a stoop with me.

"These niggers won't even let me see my girlfriend. Bitch gonna have a baby and the father can't even come in the apartment. Shit, these outlaws taking over this place . . . and I ain't even in the damn organization."

"No," interrupted Billy, "they done *took over* the place!"

Cookie's inability to visit his girlfriend has become a routine occurrence for residents of Blackstone. To visit his girlfriend, Cookie lobbied Ms. Jackson, the Council president in his building. She called the respective Council officer in Cookie's girlfriend's building, who in turn convinced the local Roaches gang leader that Cookie was a "neutron," that is, that he was not a gang member, had no allegiance to the Saints (or to the Roaches for that matter), and posed no threat. Cookie's successful use of weak ties to obtain visitation rights with his expectant girlfriend is exemplary of the streetwise efforts that are needed not only to move about freely but, in the case of youth, to sustain personal identities that are not dominated by street gang affiliations.

Similar to Cookie, other non-gang-affiliated young adults are forced to reconstitute their personal identities in reference to the gang-based social space that they inhabit. For these neutrons, gang identity has revalorized extant geographically based stigmatizations. For example, many youths feel that an address in Blackstone limits their opportunities to succeed in social institutions such as school and the mainstream labor market.

When I go out and try to get a job, I tell 'em my address and they think you know, that I'm running with a gang. It's like I can't convince them that I ain't a part of all that, you know? And, if they believe me, then they ask about all that warring going down, so like, I'm fucked if I tell 'em anything I know, 'cause then they'll ask, "How is it you know if you ain't in a gang?"

It was bad enough, before, you know, 'cause I got outta high school and I had to tell folks that I was from Blackstone but I didn't want to stay on welfare my whole life. Now, they ask me if I'm in a gang! So, I gotta work on that and tell them that we ain't all alike, not all of us are into that.

As their lamentations make clear, the stigma of their address in a public housing development has become coupled with the popular conception of Blackstone as a breeder of street gangs, thus compounding their diminished social status. . . .

In sum, due to this comprehensive presence—spatial, material, ideological—I argue that the early 1990s signaled the arrival of the street gang as an important element in the social organization of the Blackstone community. This does not mean that, after the events in December 1992, residents were held hostage by street gangs, nor that the street gangs exerted an absolute dominance over social life in Blackstone. Instead, the street gangs' modus operandi and symbolism simply became incorporated into what Bourdieu calls the "rules of the game" that defined the possibilities of social interaction, identity, and experience for residents of Blackstone. In their daily intercourse and decision making, Blackstone residents took into account the street gang, whereas in the past the gang did not have such a determinative influence.

By embedding themselves in community social organization the street gangs imposed their own expressive patterns, boundaries and territories, and symbols and markers of identity onto those already in existence. The social space that had formed decades ago based on the Council system and building-centered differentiations was challenged and partially overridden in 1992 by the territoriality of the street gang. The gang, in this sense, became more than a delinquent actor and, to the degree that it committed socially transgressive acts, it was not simply a "social band" with no other ties to the community other than periodic outbursts of disruptive behavior. It became a recognized, albeit internally contradictory, community institution, performing a range of "positive functions" while simultaneously engaging in behaviors that disrupted community social life.

CONCLUSION

In this study, I have focused on a specific historical moment in the development of an urban street gang, namely, its turn toward systematic involvement in drug economies. In the scholarship on street gangs, the process of *corporatization* has been a primary variable by which researchers differentiate entrepreneurially oriented gangs from their counterparts that are more interested in defending turf or that are motivated by symbolic factors. However, I argued in this essay that corporatization is a multifaceted social process that cannot be reduced to its economic dimensions. In the Blackstone community, developing relations with tenant leaders, building empathy from residents, and participating in nondelinquent social activities were as important in the Saints' maintenance of (informal) economic superiority as the direct control over drug distribution itself. The overly economistic understanding of corporatization has missed the ways in which symbolic issues and gang–community dynamics can affect the accumulation of revenue by street gangs. Moreover, a street gang's interest in monetary gain is not always at the expense of other motivations, which is also implied in research on street gang entrepreneurialism.

In Blackstone, the Saints street gang was not simply attempting to earn increased revenue, but in the words of its leader, "We wanted to be a part of the community, help our community, 'cause we're here to stay" (JT). That is, the Saints did not discard noneconomic motivations when they experienced greater success in drug economies. Instead, their economic gains prompted a reconsideration of their marginalized social status. Through monetary donations and the provision of law and order services, the gang tried to become a more legitimate social actor in the community. It is important to note that the redistribution of revenue by the Saints to the broader population was not their only means of winning the allegiance and support of residents. Though at its apex the Saints earned several thousand dollars per month (according to gang leaders), only a small percentage was funneled to tenant leaders, resident organizations, and other individuals who were paid off for their silence or cooperation. As important were the in-kind services that the gang provided—ranging from security escorts to recreational programming—as well as their willingness to assist households in times of need through grocery purchases, free transportation, and manpower. As I have argued, their capacity to do so was deeply linked to their successes in drug distribution. This is made clear by the demise of the Saints street gang family in the mid-1990s due to the imprisonment of their leaders from different parts of the city. As one might expect, their drug-based revenue declined precipitously at this point as did their largesse in Blackstone. To maintain a legitimate local presence, JT and other leaders used their own personal cash reserves to pay off community members, while attempting to reclaim their informal economic stature.

Little is known about such relations among gangs, community residents, and local organizations. Nor do we understand fully the ways in which patterns of association and interaction among these actors can shift over time in accordance with other social transformations. By paying attention to the varying ideological makeup and patterns of association among different actors in Blackstone, I tried to explicate the *range* of interactions that occur between a street gang and the broader community. The focus on social organization in this article allowed me to describe the varying functions, positive and negative, that street gangs can fulfill and the ways in which residents can hold ambivalent attitudes toward this social actor. Specifically, in the context of economic destitution and the lack of mainstream services, Blackstone's street gangs have become a resource as well as a harbinger of insecurity and social instability for residents.

QUESTIONS FOR DISCUSSION AND WRITING

1. When and why did the role of the street gang and their relations with the broader population change?
2. According to Clara Davis, why did the residents prefer the gangs to police?
3. What did JT and Ottie do during autumn of 1992? What did this generosity buy?

VIOLENCE

Historical Trends in Violent Crime: A Critical Review of the Evidence

TED ROBERT GURR

It is generally accepted by criminologists and other social scientists that the real incidence of serious crimes against persons and property increased substantially in the United States and most Western European societies during the 1960s and 1970s, though skepticism remains about the accuracy of official data on the precise magnitude of change. What is less widely recognized is a growing body of historical evidence, some of it examined by Lane . . . , that the incidence of serious crime has traced an irregular downward trend for a much longer period of time, in some places for a century or more. When the historical and contemporary evidence are joined together, they depict a distended U-shaped curve.

The thesis that rates of serious crime in Western societies have traced a reversing U-shaped curve is a simplification of a much more complex reality. It characterizes some but not all offenses. The evidence for it is substantial in some societies, especially the English-speaking and Scandinavian countries, but either lacking or contradictory in others.

There are severe problems in the interpretation of official data on crime compiled in different eras. Even where a reversing trend is clearly present, as in England and Wales during the past 150 years, there are substantial short-term deviations around it. For these and other reasons, the U-shaped curve is used here as a hypothesis, not received wisdom, against which to evaluate diverse evidence on trends in violent crime. . . .

This essay is limited mainly to evidence about trends in homicide and assault, with occasional reference to robbery. . . . From the perspective of the social and cultural historian, the distribution of these offenses across time, space, and social groups is of particular interest because of what it tells us about interpersonal aggression and the complex of social attitudes toward it. . . .

. . . I suggest these general guidelines for interpreting long-term trends in violent crime, with special reference to the putative period of decline that ended in the mid-twentieth century. (1) The declining historical trend in *homicide* probably is understated somewhat, because of closer official attention and a stretching of definitions to include more cases of manslaughter. Since the establishment of modern, centralized systems for recording crime and death data, official homicide data are the most accurate of all data on interpersonal violence. . . . (2) Data on robberies known are second, albeit a rather distant second, to homicide data in reliability. . . . (3) Long-run trends which show increases in assault are suspect because of increasing concern about these offenses. Long-run declining trends in assault are convincing if based on "offenses known," or on trial data for all courts, higher and lower. . . .

. . . We can be more confident about the underlying trends in interpersonal violence to the extent that there is converging evidence from different studies and different indicators. Conclusions about the directions and magnitude of change in violence are convincing to the extent that they are supported by any of the following kinds of parallel evidence: (1) Similarity in trends of indicators of an offense obtained from two different sources, for example police and coroner's records of homicides. (2) Similarity in trends of indicators of an offense registered at different stages in the criminal justice process, for example offenses known versus committals to trial or convictions. (3) Similarity in trends of indicators of an offense from different cities or regions. (4) Similarity in trends of different offenses, for example homicide and assault, or assault and robbery. . . .

The Long-Term Trend in English Homicide

. . . The general trend which emerges from the evidence is . . . unmistakable: rates of violent crime were far higher in medieval and early modern England than in the twentieth century—probably ten and possibly twenty or more times higher. . . .

There are two problematic features of the [historical] trends. One is the extraordinarily high incidence of homicide in fourteenth-century cities by comparison with the preceding century. If the handful of estimates are not grossly in error, there evidently was a tremendous upsurge in violent crime in England (or at least its cities) during the early fourteenth

century. Hanawalt suggests as much. In general the fourteenth century was more disorderly than the thirteenth. The Hundred Years War, which began in 1337, and the Black Death, which killed perhaps one-third of the population, precipitated social and economic crises of major proportions. . . .

The evidence thus clearly favors the possibility . . . that the nineteenth- and early twentieth-century decline in violent crime in England was the latest phase in a substantially longer trend. The seemingly high rates of homicide in early nineteenth- and late twentieth-century London were actually very low when contrasted with the more distant historical experience. The possibility of cyclical or wavelike movements away from the underlying trend is not ruled out, however. There probably was a surge in violent crime in fourteenth-century England. Violent crime also evidently increased in Elizabethan times. More certainly, Beattie offers evidence of several such waves during the period from 1660 to 1802, and it is likely that violent crime rates were unusually high in early nineteenth-century London.

Most of the evidence surveyed here relates only to homicide. Did assaults also decline over the long run? For the medieval and early modern period we simply cannot say because the court data on assaults are either nonexistent or unreliable. In Elizabethan times they appear in court records less often than homicide, but a century later assaults were much more numerous. Since most homicides of this period resulted from violent altercations, the real incidence of assault was presumably much higher. The infrequency of assaults in early court records almost surely reflects the fact that it ordinarily was not thought serious enough to warrant indictments unless someone died as a consequence of the assault. The higher assault rates of the period studied by Beattie, from 1660 to 1802, very likely reflect increased concern by victims and courts, not a real long-term increase in assault. During the last 150 years, however, trends and peaks in official data on assault in London and all of

England have closely paralleled those for murder and manslaughter. Thus for this period we can be reasonably confident that the incidence of assault, like murder, declined for most of the period but increased after ca. 1950.

TRENDS IN VIOLENT CRIME IN THE UNITED STATES

The Long-Term Trend in American Homicide

The composite picture of violent crime in nineteenth-century America is a stable or declining trend with a pronounced upward swing which began shortly before the Civil War and persisted into the 1870s. The evidence . . . is limited to cities, mainly on the eastern seaboard and in the Midwest, which may not be representative of what was happening in towns or on the frontier. The trends in violent crime before the Civil War are especially problematic because only Philadelphia and Boston have been studied prior to 1850. After 1900 there was a sustained rise in violent crime to the early 1930s, a thirty-year subsidence, and another increase since 1965. Current national homicide rates are higher than any recorded previously, though only slightly greater than those of the 1920s. They are also greater than any indicated by the fragmentary nineteenth-century evidence.

There is also evidence . . . that the two waves in twentieth-century homicide rates may be attributable mainly to increases in killings among blacks. White homicide rates have varied much less. The trends in black homicide arrests in Washington, D.C., are especially suggestive in this regard. . . .

In conclusion, we may ask to what extent the American evidence is consistent with the reversing U-shaped curve proposed at the outset of this essay. The dominant feature of crime trends in the United States is the occurrence of three pronounced upsurges of interpersonal violence which began roughly fifty years apart: ca. 1860, 1900, and 1960. These waves or cycles are of such amplitude that we cannot say conclusively whether the cycles are superimposed on a longer-run decline. To the extent that North America from settlement to industrialization was an extension of British culture and society, I suspect that the underlying trend was downward. At least it was for Anglo-Americans. But as Lane points out (personal communication), non-English immigrants have unquestionably added to the violence of American cities: the Irish, especially from the 1840s through the 1860s; possibly the Italians, in the early twentieth century; and inmigrating blacks throughout. In culturally heterogeneous societies the aggregate trends and cycles of interpersonal violence are instructive only about how disorderly society is, not about the social behavior of its constituent groups. . . .

SOME OBSERVATIONS

How well does the U-shaped curve of declining, then rising violent crime fit the evidence reviewed here? The English evidence on homicide covers the longest timespan and is the most convincing in documenting a sustained decline of substantial magnitude. By the same token it makes the post-1960 upturn appear to be a minor perturbation, proportionally no greater than upward swings in homicide rates in Elizabethan times and during the Napoleonic wars—swings which proved to be temporary. In the United States the occurrence of three great surges in violent crime, beginning ca. 1850, 1900, and 1960, makes it impossible to say whether these increases are superimposed on a long-term decline. My reading of the evidence is that the long-term trend in homicide rates among whites has been generally downward until recently, whereas homicide rates among blacks not only have been higher and more variable but have moved generally upward since the beginning of the twentieth century, perhaps earlier. Declines in homicidal violence also are established for nineteenth-century Stockholm, New South Wales, France, and—beginning late in the century—Germany. In general we have not seen any evidence from any country or jurisdiction that there was a sustained increase in homicides during the nineteenth century—with the important codicil that most of the time-series studies span only the second half of the century. An increase in homicide rates since the 1960s is also a common though not universal phenomenon in Western societies. . . .

The evidence on assault and robbery is more limited but in general parallels the trends in homicide. That is strikingly evident in countries which experienced the post-1960 increase in crime: robbery and assault rates usually increased much more than homicide. In the nineteenth century, however, assault rates moved contrary to homicides in France, Germany, and some American jurisdictions. There is reason to attribute this to increased official attention to minor offenses, not to real and sustained increases in assault.

The discussion of trend evidence has touched on a number of explanations for trends and variations around them. There are two separate questions for which explanation is needed. One is, What social dynamics underlie the long-term decline in violent crime? The other is, What accounts for the big deviations of crime above this trend, especially those sustained upwellings of violence that persist for ten or twenty or more years before subsiding again? I think that there is a simple and singular answer to the first question, but multiple and complex answers to the second. I also think that no special, *sui generis* explanation is needed for the late increase in violent crime. Its explanation should follow from an understanding of the dynamics of the long-term decline and of the deviations from it. In other words I propose to regard the upturn of the U-shaped curve as simply the latest, and best-documented, deviation from the underlying trend.

A plausible explanation for the long-term decline in interpersonal violence is what Norbert Elias calls "the civilizing process" and all that it implies about the restraint of aggressive impulses and the acceptance of humanistic values. By their own accounts, medieval Europeans were easily angered to the point of violence and enmeshed in a culture which accepted, even glorified, many forms of brutality and aggressive behavior. The progress of Western civilization has been marked by increasing internal and external controls on the show of violence. . . . The process is in essence a cultural one and like most cultural change had its origins in the changing values of social and intellectual elites. . . .

The cultural process of sensitization to violence, to use Soman's phrase, has not been uniform. It took root first among the urban upper and middle classes and only gradually and selectively was promulgated among rural people and the lower classes. It has been suggested, for example, that one significant social function of the new nineteenth-century police forces was to serve as missionaries of upper and middle class values to the theretofore dangerous lower classes. Be that as it may, the thesis that sensitization to violence spread from the social center to the periphery and from upper to lower classes is intrinsically plausible as an explanation of some basic features of nineteenth-century and contemporary criminality. Interpersonal violence historically may have been higher in rural than urban areas—the evidence is mixed—because of the persistence there of traditional patterns of interpersonal behavior. It tended to increase in cities during the early stages of urbanization and industrialization because new immigrants from the countryside, or from overseas, only gradually assimilated the lifeways of the city. Violence declined overall during the nineteenth century and the first half of the twentieth because Western societies became increasingly urban and formal education became universal. The further down the class and status ladder, past and present, the more common is interpersonal violence, because the lower classes did not assimilate and still have not wholly assimilated the aggression-inhibiting values of the middle and upper classes. . . .

There is one other group that may become *de*sensitized to violence: youth. The historical process of sensitization to violence must be replicated in the socialization of each new generation of children in each Western society. To the extent that socialization fails, or is incomplete because it is not reinforced by other social institutions, youth are susceptible to other kinds of values, including those which celebrate violence. . . .

The long-run downslope of interpersonal violence is irregular and some of the irregularities take the form of sharp and sustained increases. . . . Studies of France and Germany [indicate] that violent crime tends to rise in the early stages of industrialization and urbanization, though there is little evidence that the pace of urban growth in general has affected rates of violent crime. Modernization may have been one of the sources of high rates of violent crime in early nineteenth-century England and in the United States in the 1860s and 1870s. But urbanization and industrialization usually are gradual processes, not likely of themselves to create a single tidal wave of disorder except in regions and cities experiencing very rapid change.

The connection between warfare and waves of violent crime is more precise. In fact, war is the single most obvious correlate of the great historical waves of violent crime in England and the United States. Civil and foreign war contributed to the crime peak of the 1340s. . . . The upsurge of crime at the onset of the nineteenth century began while Britain was enmeshed in the Napoleonic wars, from 1793 to 1815, and continued through the severe economic depression which followed their end. In the United States the peak of urban crime in the 1860s and 1870s coincides with the social and political upheavals of the Civil War. . . . The second high wave of violent American crime crested during the decade after World War I. The third began near the onset of the Vietnam war. . . .

War may lead to increased violent crime for a number of reasons, reviewed and tested by Archer and Gartner. I opt for the interpretation, consistent with their evidence, that it does so mainly because war legitimizes violence. It does so directly for young men who become habituated to violence in military service; it does so indirectly for others who find in the patriotic gore of wartime a license to act out their own feelings of anger. . . . If the civilizing process has been accompanied by sensitization to violence, then war, including internal war, temporarily desensitizes people to violence. If there is such an effect it is probably greatest among youth who are at the most impressionable age during wartime. . . .

Another basic factor that influences the extent of personal crime is the size of the youthful population. If their relative numbers are high in a particular city or era, its crime rates are likely to be higher than in times and places where the population is older. . . .

The strands of this speculative discussion can be brought together by concluding that each great upsurge of violent crime in the histories of the societies under study has been caused by a distinctive combination of altered social forces. Some crime waves have followed from fundamental social dislocation, as a result of which significant segments of a population have been separated from the civilizing institutions which instill and reinforce the basic Western injunctions against interpersonal violence. They may be migrants, demobilized veterans, a growing population of disillusioned young people for whom there is no social or economic niche, or badly educated young black men locked in the decaying ghettoes of an affluent society. The most devastating episodes of public disorder, however, seem to occur when social dislocation coincides with changes in values which legitimate violence that was once thought to be illegitimate. Historically, wars seem to have had this effect. There is also the possibility that other factors, such as the content of popular culture or the values articulated in segmented groups, may have the same consequences.

QUESTIONS FOR DISCUSSION AND WRITING

1. When was the rate of violent crime higher, in medieval and early modern England or in the twentieth century?
2. What does the "infrequency" of assaults in early (such as Elizabethan) court records reflect?
3. What can we say about the post-1960 "upturn" when viewed as part of a long-term series of data?

Homicide: Behavioral Aspects

MARVIN E. WOLFGANG

MARGARET A. ZAHN

HOMICIDE is the killing of one human being by another. As a legal category, it can be criminal or noncriminal. Criminal homicides are generally considered first-degree murder, when one person causes the death of another with premeditation and intent, or second-degree murder, when the death is with malice and intent but is not premeditated. Voluntary manslaughter usually involves intent to inflict bodily injury without deliberate intent to kill; involuntary manslaughter is negligent or reckless killing without intent to harm.

Noncriminal forms include excusable homicide, usually in self-defense, and justifiable homicide, as when a police officer kills a felon or when a convicted offender is executed by the state. The classification of any homicide as either criminal or noncriminal, or of a death as either a homicide, an accident, or a natural death, is not uniform across all time periods or across legal jurisdictions. What is considered a homicide death varies over time by the legal code of given jurisdictions and by the interpretations and practices of agencies responsible for reporting deaths. When cars were first introduced into the United States, for example, deaths resulting from them were classified by some coroners as homicides, although now they are generally labeled accidental deaths unless caused by negligence. An abortion may be considered a criminal homicide or the exercise of women's reproductive choice. Homicide statistics, like those of many other crimes, reflect definitions and legal interpretations that vary over time and space. . . .

SOURCES OF DATA ON HOMICIDE

Homicide data generally derive from either health or police agencies. There are two major sources of international data, one compiled by the United Nations in *World Health Statistics Annual* and the other by the International Criminal Police Organization (Interpol), which was established in 1950. In addition, the national police agency of each country reports the number of that country's homicides for every two-year period. *World Health Statistics Annual* publishes the causes of death, including homicide, for each reporting country. These statistics, which have been collected since 1939, are the joint product of the health and statistical administration of many countries and the office of the United Nations and the World Health Organization. Problems in the use of these sources include lack of consistent definitions and interpretations across jurisdictions and lack of consistent reporting by all countries. Some countries, including many Communist ones, do not routinely report.

Within the United States there are two major national sources of data on homicide: the

National Center for Health Statistics (NCHS) and the Federal Bureau of Investigation's *Crime in the United States* (known as the Uniform Crime Reports and published annually). The NCHS data derive from coroners and medical examiners, who forward death certificates to the center's Division of Vital Statistics. These data focus solely on the homicide victim and generally include information on the cause of death and the age, race, and sex of the victim. Data about offenders, victim–offender relationships, and motives are not included. The various states entered this national reporting system at different times. Prior to the 1930s, when the system became fully national, the data available depended on which states and cities were included. Boston was the first entrant, and in general, there were data from East Coast cities very early. Boston had death data in 1880, Pennsylvania in 1906, and Washington, D.C., in 1880. Other states, such as Georgia and Texas, entered the registry much later—in 1922 and 1933, respectively. In establishing trends, then, there is difficulty in obtaining national data before 1930.

The Uniform Crime Reports, a voluntary national data-collection effort, began in 1930 and gradually accumulated reporting police districts. Homicide reports are detailed and include information on both victims and offenders and, since the 1970s, on victim–offender relationships. This system is the only national one with information on homicide offenders and includes information on crimes classified by size of population, state, county, and Standard Metropolitan Statistical Area. Although there are some problems with the use of the Uniform Crime Reports data, they are commonly used in studies of homicide. . . .

CROSS-NATIONAL PATTERNS OF CRIMINAL HOMICIDE

Although there are problems in using international crime statistics because of differing definitions and methods in classifying the phe-

nomenon, both Interpol and United Nations data nonetheless offer useful information on homicide rates in different countries. Of the two, data from the United Nations are more frequently used for cross-national studies. Marvin Wolfgang and Franco Ferracuti, for example, used these data in their discussion of the subcultural determinants of homicide. . . . Basing their study on data from the late 1950s and early 1960s, they found that in general, the highest rates of homicide were in Latin America and the Caribbean. Among the fifteen countries and legal dependencies constituting the top quartile, ten were Latin American; the top three were Colombia, Mexico, and Nicaragua. The lowest rates were found in northern and western European countries. Nine northern and western countries were found in the bottom quartile.

Wolfgang and Ferracuti hypothesized that the relatively high homicide rates in Latin American and Caribbean countries, as well as in urban communities and southern states in the United States, are related to subcultural values supporting violence as a means of interpersonal dispute resolution. . . . In countries with relatively weak normative supports for the resolution of violent disputes—as in many northern European, western European, and Asiatic countries—low homicide rates are found. These findings are reported for sixty-one countries and do not include many Islamic, African, and Communist countries. The last have not provided, or do not have, reportable data; hence, comparative findings reflect a select set of countries.

Marshall Clinard and Daniel Abbott, using United Nations data, presented international homicide rates for the late 1960s. Of twenty-five countries examined, nine of the thirteen highest were Hispanic; of the five lowest, three were northern or eastern European. Clinard and Abbott explained this observed variation by means of different theories of homicide. Subcultural theory was used to explain homicides in Hispanic countries that result from personal insult and extramarital involvements. . . . Homicides resulting from long-standing interfamilial or intertribal disputes were explained primarily as a function of normative or power conflicts. The authors applied this perspective to homicide in India, Ceylon, and sections of Africa . . ., introducing the concepts of tradition, obligation, and responsibility. Their formulation was used to account for certain kinds of homicide observed in tradition-bound sectors of African society—for example, those that are the outcome of failure to pay the bride-price attached to the ritual marriage contract.

Dane Archer and Rosemary Gartner compared selected cross-national homicide rates drawn from their comparative crime data file of 110 nations. Their data confirmed previous findings: Latin American and Caribbean countries are represented among the high-rate countries, and European countries are among the low-rate ones. Of the ten high-rate countries, five are Latin American, Caribbean, or Hispanic; of the ten low-rate countries, eight are northern, eastern, or western European.

Insufficient cross-national data exist on the basic demographics of criminal homicide—that is, age, sex, race, and socioeconomic distributions. The existing data, however, suggest that criminal homicide is more prevalent among the young, among males, and among racial, ethnic, and religious minorities. The United States scores substantially higher than European countries, but lower than most Latin American ones, in the rate of criminal homicide. The rate in the United States is relatively high, especially when compared to other countries of similar levels of development, affluence, and cultural heritage.

PATTERNS OF CRIMINAL HOMICIDE IN THE UNITED STATES

. . . Trend studies in the United States and comparative analyses in different time periods reveal that the overall homicide rate increased from 1900 to the early 1930s. The rate declined slowly after 1933 and was low in the 1940s and 1950s. Homicide in the United States was at a minimum in the 1950s but was followed by a modest rise and then a steep rise from 1963 through the late 1970s. The pattern held for blacks and whites and for males and females, although homicide has always been much more common among blacks and males. Reynolds Farley has reported that age-adjusted homicide rates are about six times greater for nonwhites than for whites, and four times higher for men than for women. Homicide victimization rates are highest for young adults: the highest rates generally occur between the ages of twenty-five and thirty-five. . . . There are also differences in geographic patterns of homicide, with higher rates of violence in the South. . . .

Victim–Offender Relationships

Literature on homicide since the 1960s has attempted to describe the relationship between the victim and offender and the motive for the slaying. Although many relationships occur in human affairs, only some seem to be persistently associated with homicide. Seldom, for example, is an employee–employer relationship associated with homicide, but frequently a husband–wife relationship is. . . .

In the 1940s and 1950s, the percentage of homicides between husbands and wives was more pronounced [than previously], [and] homicides between two males known to one another as friends and acquaintances were still significant. In the late 1960s and the 1970s, victims who were strangers to the offenders . . . appeared to be more prevalent than in the past. . . . [Homicides between two friends or acquaintances—usually a male killing another male within the same racial group—was the largest category in a recent study of homicide in eight major cities.] . . . Males tend to be close to the same age, generally in the early thirties, with the victim slightly older than the offender. . . .

SOCIOLOGICAL EXPLANATIONS OF VIOLENCE

There are three sociological approaches to explaining homicide: the cultural–subcultural, the structural, and the interactional. Cultural theorists explain homicide as resulting from learned, shared values and behavior specific to a given group. The basic causes are the norms and values, transmitted across generations, that are learned by members of a group. Certain subgroups exhibit higher rates of homicide because they are participants in a subculture [in which] violence [is] a norm. . . . This position asserts that there is a subculture of violence—that is, a subculture with a cluster of values that support and encourage the overt use of force in interpersonal relations and group interactions. . . .

. . . The structuralist position . . . asserts that broad-scale social forces such as lack of opportunity, institutional racism, persistent poverty, demographic transitions, and population density determine homicide rates. These forces operate independently of human cognition and do not require individual learning to explain their impact. . . . In general, structural explanations suggest variables that influence homicide rates. They do not specify, however, the conditions under which these variables lead to homicide rather than to other possible outcomes, such as passivity. With few exceptions, the explanations fail to examine whether structural forces work the same way for rates of family, friend, and stranger-to-stranger killings. . . .

Interaction theory focuses on the character of relationships that escalate into homicide. Interaction theorists see homicide as resulting from the [social] interaction process itself; they examine how the act of a participant precipitates the acts of another and how escalating [interpersonal] conflict culminates in homicide.

QUESTIONS FOR DISCUSSION AND WRITING

1. What did Wolfgang and Ferracuti hypothesize?
2. Among whom are criminal homicides "more prevalent"?
3. What do trend studies in the United States show?

DRUGS AND CRIME

Drug Use and Abuse in America

SAM STALEY

DRUGS AND CRIME

A more tangible problem associated with drug use is the connection between drugs and crime. Crime can be either drug-related or non-drug-related. Drug-related crime refers to offenses committed while the perpetrator is using drugs or criminal acts related to the use, purchase, or sale of drugs. Some crimes committed by drug users may not be directly related to drug-related activities. A drug user, for example, may commit a burglary for reasons completely independent of drug use or drug trafficking. Non-drug-related crime refers to criminal acts that are not attributable to the use of drugs or violations of drug laws.

In a study of heroin trafficking in New York, daily heroin users imposed net costs of $22,844 on victims through non-drug-related crime. Irregular users, in contrast, imposed substantially fewer costs on similar victims ($5,592). On average, non-drug-related crime committed by drug users was $14,000. A more recent study published by the RAND Corporation estimated that total non-drug-related crime in Washington, D.C., amounted to between $150 and $225 million.

From "Drugs and Crime" by Sam Staley, from *Drug Policy and the Decline of American Cities* (pp. 107–117), 1992, New Brunswick, NJ: Transaction Publishers. Copyright © 1992 by Sam Staley. Reprinted by permission of Transaction Publishers; all rights reserved.

A substantial body of research shows that drug users constitute a criminally active subpopulation. National Institute of Justice psychologist Bernard Gropper notes, "Recent studies have shown that heroin-using offenders are just *as likely* as their non-drug-using or non-heroin-using counterparts to commit violent crimes . . . and even *more likely* to commit robbery and weapons offenses" (emphasis in original). In all cases, more frequent drug users are more deeply involved in criminal activity. An increasingly prominent feature of drug-related crime is murder. In many cities, drug-related murders make up as much 50 to 80 percent of all homicides.

Yet, this observation must be tempered by a more thorough examination of the types of crimes committed. For instance, interviews with 2,285 heroin addicts in five cities from 1978 to 1981 revealed that they were criminally active. The average number of offenses over the twelve-month period, however, varied significantly among types of crimes. The average annual number of crimes against persons was 12.8, crimes against property 121.6, public order 67.9, and drug sales 162.2. Thus, even though drug users may be criminally active, they are often not involved heavily in violent crimes.

The expression "drug-related crime" does not necessarily denote crime committed while the abuser was under the influence of the drug. For example, driving under the influence

(DUI) is a crime defined by behavior induced by drug use (usually alcohol). In most cases, drug-related crime should not be construed as crime committed while the criminal is under the influence. Even when criminals commit crimes under the influence of drugs, their behavior is not a direct result of the effects of the drugs. Rather, the drugs become a tool for the criminal to induce a more "relaxed" emotional state.

A modern exception appears to be crack, which often produces erratic and sometimes violent behavior. In this respect, the effects of crack on behavior are much more similar to those of alcohol than to those of marijuana, heroin, or cocaine.

In a survey of over 215,000 convicted inmates of local jails in 1989, less than one-third (27 percent) indicated they were under the influence of a drug at the time they committed the offense. Less than 5 percent indicated they were under the influence of cocaine or crack. In contrast, 29.2 percent of convicted inmates indicated they committed the offense under the influence of alcohol. Over half of the convicted inmates, 56.6 percent, said they were under the influence of drugs or alcohol at the time of the offense. Yet, only 15.4 percent indicated they were under the influence of drugs only.

The survey also revealed that, among inmates convicted for violent offenses such as homicide, rape, assault, and robbery, less than 10 percent were under the influence of drugs only at the time of their offense. In contrast, over 30 percent were under the influence of alcohol only while 16 percent were under the influence of both. Among inmates arrested for public-order offenses such as weapons, obstruction of justice, traffic, D.U.I., etc., 54 percent indicated they were under the influence of alcohol only, and less than 7 percent indicated they were under the influence of drugs only (9.6 percent indicated they were under the influence of both).

In a summary of the literature on the connection between crime and drug use, drug-use researcher Paul J. Goldstein found drug use per se does not induce violent behavior. In particular, early reports that attempted to link violent behavior to the properties of marijuana and opiates "have now been largely discredited." In fact, drug use may cause some to become introspective and reduce violent tendencies.

Goldstein admits that the evidence on the drug use–violence connection is not extensive. Nevertheless, he finds that violence is systemic and associated with "traditionally aggressive patterns of interaction within the system of drug distribution and use." Thus, the violence and criminal activity associated with drug use is an outcome of the life-style of users and traffickers rather than an effect of the drug itself.

Clearly, then, when drawing conclusions about drug use, crime, and violence, researchers and analysts must be careful to distinguish between the statistical correlation between drug use and crime and a pharmacological correlation.

The relationship between crime and drug use is not direct. For example, Gropper observes, "The major impetus for most of [daily heroin users'] criminal behavior is the need to obtain heroin or opiates." This statement is consistent with the high correlation found between frequency of drug use and criminal activity. Yet, criminal activity may be the result of something else.

The regular user engages in criminal activity to get money to sustain his habit. The amount of criminal activity will depend on the cost of the habit. To the extent public policy restricts the supply of heroin, causing prices to rise, the heroin addict will commit more crime. Conversely, if heroin were freely available on demand, the cost of the addict's habit would approach the marginal cost of producing the drug. In this case, the drug user's habit would cost a few dollars per day.

More specifically, if a heroin addict consumed an estimated forty milligrams of heroin per day in 1986, he would have spent fifty to eighty dollars per day. Yet, the cost of supplying heroin legally would run less than twenty-five cents per day. Thus, the price of heroin is inflated by anywhere from 200 to

3,200 percent. In this case, the crime used to generate income for a heroin addict is a manifestation of its legal status rather than of heroin use per se. Thus, if drug users are committing property crimes to support their drug habit, and if accessibility is increased by allowing supply to meet demand, property crime rates should drop dramatically.

DRUGS AND PUBLIC HEALTH

Another cost of drug use is a public health concern. Drug users place themselves at risk more than nondrug users. This, of course, is true for all drug users regardless of whether the drugs are legally tolerated or not. For example, the risks of tobacco place smoking at the top of the list among potential killers. Similarly, the risks to users associated with illicit drugs may also be extremely high. While this argument plays well at first, evidence on deaths per capita by type of drug use reveals that drugs other than cocaine, heroin, and marijuana pose far greater health hazards.

James Ostrowski determined the per capita death rate for five drugs: tobacco, alcohol, heroin, cocaine, and marijuana. In his calculations, Ostrowski attempted to isolate only those deaths that were "intrinsically" connected to the drug being used. In other words, he attempted to determine whether an alcohol death was related to the use of alcohol per se

rather than to some other influence. Thus, deaths resulting from diseases directly related to alcohol use are included while others such as DUI traffic deaths are not.

The data show that tobacco remains the number one killer, claiming 650 deaths per 100,000 users (Table 1). Heroin use results in half the death rate of alcohol per capita. Not one death has been attributable to marijuana use. In fact, based on data concerning the number of repeat users of these drugs, Ostrowski notes that the illicit substances are less likely to lead to repeat use than either alcohol or tobacco.

Tallying the number of people killed through substance abuse is only one method of determining its risk. Another risk is dependence. Substantial numbers of people are psychologically dependent on drugs (although the degree of this dependence is contestable). Nevertheless, for the 10 to 20 percent of each drug user population that is dependent, the effects can be devastating.

Drug dependence, however, is manageable. Heroin addicts can lead productive lives even if they require four or five doses a day. The debilitating effects of heroin are related to the drug's availability and affordability, which in turn are due almost exclusively to its legal status.

Cocaine, in contrast to heroin, is more debilitating and interferes more with work performance. Yet, cocaine's effects typically become

TABLE 1

Estimated per Capita Death Rates for Selected Drugs

Drug	Users	Deaths Per Year	Deaths/100,000
Tobacco	60 million	390,000	650
Alcohol	100 million	150,000	150
Heroin	500,000	400	80
Cocaine	5 million	200	4

Source: James Ostrowski, "Thinking About Drug Legalization," Cato Policy Analysis No. 121 (Washington, D.C.: Cato Institute, 1989), 47, table 4.
Note: Deaths attributed to heroin and cocaine were adjusted downward to include only deaths attributed to drug use (e.g., not suicide). The unadjusted figure for heroin is 400 per 100,000 and for cocaine, 20 per 100,000.

negligible within two or three hours. After twenty-four hours, cocaine cannot be chemically traced in human urine (two days with heavy doses). Scientific evidence indicates that regular cocaine use affects the heart and causes cardiac death, heart attack, irregular heartbeat, and damage to the muscle tissue surrounding the heart. Other physical problems associated with chronic cocaine use are deterioration of the liver, high blood pressure, convulsions, respiratory failure, and destruction of the nasal passage.

Nevertheless, as Table 1 detailed, the risks of cocaine are not as significant as those of other drugs that are legally and socially tolerated. The number of chronic or compulsive users is probably very small, despite the results of the study released by the Senate Judiciary Committee. Thus, Steven Wisotsky concludes,

The data lead to one conclusion: even allowing for legitimate concerns about the health consequences of cocaine and fears about the spread of cocaine dependency, the legal prohibition of cocaine and its severe penalties cannot be justified solely on the grounds of public health. At the very least, the health and death toll of legal drugs—cigarettes and alcohol—runs far higher. . . . But for that 10–20 percent minority, . . . a destructive, accelerating pattern of compulsive use can develop over time. Approximately the same percentage fall "victim" to alcoholism or heroin addiction.

Marijuana poses a far less serious threat from addiction, although the long-term health consequences may be greater than heroin or cocaine. Small doses of marijuana appear to have negligible effects on the human body, although moderate use may produce temporary, short-term memory loss. Marijuana's "most significant adverse acute effects are [increased heart rate], impairment of short-term cognitive functioning, and impairment of motor skills." Research also indicates that long-term respiratory problems (e.g., bronchitis and general irritation) are associated with heavy marijuana use. Researchers speculate that, given higher concentrations of tars in marijuana, long-term use may place the user at higher risk of developing cancer.

THE DEMAND FOR ILLICIT DRUGS IN THE UNITED STATES

In sum, the demand for illicit drugs in the United States will continue despite their legal status. Moreover, the physical and psychological effects of the major illicit drugs—heroin, cocaine, and marijuana—appear much smaller than previously thought. A realistic assessment of the drug problem suggests that dependence on illicit drugs should be treated as a health problem similar to smoking and alcohol use. In fact, at current usage rates, the public health risks associated with illicit drug use are far lower than those for alcohol and smoking.

Moreover, unlike currently illegal drugs, the risks associated with the legal drugs will probably persist through their popularity. As James Ostrowski has noted, "not only are alcohol and tobacco inherently more dangerous than heroin and cocaine, but because they are more popular, their danger is magnified." Despite widespread access, illicit drugs appear far less popular than alcohol or cigarettes. Even those who experiment with these drugs are much less likely to use them again.

The true costs of substance abuse lies in the dependence users develop through prolonged use of the drug. In some cases, such as cigarette and alcohol abuse, the physical effects become life-threatening.

Alcohol and cigarette use, however, appear to be declining over time. The proportion of current smokers in the U.S. population has declined from 42 percent in 1955 to under one-third in the late 1980s. Moreover, recent drinking trends show a general move to beverages with lower alcohol content, such as light beer and wine.

Drug use is part of a far reaching cultural tradition. The most traditional forms of drug use manifest themselves in alcohol and tobacco consumption. These forms have been socially tolerated for centuries and have been an omnipresent fact of American life. Illicit drugs have also been around for centuries, but have received more attention in the late twentieth century.

The reasons for the resurgence of public interest in the most common illicit drugs lie principally in the perceived social devastation that lies in their wake. Indeed, social control over these drugs began in the late nineteenth century as politicians responded to heightening public criticism of cocaine and special interests sought to expand their power. Similarly, the recent trend toward widespread intolerance of psychoactive drugs reflects the rising public outcry against "soaring" addiction rates, the diffusion of drug use into schools, and the violence associated with drug trafficking. Against the backdrop of economic devastation in many American urban areas, drugs became an easy target for public criticism.

Indeed, the recent declaration of "war" against drugs can be viewed as a reaction to the rising social devastation evident in urban areas. As this chapter has detailed, while heroin, cocaine, and marijuana have addictive qualities, none of them approach the levels of use or addiction evident in socially tolerated drugs such as alcohol or tobacco. Indeed, the numbers of chronic users are substantially lower than perceptions gleaned from newspaper headlines and evening news reports. Moreover, the classification of users of illicit drugs as addicts or compulsive users is highly suspect. Many so-called addicts demonstrate substantial control over their drug intake and use.

The issue is not whether people will use drugs, but how much is demanded on the market at a given price. For the vast majority of consumers, drug use is not addictive. "Recreational" drug use, or use of drugs in the same sense that most drinkers use alcohol, is reasonably safe and enjoyable although the potentially negative long-term consequences of drug use may become important. Drug use becomes a problem only when a physical or psychological dependence emerges for the drug or individual behavior becomes individually or socially destructive. Thus, many Americans consume large amounts of psychoactive drugs legally (e.g., alcohol) and illegally (e.g., marijuana). Moreover, drug consumption is sensitive to price changes.

The illicit drug trade is accompanied by substantial social costs that are unrelated to the demand for drugs. Yet, the persistent demand for drugs ensures that producers will enter into the market to supply these drugs. Those who control their drug use so that their behavior does not interfere with their personal and work life pose a minimum threat to their lives and those of others. Rather, the "drug problem" is concerned mainly with the addict population that provides a base level of demand to fuel the drug market. Traffickers will always be able to reap large profits from the drug market as long as an addict population maintains a steady demand for the product. More important, traffickers will benefit from any policy that restricts supplies enough to maintain high prices and high profit margins.

The rules by which suppliers provide these products, however, vary significantly from the rules that exist in the legal market. As the illicit drug trade flourishes, the essential institutions of successful, productive economies founder.

QUESTIONS FOR DISCUSSION AND WRITING

1. What does a "substantial body of research show"? "In all cases," what is true?
2. What did a survey of over 215,000 convicted inmates of local jails in 1989 show?
3. What did Paul Goldstein find?

The Drug Use–Delinquency Connection in Adolescence

HELENE RASKIN WHITE

THE relationship between drug use and criminal behavior is the source of continuing speculation and debate. Researchers probing the links between drug use and crime for the past 50 years have produced an abundance of contradictory findings. These disparities have paved an erratic course for social policy. Although American drug control and crime control strategies assume that an important connection exists between drug use and crime, the precise nature of the relationship between drug use and crime remains elusive. About the only area of agreement is that substance use and crime are somehow linked.

Much of the literature supporting the drug–crime connection has been drawn from studies of criminality among narcotic addicts or alcoholics or studies of drug use among criminal offenders. This research supports the notion that alcohol use is associated with violent crime while other drug (especially heroin) use is associated with a high proportion of property crime. Proponents of the alcohol–violence model emphasize the psychopharmacological effects of alcohol intoxication as the cause for violent behavior. The drug–property crime model is based principally on the notion that heroin (and other drug) addicts commit crimes in order to secure money for drugs. Interestingly, proponents of the alcohol–violence model do not give weight to the fact that a substantial proportion of inmates convicted of property crimes were under the influence of alcohol at the time of the offense. Similarly, drug–property crime model proponents have only recently given weight to the fact that heroin-addicted individuals often are involved in violent crimes, typically committed over drug possession and sale. In advancing these separate views, some researchers have ignored the fact that distinctions between property and violent crime are often blurred. For example, some robberies have begun as property crimes purely for economic gain and have resulted in a person being hurt, thus changing categories from property to violent crime. They also have included drug-related crimes (from possession and dealing, to murder resulting from a bad drug deal) in their analyses, which inflates the associations between drug use and crime.

The value of these studies examining the drug–crime nexus in addict and criminal samples lies in their ability to detect a high degree of overlap among persons heavily involved in both behaviors. But the question still remains as to the degree of association between drug use and criminal behavior in the general population. All studies of "normal" (i.e., noncriminal, non-drug-addicted) indi-

From "The Drug Use-Delinquency Connection in Adolescence" by Helene White, from *Drugs, Crime and the Criminal Justice System* (pp. 215–255) edited by R. Weisheit, 1990, Cincinnati, Ohio: Academy of Criminal Justice Sciences and Anderson Publishing Co. Copyright © Helene R. White. Reprinted by permission of Anderson Publishing Co., Cincinnati, www.andersonpublishing.com.

viduals have been conducted on samples of adolescents and young adults. Clearly, the drug–crime connection in the adolescent population is of interest because adolescents account for a large proportion of criminal behavior. The purpose of this chapter is to review the literature on the drug–crime (delinquency) nexus among adolescents. Given that several excellent reviews have previously been written, I will not attempt to replicate these efforts, but rather highlight important conclusions from these reviews. I will also add some recent findings from several large studies of adolescents that have not been brought together in previous reviews. First, I will discuss the methodological issues in studying the drug–crime connection. Then I will present general models of the drug–crime connection and specifically discuss the spurious model among adolescents. Finally, I will describe recent results from three studies focusing on the drug–delinquency nexus in adolescence.

METHODOLOGICAL ISSUES

Definitions

In order to fully understand the data bearing on the relationship between drug use and delinquency, there are several methodological issues that need to be addressed. The first issue has to do with definitions of drug use and delinquency and the extent to which they represent two distinct types of deviant behavior. There is a history of including drug use in the early scales of delinquent behavior. In a recent issue of *Criminology*, Hill and Atkinson, for example, included six categories of drugs, as well as two drug-related offenses, among their list of 20 offenses that are combined to form a single scale of self-reported delinquency. On the other hand, several papers in this same journal reported research on drug use only or employed delinquency scales which did not include drugs.

Elliot, Huizinga, and Ageton included certain types of drug-related offenses in their self-reported delinquency scale, such as buying liquor for a minor and dealing drugs, but excluded measures of personal use. Maintaining drug selling in a delinquency scale, however, can still artificially inflate the relationship between drug use and delinquency because it has been well accepted that almost all persons who sell drugs are also regular users of those substances. In a recent interview study, Carpenter, Glassner, Johnson, and Loughlin found that virtually all adolescents who sold drugs were users of a wide variety of substances. They also found that as drug use increased, so did dealing. On the other hand, research on gangs and drug selling suggests that not all persons who sell drugs are users. The recent research on gang members and other adolescents who are involved in drug selling organizations presents strong evidence that many adolescents avoid using drugs while dealing or avoid them altogether.

Clearly illicit alcohol and other drug use fits the definition of delinquent behavior, which is generally defined as illegal acts committed by juveniles. In the basic texts on delinquency, drug use appears to be treated as a type of delinquency. For example, Jensen and Rojek stated "An interesting finding concerning female delinquency is the influence of males on female drug use." In his book on deviant behavior, Akers wrote ". . . and one form of delinquency, underage drinking . . ." Akers suggested how researchers in the drug–crime field should address this definitional problem: "Obviously, the possession and sale of illegal drugs are themselves criminal offenses, but what is the relationship between drug use and nondrug criminal behavior?"

In order to be able to clearly distinguish drug-taking behavior from criminal behavior, this chapter will focus on the connection between drug use (i.e., typical drug use patterns, as well as pattern of use at the time of commission of an offense) and *other non-drug* delinquent behaviors (i.e., excluding illicit drug use, possession, distribution, and importation, etc.).

Measures

Most of the survey research on the drug–crime connection has relied upon self-report data. Self-reports are generally accepted as a reliable indicator of delinquent behavior and alcohol and drug use. In addition, self-reports provide a more direct, sensitive, and complete measure of various forms of deviant behavior than do measures based upon official law enforcement and institutional records and avoid the problem of false negatives (i.e., "hidden" cases). According to Elliott et al., the weight of the evidence suggests that self-reports of drug use and delinquency have good to excellent levels of reliability and acceptable levels of validity, as compared to other social science measures.

Of course there are many caveats for using self-report data. First, delinquents are harder to contact than nondelinquents and when contacted are less likely to participate in research. In addition, delinquents are less likely than nondelinquents to give honest replies when they do participate. Further, there may be racial differences in reliability and validity of self-report data. According to Elliott et al., falsification is relatively rare, although there are some problems related to accuracy of recall, classification errors, and reporting of trivial events.

There also have been problems operationalizing variables. For example, in most research on the drug–crime relationship among adults, drug users have been defined as opiate addicts, and alcohol users have been defined as either alcoholics or persons who were intoxicated on alcohol at the time of the crime. For adolescents, however, a user often is anyone who has ever tried a particular substance, regardless of their frequency or extent of use. These types of contradictions have created problems for comparisons across studies.

In addition to failing to consider levels of drug use and delinquency, most researchers have also failed to distinguish among onset, continuation, and cessation of these behaviors. In fact, research on adolescents suggests that different factors contribute to the onset of drug use and delinquency than contribute to their continuation and cessation. Also, for many adolescents, behaviors such as drug use and delinquency are constantly changing, so measures tapping a static point may not represent the true behavior pattern.

There are also issues of measurement in terms of using simple dichotomies or trichotomies which could mask subtle differences between groups. As Fagan, Hansen, and Jang have suggested, crude measures can obscure critical analytic distinctions and mask etiological distinctions between various behavior patterns. Questionnaires often contain terms which lead to arbitrary interpretation, such as "often" or "occasionally," thus making comparisons among subjects unreliable. In addition, researchers often truncate scales, thus obscuring discrimination at the high end. Elliott et al. have argued that trivial forms of delinquent activity are often overrepresented and serious forms are either underrepresented or omitted.

Further, aggregate scales are often used, which have both advantages and disadvantages. Some aggregate indices of drug use combine quantitative and qualitative aspects of drug use and are sensitive to multiple drug use. However, the types of aggregate drug use scales typically used in the drug–delinquency literature are often operationalized as use of any drug other than alcohol or marijuana a certain number of times in the past year. Use of this type of scale masks the unique relationship between certain drugs (e.g., crack or cocaine) and delinquency and also disregards multiple drug use in terms of concurrent use of alcohol or marijuana and another drug. Similarly all types of delinquency are often merged into one scale obscuring distinctions between property and violent crimes or between serious and nonserious crimes.

Samples

Researchers have relied upon captive samples in prisons or in treatment programs to study the drug–crime relationship. Such samples have the advantage of providing a pool of subjects who exhibit high frequencies of the behaviors of interest, but the relationships observed may not be generalizable to the general population. At the same time, it may be these relationships that have the greatest relevance for drug control and crime control policies.

On the other hand, samples drawn from general populations have limited numbers of individuals engaging in drug use or delinquency. Drug use and delinquency are concentrated in urban areas, while some survey research is spread across wide geographic areas, hence seriously underrepresenting these behaviors and possibly attenuating the relationships observed. Further, many general surveys are administered in schools and omit dropouts who are known to have higher rates of drug use and delinquency.

Analyses

Another problem in estimating the extent of overlap between drug use and delinquency results from differences in classification schema and analytic strategies. Researchers often fail to control for age in their analyses. Given that drug use and delinquency are age-dependent, failure to take account of this phenomenon can lead to spurious findings. In addition, researchers use different analytic strategies (i.e., OLS, LISREL, path models), all of which involve differences in causal assumptions. There is conflict about whether to include Time 1 measures of the dependent variable in longitudinal models. Inclusion of these measures controls for the behavior at a prior time but also inflates the amount of variance explained.

Clayton and Tuchfeld have argued that most researchers have failed to apply the appropriate standards of proof and criteria of causality: researchers' standards of proof of causality have been unreasonably high and rigid; they have misunderstood the criteria for causality; and they have been reluctant to make causal statements for fear of the policy implications. Instead, Clayton and Tuchfeld have suggested three criteria for causality: a statistical association between two variables must be established, the causal variable must precede the effect, and the relationship must not be spuriousness.

The issues raised here provide a sample of the many conceptual and methodological ambiguities that characterize the drug–crime literature and the following review should be interpreted within these limitations. In the next section, I will present four general models that have been employed to explain the association between drug use and crime.

GENERAL ASSOCIATIVE MODELS

Four different perspectives on the drug–crime connection have been predominant in the literature. Each implies a different strategy for control policies. Here I will briefly discuss these four models and the literature on both adults and adolescents which supports or refutes each model.

Model 1—the "drugs-cause-crime" explanation assumes that drug users need to generate illicit income to support their drug habit (economic motivation), and/or that the psychopharmacological effects of drugs increase the addict's propensity toward crime, and especially violent crime. This view has been the cornerstone of U.S. narcotic and treatment policies. Recent and impressive evidence of the economic motivation explanation for the drugs-cause-crime model comes from literature on heroin addicts which indicates that raising or lowering the frequency of substance use among addicts raises or lowers their frequency of crime. Other studies demonstrate that criminal activity is significantly greater following addiction to drugs than before addiction. Heavily involved daily drug users, especially heroin users, account for a disproportionate share of criminal acts, and the containment of drug use through treatment and close supervision leads to dramatic reductions in both drug use and crime.

On the other hand, the psychopharmacological explanation for the drugs-cause-crime model has largely been refuted in the literature with regard to heroin and marijuana, but has received strong support in the alcohol literature and occasionally for other drugs such as barbiturates, amphetamines, PCP, and LSD. This model suggests that the psychopharmacological effects (including disinhibition, cognitive-perceptual distortions, etc.) of intoxication, as well as situational factors accompanying occasions of intoxication, contribute to crimes of violence.

The psychopharmacological approach, however, has received little support in the adolescent literature. While research on delinquents indicates that many have used drugs or alcohol prior to committing a crime, most youth deny that their criminal behavior is due to their substance use. For example, Carpenter et al. found that although teenagers reported being under the influence of alcohol or drugs when committing crimes, none attributed their behavior to the effects of the drugs. In fact, some youth used drugs so routinely that virtually all their activities also involved prior drug use. Among seriously delinquent drug users, the majority of drug-using episodes did not involve delinquency and the majority of delinquent events did not involve prior drug use. When drug or alcohol use occurred prior to a criminal event, subjects listed many reasons other than drug use as contributing factors. Subjects reported never being out of control from drug use when committing crimes and, in fact, they purposely regulated their drug use depending upon the nature of the crime (i.e., either to enhance an activity or to avoid interference with skillful execution of a crime). It is also possible that many youth lack insights into the reasons for their behavior and, thus, do not necessarily perceive a direct connection between their drug use and delinquent behavior.

In contrast to a pharmacological explanation for the drugs-cause-crime relationship be-tween heroin use and violent crime, Goldstein has identified a systemic violence model. He suggests that the system of drug distribution and use is inherently connected with violent crime. This model is probably not applicable to the majority of youthful drug users because few are involved in distribution at this level. In the Carpenter et al. interview study, approximately 10 percent of all youths in their random sample and one-third of their whole sample reported selling drugs. With few exceptions, nearly all of the drug dealing occurred within a loosely structured circle of friends and relatives. Only six out of 100 subjects were intensely involved in dealing. However, research on drug dealing within youth gangs partially supports Goldstein's systemic violence model. That is, some violent incidents were found to be related to disputes over drug sales or selling territories, whereas the majority of violent incidents were not drug related, but rather resulted from other issues, such as conflicts over status and "turf."

Similarly, the economic motivation explanation for the drugs-cause-crime model has not been supported among adolescents. Johnston, O'Malley, and Eveland concluded their longitudinal study of adolescents by stating that nonaddictive use of illicit drugs does not appear to play a role in causing users to become more delinquent. In accord, a reanalysis of the National Youth Survey data indicated that intensive drug users and highly delinquent youth do not report committing property crimes to raise money for drugs. Instead, the money they get from crime is used for commodities other than drugs. In the Carpenter et al. study, most of the thefts took place for direct acquisition rather than for resale. While subjects attributed alcohol or drug use as the cause of crimes for other individuals, most denied that their own crimes were related to their drug use. Subjects reported committing crimes for fun, to obtain valued goods, or to get money. They claimed to be able to obtain drugs within their usual budgets and that other commodities were more important to purchase with the profits from crime.

Hence, there is little overall support for a drugs-cause-crime model in adolescent literature. Clearly, for those who are involved in delinquency and drug use, onset of delinquency generally precedes drug use, thus refuting any hypothesis that drug use leads to initial delinquent involvement. While it is probable that for some youths under some conditions, the use of illegal drugs leads to delinquent behavior, there is little convincing evidence that this happens for the majority of youths.

A second perspective is *Model 2—"crime causes drug use."* According to this explanation, involvement in delinquency provides the context, the reference group, and definitions of the situation that are conducive to subsequent involvement with drugs. Collins, Hubbard, and Rachal's analysis of individuals in cocaine treatment programs supports this model. They found that income generated from crime provides the individual with extra money to secure drugs, and places the individual in an environment which is supportive of drug use, rather than a need for cocaine compelling the individual to commit crimes. Again, the evidence supporting this view is not conclusive. While it is indeed probable that crime leads to drug usage under certain conditions for certain persons, a direct causal path from crime to drugs is not likely to reflect the dominant pattern.

Model 3—the reciprocal model has been suggested by Elliot and Ageton and reintroduced by Watters and colleagues. This model postulates that the relationship between drug use and delinquency is bidirectional, that is, that drug use and delinquency are causally linked and mutually reinforcing. Support for this perspective is derived from several recent studies of either drug use or delinquency which have found reciprocal relationships. This perspective has also been supported by Goldstein's ethnographic research in New York City. Goldstein suggested that the relationship between drug use and crime moves in both directions even for the same individuals. When a heroin addict has an easy opportunity to obtain money illegally, he will engage in the activity and then buy drugs with the money gained, not out of a compulsion but rather as a consumer expenditure. Conversely, when the need for drugs is great, users will commit crimes to get money to buy drugs. While reciprocity is only a recently developed area, it may hold promise in clarifying causal relationships.

A final model, *Model 4—the spurious model,* is the perspective that is generating increasing research and theoretical support, especially among normal populations. Rather than being causally connected, the empirical link between drug use and crime is assumed to be spurious. Either the relationship between use and delinquency is coincident and both sets of behaviors may be elements in a concurrent cluster of other adolescent problem behaviors, or, alternatively, drug–crime relationships may be explained by a "common cause," that is, both substance use and delinquent behavior are the result of the same factor or set of factors. "Common-cause" hypotheses identify a number of social and psychological factors seemingly shared by adolescent substance users and delinquents and postulate that similar causal processes exists for both forms of deviance. Alternatively, the "coincident" hypothesis assumes that drug use and delinquency cluster together as a result of experimentation with a wide range of behaviors during the adolescent stage in the life cycle.

The empirical evidence confirms that adolescent drug use and delinquent behavior are spuriously related, and in the following sections I will present this evidence within a three-part framework similar to the one suggested by Clayton and Tuchfeld. The three sections are the *degree of association between drug use and delinquency, temporal ordering of the behaviors,* and *tests of spuriousness.*

THE ASSOCIATION BETWEEN DRUG USE AND DELINQUENCY IN ADOLESCENCE: A SPURIOUS RELATIONSHIP

Degree of Association

Elliott and Ageton's review of ten major studies exploring the drug–crime nexus among noninstitutionalized youthful populations suggested that involvement in delinquency and drug use are covariants, and the association holds for both serious and nonserious crimes. They concluded that the most plausible model for the drug–crime relationship among adolescents is a spurious model. A later review indicated that the correlations between drug use and delinquency reported in the literature generally range between .40 and .60. Although these correlations are moderate, more than 60 percent of the variance is not shared.

Research by Kandel, Simcha-Fagan, and Davies supports the association between drug use and delinquency into young adulthood. Among subjects 24–25 years of age, they found a positive relationship between involvement in drug use and delinquency indicating that current users of harder drugs were more deviant than former users and those who have used only marijuana. They also found that among males, early delinquency predicted later drug use but early drug use did not predict later delinquency. For females they found that illicit drug use in adolescence predicted delinquency in adulthood. These data, thus, indicate that there are gender differences in the association between drug use and delinquency.

In examining the degree of association between delinquency and drug use, it must be recognized that there is only a small group of youth who are both serious delinquents and problem drug users. In a national representative sample of youth, it was found that less than 5 percent of all youth reported serious crimes and used hard drugs. This small group accounted for approximately 40 percent of all delinquencies, 60 percent of all index offenses, over 50 percent of all felony assaults, over 60 percent of all felony thefts, 75 percent of all robberies, over 80 percent of all drugs sales, 30 percent of all marijuana use occasions, and 60 percent of all other drug use occasions.

Violence, especially, is concentrated among only a few youth. Most youth involved in felony assault and other felonies also commit several index offenses and many minor delinquencies per year and use drugs regularly. Carpenter and colleagues found that those youth involved in violence were also more involved in delinquency and drug use than their peers. Not only were those heavily involved individuals more often perpetrators, but also they were more often victims of violence. The most frequent type of violence was fighting primarily to defend one's honor and to test others. More serious incidents of violence occurred in the distribution of drugs, gang battles, instances of racial or ethnic antagonism, and in acts of revenge. In all of these instances it was the most heavily involved drug users and the most criminally active youth who were engaged.

The data reviewed above indicate that there is a statistical association between drug use and delinquency in adolescence, but that serious drug use and delinquency are concentrated in a small segment of the adolescent population.

Temporal Order

Almost all empirical studies report that, among those who engage in both delinquency and drug use, delinquent behavior (both serious and nonserious) developmentally precedes the use of drugs. Thus, considering the requirement of temporal sequencing, these findings do not support the "drugs-cause-crime" model.

A longitudinal analysis by Huizinga and Elliott indicated that, for the largest group of adolescents who were both users and delinquents, involvement in delinquency (especially minor offenses) preceded substance use. However, this research also identified groups of youths who displayed simultaneous initiation into drug use and delinquency and groups whose drug use preceded involvement in delinquent behavior. Only the offense of drug selling was almost always preceded by drug use. Kandel et al. also found that participation in minor forms of delinquency preceded initiation into hard liquor use and marijuana use and that participation in major forms of delinquency preceded initiation into the use of other illicit drugs.

Information about whether delinquent behavior increases with the onset of substance use among adolescents is limited and contradictory. In general, onset of drug use is not associated with increases in delinquency. The studies reviewed by Elliott and Ageton clearly indicated that differences in delinquency between drug users and nonusers existed before the onset of drug use. Huizinga and Elliott warned that "global generalizations about the drug use/delinquency relationship within the youth population are likely to be inaccurate" because of the existence of different temporal ordering of onset of both behaviors among different subgroups of youth. Their longitudinal analysis of the drug–delinquency connection led to the conclusion that for the large majority of youth, the use of drugs is not related to involvement in delinquent behavior. Whether the onset of drug use leads to increases in delinquency is dependent on the types of drugs, the quantity and frequency of use, and the subculture of the individual.

In another longitudinal analysis, Johnston and colleagues demonstrated that drug users as compared to nonusers were substantially more delinquent before they began using drugs. Thus, they concluded that level of delinquency can hardly be attributed to drug use and, if a causal relationship exists, their data supported a delinquency-causes-drug-use model. They suggested several alternative explanations for the covariation between drug use and delinquency: drug use may cause a short-term increase in delinquency, methodological artifacts may exist because the variables are measured simultaneously, drug use and delinquency may be explained by common causative factors, or other factors than drug use, per se, lead to increases in delinquency.

The literature on temporal ordering reviewed above refutes a causal model and, therefore, supports a spurious model. The following section presents explanations offered to account for the spuriousness.

Tests of Spuriousness

Evidence supporting the spurious model frequently has been derived from adolescent samples where relatively nonserious forms of substance use (cigarette smoking, occasional alcohol use, or experimentation with marijuana) appeared to occur simultaneously with relatively minor and infrequent forms of delinquent behavior. This type of association led Jessor and Jessor to identify a problem behavior syndrome in which cigarette use, precocious sexual behavior, problem drinking, use of marijuana and other drugs, stealing, and aggression clustered together. This cluster of behaviors was explained by the same set of environmental and personality variables and was negatively related to conventional behavior. Donovan and Jessor provided additional support for their hypothesis of a single dimension of deviance proneness. They advised, however, that there are several possible explanations that could account for the strong correlations among all their problem behaviors. For example, each behavior could be an interchangeable means of achieving desired goals, the behaviors could be learned together and performed together, or there might be peer pressure when engaging in one behavior to also engage in the other.

The concept of a problem behavior syndrome has been supported by other research. Having engaged in premarital sexual intercourse and driving while intoxicated were both related to a high-risk profile delineated by high sensation-seeking needs and high levels of impulsivity. This same profile was also related to drug use and delinquency.

In a cluster analysis, Hindelang and Weis found that marijuana use loaded on a general delinquency scale with alcohol use and intoxication, theft, vandalism, truancy and cheating, but other drug use (i.e., LSD, mescaline, methedrine, glue, heroin) loaded on its own scale. The fact that marijuana, as compared to other drug use, was more strongly related to delinquency may have been a statistical artifact due to a lower variation in other drug use than in marijuana. This early study, thus, suggested that marijuana use is part of a general deviance syndrome. Elliott and Ageton also concluded that marijuana use was part of a general deviance involvement, while sale of drugs and use of hard drugs were related to crime and not explained by a general involvement in delinquency.

Klein agreed that the relationship is spurious and argued that, except for drug use leading to drug selling, the relationship between delinquency and drug use is the result of a pattern of simultaneous deviant activity. He described most adolescent delinquency as cafeteria-style delinquency, meaning that most adolescents engage in a variety of delinquent behaviors rather than specialize in only one type. This style of delinquency is comparable to typical adolescent drug use patterns which often involve multiple drug use rather than use of a single substance. In fact, Klein argued that drug use is one component of cafeteria-style delinquency.

Kandel et al. identified several possible explanations for the co-occurrence of both behaviors; both behaviors could result from a common psychological trait, a common clinical disorder such as conduct disorder, a particular lifestyle, or common developmental processes. Similarly, Johnston et al. stated that the spuriousness of the relationship between drug use and delinquency may result from common personality characteristics, that is, drug users and delinquents are both deviance-prone individuals.

Common etiological roots for high rates of delinquency and drug use include: early antisocial behavior in elementary school, inconsistent parenting, lack of communication with parents, school adjustment problems, association with deviant peers, low degree of social bonding to prosocial individuals, positive attitudes toward drug use and delinquency, early onset (for drugs only), low self-esteem, high sensation-seeking, low attachments to school and family, having alcoholic parents, poor school performance, low IQ, and inadequate moral development.

There are a few noteworthy applications of theoretical common cause models to substance use and delinquency. In studies of etiology, researchers have applied traditional deviance theories to explain delinquency and drug use. The most often tested theories are control theory, differential association theory, and integrations of the two. For example, as predicted by control theory, adolescents who are not well bonded to their parents, to their teachers, or to school are more likely to engage in delinquency and in substance use. At the same time, the deviance-inducing effect of deviant peers as postulated by differential association theory has been at least equally successful in explaining adolescent substance use and delinquency.

In addition, several researchers have applied mixed or integrated theories combining differential association and control perspective to both delinquency and drug use. They have argued that attenuated bonds to parents and school, in conjunction with bonding to deviant peers, predisposes one to both drug use and delinquency.

Hawkins and Weis' Social Development Model integrates social control and social learning theory stressing the importance of early antisocial behaviors, early experiences in the family, later experiences in school, and interaction with peers. Their model has been moderately successful in predicting adolescent marijuana use and delinquency. Elliott et al. tested a social-psychological model incorporating elements of traditional strain theory, social control (bonding) theory, and social learning theory; the social learning aspect suggests that bonding to deviant persons provides the social rewards (motivations) for deviant behavior. They concluded that alcohol and marijuana use belong to a general deviance syndrome involving a wide range of minor criminal acts, and that they are predicted by a common set of causes. Their results, as well as the other tests of theory presented above, strongly support a common cause hypothesis.

On the other hand, there has been evidence which refutes common cause models suggesting that there may be independent causes for involvement in delinquency and involvement in drug use and that delinquency and drug use may represent distinctively different types of behavior. Elliott, Ageton, and Canter suggested that different causal paths could account for different types of delinquency. For example, a strain path might lead to instrumental forms of delinquency such as theft, while attenuated commitments might result in less instrumental types such as drug use.

Loeber's review of the literature on antisocial behavior also suggested that there are independent predictors of drug use and delinquency. After identifying four categories of antisocial outcomes—versatile offenders, exclusive violent offenders, exclusive property offenders, and exclusive substance abusers—he delineated the various paths to these outcomes suggesting that a history of aggressive or nonaggressive acts may determine the eventual outcome. Loeber concluded that nonaggressive rather than aggressive antisocial behaviors are predictive of later substance use or abuse, while aggression is more strongly predictive of other forms of delinquency.

Similarly, Kandel et al.'s research failed to support a common cause hypothesis. They tested a risk model combining variables from socialization, social learning, and social control theories, as well as sociodemographic variables and measures of commitment to adult roles. They compared the ability of this model to predict theft, interpersonal aggression, marijuana use, and illicit drug use among male and female young adults (24 to 25 years of age). These researchers concluded

that their results were equivocal in regard to the ability of a common cause model to predict adult participation in delinquency and use of illicit drugs. Rather, they found that prediction depended upon the type of delinquency, the type of drug used, and sex of the individual. For males they found a common etiology between illicit drug use and theft, rather than between illicit drug use and interpersonal aggression. They also found that the same factors that predicted illicit drug use among female adults predicted delinquency among males.

Differences in developmental patterns of drug use and delinquency also provide evidence against a common cause hypothesis. It is generally well-accepted that most adolescents mature out of delinquency after the age of 16 or in late adolescence. Some criminologists attribute this "maturation" to spontaneous cessation or developmental maturation. Others attribute it to the deterrent effect of perception of the differences in the criminal justice treatment of and sanctions for adolescent and adult offenders. On the other hand, for the majority of drug users, drug use persists into young adulthood. According to Chaiken and Johnson, about two-thirds of drug-using delinquents continue to use drugs into adulthood, while close to one-half stop committing crimes.

Another distinction between drug use and delinquency arguing against a common cause model has to do with the purpose of each behavior in the adolescent's lifestyle. In the study by Carpenter and her colleagues, the majority of delinquent youth were heavily involved with marijuana and alcohol and also used other substances. This substance use was a major form of self-identity, commitment, and recreation. On the other hand, their involvement in delinquency was irregular and rarely part of their self-identity.

Most of the research reviewed above supports a spurious relationship between delinquency and drug use, but is contradictory as to whether a common cause hypothesis can account for this spuriousness.

QUESTIONS FOR DISCUSSION AND WRITING

1. What "notion" does much of the literature supporting the drug–crime connection advance?
2. How does the spurious model describe the "empirical link between drug use and crime"?
3. How does "maturing out of delinquency" compare to cessation of drug use?

Data Analysis Exercise

An Exploration of Culture Conflict and Marxist Theory and a Look at Bio-Psychological Theory of Choice

INTRODUCTION

In this data analysis exercise, we will conduct three separate inquiries. First, we will use Wave VII data from the National Youth Survey (NYS) to briefly explore culture conflict theory, which is discussed in Part VII. Then, we will use the same data to briefly explore Marxist theory, which is also presented in Part VII. Finally, we will test some of the ideas in bio-psychological theory of choice, which is discussed in Part VIII.

DESCRIPTION OF THE DATASET

See the data analysis exercise for Part V for a description of the NYS dataset. Before we start our analyses, we'll need to load up the second version of our dataset, "NYSCRIM2." The reason we are switching datasets is to overcome SPSS's 50-variable-per-file limit.

Culture Conflict and Marxist Theory

GETTING A HANDLE ON THE DATA AND
USING CROSSTABULATION TABLES

Part VII presents three theories that are based on the idea that laws and ideas of deviance are created by the powerful to control the less powerful. The powerful may gain their control through political or financial clout, and then use it to their advantage (for example, the rich enact laws to protect their property from the poor).

Culture conflict theory, first published by Thorsten Sellin, acknowledges that where cultures coexist in the same area, there will be conflict and crime, even if there is no identifiable controlling entity. Although not designed to test culture conflict theory, the NYS does contain a relevant question that we can use in a brief exploration. The NYS asked respondents how much of a problem racial conflict was in the neighborhoods in which they lived. Under culture conflict theory, one would expect more crime in areas where racial conflict was a problem.

Marxist theory, on the other hand, focuses on economic factors. Marx argued that the poor were forced into crime through desperation and that they were also more likely to be victims of violent offenses. He asserted that class differences make society somewhat masochistic; that is, when a society has citizens who are much poorer than others, violence and other crimes will occur because of the desperation and frustration experienced by the poor who are continuously exploited by the rich. The NYS asked about two items that are relevant to testing Marxist theory: unemployment and victimization. We have already learned (in the exercises for Part V) that when unemployment is more of a problem, so are burglaries/thefts, but we can still check to see if respondents who live in neighborhoods characterized by greater unemployment are more likely to be victimized in violent crimes. Unfortunately, unemployment isn't the best measure of class differences, but the NYS wasn't designed to test Marxist theory.

As we learned in the exercise for Part V, the NYS did not collect actual crime rates, but it did ask respondents how much of a problem several crimes were in their neighborhoods. Among the crimes listed were two that we will examine: burglaries/thefts and assaults/muggings. We will look at burglaries first, leaving assaults/muggings for you to look at for the "further exploration" questions.

To see if culture conflict theory helps predict crime, first run a frequency of RACECONF, then run a crosstabulation table with whether or not burglaries and thefts are a problem in the respondent's neighborhood (BURGLARY) as the dependent (row) variable and RACECONF as the independent (column) variable. The frequency table shows that about one-fourth of the respondents' neighborhoods could be characterized as having some racial conflict.

What does the crosstabulation table show? In what type of neighborhood are burglaries/thefts the most problem? In what type of neighborhood are burglaries/thefts the least problem? What is the strength of the relationship shown in the table? Is it statistically significant? How can we summarize this table? Does this table support culture conflict theory?

Now, let's turn our attention to Marxist theory. I created a victimization measure for violent crime by counting as victimized anyone who experienced during the previous year at least one violent offense from a list of four crimes: threatened/beaten up by others, attacked with a weapon, sexually attacked, or sexually pressured or pushed to do more than the respondent wanted to do.

To see if Marxist theory helps us predict victimization, first run a frequency of VICTVIO, then run a crosstabulation table with whether or not the respondent was victimized by a violent offense (VICTVIO) as the dependent (row) variable and whether unemployment is a problem in the respondent's neighborhood (UNEMP) as the independent (column) variable. The frequency table shows that 20% the respondents had been the victim of a violent offense during the past year.

What does the crosstabulation table show? In what type of neighborhood was victimization the most likely? In what type of neighborhood was victimization the least likely? What is the strength of the relationship shown in the table? Is it statistically significant? How can we summarize this table? Does this table support Marxist theory?

FURTHER EXPLORATION

Remember, good theories apply in multiple situations. In the "further exploration" questions, you'll see whether culture conflict theory helps predict assaults/muggings. With respect to Marxist theory, we will see if high levels of unemployment lead to increased victimization in property crimes, although Marx argued that class differences were more likely to result in violence.

ON YOUR OWN

Now that we have explored a few tenets of the culture conflict and Marxist theories, you could devise other ways of measuring and testing the theories. For example, you could look to see if those who lived in areas characterized by racial conflict were more likely to engage in violence themselves (VIOLENCE), as would be predicted by culture conflict theory. With respect to Marxist theory, you could see whether respondents with lower incomes (INCOME) are more likely to be victimized by violent offenses.

While you are further examining culture conflict and Marxist theory, reflect on how these theories help explain why some people break the law. Think also about the theories' weaknesses, including crimes and/or situations that they cannot adequately address.

Bio-Psychological Theory of Choice

GETTING A HANDLE ON THE DATA AND
USING CROSSTABULATION TABLES

Bio-psychological theory of choice, as posed by Wilson and Herrnstein, assumes that people, when given a choice, will exercise their free will and choose the preferred course of action. Those who choose to commit crimes will do so because they perceive more benefits than drawbacks from criminal acts. Potential benefits from crime include material gains, emotional (such as the thrill of breaking the law) or sexual gratification, approval by one's peers, and the ability to enhance one's sense of justice, perhaps by getting even with someone who has somehow harmed the offender. Potential drawbacks include guilt pangs, condemnation of the act by some citizens, retaliation by the victim, and the ever-present risk of apprehension and punishment. Oh, what is a potential criminal to do? Which choice should he or she make?

Testing bio-psychological theory of choice will require us to find suitable measures, as we have done for the previous theories. Among the questions in the NYS survey are two that will work for our purposes. First, the respondents were asked to estimate their chances of arrest for a set of crimes, including theft of an item worth more than $50 (THEFT50) and violent offenses (VIOLENCE). To make our analyses easier, I have recoded the percentages into two roughly equal categories: those who perceived the chance of arrest to be 50% or less, and those who perceived it to be greater than 50%. If bio-psychological theory of choice is valid, those respondents who provide high estimates for their chances of arrest should be less likely to engage in the prohibited act.

The other relevant item asked the respondents how much guilt, remorse, or personal discomfort they would experience as the result of breaking a variety of laws. Presumably, those who would experience more guilt should be less likely to break the law in the first place. This variable was left in its original form, a rating scale from "very little" to "a great deal."

We will look at the effect of the two measures on THEFT50, leaving VIOLENCE for you to look at for the "further exploration" questions. To see if the theory holds, run frequencies for ARRTHFT and GUILTHFT, and run crosstabulation tables with THEFT50 as the dependent variable and ARRTHFT and GUILTHFT as the independent variables.

What do you notice about the ARRTHFT → THEFT50 table? Which respondents were most likely to have stolen something worth more than $50? What is the strength of the relationship shown in the table? Is it statistically significant? How can we summarize this table? Does this table support bio-psychological theory of choice?

What about the GUILTHFT → THEFT50 table? Which respondents were least likely to steal items worth $50 or more? Which respondents were most likely? What is the strength of the relationship shown in the table? Is it statistically significant? How can we summarize this table? Does this table support bio-psychological theory of choice?

POINTS TO PONDER: Does our finding with respect to the increased likelihood of thefts among those who said they would feel "not too much" versus "very little" guilt invalidate bio-psychological theory of choice? Can you come up with an explanation for why those two percentages seem reversed?

USING CONTROL VARIABLES

By now, you should be wondering if we are ever going to be able to move beyond simple bivariate analyses (analyses that involve only two variables). You may have thought to yourself, "Sure, the respondents' anticipated level of guilt may affect future involvement in crime, but what about the findings by Mears, Ploeger, and Warr (in Part IV of the text), who persuasively argued that girls are more likely than boys to rate offenses as very wrong? Could gender somehow affect the relationship between anticipated guilt and future criminality? Are males in the dataset less likely to be affected by anticipated guilt while females are more likely to be affected? I want to know!"

If you are such a person, you will be happy to know that there are options short of full-blown multivariate statistics. You can easily add control variables to your crosstabulations. That's what the third box under the Crosstabs variable boxes is for; it allows you to feed in control variables. Although you can feed in as many control variables as you wish, it is advisable to limit yourself to one or two because the nature of crosstabs. Every control variable you add makes the results harder to interpret and increases the chance of empty cells (which affect the validity of your statistics). If you want to include more than one or two control variables, you should read up on regression or other multivariate techniques that are better able to handle a lot of variables at once. Now, back to our crosstabs.

I don't know about you, but I'm dying to find out if the results found by Mears et al. might shed some light on bio-psychological theory of choice. To do that, run a crosstabulation table with whether or not the respondent stole an item worth $50 or more (THEFT50) as the dependent (row) variable, anticipated level of guilt (GUILTHFT) as the independent (column) variable, and MALE as the control variable (Layer 1 of 1). Mark the same statistics and cell choices we've been doing, because we'll need that information more than ever. You'll notice that the final table is much larger than our typical crosstabulation table. In fact, it's two tables combined into one, with the statistics and probabilities for both tables appearing in the box beneath the massive table. Spend some time looking at the resulting numbers to get the hang of tables that have control variables. Each category of the control variable has a mini-table within it, so in our case, there are two mini-tables, one for males and one for females. Within each of those tables is the GUILTHFT → THEFT50 table.

Look within the rows for males. You'll see that 20 (7.3%) of the males who anticipated a great deal of guilt had actually stolen something, compared to 6 (37.5%) of those who said they would experience very little guilt. The Cramer's V is .287, and the relationship is significant. Moving to the rows for females, we see that 8 (1.8%) of the females who anticipated a great deal of guilt had actually stolen something, compared to 4 (8.7%) of those who said they would experience some guilt. The Cramer's V is .283, and the relationship is significant. We also see the problem about which Mears et al. lamented: there are too few females who stole anything to make our comparisons more meaningful (that's why we ignored the lowest two categories of perceived guilt). From our table, we can see that fewer females participated in thefts within each of the three valid categories of anticipated guilt. In its own way, this finding supports Mears et al., but it doesn't invalidate our ideas regarding bio-psychological theory of choice (because the relationship between anticipated guilt and likelihood of committing a theft remains fairly similar within the subcategories of the control variable). In other words, the relationship we found cannot be "explained away" as due to the effects of gender rather than anticipated guilt. Among both genders, increased levels of anticipated guilt meant decreased likelihood of participating in a theft.

Now, let's turn our attention to whether gender affects the relationship between perceived chance of arrest and involvement in theft. To do that, run a crosstabulation table with whether or not the respondent stole an item worth $50 or more (THEFT50) as the dependent (row) variable, perceived chances of arrest (ARRTHFT) as the independent (column) variable, and MALE as the control variable (Layer 1 of 1). Looking within the rows for males, we see that 74 (19.8%) of the males who perceived low chances of arrest had actually stolen something, compared to 37 (11.4%) of those who perceived higher chances of arrest. The Phi value is .115, and the relationship is significant. Moving to the rows for females, we see that 13 (5.0%) of the females who perceived low chances of arrest had actually stolen something, compared to 9 (2.1%) of those who perceived higher chances of arrest. The Phi value is .079, and the relationship is significant. From our table, we can see that fewer females participated in thefts within each of the categories of perceived chance of arrest. Once again, this finding supports Mears et al.'s arguments that females are affected differently by the same forces that affect males. But as we saw above, controlling for gender does not substantially change the relationship we found between perceived risk of arrest and the likelihood of committing theft; we can still say that those who perceive higher risks of arrest are less likely to steal property.

We could run control variables forever, but we'll save this for the "on your own" exercises and for the exercises for Part X.

FURTHER EXPLORATION

We have now explored two relationships relevant to bio-psychological theory of choice as they apply to theft of items worth $50 or more. To see if the theory helps explain crimes other than theft, you will apply it to violent offenses for the "further exploration" questions.

ON YOUR OWN

Now that we have briefly examined bio-psychological theory of choice and added a few control variables, you can include control variables of your own. For example, is the relationship between likelihood of committing a crime and anticipated guilt mediated at all by income (INCOME)? Or, is the relationship between likelihood of committing a crime and perceived chances of arrest mediated at all by community size (RURAL), due in part to greater numbers of police or higher crime rates in urban areas? You can have fun with this assignment and learn a lot about theory-building as well. Although we are temporarily limited to one control variable at a time, try adding in factors you think might be important. Make sure you write down why you think they are important before trying them out, tying them to the articles you've read. With the ability to use control variables, you're now on your way to building theories of your own!

Homework for Part IX: General Questions
(Culture Conflict and Marxist Theory)

Name: _____ Date: _____

Directions: Answer the following questions by filling in the blanks or circling the appropriate responses. A couple of answers have been filled in for you to make sure you're on the right track.

1. In Wave VII of the NYS dataset, _____% of the sample said racial conflict was a big problem in their neighborhoods, _____% felt it was somewhat of a problem, and _____% felt it was not a problem. _____% of the sample had been the victim of a violent offense during the previous year.

2. In the RACECONF → BURGLARY crosstabulation, _____ (_____%) of the respondents who said racial conflict was a big problem in their neighborhoods also said that burglaries/thefts were a big problem, compared to <u>56</u> (_____%) who said racial conflict was somewhat of a problem, and _____ (_____%) who said that racial conflict was not a problem. Conversely, <u>688</u> (_____%) of those who said that racial conflict was not a problem in their neighborhoods said that burglaries/thefts were also not a problem, compared to _____ (_____%) who said racial conflict was somewhat of a problem, and _____ (_____%) who said that racial conflict was a big problem. Overall, it appears that as racial conflict becomes more of a problem in a neighborhood, burglaries/thefts go *up / down*. This relationship is *weak / moderate / strong*. This relationship *is / is not* statistically significant.

   The relationship between racial conflict and crime (as measured by burglaries/thefts) found using Wave VII of the NYS data *is similar to / differs greatly from* the findings expected under culture conflict theory.

3. In the UNEMP → VICTVIO crosstabulation, _____ (_____%) of the respondents who said unemployment was a big problem in their neighborhoods had been the victim of a violent offense during the previous years, compared to <u>88</u> (_____%) of those who said unemployment was somewhat of a problem, and _____ (_____%) of those who said that unemployment was not a problem in their neighborhoods. This relationship is *weak / moderate / strong*. This relationship *is / is not* statistically significant.

The UNEMP → VICTVIO table *does / does not* show that respondents who live in neighborhoods characterized by unemployment are more likely to be the victims of a violent offense.

The relationship between living in a neighborhood that is characterized by unemployment and victimization in a violent offense found using Wave VII of the NYS data *is similar to / differs greatly from* the findings expected under Marxist theory.

Homework for Part IX: "Further Exploration" Questions
(Culture Conflict and Marxist Theory)

Name: _____   Date: _____

Task: See if the racial conflict measure we developed for culture conflict theory helps us predict assaults/muggings (MUGGINGS); see if unemployment (the measure we used to test Marxist theory) helps us predict victimization in a property crime (VICTPROP).

Directions: Answer the following questions by filling in the blanks or circling the appropriate responses. A couple of answers have been filled in for you to make sure you're on the right track.

1. In the RACECONF → MUGGINGS crosstabulation, <u>12</u> (_____%) of the respondents who said racial conflict was a big problem in their neighborhoods also said that assaults/muggings were a big problem, compared to _____ (_____%) who said racial conflict was somewhat of a problem, and _____ (_____%) who said that racial conflict was not a problem. Conversely, _____ (_____%) of those who said that racial conflict was not a problem in their neighborhoods said that assaults/muggings were also not a problem, compared to _____ (_____%) who said racial conflict was somewhat of a problem, and _____ (_____%) who said that racial conflict was a big problem. Overall, it appears that as racial conflict becomes more of a problem in a neighborhood, assaults/muggings go *up / down*. This relationship is *weak / moderate / strong*. This relationship *is / is not* statistically significant.

   The relationship between racial conflict and crime (as measured by assaults/muggings) found using Wave VII of the NYS data *is similar to / differs greatly from* the findings expected under culture conflict theory.

2. In Wave VII of the NYS dataset, _____% of the sample had been the victim of a property crime during the previous year.

3. In the UNEMP → VICTPROP crosstabulation, <u>81</u> (_____%) of the respondents who said unemployment was a big problem in their neighborhoods had been the victim of a property offense during the previous year, compared to _____ (_____%) of those who said unemployment was somewhat of a problem, and _____ (_____%) of those

who said that unemployment was not a problem in their neighborhoods. This relationship is *weak / moderate / strong*. This relationship *is / is not* statistically significant.

The UNEMP → VICTPROP table *does / does not* show that respondents who live in neighborhoods characterized by unemployment are more likely to be the victims of a property crime.

The relationship between living in a neighborhood that is characterized by unemployment and victimization in a property offense found using Wave VII of the NYS data *is similar to / differs greatly from* the findings expected under Marxist theory.

POINTS TO PONDER: Marx argued that belonging to the lower socioeconomic strata elevated one's chances of victimization in a violent offense. Can you come up with an explanation to link belonging to lower socioeconomic strata and victimization in a property crime?

Homework for Part IX: "On Your Own" Questions
(Culture Conflict and Marxist Theory)

Name: _____ Date: _____

Task: Try to think of other ways to measure the tenets of culture conflict and Marxist theories. If any of your ideas appears in the dataset, run some analyses to test it. Otherwise, run some tables using unemployment to predict the respondents' own participation in violence (VIOLENCE). For Marxist theory, check to see whether respondents with lower incomes (INCOME) are more likely to be victimized by violent offenses.

Directions: Answer the following questions.

1. Which variable did you choose as your dependent variable for culture conflict theory, and why did you choose that variable?

2. How did unemployment (or whatever variable you chose) affect your dependent variable? Make sure to provide a description that includes the percentages, Phi or Cramer's V value, the strength of the relationship, and the significance value.

3. Can you say your testing supports culture conflict theory? Why/why not?

4. Which variable did you choose as your independent variable for Marxist theory, and why did you choose that variable?

5. How did your independent variable affect the likelihood of victimization in a violent offense? Make sure to provide a description that includes the percentages, Phi or Cramer's V value, the strength of the relationship, and the significance value.

6. Can you say your testing supports Marxist theory? Why/why not?

Homework for Part IX: General Questions
(Bio-psychological Theory of Choice)

Name: _____ Date: _____

Directions: Answer the following questions by filling in the blanks or circling the appropriate responses. A couple of answers have been filled in for you to make sure you're on the right track.

1. In Wave VII of the NYS dataset, 634 (_____%) of the sample believed their chances of arrest for committing theft were low (50% or less), and _____ (_____%) believed their chances for arrest were high (more than 50%). _____ (_____%) of the respondents said they would feel a great deal of guilt if they stole something worth $50 or more, 438 (_____%) said they would feel quite a bit of guilt, _____ (_____%) said they would feel some guilt, _____ (_____%) said they would feel "not too much" guilt, and _____ (_____%) said they would feel very little guilt.

2. In the ARRTHFT → THEFT50 crosstabulation, _____ (_____%) of the respondents who believed their chances of arrest following a theft were high (more than 50%) had actually stolen property worth $50 or more, compared to 87 (_____%) of those who believed their chances of arrest were low. This relationship is *weak / moderate / strong*. This relationship *is / is not* statistically significant.

   The relationship between perceived likelihood of arrest and thefts found using Wave VII of the NYS data *is similar to / differs greatly from* the findings expected under bio-psychological theory of choice.

3. In the GUILTHFT → THEFT50 crosstabulation, _____ (_____%) of the respondents who said they would feel a great deal of guilt if they stole something worth $50 or more had actually stolen property worth $50 or more, compared to 39 (_____%) of those said they would feel quite a bit of guilt, _____ (_____%) of those said they would feel some guilt, _____ (_____%) of those said they would feel "not too much" guilt, and _____ (_____%) of those said they would feel very little guilt. This relationship is *weak / moderate / strong*. This relationship *is / is not* statistically significant.

   The GUILTHFT → THEFT50 table *does / does not* show that respondents who say they would experience guilt after theft are less likely to steal property worth $50 or more.

The relationship between level of perceived guilt and thefts found using Wave VII of the NYS data *is similar to / differs greatly from* the findings expected under bio-psychological theory of choice.

4. In the GUILTHFT → THEFT50 crosstabulation with MALE as a control variable, 20 (7.3%) of the males who anticipated a great deal of guilt had actually stolen something, compared to _____ (_____%) of those who said they would feel quite a bit of guilt, _____ (_____%) of those who said they would feel some guilt, _____ (_____%) of those who said they would feel "not too much" guilt, and _____ (_____%) of those who said they would feel very little guilt. For males, it appears that as amount of anticipated guilt goes up, likelihood of stealing something worth $50 or more goes *up / down*. This relationship is *weak / moderate / strong*. This relationship *is / is not* statistically significant. When we turn our attention to the female rows, we see that _____ (_____%) of the females who anticipated a great deal of guilt had actually stolen something, compared to _____ (_____%) of those who said they would feel quite a bit of guilt, _____ (_____%) of those who said they would feel some guilt, and _____ (_____%) of those who said they would feel "not too much" guilt. For females, it appears that as amount of anticipated guilt goes up, likelihood of stealing something worth $50 or more goes *up / down*. This relationship is *weak / moderate / strong*. This relationship *is / is not* statistically significant. Overall, we *can / cannot* say that controlling for gender in our model substantially changes the relationship we found between anticipated guilt and likelihood of committing theft.

5. In the ARRTHFT → THEFT50 crosstabulation with MALE as a control variable, 74 (19.8%) of the males who perceived a low chance of arrest had actually stolen something, compared to _____ (_____%) of those who perceived a higher chance of arrest. For males, it appears that as perceived chance of arrest for theft goes up, likelihood of stealing something worth $50 or more goes *up / down*. This relationship is *weak / moderate / strong*. This relationship *is / is not* statistically significant. When we turn our attention to the female rows, we see that _____ (_____%) of the females who perceived a low chance of arrest for theft had actually stolen something, compared to _____ (_____%) of those who perceived a higher chance of arrest. For females, it appears that as perceived chance of arrest for theft goes up, likelihood of stealing something worth $50 or more goes *up / down*. This relationship is *weak / moderate / strong* and *is / is not* statistically significant. Overall, we *can / cannot* say that controlling for gender in our model substantially changes the relationship we found between perceived chance of arrest and likelihood of committing theft.

6. Overall, it appears that our findings using the Wave VII of the NYS *support / do not support* bio-psychological theory of choice.

Homework for Part IX: "Further Exploration" Questions
(Bio-psychological Theory of Choice)

Name: _____ Date: _____

Task: See if the two measures we developed for bio-psychological theory of choice help predict involvement in violent offenses. Make sure you substitute the measures relevant for VIOLENCE (ARRVIO and GUILVIO instead of the two theft-related measures).

Directions: Answer the following questions by filling in the blanks or circling the appropriate responses. A couple of answers have been filled in for you to make sure you're on the right track.

1. In Wave VII of the NYS dataset, <u>328</u> (_____%) of the sample believed their chances of arrest for attacking someone were low (50% or less), and _____ (_____%) believed their chances for arrest were high (more than 50%). _____ (_____%) of the respondents said they would feel a great deal of guilt if they attacked someone, <u>234</u> (_____%) said they would feel quite a bit of guilt, _____ (_____%) said they would feel some guilt, _____ (_____%) said they would feel "not too much" guilt, and _____ (_____%) said they would feel very little guilt.

2. In the ARRVIO → VIOLENCE crosstabulation, _____ (_____%) of the respondents who believed their chances of arrest for attacking someone were high (more than 50%) had actually attacked someone, compared to <u>96</u> (_____%) of those who believed their chances of arrest were low. This relationship is *weak / moderate / strong.* This relationship *is / is not* statistically significant.

   The relationship between perceived certainty of arrest and violence found using Wave VII of the NYS data *is similar to / differs greatly from* the findings expected under bio-psychological theory of choice.

3. In the GUILVIO → VIOLENCE crosstabulation, _____ (_____%) of the respondents who said they would feel a great deal of guilt if they attacked someone had actually attacked someone, compared to <u>56</u> (_____%) of those said they would feel quite a bit of guilt, _____ (_____%) of those said they would feel some guilt, _____ (_____%) of those said they would feel "not too much" guilt, and _____ (_____%) of those said

they would feel very little guilt. This relationship is *weak / moderate / strong*. This relationship *is / is not* statistically significant.

The GUILVIO → VIOLENCE table *does / does not* show that respondents who say they would experience guilt after attacking someone are less likely to actually attack someone.

The relationship between level of perceived guilt and involvement in violence found using Wave VII of the NYS data *is similar to / differs greatly from* the findings expected under bio-psychological theory of choice.

4. Overall, it appears that our findings using the Wave VII of the NYS *support / do not support* bio-psychological theory of choice.

Homework for Part IX: "On Your Own" Questions
(Bio-psychological Theory of Choice)

Name: _____ Date: _____

Task: Include some control variables of your own in your test of bio-psychological theory of choice. One idea is to insert a control variable into one of the relationships we have already examined. If you cannot find one of your own, you may use one of the two presented in the write-up for this exercise. HINT: if you stick to control variables with two or three categories, your results will be easier to interpret and you will have less of a problem with empty cells.

Directions: Answer the following questions.

1. Which control variable did you choose, and why did you choose to control that factor?

2. What was the relationship between the independent and dependent variables before the addition of the control variable?

3. Did including the control variable change the relationship between the independent and dependent variables; that is, did the relationship between the two variables vary by control variable subcategory?

4. Based on your findings, what modifications or additions would you make to the bio-psychological theory of choice?

5. Can you say your testing supports bio-psychological theory of choice? Why/why not?

If you included more than one control variable, you may summarize the findings here for future reference.

X

HOW DO WE CONTROL CRIME?

Crime and Social Control

T HIS last section ends this volume, but it also represents a beginning. Having learned about patterns and characteristics of crime and about causes of criminality, we are better prepared to begin the task of considering what a society can do to control crime.

We have seen that many social structures and forces, such as families, schools, and communities, influence levels of crime. These institutions, while not primarily concerned with controlling crime, may nonetheless effectively regulate criminal behavior. Although modern, complex, industrial societies clearly need police, courts, and means of punishing those who violate the law, many criminologists believe that other social institutions and structures, as informal mechanisms of social control, are far more important than the system of criminal justice in controlling crime. Informal structures, together with the norms and values they reinforce, are more important because they are always with us. Families and neighborhoods are ever present and constantly monitoring and supervising the individuals within them. Police and other "control agents" cannot possibly have us under surveillance at all times, nor do we want them in that role.

Unfortunately, people with a public voice, by virtue of their political position, their media platform, or even their "expert" status, tend to make pronouncements about crime and criminals, and about how we should reform the criminal justice system to make it more effective. The people who make such statements often have a rather superficial understanding of crime, criminality, or what is likely to work or not work in criminal justice. That is why we say that this chapter is in some sense a beginning. Having gained a basic understanding of crime, the reader is prepared to learn more; *Volume II: Juvenile Delinquency* presents more theory and empirical research, and also considers attempts to prevent juvenile delinquency. The reader is also better prepared to think about how we might control crime more effectively; *Volume III: Criminal Justice* presents readings that consider major issues in criminal justice and crime control.

In this section we present five papers that represent important dimensions of informed debate on controlling crime. We say "informed" because the papers reflect an understanding of crime and its causes that, unlike many ideas and arguments that students will have read and heard, is based on study and considered thinking. Nevertheless, the papers reflect radically different positions and have significant disagreements. Readers should examine each of these papers with at least three issues in mind:

1. What are the authors' recommendations for controlling crime?
2. What are the authors' underlying assumptions about the causes of crime (or factors related to trends in crime)?
3. Are the authors' assumptions about crime, its causes, and its control consistent with what we have learned from readings in the previous chapters?

The first selection, "Crime in America" from *The Economist*, calls into question American "get-tough" policies on crime in the 1980s and early 1990s. At the heart of this essay is the idea that punitive policies toward crime, such as "three strikes and you're out," make little sense in light of the data on crime trends in the United States. The relationship between rates of crime and patterns of imprisonment is far from clear; scholars currently don't understand how patterns of punishment influence rates of crime at the national level. And with crime rates dropping, should we heed calls for even longer prison sentences, particularly since incarceration is the most expensive approach to regulating criminal behavior?

Anna Baldry's piece, "Victim–Offender Mediation in the Italian Juvenile Justice System: The Role of the Social Worker," describes how one alternative to incarceration is working in Italy, and some of the challenges that emerge. Using principles of restorative justice, some courts currently bring juvenile offenders and their victims together to mediate disputes and conflicts associated with crime. Baldry's paper shows that although many caseworkers are not effectively trained as mediators, mediation can nevertheless be beneficial, even in cases involving serious violent crimes.

John Braithwaite's "The Family Model of the Criminal Process: Reintegrative Shaming" also argues for a different approach to punishing criminal offenders. Braithwaite distinguishes between punishments that are disintegrative and those that are reintegrative. Conventional punishments such as incarceration do little to restore the relationship between the offender and the community, thereby weakening social controls over the offender. In contrast, shaming the offender by expressing contempt and disapproval without severing the offender's ties to conventional society may actually enhance control and help reintegrate the offender.

James Q. Wilson and George Kelling's "Broken Windows," originally published in the *Atlantic Monthly*, sparked national debate over the role of police in crime control in the 1980s. Wilson and Kelling draw an analogy between petty crimes in communities and broken windows in abandoned buildings. They argue that petty crimes will lead to more crimes if there is no community or societal response, just as one broken window in an abandoned building will lead to more if left unrepaired. Their essay stimulated a new approach to policing that shifted the emphasis of police work from simply enforcing laws to maintaining public order in communities.

The final essay is by Steven Messner and Marcus Felson, "Strengthening Institutions and Rethinking the American Dream." Messner and Felson call into question crime control reforms over the past four decades, arguing that none have yielded major reductions in criminal behavior. In reviewing these reforms, they assert that none have achieved the fundamental social and cultural changes needed to reduce crime. Reducing crime requires that we significantly strengthen our schools and families, and also promote a culture that accords importance to individual restraint and collective interest.

We are not so much interested in whether readers agree with any of the writers, but we would like to convince those who part these pages to see the wisdom in raising the level of public debate about crime and criminal justice. We have slipped into speaking about crime in, as a former mayor of Seattle put it, "bumper sticker" phrases. The complexity of criminality means that when we reduce criminal justice reform to such slogans as "three strikes and you're out," we fail to consider fully the wisdom of such policies in light of our knowledge about crime. To confront crime more effectively, what we need is fewer bumper stickers and more reasoned debate. This debate should be informed by knowledge about the causes of crime and effective strategies for reducing criminal behavior. These five papers provide models for how that debate should proceed.

Crime in America: Violent and Irrational— and That's Just the Policy

THE ECONOMIST

Remember serial killers? A few years ago, these twisted creatures haunted not just the American imagination but, it seemed, America's real streets and parks: an official of the Justice Department was widely reported as saying that 4,000 of America's annual 24,000-or-so murders were attributable to serial killers.

America loves its myths—and that was pretty much what the "wave of serial killings" turned out to be: 4,000 people are not victims of serial murderers; 4,000 murders remain unsolved each year. According to cool-headed academic research, maybe 50 people a year are victims of serial murderers; the figure has been stable for 20 years.

Serial murderers obviously form a bizarre and special category of criminal. People might well believe extraordinary things about them. But about crime in general, surely ordinary folk have a better understanding—don't they? Well, consider two widely held beliefs:

"America has experienced a crime wave in the past 20 years." No. According to the National Crime Victimisation Survey, violent crime fell in the first half of the 1980s, rose in the second half, and has been falling in the 1990s. Over the past two decades, it has fallen

slightly. Non-violent property crimes (theft, larceny and burglary) have followed similar patterns. So has murder: its peak was in 1980.

"America is more criminal than other countries." Again, no. According to an International Crime Survey, carried out by the Ministry of Justice in the Netherlands in 1992, America is not obviously more criminal than anywhere else. You are more likely to be burgled in Australia or New Zealand. You are more likely to be robbed with violence in Spain; you are more likely to be robbed without violence in Spain, Canada, Australia and New Zealand. You are more likely to be raped or indecently assaulted in Canada, Australia or western Germany. And so on.

American misconceptions raise two questions. First, why are Americans so afraid of crime? (As according to Gallup polls, they are: in recent years Americans have put crime either first or second in their list of problems facing the country; in Britain, crime limps along between second and sixth in people's priorities.) Second, why should Americans be so punitive in their attitude to criminals? (As they also seem to be: when asked by the International Crime Survey what should happen to a young burglar who has committed more than one offence, 53% of Americans reckoned he should go to prison, compared with 37% of English and Welsh, 22% of Italians, and 13% of Germans and French.)

One possible explanation is that Americans are irrational in their attitudes to crime. But that cannot be right: crime imposes huge costs on the country and has helped turn parts of American inner cities into nightmares of violence. Given that, it is hardly surprising that Americans should fear the spread of crime. But it remains surprising that American public attitudes should be so different from those in other countries which also have dangerous inner cities. No, there seems to be something else feeding Americans' fear and loathing of criminals. More probably, two things: the violence of American crime, and its irrationality. And it is with these that America's real crime-policy problems begin.

MURDER AS PUBLIC CHOICE

America tops the developed-country crime league only in one category: murder. While you are more likely to be burgled in Sydney than in Los Angeles, you are 20 times more likely to be murdered in Los Angeles than you are in Sydney.

American crime is not only more violent; it is also irrational in its violence. Think about a person held up at gunpoint who fails to co-operate with a robber. "Since both the risk of apprehension and the potential punishment escalate when the victim is killed," says Franklin Zimring, a criminologist at the University of California, Berkeley, "the rational robber would be well advised to meet flight or refusal by avoiding conflict and seeking another victim." Yet Americans commonly get killed in these circumstances, and it is the irrationality of such violence that terrifies.

There is nothing odd or surprising in the observation that America is more violent than other countries, that Americans are more afraid of crime, and they are therefore more punitive. But the problem with America's criminal-justice policy lies in that sequence of thought. By eliding violence and crime, Americans fail to identify the problem that sets them apart from the rest of the rich world, which is violence, rather than crime generally. Americans are right to think they have a special problem

of violence. They are wrong to think their country is being overwhelmed by crime of every sort. Yet because many people do think that, they are throwing their weight behind indiscriminate policies which, at huge cost, bludgeon crime as a whole but fail to tackle the problem of violence.

America now imprisons seven times as many people (proportionately) as does the average European country, largely as a result of get-tough-on-crime laws. These are the laws other countries are now studying with admiration.

First came mandatory sentencing laws, requiring courts to impose minimum sentences on offenders for particular crimes. Michigan, for instance, has a mandatory life sentence for an offender caught with 650 grams of cocaine. A federal law condemns anybody convicted of possession of more than five grams of crack to a minimum of five years in prison.

Then came "three-strike laws," supported by Bill Clinton and adopted by 20-odd states and the federal government. These impose a mandatory life sentence on anybody convicted of a third felony. The seriousness of the felony, and therefore the impact of the law, varies from state to state. In California, in the most celebrated case, a man who stole a pizza as his third felony got life. His case was extreme, but not unique: another man got life after stealing three steaks.

THREE STEAKS AND YOU'RE OUT

Now, the fashion is for "truth-in-sentencing." Such laws require the criminal to spend most of his sentence (usually 85%) in prison, rather than making him eligible for parole after, say, four to six years of a ten-year sentence. There is much to be said for a system that does not leave the public feeling cheated about what sentences actually amount to. But, by imposing the 85% average on all offenders, "truth in sentencing" makes it impossible to discriminate between people who seem genuinely remorseful and might be let out early and the more dangerous types who should serve the whole of their sentence.

Since the early 1970s, when the first tough-sentencing laws were introduced, the prison population has risen from 200,000 to 1.1 million. If that increase were made up mostly of the violent people that have engendered America's crime panic, that could be counted as a blow against violent crime. But it is not: the biggest increase is in non-violent drug offenders.

Between 1980 and now, the proportion of those sentenced to prison for non-violent property crimes has remained about the same (two-fifths). The number of those sentenced for drugs has soared (from one-tenth to over one-third). The share sentenced for violent crimes has fallen from half to under one-third.

And so what, you might ask? Non-violent crime still matters. Even if America's crime panic is related to violence, it is right and proper that the system should be seeking to minimise all crime. The prison population is going up. The crime figures are going down. Let 'em rot. As the right says: "Prison works."

Or does it? That depends on what you mean by "works." To many people, prison can strongly influence the trend in the crime rate: putting a lot of people in prison, they believe, can achieve a long-term reversal of rising crime. This must be doubtful. Yes, crime is falling now. But it also fell in the early 1980s, rose in the late 1980s and fell again in the early 1990s. The prison population rose through the whole period.

If there is any single explanation for these changes, it would seem to lie in demographics. Young men commit by far and away the largest number of crimes, so when there are more of them around, proportionately, the crime rate goes up. That was what happened in the 1960s, the period of the big, sustained post-war rise in the crime rate. Demography also tells you that there will be more young men around in ten years' time to commit more crimes.

But demographics cannot be the only explanation. If it were, crime would have fallen in the second half of the 1980s, when there were fewer teenagers. In fact, it rose.

Why? The answer is probably drugs. What seems to have happened is that the appearance of crack in late 1985 shook up the drugs-distribution business. The number of dealers increased, kids with no capital got into the business and gangs competed murderously for market share.

This theory would account for the decline in homicides in the 1990s. Crack consumption seems to be falling—possibly just because drugs go in and out of fashion, possibly because teenagers have seen how bad the stuff is. And the market has matured as well as declined. Policemen and researchers say territories have been carved out, boundaries set. With competition less rife, murders have declined.

The significance of all this is that it loosens the connection between the rise in the prison population and the fall in the crime rate. Crime might have fallen anyway. A combination of demographic and social explanations, rather than changes in the prison population, seems to account for much of the changing pattern of crime.

VOX POPULI, VOX DEI, VOX DEMENTIAE

That said, there might still be a justification for putting more people in prison: if by doing so you lowered the overall level of crime by taking criminals out of circulation. Indeed, if a small number of young men commit a disproportionately large number of crimes, then locking up this particular group might depress crime a lot.

Liberal criminologists sometimes appear to doubt this. "It seems," says John Dilulio, the right-wing's favourite thinker on crime, "that you need a PhD in criminology to doubt the proposition that putting criminals in prison will keep down crime." Of course, the proposition is self-evidently true. If you banged up for life anyone who had ever committed a crime, however trivial, crime would plummet.

But the question is: is this sensible, even if it does work?

To many ordinary Americans, it is and politicians are happy to oblige the voters by promising to get ever tougher on crime. But what is the evidence about whether prison is an effective way of reducing crime?

Looking across the states' different crime rates and imprisonment rates, there is no correlation between the two. True, you would not necessarily expect one: states are different and tough-sentencing laws might be a reaction to a high crime rate as much as a way of bringing it down. But more sophisticated analyses confirm there is no link. Mr Zimring took the adult and juvenile crime rates in California and studied what happened over the period when tough laws were being introduced for adults, but not for juveniles. No relationship is detectable: for most crimes, offences committed by juveniles either fell or rose significantly less than did those committed by adults.

And, just as there is no convincing argument that prison effectively reduces the level of crime, nor does there seem to be a convincing cost–benefit argument in favour of prison. The problem lies in costing crime. One often-used estimate, which monetises intangibles like pain and suffering, calculates the annual costs of crime at $450 billion. This makes prison look a bargain: its annual bill is $35 billion, while the criminal-justice system, including police and courts, costs $100 billion. But if you calculate the costs of crime on the basis of physical damage—hospital bills or the cost of replacing stolen goods—the figure comes out at a mere $18 billion a year. The moral is that, while the cost of crime must be high, no one has any real idea what it is.

What you can say is that, out of the range of options for dealing with criminals, prison is among the most expensive. One currently popular alternative is the "drugs court." Under this system, people charged with possession or small dealing may opt to go through a drugs-treatment programme rather than stand trial. Treatment costs $3,500–15,000 a year, depending on whether it is residential or not;

prison costs $22,000. There is also some evidence that these courts are better than prisons at discouraging reoffending, though, since they are relatively new, the evidence is not conclusive.

Of course, get-tough policies raise questions other than that of efficacy. One is moral. Is it right to lock somebody up for life for stealing a pizza? Another is racial (see box). These concerns have not, it seems, made much of an impact on public opinion. According to Mr Dilulio, "Americans have lost interest in the Anglo-Saxon, innocent-until-proven-guilty model of justice. They want to get the bad guys."

Yet even by this measure, the get-tough policies are misfiring. Around 100,000 people go to prison for the 6 million-odd violent crimes committed a year. The system is not getting the bad guys. What it is getting is a great many drug-taking, drug-dealing, small-time thieves. Conservatives argue that most people in prison are either violent or repeat offenders. True, but many of the repeat offenders are addicts financing their habit through drug dealing or burglary. Nobody suggests that they are unfortunates for whom one should merely be sorry; but it is not clear that sending a crack-user to prison for five years is a rational solution to America's violent-crime problem.

America is awash with academics, judges, commissioners and policemen who know and study crime. The Justice Department's research arm, the National Institute of Justice, spent $53 million last year on research of a higher standard, and in a larger quantity, than goes on anywhere else in the world.

Almost all of this stuff doubts the efficacy of what is going on in criminal justice, and fears for the consequences. Almost all the professionals agree that America's problem is violence, and that the way to reduce violence is to restrict access to guns. And on this—though the point is rarely noticed—the public agrees: 62%, according to a recent Gallup poll, favour stricter gun control.

Yet none of it makes much difference to public policy. The administration promotes a

ONE-THIRD AND RISING

Blacks are more likely to commit crimes than are whites. Around 45% of those arrested for serious crimes are black. But they are also more harshly treated. Numberless studies have shown that the criminal-justice system is not colour blind. There are more unfounded arrests of blacks. Blacks pay on average twice as much bail as whites. They are more likely to be jailed before trial and get heavier sentences for the same crime.

Since the "war on drugs," the bias seems to have got worse. Blacks make up 12% of the American population, and, according to government surveys, 13% of those who say they have used drugs in the past month. But they account for 35% of arrests for drug possession, 55% of convictions and 74% of prison sentences.

Partly, that is because drug laws implicitly target blacks. Crack is a drug favoured by blacks. The mandatory federal penalty for possessing five grams of crack (a couple of days' supply for an addict) is five years in jail. Cocaine is principally a white person's drug. To get the same sentence a cocaine user has to have half a kilo in his possession.

The implementation of anti-drug laws also affects blacks disproportionately. Partly that is because the police raid black areas, not nice white suburbs, but that is not the full explanation. A study of sentencing in the 1980s, which divided blacks between "underclass" and "non-underclass," concluded that the biggest increase in the prison population was among "non-underclass" blacks convicted for drug offences.

The figures on blacks in the criminal-justice system are shocking. According to the Sentencing Project, a Washington-based penal-reform group, one-third of 20–29-year-old black men are on probation, on parole or in prison. As the prison population rises, that share will increase yet further. Think about that.

People who have been in prison have a slim chance of regular employment on release. Their families are therefore poorer than others. Their children are fatherless while they are inside. Prison becomes the norm; "normal" life abnormal. America is on a dangerous course.

---

three-strike policy even though it knows that the main effect of three-strike laws is to bung up the prison system with people long past crime-committing age.

American crime policy seems to have become an area where the arguments—admittedly often complex and finely balanced—take second place to the lobbying power of special-interest groups. The effectiveness of one, the National Rifle Association, has been well-documented. A less familiar one is the prison-building lobby.

Prisons have been likened to the defence industry as a government subsidy to the white working class. For areas hit by the end of the cold war, and by the ups and downs of agri-

culture, prisons provide attractively recession-proof employment. As the flier for the American Jail Association last year said, "Jails are BIG BUSINESS." Towns compete to get them.

The prison guards' union has also become a powerful voice. According to a study of campaign contributions in California in 1991–92, the local version, the California Correctional Peace Officers' Association, was the second-largest donor in the state. It spends around $1 million on political contributions for the governorship and the legislature in each electoral cycle.

But more important than the lobbying, and more worrying, is the failure of public debate on prison, its costs, and the alternatives. According to Bobby Scott, a Democratic congressman opposed to tough-sentencing laws, "When you call for more incarceration, you do not have to explain yourself; when you argue for effective alternatives, you do. And in politics, when you start explaining, you've lost." If that is true—and it sounds painfully accurate—something has gone badly wrong not just with American crime policy, but with America's capacity for reasoned public debate.

QUESTIONS FOR DISCUSSION AND WRITING

1. Has America experienced a "crime wave" in the past 20 years?
2. What happened "between 1980 and now"?
3. What do "sophisticated analyses" confirm regarding the link between crime and imprisonment rates?

Victim–Offender Mediation in the Italian Juvenile Justice System: The Role of the Social Worker

ANNA COSTANZA BALDRY

Vᴵᴄᴛᴵᴹ–offender mediation is an alternative way of responding to crime which contrasts with individualistic approaches, largely focused on the offender. The classical retributive approach aims to punish offenders according to the just deserts model. This way of "paying a debt to society" though, especially if it takes the form of imprisonment, can incur considerable extra expense and there is no clear evidence that it reduces recidivism rates. Moreover, it leaves victims and communities unsatisfied and unsafe. The rehabilitative justice system, which does aim to treat and reform offenders, does not take into consideration the real interests and needs of victims.

The restorative justice approach offers a different model. It considers victims and communities, rather than the state, as those primarily affected by crime. The aim of this approach is therefore to "restore victims of crime as far as possible to their state before the crime and denounce the offence by requiring offenders to take responsibility for it." This can be done by repairing the damage caused by the crime, either materially or in a symbolic way directly to the victim or to the

community, or, indirectly, through work or actions that enable offenders to regain acceptance as law-abiding members of the community and make amends to the victim.

Different aspects of the restorative approach, according to Wright, most commonly include state compensation, victim support groups, offender's reparation directly to the victim or through community work, and the recently introduced family group conferences. According to Umbreit, however, the clearest expression of this approach is victim–offender mediation. Mediation provides an opportunity to resolve conflicts that are associated with a crime.

Victim–offender mediation in Italy is still an uncommon and underdeveloped practice, and it can only take place during probation. In the limited number of cases where it does take place, youth justice social workers working as probation officers act as mediators but they lack experience and specific training. Moreover, mediators must remain neutral, so social workers should not mediate in a case where they are involved in any other capacity. According to Davis and Baldry and Scardaccione, youth justice social workers are perceived as working in the interest of offenders, and should not therefore act as mediators. Nevertheless, because social workers' skills include promoting the network between young offend-

From "Victim-Offender Mediation in the Italian Juvenile Justice System: The Role of the Social Worker" by A. Baldry, 1998, *British Journal of Social Work* 28(5):729–744. Reprinted by permission of the British Association of Social Workers.

ers, their families, the community, victims and the criminal justice system, they could in this instance play a central role, either directly as mediators or as case managers.

The first part of this paper describes the basic principles of victim–offender mediation, after which the current situation in the Italian juvenile criminal justice system is outlined. The second section presents the results of a survey of victim–offender mediation experiences in Italy and addresses the role played by social workers. A case study of an attempted murder is presented to illustrate the potential for social workers to act as mediators and the feasibility of victim–offender mediation, even for serious crimes where strong emotions are involved.

THE PRINCIPLES AND DEVELOPMENT OF VICTIM–OFFENDER MEDIATION

The principles of restorative justice involve two key elements: victim–offender mediation and reparation. These can operate either interdependently or with either one separate from the other. Wright defines mediation as "a process in which victim(s) and offenders communicate with the help of an *impartial third party*, either directly (face-to-face) or indirectly via the third party, enabling the victim(s) to express their needs and feelings, and offenders to accept and act on their responsibilities." This implies bringing the victim and offender together to reduce the conflict between these two parties. Reparation, on the other hand, in the context of victim–offender mediation, is the

contribution that can be made by the offender to the victim, to help put right the harm (physical or emotional) caused by the crime. If the victim does not wish to receive it personally, reparation may be made to the community. Reparation may include an apology, financial payment, practical work, return and/or repair of goods and undertaking of future behaviour or voluntary participation in education, treatment or training programmes.

This paper is concerned specifically with mediation and the advantages and risks it carries.

The Advantages of Mediation

A substantial proportion of the general public, as well as some victims themselves, are not, or are not solely, interested in punishing the offender or in being paid back. They would prefer that something more constructive and helpful for all parties involved were done to heal the harm caused. Others, of course, do want punishment and reparation, or to be paid back.

Criminal justice does not always need to employ coercion; procedures based on consent have advantages, such as giving victims the chance to express their feelings to offenders who can have the opportunity to make amends directly to victims or indirectly to the community.

On the basis of these principles, victim–offender mediation has developed in different ways. Victim Offender Reconciliation Programs (VORPs) started in the USA and in Canada and then spread to other countries.

These programmes are mainly community-initiated and seek to bring victims and offenders together. Referrals come mainly from the courts and probation services. In Scotland and continental European countries they are mainly referred from prosecutors. Cases are then passed to a mediation worker who gets in touch directly with the victim and the offender and arranges for them to meet or to communicate through the mediator. According to Umbreit and Coates, most current programmes in the USA are sponsored by non-profit community-based organizations which work in close connection with the courts. Yet, there too, there is a growing number of mediation programmes that are directly sponsored by the probation service or other public agencies.

Victim–offender mediation services which developed subsequently in England and in some parts of Australia are sometimes referred to as "reparation services"; they can be used when the offender has been cautioned instead of prosecuted, or after conviction and before sentence, or when disposal has already been decided. Some English mediation services are "court-based" for cases remanded on bail. The initiative in this model comes from the probation service and is administered by employees of the probation service who also act as mediators. Another model is for the probation service to refer to a voluntary organization or another informal agency. These are "community-based" programmes. In these reparation schemes, victims and offenders usually do not meet directly but communicate via the mediator who meets them separately to decide on the reparation they both agree to. Mediators may be members of staff or members of the public (either volunteers or paid on a sessional basis). The essential requirement is that they should receive specific training as mediators; social workers' responsibilities and skills differ in many ways from those of mediators.

There are no specific limitations as to which cases are best suited for mediation. According to a public opinion survey conducted by Lee, petty crimes and other non-violent crimes are those most suited to victim–offender mediation, but Umbreit illustrates how even serious and emotive crimes may be appropriately included in such schemes.

The Risks of Mediation

According to the study conducted by Smith et al., when mediation takes place before sentence, the offender might accept mediation or reparation for self-serving purposes, to lighten the sentence, although empirical evidence in this regard has not always been consistent. Moreover, some victims are afraid of being threatened or even blackmailed by offenders if they do not agree to meet them.

In other cases, especially when young offenders are involved, victims might feel obliged to meet the juveniles to give them the opportunity to make amends and to show concern about the offence, even if this is not what they think is best for themselves. To prevent this, mediators should obtain consent from both the victim and the offender, explaining the purpose of mediation to them.

Moreover, as previously mentioned, mediators should be volunteers trained for community disputes and conflict resolution who work outside the criminal justice service.

As will be seen in the next section, this is what is currently happening in Italy, where the juvenile justice system is mainly offender-oriented and mediation takes place only during the probation order. Social workers in charge of probation are responsible for the rehabilitation and welfare of young offenders but are not specifically trained in mediation skills.

THE ITALIAN JUVENILE CRIMINAL JUSTICE SYSTEM AND VICTIM–OFFENDER MEDIATION OPPORTUNITIES

According to the United Nations Standard Minimum Rules for the Administration of Juvenile Justice, all juvenile criminal justice systems of those countries conforming to these recommendations should favour the protection and promotion of the rights of young offenders by helping them to take responsibility for their actions while paying their debts to society for the crime committed. On the basis of these regulations, in 1988, the New Criminal Procedure Code for young offenders was established in Italy.

Some of the principles of the restorative justice approach were included, such as holding young offenders responsible for their actions and making them pay their debt to society or to the victim through some form of restitution or community work, but all of these changes mainly addressed the interests of the offender.

The Italian juvenile justice system allows the personality of the young offender to be taken into account at any stage of the criminal justice process, and to influence legal decisions. This principle is the opposite of the "legality principle" for adult offenders in Italy, which prevents the personality assessment of the accused from being considered in any legal action and does not allow it to influence the sentence. The assessment of the young offender's personality aims to establish the degree of responsibility of the accused based on: his or her maturity; his or her personal, social and family circumstances; and in relation to the crime committed. On the basis of all these considerations, the most appropriate sanction is recommended. This assessment is one of the responsibilities of youth justice social workers, who have to complete a report for the judge before sentencing. On the basis of the assessment, the judge can order probation as an alternative to other sanctions.

Juvenile probation is a new device in the Italian criminal juvenile justice system and differs from most existing probation orders around the world. It is based on the suspension of the trial, not of the sentence. Regardless of this distinction, it follows the same philosophical principle as probation elsewhere, aiming to avoid imposing a punitive sanction on the young offender provided that he or she behaves satisfactorily during the specified period. Moreover, in the Italian legal system, youth justice social workers are those in charge of this alternative sanction and act as probation officers. Social workers develop a plan that the offender has to agree to fulfil. This plan is based on several aims that show the complexity of this alternative disposal. Probation orders seek not only to avoid a conviction and to implement rehabilitation, but also to promote the psychological development and social adjustment of the young offender and to raise his or her own sense of responsibility. In order to achieve this, the young person is given the opportunity to restore the damage caused by the offence through "reparation" and/or "conciliation" with the victim. This is currently the only opportunity within the Italian juvenile legal system for victim–offender mediation to take place. Hence, mediation can only occur during the probation order imposed by the judge, and youth justice social workers working as probation officers are in charge of it.

What is currently happening in Italy is that juvenile courts in the country decide in each case whether to include victim–offender mediation, or any other activities, as part of the probation order.

THE RESEARCH

Aims of the Survey

There have been very few studies conducted so far in Italy on victim–offender mediation, given that it is not yet a well-established procedure and fulfils only a marginal role within the probation order. Research was therefore carried out to gather information on the current scope of victim–offender mediation in order to consider the advantages and limits of this alternative way of dealing with crimes.

The study focused special attention on the role of youth justice social workers working as probation officers given that they are the people mainly involved in mediation.

Procedure and Sample

The Central Office of Justice for Young Offenders of the Department of Criminal Justice gathers information about those cases for which the judge has ordered a "suspension of trial with probation." In some of these cases the judge has required in the probation order that social workers should consider the promotion of victim–offender mediation. Ninety cases were available in a period of one year and a half. In order to gain more detailed information, 90 questionnaires were sent to the social workers in charge of each case.

The Questionnaire

The questionnaire was divided into two parts. The first gathered information on: the offender (age, education, family background); the type of crime committed; the victim; and the victim's relationship with the offender. The second part addressed the victim–offender mediation phase: who was involved; what was done; the role played by the victim and the offender; the number of times they met and where. Another set of questions analysed the general attitudes of social workers towards mediation in terms of what they thought should be their main activities when acting as mediators.

RESULTS

All questionnaires were returned. They were completed by the youth justice social workers responsible for the probation orders. The social workers were not able to fill in all parts of the questionnaire due to a shortage of information on each case. Therefore, some of the questions relating to the family and the social background of the young offender, and almost all those regarding the victim, as well as some of those referring to mediation, were impossible to analyse.

The sample population consisted of 84 male and 6 female young offenders. Their mean age was 17 years . . . and the probation order lasted 9 months on average. . . . No results showed any significant gender differences, due partly to the small sample size of females, and therefore all results will be presented jointly for male and female offenders.

The largest number of offences committed, within a wide range, were against property. . . . Looking at the different parts of the country where the cases originated, the unequal distribution suggests that deciding whether to recommend mediation in the probation order relates more to the discretion of the judge than to the type of crime committed or to any characteristics of the young offender. . . .

In all cases analysed, social workers supervising the probation order acted as mediators. Many cases did not involve direct victim–offender mediation, with victims present in only 36 cases (40.5 per cent of the total). In these cases, both the victim and the offender were contacted and both were present during the mediation phase. In two other cases, the

victim's parents were present instead. In all remaining cases, mediation did not involve a direct meeting of the two parties. Social workers merely contacted the offenders, and in some cases, suggested to them that they should apologise to the victim by writing a letter. They did not make the process two-way by asking victims whether this was what they really wanted.

A further analysis of the 36 cases where the victim took part in the meeting revealed that, in 24 cases, victims were contacted first and, in the remaining 12 cases, the offender was contacted first. . . . This may suggest that more thought needs to be given to the way in which the initial contact is made and its effects on the victim, because, if the victim were approached first and the offender then refused mediation, the victim might feel disappointed; whereas, if the offender were approached first, then the victim might feel under pressure to accept.

Information about the mediation phase indicates that, in 15 cases (16.4 per cent), the offender made a symbolic restitution; the offender answered the victim's questions in 34 cases (37.7 per cent), in 31 of which the victim was present. In 68 cases (75.9 per cent), mediation consisted of the offender apologising to the victim, who was present in 30 cases (43.4 per cent). In 25 cases the mediation session ended with parties shaking hands. Some cases involved more than one of these options, therefore the total exceeds one hundred.

The Role of Social Workers

The next section of the questionnaire looked at the role played by social workers and evaluated their attitudes towards mediation. Social workers were asked to indicate what they thought should be their main role as mediators. This was designed as an open question in order to consider: (i) the proportion of replies which implied neutrality; (ii) the proportion of answers that implied benefits to offenders; (iii) the apparent lack of priority accorded to the interests of the victim. The answers were then divided into six categories. . . . Most of these answers implied that, in the perception of social workers, the guarantee of neutrality should be one of the main aims of the mediator.

In order to gather more information on these issues, a small sample of social workers ($n = 12$) was also interviewed by telephone on their general attitudes towards restorative justice principles, mediation, and their capacities to act as mediators.

Social workers believed that punishment has no positive effects on the young offenders nor on the community. At the same time, they thought that focusing only on treatment and rehabilitation might not serve to hold the juvenile accountable for the crime committed. Juveniles do not then have the opportunity to confront the consequences of their actions or understand the damage caused or the feelings of those affected. Social workers thought that mediation could be an excellent way of dealing with minor offences and that it could also have a potential benefit in more serious crimes.

Social workers were concerned, however, that they did not receive any specific training for conducting victim–offender mediation programmes. Although they could appreciate the advantages of a restorative means of dealing with crime, they admitted that for them it was almost impossible to act adequately as mediators because they suffered from a lack of specific skills and training as well as a lack of time. They themselves had to decide— without any guidelines to follow—how to set up a mediation session, what was the best way to conduct it, and how to approach the victim; moreover, there was no independent agency to which they could refer the case for the mediation.

This clearly shows the risks of involving as mediators youth justice social workers who are in charge of the probation order, unless they are specifically trained for this purpose. Their usual experience, duties and responsibilities are completely oriented towards the young offender. Thus, the situation in Italy is still very far from addressing one of the basic principles of a restorative justice approach, that is, to guarantee that both the interests of the victim and those of the offender are taken into consideration and that mediators are neutral.

The following case study, on the other hand, is a good example of how social workers could successfully mediate even in very serious cases like attempted murder. This case clearly shows the potential of mediation that allows all parties to have an equal opportunity to express their feelings and recognize the emotions involved. Mediation should be encouraged for serious cases where there is not continuing danger because it gives both sides the chance to express the effects of crime and enables the offender to acknowledge the suffering caused to the victim and to show willingness to make reparation.

In the example presented, a youth justice social worker in charge of probation acted as mediator according to the specific training she had received.

CASE STUDY

Giovanni (not his real name), a middle-aged man, was the victim of an attempted murder by 17-year-old Luca, who stabbed Giovanni when trying to rob him. One morning, Luca and a friend of his, both under the influence of drugs, started to vandalize telephone boxes and other public utilities. They then decided they needed money and saw Giovanni walking along the road. They followed him. Giovanni entered the front door of the building where he lived and realized that he was being followed by the two young men. Both Giovanni and Luca got inside the outer door which suddenly closed behind them. Luca, when eventually questioned by the police, said that when he realized he and Giovanni were between two closed doors, he got scared, took out a knife, and stabbed the man. Giovanni's wife, from the apartment where they lived, heard her husband screaming. She went out and saw Luca holding a knife and her injured husband on the floor. She then called the police and an ambulance.

Luca was initially sentenced to custody for attempted murder. After two months, the judge decided to suspend the trial and order probation for two years. The plan that Luca had to follow as part of the probation order was developed by the youth justice social worker in conjunction with Luca himself. It consisted of a combination of activities including: community work, attending school, and regular meetings with the social worker. Mediation with the victim was also included. The social worker first asked the young man about his willingness to meet the victim and to make his apologies. Luca did not initially understand the purpose of the meeting. He was afraid of the possible reactions of the man he had assaulted.

Once the purpose of mediation was explained, Luca showed some interest and agreed to meet Giovanni, whose consent was then asked in turn. In the first instance, Giovanni was reluctant and refused the meeting. Subsequently, he became interested and expressed a willingness to give Luca the opportunity to acknowledge the consequences of his action. He also wanted to have the opportunity for the first time to express his own feelings and to learn more about the reasons that led Luca to do what he did. Giovanni wanted to know what was in Luca's mind when he stabbed him: Did he really want to kill him? Why was he his target?

The date of the meeting was scheduled for two weeks later. Luca was extremely anxious; he was sure that Giovanni would cancel the appointment and even feared that Giovanni might want to kill him. Luca could not understand why the man he had injured and almost killed ever wanted to see him again. He could not see why Giovanni would ever accept his apologies for what he had done; it was inconceivable from his point of view that someone like that could exist.

The meeting took place in a bar in quite an informal setting. During the mediation session, Luca and Giovanni were present, as well as Giovanni's wife because she also wanted to express what she had been through. The social worker played the role of the mediator. She explained that they all had an opportunity to share their feelings and to raise and answer any questions. During the first part of the meeting, Luca never looked straight ahead. He kept his eyes lowered and made no eye contact with Giovanni. The social worker asked Giovanni if there was something he wanted to ask Luca directly. Both Giovanni and his wife talked about the physical and emotional sufferings and fears they had had to go through. Giovanni also wanted to know more about the event and to learn about the young man and what was happening in his life. Gradually, tension disappeared and Luca became able to make his apologies and answer the questions raised.

No formal agreement was made about reparation or restitution in respect of the psychological and physical damage caused. The young man clearly showed his concern to Giovanni who, like his wife, was just quite surprised to find that Luca was just a teenager like many others, with problems related to his family, social and cultural background, and the environment in which he lived.

After the mediation ended, the social worker had the opportunity of debriefing both Luca and Giovanni and his wife. Giovanni and his wife stressed the importance of having met Luca personally because it gave them the opportunity to rid themselves of the fantasies they had created about the young man as being a dangerous person. Luca, on the other hand, told the social worker that he was completely astonished to discover that there were people willing to accept apologies when you have attempted to kill them. Luca said that he had never realized the consequences of his action until he met his victim. He said that when he stabbed the man he did not realize what was going on because he was under the influence of drugs. Meeting and talking with Giovanni and his wife, however, had given him the opportunity to express his thoughts and feelings.

CONCLUSIONS

The present study shows that, in Italy, victim–offender mediation in the juvenile justice system does not take place in any uniform or structured way. In the first place, mediation is only being included in the probation order in some parts of the country. This highlights that the decision to implement mediation is reliant on the judge's discretion, given that there are no significant differences between the type of offences involved. Because there are as yet no official guidelines that establish ground-rules about the process, any initiative depends on the individual capacities of social workers in charge of young offenders during their probation orders. Youth justice social workers, moreover, hold a demanding caseload and are not always able to dedicate the time required to this work.

In addition, one of the basic principles of mediation is neutrality. It is very important for victims to have the opportunity to choose whether or not they wish to meet the offender(s) or whether they want them to restore the damage caused in any other way. When youth justice social workers are also in charge of mediation, there might be the risk that victims perceive them as acting mainly in the interest of the young offender.

Most cases analysed in the research involved petty crimes. This might suggest that Italy tends to implement mediation only for minor offences.

The case study presented is therefore interesting in going against this trend. However, it is also interesting in another respect. Some professionals think that the victims of serious crimes are too emotionally involved in what has happened, perhaps in shock, and that they do not want to have anything to do with the offender. Several research studies, however, have shown that victims can benefit from mediation even when very serious crimes are involved. The case study, although it would be inappropriate to generalize from one example, does shed some light on the ongoing debate about the potentially positive influence of mediation on both the victim and the offender. The purpose of the restorative justice approach is to develop a more human way of responding to crime: not only to punish but also to give both the offender and the victim the opportunity to play an active role. Mediation can be a way of achieving this. Advocates of mediation therefore want to make professionals more aware of the advantages of the approach. Mediation programmes should be well structured, in a way that takes into account not only the needs of the offender but also those of the victims and of the community. The risks of using these principles in a system that is offender-oriented, however, have to be considered.

Victim–offender mediation, moreover, can fit well with social work practice. Parties directly affected by the crime contribute actively towards solving their conflict. Offenders are more directly involved in the process of restoring the damage caused and can have the opportunity to admit responsibility to the victim. Victims, on the other hand, can confront their stereotypes of the offender and express their feelings and fears. Social workers can play an important role, either directly as mediators or as case managers referring the case to external agencies for mediation when they undertake the probation officer's duties.

Currently in Italy there are new guidelines for the further development of victim–offender mediation that are still under discussion by the Department of Criminal Justice. According to these new guidelines, specially trained mediators would belong to an independent group to whom social workers could refer the case. The mediator would get in touch with both parties and assess the feasibility of mediation. Once the mediation was arranged, mediators would then refer the case back to the social worker responsible for the probation order, who would subsequently include the outcome of mediation in the report to the judge. There could also be the opportunity for youth justice social workers to act directly as mediators; but, as mentioned, in such cases they could not also be responsible for the case as probation officers.

QUESTIONS FOR DISCUSSION AND WRITING

1. How does restorative justice "offer a different model"?
2. Which cases are best suited for mediation?
3. What are the risks of involving social workers as mediators?

The Family Model of the Criminal Process: Reintegrative Shaming

JOHN BRAITHWAITE

AFTER an empirical study of *The Impact of Publicity on Corporate Offenders*, Brent Fisse and I concluded:

If we are serious about controlling corporate crime, the first priority should be to create a culture in which corporate crime is not tolerated. The informal processes of shaming unwanted conduct and of praising exemplary behavior need to be emphasized.

However, in that book, and in an earlier contribution with Gilbert Geis, a sharp distinction was made between the merits of shaming for controlling corporate crime and its demerits with crime in the streets.

A major risk in apprehending the traditional criminal is that the stigmatizing process will push him further and further into a criminal self-concept. This is the contention of labeling theory. Evidence such as that from the Cambridge longitudinal study of delinquency has been interpreted as support for the labeling hypothesis. This study showed that boys who were apprehended for and convicted of delinquent offenses became more delinquent than boys who were equally delinquent to begin with but who escaped apprehension. . . . These labeling arguments cannot readily be applied to cor-

From, *Crime, Shame and Reintegration* (pp. 54–68) by J. Braithwaite, 1989, Cambridge: Cambridge University Press. Reprinted with permission of Cambridge University Press.

porate offenders. They are likely to regard themselves as unfairly maligned pillars of respectability, and no amount of stigmatization is apt to convince them otherwise. One does meet people who have a mental image of themselves as a thief, a safecracker, a prostitute, a pimp, drug runner, and even a hit man, but how often does one meet a person who sees himself as a corporate criminal? The young black offender can often enhance his status back on the street by having done some time, but the reaction of the corporate criminal to incarceration is shame and humiliation.

The purpose of this [reading] is to show that the conclusions of these two earlier works about the efficacy of shaming for controlling corporate crime do in fact apply to common crime as well. Cultural commitments to shaming are the key to controlling all types of crime. However, for all types of crime, shaming runs the risk of counterproductivity when it shades into stigmatization.

The crucial distinction is between shaming that is reintegrative and shaming that is disintegrative (stigmatization). Reintegrative shaming means that expressions of community disapproval, which may range from mild rebuke to degradation ceremonies, are followed by gestures of reacceptance into the community of law-abiding citizens. These gestures of reacceptance will vary from a simple smile expressing forgiveness and love to quite formal ceremonies to decertify the offender as deviant. Disintegrative shaming (stigmatization), in contrast, divides the community by creating a class of outcasts. Much effort is directed at labeling deviance, while little attention is paid to de-labeling, to signifying forgiveness and reintegration, to ensuring that the deviance label is applied to the behavior rather than the person, and that this is done under the assumption that the disapproved behavior is transient, performed by an essentially good person. Quoting Suchar, Page sees the defining characteristics of stigmatization as assignment of a deviant characteristics to the person as a master status.

The individual . . . is assigned a "master status trait": homosexual, drug addict, prostitute, juvenile delinquent, or others . . . this label will dominate all other "characteristics" of the individual; "good athlete," "good conversationalist," "good dancer," and the like are subordinated to or negated by this trait which is immediately felt to be more central to the "actual" identity of the individual.

One might think that, notwithstanding the criminogenic consequences of assignment to a deviant master status, stigmatization might still be more useful for crime control than reintegrative shaming because being made an outcast is a more terrible sanction than being shamed and then forgiven. The theory will come to reject this view because the nub of deterrence is not the severity of the sanction but its social embeddedness; shame is more deterring when administered by persons who continue to be of importance to us; when we become outcasts we can reject our rejectors and the shame no longer matters to us. The deterrence literature supports the view that the severity of sanctions is a poor predictor of the effectiveness of social control, while the social embeddedness of sanctions is an important predictor.

THE FAMILY MODEL

The best place to see reintegrative shaming at work is in loving families. Griffiths has described a "family model" of the criminal pro-

cess as one in which, instead of punishment being administered within the traditional framework of disharmony and fundamentally irreconcilable interests, it is imposed within a framework of reconcilable, even mutually supportive interests:

Offenses, in a family, are normal, expected occurrences. Punishment is not something a child receives in isolation from the rest of his relationship to the family; nor is it something which presupposes or carries with it a change of status from "child" to "criminal child." When a parent punishes his child, both parent and child know that afterward they will go on living together as before. The child gets his punishment, as a matter of course, within a continuum of love, after his dinner and during his toilet training and before bed-time story and in the middle of general family play, and he is punished in his own unchanged capacity as a child with failings (like all other children) rather than as some kind of distinct and dangerous outsider.

Family life teaches us that shaming and punishment are possible while maintaining bonds of respect. Two hypotheses are suggested: first, families are the most effective agents of social control in most societies partly because of this characteristics; second, those families that are disintegrative rather than reintegrative in their punishment processes, that have not learnt the trick of punishing within a continuum of love, are the families that fail at socializing their children.

The second hypothesis is consistent with the child development literature. Perhaps the classic studies in this genre are those of Baumrind. She found an "authoritative" child rearing style which combined firm control (setting clear standards and insisting on compliance with them) with nurture and encouragement more likely to secure superior control of undesirable behavior such as aggression than "authoritarian" (close control by parents who were cold and detached) or "permissive" (loose control by nurturant parents) child rearing styles.

For social learning theory reasons alone, families in which disapproval rather than approval is the normal state of affairs are incapable of socializing children by withdrawal of approval. Trasler explains why the effectiveness of shaming depends on continued social integration in a relationship sustained by social approval:

The contrast between the ordinary enjoyment of [parents'] approval and the distress of being temporarily out of favour is essential; if the child is constantly fearful and insecure in his relationship with his parents, the withdrawal-of-approval technique will not succeed in establishing a specific avoidance response.

Our theory predicts that cultures in which the "family model" is applied to crime control both within and beyond the family will be cultures with low crime rates. The family analogy forces us to think more clearly about what we mean by shaming, however.

WHAT IS SHAMING?

Developmental psychologists sometimes like to make distinctions between socialization by shaming and by guilt-induction. Shaming, according to this distinction, follows transgressions with expressions of the lower esteem the offense has produced in the eyes of external referents like parents and neighbors; guilt-induction responds to transgressions with admonitions concerning how remorseful the child should feel within herself for perpetrating such an evil act. The distinction is rather too fine for our theoretical purposes because "guilt-induction" always implies shaming by the person(s) inducing the guilt and because, as we will argue later, in broader societal terms guilt is only made possible by cultural processes of shaming. For our purposes, to induce guilt and to shame are inextricably part of the same social process. This is not to deny the distinction which Benedict and others make between guilt as a failure to live up to the standards of one's own conscience and shame as a reaction to criticism by other people. But you cannot *induce* guilt without implying criticism by others. In other words, from the perspective of the offender, guilt and shame may be distinguishable, but guilt *induction* and shaming are both criticism by others. Equally, the old distinction between shame and guilt cultures has no place in my theoretical framework because the consciences which cause us guilt are, according to the theory, formed by shaming in the culture.

Of what, then, does shaming consist? It can be subtle: a frown, a tut-tut, a snide comment, a turning of the back, a slight shaking of the head, a laugh; it can be a direct verbal confrontation in which the offender is admonished about how guilty she should feel or how shocked her relatives and friends are over her conduct; it can be indirect confrontation by gossip which gets back to the offender; it can be broadcast via the mass media or by a private medium (as when the feminist paints a slogan on the front fence of a rapist); it can be officially pronounced by a judge from the bench or by a government which names a wrongdoer in an official report or in the chamber of the legislature; it can be popularized in mass culture by a film which moralizes about a certain act of wrongdoing.

The modalities of shaming are often culturally specific: in republican Rome criminals had the doors of their house burned, and persons who had been wronged followed their offenders about dressed in mourning clothes and with dishevelled hair, sometimes chanting against the person at home or in public places. In Cuban or Chinese Peoples' Courts, ordinary citizens verbally denounce wrongdoing as part of the trial process. Freidson and Rhea showed that the almost universal sanction applied to clinic doctors who engaged in professional deviance was for colleagues and administrators to "talk to them," first "man to man," then if this did not work, by enlisting the aid of other talkers, up to the ultimate sanction of a talking-to by a formal committee of colleagues. Under the time-honored naval tradition of "Captain's mast," a seaman who fell asleep on watch, for example, could be denounced by the captain in the presence of members of the ship's company assembled on deck for the purpose of shaming him. In Crow Indian culture, shaming is effected by a polite mocking of another's inappropriate behavior called "buying-of-the-ways."

One Indian recalled a childhood occasion when he became angry and reacted by laying on the ground and pouting, not in and of itself unusual. However, another playmate laid on the ground next to him and imitated his pouting, thereby "buying his ways." Through such mimicry, the first pouting child sees his own action and is reminded of his inappropriate behavior. . . .

On occasion, and particularly among adults, the correcting scenario of ridicule is accentuated by the "buyer-of-the-ways" actually approaching the rule violator and offering a small token of money (i.e., several dollars) which is supposed to be graciously accepted, even if with embarrassment. The buyer then announces to onlookers what has taken place and what is about to take place, at which time the buyer rather dramatically repeats the inappropriate behavior.

Though shaming is often associated with a formal punishment, it does not have to be, as in this Crow example where shaming (informal punishment) is actually associated with a tangible reward.

THE UNCOUPLING OF SHAME AND PUNISHMENT

Western theorizing on deterrence often refers to the greater importance of the shame associated with punishment than of the punishment itself. Andenaes put it this way:

That the offender is subjected to the rejection and contempt of society serves as a deterrent; the thought of the shame of being caught and of the subsequent conviction is for many stronger than the thought of the punishment itself.

Andenaes continued that the ducking stool, the stocks and the pillory were "not only in-struments of corporal punishment but were used to reduce the status of the offender as well."

Yet the recent history of Western punishment practices has amounted to a systematic uncoupling of punishment and public shaming. The public visibility of the pillory and the chain-gang were replaced by penal practices to warehouse offenders away from public view. Public executions and flogging became private executions and floggings.

Viewed in a narrow historical context, this uncoupling was a good thing. Public exhibitions of state acts of brutality against other human beings perhaps did as much to legitimate brutality as it did to delegitimate crime. In differential association terms, they involved the state in communicating definitions favorable to violence. More critically to the present analysis, most of the shaming was stigmatizing rather than reintegrative, as von Hippel concluded on Continental punishment during the Middle Ages:

Public executions of capital, mutilating, corporal and dishonoring punishments, often aggravated by horrible methods of inflicting them, dulled the aim of deterrence and harmed general deterrence by brutalizing the conscience of people. Equally disastrous was the effect of this penal law from the point of view of individual prevention. The outlawed, the banished, the mutilated, the branded, the shamed, the bereft of honor or stripped of power it expelled from the community of decent people and thus drove them out on the highway. Therefore the penal law itself recruited the habitual and professional criminals, who flourished in those days.

Branding on the cheek of offenders was abandoned in eighteenth-century England because it had "not had its desired effect by deterring offenders from the further committing of crimes and offenses, but, on the contrary, such offenders, being rendered thereby unfit to be entrusted in any service or employment to get their livelihood in any honest and lawful way, become the more desperate."

While compassionate people must applaud the demise of these practices, the revulsion from them has produced a pervasive uncoupling of punishment and shaming in some Western societies. In my home state of Queensland, it used to be common for pubs which sold watered-down beer to be ordered by the court to display signs prominently indicating that the proprietor had recently been convicted of selling adulterated beer. The practice was stopped because it was regarded as "Dickensian," and because adverse publicity was regarded as having uncertain impacts that undermined the proportionality of sentences determined by the courts. Shoham has described a number of shame-based or "poetic" punishments that have now disappeared, such as a baker being required to walk in the public square with underweight loaves hung around his neck.

Shearing and Stenning have shown that one of the most important trends in contemporary criminal justice is its privatization. Private security officers are fast becoming more pervasive agents of social control than public police. A characteristic of this private enforcement is its total rejection of a moral conception of order and the control process.

Within private control, order is conceived primarily in instrumental rather than moral terms. Order is simply the set of conditions most conducive to achieving fundamental community objectives. Thus in a business corporation, for instance, order is usually whatever maximizes profit.

The corporate security division will typically respond to a detected embezzler by getting the money back and sacking the employee. No thought is given to the fact that the non-public nature of this enforcement, free of any moral content, might mean that the embezzler will be thrown back onto the labor market only to be picked up by, and to victimize, another private actor.

One contention of this [reading] is that the uncoupling of shame and punishment manifested in a wide variety of ways in many Western countries is an important factor in explaining the rising crime rates in those countries. Equally, if we look at the only clear case of a society which has experienced a downward trend in crime rates since World War II, Japan, it might be argued that this was a result of the re-establishment of cultural traditions of shaming wrongdoers, including effective coupling of shame and punishment. The decline was not simply an immediate post-war phenomenon: between 1976 and 1980 the number of murders in Japan fell 26 per cent; during the same period in the United States, murders increased by 23 per cent. The Japanese crime rate is probably the lowest of any developed country.

REINTEGRATIVE SHAMING IN JAPAN

Following World War II, the Japanese suffered from anomie, in the Durkheimian sense of a general breakdown of norms governing group and individual behavior: "The more weakened the groups to which [the individual] belongs, the less he depends on them, the more he consequently depends only on himself and recognizes no other rules of conduct than what are founded on his private interests." According to Dahrendorf, a similar anomie characterized Germany in the immediate aftermath of the humiliation of defeat in World War II. But Japan did not meekly follow the blueprint for Westernization of their criminal justice system which the occupying Americans attempted to impose following the war. In this the Japanese may have been fortunate, if one is to heed Bayley's conclusion from his comparative study of Japanese and United States police:

Searching for an explanation of the remarkably different crime rates in Japan and the United States, it is a mistake to write off as fortuitous the fact that Japanese, compared with Americans, are less combative in confrontation with authority; that offenders against the law are expected to accept the community's terms for resocialization rather than insisting on legal innocence and bargaining for the mitigation of punishment; that individual character is thought to be mutable, responsive to informal sanctions of proximate groups; that government intervention in social life is more acceptable and that individuals feel a moral obligation to assist actively in preserving moral consensus in the community.

Japan might be expected to have a high crime rate according to its demographics. It modernized at an extraordinarily rapid rate; it is highly urbanized in densely packed cities. The proportion of Japanese employed in agriculture decline from 30 per cent in 1960 to 10 per cent in 1980. On the other hand, it has enjoyed lower unemployment rates than other countries and it is culturally homogeneous. Its criminal justice system is efficient (in the sense of apprehending a high proportion of offenders) but extremely lenient (it sends very few of them to prison). George reports that in 1978 Japanese police cleared 53 per cent of known cases of theft, but only 15 per cent of the 231,403 offenders involved were arrested. Prosecution only proceeds in major cases or more minor cases where the normal process of apology, compensation and forgiveness by the victim breaks down. Fewer than 10 per cent of those offenders who are convicted receive prison sentences, and for two-thirds of these, prison sentences are suspended. Whereas 45 per cent of those convicted of a crime serve a jail sentence in the US, in Japan the percentage is under two. Even 27 per cent of murder cases result in suspended sentences of imprisonment in Japan. Moreover, the average length of sentence has reduced over the years. Recalling World War II and the modern-day exploits of the "Red Army" and other protest groups, it is difficult to argue that the Japanese have a genetic or cultural legacy of non-violence.

The conclusions of the leading scholars who have studied the social context of Japan's low and declining crime rate can be read as support for the notion of high interdependency in Japanese society (with employers and neighbors as well as families), highly developed communitarianism, and these two characteristics fostering a shaming of offenders which is reintegrative. Consider this further conclusion from Bayley:

The feeling that security consists in acceptance is transferred from the family to other groups, allowing them to discipline members through the fear of exclusion. This accounts for the ability of the police to discipline their own members so effectively. By enwrapping the officer in family-like solicitude, the organization raises the psychological costs of expulsion. Similarly, a Japanese accepts the authority of law as he would the customs of his family. The policeman is analogous to an elder brother who cautions against offending the family . . .

In psychological terms, the system relies on positive rather than negative reinforcement, emphasizing loving acceptance in exchange for genuine repentance. An analogue of what the Japanese policeman wants the offender to feel is the tearful relief of a child when confession of wrongdoing to his parents results in a gentle laugh and a warm hug. In relation to American policemen, Japanese officers want to be known for the warmth of their care rather than the strictness of their enforcement.

Here is the family model writ large. Shaming as a feature of Japanese culture is well known to even the most casual observers of Japan. What is not so widely known is the reintegrative nature of this shaming. The fact that convicted American offenders are more than twenty times as likely to be incarcerated as convicted Japanese offenders says something about the respective commitments of these societies to outcasting versus reintegration.

When an individual is shamed in Japan, the shame is often borne by the collectivity to which the individual belongs as well—the family, the company, the school—particularly by the titular head of the collectivity.

When a young constable raped a woman in Tokyo several years ago, his station chief resigned. In this way, junior and senior ranks express a shared commitment to blameless performance. This view of responsibility is part of Japanese culture more largely. When a fighter aircraft struck a commercial airliner, causing it to crash, the minister of defense resigned. Parents occasionally commit suicide when their children are arrested for heinous crimes. . . .

Japanese policeman are accountable, then, because they fear to bring shame on their police "family," and thus run the risk of losing the regard of colleagues they think of as brothers and fathers.

Families are of course the key social units which take responsibility for reintegrating the convicted offender. Beyond the family, however, are a staggering proliferation of community volunteers. Japan is covered by 540,000 local liaison units of Crime Prevention Associations and 10,725 Vocational Unions for Crime Prevention, 126,000 volunteer cooperators for Juvenile Guidance (doing street work with juveniles), 8,000 Big Brothers and Sisters for delinquents, 320,000 volunteers in the Women's Association for Rehabilitation, 80,000 members of the Voluntary Probation Officers Association, 1,640 voluntary prison visitors, 1,500 "Cooperative Employers" willing to provide jobs for probationers and parolees, 2,028 Police–School Liaison Councils, plus many others. The national commitment to reintegration is even written into Article 1 of the Offenders' Rehabilitation Law:

The objective of this law is to protect society and promote individual and public welfare by aiding the reformation and rehabilitation of offenders . . . and facilitating the activities of crime prevention. All the people are required to render help according to their position and ability, to accomplish the objective mentioned in the previous paragraph.

The crime prevention associations and other voluntary groups are linked with a system of informal local government that extends into every household, and with a neighborhood-based form of policing. Even popular culture underlines the notion of shame followed by reintegration:

Betty Latham, an American anthropologist, has shown that Japanese folktales stress repentance and reform whereas Western folktales stress punishment and often death. Western societies seem to give up more quickly on people than Eastern ones. In a Japanese translation of "Little Red Riding Hood," for example, the wicked wolf falls on his knees and tearfully promises to mend his ways. In the Western version, the wolf is simply killed.

Apology has a central place in the aftermath of Japanese legal conflicts. Ceremonies of restoration to signify the reestablishment of harmony between conflicting parties are culturally pivotal; the best way for this reconciliation to occur is by mutual apology, where even a party who is relatively unblameworthy will find some way in which he contributed to the conflict to form the basis of his apology.

There are a multitude of cultural bases for Japanese aversion to outcasting and commitment to reintegration. According to Wagatsuma and Rosett apology in Japan amounts to dissociation from the evil part of oneself that committed an unacceptable act. Japanese idiom frequently accounts for wrongdoing with possession by a "mushi" (worm or bug). Criminals are therefore not acting according to their true selves; they are victims of a "mushi" which can be "sealed off," "thus permitting people to be restored to the community without guilt." The cultural assumption of basic goodness and belief in each individual's capacity for eventual self-correction means that "nurturant acceptance" ("amayakashi") is the appropriate response to deviance once shame has been projected to and accepted by the deviant. Thus, Bayley explains the distinctive pattern of police–offender encounters in Japan:

An American accused by a policeman is very likely to respond "Why me?" A Japanese more often says "I'm sorry." The American shows anger, the Japanese shame. An American contests the accusation and tries to humble the policeman; a Japanese accepts the accusation and tries to kindle benevolence. In response, the American policeman is implacable and impersonal; the Japanese policeman is sympathetic and succoring.

Japan's crime control achievements may of course be purchased at a cost. The interdependency, the shaming, the communitarian mobilization to resocialize wrongdoers, are ingredients of a culture in which duties to the community more often than in the West overwhelm the rights of individuals. Critics also sometimes suggest that Japan's high suicide rate shows that the effective suppression of crime simply means that personal problems manifest themselves in other ways. However, the evidence of an inverse relationship between the intra-punitiveness and extra-punitiveness of societies is weak, and Clifford has shown that while the Japanese suicide rate may seem high compared to the crime rate, it is fairly average in international terms. This is in spite of the fact that Japanese culture grants a degree of approval to suicide that other cultures do not. Expanding the theory in this [reading] to other forms of deviance beyond crime would lead to the prediction that forms of deviance which are most socially approved (least subject to reintegrative shaming), like suicide in Japan, will be most common. Or, if there is less shame for women entering the mentally ill role and more shame for women in entering the criminal role, the theory could be used to predict a higher ratio of mental illness to crime for women than for men—a finding that occurs in Japan and all other societies.

SHAMING AND SUBCULTURES

[Earlier] it was argued that subcultures that provide various degrees of social support for illegal behavior do exist in all societies. Even Japan has some 2,500 highly organized criminal gangs, as well as many motorcycle gangs and other groups which transmit criminal subcultures. Sometimes these subcultures are in opposition to the mainstream culture in the sense of promoting values which are the antithesis of mainstream values; sometimes they provide a social environment which is merely more tolerant of deviations from societal norms when opportunities arise to choose between gratification and compliance; sometimes they foster a "drift" between the conventional and the deviant.

Even when all these levels of subculturalism are incorporated into the analysis, groups with strong and visible commitment to subcultural behavior patterns are numerically weak in most societies. This means that subcultural groups are not readily on tap with recruitment centers in each suburb as are the armed forces. Most citizens would know how to make contact with the army should they want to join up, but most Americans would have no idea of how to become an associate of the Mafia or to join the Hell's Angels. Consequently, even when life circumstances make criminal subcultures very attractive to individuals, more often than not those life circumstances have changed by the time the individual is exposed to an opportunity to be recruited into a subcultural group which engages in activities attractive to the individual.

If individuals were not choosy about the kind of deviant subculture they would find gratifying, subcultures would of course be more accessible in practical terms than they are. If I could imagine my own circumstances of life changing so that I would be attracted to participation in a deviant subculture, I might imagine first confronting an opportunity to participate with others in illicit drug use. But since I once had a frightening experience with marijuana interacting with alcohol, even soft drug use would not appeal to me in the least. An opportunity to smash things does not appeal either, so a vandalism opportunity would be a bore; an opportunity to rape a woman would overwhelm me with disgust rather than pleasure. On the other hand, the prospect of being $1,000 richer and my bank $1,000 poorer sounds like a result which would please me, so maybe if my life circumstances rendered me amenable to crime, fraud would appeal to my taste. The point is that criminological theory, like economic theory, systematically forgets that people have different tastes.

Just because my social controls are loosened and I encounter an illegitimate opportunity, I will not take it unless it appeals to my taste. Thus, if subcultural groups are numerically weak to start with, I will not experience opportunities to associate with many of them during my periods of suspended commitment to conventional society, and I will encounter even fewer opportunities to share in a subculture which offers those particular kinds of satisfactions which appeal to my tastes.

Stigmatization is the most important of those life circumstances that increase the attraction of individuals to criminal subcultures. As Albert Cohen told us, when a student is rejected by the status system of the school—is labeled incorrigible or a failure—he has a status problem and is in the market for a solution. Cohen suggests that he solves it collectively with other students who have similarly been rejected by the school. The outcasts band together and set up their own status system with values the exact inverse of those of the school.

Such extreme oppositional criminal subcultures as Cohen's or the Hell's Angels do not need to be invoked, though they are part of the scene, for the stigmatization hypothesis to be relevant. Young people who are constantly hammered by the family and the school with shaming that puts them in a position of mainstream rejection may find solace in a group of heroin users. Now the only thing which distinguishes that subculture from the mainstream culture may be heroin use; in all other respects those involved might be quite average in their law-abidingness, at least initially. All that is being suggested is that, when individuals are shamed so remorselessly and unforgivingly that they become outcasts, or even begin to think of themselves as outcasts it becomes more rewarding to associate with others who are perceived in some limited or total way as also at odds with mainstream standards. Once labeling and rejection have occurred, further attempts at admonishing association with the group which provides social support for deviance have no force.

However, we have said that subcultural groups, even broadly conceived as groups that provide any kind of systematic social support for illegality, are often thin on the ground. Most delinquency is at least to begin with a social rather than a solitary activity: drug use necessitates association with a supplier, vandalism or street fighting usually requires an audience, car theft needs someone to teach you the ropes. It often happens, therefore, that outcasts who are in the market for illegitimate opportunities do not encounter those opportunities, at least not opportunities of a kind which appeal to them. Either the opportunities are not encountered or a choice is made to reject them. Thus, the outcome of disintegrative shaming will often be that the outcast will reintegrate herself. We must not assume that reintegration only occurs at the hands of those who do the shaming. Individuals make choices in the light of the social structural realities they confront; they are not empty vessels totally determined by these realities.

Alternatively, outcasts who find no subcultural support for offending, or who choose to reject the subculture, remain more likely to commit crime (as lone offenders) than those who are reintegrated, though they should be less likely to become persistent offenders than those who do discover subcultural support.

In summary, then, stigmatization by the family, the school, and other sources of social control increases the attraction of outcasts to subcultural groups which provide social support for crime, and weakens social control by the former against criminal activities. However, if attractive opportunities for participation in subcultures are not encountered, stigmatization will, on balance, have a crime preventive impact. This is because there is a chance in these circumstances that the outcast will tire of a life of rejection and seek to prove himself worthy of reconciliation with the primary groups which have labeled him. Stigmatization will then have effected rehabilitation just as well as reintegrative shaming might have done. On the other hand, stigmatization still runs a risk of solitary deviance, including suicide, which is probably greater than with reintegrative shaming. At the same time, it must be remembered that irrespective of whether stigmatization is worsening or improving the prospects of crime by the outcast, at a societal level it is making a contribution to crime prevention. At a societal level shaming will still have the pluses we will discuss later of dramatizing wrongdoing for all to see, of strengthening social solidarity, of deterring others from the stigmatized conduct.

All of this means two things:

1. Reintegrative shaming is superior to stigmatization because it minimizes risks of pushing those shamed into criminal subcultures, and because social disapproval is more effective when embedded in relationships overwhelmingly characterized by social approval.
2. Whether disintegrative shaming is superior to no shaming at all is uncertain, depending largely on the density of criminal subcultures in the society.

QUESTIONS FOR DISCUSSION AND WRITING

1. What is the difference between "reintegrative shaming" and "disintegrative shaming"?
2. Why is reintegrative shaming more effective than disintegrative shaming?
3. What does "all of this mean"?

Broken Windows:
The Police and Neighborhood Safety

JAMES Q. WILSON

GEORGE L. KELLING

IN the mid-1970s, the State of New Jersey announced a "Safe and Clean Neighborhoods Program," designed to improve the quality of community life in twenty-eight cities. As part of that program, the state provided money to help cities take police officers out of their patrol cars and assign them to walking beats. The governor and other state officials were enthusiastic about using foot patrol as a way of cutting crime, but many police chiefs were skeptical. Foot patrol, in their eyes, had been pretty much discredited. It reduced the mobility of the police, who thus had difficulty responding to citizen calls for service, and it weakened headquarters control over patrol officers.

Many police officers also disliked foot patrol, but for different reasons: it was hard work, it kept them outside on cold, rainy nights, and it reduced their chances for making a "good pinch." In some departments, assigning officers to foot patrol had been used as a form of punishment. And academic experts on policing doubted that foot patrol would have any impact on crime rates: it was, in the opinion of most, little more than a sop to public opinion.

From "Broken Windows: The Police and Neighborhood Safety" by J. Wilson and G. Kelling, 1982, *The Atlantic Monthly* (March):29–83. Reprinted by permission of The Atlantic Monthly Company.

But since the state was paying for it, the local authorities were willing to go along.

Five years after the program started, the Police Foundation in Washington, D.C., published an evaluation of the foot-patrol project. Based on its analysis of a carefully controlled experiment carried out chiefly in Newark, the foundation concluded, to the surprise of hardly anyone, that foot patrol had not reduced crime rates. But residents of the foot-patrolled neighborhoods seemed to feel more secure than persons in other areas, tended to believe that crime had been reduced, and seemed to take fewer steps to protect themselves from crime (staying at home with the doors locked, for example). Moreover, citizens in the foot-patrol areas had a more favorable opinion of the police than did those living elsewhere. And officers walking beats had higher morale, greater job satisfaction, and a more favorable attitude toward citizens in their neighborhoods than did officers assigned to patrol cars.

These findings may be taken as evidence that the skeptics were right—foot patrol has no effect on crime; it merely fools the citizens into thinking that they are safer. But in our view, and in the view of the authors of the Police Foundation study (of whom Kelling was one), the citizens of Newark were not fooled at all. They knew what the foot-patrol officers were doing, they knew it was different from what motorized officers do, and they knew that having officers walk beats did in fact make their neighborhoods safer.

But how can a neighborhood be "safer" when the crime rate has not gone down—in fact, may have gone up? Finding the answer requires first that we understand what most often frightens people in public places. Many citizens, of course, are primarily frightened by crime, especially crime involving a sudden, violent attack by a stranger. This risk is very real, in Newark as in many large cities. But we tend to overlook or forget another source of fear—the fear of being bothered by disorderly people. Not violent people, nor, necessarily, criminals, but disreputable or obstreperous or unpredictable people: panhandlers, drunks, addicts, rowdy teenagers, prostitutes, loiterers, the mentally disturbed.

What foot-patrol officers did was to elevate, to the extent they could, the level of public order in these neighborhoods. Though the neighborhoods were predominantly black and the foot patrolmen were mostly white, this "order-maintenance" function of the police was performed to the general satisfaction of both parties.

One of us (Kelling) spent many hours walking with Newark foot-patrol officers to see how they defined "order" and what they did to maintain it. One beat was typical: a busy but dilapidated area in the heart of Newark, with many abandoned buildings, marginal shops (several of which prominently displayed knives and straight-edged razors in their windows), one large department store, and, most important, a train station and several major bus stops. Though the area was run-down, its streets were filled with people, because it was a major transportation center. The good order of this area was important not only to those who lived and worked there but also to many others, who had to move through it on their way home, to supermarkets, or to factories.

The people on the street were primarily black; the officer who walked the street was white. The people were made up of "regulars" and "strangers." Regulars included both "decent folk" and some drunks and derelicts who were always there but who "knew their place." Strangers were, well, strangers, and viewed suspiciously, sometimes apprehensively. The officer—call him Kelly—knew who the regulars were, and they knew him. As he saw his job, he was to keep an eye on strangers, and make certain that the disreputable regulars observed some informal but widely understood rules. Drunks and addicts could sit on the stoops, but could not lie down. People could drink on side streets, but not at the main intersection. Bottles had to be in paper bags. Talking to, bothering, or begging from people waiting at the bus stop was strictly forbidden. If a dispute erupted between a businessman and a customer, the businessman was assumed to be right, especially if the customer was a stranger. If a stranger loitered, Kelly would ask him if he had any means of support and what his business was; if he gave unsatisfactory answers, he was sent on his way. Persons who broke the informal rules, especially those who bothered people waiting at bus stops, were arrested for vagrancy. Noisy teenagers were told to keep quiet.

These rules were defined and enforced in collaboration with the "regulars" on the street. Another neighborhood might have different rules, but these, everybody understood, were the rules for this neighborhood. If someone violated them, the regulars not only turned to Kelly for help but also ridiculed the violator. Sometimes what Kelly did could be described as "enforcing the law," but just as often it involved taking informal or extralegal steps to help protect what the neighborhood had decided was the appropriate level of public order. Some of the things he did probably would not withstand a legal challenge.

A determined skeptic might acknowledge that a skilled foot-patrol officer can maintain order but still insist that this sort of "order" has little to do with the real sources of community fear—that is, with violent crime. To a degree, that is true. But two things must be borne in mind. First, outside observers should not assume that they know how much of the anxiety now endemic in many big-city neighborhoods stems from a fear of "real" crime and how much from a sense that the street is disorderly, a source of distasteful, worrisome encounters. The people of Newark, to judge from their behavior and their remarks to interviewers, apparently assign a high value to public order, and feel relieved and reassured when the police help them maintain that order.

Second, at the community level, disorder and crime are usually inextricably linked, in a kind of developmental sequence. Social psychologists and police officers tend to agree that if a window in a building is broken *and is left unrepaired*, all the rest of the windows will soon be broken. This is as true in nice neighborhoods as in run-down ones. Window-breaking does not necessarily occur on a large scale because some areas are inhabited by determined window-breakers whereas others are populated by window-lovers; rather, one unrepaired broken window is a signal that no one cares, and so breaking more windows costs nothing. (It has always been fun.)

Philip Zimbardo, a Stanford psychologist, reported in 1969 on some experiments testing the broken-window theory. He arranged to have an automobile without license plates parked with its hood up on a street in the Bronx and a comparable automobile on a street in Palo Alto, California. The car in the Bronx was attacked by "vandals" within ten minutes of its "abandonment." The first to arrive were a family—father, mother, and young son—who removed the radiator and battery. Within twenty-four hours, virtually everything of value had been removed. Then random destruction began—windows were smashed, parts torn off, upholstery ripped. Children began to use the car as a playground. Most of the adult "vandals" were well-dressed, apparently clean-cut whites. The car in Palo Alto sat untouched for more than a week. Then Zimbardo smashed part of it with a sledgehammer. Soon, passersby were joining in. Within a few hours, the

car had been turned upside down and utterly destroyed. Again, the "vandals" appeared to be primarily respectable whites.

Untended property becomes fair game for people out for fun or plunder, and even for people who ordinarily would not dream of doing such things and who probably consider themselves law-abiding. Because of the nature of community life in the Bronx—its anonymity, the frequency with which cars are abandoned and things are stolen or broken, the past experience of "no one caring"—vandalism begins much more quickly than it does in staid Palo Alto, where people have come to believe that private possessions are cared for, and that mischievous behavior is costly. But vandalism can occur anywhere once communal barriers—the sense of mutual regard and the obligations of civility—are lowered by actions that seem to signal that "no one cares."

We suggest that "untended" behavior also leads to the breakdown of community controls. A stable neighborhood of families who care for their homes, mind each other's children, and confidently frown on unwanted intruders can change, in a few years or even a few months, to an inhospitable and frightening jungle. A piece of property is abandoned, weeds grow up, a window is smashed. Adults stop scolding rowdy children; the children, emboldened, become more rowdy. Families move out, unattached adults move in. Teenagers gather in front of the corner store. The merchant asks them to move; they refuse. Fights occur. Litter accumulates. People start drinking in front of the grocery; in time, an inebriate slumps to the sidewalk and is allowed to sleep it off. Pedestrians are approached by panhandlers.

At this point it is not inevitable that serious crime will flourish or violent attacks on strangers will occur. But many residents will think that crime, especially violent crime, is on the rise, and they will modify their behavior accordingly. They will use the streets less often, and when on the streets will stay apart from their fellows moving with averted eyes, silent lips, and hurried steps. "Don't get involved."

For some residents, this growing atomization will matter little, because the neighborhood is not their "home" but "the place where they live." Their interests are elsewhere; they are cosmopolitans. But it will matter greatly to other people, whose lives derived meaning and satisfaction from local attachments rather than worldly involvement; for them, the neighborhood will cease to exist except for a few reliable friends whom they arrange to meet.

Such an area is vulnerable to criminal invasion. Though it is not inevitable, it is more likely that here, rather than in places where people are confident they can regulate public behavior by informal controls, drugs will change hands, prostitutes will solicit, and cars will be stripped. That the drunks will be robbed by boys who do it as a lark and the prostitutes' customers will be robbed by men who do it purposefully and perhaps violently. That muggings will occur.

Among those who often find it difficult to move away from this are the elderly. Surveys of citizens suggest that the elderly are much less likely to be the victims of crime than younger persons, and some have inferred from this that the well-known fear of crime voiced by the elderly is an exaggeration: perhaps we ought not to design special programs to protect older persons; perhaps we should even try to talk them out of their mistaken fears. This argument misses the point. The prospect of a confrontation with an obstreperous teenager or a drunken panhandler can be as fear-inducing for defenseless persons as the prospect of meeting an actual robber; indeed, to a defenseless person, the two kinds of confrontation are often indistinguishable. Moreover, the lower rate at which the elderly are victimized is a measure of the steps they have already taken—chiefly, staying behind locked doors—to minimize the risks they face. Young men are more frequently attacked than older women, not because they are easier or more lucrative targets but because they are on the streets more.

Nor is the connection between disorderliness and fear made only by the elderly. Susan Estrich, of the Harvard Law School, has recently gathered together a number of surveys on the sources of public fear. One, done in Portland, Oregon, indicated that three fourths of the adults interviewed cross to the other side of a street when they see a gang of teenagers; another survey, in Baltimore, discovered that nearly half would cross the street to avoid even a single strange youth. When an interviewer asked people in a housing project where the most dangerous spot was, they mentioned a place where young persons gathered to drink and play music, despite the fact that not a single crime had occurred there. In Boston public housing projects, the greatest fear was expressed by persons living in the buildings where disorderliness and incivility, not crime, were the greatest. Knowing this helps one understand the significance of such otherwise harmless displays as subway graffiti. As Nathan Glazer has written, the proliferation of graffiti, even when not obscene, confronts the subway rider with the "inescapable knowledge that the environment he must endure for an hour or more a day is uncontrolled and uncontrollable, and that anyone can invade it to do whatever damage and mischief the mind suggests."

In response to fear, people avoid one another, weakening controls. Sometimes they call the police. Patrol cars arrive, an occasional arrest occurs, but crime continues and disorder is not abated. Citizens complain to the police chief, but he explains that his department is low on personnel and that the courts do not punish petty or first-time offenders. To the residents, the police who arrive in squad cars are either ineffective or uncaring; to the police, the residents are animals who deserve each other. The citizens may soon stop calling the police, because "they can't do anything."

The process we call urban decay has occurred for centuries in every city. But what is happening today is different in at least two important respects. First, in the period before, say, World War II, city dwellers—because of money costs, transportation difficulties, familial and church connections—could rarely move away from neighborhood problems. When movement did occur, it tended to be along public-transit routes. Now mobility has become exceptionally easy for all but the poorest or those who are blocked by racial prejudice. Earlier crime waves had a kind of built-in self-correcting mechanism: the determination of a neighborhood or community to reassert control over its surf. Areas in Chicago, New York, and Boston would experience crime and gang wars, and then normalcy would return, as the families for whom no alternative residences were possible reclaimed their authority over the streets.

Second, the police in this earlier period assisted in that reassertion of authority by acting, sometimes violently, on behalf of the community. Young toughs were roughed up, people were arrested "on suspicion" or for vagrancy, and prostitutes and petty thieves were routed. "Rights" were something enjoyed by decent folk, and perhaps also by the serious professional criminal, who avoided violence and could afford a lawyer.

This pattern of policing was not an aberration or the result of occasional excess. From the earliest days of the nation, the police function was seen primarily as that of a night watchman: to maintain order against the chief threats to order—fire, wild animals, and disreputable behavior. Solving crimes was viewed not as a police responsibility but as a private one. In the March, 1969, *Atlantic*, one of us (Wilson) wrote a brief account of how the police role had slowly changed from maintaining order to fighting crimes. The change began with the creation of private detectives (often ex-criminals), who worked on a contingency-fee basis for individuals who had suffered losses. In time, the detectives were absorbed into municipal police agencies and paid a regular salary; simultaneously, the responsibility for prosecuting thieves was shifted from the aggrieved private citizen to the professional prosecutor. This process was not complete in most places until the twentieth century.

In the 1960s, when urban riots were a major problem, social scientists began to explore carefully the order-maintenance function of the police, and to suggest ways of improving it—not to make streets safer (its original function) but to reduce the incidence of mass violence. Order-maintenance became, to a degree, coterminous with "community relations." But, as the crime wave that began in the early 1960s continued without abatement throughout the decade and into the 1970s, attention shifted to the role of the police as crime-fighters. Studies of police behavior ceased, by and large, to be accounts of the order-maintenance function and became, instead, efforts to propose and test ways whereby the police could solve more crimes, make more arrests, and gather better evidence. If these things could be done, social scientist assumed, citizens would be less fearful.

A great deal was accomplished during this transition, as both police chiefs and outside experts emphasized the crime-fighting function in their plans, in the allocation of resources, and in deployment of personnel. The police may well have become better crime-fighters as a result. And doubtless they remained aware of their responsibility for order. But the link between order-maintenance and crime-prevention, so obvious to earlier generations, was forgotten.

That link is similar to the process whereby one broken window becomes many. The citizen who fears the ill-smelling drunk, the rowdy teenager, or the importuning beggar is not merely expressing his distaste for unseemly behavior, he is also giving voice to a bit of folk wisdom that happens to be a correct generalization—namely, that serious street crime flourishes in areas in which disorderly behavior goes unchecked. The unchecked panhandler is, in effect, the first broken window. Muggers and robbers, whether opportunistic or professional, believe they reduce their chances of being caught or even identified if they operate on streets where potential victims are already intimidated by prevailing conditions. If the neighborhood cannot keep a bothersome panhandler from annoying passersby, the thief may reason, it is even less likely to call the police to identify a potential mugger or to interfere if the mugging actually takes place.

Some police administrators concede that this process occurs, but argue that motorized-patrol officers can deal with it as effectively as foot-patrol officers. We are not so sure. In theory, an officer in a squad car can observe as much as an officer on foot; in theory, the former can talk to as many people as the latter. But the reality of police–citizen encounters is powerfully altered by the automobile. An officer on foot cannot separate himself from the street people; if he is approached, only his uniform and his personality can help him manage whatever is about to happen. And he can never be certain what that will be—a request for directions, a plea for help, an angry denunciation, a teasing remark, a confused babble, a threatening gesture.

In a car, an officer is more likely to deal with street people by rolling down the window and looking at them. The door and the window exclude the approaching citizen; they are a barrier. Some officers take advantage of this barrier, perhaps unconsciously, by acting differently if in the car than they would on foot. We have seen this countless times. The police car pulls up to a corner where teenagers are gathered. The window is rolled down. The officer stares at the youths. They stare back. The officer says to one, "C'mere." He saunters over, conveying to his friends by his elaborately casual style the idea that he is not intimidated by authority. "What's your name?" "Chuck." "Chuck who?" "Chuck Jones." "What'ya doing, Chuck?" "Nothing." "Got a P.O. [parole officer]?" "Nah." "Sure?" "Yeah." "Stay out of trouble, Chuckie." Meanwhile, the other boys laugh and exchange comments among themselves, probably at the officer's expense. The officer stares harder. He cannot be certain what is being said, nor can be join in and, by displaying his own skill at street banter, prove that he cannot be "put down." In the process, the officer has learned almost nothing, and the boys have decided the officer

is an alien force who can safely be disregarded, even mocked.

Our experience is that most citizens like to talk to a police officer. Such exchanges give them a sense of importance, provide them with the basis for gossip, and allow them to explain to the authorities what is worrying them (whereby they gain a modest but significant sense of having "done something" about the problem). You approach a person on foot more easily, and talk to him more readily, than you do a person in a car. Moreover, you can more easily retain some anonymity if you draw an officer aside for a private chat. Suppose you want to pass on a tip about who is stealing handbags, or who offered to sell you a stolen TV. In the inner city, the culprit, in all likelihood, lives nearby. To walk up to a marked patrol car and lean in the window is to convey a visible signal that you are a "fink."

The essence of the police role in maintaining order is to reinforce the informal control mechanisms of the community itself. The police cannot, without committing extraordinary resources, provide a substitute for that informal control. On the other hand, to reinforce those natural forces the police must accommodate them. And therein lies the problem.

Should police activity on the street be shaped, in important ways, by the standards of the neighborhood rather than by the rules of the state? Over the past two decades, the shift of police from order-maintenance to law-enforcement has brought them increasingly under the influence of legal restrictions, provoked by media complaints and enforced by court decisions and departmental orders. As a consequence, the order-maintenance functions of the police are now governed by rules developed to control police relations with suspected criminals. This is, we think, an entirely new development. For centuries, the role of the police as watchmen was judged primarily not in terms of its compliance with appropriate procedures but rather in terms of its attaining a desired objective. The objective was order, an inherently ambiguous term but a condition that people in a given community recognized when they saw it. The means were the same as those the community itself would employ, if its members were sufficiently determined, courageous, and authoritative. Detecting and apprehending criminals, by contrast, was a means to an end, not an end in itself; a judicial determination of guilt or innocence was the hoped-for result of the law-enforcement mode. From the first, the police were expected to follow rules defining that process, though states differed in how stringent the rules should be. The criminal-apprehension process was always understood to involve individual rights, the violation of which was unacceptable because it meant that the violating officer would be acting as a judge and jury—and that was not his job. Guilt or innocence was to be determined by universal standards under special procedures.

Ordinarily, no judge or jury ever sees the persons caught up in a dispute over the appropriate level of neighborhood order. That is true not only because most cases are handled informally on the street but also because no universal standards are available to settle arguments over disorder, and thus a judge may not be any wiser or more effective than a police officer. Until quite recently in many states, and even today in some places, the police make arrests on such charges as "suspicious person" or "vagrancy" or "public drunkenness"—charges with scarcely any legal meaning. These charges exist not because society wants judges to punish vagrants or drunks but because it wants an officer to have the legal tools to remove undesirable persons from a neighborhood when informal efforts to preserve order in the streets have failed.

Once we begin to think of all aspects of police work as involving the application of universal rules under special procedures, we inevitably ask what constitutes an "undesirable person" and why we should "criminalize" vagrancy or drunkenness. A strong and commendable desire to see that people are treated fairly makes us worry about allowing the police to rout persons who are undesirable by some vague or parochial standard. A growing and not-so-commendable utilitarianism leads us to doubt that any behavior that does not "hurt" another person should be made illegal. And thus many of us who watch over the police are reluctant to allow them to perform, in the only way they can, a function that every neighborhood desperately wants them to perform.

This wish to "decriminalize" disreputable behavior that "harms no one"—and thus remove the ultimate sanction the police can employ to maintain neighborhood order—is, we think, a mistake. Arresting a single drunk or a single vagrant who has harmed no identifiable person seems unjust, and in a sense it is. But failing to do anything about a score of drunks or a hundred vagrants may destroy an entire community. A particular rule that seems to make sense in the individual case makes no sense when it is made a universal rule and applied to all cases. It makes no sense because it fails to take into account the connection between one broken window left untended and a thousand broken windows. Of course, agencies rather than the police could attend to the problems posed by drunks or the mentally ill, but in most communities—especially where the "deinstitutionalization" movement has been strong—they do not.

The concern about equity is more serious. We might agree that certain behavior makes one person more undesirable than another, but how do we ensure that age or skin color or national origin or harmless mannerisms will not also become the basis for distinguishing the undesirable from the desirable? How do we ensure, in short, that the police do not become the agents of neighborhood bigotry?

We can offer no wholly satisfactory answer to this important question. We are not confident that there is a satisfactory answer, except to hope that by their selection, training, and supervision, the police will be inculcated with a clear sense of the outer limit of their discretionary authority. That limit, roughly, is this— the police exist to help regulate behavior, not to maintain the racial or ethnic purity of a neighborhood.

Consider the case of the Robert Taylor Homes in Chicago, one of the largest public-housing projects in the country. It is home for nearly 20,000 people, all black, and extends over ninety-two acres along South State Street. It was named after a distinguished black who had been, during the 1940s, chairman of the Chicago Housing Authority. Not long after it opened, in 1962, relations between project residents and the police deteriorated badly. The citizens felt that the police were insensitive or brutal; the police, in turn, complained of unprovoked attacks on them. Some Chicago officers tell of times when they were afraid to enter the Homes. Crime rates soared.

Today, the atmosphere has changed. Police–citizen relations have improved—apparently, both sides learned something from the earlier experience. Recently, a boy stole a purse and ran off. Several young persons who saw the theft voluntarily passed along to the police information of the identity and residence of the thief, and they did this publicly, with friends and neighbors looking on. But problems persist, chief among them the presence of youth gangs that terrorize residents and recruit members in the project. The people expect the police to "do something" about this, and the police are determined to do just that.

But do what? Though the police can obviously make arrests whenever a gang member breaks the law, a gang can form, recruit, and congregate without breaking the law. And only a tiny fraction of gang-related crimes can be solved by an arrest; thus, if an arrest is the only recourse for the police, the residents' fears will go unassuaged. The police will soon feel helpless, and the residents will again believe that the police "do nothing." What the police in fact do is to chase known gang members out of the project. In the words of one officer, "We kick ass." Project residents both know and approve of this. The tacit police–citizen alliance in the project is reinforced by the police view that the cops and the gangs are the two rival sources of power in the area, and that the gangs are not going to win.

None of this is easily reconciled with any conception of due process or fair treatment. Since both residents and gang members are black, race is not a factor. But it could be. Suppose a white project confronted a black gang, or vice versa. We would be apprehensive about the police taking sides. But the substantive problem remains the same: how can the police strengthen the informal social-control mechanisms of natural communities in order to minimize fear in public places? Law enforcement, per se, is no answer. A gang can weaken or destroy a community by standing about in a menacing fashion and speaking rudely to passersby without breaking the law.

We have difficulty thinking about such matters, not simply because the ethical and legal issues are so complex but because we have become accustomed to thinking of the law in essentially individualistic terms. The law defines *my* rights, punishes *his* behavior, and is applied by *that* officer because of *this* harm. We assume, in thinking this way, that what is good for the individual will be good for the community, and what doesn't matter when it happens to one person won't matter if it happens to many. Ordinarily, those are plausible assumptions. But in cases where behavior that is tolerable to one person is intolerable to many others, the reactions of the others—fear, withdrawal, flight—may ultimately make matters worse for everyone, including the individual who first professed his indifference.

It may be their greater sensitivity to communal as opposed to individual needs that helps explain why the residents of small communities are more satisfied with their police than are the residents of similar neighborhoods in big cities. Elinor Ostrom and her co-workers at Indiana University compared the perception of police services in two poor, all-black Illinois towns—Phoenix and East Chicago Heights—with those of three comparable all-black neighborhoods in Chicago. The level of criminal victimization and the quality of police–community relations appeared to be about the same in the towns and the Chicago neighborhoods. But the citizens living in their own villages were much more likely than those living in the Chicago neighborhoods to say that they do not stay at home for fear of crime, to agree that the local police have "the right to take any action necessary" to deal with problems, and to agree that the police "look out for the needs of the average citizen." It is possible that the residents and the police of the small towns saw themselves as engaged in a collaborative effort to maintain a certain standard of communal life, whereas those of the big city felt themselves to be simply requesting and supplying particular services on an individual basis.

If this is true, how should a wise police chief deploy his meager forces? The first answer is that nobody knows for certain, and the most prudent course of action would be to try further variations on the Newark experiment, to see more precisely what works in what kinds of neighborhoods. The second answer is also a hedge—many aspects of order-maintenance in neighborhoods can probably best be handled in ways that involve the police minimally, if at all. A busy, bustling shopping center and a quiet, well-tended suburb may need almost no visible police presence. In both cases, the ratio of respectable to disreputable people is ordinarily so high as to make informal social control effective.

Even in areas that are in jeopardy from disorderly elements, citizen action without substantial police involvement may be sufficient. Meetings between teenagers who like to hang out on a particular corner and adults who want to use that corner might well lead to an amicable agreement on a set of rules about how many people can be allowed to congregate, where, and when.

Where no understanding is possible—or if possible, not observed—citizen patrols may be a sufficient response. There are two traditions of communal involvement in maintaining order. One, that of the "community watchmen," is as old as the first settlement of the New World. Until well into the nineteenth century, volunteer watchmen, not policemen, patrolled their communities to keep order. They did so, by and large, without taking the law into their own hands—without, that is, punishing persons or using force. Their presence deterred disorder or alerted the community to disorder that could not be deterred. There are hundreds of such efforts today in communities all across the nation. Perhaps the best known is that of the Guardian Angels, a group of unarmed young persons in distinctive berets and T-shirts, who first came to public attention when they began patrolling the New York City subways but who claim now to have chapters in more than thirty American cities. Unfortunately, we have little information about the effect of these groups on crime. It is possible, however, that whatever their effect on crime, citizens find their presence reassuring, and that they thus contribute to maintaining a sense of order and civility.

The second tradition is that of the "vigilante." Rarely a feature of the settled communities of the East, it was primarily to be found in those frontier towns that grew up in advance of the reach of government. More than 350 vigilante groups are known to have existed; their distinctive feature was that their members did take the law into their own hands, by acting as judge, jury, and often executioner as well as policeman. Today, the vigilante movement is conspicuous by its rarity, despite the great fear expressed by citizens that the older cities are becoming "urban frontiers." But some community-watchmen groups have skirted the line, and others may cross it in the future. An ambiguous case, reported in *The Wall Street Journal*, involved a citizens' patrol in the Silver Lake area of Belleville, New Jersey. A leader told the reporter, "We look for outsiders." If a few teenagers from outside the neighborhood enter it, "we ask them their business," he said. "If they say they're going down the street to see Mrs. Jones, fine, we let them pass. But then we follow them down the block to make sure they're really going to see Mrs. Jones."

Though citizens can do a great deal, the police are plainly the key to order-maintenance. For one thing, many communities, such as the Robert Taylor Homes, cannot do the job by themselves. For another, no citizen in a neighborhood, even an organized one, is likely to feel the sense of responsibility that wearing a badge confers. Psychologists have done many studies on why people fail to go to the aid of persons being attacked or seeking help, and they have learned that the cause is not "apathy" or "selfishness" but the absence of some plausible grounds for feeling that one must personally accept responsibility. Ironically, avoiding responsibility is easier when a lot of people are standing about. On streets and in public places, where order is so important, many people are likely to be "around," a fact that reduces the chance of any one person acting as the agent of the community. The police officer's uniform singles him out as a person who must accept responsibility if asked. In addition, officers, more easily than their fellow citizens, can be expected to distinguish between what is necessary to protect the safety of the street and what merely protects its ethnic purity.

But the police forces of America are losing, not gaining, members. Some cities have suffered substantial cuts in the number of officers available for duty. These cuts are not likely to be reversed in the near future. Therefore, each department must assign its existing officers with great care. Some neighborhoods are so demoralized and crime-ridden as to make foot patrol useless; the best the police can do with limited resources is respond to the enormous number of calls for service. Other neighborhoods are so stable and serene as to make foot patrol unnecessary. The key is to identify neighborhoods at the tipping point—where the public order is deteriorating but not unreclaimable, where the streets are used frequently but by apprehensive people, where a window is likely to be broken at any time, and must quickly be fixed if all are not to be shattered.

Most police departments do not have ways of systematically identifying such areas and assigning officers to them. Officers are assigned on the basis of crime rates (meaning that marginally threatened areas are often stripped so that police can investigate crimes in areas where the situation is hopeless) or on the basis of calls for service (despite the fact that most citizens do not call the police when they are merely frightened or annoyed). To allocate patrol wisely, the department must look at the neighborhoods and decide, from first-hand evidence, where an additional officer will make the greatest difference in promoting a sense of safety.

One way to stretch limited police resources is being tried in some public-housing projects. Tenant organizations hire off-duty police officers for patrol work in their buildings. The costs are not high (at least not per resident), the officer likes the additional income, and the residents feel safer. Such arrangements are probably more successful than hiring private watchmen, and the Newark experiment helps us understand why. A private security guard may deter crime or misconduct by his presence, and he may go to the aid of persons needing help, but he may well not intervene—that is, control or drive away—someone challenging community standards. Being a sworn officer—a "real cop"—seems to give one the confidence, the sense of duty, and the aura of authority necessary to perform this difficult task.

Patrol officers might be encouraged to go to and from duty stations on public transportation and, while on the bus or subway car, enforce rules about smoking, drinking, disorderly conduct, and the like. The enforcement need involve nothing more than ejecting the offender (the offense, after all, is not one with which a booking officer or a judge wishes to be bothered). Perhaps the random but relentless maintenance of standards on buses would lead to conditions on buses that approximate the level of civility we now take for granted on airplanes.

But the most important requirement is to think that to maintain order in precarious situations is a vital job. The police know this is one of their functions, and they also believe, correctly, that it cannot be done to the exclusion of criminal investigation and responding to calls. We may have encouraged them to suppose, however, on the basis of our oft-repeated concerns about serious, violent crime, that they will be judged exclusively on their capacity as crime-fighters. To the extent that this is the case, police administrators will continue to concentrate police personnel in the highest-crime areas (though not necessarily in the areas most vulnerable to criminal invasion), emphasize their training in the law and criminal apprehension (and not their training in managing street life), and join too quickly in campaigns to decriminalize "harmless" behavior (though public drunkenness, street prostitution, and pornographic displays can destroy a community more quickly than any team of professional burglars).

Above all, we must return to our long-abandoned view that the police ought to protect communities as well as individuals. Our crime statistics and victimization surveys measure individual losses, but they do not measure communal losses. Just as physicians now recognize the importance of fostering health rather than simply treating illness, so the police—and the rest of us—ought to recognize the importance of maintaining, intact, communities without broken windows.

QUESTIONS FOR DISCUSSION AND WRITING

1. How can a neighborhood be "safer" when the crime rate does not go down?
2. What happens when a broken window is left unrepaired, and why does this happen?
3. What do the authors call a "mistake," and why do they feel this way?

Strengthening Institutions and Rethinking the American Dream

STEVEN F. MESSNER

RICHARD ROSENFELD

> It is needless to waste words in painting the situation in our country today. The headlines of any metropolitan newspaper any day do so only too clearly. Crime of the most desperate sort is so rampant that unless a robbery runs into six figures or a murder is outstandingly brutal or intriguing, we no longer even read below the headings.
>
> —James Truslow Adams, 1929

> There is a hollowness at the core of a society if its members share no common purpose, no mutual goals, no joint vision—nothing to believe in except self-aggrandizement.
>
> —Marian Wright Edelman, 1992

JAMES Truslow Adams, historian of the American Dream, never pursued a rigorous analysis of the influence of the American Dream on crime. Nonetheless, he believed that the task of reducing crime in America was urgent and that it would require alterations in basic social and cultural patterns. He also recognized the role of human agency in social change and the importance of leadership at the highest levels in mobilizing the resources necessary to reform the "very foundations" of American life. In his view, nothing less than American democracy itself was at stake. "We

From *Crime and the American Dream* (pp. 91–111) by S. Messner and R. Rosenfeld, 1994, Belmont, Calif.: Wadsworth Publishing Company. Copyright © 1994 by Wadsworth Publishing Co. Reprinted by permission of Wadsworth Publishing, a division of Thomson Learning, fax 800-730-2215.

must rule or be ruled," he wrote, because unless the crime problem is brought under control, social order will sooner or later give way to chaos, opening the way for "the dictator who inevitably 'saves society' when social insubordination and disintegration have become intolerable."

Adams directed his message for change, published originally in a 1929 essay on law observance, to Herbert Hoover. It is easy in retrospect to dismiss as futile his effort to educate President Hoover on the nature of the crime problem. However, Adams was well aware of the President's public policy limitations. Hoover may not have understood the "magnitude and the causes of the danger which we face," but at least he acknowledged that there was a crime problem. By contrast, his predecessor, Calvin Coolidge, never troubled himself over the rising tide of crime and lawlessness, beyond seeing to it that Mrs. Coolidge was accompanied on her shopping by an armed protector.

Several important lessons remain in Adams' attempts to educate the President and the public about crime. If Adams exaggerated the specter of social collapse and dictatorship, he recognized the genuine vulnerability of democratic rights and freedoms to demagogic appeals for "law and order." He also understood the importance of establishing a supportive intellectual climate for effective political leadership and public action. Hoover's moral appeals to citizens to do their "duty" by obeying the Eighteenth Amendment's prohibition against the manufacture, sale, or transportation of intoxicating liquors were ineffective, in Adams' view, because they reflected a shallow appreciation of the American crime problem:

The American problem, though complicated by Prohibition, lies far deeper; and it is the lack of understanding as to what the problem is that so greatly diminishes the force of Mr. Hoover's appeal to us as citizens anxious to do our duty toward society.

Adams also contributes very important insights regarding the causes of crime and prospects for crime policy in America. His message is organized around two themes that are central to our arguments. First, the roots of the American crime problem lie deep within our cultural and institutional history. "Lawlessness," by which Adams meant a generalized disrespect for law as such, is part of the American heritage. Prohibition may have contributed to the problem, he wrote in a 1928 article published in the *Atlantic* entitled "Our Lawless Heritage,"

but it is operating upon a population already the most lawless in spirit of any in the great modern civilized countries. Lawlessness has been and is one of the most distinctive American traits. . . . It is

needless to say that we are not going to be able to shed this heritage quickly or easily.

Second, because high rates of crime are neither recent nor ephemeral characteristics of American society, responses to crime must be equally fundamental if they are to be effective. According to Adams, the "spirit" of lawlessness, which is very similar to what we have termed the "ethic" of anomie, will give way only when the preconditions for respect for law have been established. These include knowledge of the nature and limits of law on the part of law makers and the public, and the impartial application of legal sanctions against "millionaires" and "highly placed officials in Washington," as well as against the "ordinary criminal." Most important, the American spirit of lawlessness will not abate "until the ideal of quickly accumulated wealth, by any means whatever, is made subordinate to the ideal of private and public virtue."

Adams does not describe in detail how these changes are to come about, in particular how virtue would overcome the goal of material accumulation, except to propose that the President has, if he would only seize it, an opportunity to exercise essential moral leadership. Although directed at Herbert Hoover in 1929, Adams' call for moral "regeneration" continues to be relevant to present-day political and cultural conditions, as the quotation from Marian Wright Edelman at the beginning of this [reading] suggests. If the President

will undertake to show the people what underlies their problem, and assume the leadership in a crusade to reform the very foundations of their life, . . . then he will prove the leader for whom America waits, and patriotism and nobility may again rise above efficiency and wealth. By that path only can America regain respect for law and for herself. . . . America can be saved, but it must be by regeneration, not by efficiency.

We share Adams' belief that significant reductions in crime in the United States will require fundamental changes in the social and cultural order. If our diagnosis of the problem is correct—if high levels of crime derive from the very organization of American society—the logical solution is social reorganization. This will entail, in our view, both institutional reform and cultural regeneration. Before sketching the kinds of institutional and cultural changes that might reduce crime rates, however, it is important first to consider conventional approaches to crime control and their limitations.

CONVENTIONAL STRATEGIES FOR CRIME CONTROL

The point of departure for this discussion is current policy, and proposals for alternative policies, championed by what we will call the "conservative" and "liberal" political camps. Current policy, informed largely by conservative views, has not stemmed the tide of high levels of serious crime in the United States. However, proposals from the liberal camp to complement conservative "get tough" strategies with social reforms to expand opportunities for those "locked out" of the American Dream have not been any more successful in reducing levels of serious crime. The reason for these failures, we suggest, is that both conservative and liberal strategies reinforce the very qualities of American culture that lead to high rates of crime in the first place.

The Conservative Camp: The War on Crime

Conservative crime control policies are draped explicitly in the metaphors of war. We have declared war on crime, and on drugs, which are presumed to promote crime. Criminals, according to this view, have taken the streets, blocks, and sometimes entire neighborhoods from law-abiding citizens. The function of crime control policy is to recapture the streets from criminals to make them safe for the rest of us. This is accomplished by a range of initiatives encompassing law enforcement, criminal prosecution, court decisions, and sanctions policy.

Let us summarize briefly the conservative scenario. The police will act swiftly to remove criminals from the streets; prosecutors will vigorously bring their cases to court without plea-bargaining them to charges carrying lesser penalties; judges and juries will have less discretion in determining the penalties imposed; and more criminals will serve longer sentences for their crimes. Corrections officials will thus keep offenders in prison for longer periods of time, both because offenders are serving longer sentences and because officials will have less discretion in granting parole to offenders. The cumulative effects of these "get tough" actions will be lower crime rates brought about by increases both in the deterrent effects of punishment and in what criminologists term the incapacitation effects of imprisonment. With respect to deterrence, stiffer penalties will raise the costs of crime, thereby dissuading potential offenders from committing their first crimes and convincing previous offenders that it is too costly to repeat their misdeeds. The simple logic of incapacitation is that offenders who are in prison will be unable to commit crimes against the innocent public.

Conservatives have been successful in influencing crime control policies over the course of recent decades. For the twenty-four-year period between 1968 and 1992, the White House was occupied for all but four years by Republican Presidents who proudly proclaimed their credentials as "law and order" advocates. Republican control over the Presidency resulted in the nomination of conservative justices to the Supreme Court and conservative judges to the federal judiciary, and facilitated legislative changes consistent with the conservative agenda on crime control. Among the most important of these changes was the widespread adoption during the 1980s of mandatory-minimum sentencing laws.

SENTENCING IN THE DRUG WAR Mandatory-minimum laws specify the minimum sentence for crimes and in principle prohibit court and correctional agencies from modifying them. The intent of such sentencing policy is to increase both the certainty and the severity of punishment for persons convicted of the most serious crimes. Mandatory-minimum sentencing has been applied with special force to drug trafficking, resulting in extraordinary increases in the incarceration rates of drug offenders. Data from the National Corrections Reporting Program (NCRP) indicate that over half (52 percent) of the increase in prison admissions during the 1980s were for drug offenses. According to a leading criminal justice policy analyst, the use of mandatory-minimum sentencing in the war on drugs has "elevated the severity of punishment for drug sales to a level comparable to that for homicide."

By any reasonable standard, the policies associated with the war on crime and drugs have been a dismal failure. There have been no appreciable changes in rates of serious crime in America that can be unambiguously attributed to conservative policies. Moreover, Americans do not perceive themselves to be safer than in the past. If anything, fear of crime and preoccupation with personal safety have intensified over the past twenty-five years.

THE EXPANSION OF PUNITIVE SOCIAL CONTROL The war on crime has achieved one noteworthy victory, suggested in our discussion of mandatory-minimum sentencing, although it is surely a pyrrhic one: Incarceration levels have soared. The number of persons sentenced to more than one year in state and federal prisons increased to 823,414 in 1991 (a rate of 310 persons per 100,000 population) from 315,974 (139 per 100,000 population) in 1980. The rapid escalation of incarceration has produced a costly and potentially very dangerous "capacity crisis" in the correctional system. As incarceration rates increased throughout the 1970s and 1980s, national attention began to focus on the problem of over-crowding in prisons and jails. By the end of 1991, state prisons were operating with inmate populations that averaged 116 percent of their "highest" capacity, which is the capacity level required to maintain basic custody, security, and custodial operations, limited programming, and little else. The federal system operated at 146 percent of inmate capacity. The American Correctional Association, meanwhile, recommends that a prison never run at greater than 90 percent of capacity, to allow for administrative flexibility and response to emergencies. Only six states met this "industry standard" in 1991, and thirty-six states operated above 100 percent of "highest" capacity. The situation in local jails is no better, in part because thousands of state prisoners are held in local jails due to crowding in state facilities.

The extraordinary increase in the population of prisons and jails is only part of a larger expansion of formal, punitive social control in the United States. As of the end of 1989, over 4 million Americans, 2.2 percent of all adults, were under some form of correctional sanction. Roughly 1 million were in prison or jail, and the remaining 3 million were under supervision in the community (roughly 2.5 million on probation and 0.5 million on parole). Between 1984 and 1988 alone, the number of adults under some form of correctional sanction in the United States increased by 39 percent. At present rates of growth, 6 percent of the adult population will be subject to some form of correctional supervision by the year 2000, and 10 percent of American adults will be under correctional control by 2006.

. . . African Americans currently are subject to levels of punitive social control that are much higher than these projected estimates for the population as a whole. African Americans have been hit hard by the war against crime—and especially by the war against drugs. In his 1992 presidential address to the American Society of Criminology, Alfred Blumstein characterized rising levels of arrest and incarceration of black Americans as nothing less than a major assault on the black community. One can be reasonably confident that if a similar assault was affecting the white community, there would be a strong and effective effort to change either the laws or the enforcement policy.

Whether or not black Americans have been targeted explicitly, there are disturbing parallels between the massive expansion in formal social control during the 1980s and the infamous "black codes" of the post–Civil War South. Most of the southern states passed such vagrancy laws, allowing for the arrest of unemployed and "idle" blacks. However, the aggressive sanctions policies of recent years have not resulted in declines in offending among blacks. On the contrary, rates of violent crime and drug offending among young blacks increased sharply during the last half of the 1980s.

UNINTENDED CONSEQUENCES OF EXPANDED CONTROL Not only has the extension of the reach of the criminal justice system failed to reduce crime, it tends to undermine the capacity of the system to realize an equally important objective: justice. Excessive case loads put pressure on the major participants in the adjudication process—district attorneys, defense lawyers (especially public defenders), and judges—to dispense with cases quickly. The result is a preoccupation with efficiency rather than with the rights of criminal defendants. A concern with the simple management of large numbers of cases also pervades the correctional system. Indeed, criminologists Malcolm Feeley and Jonathan Simon have recently argued that a new way of perceiving the very functions of criminal sanctions has become dominant in criminology and criminal justice. According to this "new penology," the focus of corrections has shifted away from a concern with administering levels of punishment that individuals deserve, or a concern with rehabilitating these offenders, to a preoccupation with more efficient "risk management" of dangerous populations.

The unfortunate and unintended consequences of the war on crime, however, extend far beyond the criminal justice system itself. Crackdowns on crime are directed at those populations considered to be most dangerous to society. This implies that minority groups will be affected disproportionately by these efforts. As we have seen, this has been precisely the case for black Americans, many of whom quite understandably resent the differential treatment imposed on them by vigorous law enforcement efforts. It should come as little surprise, therefore, that police–citizen confrontations involving minority group members are likely to be filled with tension and hostility, and can ignite episodes of collective disorder.

In addition, given the greater criminal involvement of males in comparison with females, and of young males in particular, extremely high levels of incarceration can have devastating implications for the sex ratio of a community and, in turn, for family relations. The large-scale removal of young males from the general population depletes the supply of potential marriage partners for young females. In so doing, expansive incarceration policies impede the formation of traditional families and thereby encourage, indirectly, higher rates of female-headed households and illegitimacy—precisely the types of family conditions that have been linked with high rates of crime. Thus the war on crime has not only failed to realize the goal of significant crime reduction; it has exacerbated the very problem that it is supposed to solve.

The failure of conservative crime control policies reflects the warfare mentality that provides their justification. This is why it is so politically dangerous to call for an end to current policy, even for those who are willing to acknowledge its limitations. It appears defeatist to advocate limits on the costs of criminal sanctions, or on the proportion of the population it is reasonable or desirable to place under correctional control, when crime control is imbued with the metaphors of war. A former official in the current drug war is said to have compared the drug problem with Humpty Dumpty:

When all the King's horses and all the King's men couldn't put Humpty together again, the response was merely to double the number of horses and men, rather than to recognize at some point the futility of the effort.

However, reports of violent conflict from the "battle zones" of American cities suggest that the war on crime is more than just a rhetorical device: It is a classic instance of the sociological self-fulfilling prophesy. It begins with a definition of the situation that likens the crime problem to war. The war on crime, in turn, reinforces the cultural and social arrangements that produce warlike conditions in the society. The response is to intensify the war on crime. An alternative response would be to change the initial definition of crime as war and criminals as "enemies." This is the approach to crime control taken by the liberal camp, although it too ends up reproducing social and cultural conditions conducive to crime.

The Liberal Camp: The War on Poverty and on Inequality of Opportunity

In contrast to conservative crackdowns on criminals, the liberal approach to crime control emphasizes correctional policies and broader social reforms intended to expand opportunities for those "locked out" of the American Dream. This approach is based on the premise that the poor and disadvantaged want to conform to the law and that they commit crimes only when doing so is necessary to achieve goals that cannot be achieved through conformity. The temptations for crime can thus be lessened by providing access to the legitimate means of success for those who lack opportunities. For those who have already become enmeshed in the criminal justice system,

liberals call for rehabilitation and reform, with a heavy emphasis on training and skill development to allow offenders to compete more effectively for jobs upon reentry into society.

Liberals, like conservatives, have enjoyed some notable successes in getting their policies implemented. A good example of liberal strategies for general social reform is provided by the War on Poverty during the 1960s. Many of the programs associated with this initiative were justified with explicit reference to crime reduction. Perhaps the most famous of these was the Mobilization for Youth program, which sought to reduce crime and delinquency in a depressed area of Manhattan by expanding educational and employment opportunities. This program was organized in part by Richard Cloward, one of the leading figures associated with the anomie perspective on crime and delinquency.

EFFECTS OF LIBERAL POLICIES ON CRIME RATES
There is little evidence to suggest that the liberal strategies, including the Mobilization for Youth program, have been any more effective than the conservative approaches in reducing levels of crime. Crime rates increased markedly during the height of liberal social reform in the 1960s and early 1970s. Some liberal advocates have argued that their approach was never really tried, that the War on Poverty was underfunded, that it was more image than reality, or that it was quickly overwhelmed by other issues, such as the Vietnam War. Typical of this view is Ruth Sidel's comment:

The War on Poverty was woefully inadequate to reverse the damage that was done, particularly to blacks, in our society; and no sooner did it get started than Vietnam, inflation, and the Nixon administration had begun to subvert it.

However, the fact is that poverty rates in the United States did decline during the 1960s and most of the 1970s. Unless official poverty rates are rejected as grossly invalid indicators of impediments to economic opportunity, then, based on the liberal view, some relief from serious crime should have coincided with the realization of genuine social reform.

There are additional reasons to question the liberal approach to crime control. First, it is difficult to see how the liberal explanation of crime and the policies based on it would apply to the crimes committed by persons at the top of the opportunity structure, crimes that are far from rare and that are very costly to society. Second, although certain forms of serious crime are disproportionately committed by the poor, crime rates do not rise and fall in a direct way with poverty rates, unemployment rates, or other indicators of economic deprivation. In fact, the opposite is the case for certain historical periods.

Crime rates fell during the Great Depression of the 1930s and rose dramatically during the prosperous 1960s. Crime rates declined during the mid-1970s and then again during the early 1980s, but in both instances the reductions coincided with periods of economic recession. A full assessment of changes in levels of serious crime must, of course, encompass a wide range of causal factors in addition to economic opportunities, such as changes in the age composition of the population and in the routine activities that make people and property more or less vulnerable or attractive targets for crime. Even so, the evidence fails to support the proposition that reductions in crime follow directly from an expansion of economic opportunities.

The failure of the liberal approach to crime control is not surprising given our thesis that widespread crime is a product of cultural pressures for the unrestrained pursuit of monetary success and weak social control deriving from an imbalanced institutional structure. Greater equality of opportunity will not alter in any appreciable way either of these cultural and structural conditions. Genuine equality of opportunity would undoubtedly redistribute the economic winners and losers, but it would not by itself diminish either the importance of winning and losing or the concomitant pressures to try to win by any means necessary.

UNINTENDED CONSEQUENCES OF LIBERAL REFORM Not only do liberal crime control strategies fail to target the underlying cultural and structural causes of high crime rates in the United States, but like conservative strategies, they are self-defeating when enacted in the absence of more fundamental social change. Policies that reduce discriminatory barriers to occupational achievement and broaden access to education, to the extent that they are successful, promote social mobility and extend the reach of the American Dream to persons and groups who have historically been excluded from its benefits. This is, of course the very point of much liberal social policy. But in so doing, these policies reinforce the commitment to the American Dream itself and hence sustain its criminogenic consequences. A population would not long remain wedded to the idea that everyone should struggle relentlessly to get ahead if hardly anyone actually ever did get ahead.

In addition, the social mobility fostered by liberal social reform may aggravate the crime problem in another way, as suggested by the sociologist William Julius Wilson. Wilson describes the process through which poverty, crime, and other social problems become concentrated in urban neighborhoods. When better-off residents depart for other areas of the city or for the suburbs, they take with them skills, resources, and models of conventional behavior that contribute to community stability. They leave behind, all else equal, a community that is less able to exercise informal social control over its members, less able to protect itself from outsiders, and therefore more vulnerable to crime. As crime rates rise, more residents depart, again those with the best "prospects" being the first to go. The concentration of economic and social disadvantage increases, and crime rates continue to climb.

Wilson's analysis of neighborhood transition draws heavily on the social disorganization tradition associated with the Chicago school in urban sociology; in fact, he illustrates his argument with data from Chicago community areas. Writing in the 1980s, however, Wilson supplements his analysis with an account of the growth in mobility opportunities for middle- and working-class blacks that accompanied declines in discriminatory barriers in education and work, and, to a more limited degree, in housing during the previous two decades. The opening of the opportunity structure enabled many, though far from all, blacks to join the urban exodus of the previous thirty years. Even blacks who did not leave the central city because of continuing residential discrimination in suburban areas were able in greater numbers than ever before to move away from "declining" neighborhoods. As whites had been able to do for decades, blacks could now abandon old and declining neighborhoods for new, more stable ones. They could participate in the American tradition of linking geographic and social mobility. Now, like other Americans, when they moved up, they could move out. As a result, unintentional to be sure, expansions in opportunities for some black Americans led to expansions in crime rates for others.

We do not mean to exaggerate either the effects on neighborhood crime rates of the outmigration of better-off residents or, for that matter, the number of black Americans who have benefited from equal-opportunity policies. Nor do we condone in any way the racial discrimination that "kept blacks in their place" in earlier periods. Further, it would be absurd to blame those who flee crime-ridden communities in search of greater personal security. Their decisions and actions are understandable and from an individual point of view entirely justifiable.

We also do not mean to belittle the achievements of liberal social reform. The expansion of opportunities produces a broad range of benefits regardless of any impact on crime rates; there is more to improving the quality of life in a society than reducing the risks of criminal victimization. Finally, we personally believe that providing everyone with the maximum feasible degree of opportunity for the realization of human potential is a worthy cultural goal as a matter of simple justice. Our point is simply that a war on poverty or on inequality of opportunity is not likely to be an effective strategy for *crime control* in the absence of other cultural and structural changes.

Beyond Liberalism and Conservatism

The failure of both liberals and conservatives to offer effective solutions to the crime problem ultimately reflects the inability, or unwillingness, of advocates of either approach to question the fundamental features of American society. In a sense, both are prisoners of the dominant culture. Conservatives and liberals alike embrace the American Dream without reservation and search for an external "enemy" with which to engage in a war. Conservatives direct the war against the "wicked" persons who are held to represent a danger to society. The enemies for liberals are not bad persons but bad social conditions, imperfections of the social structure that make it difficult or impossible for some people to conform to dominant norms. These social imperfections, including poverty, racial discrimination, and lack of education, are typically viewed by liberals as a "betrayal" of the American Dream. Neither group entertains the possibility that the enemy comes from within, that the causes of crime lie within the dominant culture itself.

As a consequence of this intellectual blind spot, the policies of both conservatives and liberals are severely constrained by the logic of the existing culture and, in ironic ways, reflect this logic. The conservative approach promotes crime control policies without limits and at any cost. This expansive and expensive strategy for controlling crime embodies the anomic quality of American culture: the cultural imperative to pursue goals by any means necessary. Liberal policies, in contrast, strengthen the other element of American culture that is criminogenic—the excessive emphasis on the competitive struggle for monetary success. Liberals propose, in effect, that strengthening the American Dream will solve the problems caused by the American Dream. In short, both liberal and conservative policies for crime control are ultimately self-defeating because they reproduce the very cultural and social conditions that generate the distinctively high levels of crime for which the United States is known throughout the world.

Any significant reduction in crime will require moving beyond the failed ideas and policies associated with both ends of the conventional political spectrum. However, the policies that we suggest are also not likely to bring about substantial reductions in crime in the short run. We are not aware of any policy solutions for the crime problem that could have this effect. This is not simply because past and present policies have been hamstrung by the liberal and conservative alternatives; it is also because the conditions that lead to crime cannot be ameliorated by "policy" as such, or at least by policy that is politically feasible. In the United States, substantial crime reductions require *social change*, and not simply new social policy. Policy, on the other hand, is most often concerned with making existing arrangements more "efficient." The function of policy is to improve existing means of achieving collective goals; rarely does policy seek to alter the goals themselves. As one analyst suggests, addressing the "basic causes" of a problem may be of little interest to policymakers, because they are under strong political pressures to define problems in terms of available solutions, and they typically lack the material or political resources to alter basic causes.

Genuine crime control requires transformation from within, a reorganization of social institutions and a regeneration of cultural commitments. This is certainly a formidable task, given the powerful influence of existing cultural beliefs and structural arrangements. The task is not, however, an impossible one. Culture and social structure inevitably place constraints on human action, but these constraints are of a unique type. Unlike the limits imposed by the natural world, the social world is ultimately created and recreated by the participants themselves.

Sociologist Peter Berger uses the metaphor of a puppet to describe the paradox of constraint and potentiality in human action. He compares the expectations and requirements of social roles to the strings that regulate the movements of a puppet. The puppet's movements are, of course, constrained by the strings. At the same time, Berger cautions that the puppet metaphor should not be stretched too far. Human beings are not mindless puppets. Each of us individually is able to look up and examine the mechanism from which the strings hang, and, collectively, we can redesign the mechanism. Human actors, in other words, have the capacity to become aware of the social constraints on action and to change these constraints. In the section that follows, we sketch the kinds of changes in the institutional and cultural "mechanism" of American society that offer some promise of meaningful reductions in levels of serious crime.

CRIME REDUCTION THROUGH SOCIAL REORGANIZATION

Our prescriptions for crime reduction follow logically from our analysis of the causes of high levels of crime. To recapitulate very briefly: We contend that criminal activity is stimulated by strong cultural pressures for monetary success combined with anomie, a normative order with weak restraints on the selection of the means to pursue success. This anomic cultural condition is accompanied by an institutional balance of power in which the economy assumes dominance over other social institutions. Economic dominance diminishes the attractiveness of alternatives to the goal of monetary success and impedes the capacity of other institutions to perform their distinctive functions, including social control. High levels of crime thus reflect intrinsic elements of American culture and the corrosive impact of these cultural elements on social structure.

It follows from this analysis, moving back up the causal chain from high levels of crime through social structure and culture, that crime reductions would result from policies that strengthen social structure and weaken the criminogenic qualities of American culture. More specifically, crime reductions would follow from policies and social changes that vitalize families, schools, and the political system, thereby enhancing the "drawing power" of the distinctive goals associated with these institutions and strengthening their capacity to exercise social control. This institutional vitalization would, in turn, temper the anomic qualities and the intense pressures for monetary success associated with the American Dream. Finally, cultural regeneration—modifications in the American Dream itself—would promote and sustain institutional change, and would reduce cultural pressures for crime. We begin our discussion of social reorganization with a consideration of the structural dimension: institutional reform.

Institutional Reform

THE FAMILY AND SCHOOLS Initiatives such as the provision of family leave, job sharing for husbands and wives, flexible work schedules, employer-provided child care, and a host of other "pro-family" economic policies should help to alter the balance between the economic demands faced by parents and their obligations and opportunities to devote more time and energy to exclusively "family" concerns. In many families, parents and children spend very little time with each other. In a 1990 survey of American students in the sixth through the twelfth grades, half of the high school students reported that they did not share evening meals with their parents on a daily basis, and nearly half of the sixth-graders reported that they spent two or more hours a day at home without an adult present.

Policies that enable parents to spend more time with their children should not only strengthen family controls over children's behavior but should also enable the schools to carry out their control functions more effec-

tively. School teachers and educational researchers alike maintain that the absence of parental support for education handicaps the schools in their efforts to motivate learning and keep children engaged in the educational process. Yet only about half of the ninth- and twelfth-graders in the survey cited above reported that their parents "talk with me about school." Only one-third reported that their parents attended school meetings or events.

These examples illustrate the interdependent nature of social institutions: The capacity of any institution to fulfill its distinctive function is dependent on the effective functioning of the others. Not surprisingly, then, the lack of articulation between the family and the schools has unfortunate consequences for society at large. As one educational researcher observes, the poor articulation between the home and the school reflects and reinforces a "serious erosion of social capital" in American communities. If children do not see adults often, if their relationships with adults are "fleeting," adults cannot serve as effective deterrents and as positive influences on children's behavior. The social bonds necessary for discipline, emanating from both the family and the schools, are weakened as a result.

Policies aimed at strengthening the schools, then, must proceed in concert with those designed to improve family functioning. These policies must confront two interrelated problems: (1) strengthening external controls; and (2) strengthening the engagement of people—parents and teachers, as well as children and students—in the distinctive goals and "logics" of these institutions. It is worth pondering the mixed messages that our society currently sends regarding the best way to repair and strengthen families and schools.

The message regarding families is to avoid having one as long as possible. It is difficult to think of a single source of cultural encouragement in the United States today for young people to get married and to have children—in either order. In the current obsession with out-of-wedlock births, it is scarcely noticed that birth rates among young women have declined sharply since 1960. The proportion of births to unmarried women has risen, but this is because marriage rates have fallen even faster than birth rates. Over 75 percent of males and more than 60 percent of females between the ages of twenty and twenty-four were single (i.e., never married) in 1989, compared with 55 percent of males and 36 percent of females in this age group in 1970. Over the same period, the percentage of males in their late twenties who were single grew from 19 percent to 46 percent. Over 25 percent of males in their early thirties were single in 1989, compared with less than 10 percent two decades earlier. Although in each age group females were more likely than males to be married, the fraction remaining single grew just as rapidly.

Yet the loud message to young people is to stop having children rather than to start having families. Whatever the salutary effects of this message, it serves to reinforce the view of families as "burdens" to be shouldered only after a long period of economic preparation. We do not necessarily advocate early marriage as a form of crime control, but it seems that a society with a professed commitment to "family values" should provide more cultural and social support for family formation. As a practical matter, this support will require lessening the dependence of marital and family decision-making on purely economic considerations.

With respect to schools, a popular message of the 1990s sounds the market-oriented theme of "choice": Bad schools will be driven out of business by good ones if obstacles blocking open markets in schooling are eliminated. This will occur if people are given the options of purchasing their educations in either public or private schools and of enrolling in schools outside of specific attendance areas or districts. Again, although such proposals may have particular merits, their general effect is to reinforce the market mentality of American education. One can scarcely blame students for asking whether this or that aspect of their education "pays" when this is exactly the question that dominates current educational policy discussion.

A rather different type of policy for schools is suggested by our argument. Schools should be enabled to devote themselves to their distinctive goal of formal learning. This requires, as we have suggested, stronger parental support for the educational function. However, it also requires that children's economic prospects become tied less closely to their performance in school.

Those who look back fondly to the "good old days" of strict discipline and respect for learning that are supposed to have once characterized the American public school system often forget that one reason the schools could educate more effectively in the past is because they did not have to educate as universally. In a world where labor markets offered jobs that did not require a high school education, the public schools operated much more selectively than they do now. Students who flunked out or who were expelled for disciplinary reasons, or who left because they simply did not like school, did not as a rule end up in the streets; they went to work, they formed families, or they joined the military.

Not long ago, Americans depended less on schools for economic rewards. In 1940, 39 percent of whites and 11 percent of blacks between the ages of 25 and 34 had completed four or more years of high school. By 1970, 75 percent of whites and 52 percent of blacks in this age group had completed high school. In a society where "good jobs" require a college degree or some other form of training beyond high school, and where military service requires a high school diploma, schools will daily confront students who, at best, calculate their "investment" in education according to future earnings. At worst, they will find themselves in chronic conflicts with students made hopeless by the knowledge that education is a necessary—but far from sufficient—condition for economic success.

THE POLITY Turning to the institution of the polity, our analysis points to two types of policy shifts: (1) reform of the formal system of crime control, particularly the correctional system; and (2) the creation of broader patterns of social participation and social control beyond the criminal justice system.

Correctional policy that is consistent with our analysis of the crime problem begins with a fundamental question that neither the liberal nor the conservative camp addresses: What is the optimum proportion of the population that should be under the jurisdiction of correctional agencies? One may be tempted to answer zero to this question, but unless we are willing to assume a crime rate of zero or are willing to let all convicted offenders go unpunished, some proportion of the population must be under some form of correctional control at all times. So, again, what is the optimum proportion?

This is not a "policy question" narrowly defined; it is a question designed to stimulate a different way of thinking about crime control policy. It is a political question, and it most certainly is a moral question, because it requires judgments about the goals of crime control and not simply choices among more efficient or less efficient means to achieve a predefined goal or, as in current policy, among several ill-defined and conflicting goals. A central goal of any approach to crime control that is based on our analysis is to reduce cultural support for crime. A prerequisite for accomplishing this objective is to end the war on crime. We are not proposing, of course, to end efforts at crime control. On the contrary, we believe that effective crime control can begin only when control is gained over current crime policy. Achieving control of crime policy requires placing limits on the costs of crime control, especially the costs of corrections. Although cost containment will not be easy, it is essential if the anomic and perverse consequences of the war on crime are to be halted.

The idea of *intermediate sanctions*, which are community-based punishments situated between ordinary probation and prison, has been promoted by correctional reformers as a way to reduce the costs and crowding of correctional supervision while maintaining a high level of public safety. Sentencing policy based on the principle of intermediate sanctions would impose the kinds of limits on crime control that are consistent with our analysis. We question, however, whether the intensified supervision associated with most intermediate sanctions will produce the cost savings claimed by some advocates.

A key issue is whether the flow of offenders into the new community programs consists primarily of those who would have gone to prison or those who would have been placed on ordinary probation. If intermediate sanctions programs draw primarily from the pool of prison-bound offenders, they can help to lower correctional costs and to relieve overcrowding in correctional facilities. However, the great majority of persons serving time in prison have been convicted of violent crimes, have committed violent crimes in the past, or are repeat felony offenders. These offenders are not likely to be deemed suitable candidates for community-based programs, no matter how intensive the supervision. If, on the other hand, offenders who would otherwise have received ordinary probation are the main recipients of intermediate sanctions, then the cost savings of these intermediate punishments are greatly reduced in order to pay for heightened supervision of offenders in the community.

The net impact of intermediate sanctions is, then, difficult to discern. Interestingly, however, this is one of their great advantages over current policy. Reconciling tough choices regarding cost, safety, and justice presupposes some agreement over the priorities of the criminal justice system. Current policy is politically pleasing because it does not require consensus building or difficult tradeoffs among competing values and interests; there are no limits in a war on crime. The system we prefer does not have this spurious benefit, because, by introducing a measure of restraint into crime control policy, it would make explicit both the scope and the purposes of punishment.

Reforms that are limited to the criminal justice system, however, will not by themselves produce appreciable reductions in crime. Broader changes within the polity are necessary to nurture the sense of collective obligation and individual duty essential for the effective functioning of formal social controls. One proposal that appears especially promising in this respect is the creation of a national service corps. If it is to contribute to crime control, such a system must be universalistic and involve an array of opportunities and obligations to serve local communities and the society as a whole. It can perform a particularly important integrative function by providing education, training in needed skills, and meaningful social controls for adolescents and young adults who have graduated from or dropped out of school, have not found work that will lead to a career, and who have outgrown the reach of their parents but have not yet formed families of their own. In short, by offering an institutional mooring for young people during the transition to adulthood, national service promises to bolster social control and to facilitate "maturational reform," i.e., the process through which young people involved in common forms of delinquency turn away from illegal behavior as they mature and assume adult obligations.

A specific form of national service with direct relevance to crime control policy is a Police Corps of young people trained as police officers who would serve on local forces for periods of two to four years. The concept was endorsed by President Bill Clinton as part of his proposal to provide college assistance in return for community service. One commentator suggested that the Police Corps might serve as the basis for President Clinton's efforts to build support for his broader philosophy of national service:

It's the logical place to start now, as the new President embarks on his most ambitious goal—to rebuild a national sense of community, responsibility, and public altruism.

SOCIAL STRATIFICATION AND THE ECONOMY Finally, our analysis has important implications for the system of social stratification and the interrelations between this system and the economy. The relationship between stratification and crime has been the focus of extensive research and theorizing in modern criminology. Conventional approaches to the stratification–crime relationship, however, direct attention almost exclusively to a single feature of the stratification system: the distribution of opportunities for economic rewards. These explanations typically attribute crime to inequality in economic opportunities. We have maintained that greater equality of opportunity is not likely to eliminate, and in fact may aggravate, pressures to turn to illegitimate means to realize the goal of economic success. The mere existence of unequal *outcomes* is likely to generate such pressures, regardless of the openness of the stratification system, if monetary success reigns supreme as a cultural goal and the economy dominates the institutional structure of society.

It might seem on the surface that the solution to the crime problem lies in greater equality of results. However, it is not merely the shape of the distribution of material and symbolic rewards in America that contributes to crime but rather the mechanism by which rewards are distributed. In this respect, our analysis is informed by Marx's insight that the distribution of the means of consumption is ultimately dependent on the "conditions of production themselves." The conditions of production in American society dictate that the distribution of rewards be tied to economic functions: either the performance of economic roles or the possession of capital. In other words, the wealth that is produced within the economy is also distributed almost exclusively in accordance with economic criteria by labor and capital markets. To shore up such other institutions as the family, schools, and the polity relative to the economy, a greater share of the national wealth will have to be allocated on the basis of noneconomic criteria.

We are not endorsing the nationalization of the means of production to rebalance institutions. The political and economic failures of state socialist societies have been made glaringly apparent by recent history. Rather, the model that appears promising is that of the mixed economies in Europe and Japan. These nations have implemented a wide range of social policies and programs to ensure that material well-being is not strictly tied to economic functions and to guarantee that noneconomic roles receive meaningful financial support from collective resources.

To summarize: The structural changes that could lead to significant reductions in crime are those that promote a rebalancing of social institutions. These changes would involve reducing the subordination to the economy of the family, schools, the polity, and the general system of social stratification. Most of the specific proposals for institutional change that we have put forth are not particularly novel. They have been advanced by others in different contexts and with different agendas. These proposals, however, typically are considered in isolation from one another. For example, conservatives who bemoan the demise of the family and call for its rejuvenation rarely pursue the logical implications of their analyses and proposals. They fail to recognize or acknowledge that the vitalization of the family requires changes in the economy that are likely to be very distasteful to conservatives on ideological grounds.

The distinctive and powerful feature of the sociological paradigm is that it directs attention to the interconnections among social institutions. Because of these interconnections, piecemeal reforms are likely to be ineffective. Moreover, our analytical framework implies that institutional reforms must go hand in hand with cultural change, because culture and institutional structure are themselves inextricably bound. It is to the matter of cultural change that we now turn.

The Task of Cultural Regeneration

A basic premise of this book is that the beliefs, values, and goals associated with the American Dream are firmly entrenched in the American historical experience and consciousness. If this premise is correct, it would be fanciful to entertain the possibility of any wholesale rejection of the American Dream. Such a radical cultural transformation is not required, however, to vitalize noneconomic institutions. Instead, by moderating the excesses of the dominant cultural ethos, and emphasizing its useful features, institutional reform can be stimulated and significant reductions in crime can be realized.

We have characterized the American Dream as the commitment to the goal of monetary success, to be pursued by all members of society under conditions of open, individual competition. The most important and valuable theme running through this cultural ethos is that of a universal entitlement to strive for a better life, which can be attained as a consequence of one's own achievements. In other words, the American Dream empowers everyone to dream about a brighter future and about participating in the creation of that future. This vision of possibilities, of hope, is liberating, and it serves the interests of both individuals and the larger society by inspiring people to develop their talents and abilities.

The criminogenic tendencies of the American Dream derive from its *exaggerated* emphasis on monetary success and its resistance to limits on the means for the pursuit of success. Any significant lessening of the criminogenic consequences of the dominant culture thus requires the taming of its strong materialistic pressures and the creation of a greater receptivity to socially imposed restraints. To dampen the materialistic pressures, goals other than the accumulation of wealth will have to be elevated to a position of prominence in the cultural hierarchy. This implies greater recognition of and appreciation for the institutional realms that are currently subservient to the economy. More specifically, social roles such as parenting, "spousing," teaching, learning, and serving the community will have to become, as ends in themselves, meaningful alternatives to material acquisition. Furthermore, enhancing the respect for these noneconomic roles implies that money will no longer serve as the principal gauge of social achievement and personal worth. Money will not be, in the words of Marian Wright Edelman, the preeminent "measure of our success."

The other, complementary task of cultural regeneration will involve fostering a cultural receptivity to restraints. The dominant cultural ethos glorifies the individual pursuit of material well-being. People are encouraged to maximize personal utility, to be guided by self-interest, and to regard others as potential competitors in the race for economic rewards. However, many of the institutional reforms to which we point entail the subordination of individual interests to larger collectivities, such as the family and the community. In short, it seems unlikely that social change conducive to lower levels of crime will occur in the absence of a cultural reorientation that encompasses an enhanced emphasis on the importance of mutual support and collective obligations and a decreased emphasis on individual rights, interests, and privileges.

An Intellectual Foundation for Change

An important intellectual component accompanies the task of balancing social obligations with individual interests. The extreme individualism of American culture impedes a full understanding of the interdependencies between the individual and society. Human beings are inherently social beings. As a consequence, their individual development and maturation presuppose social relationships that are necessarily constraining. To borrow from Marx once again:

Only in association with others has each individual the means of cultivating his [or her] talents in all directions.

The idea that individual growth requires social motivation, support, and regulation forms part of the distinctive corpus of classical sociological thought. It figures significantly not only in Marx's analysis of capitalist society but also in George Herbert Mead's theory of the social formation of the self and in Emile Durkheim's conception of the collective conscience. It is one of the few ideas in the history of sociological thought that is not readily identified as belonging to one or another intellectual or ideological camp. It links the micro and the macro levels of analysis, and informs conflict theories of social change as well as consensus theories of social order. As a defining element in the common heritage of the discipline, it prepares the conceptual ground for a sociological reappraisal of the American Dream.

This reappraisal suggests that different parts of the American Dream work at cross-purposes. Its universalism and achievement orientation inspire ambition and in so doing stimulate the motivational dynamic necessary for the realization of human potential. However, its exaggerated materialism and extreme individualism narrow the range of human capacities that receive cultural respect and social support and discourage people from assuming obligations that in principle could be liberating. By helping to clarify this internal contradiction, a sociological understanding of the American Dream can perhaps lay the intellectual groundwork for the cultural and institutional changes necessary for reducing crime in our society.

Toward a Mature Society

In closing, we return to James Truslow Adams for a final observation of the legacy and the future of the American Dream. Adams traces the possibilities of the Dream to the American Revolution. The cultural significance of the revolt lay in "the breaking down of all spiritual barriers to the complete development of whatever might prove to be fertile, true, and lasting in the American dream." However, Adam lamented the fact that this developmental potential was inhibited by the "debilitating doctrine" that, two centuries after its birth, the United States is still a "young" nation. He asked:

Is it not time to proclaim that we are not children but men [and women] who must put away childish things; that we have overlooked that fact too long; that we have busied ourselves overmuch with fixing up the new place we moved into 300 years ago, with making money in the new neighborhood; and that we should begin to live a sane, maturely civilized life?

The promise of a mature America is the cultural encouragement for all persons to develop their full range of talents and capacities on the basis of mutual support and collective obligations. James Truslow Adams' American Dream, and ours, must be reinvented so that its destructive consequences can be curbed, and so that its fertile, true, and lasting promise of human development can be fulfilled.

QUESTIONS FOR DISCUSSION AND WRITING

1. Which belief of Adams' do the authors "share"?
2. How do both the conservative and liberal policies reflect the fact that American culture is the cause of crime?
3. What "follows from this analysis"?

Data Analysis Exercise

A Brief Look at Routine Activities Theory and an Exploration of Low Self-Control Theory

INTRODUCTION

In this data analysis exercise, we will use Wave VII data from the National Youth Survey (NYS) to look at routine activities theory, which is discussed in Part VIII. Then, we will use the same data to explore low self-control theory, also presented in Part VIII.

DESCRIPTION OF THE DATASET

See the data analysis exercise for Part V for a description of the NYS dataset. Before we start our analyses, we'll need to load up the second version of our dataset, "NYSCRIM2."

Routine Activities Theory

GETTING A HANDLE ON THE DATA AND USING CROSSTABULATION TABLES

Part VIII presents a number of relatively recently minted theories, one of which is routine activities theory. Proposed by Lawrence Cohen and Marcus Felson, this commonsensical theory appears to be quite helpful in explaining otherwise bizarre crime rates. Routine activities theory, for example, predicts that property crimes should go down as unemployment goes up because unemployed people are more likely to be at home, where they can serve as effective guardians over their property. However, while crimes between strangers may go down, crimes between intimates may increase because the parties are spending more time in one another's proximity.

These changes are due to variations in the convergence in time and place of the three essential elements of any predatory offense. First, one needs a motivated offender. Second, one needs a suitable target. The third requirement is an absence of capable guardians that could prevent the offense. Neighbors, for example, often serve as effective guardians of their co-residents' property. Routine activities such as work and school serve to prevent people from protecting their own property. At the same time, they also serve to bring together individuals in the workplace/school where they can engage in violence against one another. The mere fact of employment, then, can increase crime.

Testing routine activities theory requires that we find suitable measures, as we have done for the previous theories. Among the questions in the NYS survey are several that will work for our purposes. The respondents were asked to estimate how many hours they worked and how many hours they spent with friends. Under routine activities theory, we would posit that those who spent more hours at work or with their friends would be more likely to be out where they could become victims of violent crimes and less likely to be at home where they could protect their possessions (thus, they would also be more likely to be property crime victims, too). Along these lines, I created a variable (TOTHRS) that represented the total number of hours the respondents spent at work and with friends, then recoded the variable into three categories: (1) those who spent 10 or fewer hours a week engaged in these activities; (2) those who spent 11 to 30 hours a week at work or with their friends; and (3) those who spent 31 or more hours a week in these activities. Although there was also a question about how many hours a week the respondent spent studying, the answers were not broken down into the number of hours spent studying at home versus in other locations. For this reason, I relied only on the two questions that were most appropriate for routine activities theory.

We will look at the effect of our new measure on whether the respondent was a victim of a property crime (VICTPROP), leaving victimization in violent offense (VICTVIO) for you to examine in the "further explorations" questions. To see if the theory holds, run a frequency table for TOTHRS, then run a crosstabulation table with VICTPROP as the dependent variable and TOTHRS as the independent variable.

What do you notice about the TOTHRS → VICTPROP table? Which respondents were most likely to have been the victims of a property crime? What is the strength of the relationship shown in the table? Is it statistically significant? How can we summarize this table? Does this table support routine activities theory?

USING CONTROL VARIABLES

You might be wondering if routine activities theory applies to all types of neighborhoods, including those in which unemployment is (or is not) a problem. Let's find out by running a crosstabulation table with VICTPROP as the dependent variable, TOTHRS as the independent variable, and UNEMP as the control variable. Look within the rows for UNEMP. You'll see that the relationship between time spent outside the home (working or with friends) and victimization is not statistically significant for any of the three categories of unemployment. The cell sizes are all adequate, and the percentages increase in the predicted direction, but the findings are not significant, so we cannot use them to support our theory. Does this mean routine activities theory is bunk? Since we would never throw out a theory based on one study (especially given that our data show increases in the predicted direction), our finding doesn't disprove the theory. The finding does, however, pique my interest regarding what's going on, and I'm assuming it piques yours, too.

To further explore this finding, let's control for TOTHRS instead. We know from the exercises for Marxist theory that high neighborhood unemployment is tied to victimization. It's possible that neighborhood unemployment and hours spent by respondents at work or with friends are related in some unexpected way that negates our relationship. To find out, run a crosstabulation table with VICTPROP as the dependent variable, UNEMP as the independent variable, and TOTHRS as the control variable.

Isn't the resulting table interesting? When we look within the rows for TOTHRS, we see that the relationship between neighborhood unemployment and victimization is not statistically significant for the first two categories of TOTHRS (those who spent 10 or fewer hours a week at work or with friends and those who spent 11 to 30 hours a week at those activities). But when we look at the respondents who spent more than 30 hours a week at work (and/or with friends), we see that victimization is more likely for respondents who live in neighborhoods in which unemployment is more of a problem. It appears, then, that living in a high unemployment area isn't statistically related to victimization unless the respondent spends a greater amount of time outside the home, where she or he is presumably less able to protect her or his belongings. Routine activities theory is supported by our data, and we can also add to the theory by specifying that hours spent outside the home may interact with level of unemployment in one's neighborhood to produce crime. This addition makes sense, too. Remember that we need a motivated offender, a suitable target, *and* an absence of guardians in order to have a predatory violation. Potential offenders who are motivated by unemployment are unable to act on their motivations if their potential victims stay at home where they can protect their belongings. When the capable guardians are at work or out with friends, however, motivated offenders may commit their crimes. Similarly, just because a person is outside his or her home doesn't mean that he or she will be the victim of a property crime; if there are no motivated offenders, no crime will take place. Together, we have contributed to a theory to make it more useful in predicting crime. This is exciting!

FURTHER EXPLORATION

We have now explored an idea relevant to routine activities theory as it applies to victimization in a property crime. To see if the theory applies to victimization in a violent offense, you will apply it to VICTVIO for the "further exploration" questions.

ON YOUR OWN

Now that we have briefly examined routine activities theory and added a control variable, you can include other control variables. By now, you should have some ideas of important variables to include (for example, victimization may vary by income level or gender of respondents). While you are choosing variables, you'll be learning a lot about theory building as well. Make sure you write down why you think they are important before trying them out, tying them to the articles you've read.

Low Self-Control Theory

GETTING A HANDLE ON THE DATA AND USING CROSSTABULATION TABLES

Another relatively recent theory is low self-control theory. Proposed by Michael Gottfredson and Travis Hirschi, this theory focuses on the personality and character weaknesses of offenders. Individuals with low self-control are more likely to commit crimes because of their tendency to respond immediately to stimuli rather than reasoning things out. As described by Gottfredson and Hirschi, these individuals tend to engage in illicit sexual intercourse, be adventuresome, find it difficult to maintain stable work and interpersonal relationships, lack perseverance, and be uninterested in long-term work and educational goals. With respect to crime, those with less self-control are more likely to resort to violence to resolve conflicts and to commit property (and other) crimes when they become convenient means to an end. Gottfredson and Hirschi also argue that people who engage in quasi-deviant behavior such as smoking or drinking are more likely to participate in outlawed behavior as well, because smoking and drinking also reflect their low self-control.

Testing low self-control theory requires that we find suitable measures, as we have done for the previous theories. Among the questions in the NYS survey are a large number that will work for our purposes. First, the respondents were asked whether they smoked and how much they drank. Smoking was used "as is," but alcohol consumption had to be recoded to make it easier to use in our crosstabulations. The new variable, ALCO13X, was coded as "0" for those who reported drinking on 12 or fewer occasions (an average of once a month or less) and as "1" for those who reported drinking on a more frequent basis.

Gottfredson and Hirschi argued that participation in illicit sexual activity was correlated with criminality as well. The respondents were asked a series of questions regarding their sexual behavior, including whether they had ever had a venereal disease (which could serve as a proxy for non-use of protection during intercourse or an inability to properly screen sexual partners), whether they had ever paid for sex, whether they had ever been paid for sex, and their number of sexual partners during the previous year. I created a new variable, SEXDEVI, that represented participation in sexual deviance. SEXDEVI was coded "1" for any respondent who had ever had a venereal disease, had ever paid or been paid for sex, or who had had more than three sexual partners during the year (I chose that number because 90% of the sample had 3 or fewer partners, so those who had more partners were on the outer fringes of the sample). SEXDEVI was coded as "0" for the remaining respondents.

Finally, I created a composite factor, LIE_OKAY, that represented the average of the answers to four lie-related questions ("Sometimes you need to lie in order to get a job," "Making a good impression is more important than telling the truth to friends," "Making a good impression is more important than telling the truth to parents," and "If you want your fellow workers to like you, you may have to cover up for them"). This measure was designed to represent impulsiveness, because Gottfredson and Hirschi proposed those with low self-control have a "here and now" orientation that makes them impulsive, and that such individuals are always on the lookout for the easy way out of potentially difficult situations. Because the measure represents the average of the respondents' responses to four different scenarios, a higher score means that a given respondent agrees with the statements (and thus considers lying acceptable).[1]

To see if the ideas proposed by Gottfredson and Hirschi are supported by the NYS data, we will look at the effect of our new measures on whether the respondent had ever stolen an item worth $50 or more (THEFT50), leaving violent offenses (VIOLENCE) for you to examine in the "further explorations" questions. To see if the theory holds, run frequencies for SMOKES, ALCO13X, SEXDEVI, and LIE_OKAY; then run crosstabulation tables with THEFT50 as the dependent variable and our four new measures as the independent variables.

What do you notice about the SMOKES → THEFT50 table? Which respondents were most likely to have stolen an item worth more than $50? What is the strength of the relationship shown in the table? Is it statistically significant? How can we summarize this table? Does this table support low self-control theory?

What about the ALCO13X → THEFT50 table? Which respondents were most likely to have stolen an item worth more than $50? What is the strength of the relationship shown in the table? Is it statistically significant? How can we summarize this table? Does this table support low self-control theory?

What do you notice about the SEXDEVI → THEFT50 table? Which respondents were most likely to have stolen an item worth more than $50? What is the strength of the relationship shown in the table? Is it statistically significant? How can we summarize this table? Does this table support low self-control theory?

Finally, what is going on in the LIE_OKAY → THEFT50 table? Which respondents were most likely to have stolen an item worth more than $50? What is the strength of the relationship shown in the table? Is it statistically significant? How can we summarize this table? Does this table support low self-control theory?

USING CONTROL VARIABLES

You might be wondering if low self-control theory applies equally to various groupings of respondents—for example, whether the criminality of males and females are differently affected by sexual deviance. Let's find

---

[1]Because of the small number of individuals who scored "4" on the scale, I recoded those individuals into the "3" category.

out by running a crosstabulation table with THEFT50 as the dependent variable, SEXDEVI as the independent variable, and MALE as the control variable. Look within the rows for MALE. You'll see that the relationship between participation in atypical sexual activities and stealing something worth $50 or more is statistically significant for both males and females, and shows increased percentages of thefts among those who participated in atypical sexual activities. The relationship we found cannot be "explained away" as due to the effects of gender rather than participation in atypical sexual activities. Among both genders, increased levels of sexual deviance meant increased chances of participating in a theft.

POINTS TO PONDER: Can we say that smoking (or participation in deviant sexual behaviors or any other measure of low self-control) "causes" criminality, or should we argue that the factors coexist (that is, they are related to one another)?

FURTHER EXPLORATION

We have now explored the relationship between each of four variables relevant to low self-control theory and thefts of property worth $50 or more. To see if the theory applies to violent offenses, you will apply it to VIOLENCE for the "further exploration" questions.

ON YOUR OWN

Now that we have briefly examined low self-control theory and added a control variable, you can include other control variables. By now, you should have some ideas of important variables you would like to include (for example, the relationship between atypical sexual behavior and participation in crime may vary by income category because of the increased freedom accorded to those in the higher classes, an idea proposed under power-control theory). You could also look at the effects of the other "low self-control" measures developed for these exercises, adding in control variables that you consider important. While you are choosing control variables, make sure you write down why you think they are important before trying them out, tying them to the articles you've read.

Although this concludes our last exercise together, I invite you to obtain and work with different datasets to further explore the theories we have examined in the exercises or to expand your understanding of the other theories in the book. You could start by downloading the full NYS dataset from the ICPSR web page or by obtaining the full version of the GSS for whatever years you want to use. Watch out, though, because data analysis is just as addictive as Tetris or other computer games! Maybe someday I'll read a research article written by you. (If you think that idea is ludicrous, just remember that the professors who taught the authors included in this book probably wondered the same thing about them.)

Homework for Part X: General Questions
(Routine Activities Theory)

Name: _____ Date: _____

Directions: Answer the following questions by filling in the blanks or circling the appropriate responses. A couple of answers have been filled in for you to make sure you're on the right track.

1. In Wave VII of the NYS dataset, _____% of the sample said they spent 10 or fewer hours at work or with friends, _____% spent between 11 and 30 hours engaged in those activities, and _____% spent 31 or more hours at work or with friends.

2. In the TOTHRS → VICTPROP crosstabulation, _____ (_____%) of the respondents who spent 31 or more hours at work or with their friends were also victims of property crimes, compared to <u>70</u> (_____%) who spent 11 to 30 hours engaged in those activities, and _____ (_____%) of those who spent 10 or fewer hours at work or with friends. It appears that as number of hours spent outside the home goes up, risk of victimization goes *up / down*. This relationship is *weak / moderate / strong*. This relationship *is / is not* statistically significant.

   The relationship between time spent outside the home (as measured by time spent at work or with friends) found using Wave VII of the NYS data *is similar to / differs greatly from* the findings expected under routine activities theory.

3. In the TOTHRS → VICTPROP crosstabulation with UNEMP as a control variable, <u>53</u> (_____%) of the respondents who both lived in neighborhoods where unemployment was a big problem and spent 31 or more hours at work or with friends were the victims of property crimes, compared to <u>3</u> (_____%) of those who spent 10 or fewer hours at work or with friends. This relationship is *weak / moderate / strong*, and *is / is not* statistically significant. Among those who lived in neighborhoods where unemployment was somewhat of a problem, _____ (_____%) of the respondents who spent 31 or more hours at work or with friends were the victims of property crimes, compared to _____ (_____%) of those who spent 10 or fewer hours at work or with friends. This relationship is *weak / moderate / strong*, and *is / is not* statistically significant. Among those who lived in neighborhoods where unemployment was not a problem, _____ (_____%) of the respondents who spent 31 or more hours at

work or with friends were the victims of property crimes, compared to _____ (_____%) of those who spent 10 or fewer hours at work or with friends. This relationship is *weak / moderate / strong*, and *is / is not* statistically significant.

The relationship between victimization in a property crime and time spent outside the home (as measured by time spent at work or with friends) found using Wave VII of the NYS data *is similar to / differs from* the findings expected under routine activities theory.

4. In the UNEMP → VICTPROP crosstabulation with TOTHRS as a control variable, 53 (_____%) of the respondents who both spent 31 or more hours at work or with friends and who lived in neighborhoods where unemployment was a big problem were the victims of property crimes, compared to 204 (_____%) of those who lived in neighborhoods where unemployment was less of a problem. This relationship is *weak / moderate / strong*, and *is / is not* statistically significant. Among those who spent between 11 and 30 hours at work or with friends, _____ (_____%) of the respondents who lived in neighborhoods where unemployment was a big problem were the victims of property crimes, compared to _____ (_____%) of those who lived in neighborhoods where unemployment was not a problem. This relationship is *weak / moderate / strong*, and *is / is not* statistically significant. Among those who spent 10 or fewer hours at work or with friends, _____ (_____%) of the respondents who lived in neighborhoods where unemployment was a big problem were the victims of property crimes, compared to _____ (_____%) of those who lived in neighborhoods where unemployment was not a problem. This relationship is *weak / moderate / strong*, and *is / is not* statistically significant.

The relationship revealed by this table demonstrates that unemployment and time spent outside the home (as measured by time spent at work or with friends) *are / are not* related in such a way that our findings support routine activities theory.

Homework for Part X: "Further Exploration" Questions
(Routine Activities Theory)

Name: _____   Date: _____

Task: See if the time-spent-away-from-home measure we developed for routine activities theory helps us predict victimization in a violent offense (VICTVIO).

Directions: Answer the following questions by filling in the blanks or circling the appropriate responses. A couple of answers have been filled in for you to make sure you're on the right track.

1. In Wave VII of the NYS dataset, _____% of the sample had been the victim of a violent offense during the previous year.

2. In the TOTHRS → VICTVIO crosstabulation, _____ (_____%) of the respondents who spent 31 or more hours at work or with their friends were also victims of violent offenses, compared to <u>36</u> (_____%) who spent 11 to 30 hours engaged in those activities, and _____ (_____%) of those who spent 10 or fewer hours at work or with friends. It appears that as number of hours spent outside the home goes up, risk of victimization in violent offenses goes *up / down*. This relationship is *weak / moderate / strong*. This relationship *is / is not* statistically significant.

    The relationship between violent victimization and time spent outside the home (as measured by time spent at work or with friends) found using Wave VII of the NYS data *is similar to / differs greatly from* the findings expected under routine activities theory.

Homework for Part X: "On Your Own" Questions
(Routine Activities Theory)

Name: _____ Date: _____

Task: Include some control variables of your own in your test of routine activities theory. For example, does victimization in a property or violent crime vary by income level or gender of the respondents?

Directions: Answer the following questions.

1. Which control variable did you choose, and why did you choose to control that factor?

2. What was the relationship between the independent and dependent variables before the addition of the control variable?

3. Did including the control variable change the relationship between the independent and dependent variables; that is, did the relationship between the two variables vary by control variable subcategory? In what way?

4. Based on your findings, what modifications or additions would you make to routine activities theory?

5. Can you say that your testing supports routine activities theory? Why/why not?

If you included more than one control variable, you may summarize the findings here for future reference.

Homework for Part X: General Questions
(Low Self-Control Theory)

Name: _____   Date: _____

Directions: Answer the following questions by filling in the blanks or circling the appropriate responses. A couple of answers have been filled in for you to make sure you're on the right track.

1. In Wave VII of the NYS dataset, 642 (_____%) of the sample smoked cigarettes, _____ (_____%) consumed alcohol more than 12 times a year, and _____ (_____%) participated in what could be labeled deviant sexual activities. On the LIE_OKAY scale, _____ (_____%) scored 3 (meaning that they felt it was acceptable to lie in the four scenarios), _____ (_____%) scored 2, and _____ (_____%) scored 1 (the lowest score).

2. In the SMOKES → THEFT50 crosstabulation, _____ (_____%) of the respondents who smoked had stolen property worth $50 or more, compared to 46 (_____%) of those who did not smoke. This relationship is *weak / moderate / strong*. This relationship *is / is not* statistically significant.

    The SMOKES → THEFT50 table *does / does not* show that respondents who smoked are more likely to steal property worth $50 or more. The relationship between smoking and thefts found using Wave VII of the NYS data *is similar to / differs greatly from* the findings expected under low self-control theory.

3. In the ALCO13X → THEFT50 crosstabulation, _____ (_____%) of the respondents who drank on 13 or more occasions during the previous year had stolen property worth $50 or more, compared to _____ (_____%) of those who did not drink as much alcohol. This relationship is *weak / moderate / strong*. This relationship *is / is not* statistically significant.

    The ALCO13X → THEFT50 table *does / does not* show that respondents who consumed alcohol 13 or more times are more likely to steal property worth $50 or more. The relationship between alcohol consumption and thefts found using Wave VII of the NYS data *is similar to / differs greatly from* the findings expected under low self-control theory.

4. In the SEXDEVI → THEFT50 crosstabulation, _____ (_____%) of the respondents who participated in what could be labeled deviant sexual activities had stolen property worth $50 or more, compared to _____ (_____%) of those whose sexual activities were less atypical. This relationship is *weak / moderate / strong*. This relationship *is / is not* statistically significant.

   The SEXDEVI → THEFT50 table *does / does not* show that respondents who engaged in deviant sexual activities are more likely to steal property worth $50 or more. The relationship between deviant sexual activities and thefts found using Wave VII of the NYS data *is similar to / differs greatly from* the findings expected under low self-control theory.

5. In the LIE_OKAY → THEFT50 crosstabulation, _____ (_____%) of the respondents who scored highest on the lying scale had stolen property worth $50 or more, compared to _____ (_____%) of those who scored 2 on the lying scale, and _____ (_____%) of those who scored the lowest on the lying scale. This relationship is *weak / moderate / strong*. This relationship *is / is not* statistically significant.

   The LIE_OKAY → THEFT50 table *does / does not* show that respondents who consider lying acceptable (an indicator of impulsiveness) are more likely to steal property worth $50 or more. The relationship between attitudes toward lying and thefts found using Wave VII of the NYS data *is similar to / differs greatly from* the findings expected under low self-control theory.

6. In the SEXDEVI → THEFT50 crosstabulation with MALE as a control variable, _____ (_____%) of the males who participated in atypical sexual activities committed thefts of property worth $50 or more, compared to _____ (_____%) of the males who did not participate in atypical sexual activities. For males, it appears that those who participate in deviant sexual activities are *more / less* likely to commit theft. This relationship is *weak / moderate / strong*, and *is / is not* statistically significant. When we turn our attention to the female rows, we see that _____ (_____%) of the females who participated in atypical sexual activities committed thefts of property worth $50 or more, compared to _____ (_____%) of those who did not participate in atypical sexual activities. For females, it appears that those who participate in deviant sexual activities are *more / less* likely to commit theft. This relationship is *weak / moderate / strong*, and *is / is not* statistically significant. Overall, we *can / cannot* say that controlling for gender in our model substantially changes the relationship we found between participation in deviant sexual activities and likelihood of committing theft.

7. Overall, it appears that our findings using the Wave VII of the NYS *support / do not support* low self-control theory.

Homework for Part X: "Further Exploration" Questions
(Low Self-Control Theory)

Name: _____   Date: _____

Task: See if the two measures we developed for low self-control theory help us predict involvement in violent offenses (VIOLENCE).

Directions: Answer the following questions by filling in the blanks or circling the appropriate responses.

1. In the SMOKES → VIOLENCE crosstabulation, _____ (_____%) of the respondents who smoked had committed a violent offense, compared to _____ (_____%) of those who did not smoke. This relationship is *weak / moderate / strong*. This relationship *is / is not* statistically significant.

   The SMOKES → VIOLENCE table *does / does not* show that respondents who smoked are more likely to engage in violence. The relationship between smoking and violence found using Wave VII of the NYS data *is similar to / differs greatly from* the findings expected under low self-control theory.

2. In the ALCO13X → VIOLENCE crosstabulation, _____ (_____%) of the respondents who drank on 13 or more occasions during the previous year had committed a violent offense, compared to _____ (_____%) of those who did not consume as much alcohol. This relationship is *weak / moderate / strong*. This relationship *is / is not* statistically significant.

   The ALCO13X → VIOLENCE table *does / does not* show that respondents who consumed alcohol 13 or more times are more likely to engage in violence. The relationship between alcohol consumption and violence found using Wave VII of the NYS data *is similar to / differs greatly from* the findings expected under low self-control theory.

3. In the SEXDEVI → VIOLENCE crosstabulation, _____ (_____%) of the respondents who participated in what could be labeled deviant sexual activities had committed a violent offense, compared to _____ (_____%) of those whose sexual activities were less atypical. This relationship is *weak / moderate / strong*. This relationship *is / is not* statistically significant.

The SEXDEVI → VIOLENCE table *does / does not* show that respondents who engaged in deviant sexual activities are more likely to engage in violence. The relationship between deviant sexual activities and violence found using Wave VII of the NYS data *is similar to / differs greatly from* the findings expected under low self-control theory.

4. In the LIE_OKAY → VIOLENCE crosstabulation, _____ (_____%) of the respondents who scored highest on the lying scale had committed a violent offense, compared to _____ (_____%) of those who scored 2 on the lying scale, and _____ (_____%) of those who scored the lowest on the lying scale. This relationship is *weak / moderate / strong*. This relationship *is / is not* statistically significant.

   The LIE_OKAY → VIOLENCE table *does / does not* show that respondents who consider lying acceptable (an indicator of impulsiveness) are more likely to engage in violence. The relationship between attitudes toward lying and violence found using Wave VII of the NYS data *is similar to / differs greatly from* the findings expected under low self-control theory.

5. Overall, it appears that our findings using the Wave VII of the NYS *support / do not support* low self-control theory.

Homework for Part X: "On Your Own" Questions
(Low Self-Control Theory)

Name: _____   Date: _____

Task: Include some control variables of your own in your test of low self-control theory. For example, does the relationship between atypical sexual behavior and participation in crime vary by income category?

Directions: Answer the following questions.

1. Which control variable did you choose, and why did you choose to control that factor?

2. What was the relationship between the independent and dependent variables before the addition of the control variable?

3. Did including the control variable change the relationship between the independent and dependent variables; that is, did the relationship between the two variables vary by control variable subcategory? In what way?

4. Based on your findings, what modifications or additions would you make to the low self-control theory?

5. Can you say that your testing supports low self-control theory? Why/why not?

If you included more than one control variable, you may summarize the findings here for future reference.

Selected Bibliography

Defining Crime: An Issue of Morality (Hagan)

Chambliss, William and Robert Seidman. 1982. *Law, Order, and Power*. Reading, MA: Addison-Wesley.

Morris, Norval and Gordon Hawkins. 1970. *The Honest Politicians' Guide to Crime Control*. Chicago, IL: University of Chicago Press.

Quinney, Richard. 1974. *Critique of Legal Order: Crime Control in Capitalist Society*. Boston, MA: Little, Brown.

Schur, Edwin. 1965. *Crimes Without Victims: Deviant Behavior and Public Policy*. Englewood Cliffs, NJ: Prentice Hall.

Turk, Austin. 1969. *Criminality and Legal Order*. Chicago, IL: Rand McNally.

Historical Explanations of Crime: From Demons to Politics (Huff)

Beccaria, Cesare. 1996. *Of Crimes and Punishments*. New York: Marsilio Publishers.

Becker, Howard. 1963. *Outsiders: Studies in the Sociology of Deviance*. New York: Free Press.

Bonger, Willem. 1916. *Criminality and Economic Conditions*. Boston, MA: Little, Brown.

Goring, Charles. 1972. *The English Convict: A Statistical Study*. Montclair, NJ: Patterson Smith.

Merton, Robert. 1957. *Social Theory and Social Structure*. Glencoe, IL: Free Press.

Quinney, Richard. 1974. *Critique of Legal Order: Crime Control in Capitalist Society*. Boston, MA: Little, Brown.

Racial Composition of Neighborhood and Fear of Crime (Chiricos, Hogan, and Gertz)

Covington, Jeanette and Ralph Taylor. 1991. "Fear of Crime in Urban Residential Neighborhoods: Implications of Between- and Within-Neighborhood Sources for Current Models." *The Sociological Quarterly* 32: 231–249.

Ferraro, Kenneth. 1995. *Fear of Crime: Interpreting Victimization Risk*. Albany, NY: SUNY Press.

Jackson, Pamela. 1989. *Minority Group Threat, Crime and Policing*. New York: Praeger.

LaGrange, Randy, Kenneth Ferraro, and Michael Supancic. 1992. "Perceived Risk and Fear of Crime: Role of Social and Physical Incivilities." *Journal of Research in Crime and Delinquency* 29: 311–334.

Moeller, Gertrude. 1989. "Fear of Criminal Victimization: The Effect of Neighborhood Racial Composition." *Sociological Inquiry* 59: 208–221.

Oretga, Suzanne and Jessie Myles. "Race and Gender Effects on the Fear of Crime: An Interactive Model with Age." *Criminology* 25: 133–152.

A Murder "Wave"? Trends in American Serial Homicide, 1940–1990 (Jenkins)

Best, Joel (Ed.). 1989. *Images of Issues*. New York: Aldine de Gruyter.

Goode, Erich. 1989. "The American Drug Panic of the 1980s." *Violence-Aggression-Terrorism* 3(4): 327–348.

Jenkins, Phillip. 1988. "Myth and Murder: The Serial Murder Panic of 1983–1985." *Criminal Justice Research Bulletin* 3(11): 1–7.

Levin, Jack and James Fox. 1985. *Mass Murder: America's Growing Menace*. New York: Plenum.

Leyton, Elliott. 1986. *Compulsive Killers*. New York: New York University Press.

Crack in Context: Politics and Media in the Making of a Drug Scare (Reinarman and Levine)

Bakalar, James and Lesten Grinspoon. 1987. *Drug Control in a Free Society*. Cambridge: Cambridge University Press.

Duster, Troy. 1970. *The Legislation of Morality*. New York: Free Press.

Gusfield, Joseph. 1963. *Symbolic Crusade*. Urbana: University of Illinois Press.

Lindesmith, Alfred. 1965. *The Addict and the Law*. Bloomington: Indiana University Press.

Morgan, Patricia. 1978. "The Legislation of Drug Law: Economic Crisis and Social Control." *Journal of Drug Issues* 8: 53–62.

Zinberg, Norman. 1984. *Drug Set and Setting: The Basis for Controlled Drug Use*. New Haven, CT: Yale University Press.

Did Crime Rise or Fall During the Reagan Presidency? (Steffensmeier and Harer)

Kamisar, Yale. 1972. "How to Use, Abuse—and Fight Back with—Crime Statistics." *Oklahoma Law Review* 25: 239–258.

O'Brien, Robert. 1985. *Crime and Victimization Data*. Beverly Hills, CA: Sage.

Osgood, D. Wayne, Patrick O'Malley, Jerald Bachman, and Lloyd Johnston. 1989. "Time Trends and Age Trends in Arrests and Self-Reported Illegal Behavior." *Criminology* 27: 389–416.

Smith, Dwayne. 1986. "The Era of Increased Violence in the United States: Age, Period, or Cohort Effect?" *Sociological Quarterly* 27: 239–251.

Steffensmeier, Darrell and Miles Harer. 1987. "Is the Crime Rate Really Falling? An Aging U.S. Population and Its Impact on the Nation's Crime Rate." *Journal of Research in Crime and Delinquency* 24: 23–48.

Reconciling Race and Class Differences in Self-Reported and Official Estimates of Delinquency (Elliott and Ageton)

Farrington, David. 1973. "Self-Reports of Deviant Behavior: Predictive and Stable?" *Journal of Criminal Law and Criminology* 64: 99–110.

Gold, Martin. "Undetected Delinquent Behavior." *Journal of Research in Crime and Delinquency* 3: 27–46.

Hardt, Robert and Sandra Peterson-Hardt. 1977. "On Determining the Quality of the Delinquency Self-Report Method." *Journal of Research in Crime and Delinquency* 14: 247–261.

Hindelang, Michael. 1978. "Race and Involvement in Common Law Personal Crimes." *American Sociological Review* 43: 93–109.

Short, James and Ivan Nye. 1958. "Extent of Unrecorded Juvenile Delinquency: Tentative Conclusions." *Journal of Criminal Law, Criminology, and Police Science* 49.

Williams, Jay and Martin Gold. 1972. "From Delinquent Behavior to Official Delinquency." *Social Problems* 20: 209–229.

You Can Get Anything You Want If You've Got the Bread (Chambliss)

Block, Alan and William Chambliss. 1981. *Organizing Crime*. New York: Elsevier.

Chambliss, William and Robert Seidman. 1971. *Law, Order and Power*. Reading, MA: Addison Wesley.

Cressey, Donald. 1969. *Theft of the Nation*. New York: Harper & Row.

Morgan, Murray. 1951. *Skid Road*. New York: Ballantine Books.

A Snowball's Chance in Hell: Doing Fieldwork with Active Residential Burglars (Wright et al.)

Berk, Richard and Joseph Adams. 1970. "Establishing Rapport with Deviant Groups." *Social Problems* 18: 102–117.

Cromwell, Paul, James Olson, and D'Aunn Avary. 1991. *Breaking and Entering: An Ethnographic Analysis of Burglary.* Newbury Park, CA: Sage.

Dunlap, Eloise, Bruce Johnson, Harry Sanabria, Elbert Holliday, Vicki Lipsey, Maurice Barnett, William Hopkins, Ira Sobel, Doris Randolph, and Ko-Lin Chin. 1990. "Studying Crack Users and Their Criminal Careers: The Scientific and Artistic Apsects of Locating Hard-to-Reach Subjects and Interviewing Them About Sensitive Topics." *Contemporary Drug Problems* 17: 121–144.

Hagedorn, John. 1990. "Back in the Field Again: Gang Research in the Nineties." Pp. 240–259 in *Gangs in America,* edited by C. Ronald Huff. Newbury Park, CA: Sage.

West, Gordon. 1980. "Access to Adolescent Deviants and Deviance." Pp. 31–44 in *Fieldwork Experience: Qualitative Approaches to Social Research,* edited by William Shaffir, Robert Stebbins, and Allan Turowitz. New York: St. Martin's.

Wright, Richard and Trevor Bennett. 1990. "Exploring the Offender's Persective: Observing and Interviewing Criminals." Pp. 138–151 in *Measurement Issues in Criminology,* edited by Kimberly Kempf. New York: Springer-Verlag.

The Poverty of a Classless Criminology: The American Society of Criminology 1991 Presidential Address (Hagan)

Brownfield, David. 1986. "Social Class and Violent Behavior." *Criminology* 24: 421–471.

Colvin, Mark and John Pauly. 1983. "A Critique of Criminology: Toward an Integrated Structural-Marxist Theory of Delinquency Production." *American Journal of Sociology* 89: 513–551.

Hagan, John, A. R. Gillis, and John Simpson. 1985. "The Class Structure of Gender and Delinquency: Toward a Power-Control Theory of Common Delinquent Behavior." *American Journal of Sociology* 90: 1151–1178.

Johnson, Richard. 1980. "Social Class and Delinquent Behavior: A New Test." *Criminology* 18: 86–93.

Tittle, Charles and Robert Meier. 1990. "Specifying the SES Delinquency Relationship." *Criminology* 28: 271–299.

Weis, Joseph. 1987. "Social Class and Crime." In *Positive Criminology,* edited by Michael Gottfredson and Travis Hirschi. Beverly Hills, CA: Sage.

Toward a Theory of Race, Crime, and Urban Inequality (Sampson and Wilson)

Sampson, Robert. 1987. "Urban Black Violence: The Effect of Male Joblessness and Family Disruption." *American Journal of Sociology* 93: 348–382.

Sampson, Robert and W. B. Groves. 1989. "Community Structure and Crime: Testing Social Disorganization Theory." *American Journal of Sociology* 94: 774–802.

Shaw, Clifford and Henry McKay. 1942. *Juvenile Delinquency and Urban Areas.* Chicago: University of Chicago Press.

Wilson, William Julius. 1986. "The Urban Underclass in Advanced Industrial Society." In *The New Urban Reality,* edited by Paul E. Peterson. Washington, DC: Brookings Institution.

Wilson, William Julius. 1987. *The Truly Disadvantaged: The Inner City, the Underclass, and Public Policy.* Chicago: University of Chicago Press.

Age and the Explanation of Crime (Hirschi and Gottfredson)

Blumstein, Alfred and Jacqueline Cohen. 1979. "Estimation of Individual Crime Rates from Arrest Records." *Journal of Criminal Law and Criminology* 70:4.

Elliott, Delbert, Suzanne Ageton, and Rachelle Canter. 1979. "An Integrated Theoretical Perspective on Delinquent Behavior." *Journal of Research in Crime and Delinquency* 16: 3–27.

Empey, LaMar. 1978. *American Delinquency*. Homewood, IL: Dorsey.

Greenberg, David. 1979. "Delinquency and the Age Structure of Society." Pp. 586–620 in *Criminology Review Yearbook*, edited by Sheldon L. Messinger and Egon Bittner. Beverly Hills, CA: Sage.

Petersilia, Joan. 1980. "Criminal Career Research: A Review of Recent Evidence." *Crime and Justice: An Annual Review of Research*, Vol. 2, edited by Norval Morris and Michael Tonry. Chicago: University of Chicago Press.

Explaining the Gender Gap in Delinquency: Peer Influence and Moral Evaluations of Behavior (Mears, Ploeger, and Warr)

Caspi, Avshalom, Donald Lynam, Terrie Moffitt, and Phil Silva. 1993. "Unraveling Girls' Delinquency: Biological, Dispositional, and Contextual Contributions to Adolescent Misbehavior." *Developmental Psychology* 29: 19–30.

Gibbs, John, Kevin Arnold, and Jennifer Burkhard. 1984. "Sex Differences in the Expression of Moral Judgment." *Child Development* 55: 1040–1043.

Gilligan, Carol. 1982. *In a Different Voice: Psychological Theory and Women's Development*. Cambridge, MA: Harvard University Press.

Sutherland, Edwin. 1947. *Principles of Criminology*. 4th ed. Philadelphia, Lippincott.

Warr, Mark and Mark Stafford. 1991. "The Influence of Delinquent Peers: What They Think or What They Do?" *Criminology* 29: 851–866.

Juvenile Delinquency and Urban Areas (Shaw and McKay)

Park, Robert, Ernest Burgess, and Roderick McKenzie. 1925. *The City*. Chicago, IL: University of Chicago Press.

Shaw, Clifford. 1929. *Delinquency Areas*. Chicago, IL: University of Chicago Press.

Wirth, Louis. 1928. *The Ghetto*. Chicago, IL: University of Chicago Press.

Social Interaction and Community Crime: Examining the Importance of Neighborhood Networks (Bellair)

Bursik, Robert, Jr. 1988. "Social Disorganization and Theories of Crime and Delinquency: Problems and Prospects." *Criminology* 26: 519–551.

Bursik, Robert, Jr. and Harold Grasmick. 1993. *Neighborhoods and Crime*. New York: Lexington Books.

Granovetter, Mark. 1973. "The Strength of Weak Ties." *American Journal of Sociology* 78: 1360–1380.

Heitgard, Janet and Robert Bursik, Jr. 1987. "Extra-Community Dynamics and the Ecology of Delinquency." *American Journal of Sociology* 92: 775–787.

Sampson, Robert and W. Byron Groves. 1989. "Community Structure and Crime: Testing Social-Disorganization Theory." *American Journal of Sociology* 94: 774–802.

A Theory of Crime: Differential Association (Sutherland)

Bordua, David. 1962. "Some Comments on Theories of Group Delinquency." *Sociological Inquiry* 32: 245–260.

Cressey, Donald. 1952. "Application and Verification of the Differential Association Theory." *Journal of Criminal Law, Criminology, and Police Science* 43: 43–52.

Eynon, Thomas and Walter Reckless. 1961. "Companionship at Delinquency Onset." *British Journal of Criminology* 13: 162–170.

Glaser, Daniel. 1956. "Criminological Theories and Behavioral Images." *American Journal of Sociology* 61: 433–444.

Reiss, Albert, Jr. and Lewis Rhodes. 1964. "An Empirical Test of Differential Association

Theory." *Journal of Research in Crime and Delinquency* 1: 5–18.

Short, James, Jr. 1960. "Differential Association as a Hypothesis: Problems of Empirical Testing." *Social Problems* 8: 14–25.

The Current State of Differential Association Theory (Matsueda)

Akers, Ronald, Marvin Krohn, Lonn Lanza-Kaduce, and Marcia Radosevich. 1979. "Social Learning and Deviant Behavior: A General Test of a Specific Theory." *American Sociological Review* 44: 635–655.

Cloward, Richard and Lloyd Ohlin. 1960. *Delinquency and Opportunity*. New York: Free Press.

Cressey, Donald. 1954. "The Differential Association Theory and Compulsive Crimes." *Journal of Criminal Law and Criminology* 45: 29–40.

Matsueda, Ross. 1982. "Testing Control Theory and Differential Association: A Causal Modeling Approach." *American Sociological Review* 47: 489–504.

Sutherland, Edwin. 1947. *Principles of Criminology*. 4th ed. Philadelphia, PA: Lippincott.

Sutherland, Edwin and Donald Cressey. 1978. *Criminology*. 10th ed. Philadelphia, PA: Lippincott.

Sykes, Gresham and David Matza. 1957. Techniques of Neutralization: A Theory of Delinquency." *American Sociological Review* 22: 664–670.

Social Structure and Anomie (Merton)

Durkheim, Emile. 1951. *Suicide: A Study in Sociology*. New York: Free Press.

Horney, Karen. 1937. *The Neurotic Personality of Our Time*. New York: W. W. Norton and Company Inc.

Mayo, Elton. 1933. *The Human Problems of an Industrial Civilization*. New York: The Macmillan Company.

Plant, James. 1937. *Personality and the Cultural Pattern*. London: Oxford University Press.

Siegfried, Andre. 1927. *America Comes of Age: A French Analysis*. New York: Harcourt, Brace and Company.

General Strain Theory and Delinquency: A Replication and Extension (Paternoster and Mazerolle)

Agnew, Robert. 1992. "Foundation for a General Strain Theory of Crime and Delinquency." *Criminology* 30: 47–87.

Agnew, Robert and Helene White. 1992. "An Empirical Test of General Strain Theory." *Criminology* 30: 475–499.

Clinard, Marshall. 1964. *Anomie and Deviant Behavior*. New York: Free Press.

Cloward, Richard and Lloyd Ohlin. 1960. *Delinquency and Opportunity*. New York: Free Press.

Merton, Robert. 1938. "Social Structure and Anomie." *American Sociological Review* 3: 672–682.

The Subculture of Violence (Wolfgang)

Bandura, Albert and R. H. Walters. 1959. *Adolescent Aggression*. New York: Ronald Press.

Berkowitz, Leonard. 1962. *Aggression*. New York: McGraw Hill.

Lawson, Reed. 1965. *Frustration: The Development of a Scientific Concept*. New York: MacMillan.

Reckless, Walter. 1961. *The Crime Problem*. 3rd ed. New York: Appleton Century Crofts.

Trasler, Gordon. 1962. *The Explanation of Criminality*. London: Routledge and Kegan Paul.

Racial Inequality and Homicide Rates (Messner and Golden)

Balkwell, James. 1983. "Ethnic Inequality and the Rate of Homicide." *Social Forces* 69: 53–70.

Blau, Judith and Peter Blau. 1982. "The Cost of Inequality: Metropolitan Structure and Criminal Violence." *American Sociological Review* 47: 114–129.

Blau, Peter and Schwartz, Joseph. 1984. *Crosscutting Social Circles*. New York: Academic Press.

Golden, Reid and Steven Messner. 1987. "Dimensions of Racial Inequality and Rates of Violent Crime." *Criminology* 25: 525–541.

Land, Kenneth, Patricia McCall, and Lawrence Cohen. 1990. "Structural Covariates of Homicide Rates." *American Journal of Sociology* 95: 922–963.

Logan, John and Steven Messner. 1987. "Racial Residential Segregation and Suburban Violent Crime." *Social Science Quarterly* 68: 922–963.

Messner, Steven. 1989. "Economic Discrimination and Societal Homicide Rates: Further Evidence on the Cost of Inequality." *American Sociological Review* 54: 597–611.

Sampson, Robert. 1987. "Urban Black Violence." *American Journal of Sociology* 93: 348–382.

Wilson, William Julius. 1987. *The Truly Disadvantaged: The Inner City, the Underclass, and Public Policy*. Chicago: University of Chicago Press.

Causes and Prevention of Juvenile Delinquency (Hirschi)

Hirschi, Travis. 1969. *Causes of Delinquency*. Berkeley: University of California Press.

Matza, David. 1964. *Delinquency and Drift*. New York: Wiley.

Thrasher, Frederick. 1963. *The Gang*. Chicago: University of Chicago Press.

Toby, Jackson. 1957. "Social Disorgaization and Stake in Conformity: Complementary Factors in the Predatory Behavior of Young Hoodlums." *Journal of Criminal Law, Criminology, and Police Science* 48: 12–17.

Wilson, James. 1975. *Thinking About Crime*. New York: Vintage.

School Delinquency and the School Social Bond (Jenkins)

Fehrmann, P., T. Keith, and T. Reimers. 1987. "Home Influence on School Learning: Direct and Indirect Effects of Parental Involvement on High School Grades." *Journal of Educational Research* 80: 330–337.

Gold, M. 1978. "Scholastic Experiences, Self-Esteem, and Delinquent Behavior: A Theory of Alternative Schools." *Crime and Delinquency* 24: 290–308.

Hirschi, Travis. 1969. *Causes of Delinquency*. Berkeley: University of California Press.

Krohn, Marvin and J. Massey. 1980. "Social Control and Delinquent Behavior: An Examination of the Elements of the Social Bond." *The Sociological Quarterly* 21: 529–543.

Thornberry, Terrance, A. Lizotte, Marvin Krohn, M. Farnworth, and S. Jang. 1991. "Testing Interactional Theory: An Examination of Reciprocal Causal Relationships among Family, School, and Delinquency." *Journal of Criminal Law and Criminology* 82: 3–35.

Labeling Criminals (Schur)

Becker, Howard. 1963. *Outsiders: Studies in the Sociology of Deviance*. New York: Free Press.

Lemert, Edwin. 1951. *Social Pathology*. New York: McGraw-Hill Book Company.

Merton, Robert. 1961. "Social Problems and Sociological Theory." In *Contemporary Social Problems*, edited by R. Merton and R. Nisbet. New York: Harcourt, Brace and World, Inc.

Schur, Edwin. 1963. "Recent Social Problems Texts: An Essay-Review." *Social Problems* 10: 287–292.

Tannenbaum, Frank. 1938. *Crime and the Community*. New York: Ginn and Company.

Deviance on Record: Techniques for Labeling Child Abusers in Official Documents (Margolin)

Best, Joel. 1990. *Threatened Children: Rhetoric and Concern about Child-Victims*. Chicago: The University of Chicago Press.

Cicourel, Aaron. 1968. *The Social Organization of Juvenile Justice*. New York: John Wiley and Sons.

Conrad, Peter and Joseph Schneider. 1980. *Deviance and Medicalization*. St. Louis, MO: C. V. Mosby.

Pride, Mary. 1986. *The Child Abuse Industry.* Westchester, IL: Crossway.

Rosenhan, D. L. 1973. "On Being Sane in Insane Places." *Science* 179: 250–258.

Culture Conflict and Crime (Sellin)

Glueck, Eleanor. 1937. "Culture Conflict and Delinquency." *Mental Hygiene* 21: 46–66.

Shaw, Clifford. 1930. *The Jack-Roller.* Chicago: University of Chicago Press.

White, William. 1933. *Crimes and Criminals.* New York: Farrar and Rinehart.

Wirth, Louis. 1931. "Culture Conflict and Misconduct." *Social Forces* 9: 484–492.

Young, Pauline. 1936. "Social Problems in the Education of the Immigrant Child." *American Sociological Review* 1: 419–429.

The Code of the Streets (Anderson)

Anderson, Elijah. 1978. *A Place on the Corner.* Chicago: University of Chicago Press.

Anderson, Elijah. 1989. "Sex Codes and Family Life Among Poor Inner-City Youths." In *The Ghetto Underclass: Social Science Perspectives,* edited by William Julius Wilson. Special edition of *The Annals of the American Academy of Political and Social Science* 501: 59–78.

Anderson, Elijah. 1990. *Streetwise: Race, Class and Change in an Urban Community.* Chicago: University of Chicago Press.

Drake, St. Clair and Horace Cayton. 1962. *Black Metropolis.* New York: Harper & Row.

Wolfgang, Marvin and Franco Ferracuti. 1967. *The Subculture of Violence.* London: Tavistock.

Conflict and Criminality (Turk)

Becker, Howard. 1963. *Outsiders: Studies in the Sociology of Deviance.* New York: The Free Press of Glencoe.

Bonger, William. 1916. *Criminality and Economic Conditions.* Boston, MA: Little, Brown.

Sellin, Thorsten. 1938. *Culture Conflict and Crime.* New York: Social Science Research Council.

Simmel, Georg. 1955. *Conflict.* Glencoe, IL: Free Press.

Sutherland, Edwin. 1949. *White Collar Crime.* New York: Dryden.

Vold, George. 1958. *Theoretical Criminology.* New York: Oxford University Press.

A Tale of Three Cities: Labor Markets and Homicide (Crutchfield, Glusker, and Bridges)

Chiricos, Theodore. 1987. "Rates of Crime and Unemployment: An Analysis of Aggregate Research Evidence." *Social Problems* 34: 187–211.

Crutchfield, Robert. 1989. "Labor Stratification and Violent Crime." *Social Forces* 68: 489–512.

Crutchfield, Robert and Susan Pitchford. 1997. "Work and Crime: The Effects of Labor Stratification." *Social Forces* 76: 93–118.

Kalleberg, Arne and Aage Sorenson. 1979. "The Sociology of Labor Markets." *Annual Review of Sociology* 5: 351–379.

Wilson, William Julius. 1987. *The Truly Disadvantaged: The Inner City, the Underclass, and Public Policy.* Chicago: University of Chicago Press.

Toward a Political Economy of Crime (Chambliss)

Chambliss, William. 1973. *Sociological Readings in the Conflict Perspective.* Reading, MA: Addison-Wesley.

Chambliss, William. 1974. "The State, the Law and the Definition of Behavior as Criminal or Delinquent." In *Handbook of Criminology,* edited by Daniel Glaser. Chicago: Rand McNally.

Duster, Troy. 1970. *The Legislation of Morality: Law, Drugs and Moral Judgement.* New York: Free Press.

Gusfield, Joseph. 1963. *Symbolic Crusade: Status Politics and the American Temperance Movement.* Urbana: University of Illinois Press.

Hall, Jerome. 1952. *Theft, Law and Society*. Indianapolis, IN: Bobbs-Merrill and Co.

Causes of Crime: A Radical View
(Lynch and Groves)

Blau, Judith and Peter Blau. 1982. "The Cost of Inequality: Metropolitan Structure and Criminal Violence." *American Sociological Review* 47: 114–129.

Daly, Kathleen and Meda Chesney-Lind. 1988. "Feminism and Criminology." *Justice Quarterly* 5(4): 497–538.

Hagan, John, A. R. Gillis, and John Simpson. 1985. "The Class Structure of Gender and Delinquency: Toward a Power-Control Theory of Common Delinquent Behavior." *American Journal of Sociology* 90(6): 1151–1178.

Messerschmidt, James. 1986. *Capitalism, Patriarchy, and Crime: Toward a Socialist Feminist Criminology*. Totowa, NJ: Rowman and Littlefield.

Schur, Edwin. 1984. *Labeling Women Deviant: Gender, Stigma, and Social Control*. New York: McGraw Hill.

Taylor, Ian, Paul Walton, and Jock Young. 1973. *The New Criminology*. London: Routledge and Kegan Paul.

Social Change and Crime Rate Trends: A Routine Activity Approach
(Cohen and Felson)

Ferdinand, Theodore. 1970. "Demographic Shifts and Criminality." *British Journal of Criminology* 10: 169–175.

Gould, Leroy. 1969. "The Changing Structure of Property Crime in an Affluent Society." *Social Forces* 48: 50–59.

Hindelang, Michael. 1976. *Criminal Victimization in Eight American Cities: A Descriptive Analysis of Common Theft and Assault*. Cambridge: Ballinger.

Kobrin, Frances. 1976. "The Primary Individual and the Family: Changes in Living Arrangements in the U.S. Since 1940." *Journal of Marriage and the Family* 38: 233–239.

Land, Kenneth and Marcus Felson. 1976. "A General Framework for Building Dynamic Macro Social Indicator Models." *American Journal of Sociology* 85: 565–604.

A Power-Control Theory of Common Delinquent Behavior
(Hagan, Simpson, and Gillis)

Colvin, Mark and John Pauly. 1983. "A Critique of Criminology: Toward an Integrated Structural-Marxist Theory of Delinquency Production." *American Journal of Sociology* 89: 513–552.

Elliott, Delbert and Swan Ageton. 1980. "Reconciling Race and Class Differences in Self-Reported and Official Estimates of Delinquency." *American Sociological Review* 45: 95–110.

Hagan, John, John Simpson, and A. R. Gillis. 1979. "The Sexual Stratification of Social Control." *British Journal of Sociology* 30: 25–38.

Jensen, Gary, M. L. Erickson, and Jack Gibbs. 1978. "Perceived Risk of Punishment and Self-Report Delinquency." *Social Forces* 57: 57–78.

Robinson, Robert and Jonathan Kelly. 1974. "Class as Conceived by Marx and Dahrendorf." *American Sociological Review* 44: 38–58.

A Bio-Psychological Theory of Choice
(Wilson and Herrnstein)

Beccaria, Cesare. 1963 (1764). *On Crimes and Punishments*. Trans. Henry Paolucci. Indianapolis, IN: Library of Liberal Arts/Bobbs-Merrill.

Herrnstein, Richard. 1983. "Some Criminogenic Traits of Offenders." In *Crime and Public Policy*, edited by James Q. Wilson. San Francisco, CA: ICS Press.

Wilson, James Q. 1983. *Thinking About Crime*. New York: Basic Books.

Feminist Theory, Crime, and Justice (Simpson)

Daly, Kathleen. 1989. "Neither Conflict nor Labeling nor Paternalism Will Suffice: Intersections of Race, Ethnicity, Gender, and Family in Criminal Court Decisions." *Crime and Delinquency* 35: 136–168.

Daly, Kathleen and Meda Chesney-Lind. 1988. "Feminism and Criminology." *Justice Quarterly* 5: 497–538.

Glueck, Sheldon and Eleanor Glueck. 1934. *Five Hundred Delinquent Women*. New York: Alfred A. Knopf.

Hagan, John, John Simpson, and A. R. Gillis. 1979. "The Sexual Stratification of Social Control: A Gender-Based Perspective on Crime and Delinquency." *British Journal of Sociology* 92: 788–816.

Klein, Dorie. 1973. "The Etiology of Female Crime: A Review of the Literature." *Issues in Criminology* 8: 3–29.

Laub, John and M. Joan McDermott. 1985. "An Analysis of Serious Crime by Young Black Women." *Criminology* 23: 81–98.

Nagel, Ilene. 1981. "Sex Differences in the Processing of Criminal Defendants." In A. Morris and L. Gelsthorpe (eds.), *Women and Crime*. Cambridge: Cambridge Institute of Criminology.

Visher, Christy. 1983. "Gender, Police Arrest Decisions, and Notions of Chivalry." *Criminology* 21: 5–28.

The Nature of Criminality: Low Self-Control (Gottfredson and Hirschi)

Bentham, Jeremy. 1970 (1789). *An Introduction to the Principles of Morals and Legislation*. London: The Athlone Press.

Glueck, Sheldon and Eleanor Glueck. 1950. *Unraveling Juvenile Delinquency*. Cambridge, MA: Harvard University Press.

Gottfredson, Michael. 1984. *Victims of Crime: The Dimensions of Risk*. London: HMSO.

Robins, Lee. 1966. *Deviant Children Grown Up*. Baltimore: Williams and Wilkins.

West, Donald and David Farrington. 1973. *Who Becomes Delinquent?* London: Heinemann.

Toward an Age-Graded Theory of Informal Social Control (Sampson and Laub)

Blumstein, Alfred, Jacqueline Cohen, Jeffrey Roth, and Christy Visher (Eds.). 1986. *Criminal Careers and Career Criminals*. Washington, DC: National Academy Press.

Coleman, James. 1988. "Social Capital in the Creation of Human Capital." *American Journal of Sociology* 94: 95–120.

Elder, Glen. 1975. "Age Differentiation and the Life Course." Pp. 165–190 in *Annual Review of Sociology*, Vol. 1, edited by Alex Inkeles. Palo Alto, CA: Annual Reviews.

Kornhauser, Ruth. 1978. *Social Sources of Delinquency*. Chicago: University of Chicago Press.

Loeber, Rolf and Marc LeBlanc. 1990. "Toward a Developmental Criminology." Pp. 375–437 in *Crime and Justice*, Vol. 12, edited by Michael Tonry and Norval Morris. Chicago: University of Chicago Press.

Rutter, Michael, D. Quinton, and J. Hill. 1990. "Adult Outcomes of Institution-Reared Children: Males and Females Compared." Pp. 135–157 in *Straight and Devious Pathways from Childhood to Adulthood*, edited by Lee N. Robbins and Michael Rutter. Cambridge: Cambridge University Press.

Control Balance Theory (Tittle)

Elliott, Delbert. 1985. "The Assumption That Theories Can Be Combined with Increasing Explanatory Power: Theoretical Integrations." Pp. 123–149 in *Theoretical Methods in Criminology*, edited by Robert Meier. Beverly Hills, CA: Sage.

Hagan, John, A. R. Gillis, and John Simpson. 1985. "The Class Structure of Gender and Delinquency: Toward a Power-Control Theory of Common Delinquent Behavior." *American Journal of Sociology* 90: 1151–1178.

Hirschi, Travis. 1969. *Causes of Delinquency.* Berkeley: University of California Press.

Messner, Steven, Marvin Krohn, and Allen Liska (Eds.). 1989. *Theoretical Integration in the Study of Deviance and Crime: Problems and Prospects.* Albany: SUNY Press.

Messner, Steven and Richard Rosenfeld. 1994. *Crime and the American Dream.* Belmont, CA: Wadsworth.

White-Collar Criminality (Sutherland)

Cohen, Albert, Alfred Lindesmith, and Karl Schuessler (Eds.). 1956. *The Sutherland Papers.* Bloomington: Indiana University Press.

Sutherland, Edwin. 1945. "Is 'White-Collar Crime' Crime?" *American Sociological Review* 10: 132–139.

Sutherland, Edwin. 1949. *White Collar Crime.* New York: Dryden Press.

The Criminal Elite (Coleman)

Braithwaite, John. 1984. *Corporate Crime in the Pharmaceutical Industry.* London: Routledge and Kegan Paul.

Duster, Troy. 1970. *The Legislation of Morality.* New York: Free Press.

Schur, Edwin. 1965. *Crimes Without Victims.* Englewood Cliffs, NJ: Prentice-Hall.

Stone, Christopher. 1975. *Where the Law Ends: The Social Control of Corporate Behavior.* New York: Harper & Row.

From Mafia to Cosa Nostra (Cressey)

Anderson, Robert. 1965. "From Mafia to Cosa Nostra." *American Journal of Sociology* 61: 302–310.

Becker, Howard. 1963. *Outsiders: Studies in the Sociology of Deviance.* New York: Free Press.

Johnson, Earl. 1962. "Organized Crime: Challenge to the American Legal System." *Journal of Criminal Law, Criminology, and Police Science* 53: 399–425.

Tyler, Gus. 1962. "The Roots of Organized Crime." *Crime and Delinquency* 8: 325–338.

Myths and Organized Crime: Is There a Mafia, and Does It Really Matter? (Kenny and Finckenauer)

Albini, J. 1976. "Syndicated Crime: Its Structure, Function and Modus Operandi." In *The Crime Society: Organized Crime and Corruption in America,* edited by F. Ianni and E. Ruess-Ianni. New York: Times-Mirror.

Bell, Daniel. 1953. "Crime as an American Way of Life." In *The Sociology of Crime and Delinquency,* edited by Marvin E. Wolfgang, Leonard Savitz, and Norman Johnston. New York: John Wiley and Sons.

Hawkins, Gordon. 1969. "God and the Mafia." *The Public Interest* 14: 24–51.

Jenkins, Philip and Gary Potter. 1987. "The Politics and Mythology of Organized Crime: A Philidelphia Case Study." *Journal of Criminal Justice* 15: 473–484.

Smith, Dwight. 1975. *The Mafia Mystique.* New York: Basic Books.

Ganging (Thrasher)

Cloward, Richard and Lloyd Ohlin. 1960. *Delinquency and Opportunity: A Theory of Delinquent Gangs.* Glencoe, IL: Free Press.

Cohen, Albert. 1955. *Delinquent Boys.* Glencoe, IL: Free Press.

Puffer, J. Adams. 1912. *The Boy and His Gang.* Boston: Houghton Mifflin Company.

Whyte, William Foote. 1943. *Street Corner Society: The Social Structure of an Italian Slum.* Chicago: University of Chicago Press.

Wirth, Louis. 1928. *The Ghetto.* Chicago: University of Chicago Press.

The Social Organization of Street Gang Activity in an Urban Ghetto (Venkatesh)

Bursik, Robert, Jr. and Harold Grasmick. 1993. *Neighborhoods and Crime.* New York: Lexington.

Curry, David and Irving Spergel. 1992. "Gang Involvement and Delinquency among Hispanic and African-American Males." *Journal of Research in Crime and Delinquency* 29(3): 273–292.

Fagan, Jeffrey. 1996. "Gangs, Drugs, and Neighborhood Change." Pp. 39–74 in *Gangs in America*, 2nd ed., edited by C. Ronald Huff. Newbury Park, CA: Sage.

Horowitz, Ruth. 1987. "Community Tolerance of Gang Violence." *Social Problems* 38(4): 52–65.

Jankowski, Martin. 1991. *Islands in the Street: Gangs and the American Urban Society*. Berkeley: University of California Press.

Klein, Malcolm. 1995. *The American Street Gang: Its Nature, Prevalence and Control*. New York: Oxford University Press.

Historical Trends in Violent Crime: A Critical Review of the Evidence (Gurr)

Archer, Dane and Rosemary Gartner. 1976. "Violent Acts and Violent Times: A Comparative Approach to Postwar Homicide Rates." *American Sociological Review* 41: 937–963.

Block, Richard. 1977. *Violent Crime: Environment, Interaction, and Death*. Lexington, MA: Lexington Books.

Brearley, H. C. 1932. *Homicide in the United States*. Chapel Hill: University of North Carolina Press.

Given, James. 1977. *Society and Homicide in Thirteenth-Century England*. Stanford: Stanford University Press.

Hoffman, F. L. 1925. *The Homicide Problem*. Newark, NJ: Prudential Press.

Homicide and Aggravated Assault (Wolfgang and Zahn)

Archer, Dane and Rosemary Gartner. 1977. "Homicide in 110 Nations: The Development of the Comparative Crime Data File." *International Annals of Criminology* 16: 109–139.

Farley, Reynolds. 1980. "Homicide Trends in the United States." *Demography* 17: 177–188.

Wolfgang, Marvin. 1958. *Patterns in Criminal Homicide*. New York: Wiley.

Zahn, Margaret. "Homicide in the Twentieth-Century United States." Pp. 111–131 in *History and Crime*, edited by James Inciardi and Charles Faupel. Beverly Hills, CA: Sage.

Drug Use and Abuse in America (Staley)

Barnett, Randy. 1987. "Curing the Drug-Law Addiction." In *Dealing With Drugs: Consequences of Government Control*, edited by Ronald Hamowy. Lexington, MA: Lexington Books.

Faupel, Charles. 1988. "Heroin Use, Crime, and Employment Status." *Journal of Drug Issues* 18(3): 467–479.

Goldstein, Paul. 1985. "The Drugs/Violence Nexus: A Tripartite Conceptual Framework." *Journal of Drug Issues* 15(4): 493–506.

Liska, Ken. 1990. *Drugs and the Human Body: With Implications for Society*. 3rd ed. New York: Macmillan.

McBride, Duane and Clyde McCoy. 1982. "Crime and Drugs: The Issues and Literature." *Journal of Drug Issues* 12(2): 137–152.

The Drug Use–Delinquency Connection in Adolescence (White)

Anglin, M. D. and G. Speckart. 1988. "Narcotics Use and Crime: A Multisample, Multimethod Analysis." *Criminology* 26: 197–233.

Blumstein, Alfred, D. P. Farrington, and S. Moitra. 1985. "Delinquency Careers: Innocents, Desisters, and Persisters." In *Crime and Justice: An Annual Review of Research*, Vol. 7, edited by M. H. Tonry and N. Morris. Chicago: University Press.

Carpenter, C., B. Glassner, B. D. Johnson, and J. Loughlin. 1988. *Kids, Drugs, and Crime*. Lexington, MA: Lexington Books.

Elliott, Delbert and Suzanne Ageton. 1981. *The Epidemiology of Delinquent Behavior and Drug Use Among American Adolescents, 1976–78*. Boulder, CO: Behavioral Research Institute.

Elliott, Delbert, D. H. Huizinga, and Suzanne Ageton. 1985. *Explaining Delinquency and Drug Use*. Beverly Hills, CA: Sage.

Kandel, D. B. 1975. "Stages in Adolescent Involvement in Drug Use." *Science* 190: 912–914.

Victim-Offender Mediation in the Italian Juvenile Justice System: The Role of the Social Worker (Baldry)

Braithwaite, John and P. Pettit. 1990. *Not Just Desserts. A Republican Theory of Criminal Justice.* Oxford: Claredon Press.

Davis, G. 1992. *Making Amends: Mediation and Reparation in Criminal Justice.* London: Routledge.

Galaway, B. 1988. "Crime Victims and Offender Mediation as a Social Work Strategy." *Social Service Review* 62: 668–683.

Umbreit, M. and R. Coates. 1993. "Cross-Site Analysis of Victim-Offender Mediation in Four States." *Crime and Delinquency* 39: 565–585.

Wright, M. and B. Galaway. 1989. *Mediation and Criminal Justice: Victims, Offenders and Community.* London: Sage.

The Family Model of the Criminal Process: Reintegrative Shaming (Braithwaite)

Andenaes, J. 1974. *Punishment and Deterrence.* Ann Arbor: University of Michigan Press.

Bayley, D. H. 1976. *Forces of Order: Police Behavior in Japan and the United States.* Berkeley: University of California Press.

Bott, E. 1971. *Family and Social Network: Roles, Norms and External Relationships in Ordinary Urban Families.* 2nd ed. New York: Free Press.

Canter, R. J. 1982. "Family Correlates of Male and Female Delinquency." *Criminology* 20: 149–167.

Shearing, C. D. and P. C. Stenning. 1984. "From Panopticon to Disney World: The Development of Discipline." In *Perspectives in Criminal Law: Essays in Honor of John L. J. Edwards,* edited by A. N. Doob and E. L. Greenspoon. Aurora, Ontario: Canada Law Book Inc.

Strengthening Institutions and Rethinking the American Dream (Messner and Rosenfeld)

Adams, James. 1931. *Epic of America.* Boston: Little, Brown.

Blumstein, Alfred. 1993. "Making Rationality Relevant: The American Society of Criminology 1992 Presidential Address." *Criminology* 31: 1–16.

Braithwaite, John. 1989. *Crime, Shame and Reintegration.* New York: Cambridge University Press.

Feeley, Malcolm and Jonathan Simon. 1992. "The New Penology: Notes on the Emerging Strategy of Corrections and Its Implications." *Criminology* 30: 449–474.

Rosenfeld, Richard and Kimberly Kempf. 1991. "The Scope and Purposes of Corrections: Exploring Alternative Responses to Crowding." *Crime and Delinquency* 37: 481–505.

Index

A

Abandoned houses, 225, 227
Abbott, Daniel, 494
Accessories to crime, 433
Adams, Charles Francis, 430
Adams, James Truslow, 574–575, 588–589
Adolescent criminals. *See* Juvenile delinquency
African-Americans. *See* Blacks
Africville, 8–9
Age
  crime rates and, 61–62, 64–65, 540
  criminal behavior and, 115, 138–142
  crosstabulation tables for, 101
  drug use and, 505
  fear of crime and, 101
  frequency tables for, 94, 219
  juvenile delinquency and, 139–140, 164, 166, 271–272, 273–274, 275–276
  life-course events and, 140–141
  subculture of violence theory and, 255
  theories of crime and, 138–141
  types of crimes and, 139–140
Ageton, Suzanne, 59, 67
Aggression
  black culture and, 252
  street culture and, 303–313
  subculture of violence theory and, 252, 256, 257
  See also Violence
Agnew, Spiro, 332
Alcohol consumption
  current trends in, 500
  driving under the influence of, 497–498
  low self-control theory and, 595

public health concerns and, 499
violent crime and, 498, 502
See also Drug use
Alito, Samuel A., Jr., 468
America. *See* United States
American Correctional Association, 577
American Criminal, The (Hooton), 19
American Dream
  conventional crime policies and, 581–582
  cultural regeneration and, 587–588
  resolving contradictions in, 588
  societal maturation and, 588–589
American Jail Association, 542
Anderson, Annelise Graebner, 462
Anderson, Elijah, 298, 303
Anger
  general strain theory and, 214, 215
  See also Aggression
Anomie theory, 152–153, 201–215
  overview of, 201–206
  racial inequality and, 263
  social class and, 205–206
  strain theory and, 207–215
  subculture of violence theory and, 250
Anslinger, Harry, 458
Antisocial behavior, 511
Archer, Dane, 495
Arrest rates
  juvenile delinquents, 177–182
  white-collar criminals, 439
Ascriptive inequalities, 260
Assault, 488
Atlantic Monthly, 536
Auditors, 445

Autonomous deviance, 411–412, 417–418

B

Baby boom generation, 64, 65
Babysitters, 285–293
Baldry, Anna, 536, 544
Barnes, Harry Elmer, 14
Barzini, Luigi, 461
Beccaria, Cesare, 15–16
Beck, James M., 431
Becker, Howard, 23, 281
Belief systems
  juvenile delinquency and, 271
  school rules and, 278
Bell, Daniel, 463–464, 466
Bellair, Paul, 152, 183
Bentham, Jeremy, 15, 16
Berger, Peter, 582
Bio-psychological theory of choice, 386–388
  data analysis exercise on, 516–520
  homework assignments on, 527–532
Bird, Jake, 40, 41
Bivariate analyses, 517
Blacks
  aggression and, 252
  crime rate and, 126–137, 324–326, 542
  economic stratification and, 337, 339
  fear of crimes by, 30–35, 100
  incarceration of, 393–394, 542, 577–578
  neighbor networks among, 183–184
  police behavior toward, 392
  poverty among, 127–131

Blacks (*continued*)
    serial killers as, 41–42
    sexual assault and, 391
    street culture and, 303–313
    violent crimes and, 126–137,
      324–326
    See also Race/ethnicity
Blackstone community study, 473–
    486
Blau, Judith and Peter, 246
Blumstein, Alfred, 577
Bonger, Willem, 21, 23, 299, 342,
    381
Bootlegging gangs, 451
Brace, Charles, 116
Bradley, Bill, 30
Braithwaite, John, 447, 536, 553
Brecher, Edward, 52
Bribery, 431, 433
Bridges, George, 299, 321
Brokaw, Tom, 50
Broken-window theory, 565
Brown, Dee, 123
Bundy, Ted, 37–38, 39
Burgess, Ernest, 152
Burglary
    control deficits and, 409–410
    drug use and, 506–507, 511
    field research on, 83–89
    routine activity studies on, 376–
      377
    social disorganization and, 224–
      229

C

Cafeteria-style delinquency, 510
Cain, James A., 463
Campaign reforms, 448
Capitalist societies, 330–334
    crime causation and, 341–342
    public corruption in, 332–333
    street crime in, 334
    structural contradictions in,
      330–332
    surplus value in, 340–341
    white-collar crime and, 438
Capone, Al, 430
Catoe, Jarvis, 39, 41
Causation vs. correlation, 113
Chain referral sampling technique,
    84
Chambliss, William, 59, 74, 300,
    328
Chase, Richard Trenton, 45

Chessman, Caryl, 41
Chicago Cook County delinquency
    study, 154–182
Chicago Tribune, 38
Child abuse
    determining intentionality in,
      290–292
    labeling theory and, 285–293
    physical violence as, 286
    sexual abuse as, 286–288
    street culture and, 305–306
    witnesses to, 288–290
Child criminals. *See* Juvenile
    delinquency
Chiricos, Ted, 28, 30
Choice, bio-psychological theory
    of, 386–388, 516–520
Civilizing process, 490
Clairmont, Donald, 8
Classical criminology, 15–17
Clinard, Marshall, 494
Clinton, Bill, 539, 586
Cloward, Richard, 22, 579
Cocaine
    media attention on, 47–52
    public health concerns and,
      499–500
    racial data on use of, 542
    See also Crack cocaine; Drug use
Code of the streets, 303–313
Cognitive landscapes, 135
Cohen, Albert, 22, 561
Cohen, Lawrence, 370, 373, 591
Coincident hypotheses, 507
Cole, Carroll E., 45
Coleman, James, 426, 438
Collins, Carol, 480, 481
Colombia, 251
Colquhoun, Pat, 377
Common-cause hypotheses, 507,
    511
Community relations
    breakdown of, 566
    crime rates and, 183–189
    street gangs and, 473–486
    See also Neighborhoods; Social
      interaction
Comparative Homicide File
    (CHF), 262
Comte, Auguste, 17
Concentration effects, 129
Conflict
    contradictions as basis for, 328–
      330
    criminal behavior and, 314–320

    culture-based, 301–302
    law as product of, 7–8
Conflict theory, 314–327
    contemporary research in, 321–
      327
    overview of, 314–320
    See also Culture conflict theory
Conformity, 396
Consensus, law as product of, 7
Conservative crime policies, 576–
    579
Contradictions
    conflicts and, 328–330
    structural, 328–334
Control balance theory, 408–420
    basic assumptions of, 412–415
    manifestations of deviance and,
      416–418
    mechanics of cause in, 415–416
    probabilities of deviance and,
      408–412
    summary of, 418–420
Control deficits, 409–411
Controlling crime, 535–589
    America's policies on, 538–543
    conventional strategies for,
      576–582
    reintegrative shaming for, 553–
      562
    role of police in, 563–573
    social reorganization as means
      of, 582–589
    victim–offender mediation for,
      544–552
Control surpluses, 411–412
Control theory, 266–280
    belief systems and, 271
    contemporary research in, 273–
      280
    data analysis exercise on, 248–
      249
    differential association theory
      vs., 200
    family attachments and, 267–
      269
    gangs and, 270–271
    general strain theory vs., 211
    homework assignments on,
      361–366
    juvenile delinquency and, 266–
      280
    overview of, 266–267
    peer groups and, 270–271
    school bonding and, 269–270,
      273–279

Crosstabulation tables *(continued)*
  on differential association
    theory, 343–347
  on fear of crime, 96–102
  on Marxist theory, 514–515
  on routine activity theory, 591–
    594
  on self-control theory, 594–596
  on social disorganization, 226–
    229
  steps for running in SPSS, 97–
    98
  See also Data analysis exercises;
    Frequency tables
Crowding, and homicide rates,
    324–326
Crude crime rates, 61
Crutchfield, Robert, 299, 321
Culture
  conflicts based on, 301–302
  criminal behavior and, 249–265
  homicide and, 496
  national regeneration of, 587–
    588
  organized crime and, 459–460
  shaming process and, 557–562
Culture Conflict and Crime (Sellin),
    298
Culture conflict theory, 301–313
  code of the streets and, 303–313
  contemporary research in, 303–
    313
  data analysis exercise on, 513–
    516
  homework assignments on,
    521–526
  overview of, 301–302
  See also Conflict theory;
    Subculture of violence
    theory
Customs, law as product of, 7

D
Dahrendorf, Ralf, 23
D'Amato, Alphonse, 49
Dangerous Classes of New York, The
    (Brace), 116–117
Data analysis exercises
  on bio-psychological theory of
    choice, 516–520
  on control theory, 248–249
  on correlates of crime, 217–224
  on culture conflict theory, 513–
    516

  on differential association
    theory, 343–347
  on fear of crime, 91–103
  on Marxist theory, 513–516
  on routine activity theory, 591–
    594
  on self-control theory, 594–598
  on social disorganization
    theory, 224–229
  See also Homework assign-
    ments
Decent-family model, 304–306
Decker, Scott, 59, 83
Defiant behavior, 417
Defoe, Daniel, 116
Delinquency Areas (Shaw and
    McKay), 374
DeSalvo, Albert, 40, 41, 42
Determinism, 17–22
Deterrence studies, 396–397, 414
Deviant behavior
  autonomous, 411–412, 417–418
  control balance theory of, 408–
    420
  criminal behavior vs., 315
  female, 389–390
  labeling of, 281–283
  peer relationships and,
    510–511
  probabilities of, 408–412
  repressive, 409–411, 416–417
  stigmatization and, 554, 561–
    562
  types of, 416–418
  See also Criminal behavior
Deviant Children Grown Up
    (Robins), 120
Devlin, Lord Patrick, 5, 6
Differential association theory, 152,
    190–200
  contemporary research in, 194–
    200
  criticisms of, 195
  data analysis exercise on, 343–
    347
  directions for future research
    on, 197–200
  empirical testing of, 195–196
  homework assignments on,
    351–360
  Marxist theories and, 199–200
  overview of, 190–193
  peer relationships and, 344–346
  revisions to, 196–197
  social control theory vs., 200

  social disorganization and, 192–
    193
Differential opportunity theory,
    153
Differential social disorganization,
    192–193
Dilulio, John, 540
Direct-contact predatory viola-
    tions, 373–374
  ecological analysis of, 375–376
  minimal elements of, 375
Disintegrative shaming, 553–554,
    561, 562
Drew, Daniel, 434
Driving under the influence (DUI),
    497–498
*Drug Policy and the Decline of
    American Cities* (Staley), 428
Drug sales and distribution
  demand for illicit drugs and,
    500–501
  gangs and, 474, 477–478, 540
  juvenile delinquency and, 503
  mandatory-minimum sentenc-
    ing for, 577
  violent crime associated with,
    506, 540
Drug use, 497–512
  criminal behavior and, 220,
    497–499, 502–511, 540
  gender-based research on, 221
  incarceration rates for, 540
  income and, 223
  juvenile delinquency and, 502–
    511
  media exploitation of, 47–52
  peer relationships and, 344–
    347
  police corruption and, 9–11
  public health and, 499–500
  racial data on, 542
  social bonds and, 348–349
  treatment and prevention of, 50
  violent behavior and, 498, 508,
    540
  See also Alcohol consumption
Dual labor market theory, 321–327
Dugdale, Richard, 20
Durkheim, Emile, 22, 246, 441, 588

E
Ecological theory, 374–376
Economic stratification
  capitalism and, 330–334

Victim–offender mediation
(*continued*)
    research study on, 547–548
    risks of, 546
    role of social workers in, 548–549
Victim Offender Reconciliation Programs (VORPs), 545
Vigilante movement, 571
Violence, 487–496
    child abuse and, 286–293
    drug-related, 497, 502, 506, 508
    foot-patrol police officers and, 563–565
    historical trends in, 487–491
    labor markets and, 321–327
    neighborhood crime programs and, 563–573
    race and, 126–137, 259–265
    research data on, 493–496
    sensitization to, 490–491
    sociological explanations for, 496
    street culture and, 305–306
    subculture of violence theory and, 249–265
    unemployment and, 128–129
    in the United States, 539
    war and, 253
    See also Aggression; Homicide; Person crimes

W

Wall Street Journal, The, 571
Walton, Paul, 23
War
    crime waves and, 491
    violence in, 253, 491

Warr, Mark, 115
Wealth. *See* Economic stratification; Income; Social class
Weapons, 255, 541
Weber, Max, 337
Wertham, Fredric, 41
Wheeler, Stanton, 121
White, Helene Raskin, 428, 502
White, Richard, 301
White-collar crime, 121–122, 429–449
    criminal justice system and, 432, 439–440, 442–446
    criterion for, 432–434
    ethical standards and, 441–442
    female participation in, 395–396
    feminist theory and, 395–396
    financial cost of, 431–432
    history of, 430
    legislation and, 433–434, 438–439
    political system and, 431, 448–449
    power-control theory and, 382
    prevention of, 444–446
    punishments and penalties for, 442–444
    shaming process and, 553
    social class and, 121–122, 434, 438
    social disorganization theory and, 436
    structural reforms and, 446–448
    theory of, 435–436
    types of, 430–431
    victims of, 434–435
Whitman, Charles, 42

Wilson, Corey, 483
Wilson, James Q., 30, 35, 370, 386, 536, 563
Wilson, William Julius, 114, 117, 126, 129, 137, 222, 475, 580–581
Window breaking, 565
Wiretapping, 467
Wisotsky, Steven, 500
Witnesses, juvenile, 288–290
Wolfgang, Marvin, 245, 249, 427, 493, 494
Women
    criminality and, 143–148, 389–390
    incarceration of, 393–394
    justice system and, 391–394
    victimization of, 390–391
    See also Feminist theory; Gender
Women and Crime (Simon), 390
Work. *See* Employment; Labor markets
World Health Statistics Annual, 493
Wright, Richard, 59, 83

Y

Young, Jock, 23
Youth-based crime. *See* Juvenile delinquency

Z

Zahn, Margaret, 427, 493
Zimbardo, Philip, 565
Zimring, Franklin, 539